A Sample HTML 2.0 Document

This shows you that H

- Create Large H
- Create Lists
- Smoothly Integ
- Display various
- Display such at

Document: Done

Running a Perfect
Web Site with
Windows®

e Gover

of Congress

Sports Menu

Comments on this object

Link to the White House

The
White
House

amazing how c
Not long ago M
recognized per
for beating
shorts. He stole the title
de-da football
acted with a
recall the guys name -- but the horse is still famous.
-- wonder if you could train that horse to box

QUE

MICROSOFT INVITES YOU TO

Explore
THE INTERNET

Graphi
For

Version

Micrograf
All Rights R

MICROGRAFX
Picture Pub

Selector tool

TUTORIA

SEARCH

SERVICE

LINKS

ABOUT

PRODUCT
SUPPORT

SOFTWARE
DOWNLOADS

Running a Perfect Web Site with Windows®

*Written by Mark Surfas
and David M. Chandler
with*

Tobin Anthony	Eric Ladd
Rick Darnell	Robert Parker
Noel Estabrook	Kannan Ramasubramanian
Jeffrey Graber	David A. Schramm
Chris Hubbard	Crispen A. Scott

Accompanied by CD-ROM. Inquire at
the Multimedia Center Service Desk.

que®

Running a Perfect Web Site with Windows

Copyright© 1996 by Que® Corporation

Library of Congress Catalog No.: 96-67568

ISBN: 0-7897-0763-2

98 97 96   6 5 4 3 2 1

Interpretation of the printing code: the rightmost double-digit number is the year of the book's printing; the rightmost single-digit number, the number of the book's printing. For example, a printing code of 96-1 shows that the first printing of the book occurred in 1996.

Screen reproductions in this book were created using Collage Plus from Inner Media, Inc., Hollis, NH.

Composed in *Stone Serif* and *MCPdigital* by Que Corporation

Credits

President
Roland Elgey

Publisher
Joseph B. Wikert

Editorial Services Director
Elizabeth Keaffaber

Managing Editor
Sandy Doell

Director of Marketing
Lynn E. Zingraf

Title Manager
Jim Minatel

Acquisitions Manager
Cheryl D. Willoughby

Acquisitions Editor
Doshia Stewart

Product Director
Benjamin Milstead

Software Specialist
Oran J. Sands

Production Editor
Danielle Bird

Copy Editor
Noelle Gasco

Product Marketing Manager
Kim Margolius

Technical Editors
Mark Brown
Todd Brown
Paul Ehteridge
Faisal Jawdat
Greg Newman
Paolo Papalardo

Acquisitions Coordinators
Jane Brownlow
Ruth Slates

Operations Coordinator
Patricia J. Brooks

Editorial Assistant
Andrea Duvall

Book Designer
Ruth Harvey

Cover Designer
Dan Armstrong

Production Team
Steve Adams, Brian Buschkill,
Jason Carr, Chad Dressler,
Jenny Earhart, Bryan Flores,
Jason Hand, Sonja Hart,
Daryl Kessler, Clint Lahnen,
Bob LaRoche, Michelle Lee,
Julie Quinn, Bobbi Satterfield,
Kelly Warner, Paul Wilson, Jeff Yesh

Indexer
Tom Dinse

To my Dad, "Hey dude—you're the coolest!"

To all those who aspire to find a higher plane, and then work their tails off to get there.

—Mark Surfas

About the Authors

Mark Surfas has been involved in computer networks and online computing for over ten years through both entrepreneurial startups and corporate positions. Surfas is currently technical director for Critical Mass Communications, an online services company. Critical Mass Communications both consults on Internet and online communications and develops new online technologies. Current high-profile projects include Virtual Casino World and The Red-Ribbon Network, a joint venture with NETCOM, Inc. Prior to this, Surfas was director of online communications at Coldwell Banker Corporation in Mission Viejo, California. For several years, Coldwell Banker led the real estate industry in communications technology with an online system linking over 2,300 offices and 50,000 sales agents. Other systems Surfas has developed include a statewide real estate information system for the 120,000-member California Association of Realtors and a national commercial real estate system for Grubb & Ellis Corporation. Surfas has consulted for many Fortune 1000 corporations including Bank of America, Wells Fargo Bank, Freedom Communications, American Health Care Systems, CB Commercial Real Estate, and the Automobile Club of Southern California.

David M. Chandler is a World Wide Web enthusiast in Cedar Rapids, Iowa. He currently runs Internet At Work, a Midwestern consulting firm specializing in network security, Intranet development, and advanced Web applications. Chandler previously managed Web servers for the Collins Avionics & Communications Division of Rockwell International. He has programmed computers since 1982 when he received a TI-99/4A as a gift. Chandler holds a degree in Electrical Engineering from the University of Kansas. When he's not at his computer, he enjoys the mountains and flying as a private pilot. You can reach Chandler via e-mail at **chandler@iwork.net** or on the Web at **http://www.iwork.net/~chandler**.

Tobin Anthony holds a Ph.D. in aerospace engineering but has been tinkering with computers for over 18 years specializing in the UNIX and MacOS environments. A strict vegetarian, devout Roman Catholic, and lapsed private pilot, Anthony spends what little spare time he has with his wife Sharon and three children, Michelle, Austin, and Evan. Anthony works as a spacecraft control systems engineer at NASA's Goddard Space Flight Center in Greenbelt, MD. E-mail and Web stops are welcome at **tobin@pobox.com** and **http://pobox.com/~tobin**.

Rick Darnell is a midwest native who lives with his wife and two daughters in Missoula, MT. He began his career in print at a small weekly newspaper after graduating from Kansas State University with a degree in broadcasting. While spending time as a freelance journalist and writer, Rick has seen the full gamut of personal computers since starting out with a Radio Shack Model I in the late 1970s. Darnell serves as a volunteer firefighter and a member of a regional hazardous materials response team.

Noel Estabrook is currently a faculty member of the College of Education at Michigan State University after having obtained degrees in Psychology, Education, and Instructional Technology. He is heavily involved in delivering Internet Training and technical support to educators, professionals, and laymen. In addition to writing, he also runs his own training business part-time. Most recently, Estabrook has been involved in authoring on the Web and coauthored Que's *Using UseNet Newsgroups* and *Using FTP*. His e-mail address is **noele@msu.edu**.

Jeffrey Graber is a technical consultant for Compuware Corp. at its Washington, DC branch. There, Graber is responsible for management and development of Internet services and businesses. In addition, he manages a major client Internet site at the National Science Foundation. Graber has been involved in Web development almost since it began. He has developed several sites for other government agencies. Graber has spoken on the topic of the WWW at the 2nd and 4th International WWW conferences (sponsored by the official W3.org) as well as MecklerMedia's WebDev Conference. He is also founder and chair of the DC area Internet Developers Association (**http://www.shirenet.com/dcida/**). Over the years, Graber has taught numerous computer science courses and given presentations at numerous conferences.

Chris Hubbard is an Internet veteran and technical supervisor with Questar Microsystems, responsible for documentation, testing, and implementation of WebQuest products. His broad professional experience and a wide range of outside interests uniquely qualify him to discuss the World Wide Web in general and WebQuest in particular. A member of the HTML Writers Guild, Hubbard has consulted and built HTML pages for numerous high-profile clients. For recreation, Hubbard surfs the Web discovering and correcting defective Web pages. You can e-mail him at **chris.hubbard@questar.com**.

Eric Ladd is a "math teacher turned Internet teacher" and currently works as an Internet training coordinator for Walcoff and Associates, Inc., a communications and technology firm in Fairfax, Virginia. He holds B.S. and M.S. degrees in mathematics from Rensselaer Polytechnic Institute in Troy, New York, where he also taught calculus, linear algebra, and differential equations for six years. Rensselaer also taught Ladd a thing or two about running a newspaper, engineering late-night angst radio shows, and managing a bar. Away from work and writing, he enjoys running, ice hockey, and spending far too much time playing with his new computer.

Robert Parker first caught the writing bug in the machine room of the Yale Computer Science Facility, tending mainframe systems equipped with an awesome 256K of core memory. He has crafted technical publications for such firms as Compu-Teach, DAK Industries, and most recently Quarterdeck Corporation; scripted and narrated educational videotapes, radio theater, and commercials; and is currently on the faculty at Glendale College, where both he and his father teach courses in the same division. Parker is currently completing his doctorate in conducting, and hopes someday to retire from a successful career as a beloved professor of music.

Kannan Ramasubramanian graduated in 1990 from the Government College of Technology, India with a B.S. in Computer Technology. Currently working with Aslan Computing Inc., located in Palo Alto, California, as a network consultant, he provides Internet connectivity and Web-related services to clients. Ramasubramanian worked for International General Electric India Ltd., Bombay, India, where he set up a national network based on X.25 PDNs. He also has worked with the Supercomputer Education and Research Centre at the Indian Institute of Science, Bangalore, India. Ramasubramanian has published a paper on the conference proceeds of the South East Asian Regional Computer Confederation, titled *A Multiple NMS Based Network Management System*.

David A. Schramm is the founder and president of Internet Productions, Inc. of Florida. He has over 25 years experience in advanced information systems technologies. Schramm's experience includes 15 years at IBM, culminating as the lead service and business system architect of what is now Advantis. Upon leaving IBM in 1983, he began applying Object-Oriented concepts and technologies to the delivery of business information systems. He has been instrumental in the delivery of Object-Oriented business systems in manufacturing, healthcare, automotive, and services industries. Schramm has over four years of experience running his own company and an MBA degree with high honors. Internet Productions, Inc. was founded in 1995 with the mission to know about and exploit advanced technologies such as OMG COSS services, OLE, the Internet, World Wide Web (WWW), multimedia, transport protocols, database management, etc. on behalf of its customers to facilitate the delivery of advanced business solutions. You can find additional information about Internet Productions at **http://www.ipworld.com/company/about.htm**.

Crispen A. Scott is an independent hardware and software engineering consultant who lists among his accomplishments such varied projects as the digital anti-skid braking system for the B-2 Stealth Bomber, various Windows drivers and applications, and embedded control systems for the medical and industrial control fields. Scott is currently developing home pages, CGI applications, and establishing Web sites for Chicago-based customers of his Commercial, Residential, and Institutional Software Corporation [YEP, CRIS Corporation—said with much tongue-in-cheek! :)]. In addition, Scott also lectures, conducts seminars, and presents training reviews nationally. Scott is a continuing, lifelong student who barely remembers graduation from UT (Go Vols), and ardently follows his favorite sports: football and lacrosse. In his "spare" time, Scott is continuing to polish his writing skills in both the poetry and science fiction genres. Scott can currently be reached at **crisin19@starnetinc.com**, and, in the near future, at his Web site. Search for "Chicago Developments" using your favorite search engine.

Acknowledgments

First off—my great thanks to all the geniuses at Critical Mass Communications who have both deftly handled a sizable share of my duties and have skillfully deflected my grumpiness from all the late nights. You are a great team and have many exciting times in store for you! Amy, Steve, Steve, Jason, Jan, and Cathy; thanks for being there! You make it great to come in everyday and turn on the lights.

Second, my thanks to Cathy (I'm not shmoopy, YOU'RE shmoopy!) for your unwavering support and help when I have needed it most.

Special thanks to Doshia Stewart at Que, without whom I would never have dared to take on this ambitious task! Doshia—you have the patience of a saint and I am glad we have had this opportunity to work together. My thanks as well to the great team at Que; I have enjoyed working with you.

Many thanks to Steve Cyrkin, without whom I would not have been in a position to write even a single sentence.

Thanks to Kendell Lang; may we continue to learn from each other as we create the next great online services. World class!

My great thanks to Andre Durand, a visionary who will create an industry with a little help from the rest of us, as well as the entire team at Durand Communications.

Thanks as well to my long lost friends, will you remember me? Deborah & Danny, Piero & Mary, Lance & Penny, Brian, Ken & Chrissy J., Kevin & Julie, Mike & Janice, Topper, Mary & Don, Eric, and Peter & The Great Ragu. Jonas will return!

Finally, I would be remiss if I failed to mention my friends at Monacall, in Monte Carlo—Monaco (yes, part of this book was written in the beautiful principality of Monaco!). Bernard, Laurie, Vincent, Marie-Helene, Jil, Philippe (one more audition, please?) & Carmen (the swimmer!). Thank you for your help and perspectives. Oui! Oui!

We'd Like To Hear From You!

As part of our continuing effort to produce books of the highest possible quality, Que would like to hear your comments. To stay competitive, we *really* want you, as a computer book reader and user, to let us know what you like or dislike most about this book or other Que products.

You can mail comments, ideas, or suggestions for improving future editions to the address below, or send us a fax at (317) 581-4663. For the online inclined, Macmillan Computer Publishing has a forum on CompuServe (type **GO QUEBOOKS** at any prompt) through which our staff and authors are available for questions and comments. The address of our Internet site is **http://www.mcp.com** (World Wide Web).

In addition to exploring our forum, please feel free to contact me personally to discuss your opinions of this book: I'm **102121,1324** on CompuServe, and **bmilstead.que.mcp.com** on the Internet.

Thanks in advance—your comments will help us to continue publishing the best books available on computer topics in today's market.

Benjamin Milstead
Product Director
Que Corporation
201 W. 103rd Street
Indianapolis, Indiana 46290
USA

Contents at a Glance

Planning Your Web Server

Setting Up a Web Server

Doing HTML

Forms and Scripting

Applications

Contents

8 Managing an Internet Web Server — 181

9 Creating and Managing an Intranet Web Server   197

III Doing HTML   235

10 Basic HTML: Understanding Hypertext   237

11 HTML 2.0, HTML 3.0, and Extensions

12 HTML Editors and Tools   311

15 CGI Scripts, Server Side Includes, and Server APIs 415

Introduction

This book is your guide to the two most significant events in computing today; the emergence of the Internet, and the emergence of Microsoft Windows as the most important platform for both client use and hosting services. This is happening quickly, but for those of us involved in Internet services it has been a long wait.

Rejoice! Providing information and services on the Internet is no longer the exclusive domain of UNIX gurus and educational institutions! Corporations and individuals are now free to publish and create their own presence without the need to learn or adapt to the freakish UNIX Operating System. (Okay, *freakish* is a little strong. How about *ornery*?) Publish your own home page! Create an online store! Set up an online club for fellow enthusiasts of whatever hobby it is that you love! Whatever your needs, views or interests, go forth and publish!

The Corporate World has long been migrating to Windows NT as a server platform of choice. Windows NT is a robust operating platform for Internet services. If you're at home with the Windows 3.1 or 95 operating platform, Windows NT is an easy step up for you to make.

The spectacle of the Windows 95 marketing campaign marked the breakthrough of computers as a true consumer item. Heck, operating systems are almost trendy! Fortunately, behind the hype is a real gem of an operating system that is powerful enough to serve as client computing platform and as a base for small server applications.

This book is the right tool at the right time. It's been extremely difficult in the past for people to find information to enable them to run their own Internet services on Windows 95 or Windows NT. This book provides step-by-step advice and guides users through the rigors of setting up online presences on the World Wide Web.

What This Book Is

This book is a comprehensive guide to designing, setting up, and managing a Web site using either Windows 95 or Windows NT. From getting an Internet connection to selecting a server software to writing HTML, it's all here. Most importantly, we have stretched beyond the issue of setting up a simple site to explain the options and availability of more sophisticated Webs and Web tools. For the budding infopreneur, we discuss the financial systems and resources available for online transactions.

Included with this book is the excellent WebQuest server for Windows NT and 95 for anyone who needs a robust server with excellent (and easy!) programming options and database hooks. If you need to put a database online, you will love WebQuest! In addition to the WebQuest server, you will find a rich selection of tools and information that will speed you on your way to running a perfect Web site with Windows.

Overview of each chapter:

- Chapter 1, "The State of the World Wide Web," introduces you to the history of the Web and tells you what's made it popular and where it's going.

- Chapter 2, "Introduction to Web Servers," discusses the basics of the Web: how it works, what kind of content can be delivered, and how security is implemented.

- Chapter 3, "Setting Up a Web Presence," presents the advantages and disadvantages of building your own server versus leasing space, how to find an Internet service provider, the options available for connecting to the Net, and what hardware and software are best for the job.

- Chapter 4, "Getting Started with Your NT/Windows 95 Web Server," covers the all-important issues of server software—what's available and what to look for. This chapter also introduces the installation of both the WebQuest server and the Microsoft Internet Information Server.

- Chapter 5, "Server Configuration," teaches you about all aspects of server configuration, including log files, document directories, MIME types, and security features.

- Chapter 6, "Configuring and Managing the Microsoft Internet Information Server" gives a detailed explanation of the setup and management of the new NT server-based Internet Server package from Microsoft.

- Chapter 7, "Configuring Your Questar WebQuest Server," is a guide to setting up and managing both the Windows 95 and Windows NT versions of the WebQuest servers included with this book.

- Chapter 8, "Managing an Internet Web Server," explains how to build a successful Internet Web server. It includes instructions on how to develop a fun and useful server, attract and keep visitors, protect your data, and promote your server. This chapter also lists popular features and overviews secure transactions.

■ Chapter 9, "Creating and Managing an Intranet Web Server," describes how to maximize the effectiveness of your internal server. It explains how you can manage server content, provide useful features, and protect your internal network from hostile access.

■ Chapter 10, "Basic HTML: Understanding Hypertext," includes a hands-on tutorial that will transform you into a bona fide Webmaster. It teaches you everything you need to know about writing attractive and functional HTML documents, including how to use text and graphics features, use hypertext, and create clickable images.

■ Chapter 11, "HTML 2.0, HTML 3.0, and Extensions," enriches your HTML knowledge to include all of the new standards that are transforming the Web from a simple medium to a rich page layout environment. Tables, frames, and even Virtual Reality Markup Language are covered!

■ Chapter 12, "HTML Editors and Tools," teaches you to create HTML using the latest generation of HTML editors and word processor add-ins. Also included is extensive coverage of how to convert to HTML from other document and spreadsheet formats. The chapter ends with a study of the analysis tools available to help make your HTML error-free.

■ Chapter 13, "Graphics and Imagemaps," uncovers the mysteries of why some Web page graphics look so great and yet take so little time to download! It covers the graphic formats you need to know about and the tools you should use to create them. It also covers the ins and outs of imagemaps: what they are, how to create them, and the best tools to use.

■ Chapter 14, "HTML Forms," gives you all the information you need about forms, which allow users to send data back to Web servers. It teaches you about all the elements of forms, including text boxes, check boxes, option buttons, pull-down menus, and push buttons. Advanced uses of forms to manage data are covered, as well as innovative uses of forms on the Web today. The chapter follows with an in-depth look at server side includes as implemented with the WebQuest Server. Finally, this chapter looks at the emerging server APIs, which are challenging CGI scripting as the most efficient means of extending your Web server.

■ Chapter 15, "CGI Scripts, Server Side Includes, and Server APIs," covers the programs that process form data as well as the scripting options that provide power without programming. It describes which scripting languages are best-suited to your needs, the general principles of scripting, and how to write scripts.

- Chapter 16, "More Scripting Options," covers the powerful new language everyone is talking about: Java! It explains at Java apps and applets and their current state of implementation. It also covers Microsoft's VB Script and OLE controls.

- Chapter 17, "Search Engines and Annotation Systems," looks at the newly available Web search engines and teaches how to utilize them. It also shows you how to write scripts to search simple text databases and how to efficiently search your entire server for information. The chapter wraps up with a look at systems for annotating Web documents.

- Chapter 18, "Usage Statistics and Maintaining HTML," covers tools for analyzing usage data and tools for checking to see that your HTML files are all intact. It shows you the tools to use for reporting usage data to users on the Web. This chapter also helps you handle the maintenance activity involved once your server is up and running.

- Chapter 19, "Database Access and Applications Integration," presents techniques for accessing data in databases and corporate data warehouses. More and more Web sites are database-driven—for good reason: this is where your data lives! This powerful technique is explored and the options available are surveyed.

- Chapter 20, "Integrating Microsoft BackOffice," covers the issues of utilizing the myriad of Microsoft NT support software to create a powerful extension to the corporate LAN. Security and remote management are implemented here as well as messaging and database management.

- Chapter 21, "Financial Transactions," discusses the potential traps and pitfalls that every infopreneur needs to know about. It gives you a history of electronic commerce, detailed notes about the state of commerce today, and some great ideas about how to safely proceed to your first million cyber-bucks!

- Chapter 22, "Interactive and Live Applications," talks about the new technologies coming that will take the Web and the Internet beyond the static page you see today into a fully interactive experience. It covers what is happening today and what's coming tomorrow.

What This Book Is Not

This book is not an introduction to Microsoft Windows NT or Windows 95. You should already be proficient with the Windows operating system to utilize this book (and the software included with it) effectively.

This book is not specifically an introduction to the World Wide Web. It is recommended that you have some familiarity with the World Wide Web and Web browsing in general. While this book covers most Web fundamentals, you will benefit from already having firsthand experience using the Web.

WebmasterCD: Your One-Stop Web Resource

To help ensure your successful launch into the world of Web, this book includes an incredible resource: the WebmasterCD. You'll find all of the crucial tools you need to get started as a Webmaster. This resource includes HTML authoring tools, graphics tools, and even the powerful Web server software you need to run a superior site!

This book also includes a large collection of useful documents about the Internet. You'll find all the RFCs (Request for Comments) used to create Internet standards, STDs, and FYIs on the WebmasterCD. Look for samples of HTML and code from the book, FAQs, and other documents of interest to aspiring Webmasters.

Conventions Used in This Book

Certain conventions are used in *Running a Perfect Web Site with Windows* to help you absorb the ideas easily.

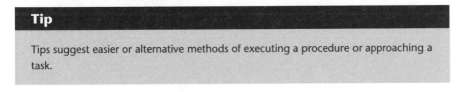

> **Tip**
>
> Tips suggest easier or alternative methods of executing a procedure or approaching a task.

Text that is part of an HTML document will look like this: `<TAG>content</TAG>`. This type of text will appear in the figures and samples of HTML you see throughout the book.

New terms are introduced in *italic,* and text you type appears in **boldface**. World Wide Web URLs (essentially document addresses) are also presented in **boldface**.

> **Note**
>
> This paragraph format indicates additional information that might help you avoid problems, or that might be considered when using the described features.

> **Caution**
>
> This paragraph format warns you of potentially hazardous procedures.

▶ See "Section
Title," p. xx

▶ See "Chapter
Title," p. xx

Running a Perfect Web Site with Windows uses marginal cross-references so you can quickly find related information in the book. These are listed by section or chapter title and page number.

Throughout the book, you'll also see the WebmasterCD icon (shown beside this paragraph) in the margins. Where you see this icon, the text is discussing software or a document on the CD-ROM that is included with this book.

Part I

Planning Your Web Server

## CHAPTER 1

The State of the World Wide Web

The World Wide Web continues to grow faster than any other segment of the Internet. Its graphical interface and hypertext capabilities have caught the fancy of Internet users and the media like no other Internet tool in history. Businesses, schools, government, and nonprofit organizations (in addition to millions of individuals) are flocking to the Web to promote themselves and their products in front of an audience spanning the entire planet.

It's difficult to watch a sporting event, a commercial, or even the news without seeing that increasingly familiar *http://* telling us of yet another enterprise on the Web. Because of the Web's popularity and its cost-effectiveness as a marketing tool, the World Wide Web is quickly becoming the electronic marketplace of the decade.

In this chapter, you learn:

- Where the Web has been
- How Web usage is changing
- How you can do business on the Web
- Where the Web is going

The Web's Phenomenal Growth

The Web is now accessible in over 100 countries on all seven continents, and its information and services range from the esoteric to the absurd. Web sites are maintained by universities, companies, public institutions, states, cities, and even high schools. A number of powerful search engines allow rapid information location and retrieval, making the Web the ultimate tool for research, interactive entertainment and, yes, even advertising.

The cutting edge of Web technology attacks two distinct problems. The first, with the most exciting prospects for end users, deals with adding movement—animation—to Web pages; unlike today's static page, tomorrow's Web page may feature animated characters, marquees that scroll across the browser window, even full-motion videos. The second, and of most interest to Web-based businesses, deals with how to send confidential information (specifically, credit card numbers) safely and secretly across the Internet, a network not originally designed for open transactions. Progress is being made on both fronts daily; watch the Web for the latest news!

In January 1993, there were only 50 known Web servers in existence. Today, the Web has become the largest source of traffic on the Internet. Table 1.1 shows the growth of the Web relative to other Internet services on the Internet. You can find more details about Internet usage from Nielsen Interactive Services at **http://www.nielsenmedia.com/whatsnew/** and **http://www.nielsenmedia.com/demo.htm**. As was mentioned earlier, Web servers are in almost every developed country in the world.

Table 1.1 measures Web traffic three different ways. *Ports* provide a means to route network data to the appropriate service on a network computer (you can think of ports like numbered portals at a ballpark—they direct ticket holders to the appropriate section of the stadium). Each network service uses a standard port; by noting how much traffic is directed to port 80 (the Web port), you can gauge how much network traffic is Web traffic. *Pkts*, or *Packets*, are discrete packages of data sent across the Internet (you can think of them roughly as individual words in the dialog between computers over a network). Counting the packets gives you an idea of how heavily a network is being used. *Bytes* are another means of measuring the amount of data flowing through a network.

In table 1.1, notice that in a four-month period, the Web overthrew ftp-data as the most-used service, going from 13.12 to 21.44 packets and from 17.69 to 26.25 bytes.

> **Note**
>
> If you're interested, a list of all registered servers is available from **http://www.w3.org/hypertext/DataSources/WWW/Servers.html**.

Table 1.1   Growth of World Wide Web Traffic (Percentage of Total Byte Traffic Change on the NSF Backbone in a Four-Month Period)

Service Name	Port	Rank %	Pkts	Rank %	Bytes
Beginning of Study					
ftp-data	20	1	18.758	1	30.251
www	80	2	13.122	2	17.693
telnet	23	3	10.357	6	3.715
End of Study					
www	80	1	21.443	1	26.250
ftp-data	20	2	14.023	2	21.535
nntp	119	3	8.119	3	8.657

As table 1.1 illustrates, the World Wide Web already comprises more traffic than any other Internet function. Despite the fact that the Web has been in operation for several years now, it's still able to grow at a rate of almost 20 percent a year. By the end of 1996, it's quite possible that the Web will account for more traffic than all other Internet activity combined!

> **Note**
>
> The World Wide Web traffic in table 1.1 reflects only connections to World Wide Web servers. Web browsers can also connect to FTP (File Transfer Protocol), Gopher, and other types of servers.

Do we know anything else about who is actually on the Web? The Nielsen study mentioned in earlier tells us quite a bit about who is on the Net. Among the findings:

- 56 percent of WWW users were between 25-44 years old.
- 64.5 percent of users were male.
- 88 percent had at least some college education.

The Growing Marketplace of Web Servers

As a recent survey of Web servers indicates, last year's most popular servers were free UNIX-based servers. Just four months later, more and more users were willing to pay for their servers, turning to Netscape, WebSTAR, and WebSite among others. There is also a wide range of individual sites being powered by a wide variety of other servers not shown in the table below; in January 1996 alone, 12 different PC-based Web servers were released.

Table 1.2 Growth of Commercial Web Servers		
Server	**9/95**	**1/96**
Percent Change in Free versus Commercial Servers Used at Active Web Sites over a Four-Month Period		
NCSA (free)	54	41
Apache (free)	7	17
Netscape	8	13
CERN (free)	17	11
WebSTAR/MacHTTP	5	6
WebSite	1	4
BESTWWWD (best.com)	<1	2
OSU (Region 6)	<1	1
Purveyor	<1	1

> **Note**
>
> This information comes from Paul E. Hoffman's survey of the servers used on the Web, available at **http://www.proper.com/**.

The Web Offers a Wealth of Opportunities

Although the next section talks about specific opportunities for business on the Internet, there is little doubt that there are some huge benefits to being on the Web today. In business, numbers speak volumes. There is no doubt that the Web has them. Web users are generally educated, professional middle to upper-middle class people who want to use the Web for information, research, fun, and even for shopping.

In addition to the obvious opportunities on the Web are its inherent advantages to other media. Instant access is probably the biggest. Many commercial sites report thousands of visitors within the first days of operation. Electronic malls are appearing everywhere, and financial transactions are becoming safer all the time.

The best thing about the Web, of course, is that it isn't going to go away. It's only going to get bigger and bigger. Connections will get faster, computers will get better, programming will get slicker, and access will get better.

Conducting Business on the Web

So, you're convinced. The Web is the greatest thing since tail fins, right? Well, almost. There are definitely a lot of advantages to doing business on the Net (as well as some pitfalls), and it will definitely be helpful to know about some of them. Who's out there? What are they like? Are they ready to buy your product? Who's doing business on the Web?

Some of those questions are easy to answer. We know that there are a lot of educated professionals on the Internet. We also know that many of them are involved in education, research, and industry. It's time to dig a little deeper and find out a little bit about how the Web can serve businesses and consumers of all kinds.

Generating Sales

The Web has proven that people will come—in droves—to the Internet if it's easy to use, accessible, and useful (and, well, sometimes even if it's not so useful). For those in business for profit, a "presence on the Web" (that is, putting pages on the Web) has one basic goal: increasing sales. However, most companies don't use the Web for direct sales (although many do). A Web presence can be used to *indirectly* increase sales, by offering information about a product or service that must be purchased elsewhere, or just by increasing customer awareness of the company or its offerings.

This section gives you three examples of different ways that companies use Web pages to directly—or indirectly—generate sales.

Many companies, such as CD-Now, are concerned with marketing a specific product (see fig. 1.1). Very little "advertising" or name-recognition is involved. They offer a product, and they hope people buy it.

Fig. 1.1
CD-Now is a Web-based company that sells music on the Internet

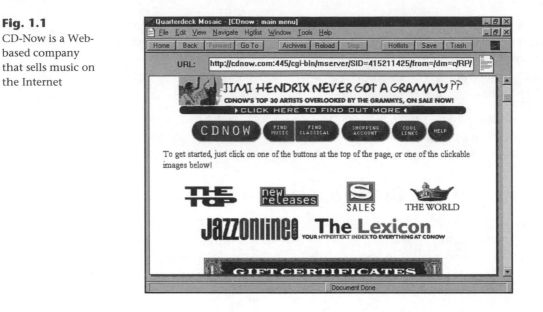

Many companies maintain a Web presence, but do not sell products directly over the Internet (see fig. 1.2). They hope that you will read about their products or services on their Web page, and make your purchasing decision based on that information.

Fig. 1.2
GISD is a Michigan company that provides Internet training and other services.

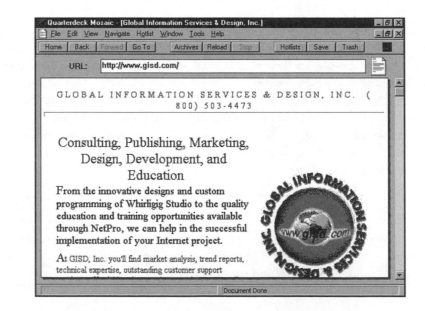

A site on the Web also enables companies to keep their name before the public. Even major movie and television studios, car companies, and beverage companies that already have wide (or global) name recognition use the Web to further their corporate image and sales (see fig. 1.3).

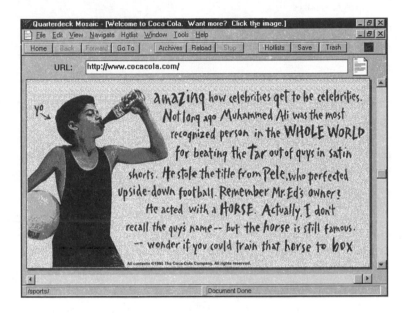

Fig. 1.3
Even Coca-Cola, known the world around, advertises on the Web.

Companies who use the Web for this purpose are often service-based businesses, such as Global Information Services & Design in Michigan. Still others offer products that are just very difficult to sell over the Web and for whom product familiarity is of utmost importance. Again, these types of companies are generally national in nature or are service providers of some sort.

Table 1.3 shows what businesses reported when asked what they used the Web for. As you can see, many of the functions already being employed through other media are being utilized on the Web today.

Table 1.3 Business Usage of the Web	
Percent of Business WWW Users Who Have Used Web Pages To...	
Collaborate with others	54
Publish information	33
Gather information	77

(continues)

Table 1.3 Continued	
Percent of Business WWW Users Who Have Used Web Pages To...	
Research competitors	46
Sell products or services	13
Purchase products or services	23
Provide customer service and support	38
Communicate internally	44
Provide vendor support and communications	50

Who Is Your Audience?

It's time to mention a few specifics about who exactly is on the Internet, and whether they actually buy what a business has to sell. We're going to return to the Nielsen survey for some more statistics that were gathered from 280,000 telephone interviews nationwide.

If you're interested in getting a copy of the full report, The Final Report is available for purchase from CommerceNet (phone: 415-617-8790; e-mail: **survey@commerce.net**) and Nielsen Media Research (phone: 813-738-3125; e-mail: **interactive@nielsenmedia.com**).

So, what did the Nielsen survey find? Well, over 2.5 million Americans have purchased products and services over the WWW. Again, these numbers will continue to grow. Earlier in the chapter, you were given a glimpse of some general demographics of users. The survey showed specific results important for businesses:

- 25 percent of WWW users had incomes over $80,000 a year.
- 55 percent of users have used the Web to research products or services and 14 percent have actually purchased them.
- There was a user base of 18 million Web users in the United States and Canada.

Cautionary Note

As rosy a picture as the Web paints, there are some downsides. The biggest is that Internet surveys or usage statistics fail to take into account the still large majority of people who do not access the Internet. Even with 18 million users online, that still leaves over 300 million people in the U.S. and Canada alone who are not yet online—plus the countless millions around the world who have yet to join the Internet community either because they don't have access, or because the vast majority of Web traffic is conducted in English only.

This brings up another point. There is a danger in marketing exclusively to those who use the Internet. The users of the Internet make up an affluent minority; people who don't own computers or who don't use them for Internet access are still responsible for most of the purchases made in the U.S. today. The Internet won't be a universal marketing medium like television or radio until the still-unconnected majority comes online.

The Internet is not yet (nor will it likely ever be) a panacea for everyone's advertising and marketing woes. It's another tool that can, and should, be utilized along with other, more traditional media.

The Future of the Web

Now that you have a better idea of where the Web has been and where it is—wouldn't you like to know where it's going? Wouldn't we all? A popular TV commercial shows all sorts of fanciful futuristic gadgets as being the future. The commercial sends a message that each possibility is likely and that it's sheer guesswork as to what the future will actually hold. To an extent, that commercial is right, but we can make some educated guesses.

We know that many advances are being made in technology that are now used on the cutting edge. Although we can't know exactly what everything will be like later, we can draw some general conclusions.

Room for Improvement

There's no doubt the Web's popularity has benefited in no small part from increased public awareness and the availability of dial-up Internet connections. But, let's face it—every time you have to wait while your modem slowly downloads particularly complex Web-site graphics, you know that the Web still has a long way to go.

Not only are there problems with access speed, but, as was mentioned in the last section, a large segment of the population remains unconnected. And, as with most computer endeavors, the Internet has, up until the last year or so, been dominated by those in the computer field. Only now is this fact beginning to radically change as the Internet becomes more of a mass media.

Note

The old maxim of one bad apple spoiling it for everyone also holds true on the Internet. Problems with credit card commerce on the Internet have become popular targets for media attention—not all of it balanced or accurate. Credit card owners face risks every time a card is used (Did the waiter make a copy of the number? Can I trust the telemarketer not to steal my number?) far greater than the possibility that someone may siphon a card number off an Internet transaction. Internet commerce is still risky—but in the context of other, everyday risks, it's much safer than popular wisdom may suggest.

Less Expensive, Faster Internet Connections

In the past, getting a full connection to the Internet required a high-speed leased telephone line and expensive networking hardware. As a result, only businesses and large institutions could afford Internet access. This limited the Internet's usefulness for commercial purposes. However, the introduction of high-speed modems and dial-up Internet Service Providers (ISPs) has made WWW access from home both possible and practical.

The breakthrough that made a connection to the Internet as close as your telephone was the development of Serial Line Internet Protocol and Point-to-Point Protocol (SLIP and PPP). These protocols enable you to connect your home computer to the Internet via an ordinary modem, avoiding the expense of a leased line and connecting hardware (albeit at a significant cost of speed).

Note

"SL/IP" is equivalent to "SLIP." Both refer to Serial Line Internet Protocol; this book uses SLIP.

But, as we expect more from the Net, standard computer modems often don't do the job. The use of ISDN (Integrated Services Digital Network) lines has recently become more popular, but even this solution brings up the problem of needing specialized add-on cards and protocols. ISDN is more expensive than standard phone lines, and is not available in many areas. As an example, at the time this chapter was written, a typical ISDN line in North Carolina cost over $200 for installation, plus an additional $75 per month to maintain (for more on ISDN, go to **http://www.bst.bls.com/bbs/isdnintr.htm**).

Two areas that seem to hold a lot of promise in our quest for cheap, fast Internet connections are cable and satellite. Satellite transmission is probably further away, but some cable companies in the United States are already offering Internet through the same line through which you receive your TV stations. One example is TCI in East Lansing, which already offers 10Mbps Internet connections (that's *mega*bits per second, versus the current 28.8 *kilo*-bits per second of an ordinary modem) for under $50 a month. It's expected that these types of connections will only get cheaper and more widespread in the future.

A Larger, More Diverse Audience

Undoubtedly, the people that use the Internet will also change. Many factors will cause the number and types of Internet users to expand in the future.

As more and more schools, libraries, community colleges, and other public institutions get connected, those who use these facilities will also become users. In addition, ISP rates will continue to fall and, as Internet Service be-comes available through more accessible and accepted means (such as cable) people's fear of technology will also continue to decrease.

One of the last factors involved in increased usage will stem from a not-so-obvious source. In the past, if you wanted Internet service, you had to con-tact the provider, install the software, make the connection, and basically go through a lot of trouble to get online. However, with the breakout of Windows 95, OS/2 Warp, and other Operating Systems, the Internet is now built-in (see fig. 1.4). When Internet access becomes as easy as buying your computer, plugging it in, and getting online, a large barrier to access will have been removed.

Customized Service

It's not science fiction anymore. Click on your computer screen to order your favorite movie and watch it appear on your TV (or computer monitor) 30 sec-onds later. Get e-mail from companies who know just what you like and don't like and who offer you "tailor-made" products and services. Fire up your Web browser and talk live, with video, to your brother in California. These services, and more, are either already here or will soon be here.

With Internet connectivity, users and businesses will be able to teleconfer-ence with multiple sites at the same time at a comparatively inexpensive price. Several colleges have begun to offer radio broadcasts of their school's sports games over the Web so that alumni across the nation can catch the games. There is much more, and the Internet will bring it to you.

Fig. 1.4
Microsoft's
Internet Explorer
incorporates the
same functionality
as Netscape right
out of the box.

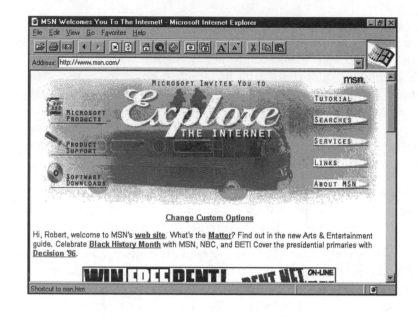

Super Web Page Design

Even as this book goes to press, exciting new possibilities are emerging for
Web designers—ways to make Web pages literally come to life.

VRML—Virtual Reality Modeling Language—is an exciting new development
that enables you to create three-dimensional "virtual worlds" to be viewed
with a VRML-capable Web browser (such as Microsoft's Internet Explorer).
For example, you can create VRML tours through buildings or landscapes, or
view 3-D models of vehicles or devices. VRML is only in the earliest stages of
development; the virtual worlds you can create are still very basic. Even so,
VRML worlds are popping up like weeds all over the landscape of the Web.

Another exciting addition to the Web is Java (which was probably named in
honor of the beverage that keeps the computer industry running twenty-four
hours a day). Java is a system that enables you to create animated images on
a Web page. The first Java applications will be used to create animated logos
on corporate Web pages (for example, Netscape has a sample animation fea-
turing its Mozilla mascot). Other applications will enable users to include
marquees that "chase" across the browser window, make product demonstrations—and, sooner than you think, create animated pictures!

Webmaster Duties Increase

All these new technologies put even greater demands on the Webmaster, who must not only provide the care and feeding of the Web site—tending the server, creating and implementing new documents or applications, answering e-mail from remote users—but must also keep abreast of the ever-changing face of the Web.

Security alone takes up a great deal of a Webmaster's attention—staying a step ahead of the "hacker" by keeping up with the latest hardware and software is vital to any site concerned with protecting its resources. The newest Web technologies like VRML and Java aren't just add-ons that Web document writers can cut and paste into their pages—they require a great deal of cooperation from the Webmaster as well. Businesses that rely on the Web will put the greatest demands on their Webmasters—after all, who wants to be seen using yesterday's technology on tomorrow's Web?

Conclusion: The Web Has a Great Future

The future really is bright. We've already looked at many of the things that are available or soon will be that will make using the Web more efficient, profitable, and sensible. Perhaps one of the biggest benefits of all these changes is in the opportunity presented to small organizations without a lot of computer expertise or a lot of money to establish a presence on the Web.

Thanks to dial-up SLIP and PPP, the cost can be as little as $30 per month. Because the Web server software included with this book can run using a SLIP or PPP connection, any home computer enthusiast can run a World Wide Web server from home for a small monthly fee. This will serve to open whole new markets to Web usage. Nonprofit organizations, local businesses, small niche-market businesses, or just an individual with something interesting to say—*anyone* can have a presence on the Web.

The types of media becoming available to users and providers of all types will continue to rapidly expand to allow individuals and enterprises to deliver (and receive) information much more quickly and efficiently. No longer are just simple text and pictures available over the Internet. Many companies are already working on ways to deliver low-bandwidth audio and video over the Web that can be accessed by even high-speed modem connections.

Many companies advertise on the radio. What if you didn't have to buy 30-second commercials on radio stations all over town—instead, imagine that you could broadcast a 30-minute show about your business, every day, to anyone connected to the Internet? This may not be practical today in terms of how many may actually listen, but it isn't far off. Some have even pronounced the death of broadcast radio as sound transmission through the Internet becomes seamless and practical. Figure 1.5 shows an example of one company that is already taking advantage of the Internet for live broadcasts.

Fig. 1.5
Sportline USA
offers one of its
popular talk shows
live on the Web.

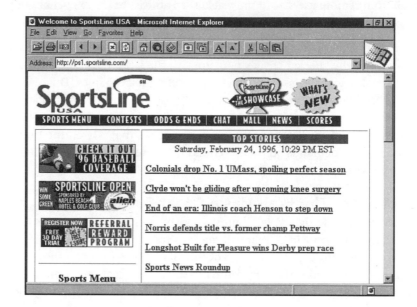

Compression techniques also continue to increase the feasibility of using video transmissions over the Web. Uses can range from video-conferencing (thereby drastically cutting the costs of doing business), to advertising, to product demonstrations, and more.

Even Internet-savvy veterans are often lulled into thinking *how* they get information will continue to be the same. However, this area is not immune to change, either. *How* we get information may change as much as the information we receive does. We've already talked some about Internet transmission coming through our local cable. Also, the possibilities for satellite transmission may not be too far off. Searching on the Web for information on wireless communications already yields hundreds to thousands of hits. It may not be long before you get your e-mail from the same dish as ESPN.

Lastly, it may even become unnecessary to read Internet information. Many companies have already integrated e-mail and voice-mail to be delivered audially. Can it be that one day you'll turn on your TV and, instead of channel surfing with your remote control, you'll Web surf instead? Don't be surprised if it happens.

The Web has experienced terrific growth in the first several years of existence. Fueled by applications in business, government, education, and research, all made available from home computers, the Web is poised to become *the* electronic marketplace and information source of the century. ❖

## CHAPTER 2

Introduction to Web Servers

The World Wide Web is an evolving paradigm. The Web sports a different look today than it did at its inception only a few short years ago. This chapter describes some Web nomenclature; and, some types of data you can convey via the Web. There is almost no limit to the type of data you can provide to your Web users.

You'll want to provide Web services that are both innovative and useful. You can accomplish this by first understanding some of the terminology associated with the Web; furthermore, you will develop an appreciation for the type of material available through the Web by visiting some popular sites. This chapter provides:

- Definitions of terms associated with the World Wide Web
- An introduction to the HyperText Transport Protocol
- A discussion of some of the Internet protocols that predate the World Wide Web
- The types of data that you can serve via the World Wide Web
- Methods used to secure Web servers

Defining WWW Terminology

Before covering the types of services you can offer through the Web, this section covers some of the terminology that is used in this book. In addition, it describes some of the underlying protocols that make data transfer using the World Wide Web possible.

Definitions

The *World Wide Web* describes a cross-platform, interactive network of Internet sites that offer interconnected document access. Also known as *the WWW* or simply *the Web,* the World Wide Web supports a variety of data formats. The Web was initially developed to allow researchers to access documents of similar subjects. While viewing these documents online, the Web allowed users to click on a highlighted section of text, bringing up a document linked to that passage. This document could reside on the same host computer or on a computer located in another part of the world. The portions of text linked to remote documents are known as *hypertext.*

HyperText Transport Protocol, more commonly known as *HTTP,* is the Internet protocol that allows data transfer through the World Wide Web. It's a stateless protocol similar to Gopher; connections are opened and closed as data is transferred between hosts. FTP connections differ because they are held open at the users' discretion.

▶ See "Graphics Standards," p. 362, for more information on graphic data types supported by Web servers.

A *Web browser* is an application that allows users to view documents within a hypertext context. Web browsers allow text and graphics to be viewed and formatted beside each other. The Web supports transfer of files of many different data types; some data types supported by the Web include text, graphics, and multimedia. When a Web browser encounters a data type that it cannot display, it can launch external applications to display those files.

A *Web server* is a computer that responds to requests from Web browsers via HTTP. Servers transfer text files and corresponding graphics and transfer this data via HTTP to remote computers that are running Web browsers.

HyperText Markup Language, or *HTML,* is the foundation of the World Wide Web. Text and graphics are formatted in WWW documents using HTML; Web browsers process these documents transferring the HTML commands into the desired format in the Web browser display window. The content of HTML is subject to a standards process monitored by the World Wide Web Consortium (W3C). As of this writing, HTML 2.0 is the accepted standard; HTML 3.0 is a backwards-compatible proposal containing enhanced functionality. Members of the Consortium are tasked with defining the features of the language.

Helper applications are those applications defined within Web browsers that display nonstandard file formats. Browsers such as Netscape and Mosaic can display text and graphics. However, such file formats as MPEG, audio, and PostScript are not supported within all Web browsers. Therefore, the browser hands the file off to the requisite helper application so that the user can view the file.

The Client-Server Model

As with most other enterprise systems, the World Wide Web works within a *client-server* paradigm. The Web operates through exchange of data between Web clients, or browsers, and Web servers. Web servers usually run on computers that employ fast microprocessors and high-speed Ethernet or FDDI network connections. These servers field requests from Web browsers for certain files that can be comprised of almost an unlimited number of data types.

Figure 2.1 details a schematic of how Web browsers interact with a single Web server. Several browsers can simultaneously request files from a single server. This server, depending on its processing and networking resources, processes these requests and returns requisite files to the browsers.

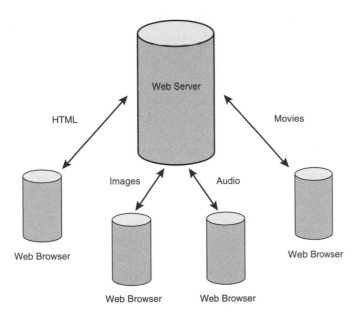

Fig. 2.1
World Wide Web servers interact with requests from various Web browsers. A single server can transfer several types of files to multiple browsers.

Web Protocols

The HyperText Transport Protocol (HTTP) is the most common method of transporting data between WWW browsers and clients. The protocol was developed in 1989 for the purpose of transporting documents along the Internet via a hypertext interface. HTTP has its origins in the Gopher protocol. In contrast to a connection made using the File Transfer Protocol (FTP), an HTTP connection between computers requires few resources. The protocol was designed to very nimbly recover text and other data from HTTP servers with very little overhead required from the browser or server computers.

The HTTP specifications undergo periodic review by a committee of Internet specialists. The current standard is HTTP/1.0 which supersedes the original HTTP/0.9. Further versions of HTTP are under review; they will provide greater capabilities to Web browsers in the areas of performance and security.

An HTTP connection between a Web client and server can be separated into four separate actions:

- *Connection Launch*   The HTTP server constantly listens on a certain Internet port for a request from a Web browser. This port is usually specified as port 80 but other port numbers can be included in the URL.

> **Note**
>
> A *port* is similar to a TV channel but is implemented in software rather than as a physical channel. Most Web servers receive HTTP traffic on a single network connection. Ports are used to differentiate the different Internet packets depending on protocol (HTTP, FTP, etc.) to which they adhere. Traffic on a particular port is relayed to a relevant application such as a Web or FTP server. It is possible to set a port to any number from 0 to 65535.

- *Client Request*   After a connection is established, the browser sends a request to the server. In addition to querying the server regarding a CGI script or a certain image, sound, or HTML file, the browser sends information about itself including what kind of file formats it can understand.
- *Server Response*   The server, having digested the request from the browser, sends an HTTP message to the browser. This server tells the browser what level of HTTP is being supported, what format is used to convey the response, and the response itself.
- *Connection Close*   Having sent the message, the connection is terminated by either the client or server.

As you can see, as opposed to FTP or Telnet connections, the HTTP connection does not normally stay open. As a result, a server can maintain many more HTTP connections for a given length of time than it can support remote logins.

> **Tip**
>
> For more specific information on HTTP, visit the World Wide Web Consortium HTTP draft specification at **http://www.w3.org/hypertext/WWW/Protocols/HTTP/HTTP2.html**.

Understanding MIME

The Multimedia Internet Mail Exchange (MIME) message representation protocol is a means of conveying information about a file that is being sent through the Internet. This protocol conveys information about the message through MIME headers but leaves the message content or body in the form of plain ASCII text. For this reason, MIME is an excellent means of transferring files between different platforms. For example, you can use the e-mail program Eudora to send a graphics file from your Macintosh to a PC user. If the PC user is also running Eudora, or any other MIME-capable mail reader, the program will read the MIME header and attach the relevant tag to the file to make it readable by the correct application.

Much like HTTP, MIME content headers are under a standards process. The key information in the header is the MIME type and subtype that identify the type of message content. The MIME type will usually consist of one of the types listed in table 2.1.

Table 2.1	Common MIME Types
Type	**Function**
application	Defines client applications
audio	Defines audio formats
image	Defines image formats
message	Used for electronic mail messages
multipart	Used for transmission with multiple parts
text	Defines text formats
video	Defines video formats
x-"string"	Denotes an experimental MIME type not recognized as a standard

The content header is comprised of a type and subtype. The subtype specifically defines the message content within the context of the MIME type. For example, an HTTP server will send the following MIME type/subtype in response to a Web client query

```
text/html
```

This header information tells the browser to expect some text and specifically some HTML text. Web browsers, as opposed to other applications, understand that MIME types need to be interpreted as HTML and displayed accordingly. Similarly, a MIME header containing the information

```
image/gif
```

would tell the browser the following ASCII text is actually a GIF image. The browser then displays the GIF within the window or launches a GIF-viewing application.

There are a variety of MIME subtypes defined for each type. The HTTP server needs to correlate the type of information it's serving to a certain MIME type. For example, if it's serving a JPEG file as part of a Web page, the server needs to somehow know that

- The file is a JPEG formatted-file
- Image/jpeg is the standard MIME classification for that file

The Web server needs to have some means of identifying files and the relevant MIME types in order to tell the browsers what to expect. This chapter describes how to do this for the various server applications.

Pre-WWW Protocols

One reason for the success of the WWW is the ability of Web browsers to transfer data using protocols other than HTTP. Hence, Web clients such as Mosaic and Netscape Navigator can serve as FTP and Gopher clients in addition to interpreting HTTP. Modern Web clients have positioned themselves as all-in-one Internet tools. There are more uses for an Internet server than just serving Web pages.

The *Transmission Control Protocol/Internet Protocol (TCP/IP)* is comprised of many protocols and while HTTP is the 800-lb gorilla of the bunch, there are other useful capabilities that you may want to offer on your server. The File Transfer Protocol is useful for quickly transferring large amounts of data. Many shareware and freeware applications are available on Internet servers through FTP connections. Gopher offers an even more intuitive and flexible means of transferring files. Furthermore, you may want to set up your Internet site as an e-mail server for your organization. In this manner, users will be able to exchange mail with one another as well as with other users on the Internet. Finally, you may want to offer UseNet newsgroup access to your organization. In addition to offering UseNet groups, many large organizations, such as corporations and universities, often establish newsgroups of local interest to the organization.

Data You Can Serve via the Web

As mentioned earlier in this chapter, a variety of file types can be served via the World Wide Web. This section covers some of the types of files that modern Web browsers support.

Text

The World Wide Web was originally conceived as a means of displaying text documents with hypertext links to other documents. These hypertext links allow users to refer to documents that are located throughout the Internet. This "Web" of documents extends throughout the Net. While many file types are either displayed within Web browsers or viewed with helper applications, most of the information on Web pages is displayed as text.

Web servers use HTML to store text files for the purpose of formatting text and graphics within a Web browser. Figure 2.2 shows how text and graphics can be formatted to appear within a Web browser window. The use of HTML allows Web designers to apply a variety of styles and formatting to the text within a browser window.

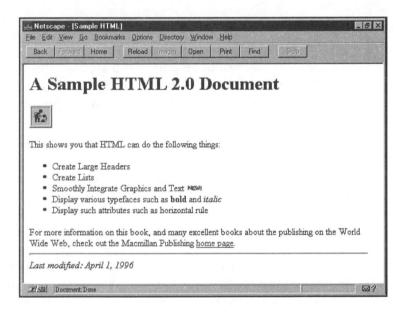

Fig. 2.2
Web files are often constructed using HTML to allow formatting of text and graphics within a Web browser.

Graphics

Figure 2.2 shows how text and graphics can be displayed in the same browser window. Displaying graphics is one of the most appealing features of using the Web. Photographs, clip art, and cartoons can be easily downloaded by Web users. The various features of HTML allow you to display graphics and text in a manner not unlike printed media. This is one reason why the Web is competing with more conventional media for the public's attention.

In the early days of the Web, the Mosaic browser could only display files using the *Graphic Interchange Format* (GIF). This format allows accurate display of simple images such as clip art, cartoons, or text. With the advent of Netscape, an additional graphic format was supported for inline imaging. The *Joint Photographic Expert Group* (JPEG) format is more useful for displaying complicated images, such as photographs and intricate line art, more accurately and in smaller files than can GIF.

> **Tip**
>
> For more information on the pros and cons of using JPEG and GIF images, consult the JPEG FAQ at **http://www.cis.ohio-state.edu/hypertext/faq/usenet/ jpeg-faq/top.html**

Audio

The capability to download audio files using the World Wide Web adds an exciting new dimension to the Internet. Almost any computer with the appropriate software can download sound files from sites that publish them. High-fidelity sound files, such as those sampled from an audio CD, can be quite large even for a few seconds' recording. Some home pages publish greetings from the Webmaster or even the head of the sponsoring organization.

Not all browsers support sounds; helper applications are needed to play the sound files. Sun Microsystems' AU format is a popular means of storing sounds and there are several AU sound players for the Windows platform. Microsoft's Internet Explorer, however, allows you to define a sound to be played when a user accesses one of your pages.

Video

Much like sound, downloading video files through the Web is an exciting means of transferring information. However, like sound files, video files take an enormous amount of space and require a long time to transmit over even high-speed network connections. Downloading movies over a modem connection is nothing short of a tortuous exercise in patience.

Most browsers cannot display movies within the browser; an appropriate helper application is required. Two common formats are the *Motion Pictures Expert Group* (MPEG) and *QuickTime*. More often than not, movie files served via the Web take up a small portion of the desktop so as to conserve file size. Figure 2.3 shows an example of how movie files can be served via the Web. In this example, movies of the same sequence are stored in a variety of formats.

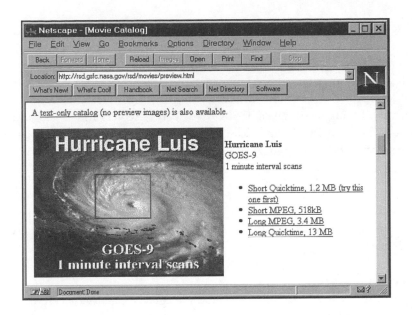

Fig. 2.3
Sites containing weather-related movie files are popular with many Web users. Note the large size of some movie files.

Forms

Soon after the introduction of Mosaic, the HTML 2.0 standard was revised by the W3C to include several new capabilities. The capability to develop interactive forms on a Web page is one of those. Figure 2.4 shows the types of forms that you can use on a Web page to retrieve information from Web users. Users can enter text in text fields and can select options using radio buttons and checkboxes. These devices are available as familiar graphical user interface features on many Windows applications.

▶ See Chapter 14, "HTML Forms," p. 393, for more information on developing your own HTML forms.

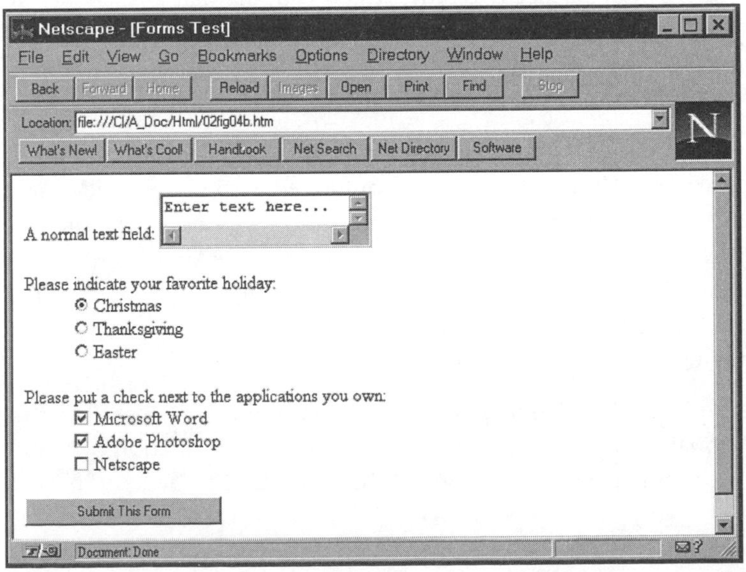

Fig. 2.4
There are several types of HTML forms you can use to retrieve information from Web users.

▶ See "Java," p. 432, for more information about Java.

These forms do not process any of the information they contain. They merely act as a conduit for conveying information to a third-party application on the server. These scripts adhere to the Common Gateway Interface standard and represent a means of processing information retrieved from HTML forms. CGI scripts can be written in almost any language with Perl, C/C++, and UNIX shell being prevalent on UNIX-based WWW servers and C/C++ and Visual Basic being heavily used as scripting languages under Windows-based Web servers. The Java language is also receiving heavy use as a means of customizing Web content.

Using information gleaned from a page containing HTML forms, CGI scripts can send e-mail, search databases, or even create HTML pages to present back to the user. These functions are prevalent throughout the Web in a variety of implementations.

Virtual Reality

One alternative to HTML is the *Virtual Reality Modeling Language* (VRML—rhymes with "thermal")—a draft specification for a language that would publish three-dimensional data over the Internet. HTML allows you to construct a two-dimensional publishing metaphor for graphics and text, but VRML is a totally separate language designed to extend the metaphor to a third dimension. With Netscape and HTML, you meander across a page and click on links and graphics as you see fit. A VRML browser allows you to traverse a hypothetical third-dimension as well. Instead of two-dimensional imagemaps, VRML browsers have hallways that you can traverse much like you would in a virtual reality simulation. You can display information from a variety of three-dimensional perspectives rather than from the rigid display defined by a two-dimensional Web browser. VRML worlds can be supplement HTML documents on the Web. In fact, Microsoft's Internet Explorer Web browser supports VRML through a supplementary plug-in.

Whereas you jump from page to page using HTML, VRML users jump between "worlds." These worlds can be configured with various VRML editors. Loading a world over the Internet requires not much more time than a large graphic does over using HTML. It's possible that with Apple recently releasing QuickDraw 3D, a new 3-D rendering technology, three-dimensional graphics will become more prevalent in the Macintosh environment. Apple is also releasing QuickDraw 3D for Windows.

Programming in VRML is analogous to programming in HTML. The three-dimensional interface leads to new possibilities in information publishing. If you have ever played Doom or one of the 3-D action games, you have seen some of the applications of three-dimensional graphics under Windows. As you explore other VRML worlds, you can think of ways that you can use the three-dimensional metaphor to present information to your users. Examples of this metaphor can include a VR implementation of a library where users can navigate through virtual stacks to browse some of the library selections.

Figure 2.5 shows a sample VRML world in which we see the familiar Netscape "N" in a seemingly three-dimensional perspective. While VRML browsers exist, which interpret the VRML language similar to how Web browsers work with HTML, the world in this figure is displayed using the WebFX plug-in for the Netscape browser. When accessing a VRML world, Netscape launches the plug-in and the navigation bar is displayed at the bottom of the browser window. By operating these controls, a user can traverse the world and access information associated with various aspects of the world.

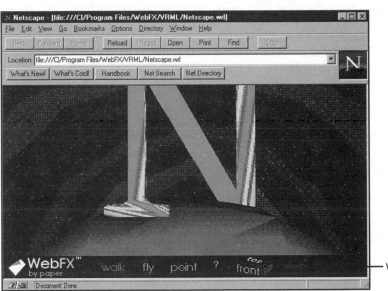

Fig. 2.5
The familiar Netscape "N" is the main attraction in this VRML world. This world is viewed within the Netscape browser using the WebFX Netscape plug-in.

WebFX navigation bar

The application VRserver, by Webmaster, Inc., is a means of transforming your Web file structure into a customized VRML world. VRserver processes your HTML files and directory structure and creates a corresponding world viewable by any VRML browser or VRML-enabled Web browser. The world created by VRserver is an alternative means of presenting your HTML content. The server supports the use of themes that allow you to display your server file structure as a medieval castle or futuristic starship with doors and rooms corresponding to directories and documents.

Custom Web Scripting

▶ See Chapter 16, "More Scripting Options," p. 443, for more discussion on Web scripting including information on using JavaScript and VBScript.

As mentioned above, CGI scripts stand together with HTML and HTTP as the three major components of the World Wide Web. Using CGI scripts, you can customize the type of information you serve to users. The server doesn't process the script instructions but instead passes data from the browser to the script residing on your NT server. The script receives the data, parses the commands into a comprehensible format, and then returns the results in the form of a Web page. Many powerful search engines and other popular devices found on the Web are constructed using CGI scripts.

Binary Data Files

Like other Internet protocols, HTTP is primarily a mechanism for transporting data between two computers. With FTP, a user transfers files and data. Users transfer electronic mail using the Simple Mail Transport Protocol (SMTP). Similarly, graphics, text, and other formatted files are transported via HTTP between Web servers and Web browsers.

You may wish to serve other types of files from the standard JPEG, GIF, HTML, audio formats. For example, you may want to serve Microsoft Word documents or Microsoft Excel spreadsheets to both Macintosh or Windows users. In order to do this, you must tell the browser how to handle these data types. This is accomplished by matching various external applications to the suffixes of the file names.

For example, if you wanted to publish a Microsoft Word file, you would have to tell your server to attach a customized MIME type to the file when responding to a browser request.

The standard MIME type for Microsoft Word files is "application/msword." The browser will have to have this MIME type defined and will have to define Microsoft Word as a helper application for files of this type. Clicking on a link which serves a "*.msw" file causes the server to send the file down to the browser; the browser then launches Microsoft Word to view the document. You can do this for any file for which the browser has a defined MIME type/ subtype.

> **Tip**
>
> You can define other nonstandard MIME types to serve Windows files. The convention is to append an "x" at the front of the MIME subtype. For example, a sample MIME header for a Canvas document would be "application/x-canvas."

Security

Possibly no other aspect of your WWW server requires more attention than security. Depending on whether you wish to provide secure communication through your server or whether you wish to protect certain areas of your server from individuals within your organization, securing your server requires a great deal of planning and forethought. There are hardware options for ensuring secure access to your server, but the measures discussed here are implemented in software.

Securing your server transactions allows you to provide a variety of transactions. For example, you can conduct online business by allowing transmission of financial data such as credit card numbers. You can also protect various documents for viewing by authorized personnel within your organization. The fact that members of your organization can exist outside your local-area network or wide-area network complicates your security concerns.

The security schemes described in this section are new and not yet widely implemented throughout the Web. For this reason, financial transactions over the Web are not occurring in a widespread fashion. Implementation of these schemes will enable a burgeoning world of commerce to develop.

Tip

For a look at how some online transactions are conducted, visit First Virtual at **http://www.fv.com**.

The WWW Security Model

You have several options with which to restrict access to your server. You may wish to restrict access to certain documents to certain users. You may also want to enable access to groups of users. The following sections discuss these options.

Domain Restrictions

By restricting access to your server by domain, you can enable or deny access to large groups of people. For example, if your organization has the Internet address "anywhere.com," you can enable access to your server only to those computers within the "anywhere.com" domain. Users with computers outside this domain could be restricted from accessing your server.

User Authentication

If you desire to further restrict access to your server to smaller groups of users, you can employ some means of authentication. Much like a remote Telnet session, you can require users to enter an account name and password upon accessing certain documents on the server. You can store and access sensitive documents in this manner.

Data Encryption

One way of securing the data on your server is not to alter the data but to encrypt the communication between your server and various Web browsers. The algorithms discussed in this section are used to encrypt HTTP transactions using a variety of methods. Not only does your server need to support these methods but Web browsers must adhere to these standards.

The Secure Sockets Layer Protocol

The Secure Sockets Layer (SSL) Protocol is designed to provide accurate and secure communication between two applications such as your Web server and a Web browser. Implemented by several servers such as WebSite and the Netscape Commerce Server, SSL allows secure communication of financial transactions or a variety of other connection types. SSL is an open protocol and Netscape has recently proposed a standard implementation to the Internet Engineering Task Force.

The SSL protocol is composed of two layers: the SSL Record Protocol and the SSL Handshake Protocol. The *SSL Record Protocol* is used for encapsulation of various higher level protocols. One such encapsulated protocol, the *SSL Handshake Protocol,* allows the WWW server and client to authenticate each other and to negotiate an encryption algorithm and cryptographic keys before the application protocol transmits or receives its first byte of secure data. The advantage of SSL is that it is application-protocol independent. A higher level protocol can layer on top of the SSL Protocol transparently.

The SSL protocol provides connection security with three basic properties:

■ The transmission is private as encryption is used after an initial handshake to define a secret key

■ The connection can be authenticated using popular cryptographic schemes such as RSA or DSS

■ The connection is reliable—a message integrity check is included with the transmission

The advantage of using SSL is that it's a layered protocol. For your Web site, you may want to use SSL to secure your Web connections. However, you could also use SSL to secure UseNet transactions via NNTP. Furthermore, you could use SSL to secure e-mail traffic via SMTP or file transfer via FTP.

Secure-HTTP

Secure-HTTP, or S-HTTP, is an encryption standard designed solely for the purpose of securing HTTP transactions. S-HTTP acts to secure Web connections in three chief ways: signature, encryption, and authentication. You can attach digital signatures to documents using a CGI script. You can encrypt messages using a variety of encryption algorithms, including the very popular PGP. However, one advantage of S-HTTP is that encryption can occur between a server and a client without necessarily requiring a predetermined encryption key. In contrast to a less comprehensive password authentication scheme, S-HTTP authentication requires the unique identifier upon request. Such an authentication scheme might be employed to complete financial transactions.

Overview of Popular Web Browsers

The wild growth of the World Wide Web was spurred by the introduction of the Web browser Mosaic in late 1993 by the National Center for Supercomputing Applications (NCSA) at the University of Illinois. Until the introduction of Mosaic, the Web had languished as a novel but arcane protocol used by academicians. Like the Web itself, Web browser technology has changed rapidly in these last few years. In this section, we'll look at the various Web browsers available to your users.

NCSA Mosaic

As mentioned above, NCSA Mosaic has been in use more than any other browser. Mosaic first introduced millions of Internet users to the linking of graphics and text in a browser window to documents located throughout the Internet. Mosaic's popularity was aided by its cross-platform presence; versions were available for the Windows and MacOS environments in addition to several flavors of UNIX. Mosaic is still maintained by the NCSA and is free to users; the NCSA licenses Mosaic to large institutions. Many browsers are based on the original Mosaic code. However, other commercial browsers, such as Netscape Navigator and Microsoft Internet Explorer, have surpassed Mosaic in terms of speed, versatility, and HTML support. Figure 2.6 shows a sample Mosaic browser window; you can see in this figure that Mosaic supports tables as defined by HTML 2.0.

▶ See "Tables," p. 280, for a discussion of HTML tables.

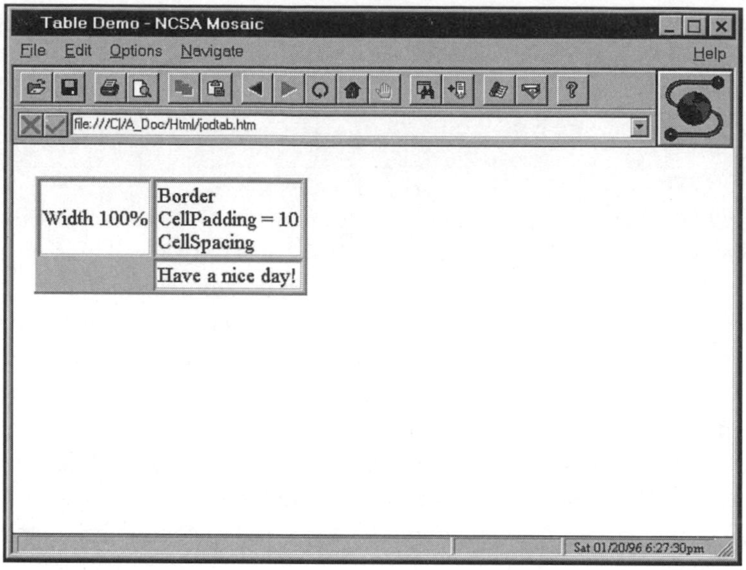

Fig. 2.6
NCSA Mosaic has a similar appearance to other browsers but does not support many of the HTML extensions supported by the Netscape Navigator and Microsoft Internet Explorer browsers.

Netscape

The original developers of Mosaic left the NCSA in 1994 to form what eventually became Wall Street and media darling Netscape Communications. The company's flagship product, the Netscape Navigator Web browser, is estimated to be used by up to 70 percent of all users of the Web. Netscape Navigator was the first browser to allow inline display of graphics written in the JPEG format. Furthermore, the browser originally supported many features contained in the HTML 2.0 proposals. Currently, Navigator supports several of the proposed features described in the HTML 3.0 proposals such as client-side imagemaps and background colors for browser windows. Netscape Navigator also supports encrypted HTTP connections thereby facilitating growth of a booming online transaction market. Using the browser, users are able to send encrypted information for use in online purchases of goods and services.

▶ See "Chapter 11, "HTML 2.0, HTML 3.0, and Extensions," p. 269, for a discussion of frames and other Netscape HTML extensions.

In addition to features outlined in the HTML standards, Netscape has introduced several of their own HTML extensions. For example, with Netscape Navigator, it's possible to arrange your browser windows into partitions or *frames*. As shown in figure 2.7, you can display hypertext and graphics in each of these frames. Browser frames give Web designers yet another means of customizing their pages.

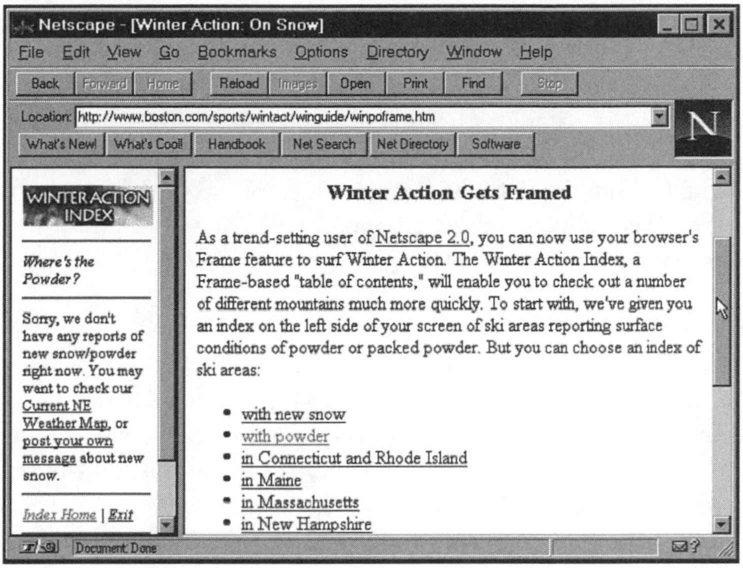

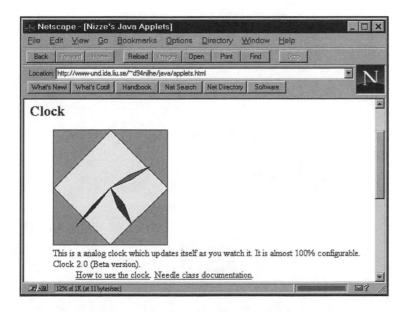

Fig. 2.7
Netscape Navigator frame support allows HTML documents to be split into sections and viewed separately.

Netscape Navigator was also the first Web browser to support the use of Java applets. Few advances in computing have been as hotly anticipated as Sun Microsystem's Java. Using Java, a programming language much like C++, Web designers can develop small applications or *applets* that can interact with a Web browser and perform specific functions. An example of a Java applet is shown in figure 2.8.

Fig. 2.8
Netscape Navigator's support for Java applets allow interactive and dynamic applications such as this analog clock to be built into Web pages.

In this example, there's a large clock in the Web browser window. This image is neither a static GIF nor JPEG images but is instead a dynamic display programmed using the Java language. The applet that created this clock is sent down to the browser along with the HTML code that constructs the page. More complicated Java applets can be developed that will allow users to perform complicated tasks within the browser window. As of this writing, the raw utility of Java applets appears untapped; Java holds great promise as a supplementary extension to HTML.

Internet Explorer

With Netscape dominating the Web browser and server market, slumbering industry giant Microsoft awoke in early 1996 introducing a new Web browser and server to the Internet community. Microsoft Internet Explorer is destined to be one of the more popular Web browsers for several reasons. Not only is the browser easy to use and supported by the world's largest software company, but as a shot across Netscape's bow, it is offered free of charge. In fact, Internet Explorer is bundled with Microsoft Windows 95.

Internet Explorer supports many of the same HTML extensions that Netscape Navigator supports as shown in figure 2.9. The browser also supports many of the HTML 3.0 proposals. In addition, Internet Explorer supports several other specific HTML extensions. These include the following:

- Background sounds played automatically when the Web page is loaded
- Inline animations of AVI files instead of graphic images
- Marquees that scroll across the browser window

Fig. 2.9
Microsoft's Internet Explorer demo page for the fictional "Volcano Coffee Company" shows off many Microsoft-specific HTML enhancements.

Internet Explorer does not support Java (as of this writing) but Microsoft has pledged support for the language in future versions of the browser. Microsoft is also pledging support for its own Visual Basic language as a Java-like support environment.

Other Browsers

Mosaic, Netscape Navigator, and Internet Explorer are by no-means the only entries in the Web browser field. Other members of the NCSA Mosaic team left and formed ventures. Spry and Quarterdeck also maintain popular browsers. Furthermore, the major online services such as America Online, Prodigy, and CompuServe also sport Web browsers for their customers. To some degree, even the pre-Mosaic, text-only browser Lynx is used by Internet users who do not have access to graphical terminals. As both Microsoft and Netscape produce popular browser/server combinations, the Web's near future will likely be charactarized as a struggle between these two companies.

Browser Directions

Not only have the number of browsers multiplied in the years since the introduction of Mosaic, but sophistication of browser technology has grown at a similar breakneck pace. In the early days, browsers simply downloaded text and graphics. Capabilities exist for users to display movies, sounds, Java applets, and other advanced features to the desktop. This section looks at some of this technology.

Plug-In Technology

Netscape Navigator introduced the use of *plug-in* technology to the Web browser market. A *plug-in* is a software module that adds functionality to a larger application. Navigator did not introduce the plug-in concept to the software industry; applications such as Adobe PhotoShop had employed plug-ins long before Navigator. Navigator plug-ins are often developed by third-party programmers for the purposes of adding specific functionality to the browser. For example, Adobe provides the Amber plug-in to provide users with the capability of reading Adobe Acrobat files within the browser window. Apple Computer provides a QuickTime Navigator plug-in allowing Web users to play QuickTime movies. Plug-in technology was introduced with Netscape 2.0 in early 1996 so the limits in range and sophistication of browser plug-in modules are nowhere in sight.

> **Tip**
>
> Examples and listings of available Netscape plug-ins are available at
> **http://home.netscape.com/comprod/products/navigator/version_2.0/
> plugins/index.html**

HTML Versions

As mentioned earlier, HTML is subject to a rigorous standards process sponsored by the W3C. HTML 1.0 was developed in the late 1980s with the dawn of the World Wide Web. The popularity of Mosaic and the Internet in general has accelerated the standards process to some degree. For example, HTML 2.0, which introduced the concepts of HTML forms and other features, was approved in 1994. HTML 3.0 includes many more features such as tables and client-side imagemaps; however, support for these features have already begun to be included in browsers such as Netscape Navigator and Internet Explorer. As of this writing, the HTML 3.0 proposals have not been ratified into a standard implementation.

▶ Refer to Chapter 11, "HTML 2.0, HTML 3.0, and Extensions," p. 269, for more discussion of features included in the different HTML versions.

HTML is a very limited and primitive programming language yielding few capabilities that were not available by 1980s-era word processing applications. It remains to be seen whether the glacial tempo of the HTML standards process will be able to keep pace with the lightning pace of the Web browser market. As seen with Netscape and Microsoft, browser developers may introduce their own features to browsers thereby circumventing or influencing the standards process. The HTML standards may become less of an issue as customized environments using Java applets and plug-in modules become more prevalent. With these extensions, browsers today rely soley on HTML much less than they did before Navigator 2.0. Once again, the relative importance of HTML with respect to advances such as Java and browser plug-ins remains to be seen in the near future.

Graphics and Media

Netscape made a big splash by introducing JPEG inline support for its browser. This was relevant because JPEG provides a better mechanism with which to store photographs and complicated graphical images. Along with graphical images, many Web administrators are posting QuickTime and AVI movies on their systems; in addition, audio files are often used to supplement Web sites. However, the future direction of multimedia support within the browser environment lies with the use of plug-in modules. Multimedia standards come and go and there's a lot of overhead in configuring a browser to natively support each and every one of them. However, the explosive growth of browser plug-in modules provides browser vendors, as well as third-party developers, a means of adding multimedia support to the application. As a Web administrator, you will have many options as to the type of data you wish to make available to your users. However, you will need to keep abreast of the plug-in technology that will allow you to serve multimedia files.

Concerns and Considerations

It's a ruthless Web out there. The viability of your server will depend on your ability to stay current on certain trends and to be aware of various concerns. Some of these issues are discussed below.

Standards

One advantage of a medium like the World Wide Web is its adherence to standards. HTML 2.0 is supported by all major browsers. Similarly, most browsers can interpret GIF and JPEG images within the browser window. The use of standards ensures that a large majority of Web users will be able to access and comprehend your Web pages. The Netscape HTML extensions, and later the extensions introduced by Internet Explorer, show the danger of using such nonstandard features. For example, Netscape users will not be able to see the scrolling marquee you have bouncing back and forth on your Web pages. The balkanization of HTML and other standards is an ominous development that may diminish the Web as a utilitarian platform.

As a Web administrator, your job will be to ensure that your content will be accessible to the widest number of users. Many administrators eschew the use of nonstandard HTML extensions while others leave remarks on their pages denoting the Netscape-specific or Internet Explorer-specific features. As labor-intensive as this may seem, you may be forced to employ such measures to allow full usability of your pages. It will be interesting if, in the near future, Web standards converge or diverge depending on trends and market forces.

Security

The introduction of secure connections using the Web has held out the promise of online transactions. Such transactions would allow financial data to be transferred between a vendor and a buyer. Online catalogs are already in-place where consumers can browse, select, and purchase items through their browser window. However, the general consumer confidence in these transactions is not evident at this time. The methods described above and later in this book are attempts to overcome this concern but the future of online commerce and content security rides on the ability of the Web community to develop secure connections.

▶ See "Protecting Your Data and Your Image," p. 189, for more discussion on server security.

Graphics, Network Speed, and the Web

The explosive popularity of Mosaic largely resulted from its capability to display graphics and text in the same browser window. Using graphics on the World Wide Web added a new dimension of usability to the system. However, the use of graphics was, and still is, restricted by the speed of the user's connection to the Internet. More of a percentage of Internet users are connected by modem than by direct Ethernet, meaning that limitation in network speed is actually more of a concern now than before. Files containing graphic images and other media such as movies and audio files are larger than standard HTML files. Hence, use of these media can be problematic for users with slow network connections.

With telecommuncations reform on the horizon, the promise of high-speed network access seems imminent for many domestic Internet users. Furthermore, new technology may improve network performance for even those users with direct Internet connections. With the immense popularity of the Web and the Internet in general, it's likely that new technologies will be introduced that will exploit this enhanced network performance. ❖

## CHAPTER 3

Setting Up a Web Presence

This chapter discusses the first steps you need to take to create a presence on the Web: getting the connection to the Internet itself, and selecting a system to host your presence. You can follow two basic paths to put your site on the Internet: the first part of this chapter discusses the benefits and costs of each. The second part of the chapter discusses the choices you'll need to make when building the Web server itself. Even if you're setting up an internal Web server with no connection to the Internet, take a look through the section about building the perfect Web server. This chapter also contains some estimates of how much your Web presence can cost; the prices discussed reflect the approximate range of prices these services and systems cost when this chapter was written.

Setting up an Internet Web server can be quite a complex undertaking, and the detailed knowledge required would fill far more than just a single book. This chapter describes important parts of the process and outlines the choices you need to make.

In this chapter, you learn:

- The advantages and disadvantages of hosting your own site or leasing space from a provider
- What kind of Internet connections are available and the hardware they require
- How to select the operating system and hardware for your Web server

Establishing a Presence

There are two basic ways to create a presence on the Web. You can host the site on your own system, or you can have your Internet provider host the site. Each method has its own benefits and costs; the method you choose depends on your needs.

Key Considerations

Putting information on the Web requires a Web server and a system to host that information. The first choice you need to make is whether to support that system yourself—including tending the hardware, configuring and monitoring the server, and installing all the information or services you want to provide to the world—or to lease Web space from your Internet provider and let your provider do all nitty-gritty of running the server. It may sound like a simple choice—after all, why not just sit back and let someone else do all the dirty work? But actually, the choice is a little more complex. The main trade-offs you make when you decide whether to have your provider host your Web site or whether you host the site yourself are *cost* and *control*.

Reviewing and Comparing the Alternatives

When your provider hosts your Web site, the provider takes care of obtaining the hardware, maintaining the system, worrying about security, and may even be able to design and produce your Web pages. Depending on the complexity of your Web site, creating a Web site can be a considerable effort, especially if you need to integrate it with an existing network. Having your provider do all the work can certainly be very convenient. It can, however, also be costly, depending on the number of conveniences you require and the rates your provider charges. When you rely totally on the provider, aside from the content of the information you supply for the Web, you have absolutely no control over your Web site. Your provider may regulate how often you can update your HTML pages, or may prohibit access counters (the "you are visitor number so-and-so" that appears at the bottom of many Web pages) or other on-the-fly page customizations because of system concerns or capabilities. Your provider takes care of all the hardware, including a high-speed 24-hour-a-day connection to the Internet, but if your provider's system goes "off the air," there's nothing you can do about restoring your Web presence.

▶ For more information about writing CGI scripts, see "CGI Scripting," p. 430.

> **Note**
>
> If you're thinking about having your provider host your Web site and you want to provide HTML forms that use CGI scripts, be sure to ask whether your provider will allow you to provide your own scripts. For security reasons, many providers will only host scripts they produce themselves—and will charge you for the time required to develop them.

WebmasterCD

When you host your own Web site, you have total control over all aspects of your site; its features, its services, its hours of operation. You also have total responsibility for its operation (or lack thereof if you run into problems). The highest costs are in setting up the server and the network connection; once the server is up and running, all you'll need to pay will be your Internet connection charge and whatever fees are involved in making the physical connection between your system and the Internet. Your initial cost can be very low—after all, your most crucial software, including the Web server itself, is included on the CD-ROM with this book—or quite high, if you have complex security requirements.

There are a few other factors to consider. If you already have a full-time Internet connection for other purposes (such as FTP or e-mail), you should host your own Web site—most of the hard work of integrating the Internet and your internal network will already have been done. If your needs are very simple—for example, if you just want to host a few pages, want to run the Web server only for limited hours, or if you don't want to connect your Web server to an internal network—you're also a good candidate for your own Web site. Once you have a connection established, setting up the Web server itself is simple.

Finally, you need to consider what kind of information your server might gather as well as what kind it will distribute. If you want to collect sensitive or confidential information (for example, credit card numbers or customer names and addresses), your provider must support secure Web transactions. More importantly, you must be able to trust your provider to keep your confidential information secret. If you don't want to trust your provider with your secrets, you'll need to operate the secure server yourself, which is not a small task.

▶ For more information about transacting business over the Web, see Chapter 21, "Financial Transactions," p. 591.

Credit Card Transactions

Want to take orders using credit card numbers on the Web? It's not as simple as it sounds. You need a server that provides special protection for information exchange (called *secure transport*) using a protocol like SSL or SHTTP. Internet standards for secure transport are still evolving, and security for credit card transactions is a technically thorny issue. If you need this kind of service, think carefully before hosting the site yourself.

Here's a summary of the advantages and disadvantages to hosting your own Web site.

Issue	Your Own Server	Leased Space
Cost	Low to moderate; initially low upkeep (not counting Internet costs, which can run quite high)	Varies widely
Control	You have total control	They have total control
Features	Your site has any features you want	Your site only has features they allow
Security	You must configure; can be extremely difficult	They do it for you
Setting up the Server	Simple to moderately difficult	They do it for you
Setting up the hardware	Can be *very* complicated, especially the Internet connection	They do it for you

Note

There is also a happy medium between having your provider do *all* the work at his own server and setting up a Web site by yourself. Some providers (or other specialists) can assist in the initial setup of the server, including designing Web pages. You can then take over server operations.

The next few sections cover some of the details involved in getting the Internet connection. Leasing space from a provider is explained more fully and the hardware you'll need to make the connection to the Internet yourself is described.

Leasing Space

Leasing space is a popular, easy way to get your presence on the Web quickly. The greatest appeal of leased space is that your provider gives you a high-speed Internet connection, all day, every day. However, your provider's charge for this service may be as much as, or more than, what it would cost you to provide a satisfactory Internet connection, but with the added flexibility that your own server provides.

Working with Leased Space

When you have a leased Web site, you either tell your provider how you want your pages set up, or you create them yourself and send them to your provider, most frequently via FTP.

As was mentioned earlier, a leased Web site can only provide those services that your provider allows. Will your provider allow you to use the forms and scripts you want to use to collect information or provide services? Some don't, for security reasons. Will your provider allow you to use programs (called *server side includes*) or programs such as Java that enable you to create custom Web pages on-the-fly?

Finding a Provider

Finding a provider today is extremely simple, just by using the Internet itself. A search of the Yahoo Web site for "Internet Providers" yields a dizzying array of Internet access providers, Web page designers, and network specialty firms, in every locale and every price range. Some firms provide browser forms for price quotes, or just descriptions of services; others provide full pricing schedules. The following table contains a list of Internet access providers (by the time this book is printed, more providers may be available).

Finding service providers on the Web is relatively easy. The National Center for Supercomputing Applications, which developed Mosaic, maintains a list of Web service providers at **http:// union.ncsa.uiuc.edu/HyperNews/get/www/leasing.html**. The Directory of WWW Service Providers at **ftp://ftp.einet.net/ pub/INET-MARKETING/www-svc-providers** is another excellent resource containing Web consultants as well as service providers. This list is included as PROVIDER.HTM on WebmasterCD; table 3.1 summarizes the list. All providers in the U.S. who offer basic Web page serving and listed a Web address are included, along with the area codes they serve if local dial-up Internet access is also offered. Because the Web is growing so rapidly, it would be a good idea to check these lists often.

Table 3.1 WWW Service Providers

H=HTML Authoring/Web Application Development
C=CGI Script Processing
S=WAIS or other search capabilities offered
P=Prebuilt applications
Speed=Speed of service provider's connection to the Internet
Area=Area code(s) served in part or in whole by local dial-up
access. If no area code is listed, provider either offers national
dial-up access or none at all.

Name and URL	Services	Speed	Area
Computer Solutions by Hawkinson **http://www.mhv.net/**	HP	T1	914
Telerama Public Access Internet **http://www.lm.com/**	HCSP	T1	412
Quantum Networking Solutions **http://www.gcr.com**	HC	14K	
Internet Presence & Publishing, Inc. **http://www.ip.net/**	HCSP	T1	804
Computing Engineers, Inc. **http://www.wwa.com/**	HCSP	56K	312, 708
South Valley Internet **http://www.garlic.com**	CS	56K	408
Branch Information Services **http://branch.com**	HCSP	T1	313
APK, Public Access UNI*. **http://www.wariat.org**	HS		216
Internet Distribution Services, Inc. **http://www.service.com/**	HCSP	T1	415
Cyberspace Development, Inc. **http://marketplace.com**	HS	T1	
BEDROCK Information Solutions, Inc. **http://www.bedrock.com/**	HCS	T1	
Electric Press, Inc. **http://www.elpress.com**	HCSP	T1	
Quadralay Corporation **http://www.quadralay.com/ home.html**	HCSP	T1	
Downtown Anywhere Inc. **http://www.awa.com/**	HCSP	frac. T1	

Name and URL	Services	Speed	Area
Internet Marketing Inc. **http://cybersight.com/** **cgi-bin/imi/s?main.gmml**	HCS	T1	
The New York Web **http://nyweb.com**	HCSP	T1	
The Sphere Information Services **http://www.thesphere.com**	HC	56K	
The Computing Support Team, Inc. **http://www.gems.com/**	HCS	T1	
The Internet Group **http://www.tig.com/**	HCS	T1	
Lighthouse Productions **http://netcenter.com**	HP	115K	
Catalog.Com Internet Services **http://www.catalog.com**	T1		
Great Basin Internet Services **http://www.greatbasin.net/**	HCSP	56K	702
Net+Effects **http://www.net.effects.com**	HCSP	14K	
XOR Network Engineering **http://plaza.xor.com/**	HCS		
BizNet Technologies **http://www.biznet.com.** **blacksburg.va.us/**	HCSP	T1	
Sell-it on the WWW **http://www.electriciti.com/**	H	T1	
RTD Systems & Networking, Inc. **http://www.rtd.com/**	HCP	T1	602
Atlantic Computing Technology Corporation **http://www.atlantic.com/**	HCSP	56K	
InterNex Information Services, Inc. **http://www.internex.net/**	HCS	T1	510, 415, 408
Teleport, Inc. **http://www.teleport.com**	56k	503, 206	
QuakeNet **http://www.quake.net/**	H	T1	415
Internet Information Services, Inc. **http://www.iis.com**	HCSP	T1	301, 410, 703
CyberBeach Publishing **http://www.gate.net/**	HCSP	T1	305, 407, 813, 904

(continues)

Table 3.1   Continued

Name and URL	Services	Speed	Area
Primenet **http://www.primenet.com/**	HCP	T1	602
TAG Systems inc. **http://www.tagsys.com/**	HC	56K	
Internet Information Systems **http://www.internet-is.com/**	HCS	frac. T1	
Stelcom, Inc. **http://www.webscope.com**	HC	frac. T1	
Coolware Inc. **http://none.coolware.com/**	HCS	56K	
IDS World Network Internet Access Services **http://www.ids.net**	HCSP	T1	401, 305, 407, 914
SenseMedia Publishing **http://www.picosof.com**	H	T1	408
Home Pages, Inc. **http://www.homepages.com**	HCSP	128K	
TeleVisions Inc. **http://www.tvisions.com**	H	T1	
Internet Services Corporation **http://www.netservices.com/**	HCSP	T1	
EarthLink Network, Inc. **http://www.earthlink.net**	HC	T1	213, 310, 818
New Jersey Computer Connection **http://www.njcc.com**	H	56K	609
CTS Network Services **http://www.cts.com**	HCSP	T1	619
The Tenagra Corporation **http://arganet.tenagra.com/** **Tenagra/tenagra.html**	HCS	T1	

Costs

The recent competition for Internet services, and the (relatively) low cost of the necessary technology, has lowered the prices and raised the quality of Internet service in general, but prices and services vary widely from provider to provider. For example, one provider offers a wide range of prices, from an extremely low rate for very small businesses (a little over $200 setup charge and around $30 per month) to a high rate for large, high-volume sites (almost $6,000 setup and nearly $2,000 per month). Some providers have fixed rates; others charge by the number of page accesses or by the amount of data the server transmits. Providers also have a range of "package deals" with varying degrees of flexibility and services, ranging from a simple "you upload it, we publish it" to page design and application programming.

> **Tip**
>
> It definitely pays to shop around for Internet services, even for simple personal access. A savings of even $20 per month adds up quickly. And don't be afraid to look outside your geographical area for low-cost services. Remember, it's the *World Wide* Web, and if you have local Internet access yourself, you can FTP your pages to a provider's server in another state as easily as you can to one across the street.

Concerns and Advantages

Leasing your presence on a provider's Web server provides an easy way to establish your presence on the Web, but one with many constraints and one that may not be cost-effective for your needs. If you don't want to hassle with network connections, server security, and system maintenance, and don't mind giving up control of your Web presence, this is definitely the way to go. If you already have the Internet connection, or can't find a provider package that suits your needs or your budget, consider running your own server.

Connecting Your Own Web Server

If you decide to host your own Internet server, you will need to provide your own Internet connection. Again, this is something that is best done by professionals, and a good Internet access provider will be able to do most of the dirty work for you. This section is intended to give you an overview of some of your choices.

All Internet connections have several costs, all of which add up alarmingly quickly:

- The hardware required to make the connection itself—ranging from a simple plug-in modem to multiple routers and other network connectivity devices
- The provider's setup cost (sometimes includes the service charge for installing equipment at your site, sometimes doesn't)
- The cost of the Internet service itself
- The price of the physical connection to the Internet—ranging from an ordinary phone line to special data lines

Of course, the faster and the more complex the connection, the more expensive it will be.

Connection Types: Switched versus Leased

There are two basic types of Internet connection: *switched connections,* which use some sort of intermediary technology between your system and the Internet, and *leased lines,* a direct network connection to the Internet itself.

Leased lines are the method of choice for anyone needing full-time high-speed connections. Leased lines are the fastest type of Internet connection— they are also the most expensive. Connecting a high-speed leased line to your system is probably the single-most complicated operation in the entire Web server setup process, and you will need to budget plenty of time–and money to make that connection.

A slow leased line (56 kbps, about twice as fast as a standard 28.8 kbps modem) provides more than enough bandwidth for e-mail and news, but is not much faster than a regular home dial-up connection when transmitting heavy graphics.

The most common leased-line connection is a T1, which has a very respectable data rate of 1,544 kbps (more than 50 times faster than a 28.8 kbps modem). T1s provide enough bandwidth for dozens of Web servers, so several users can each use only a part of the T1, sharing the bandwidth as well as the cost. A full T1 connection costs between $1,000 and $3,000 per month, not including the cost of the leased line (which can be as much again as the Internet access charge). Many providers offer fractional T1 lines in 256 kbps increments. There are other connections available (such as T2 or T3), but these ultra-high traffic lines are used only in special installations or between Internet access providers on the Internet backbone.

Leased lines can't just be plugged into a network card on the back of your computer; they require additional hardware, the most important being a *router,* a device that controls the flow of data between the Internet and your local network or system. Cost for routers (not always including installation and support) range from $1,000 to $4,000. Routers can be crucial components in your network security system, and the more protection your internal network requires, the more important your routers become.

Leased lines also require a *Channel Service Unit/Data Service Unit* (CSU/DSU or just CSU) installed between the leased line and the router. CSUs run from around $300 to around $3,000, depending on the speed you require.

> **Tip**
>
> Leave a little "room to grow" when you purchase your router and CSU; you can often save upgrade costs later by spending a little more up front for higher speed equipment.

If you want to run a high-volume server with heavy graphics, you will probably need a leased line of some kind. However, in addition to these traditional solutions, there are several alternative technologies that you might explore if you don't require leased lines' ultra-high speeds (or can't afford leased lines' high costs). Table 3.2 has a list of leased-line providers; be sure to shop around for the best rates.

Table 3.2   Leased Line Providers in the United States

The following information is taken from the InterNIC Leased Line Providers List that is published by the InterNIC, a project of the National Science Foundation, and is reprinted here with permission. Some of the entries have been modified to reflect new information and addresses.

===

InterNIC Information Services E-mail: info@internic.net
General Atomics (GA)   Phone: (619) 455-4600
P.O. Box #85608   Fax: (619) 455-4640
San Diego, CA 92186-9784

InterNIC Internet Service Providers List: Leased Line Only (United States)

Permission for noncommercial distributions is granted, provided that this file is distributed intact, including the acknowledgment, disclaimer, and copyright notice found at the end of this document.

****

Adhesive Media, Inc.
Eden Matrix Online Service
Aubrey McAuley
adhesive-media@eden.com

Texas
(512) 478-9900 x200 (PHONE)
(512) 478-9934 (FAX)

AlterNet
alternet-info@uunet.uu.net

United States and International
(800) 4UUNET3 (PHONE)

American Information Systems
Josh Schneider
schneid@ais.net

Illinois
(708) 413-8400 (PHONE)
(708) 413-8401 (FAX)

ANS
Sales and Information
info@ans.net
http://www.ans.net

United States and International
(800) 456-8267 (PHONE)
(703) 758-7717 (FAX)

APK Public Access
Zbigniew Tyrlik
support@wariat.org

Ohio
(216) 481-9428 (PHONE)

BBN BARRNet, Inc
John Toth
info@barrnet.net

California, Nevada
(415) 528-7111 (PHONE)
(415) 934-2665 (FAX)

(continues)

Table 3.2   Continued

Beckemeyer Development Sales **info@bdt.com**	California (510) 530-9637 (PHONE) (510) 530-0451 (FAX)
CCnet Communications Information **info@ccnet.com**	California (510) 988-0680 (PHONE) (510) 988-0689 (FAX)
CERFnet CERFnet Hotline **sales@cerf.net**	Western US and International (800) 876-2373 (PHONE) (619) 455-3900 (PHONE) (619) 455-3990 (FAX)
CICnet Marketing and Sales Dept. **info@cic.net**	Midwestern United States (800) 947-4754 (PHONE) (313) 998-6703 (PHONE) (313) 998-6105 (FAX)
Clark Internet Services ClarkNet Office **info@clark.net**	Northeastern United States (800) 735-2258 (PHONE) (410) 254-3900 (PHONE) (410) 730-9765 (FAX)
Cloud 9 Internet Scott Drassinower **scottd@cloud9.net**	New York (914) 696-4000 (PHONE) (914) 696-4050 (FAX)
Supernet, Inc Anthony Rael **info@csn.net** **www.csn.net**	Colorado (303) 296-8202 x124 (PHONE) (303) 296-8224(FAX)
Connix Jim Hogue **office@connix.com**	Connecticut (860) 349-7059 (PHONE)
CRL Network Services Sales **sales@crl.com** **info@crl.com**	California (415) 837-5300 (PHONE)
CTS Network Services Sales **support@cts.com**	California (619) 637-3637 (PHONE) (619) 637-3630 (FAX)
CyberGate, Inc. Dan Sullivan **sales@gate.net**	Florida (305) 428-4283 (PHONE) (305) 428-7977 (FAX)
DFW Internet Services, Inc. Jack Beech **sales@dfw.net**	Texas (817) 332-5116 (PHONE) (817) 870-1501 (FAX)
DIGEX Sales **sales@digex.net** **info@digex.net**	United States/International (800) 99DIGIX (PHONE) (301) 847-5000 (PHONE) (301) 847-5215 (FAX)
EarthLink Network, Inc. Sky Dayton **info@earthlink.net**	California (213) 644-9500 (PHONE) (213) 644-9510 (FAX)

Edge Internet Services
Tim Choate
info@edge.net
tchoate@edge.net

Escape (Kazan Corp)
Sales
info@escape.com

Evergreen Internet
Phil Broadbent
sales@libre.com

Florida Online
Jerry Russell
jerry@digital.net

HoloNet
HoloNet Staff
support@holonet.net
http://www.holonet.net/

Global Internet Network Services
Network Information Center
info@gi.net

Global Enterprise Services
Sergio Heker, President
market@jvnc.net

IACNet
Devon Sean McCullough
info@iac.net

ICNet
Ivars Upatnieks
info@ic.net

IDS World Network
Information
info@ids.net

Innovative Data Services
Sales
info@id.net

INTAC Access Corporation
Sales
info@intac.com

InterAccess
Lev Kaye
info@interaccess.com

The Internet Access Company
Sales
info@tiac.net

Internet Atlanta
Dorn Hetzel
info@atlanta.com

Tennessee
(615) 726-8700 (PHONE)
(615) 726-0665 (FAX)

New York
(212) 888-8780 (PHONE)
(212) 832-0344 (FAX)

Arizona
(602) 230-9330 (PHONE)
(602) 230-9773 (FAX)

Florida
(407) 635-8888 (PHONE)
(407) 635-9050 (FAX)

North America
(510) 704-0160 (PHONE)
(510) 704-8019 (FAX)

(800) 682-5550 (PHONE)
(402) 436-3030 (FAX)

United States and International
(800) 35-TIGER (PHONE)
(609) 897-7310 (FAX)

Ohio
(513) 887-8877 (PHONE)

Michigan, Ohio
(313) 998-0090 (PHONE)

Northeastern United States
(800) IDS-1680 (PHONE)

Michigan
(810) 478-3554 (PHONE)
(810) 478-2950 (FAX)

New Jersey
(201) 944-1417 (PHONE)
(201) 944-1434 (FAX)

Illinois
(800) 967-1580 (PHONE)
(708) 498-3289 (FAX)

Massachusetts
(617) 276-7200 (PHONE)
(617) 275-2224 (FAX)

Georgia
(404) 410-9000 (PHONE)
(404) 410-9005 (FAX)

(continues)

Table 3.2   Continued

Internet Channel, Inc. Tony Walters **sales@internet-channel.net**	U.S./Worldwide (803) 722-7900 (PHONE) (803) 722-4488 (FAX)
Internet Express Customer Service **service@usa.net**	Colorado (800) 592-1240 (PHONE) (719) 592-1201 (FAX)
Internet On-Ramp, Inc. Sales **sales@on-ramp.ior.com**	Washington (509) 624-RAMP (PHONE) (509) 323-0116 (FAX)
Internetworks Internetworks, Inc. **info@i.net** **ftp.i.net:/pub/internetworks**	United States and Pacific Rim (503) 233-4774 (PHONE) (503) 614-0344 (FAX)
Interport Communications Corp Sales and Information **info@interport.net** **http://www.interport.net**	New York (212) 989-1128 (PHONE)
IQuest Network Services Robert Hoquim **info@iquest.net**	Indiana (800) 844-UNIX (PHONE) (317) 259-5050 (PHONE) (317) 259-7289 (FAX)
KAIWAN Internet **info@kaiwan.com**	California (714) 260-8888 (PHONE) (714) 260-8877 (FAX)
LI Net, Inc. Michael Reilly **questions@li.net**	New York (516) 265-0997 x101 (PHONE)
Lightside, Inc. Fred Condo **lightside@lightside.com** **http://www.lightside.net/**	California (818) 858-9261 (PHONE) (818) 858-8982 (FAX)
Los Nettos Joe Kemp **los-nettos-info@isi.edu** **http://www.isi.edu/ln**	Southern California (310) 822-1511 (PHONE) (310) 823-6714 (FAX)
netMAINE, Inc. Andy Robinson **sales@maine.net**	Maine (207) 780-6381 (PHONE) (207) 780-6301 (FAX)
MCSNet Karl Denninger **info@mcs.net**	Illinois (312) 248-8649 (PHONE) (312) 248-9865 (FAX)
MichNet/Merit Recruiting Staff **info@merit.edu**	Michigan (800) 682-5550 (PHONE) (313) 764-9430 (PHONE) (313) 747-3185 (FAX)
Minnesota Regional Network (MRNet) Dennis Fazio **info@mr.net**	Minnesota (612) 342-2570 (PHONE) (612) 342-2873 (FAX)

MSEN
Owen S. Medd
info@msen.com

Michigan
(313) 998-4562 (PHONE)
(313) 998-4563 (FAX)

MV Communications
Sales
info@mv.mv.com

New Hampshire
(603) 429-2223 (PHONE)

NEARNET
NEARNET Information Hotline
nearnet-join@near.net

Northeastern United States
(617) 873-8730 (PHONE)
(617) 873-5620 (FAX)

NetAxis
Luis Hernandez
luis@eliza.netaxis.com

Connecticut
(203) 969-0618 (PHONE)
(203) 921-1544 (FAX)

NETCOM On-line Communications Services
Business or Personal Sales
info@netcom.com

United States
(800) 353-6600 (PHONE)
(408) 983-5950 (PHONE)
(408) 241-9145 (FAX)

netILLINOIS
Peter Roll
info@illinois.net

Illinois
(708) 866-1804 (PHONE)
(708) 866-1857 (FAX)

Network Intensive
Sales and Information
info@ni.net
http://www.ni.net/

California and New Mexico
(714) 450-8400 (PHONE)
(800) 273-5600 (PHONE)
(714) 450-8410 (FAX)

New Mexico Technet, Inc.
Marianne Granoff
granoff@technet.nm.org

New Mexico and Navajo Reservation
(incl: AZ, UT, CO Reservations)
(505) 345-6555 (PHONE)
(505) 345-6559 (FAX)

New York Net
Bob Tinkelman
sales@new-york.net

New York
(718) 776-6811 (PHONE)
(718) 217-9407 (FAX)

Northcoast Internet
support@northcoast.com

California
(707) 443-8696 (PHONE)
(707) 441-0321 (FAX)

NorthWest CommLink
Garlend Tyacke
gtyacke@nwcl.net

Washington
(206) 336-0103 (PHONE)
(206) 336-2339 (FAX)

Northwest Nexus, Inc.
Information
info@nwnexus.wa.com
support@halcyon.com

Washington
(206) 455-3505 (PHONE)
(206) 455-4672 (FAX)

NorthwestNet
Sales and Information
info@nwnet.net

Northwestern United States
(206) 649-7400 (PHONE)
(206) 649-7451 (FAX)

NYSERNet
Sales
info@nysernet.org

New York
(315) 453-2912 (PHONE)
(315) 453-3052 (FAX)

OARnet
Larry L. Buell
info@oar.net

Ohio
(614) 728-8100 (PHONE)
(614) 728-8110 (FAX)

(continues)

Table 3.2   Continued

Old Colorado City Communications L.S. Fox **thefox@oldcolo.com**	Colorado (719) 528-5849 (PHONE) (719) 528-5869 (FAX)
Panix New User Staff **info-person@panix.com**	New York City, Nassau County in Long Island, Jersey City, NJ (212) 741-4400 (PHONE) (212) 741-5311 (FAX)
Ping Brett Koller **bdk@ping.com**	Georgia (404) 399-1670 (PHONE) (404) 399-1671 (FAX)
Pioneer Global Craig Komins **sales@pn.com** **http://www.pn.com**	Massachusetts (617) 375-0200 (PHONE) (617) 375-0201 (FAX)
Planet Access Networks Fred Laparo **fred@planet.net** **http://www.planet.net**	New Jersey (201) 691-4704 (PHONE) (201) 691-7588 (FAX)
PREPnet **nic@prep.net** **http://www.prep.net**	Pennsylvania (412) 268-7870 (PHONE) (412) 268-7875 (FAX)
Primenet Clay Johnston **info@primenet.com**	Arizona (602) 870-1010 x109 (PHONE) (602) 870-1010 (FAX)
PSINet PSI, Inc. **info@psi.com**	United States and International (800) 82PSI82 (PHONE) (703) 709-0300 (PHONE) (800) FAXPSI1 (FAX)
QuakeNet Sales **info@quake.net**	California (415) 655-6607 (PHONE) (415) 377-0635 (FAX)
The Rabbit Network, Inc. Customer Liaison Services **info@rabbit.net**	Michigan (800) 456-0094 (PHONE) (810) 790-0156 (FAX)
Red River Net Craig Lien **lien@rrnet.com**	Minnesota, North and South Dakota (701) 232-2227 (PHONE)
Rocky Mountain Internet, Inc. Rick Mount **info@rmii.com**	Colorado (800) 900-RMII (PHONE) (719) 576-0301 (FAX)
Scruz-Net Matthew Kaufman **info@scruz.net**	California (800) 319-5555 (PHONE) (408) 457-5050 (PHONE) (408) 457-1020 (FAX)
SeaNet Igor Klimenko **igor@seanet.com**	Seattle (206) 343-7828 (PHONE) (206) 628-0722 (FAX)

Sibylline, Inc.
Dan Faules
info@sibylline.com

Arkansas
(501) 521-4660 (PHONE)
(501) 521-4659 (FAX)

SIMS, Inc.
Natalie Carrigan
info@sims.net

South Carolina
(803) 853-4333 (PHONE)
(803) 722-4488 (FAX)

South Coast Computing Services, Inc.
Sales
sales@sccsi.com

Texas
(713) 917-5000 (PHONE)
(713) 917-5005 (FAX)

SprintLink
SprintLink
info@sprintlink.net

United States and International
(800) 817-7755 (PHONE)
(703) 904-2680 (FAX)

SuperNet, Inc.
Anthony Rael
info@csn.net
www.csn.net

Colorado
(303) 296-8202 x124 (PHONE)
(303) 296-8224 (FAX)

SURAnet
Kimberly Donaldson
kdonalds@sura.net

Southeastern US, South America,
Puerto Rico
(301) 982-4600 (PHONE)
(301) 982-4605 (FAX)

Synergy Communications
Sales Department
info@synergy.net

United States
(402) 346-4638 (PHONE)
(402) 346-0208 (FAX)

Telerama Public Access Internet
Scott Brown
sysop@telerama.lm.com
http://www.lm.com/~scott

Pennsylvania
(412) 481-3505 (PHONE)
(412) 481-8568 (FAX)

THEnet (Connectivity for
education and government)
Frank Sayre
f.sayre@utexas.edu

Texas
(512) 471-2444 (PHONE)
(512) 471-2449 (FAX)

ThoughtPort Authority Inc.
David Bartlett
info@thoughtport.com

National
(314) 474-6870 (PHONE)
(800) ISP-6870 (PHONE)
(314) 474-4122 (FAX)

UltraNet Communications, Inc.
Sales
info@ultranet.com

Massachusetts
(508) 229-8400 (PHONE)
(800) 763-8111 (PHONE)
(508) 229-2375 (FAX)

US Net, Inc.
Services
info@us.net

Eastern United States
(301) 572-5926 (PHONE)
(301) 572-5201 (FAX)

VERnet
James Jokl
net-info@ver.net

Virginia
(804) 924-0616 (PHONE)
(804) 982-4715 (FAX)

ViaNet Communications
Joe McGuckin
info@via.net

California
(415) 903-2242 (PHONE)
(415) 903-2241 (FAX)

(continues)

Table 3.2 Continued

VNET Internet Access, Inc. PO Box 31474 Charlotte, NC 28231 **info@vnet.net**	National (800) 377-3282 (PHONE)
WestNet Lillian or Chris **staff@westnet.com**	Western United States (914) 967-7816 (PHONE)
WiscNet Network Information Center **wn-info@nic.wiscnet.net**	Wisconsin (608) 262-4241 (PHONE) (608) 262-4679 (FAX)
WLN (Western Library Network) Kate Wakefield **info@wln.com** **http://www.wln.com/**	Washington (800) DIAL-WLN (PHONE) (360) 923-4000 (PHONE) (360) 923-4009 (FAX)
WorldWide Access Stephen Moscarelli **sales@wwa.com**	Illinois (312) 803-9921 (PHONE) (312) 803-9923 (FAX)
XMission Support **support@xmission.com**	Utah (801) 539-0852 (PHONE) (801) 539-0853 (FAX)

****

Acknowledgment and Disclaimer

This material is based on work sponsored by the National Science Foundation under Cooperative Agreement No. NCR-9218749. The Government has certain rights in this material. Any opinions, findings, and conclusions or recommendations expressed in this material are those of the author(s) and do not necessarily reflect the views of the National Science Foundation, General Atomics, AT&T, or Network Solutions Inc.

Frame Relay

Frame relay is an interesting new technology that attempts to maximize the way systems use communications bandwidth. Here's an extremely simplified example of how frame relay works. Imagine a typical telephone conversation: at some point in the conversation, you pause a moment to collect your thoughts. While you're *not* speaking, the phone line is still dedicated to your conversation; while you're silent, your telephone is still sending data (it's just silent data, if you will).

In a frame relay system, while you were pausing to think, the system "loans" your phone line to another conversation, and restores your connection as soon as you began talking again. This way, the phone circuits can be kept busy, even while you're not using them. Now imagine that instead of waiting for a long pause in the conversation, the frame relay system was able to "borrow" the phone line between the sentences, even the words, of your conversation. By switching rapidly during the pauses between several conversations, the same phone line can carry several conversations at once, while maintaining the integrity of each conversation.

Frame relay systems are fast and efficient, and can run between 56 mbps and 512 mbps (equivalent to about half a T1). Some of its proponents claim that frame relay can support speeds up to 50 mbps, about the same speed as the Internet backbone itself.

Tip

For more information about frame relay technology, see the Frame Relay Forum's Web site at **http://frame-relay.indiana.edu/**.

Hardware/Software. Frame relay is a cooperative system; not only do you need the appropriate frame relay access equipment, but your provider must be able to support the system. To use a frame relay system, you'll need a router and possibly other hardware. Some routers are frame-relay compliant, as are some network switches. You don't need any additional network software on your server machine besides Windows' built-in network support.

Costs. Costs vary significantly, as do pricing schemes, ranging from fixed price for a particular amount of service, or a per-data-transmitted price. Initial costs can run to more than $5,000; the frame relay connection fee itself can vary from around $200 to $1,000, depending on the provider and the speed of the connection you select—and of course, there's also the cost of the physical frame relay line, which varies from region to region.

Concerns. Frame Relay is becoming a stable and reliable alternative to leased-line technology. The major concern working with frame relay is whether your provider supports it, and whether you can support its cost.

ISDN

Unlike the other technologies discussed so far, *ISDN* (Integrated Services Digital Network) is a dial-up service. The technology has been around for years, but it is recently becoming popular, especially for users that need a high-speed on-demand Internet connection. ISDN service provides two channels, each of which can be used for voice or data. By combining both channels, it's possible to achieve a total data rate of 128 kbps (about four times faster than an ordinary 28.8 kbps modem).

Hardware/Software. ISDN requires a special ISDN modem, but not necessarily a special line; usually, an ordinary phone line will work. The ISDN modem replaces the ordinary modem, and plugs right into your system.

Costs. ISDN modems cost significantly less than router systems—you can get ISDN modems for between $200 and $300. There is a monthly charge for the ISDN service, and a charge per minute. Essentially, ISDN service is just an extremely expensive phone call, and is billed as such.

Concerns. ISDN is extremely cost-effective for brief, high-speed connections, but a poor choice for full-time Web servers. A 24-hour ISDN connection would run charges up quickly. At just $2 per hour, ISDN costs $48 per day, $336 per week, $1,344 per month—which turns out to be about as much as the initial set-up charge for some leased-line services. If you want to operate your server for just a few hours a day, ISDN may be a good idea—if you plan to keep the connection open longer than that, you should probably investigate a leased-line solution. ISDN is also not a universally offered service, even by the major providers.

Analog Modem

The analog modem is the workhorse of the typical Web user; fast, inexpensive analog modems have made the wide audience of the Web possible. And, yes indeed, you can run a Web server with just a basic analog modem—but at a price of performance.

Hardware/Software. Modems are extremely inexpensive for their capabilities. Prices being as low as they are, you should get the fastest modem you can: 28.8 kbps. You need no additional software other than that supplied by Windows or NT (although Windows 95 Plus! package does make dial-up networking significantly easier).

Costs. Fast analog modems at this writing were available in the $140-300 range. If you are selecting a modem for a Web server, don't pay extra for voice mail or fax capabilities—you won't be using them.

Given the popularity of the home and home-business Web server, some providers are beginning to offer 24-hour SLIP/PPP access, as low as $50-60 per month. A single dedicated phone line is usually very inexpensive, but you might want to speak to your phone company about whether a special rate is available for 24-hour calls.

Concerns. The single greatest concern of the modem-based server is speed. How many times have you sat watching the download counter on your personal Internet account, wishing that your 28.8 kbps modem was faster? You may be able to run a very simple text-only Web site over a 28.8 kbps modem, but if you intend to offer high graphics or multimedia-like imagemaps, an ordinary modem is just too slow.

Building the Perfect Server

If you're going to host your own Web site (whether on an internal network or on the Internet), you will need a system to run the server and to store whatever Web pages you want to provide. If you've done any computer shopping recently, you know that getting the "latest and greatest" can run up costs in a hurry. However, with careful shopping—and careful consideration of your needs, you can obtain a more-than-satisfactory system at a very reasonable price.

Key Considerations

There are two main considerations in building a server system:

- How much traffic do you expect to support?
- Can your system grow as your needs grow?

The capacity of your system must be matched to the amount of traffic you expect to support. If you're running an Internet server, response to customer's requests is crucial; a slow server makes a poor impression. You must also look at your future needs and select a path you can follow if you need to upgrade to a larger system.

Operating System

The first choice you will need to make is what operating system to use. All three systems are multitasking 32-bit operating systems, and the server software itself will run just as well on Windows 95, Windows NT Workstation, and Windows NT Server. There are, however, several other considerations.

Windows 95 is the least expensive of the three systems; it's the fastest, has a very zoomy user interface, supports long file and folder names, is reasonably easy to configure, and provides many other conveniences that make it an enjoyable user platform. Windows 95 is also the youngest of the three systems, and it's having its fair share of growing pains, both on the hardware and software level. It's designed primarily as a personal system, and as such, does not have heavy emphasis on security. If you're on an extremely tight budget, you can run a Web server quite acceptably on a Windows 95 system, but you make a tradeoff in not having the sort of robust system that Windows NT can provide.

"Robust" is a very good word for Windows NT Workstation. Its user interface is almost identical to Windows 3.1, and if you're used to Windows 95, you may feel as if you're taking a step backwards to Windows NT—not so! Moving to NT, you pay a small price in speed and interface, but it's more than made up in sturdiness. One NT user on the Internet reported that he had not rebooted his machine once in the last two *years*. Windows NT has superior multitasking capabilities, supports multiple CPUs, and has an extremely configurable security system (which can be extremely important in an internal network environment). Windows NT installs simply, but, unlike its humbler relatives, Windows 3.1 and Windows 95, Windows NT is very hard to fine-tune, and optimizing Windows NT can be a quite arcane art. Windows NT Workstation requires more memory than Windows 95 to affect the same speed of performance, but your investment is more than returned in the stability of the system.

> **Caution**
>
> There is currently a Windows 95 "shell" you can run under regular Windows NT. Some users have reported difficulties with this add-on shell. We recommend that you do not use this add-on; the price you pay in convenience in using NT's "old" Windows interface is more than made up in the stability of a proven system.
>
> Microsoft is currently developing a new version of Windows NT with more of a Windows 95 "feel;" upgrades should be available in just a few months.

Windows NT Server has the same iron-clad constitution as Windows NT, but with several additional services. Windows NT Server is designed to run on a network's central hardware platform, and as such supports many remote access and administration services.

The price difference between each platform is significant. You can buy Windows 95 almost anywhere for $89; Windows NT Workstation retails for around $500; and Windows NT Server costs over $1,600.

For most Web server applications, Windows NT Workstation is the recommended platform. Windows NT Server has more power than most Web installations require, unless you need to use the same system as a server for several different applications. Windows 95 is sufficient for home or small servers; but Windows NT's muscle and reliability are worth the extra investment.

Once you select your operating system, you need to select the hardware to run that system.

> **Caution**
>
> Microsoft provides a hardware compatibility list for Windows NT. We strongly recommend that you follow Microsoft's recommendations when selecting hardware for an NT system. Windows NT functions *very unpredictably* on incompatible hardware.

CPU

The CPU is the heart of your system; it determines not just the speed of your system, but the path you will take for future upgrades. There are really only two choices for the CPU: a 486-class CPU, or a Pentium-class CPU.

The 486-class CPU is by far the cheaper solution; a 486DX4/100 can cost just a little over $100. 486 systems are well-suited for smaller, low-traffic servers, where raw computing power isn't a necessity. Any system is only as fast as its slowest component, and if you have a slow network connection (such as a dial-up connection) a "slow" 486 will handle requests much faster than the connection can transmit them. A downside to the 486-class CPU is that it has already become a technological dead end; with the Pentium already on the market, there's no call for further development of the 486. If you have a slow 486 (like a 486/33), you can upgrade to a fast 486 just by installing a new CPU. Unfortunately, you can't upgrade to Pentium just by installing a new CPU—you'll need a whole new motherboard (and possibly new memory as well). If cost is a serious concern but speed or growth is not, a 486 CPU can provide a very satisfactory answer.

The Pentium CPU is fast becoming the industry standard. Pentium CPUs come in a wide range of speeds, from the P-60 and -75 at the low end to -120 and -133 at the high end. Pentium CPUs seem to be released almost monthly at newer and higher speeds—the Pentium 133, clearly the top of the line only a short time ago, will soon be surpassed by the P-160, an even faster chip. High-speed Pentium systems are the platform of choice for high-demand servers; if you expect serious traffic on your server, it is worth investing in a serious system. For extremely high volumes, you can get an extremely powerful system with multiple CPUs (such systems require Windows NT, which has special support for such machines).

If you need to run under the Windows NT platform, we recommend a Pentium system. The robustness and security of Windows NT comes at a small cost of desktop performance over Windows 95; but you will more than make up that cost by using a Pentium system.

Tip

If you want to invest in Pentium power but can't afford a high-speed CPU, get a low-speed CPU (such as a P-75) on a motherboard that will support a high-speed CPU (such as a P-133). You can then upgrade the system later only for the cost of a new CPU.

One last note: There is a very small (and, some would say, shaky) middle ground between the 486 and Pentium systems. One choice is the "overdrive processor," which offers speeds of up to P-80 on a 486 system; but these CPUs cost almost as much as true Pentiums of the same speed, and are really only appropriate if you have an existing 486 system that you want to upgrade. Another system called "Next Generation" consists of a special "Next Generation" CPU on its own special motherboard. Its manufacturers suggest that the system offers Pentium performance at less-than-Pentium price. The computing community at large has not yet returned a verdict on this system; some regard it as a hobbyists system, while others suggest it's an economical choice for certain applications. We only recommend that if you're interested in this option, you investigate it *very* carefully.

Bus Architecture

There have been several bus architectures through the history of the PC, but the three that have survived the test of the marketplace are ISA (Industry Standard Architecture), Extended ISA (sometimes also called VESA), and PCI (Peripheral Component Interconnect), with the last architecture currently enjoying a meteoric rise to prominence, due no doubt in part to the extremely fast video cards it makes possible.

Market trends today suggest that a PCI motherboard is the wisest investment; it's the native architecture for the Pentium chip, and more and more peripherals are being manufactured on PCI cards. If you have existing EISA peripherals (such as CD-ROM control cards) you were hoping to use in your new server system, you can get PCI boards with some EISA slots.

Tip

If you can't afford a Pentium system, but may want someday to upgrade to that platform, you might consider basing your 486 system on a PCI motherboard. Not only will this give you a faster system, but you won't need to upgrade any of your PCI peripherals when you migrate them to the Pentium PCI system.

Memory & Disk

Memory continues to be the most expensive single component in any computer system, ranging roughly from $40 to $70 per megabyte (MB)—which translates on a 36 MB system to between $1440 and $2520. Microsoft's minimum for Windows 95 is 8 MB, and for Windows NT, 12 MB for Workstation and 16 MB for Server. Some have suggested that performance improves quite noticeably as you add memory up to 20 or 24 MB; the improvement as you add memory from 24 to 32 MB is much smaller.

If you plan to run even a small to moderate server, you will need a *minimum* of 16 MB to insure server response; if you intend to serve graphic files, you should plan on installing even more. If you expect to support more than a moderate volume of server traffic, you should consider getting at least 24 MB; for high volumes, at least 32 MB.

Memory prices change constantly, and vary widely from one source to another. Some shops don't even print their memory prices on flyers—only "call for daily price." Wise shopping may save you enough to buy a few crucial extra megabytes.

Tip

One good rule of thumb is to budget for memory *first*. Be sure you can get at least 16 or 20 MB; and then get the fastest system you can afford with the remainder of your budget.

Unlike memory, hard disks are rapidly becoming the most *economical* component of your system, at an average cost of around $3 per megabyte.

When you select a disk, you must also select the type of controller which the disk requires. The most common controller today on PCs today is IDE (Integrated Drive Electronics). Many motherboards, especially PCI motherboards, now come with IDE disk controllers on board. Another very popular option is SCSI (Small Computer System Interface), which is faster and more expandable (you can easily add up to seven disks on a single controller). If you do decide to go to SCSI, be sure to select a controller that fits your motherboard (EISA or PCI).

Not all disks are created equal; a faster disk will substantially improve your overall system performance. There are a lot of measurements of hard disk performance: two of the basic ones are rotational speed (how fast the disk spins) and average seek time (the average amount of time it takes for the disk to locate specific data). A good IDE drive has a rotational speed of at least 4,500 RPM; the newest SCSI-2 drives can spin at 7,200 RPM. Average seek times range from 15 milliseconds (too slow) to 9 milliseconds or less (very fast). Speed, of course, is a big factor in the cost of the hard drive. If you can, get a drive with at least a 10-millisecond seek rate—faster if you can afford it—or, if your budget is tight, as close to that speed as affordable. If you've been able to fit 16 MB of memory into your budget, buy a faster disk drive before you buy more memory.

Given the amount of disk space Windows requires—50+ MB for Windows 95, and 70–90 MB for Windows NT—plus the space required for the server, log files (which on high-traffic systems can grow by 2 MB per day), and the information or applications you want to provide, we recommend you select a disk with at least a gigabyte of storage.

Other Components

To complete your server, you'll need a few other components:

■ *Video card*   This is the one component you can scrimp on with a clear conscience. Since you won't be using your server as a desktop system (at least, we don't recommend that you do), you won't need a high-price "Windows accelerator." Get the least expensive card you can find that's compatible with your version of Windows. If you just can't live without good video response on your server, you can still get an acceptable card for under $100.

■ *CD-ROM drive*   This is an absolute must, especially if you plan on using Windows NT. Installing Windows 95 from diskette (13 diskettes) is no fun at all—installing Windows NT from diskette (20+) is worse. But again, since you won't need snappy multimedia performance, this can be another low-budget item—a double-speed CD-ROM will more than suffice.

■ *Backup device*   Take the money you saved on the video card and the double-speed CD-ROM drive and get a good tape backup system. Backup systems are generally rated by the style and capacity of tape they use. Obviously, systems that take higher-capacity tapes will require less intervention (that is, tape changes), enabling you to run backups overnight or at other unattended times. The first time you truly need your backup system, you will be glad you have it.

■ *Removable disk drive*   such as the Iomega Corporation's Zip drive, is an optional feature you might consider, especially for an Internet server isolated from the rest of your network for security reasons. You can develop an entire Web site on your local network, copy it to the removable disk, and then copy it from that disk onto your server.

We recommend that you shop mercilessly for your system. There are a huge number of small computer firms that can custom-build a perfect system for the same price as a fully-loaded off-the-shelf system that's full of equipment you just don't need. Your server doesn't need sound cards, speakers, cameras, six-speed CD-ROM drives, a flat-screen monitor, or any of the other glitzy components included in most packaged systems. If you need to produce multimedia files, equip a different system for that purpose—your server should be optimized to do one thing only: *serve.* ❖

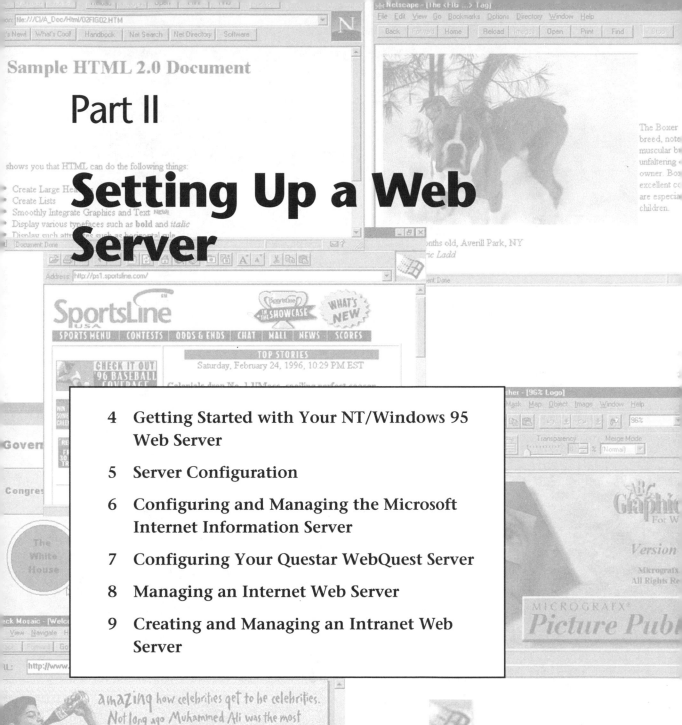

Part II

Setting Up a Web Server

## CHAPTER 4

Getting Started with Your NT/Windows 95 Web Server

This chapter reviews many of the more popular Web servers. It covers their unique features and comments on the usability of each program. You'll find a handy chart of server software packages and their features. You'll also find some guidelines to follow in choosing the right Web server for you.

The chapter then guides you through the process of installing, configuring, and starting two of the reviewed Web servers: Microsoft's Internet Information Server, and Questar's WebQuest NT.

Specifically, you learn the following for Windows NT and Windows 95:

- What to look for in a Web Server
- What servers are available and where
- How to install the WebQuest server software included with this book
- How to install the Microsoft Internet Information Server
- How to start and stop the servers

Overview of WWW Server Software

As the growth of the Internet progresses, so does the number of companies producing software applications for Internet implementation. Nowhere is this more evident than in the market for Windows NT and 95 based WWW server software. There are more than twenty Web servers and more on the horizon.

For both the corporate-level publishing site and the home hobbyist, the availability of professional server software is clearly good news. The progression of the Internet from a domain of UNIX gurus and hackers to one that is accessible to Microsoft Windows users for both browsing and publishing is a significant breakthrough. The barrier for entry to publishing and communicating via the Web has fallen.

The original standard for Web servers comes from the NCSA (National Center for Supercomputing Applications) server software originally developed for the UNIX operating system. You can read more about NCSA and their server platform at **http://hoohoo.ncsa.uiuc.edu**. Some Web servers, like EMWAC, are ported versions of this server.

Most commercial servers now seek to differentiate themselves from the pack and often endeavor to set a new standard for others to follow. You need to decide which features are the most valuable for your organization as well as which features are likely to become irrelevant as development of Web servers progresses.

Available Server Software

A number of excellent lists of available server software are out on the Web.

- *Webcompare*   Visit Webcompare to find an up-to-date and intensive list of server software, categorized by features. This site is the most brutally honest server comparison, literally feature for feature, that you find on the Net or anywhere else. Go to **http://www.webcompare.com/server-main.html**.

- *Yahoo Internet Directory*   Here you'll find links to commercial server software packages that have elected to register. You will also find terrific links to additional utilities and services that will help speed you on your way to running a perfect Web site. Go to **http://www.yahoo.com/Computers_and_Internet/Internet/World_Wide_Web/HTTP/**.

- *The World Wide Web Consortium (W3C)*   You'll find in-depth information, white papers, and links to additional resources regarding all facets of the Web. Go to **http://www.w3.org/pub/WWW/**.

Survey of Server Software

As the demand for Windows-based 32-bit Web servers has exploded so has the dividing list of features. This section offers a list of many of the top packages in terms of both market presence and popularity.

Windows NT or Windows 95?

Some of the Web servers listed here have two versions, one for Windows NT and one for Windows 95. Others have only a Windows NT version. Most of Windows NT Web server will run on Windows NT Workstation. One exception, the Microsoft Internet Information Server, is available only for Windows NT Server. For low-volume Web sites, Windows 95 can be adequate. If your Web site needs to handle transaction processing or has extensive database links, you need to consider Windows NT. Also, you can only perform multihoming or virtual servers under Windows NT. Windows 95 does not support multiple IPs assigned to a single machine.

Windows NT is a true 32-bit multithreaded environment that is perfect for serving large quantities of transactions. Windows 95 is a 32-bit operating system that still relies on a 16-bit base. While Windows 95 is a remarkable operating system, it is not as rock-solid as Windows NT.

WebQuest NT and 95

www.questar.com

WebQuest 95 and WebQuest NT are published by Questar Microsystems and are included with this book. Both these servers feature a simple GUI-driven installation and management software and many additional features. WebQuest has the only implementation of the Server Side Includes+ (SSI+) 1.0 specification. SSI as an Internet standard allows powerful interactive functions that don't require programming or CGI scripts. SSI+ enhances the functionality of SSI by providing even more options to the Web developer. Server Side Includes+ allows Web browsers to serve as platform-independent front ends to live databases and can therefore provides the user with up-to-the-minute information. SSI+ 1.0 provides a major enhancement to SSI+ with a programming front end: Cscript.

Cscript provides a complete C-like object-oriented language to HTML pages. Very complex operations may now be performed right on the HTML page without any compiler or external programs. In many ways this feature allows any browser to run a C program within the browser. Cscript is similar to JavaScript and other proposed scripting languages, except that Cscript is the C programming language implemented within HTML. A Web page author does not need to learn how to use SSI+ to create standard HTML pages. The power and flexibility of SSI+ becomes apparent when creating complex functions with the Web page—back ends to forms, database connections, and complex WAIS Web space indexing with graphical generation and administration.

The graphical configuration and maintenance utility that comes with WebQuest is called *WebMeister*. With WebMeister, you can manage all the functions and features of WebQuest. You can set up multiple independent proxy servers, administer, and monitor your Webspaces on remote machines and mounted drives. The Load Sensor technology with WebQuest intelligently maximizes the balance between resources and speed.

WebQuest offers many programming interfaces including: built-in PERL, Win-CGI (supports legacy Windows 3.1 WinCGI scripts), OLE2 calls directly from HTML pages, and direct access to any DLL. DLLs may be accessed instead of CGI programs. The DLL interface is much easier to develop and

II

Setting Up a Web Server

debug than is the CGI interface, and in order of magnitude faster and more efficient. All existing system and application DLLs may be accessed, or new DLLs may be created. The DLLGI (DLL Gateway Interface) allows calls to DLLs directly from a URL.

WebPak support allows plug-in extensibility of the WebQuest server. WebPaks available from Questar Microsystems, third parties, or even developed in house may be plugged in to WebQuest to provide almost any desired custom feature to your Web space. WebPak SDK is available to help you create WebPaks for internal use or resale.

WebSite

website.ora.com.
WebSite, from O'Reilly & Associates, was written by Bob Denny. This is a 32-bit multithreaded server that allows you to use standard Windows programming languages to access Excel, FoxPro, and other data sources from within a Web document. Additional features include:

- WebSite 1.1 supports a Visual Basic 4 framework (CGI32.BAS) with sample applications as well as server-push applications
- A graphical interface for creating virtual servers and it supports remote administration, password authentication, and access control
- WebSite Pro features SSL for encrypted transactions
- A GUI tool, Webview, which provides a tree-like display of the documents and links on your server
- Wizards that automatically create common Web documents
- Indexing and search tools to locate items anywhere on your site
- Server Side Includes (SSI) so you can combine static and programmed documents on-the-fly, and common document components are easier to maintain

EMWACs HTTPS for NT

emwac.ed.ac.uk
The only freeware server on our list, this server has been available for over a year, courtesy of the European Microsoft Windows Academic Center. This server has been used widely across the Internet—the Purveyor Server (covered next) is a commercial adaptation of the HTTPS server.

The EMWACS server is well-suited to the simple serving of Web pages. It lacks any administration utilities and has only the most basic of features. If you're running a simple low-volume site and don't mind editing a few configuration files, be sure to take a look at EMWACS. Features include:

- MAP file support
- Automatic Directory indexing
- CGI support
- Runs as a Windows Service
- Links to the WAIS toolkit for text searching and retrieval

Purveyor for Windows NT and 95

www.process.com

The Purveyor Web server from Process Software has its origins in the EMWACs server listed above, but has quickly grown to become a full-featured server with advanced administration tools. Purveyor was one of the earliest commercial strength NT Web servers and is highly regarded. One of the three servers to offer Proxy services, Purveyor also features advanced database publishing capabilities. The Purveyor product line spans Windows NT, Windows 95, NetWare, and VMS. An SSL enhanced server for secure transactions is in the works as well. Features include:

- Data Wizard simplifies integration of ODBC/SQL databases
- Internet Server API
- Advanced Proxy Services
- Advanced Logging features
- Remote Server Management
- Security implemented via Microsoft File Manager

Netscape Communication/Commerce Servers for NT

home.netscape.com/comprod/netscape_commun.html

Netscape, the company that publishes the popular Netscape browser also (surprise!) publishes a line of Web servers and related products. While Netscape was founded less than two years ago, the Netscape server development team includes many of the original members of the NCSA team.

The Netscape server family is split into two components. The Communication server is a high performance server for Windows NT. The Commerce Server includes the features of the Communication server and also supplies the means for secure data transmission. The Netscape servers are leading edge and have been priced accordingly. Features include:

- Virtual Server hosting
- Remote graphical management via HTML forms
- Netscape Server Application Programming Interface (NSAPI) for programmable access to a suite of server application functions and a dynamic loading interface

- Integrated security using SSL, which incorporates public key cryptographic technology from RSA Data Security
- Remote administration using a Web browser
- Easy setup via Web forms based tools

Oracle Web System

www.oracle.com/info/products/servprod.html

The Oracle Web system is from renowned database software developer Oracle Corporation. The Web System is from the newly evolving group of servers that are not based on static documents, but rather on dynamically created documents served up by a database. The Oracle 7 RDBMS is queried by the Web Server and responds with pages created on-the-fly. Features include database-driven Web pages and graphical Web and database administration.

	WebQuest	WebSite	EMWAC
Remote Admin	Yes	Yes	No
GUI Interface	Yes	Yes	No
Proxy	Yes	No	No
SSI	Enhanced	Yes	No
Map support	CERN	Yes Registry	Yes
SSL	No	Yes	No
WAIS	Yes	Yes	Yes
OS	NT w&s 95	NT & 95	NT w&S
ODBC links	Yes	Yes	No
CGI	Yes	Yes	Yes
Logging	Yes	Yes	Yes
Multihoming	Yes	Yes	No
Virtual roots	No	Yes	No
HTML Editor	WebEdit	WebEdit	No
Other	DLL calls		

CompuServe Spry Web/Safety Web Servers for NT and 95

support.spry.com/public/iosws/

This robust Web server from the SPRY Internet division of CompuServe supports SSL for secure transactions, is highly configurable, and includes proxy services. Download an evaluation copy at the Spry Web site. Features include:

- Remote Administration from NT or Windows 95
- Virtual Server Hosting
- Extended logging to ASCII files and ODBC databases
- Direct Database Access to ODBC Compliant databases
- Caching Proxy Server to facilitate use with a firewall
- Supports compiled Windows DLLs for scalability and high performance

Purveyor	Netscape	Oracle	Spry	IIS
Yes	Yes			Yes
Yes	Yes			Yes
Yes	Yes			No
Yes	Yes			No
Yes	Yes			Yes
Yes	Yes			Yes
Yes				No
NT w&s	NT w&s		NT 95	NT s
Yes		Yes	Yes	Yes
Yes	Yes		Yes	Yes
Yes	Yes		Yes	Yes
Yes	Yes			Yes
Yes	Yes			Yes
HotMetal	No			No
	NSAPI	Database based		Adv. API sets

Microsoft Internet Information Server

www.microsoft.com/InfoServ/

The Microsoft Internet Information Server (IIS) for NT is a powerful and flexible tool for serving up Web pages. The IIS is actually three servers: WWW, FTP, and Gopher. The IIS is in its infancy and doesn't have all the features you may desire, but it *is* free. Features include:

- GUI administration tool
- Remote server management
- ODBC Database access
- Advanced Internet Server Application Program Interface (ISAPI) set
- Utilizes Windows NT Security System
- Extremely fast server platform

Key Considerations for Server Selection

The cornucopia of server software leaves you with the happy dilemma of deciding which software to base your publishing enterprise on. There are a myriad of issues to consider, including:

- Features
- Administration
- Cost
- Standards implementations
- Ease of use
- Stability, reliability
- Technical support

Selecting your Windows-based Web server is a simple matter of selecting the features you need and matching them up with a reputable company. Cost is also a factor, but you should consider it only after you define your needs.

Features

First define the features you need in a Web server. Start this process by defining the main purpose of the Web server: Is it document publishing? Database access? Financial transactions? Custom programming? Next, consider the overall environment that you will expose the server to. Will you need to service large numbers of users? You'll need a server that can handle the load.

Will you need to manage and administer these users extensively? You'll want a server with extensive administration tools.

Steps to take:

1. Examine your goals
2. Determine what features your software will need
3. Align your needs with the server software available
4. Select the server software package that best meets your needs

Volume of Activity

The volume of activity for your server should first dictate your choice of operating system, and then your Web server. Use the following chart as a good rule of thumb:

Activity Level	Operating System
Low (< 100 hits/hr)	Windows 95
Medium (100- 400 hits/hr)	Windows NT Workstation
High (400- 1000 hits/hr)	Windows NT Server
Very high (>1000 hits/hr)	Windows NT Server

Administration

The new generation of Windows-based Web servers now offer graphical administration tools. These tools make it much easier for you to set up and administer your server. If you're nontechnical consider this a high priority. It will help you avoid wasted time and consultant fees.

Cost

The price of Web servers varies from free of charge for the Emwacs and IIS to several thousand dollars for the Netscape Commerce Server. Generally, the more features, the more expensive the server. Fortunately, as the market matures, prices drop.

Company Strength and Commitment

In a rapidly maturing software market there will be many winners and losers. If your project requires a large resource commitment, take a close look at the vendor of your software. Do they have the financial wherewithal to ride out the storm? Or are they a one product company in a crowded market? Building and maintaining a large Web site is a complicated process in and of itself. Access to bug fixes, upgrades, and technical support can prove to be extremely vital.

Extending Web Server Capabilities

It's important to understand that you don't need to look to your server software as a complete solution. You can (and probably will) enhance your server with add-on software.

A relatively new cadre of products are now available for use in extending the power and capabilities of your Web server. These products can be divided into roughly three categories that are covered below: Database, Programming/Scripting, and Development Aids.

Databases

Large amounts of corporate data are stored in databases in addition to documents, spreadsheets, and so on. The latest trend in Web services to provide access to corporate databases either directly from your Web server or via a database into which you have imported this information. The direction in NT and 95 database add-ons is to implement a direct connection to an already existing ODBC compliant database.

A world of possibilities opens up when a Web server can access a database. For example, consider that you can store your HTML pages in a database. This can make for easy site maintenance! When database access is combined with scripting capabilities—almost anything is possible. The best products combine database access with the ability to create and include HTML and graphics on-the-fly.

Two excellent examples of third-party Web server database enhancements are:

- *WEBDBC from Nomad Development Corp*   WEBDBC is an add-on built specifically to facilitate access to data stored in an SQL server. WEBDBC is available for both Windows NT and Windows 95. Check it out (and get the demo) at: **http://www.ndev.com/**.
- *Cold Fusion from Allaire*   A popular database connectivity add-on, Cold Fusion is built specifically for the Windows NT platform. Take it for a test drive at: **http://www.allaire.com/**.

> **Note**
>
> ODBC is an acronym for *Open Database Connectivity*, a Microsoft strategy to provide a standard interface for accessing heterogeneous databases. ODBC uses Structured Query Language (SQL) as a standard for accessing data. This interface provides maximum interoperability; a single application can access different database management systems through a common set of code. This allows a developer to build and distribute a client/server application without targeting a specific database management system.
>
> You can learn more about ODBC and other Microsoft development strategies at **http://www.microsoft.com/DEVONLY/strategy/**.

The value of Web services often rises dramatically when a company realizes that this is a terrific new tool for deploying a client server database system.

Programming/Scripting

A new selection of products on the market enables you to provide sophisticated interaction with users via the Web. Instead of merely serving up pages and forms, you can build entire systems that bear little resemblance to their HTML forefathers. For several years, scripting has been accommodated through a standard known as the *Common Gateway Interface (CGI)*. This is a powerful means of providing a way to send data from a browser to a program that runs on the Web server.

Since the original Web servers existed solely in the UNIX environment, most of the tools used are foreign to our NT universe. The largest number of currently existing CGI programs were written using PERL and run on UNIX servers. Fortunately for us, now more options utilize languages more common to the Windows and Windows NT world.

> **Note**
>
> PERL is an acronym for *Practical Extraction and Report Language* and has achieved high popularity for ease of use in creating CGI programs. PERL has been ported to NT, so you can now make use of the many PERL programs that are in the public domain. You can pick up the latest version of NT PERL at **http://www.bhs.com**

> **Tip**
>
> The Windows NT Resource Center at **http://www.bhs.com** contains a wealth of information for anyone using or considering using Windows NT. The software library contains many great freeware, shareware, and evaluation programs for use with Windows NT and Windows 95.

Interestingly, CGI evolved as a superior method of enhancing Web servers over the method commonly referred to as a Server Include. The Server Include method is a powerful means of enhancing your server but also has a number of potential security holes. Server Includes are now offered in many of the servers discussed here. The WebQuest server offers an enhanced specification referred to as SSI+. You can read more about this in Chapter 14 or online at: **http://www.questar.com/ssiplus.htm**.

Java and VBScript: Pump Up the Volume!

▶ See "Java," p. 432.

A new direction that you have probably heard about involves *scripts that execute at the browser, not at the server*. This is a tremendous increase in browser functionality. Java from Sun Microsystems (**http://java.sun.com**) has received a lot of attention and is covered in Chapter 15 of this book. There are two types of Java currently being implemented, Java and JavaScript. Java is a compiled executable, while JavaScript is scripting that is interpreted on-the-fly at the browser.

VBScript from Microsoft (**http://www.microsoft.com/intdev/vbs/vbs.htm**) is an easy way for the current masses of Visual Basic programmers to become Web programmers. VBScript combined with additional Microsoft offerings portends to be a significant force for Internet and Web based development.

Development Aids

Now, a number of products conform to the CGI specification and provide a framework for programmers to utilize the languages in which they are most comfortable. If your needs include extensive scripting, be sure to contact your programming software vendor to explore the available options. This area of software development is a quickly growing industry.

An excellent example of this type of product is the WebHub framework for Borland's Delphi language from HREF Corp. Using Object Pascal you can create dynamic Web sites based on pieces of code, chunks of HTML, and database access. Powerful stuff! Learn more at **http://www.href.com**.

Another example of this type of product is Web Objects from Next Software, Inc. (**http://www.next.com**). NEXT, the brainchild of Steve Jobs of Apple Computer fame has gotten out of hardware and into software. Web Objects is an object-oriented framework for adding interactive Web functionality to your NT-based Web site. Download the free demo and taste the future of Web development.

Installing a Windows NT Web Server: Security Checklist

Before you get started installing the server, you should review a quick check-list of items. Remember, you're exposing this Web server software and the computer it's running on to the vast reaches of the Internet. This means that every 13-year-old computer hacker in the world has access to this computer.

Consider the following quick list of items before you turn the key and give the world access to your site.

▶ See "Securely Configuring Windows NT Server," p. 136, for a more in-depth look at security.

User Accounts

Create an account for the Web server to run under. Review the account's rights.

Choose difficult passwords.

Rules for Setting Passwords

Security experts believe that the easiest and most common way into a computer system is through the front door—a valid user name and a password. Set up a pass-word policy that requires your users to utilize the following rules:

Use passwords that are combinations of unrelated words, separated by delimiters. Example: Lobster&Basketball Elmer@#carapice

Do not use passwords that are:

- Shorter than six characters
- A name of someone you care about (or don't care about)
- A date that it is significant to you
- A "swear" word (hey, you're too good to work blue!)

Additionally, *never* use the same password in multiple locations. This is a common mistake. Yes, it's hard to remember all these passwords, but it's common for a hacker to breach the security of an unimportant system and use information gleaned there to access high-security installations—like your bank account.

Of course, it goes without saying that you should never write your passwords down where someone may discover them.

II

Setting Up a Web Server

Maintain strict account policies. The User Manager utility provides a way for the system administrator to specify how quickly account passwords expire (which forces users to regularly change passwords), and other policies such as how many bad logon attempts will be tolerated before locking a user out. Use these policies to manage your accounts, particularly those with administrative access, to prevent exhaustive or random password attacks.

Limit the membership of the Administrators group to those accounts that MUST absolutely have it. The fewer high-level accounts, the lower the risk that someone will breach your security and wreak havoc.

File Security

If your NT server is attached to the Internet, use NTFS. NTFS is a powerful disk storage allocation system, much more powerful than DOS. By utilizing NTFS, you can create file-level security restrictions and use auditing.

Enable NTFS Auditing.

Other Network Services

Run only the services that you need. Do *not* leave that experimental telnet server running that you downloaded last week.

Unbind unnecessary services from your Internet adapter cards. If you're running a server purely for Internet services, disable NetBeui and IPX/SPX.

Go through your entire system and check all permissions on network shares. Are they appropriate?

Getting Started with Your Microsoft Internet Information Server

The Microsoft Internet Information server is predestined to become one of the most popular Web servers on the Internet and on corporate intranets. The reasons for this are simple: It's powerful. It's fast. It runs on the most popular corporate server operating system today, Windows NT Server. And it's free.

You can get Internet Information Server in four ways:

- Customers who don't own Windows NT Server can get Internet Information Server as part of the Windows NT Server Value Pack that also includes Windows NT Server 3.51 and 10 Client Access Licenses, available for approximately $999.

- Customers who already own Windows NT Server can get Internet Information Server on disk for approximately $99.
- You can sign up for the Microsoft Developer Network (MSDN) program.
- You can download it for *free* from the Microsoft WWW site.

Requirements

The IIS server is available only for Windows NT Server.

A computer with at least the minimum configuration to support Windows NT Server.

Windows NT Server version 3.51 or later. Windows NT Server version 3.51 must include Service Pack 3, which is provided on the Internet Information Server compact disc.

Note
Remote administration of Internet Information Server can be performed from a computer running Windows NT Workstation version 3.51 and Service Pack 3.

A CD-ROM drive for the installation compact disc.

How To Install Internet Information Server

To install the Internet Information Server services, you must be logged on with administrator privileges. In addition, to configure the Internet Information Server services by using the Internet Service Manager, your user account must be a member of the Administrators group on the target computer.

Tip
Before beginning installation, close all running applications. This will reduce the chance that an application is keeping a file open that the installation process will need to update.

1. To start Setup from File Manager, double-click the file named Setup.exe in the root directory of either the compact disk or the directory you have expanded the downloaded server to.

> **Note**
>
> During setup, you can choose the Help button in any dialog box to get assistance. When you do, a Help topic is displayed that explains the choices you have at that point and the procedure to complete the dialog box.

2. If you haven't installed Service Pack 3 for Windows NT version 3.51, a dialog box will appear and offer to install the service pack automatically at the conclusion of setup. The Microsoft Internet Information Server will not operate without Service Pack 3 installed. Choose the Yes button to install Service Pack 3. Note that at the conclusion of the Service Pack Update you must restart your computer.

3. The Microsoft Internet Information Server Welcome dialog box appears (see fig. 4.1). Choose the OK button.

Fig. 4.1

The installation welcome dialog box.

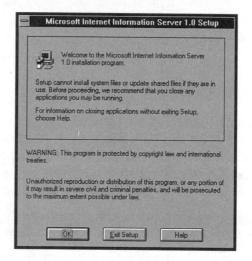

The second dialog box appears, displaying the installation options shown in figure 4.2.

4. The installation dialog box displays a dialog for three types of Internet Servers, and some support systems. All of the items are selected for installation by default. Here's a brief description of each option:

■ Internet Service Manager installs the administration program for managing the services. This is necessary for system setup and maintenance.

■ World Wide Web services for HTML publishing.

- Gopher Service creates a Gopher server.

- FTP Service creates an FTP publishing server.

- ODBC Drivers and Administration installs Open Data Base Connectivity (ODBC) drivers. These are required for logging to ODBC files and for enabling ODBC access from the WWW service.

- Help and Sample files installs online Help and sample HyperText Markup Language (HTML) files.

- Microsoft Internet Explorer installs the Web browser, Microsoft Internet Explorer.

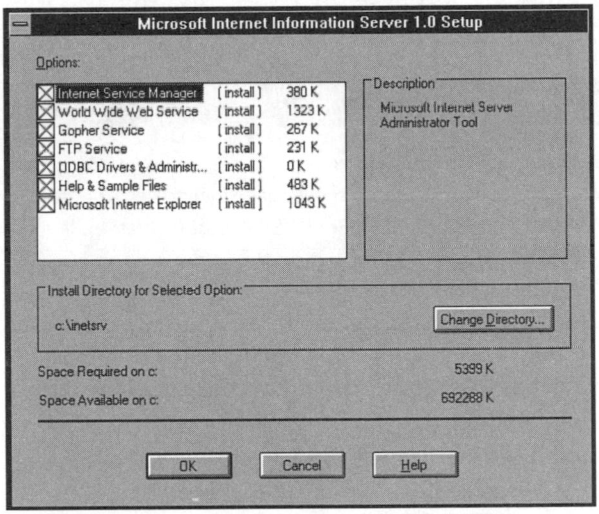

Fig. 4.2
The Installation option dialog box.

Setting Up a Web Server

Note

The Gopher service is a powerful system for accessing textual information. Gopher existed before HTTP, but has not seen the same popularity. Here's a snippet from the gopher FAQ (**http://www.cis.ohio-state.edu/ hypertext/faq/usenet/gopher-faq/faq.html**):

Internet Gopher is a distributed document search and retrieval system. It combines the best features of browsing through collections of information and fully indexed databases. The protocol and software follows a client-server model, and permits users on a heterogeneous mix of desktop systems to browse, search, and retrieve documents residing on multiple distributed server machines.

> **Note**
>
> If you have an application running that uses ODBC, you may see an error message telling you that one or more components are in use. Before continuing, close all applications and services that use ODBC.

You can also use the Setup program later to add or remove components. Setup can also be used to remove all Internet Information Server components. You can accept the default installation directory (C:\Inetsrv) or click the Change Directory button and enter a new directory. Be sure to check this directory against your security setup to ensure that you aren't creating any holes for mischief.

> **Caution**
>
> If you've installed Internet Information Server, but want to reinstall it into another directory, you must remove the following key from the Registry: \HKEY_LOCAL_MACHINE\SOFTWARE\Microsoft\INetStp. If you don't delete this key, the Change Directory button will be dimmed and you will be unable to change the default directory.

5. The Publishing Directories dialog box will appear next and will offer default directories for each type of service you are installing. To change the directories, click Browse (see fig. 4.3).

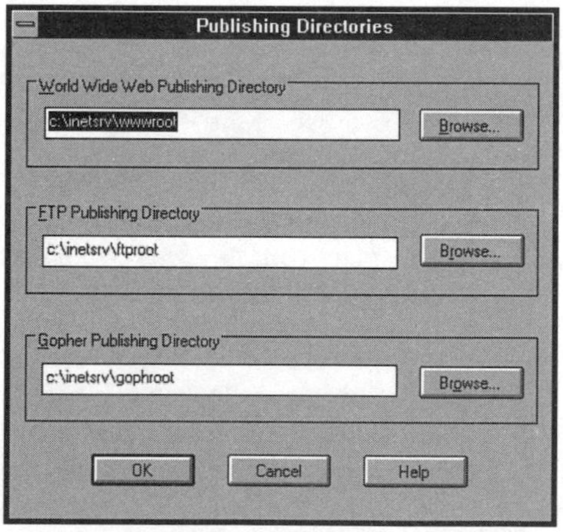

Fig. 4.3
The IIS Publishing Directories dialog box.

6. If you already have files ready to publish, you can enter the full path to their current location, or move them into the default directories later. If your files are on a network drive, you should accept the default directory. After setup is completed, use Internet Service Manager to change your default home directory to the path for the network directory containing your files; for example, \\Servername\Sharename\WWWfiles. Be sure to carefully check the permissions on the network drive; there may be security implications.

7. When prompted to create the service directories (Wwwroot, Gophroot, and Ftproot by default), click Yes.

8. The Create Internet Account dialog box appears. This is the account used for all anonymous access to the Internet Information Server. The access permissions for this account must be monitored carefully. Enter a password and confirm the password for this account. Choose OK and the installation copies all remaining Internet Information Server files.

9. If the ODBC Drivers and Administration option box was selected, the Install Drivers dialog box appears.

10. To install the SQL Server driver, select the SQL Server driver from the Available ODBC Drivers list box, and choose the OK button.

11. If, during Setup, you were prompted to install the Service Pack 3 update and you answered Yes, the Service Pack 3 update program will start automatically after setup. At the conclusion of the update, you must restart your computer.

The preceding steps are all that is required for a simple installation. You're now ready to publish on the Internet or your intranet. The server is now up and running! You can use the Services applet in Control Panel to confirm successful installation of the World Wide Web publishing service (see fig. 4.4).

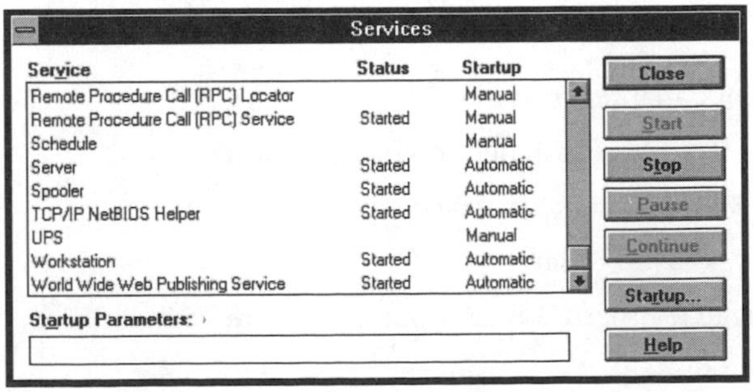

Fig. 4.4
The Control Panel Services applet.

There is no need to start Internet Service Manager unless you want to make advanced configuration changes.

II

Setting Up a Web Server

Getting Started with the Questar WebQuest Server for Windows NT and Windows 95

WebQuest is published in two versions, one for Windows 95 and another for Windows NT. If you're just getting your feet wet in the pool of Web publishing, the Windows 95 version is a great start. There are some significant differences between the two versions, most notable is that the Windows 95 version cannot serve more than one Web space.

Again, if you're serving Web in a production mode with high volume, Windows NT is the clear choice.

Requirements for WebQuest NT

Minimum recommended configuration for Windows NT version are:

- *Processor*   486 DX2 66
- *RAM*   16 Megabytes
- *Hard disk*   4 Megabytes
- *Operating System*   Windows NT Server or Workstation V3.51 with service pack 3 or higher

- *ODBC*   Must be installed with 32-bit drivers (An install is provided on the CD-ROM)
- *Network*   A Network card configured for TCP/IP with a static IP address assigned to the computer.

There are no special requirements for WebQuest NT, if your computer will run Windows NT, it will also run WebQuest NT.

Requirements for Windows 95 Version

The minimum system requirements for WebQuest95 to run on your system are:

- A network adapter configured to support TCP/IP
- A static IP address assigned to your computer
- ODBC 32-bit driver(s) installed on your system
- Windows 95 1.0 or later
- 3 MB available hard drive space for WebQuest95
- 486 DX2 66
- 8 MB of RAM

ODBC

As mentioned in the System Requirements, you must have a 32-bit version of ODBC installed and properly configured on your system to install and run both WebQuest NT and 95. If you don't know whether you have ODBC installed on your system, do a search on your hard drive for ODBC32.DLL. If you don't have this file, you either have a 16-bit version of ODBC or you don't have ODBC. In either case you must install ODBC before WebQuest.

Close all programs that are running on your workstation or server before installation. Only Program Manager should be running. If ODBC is being used by another application, WebQuest NT will not install properly.

If you receive a login error after installing WebQuest NT for the first time, you will need to go into Control Panel, Services. Highlight WebQuest, select Startup and log on as System Account or the same account that WebQuestNT will be using. ODBC and WebQuest need to be using the same account and password.

Installation of WebQuest NT

To prepare for installation, you must close all programs that are running on your workstation or server. Only Program Manager should be running. If ODBC is being used by another application, WebQuest will not install properly.

1. To install WebQuestNT, log onto the Windows NT server or workstation as the Administrator.

2. Copy the file WQ20BETA.ZIP from the CDROM into a temporary directory and extract it.

3. After reading the various text files that are included with WebQuest 2.0, run the SETUP.EXE file. See figure 4.5.

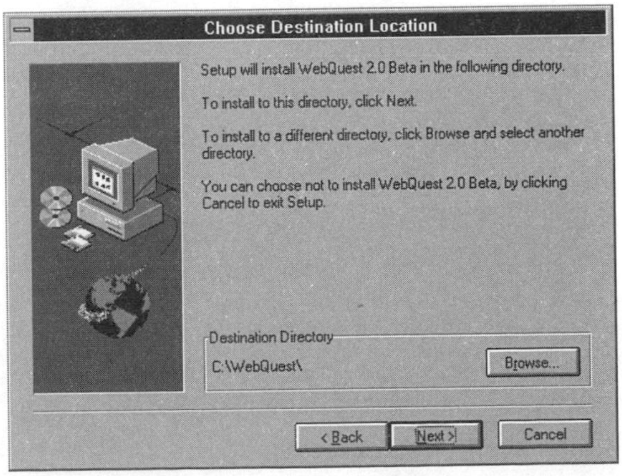

Fig. 4.5
WebQuest Directory Installation dialog box.

You will be prompted to enter the password for the Administrator account for this NT system (see fig. 4.6). The Administrator account is a standard, "built-in" account that can alter all aspects of system setup and security. Guard this password carefully.

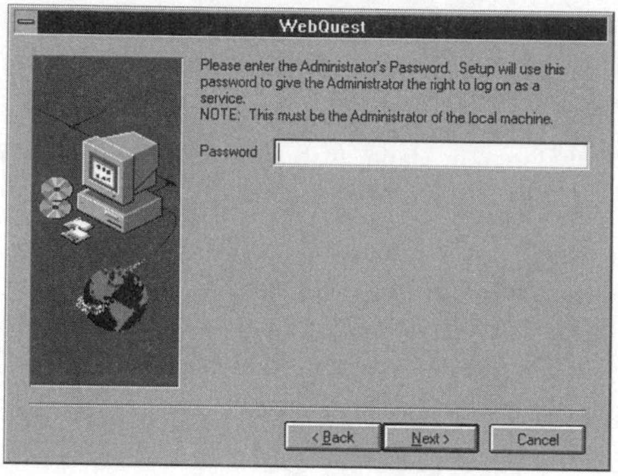

Fig. 4.6
Enter the Administrator Account password.

Note

Many Web servers will give you the option to run them as either a service or a program. There are advantages (and disadvantages) to both. One significant benefit of running your server as a service is that the server will run without a user having to be logged in at the console.

If you select Automatic Startup, the WebQuest server will launch immediately upon boot-up (see fig. 4.7). This is handy if your server restarts due to loss of power or some other reason that causes a system reboot.

Fig. 4.7
Manual or Automatic?

When installed, WebQuest creates its own Common Group called WebQuest (see fig. 4.8). All files relevant to WebQuest NT are located in this Group. Double-click on WebMeister to launch the graphical interface for WebQuest NT. When WebQuest installs, it creates a default home page with files included with this program.

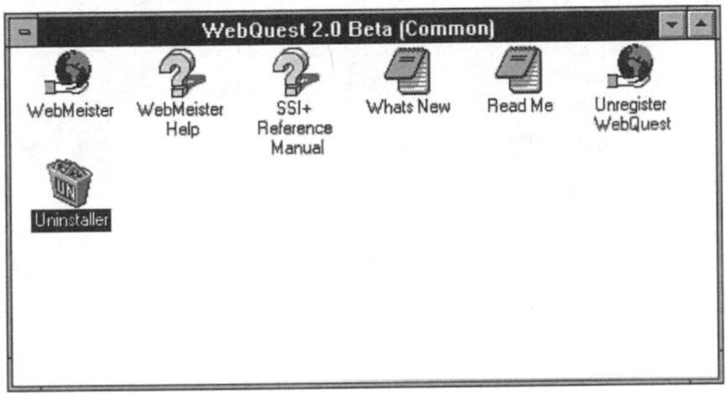

Fig. 4.8
The WebQuest program group.

Starting and Stopping the WebQuest NT Server

The WebQuest server can be started and stopped directly through the Control Panel, Services option (see fig. 4.9). Click on Start or Stop as required. You can also start and stop WebQuest NT through the WebMeister administration utility.

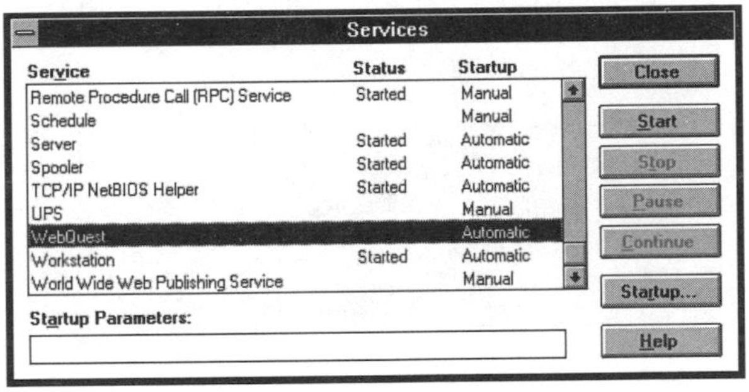

Fig. 4.9
The Control Panel Services applet.

Installation of WebQuest for Windows 95

To prepare for installation you must close all programs that are running on your workstation or server. Only Program Manager should be running. If ODBC is being used by another application, WebQuest will not install properly.

To install WebQuest 95, simply launch SETUP.EXE and follow the dialog prompts. See fig. 4.10.

II

Setting Up a Web Server

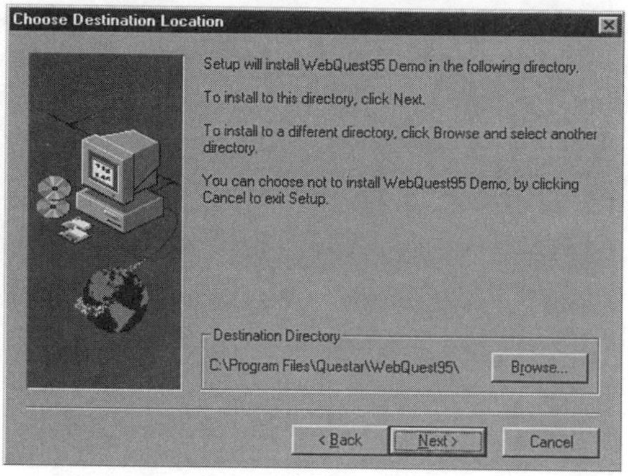

Fig. 4.10
The WebQuest 95
Directory dialog
box.

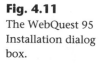

WebQuest 95 follows standard Windows 95 conventions and the server installation is configured exactly the same as any standard Windows 95 program installation (see fig. 4.11)

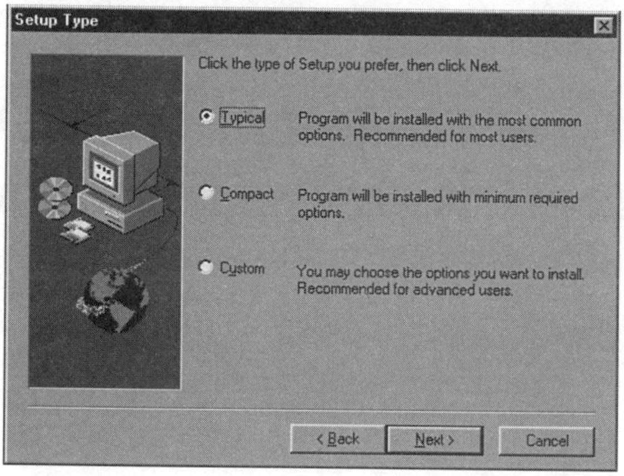

Fig. 4.11
The WebQuest 95
Installation dialog
box.

Unless you are reinstalling the software, select the Typical option in the Setup Type dialog box.

When complete, WebQuest will have installed its own program group called WebQuest 95 (see fig. 4.12). All files relevant to WebQuest 95 are located in this group.

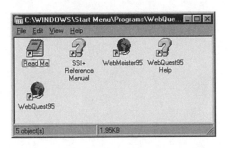

Fig. 4.12
The WebQuest 95 program group.

Starting and Stopping the WebQuest 95 Server

Starting the WebQuest 95 server is a two-part operation. Load the WebQuest server into the Windows 95 environment by double-clicking on the WebQuest 95 icon in the WebQuest 95 program group as shown in figure 4.12.

After double-clicking the WebQuest 95 icon, you will see the WebQuest 95 icon in the bottom right-hand corner of your screen (see fig. 4.13). This does not mean that the server is actually running!

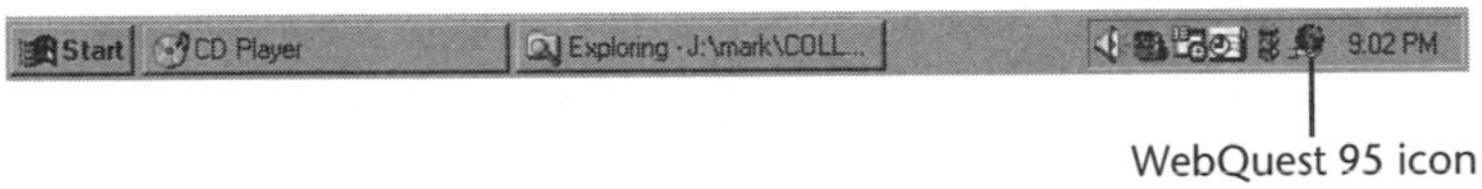

![WebQuest 95 taskbar](WebQuest 95 icon)

WebQuest 95 icon

Fig. 4.13
Note the WebQuest icon in the lower right-hand corner of your screen.

To actually run the server you must right click on the icon to bring up the WebQuest 95 start menu (see fig. 4.14).

Fig. 4.14
The WebQuest start menu.

To start the server using the default Web setup simply click on Start WebQuest 95. Your server is now up and running! To verify this, right click again on the WebQuest icon and note that the top menu selection now reads "Stop WebQuest 95." See figure. 4.15. This is your indication that the server is in fact running.

Fig. 4.15
This time the menu reads "stop," not "start."

II

Setting Up a Web Server

CHAPTER 5

Server Configuration

The previous chapter presented an overview of NT Servers and got us started with the WebQuest and Microsoft IIS servers. Fortunately for us, these servers use GUI-based tools for configuration and maintenance. While most servers are migrating in this direction, many are still based on configuration files. These files control the behavior, the operational parameters, of the server. The new generation of 32-bit Windows servers tend to store this configuration information in the registry, not text files.

That said, this chapter uses the old-style configuration files as a reference point. The new generation of Windows-based servers are seeking to differentiate themselves from each other and are using different terminology to express the same points. Use this chapter as a point of reference to refer to for the configuration commands of your server software.

This chapter covers in detail all standard server configuration commands and how to use them, including those related to access control, directory indexing, and MIME types. This will provide a solid base of information that you will use to understand the different configuration steps, although they may be referred to differently by each server software package. This chapter takes you step-by-step through each file and the myriad of configuration possibilities.

Our demonstration files come from the standard NCSA server originally created for the UNIX environment. The NCSA Server uses four primary configuration files that you may view as a set of toolboxes. With most servers you can use as many or as few features as you like. If you want to get a plain-vanilla Web server up and running quickly, the configuration files usually require very little editing. However, the power is always there to get your tools out and create the additional features that you need.

In this chapter, you learn the essentials of how to:

- Set up the server's physical network parameters
- Serve documents from multiple directories
- Use and configure server-generated directory indexes
- Configure MIME types for launching viewers
- Implement password security and access control
- Set up Windows NT and Windows 95 for Internet Networking

Overview of Configuration

This chapter presents information on using the NCSA server configuration files. Table 5.1 lists the four primary server configuration files.

Table 5.1 Server Configuration Files	
File	**Description**
httpd.conf	Primary server configuration file
srm.conf	Server resource map
access.conf	Security configuration
mime.types	Information on document types

> **Note**
>
> The WebQuest Servers included on the WebmasterCD use a GUI administration program and store all associated configurations in the Windows registry.

General Principles

Making any server configuration change requires editing one or more of the server configuration files. All configuration files are simply plain ASCII text that you con modify in any text editor (Notepad, Wordpad, and so on). All of the files follow these rules:

- All files are case-insensitive ("ALL" is the same as "all").
- Comment lines begin with the number sign (#). Comments must be on a line by themselves.
- Except in the access configuration file, the order of statements is not important.

> **Note**
>
> File and path names in the configuration files must be given in UNIX format using the forward slash (/).

When you start the server, it reads the configuration files and loads them into memory for as long as the server is running. In order for changes made to the configuration files to take effect, you must restart the server (just the software, not the whole machine). This means that you can edit the files while the server is running without having any effect on the server. Only when the server is restarted do changes take effect.

Terminology

Many of the server configuration commands specify a path to a directory or file. This path can be one of two types, a physical or virtual path. In some cases, either can be specified.

A *virtual path* is the document path specified in a URL. In the URL **http://www.xyz.com/sales/intro.txt**, the virtual path is sales/intro.txt. This may or may not correspond to an actual path on the server. One of the server functions is to map a virtual path to a physical path on the server. The *physical path* is the actual location on disk, such as C:\WINDOWS\MM.BMP.

A physical path can either be absolute or relative. In Windows, *absolute paths* begin with a drive letter (like C:) or backslash (\). *Relative paths* begin with the name of a file or directory, like wedding/gowns/white.txt. Two special symbols can also be used in relative paths. A single dot (.) stands for the current directory, and two dots (..) means the parent directory. The previous example could also be written ./weddings/gowns/white.txt. The path ../birthdays points to the birthdays directory underneath the parent directory.

The Server Configuration File

The *server configuration file* is the main configuration file. By default, it resides in a file called HTTPD.CNF. This is the starting place for configuration. It contains information about the server itself, the locations of log files, and the locations of other configuration files. This section shows you how to configure the server's primary configuration file.

> **Tip**
>
> If your server supports configuration files, it's a good idea to make backup copies of all configuration files before you begin editing.

Server Information

Several types of server information are specified in the server configuration file. These include parameters directly affecting the server's operation such as the server's port and time-out. Elements in the server configuration file used in error reporting include the server administrator name.

To define basic server information, you use the following directives:

```
Port

TimeOut

User

ServerAdmin

ServerRoot

ServerName
```

Setting the Server Port

In order for your Web server to run properly, it must know what port to listen to for information. A port is somewhat like a CB channel, but it is implemented in software rather than physical channels. All Internet traffic to the server is carried on a single network cable; there are not really multiple channels. Every information packet contains a destination port number that is read by the receiving machine so that the data can be sent to the right program. Different types of Internet traffic are carried on different ports. Table 5.2 lists commonly used Internet ports. To set the server's port, use the `Port` directive:

Port

Usage:	Port *number*
Example:	Port 80
Default:	Port 80

The `Port` directive sets the port number that the server listens to for incoming requests. Most Web (HTTP) traffic is on port 80, but it is possible to set the port to any number from 0 to 65535. Ports under 1024 are reserved for the most common types of Internet traffic, so it is recommended that you use a number above 1024 if you need an alternate port. As a rule, experimental Web servers are often run on port 8080.

> **Note**
>
> Some network routers are configured by default to allow all incoming and outgoing Internet traffic on ports greater that 8000. It is very easy, therefore, for a PC or work-station on an internal network to bypass Internet security mechanisms by running a Web server on a high-numbered port.

Table 5.2   Commonly Used Internet Ports

Service	Port
FTP	21
Telnet	23
NNTP	119
SMTP	25
HTTP	80
Gopher	70
IRC	6667
Talk	517
Finger	79

Setting the Server's Time-out

All Internet data is sent in short bursts called *packets*. By breaking up each transmission into small packets, it is necessary to resend only a small amount of information (one packet) when there is a problem with the data transmission. Normally, a client receives a steady stream of packets from an Internet server. However, if the stream is interrupted for a significant time interval, the client or server can *time out* and abort the connection. To set the server's time-out interval, use the TimeOut directive:

TimeOut

> Usage: TimeOut *seconds*
>
> Example: TimeOut 30
>
> Default: 30 seconds

The TimeOut directive is used primarily to facilitate more reliable connections between sending or receiving successive data packets. If, due to a busy or slow link, successive data packets are not sent or received within the allotted time, the server times out and reports an error. It may be necessary to set the timeout to 60 seconds to accommodate slow PPP or SLIP dial-up links on either the server or client end.

II

Setting Up a Web Server

Locations of Other Configuration Files

Because the server configuration file is the main configuration file, it defines the location of all the other configuration files, including the global access configuration file, server resource map, and MIME types configuration file.

You can specify the names of these files as absolute system paths or relative to the server root directory by using the `ServerRoot` directive.

ServerRoot

Usage:	ServerRoot *directory*
Example:	ServerRoot /test/httpd
Default:	C:\HTTPD

The `ServerRoot` directive specifies the path to the top-level directory containing the configuration, support, and document directories and files.

Locations of Log Files

▶ See Chapter 18, "Usage Statistics and Maintaining HTML," p. 497.

Most servers can log every document access and every error. You can use several different utilities to collate and graph these statistics after they are collected.

Two directives specify the location of log files: `AccessLog` and `ErrorLog`

ErrorLog

Usage:	ErrorLog *file*
Example:	ErrorLog /errors/web.err
Default:	logs/error.log

The `ErrorLog` directive specifies the location of the file that records server errors, including:

- Documents that could not be found
- Timeouts due to slow connection links
- Connections that have been interrupted
- Script errors
- Invalid configuration files

ReverseDNSLookup

One final directive in the server configuration file doesn't fall neatly into any other category. You can use the `ReverseDNSLookup` directive to determine the computer names of those accessing server documents.

Usage: `DNSLookup {on¦off}`

Example: `DNSLookup off`

Default: off

The `ReverseDNSLookup` directive determines whether the server will attempt to find the user name of the remote client for every document requested. The remote user name is only available if that TCP/IP address is referenced by a DNS server. Unless you really need to know computer names, leave this option off because it requires considerable overhead.

> **Note**
>
> Most Webmasters don't really need to know the computer name of the client until it comes time to look at statistics. Today's statistic packages will look up the client names for you as they compile the statistics.

> **Caution**
>
> Remote Identity checking is intended to be for information purposes only. It is not a secure mechanism for identifying a client. The information returned can be misleading or wrong.

MIME Types

Multimedia Internet Mail Exchange (MIME) types provide a way for Web browsers to automatically launch a viewing program associated with the file received. For example, the server MIME types file maps an image file in the JPEG format that has the extension JPG to type "image/jpeg." This type is then sent to the browser, which you can configure to launch a JPEG viewer when it receives a file of type "image/jpeg." You can use the MIME types to launch word processors, spreadsheets, or any program that resides on the client's machine, as well as to launch multimedia viewers.

The MIME Types Configuration File

A list of registered MIME types is contained in the MIME types configuration file that comes with the server. By default, this file is often named MIME.TYP.

Each line in the MIME types file contains one MIME type/subtype and a list of file extensions to map to that type. Image, audio, and video types launch their respective multimedia viewers. Text types are for documents written in plain text, but can also be interpreted using formatted tags (like HTML). Application types are defined for most everything else. Subtypes containing x- are experimental types. Listing 5.1 is the standard MIME types file that comes with NCSA httpd.

Listing 5.1   Standard MIME Types File

```
application/activemessage
application/andrew-inset
application/applefile
application/atomicmail
application/dca-rft
application/dec-dx
application/mac-binhex40
application/macwriteii
application/msword             doc
application/news-message-id
application/news-transmission
application/octet-stream       bin
application/oda                oda
application/pdf                pdf
application/postscript         ai       eps      ps
application/remote-printing
application/rtf                rtf
application/slate
application/mif                mif
application/wita
application/wordperfect5.1
application/x-csh              csh
application/x-dvi              dvi
application/x-hdf              hdf
application/x-latex            latex    ltx
application/x-netcdf           nc       cdf
application/x-sh               sh
application/zip                zip
application/x-lzh              lzh
application/x-gzip             gz
audio/basic                    au       snd
audio/x-aiff                   aif      aiff     aifc
audio/wav                      wav
image/gif                      gif
image/ief                      ief
image/jpeg                     jpeg     jpg      jpe
image/tiff                     tiff     tif
image/x-cmu-raster             ras
image/x-portable-anymap        pnm
image/x-portable-bitmap        pbm
image/x-portable-graymap       pgm
```

```
image/x-portable-pixmap          ppm
image/x-rgb                      rgb
image/x-xbitmap                  xbm
image/x-xpixmap                  xpm
image/x-xwindowdump              xwd
message/external-body
message/news
message/partial
message/rfc822
multipart/alternative
multipart/appledouble
multipart/digest
multipart/mixed
multipart/parallel
text/html                        html    htm
text/plain                       txt     log
text/richtext                    rtx
text/tab-separated-values        tsv
text/x-setext                    etx
video/mpeg                       mpeg    mpg    mpe
video/quicktime                  qt      mov
video/msvideo                    avi
video/x-sgi-movie                movie
```

Creating New MIME Types

In some cases, you may wish to create a new MIME type in order to automatically launch an application not defined in the standard configuration file. This is frequently useful on an internal Web server, where the appropriate viewer application for the new type is available on the network. However, it is less useful on a public Web server because browsers have to be specially configured for your new type. Typically, this means you have to tell users what the new type is and provide the view application. This is time consuming and inconvenient; therefore, use new MIME types sparingly on public Web servers.

You can use several methods to create new MIME types for document types not defined in the default MIME types configuration file. You can edit the MIME types file directly but this is not recommended. A better method is to use the AddType directive in the server resource map (covered in the next section) to create a new MIME type for all documents on the server.

In addition you can add MIME types for files only in certain directories by using the AddType directive in *local directory access configuration files*. The "Local Directory ACF's" section later in this chapter covers this type of file.

II

Setting Up a Web Server

> **Note**
>
> Do not modify the MIME types file provided with the server, because you might accidentally modify standard MIME types. If you do edit the MIME types file directly, be sure to make all changes with comments so that you can find them later.

The Server Resource Map

The server resource map file controls server content-related features, including the location of document directories, MIME types for launching viewers, and automatic directory indexing features. By default, the server resource map is located in C:\HTTPD\CONF\SRM.CNF.

Establishing Document Directories

By default, all documents are served from a single directory tree called the *document root,* which is defined by the `DocumentRoot` directive. However, it is possible to serve documents from many other directory trees defining aliases to these directories in the server resource map.

You can create simple directory aliases using the `Alias` directive, which maps a virtual path to a physical path on the server. You also can use the `Alias` directive to serve documents from locations on other servers; `Redirect` redirects requests for documents in a given directory to another location. In addition, you can serve documents from users' personal directories on a network with the `UserDir` directive.

The following directives apply to document directories and scripts:

```
DocumentRoot

Alias

ScriptAlias

WinscriptAlias

Redirect

UserDir
```

By default, all documents are served from a single directory tree specified by the `DocumentRoot` directive. As far as the Web server is concerned, the document root directory is the highest level directory possible. Users of the server cannot specify a higher-level directory using the `..` relative path that normally points to parent directories. This is vital for security, because all Web server security mechanisms are built upon the notion that documents are located only in those directory trees explicitly defined in the server resource map.

DocumentRoot

Usage: `DocumentRoot directory`

Example: `DocumentRoot c:\httpd\documents`

Default: none

The document directory is the directory in which the server looks when it receives a URL without any path information, like http://www.xyz.com/home_page.html. Only one `DocumentRoot` may be specified in the server resource map. You can define additional directory trees with the `Alias` directive.

Creating Aliases

You can serve documents from directory trees outside the document root directory by defining aliases to them with the `Alias` directive. An *alias* maps a virtual path in a URL to a physical path on the server.

Alias

Usage: `Alias virtual_path physical_path`

Example: `Alias /sales c:\documents\sales\data`

Default: none

The `Alias` directive provides a way to serve documents from directories other than the document root directory. By default, the server looks for documents in the root directory only. Using aliases allows other virtual directories to be created. In this example, if a request was received for http://www.xyz.com/sales/march.gif, the server would look for c:\documents\sales\data\march.gif. You can define as many aliases as you like in the server resource map.

> ### Tip
>
> In addition to serving documents from directories other than `DocumentRoot`, aliases can be used to shorten long path names. For example, "c:\xyzcorp\a1division\finance\data\sales" can be shortened to just "/a1sales" by defining an alias.

Aliases can point only to directory trees accessible on the server. This includes all drives physically located on the server and those accessible via a network. Aliases cannot be used to point to other servers. This is the function of the `Redirect` directive.

II

Setting Up a Web Server

Redirect

Usage:	Redirect *virtual_path new_URL*
Example:	Redirect /data/finance http://xyz.finance.com/data
Default:	none

The Redirect directive is similar to the Alias directive, but causes URLs beginning with the special path to be redirected to a new location, which can be any other site on the Internet. The Alias directive defines an alias for a physical path, whereas redirect defines an alias to a virtual path, which can be any valid URL.

> **Tip**
>
> If a document has moved, you can use Redirect to point to the new location so that browsers and HTML files at other sites on the Internet do not all have to be updated to point to the new location. However, if the referring server is unavailable the browser will be unable to locate the document. Use referral only as a temporary measure.

Establishing Script Directories

Closely related to document aliases are *script aliases*, which define directories containing executables scripts instead of documents. When the server reads a document from a script directory, it attempts to run the file rather than to send it on to the client. Script directories are defined with several variations of the ScriptAlias directive, depending on which environment the scripts are written for.

ScriptAlias

Usage:	ScriptAlias *virtual_path physical_path*
Example:	ScriptAlias /cgi-bin/ /usr/local/etc/httpd/cgi-bin

▶ See "CGI Scripting," p. 430.

The ScriptAlias directive is used to define a directory as containing executable CGI (Common Gateway Interface) scripts rather than files to be sent to the client. It also creates a virtual path to the specified directory just like the Alias directive. Files in script directories are not sent to the client. Instead, they are executed and the resulting output is sent to the client. You can define multiple script directories.

WinScriptAlias

Usage:	WinScriptAlias *virtual_path physical_path*
Example:	WinScriptAlias /WIN-CGI/ C:/WINDOWS/CGI/
Default:	none

The WinScriptAlias directive is identical to the ScriptAlias directive except that it identifies directories containing Windows scripts rather than DOS scripts. You can define multiple WinScriptAliases.

MIME Types and Encoding

As discussed in a previous section of this chapter, MIME types provide a way to launch viewers and applications from within a Web browser. The server implements this by sending MIME type information with each document.

Defining MIME types

Normally, the server uses file extensions to map documents being served to their appropriate MIME types. If a file has no extension or an extension that can't be found in the MIME types file, the server sends the default MIME type, txt/html. In certain instances, you may wish to change the default MIME type. You might want to do this, for example, if you have many formatted plain text documents without extensions. To avoid renaming all the documents to end in TXT, you can simply change the default MIME type to text/plain so that the documents are viewed correctly in Web browsers. Change the default MIME type with the DefaultType directive.

DefaultType

Usage:	DefaultType *type*/*subtype*
Example:	DefaultType text/plain
Default:	text/html

The DefaultType directive in the server resource map specifies the default MIME type for all documents on the server.

> **Tip**
>
> If your server contains many nonHTML files that have no extension, it is important to use the DefaultType directive to specify the correct document type. Otherwise, the server assumes they are HTML files (type "text/html").

You can create MIME types that are not currently registered in the MIME types configuration file with the AddType directive. In general, you should not add new MIME types unless absolutely necessary because of the work involved in configuring clients for new MIME types. This is especially true on public Web servers. Like the DefaultType directive, the AddType directive can be used to add a MIME type just for one directory by placing it in a local directory access configuration file. For more information about these files, see the later section, "Local Directory ACFs."

AddType

Usage: AddType *type/subtype* {*extension¦file¦physical_path*}

Example: AddType application/msword doc

Default: none

Using the AddType directive is the preferred method of adding MIME types to the server (as opposed to editing the MIME types configuration file). All documents having the specified extension are mapped to the specified type. The extension argument can be a file name or full path name to a single file as well as a file extension. For example, the statement AddType image/jpeg sat001.dat maps all files named sat001.dat to type "image/jpeg." The statement AddType image/jpeg /pictures/earth_view/sat001.dat maps only the file sat001.dat to type "image/jpeg." Any number of these directives may appear in the server resource map.

A capability similar to MIME types is *encoding*, in which the server can mark compressed documents as being encoded in a specified format. Browsers that support automatic decoding can then use the encoding type information to automatically decode the file when it is received. You indicate encoding types with the AddEncoding directive.

AddEncoding

Usage: AddEncoding *encoding extension*

Example: AddEncoding x-gzip gz

Default: none

You can use the AddEncoding directive to conserve bandwidth on a busy network; however, few clients currently support automatic decoding, so it is not commonly used.

Note

You can achieve automatic decoding using MIME types even on clients that do not support the HTTP encoding extensions. The types "application/zip" and "application/x-gzip" (x means experimental) are already defined in the standard MIME types file. To automatically uncompress ZIP files, users simply configure their browsers to run PKUNZIP after receiving files of type "application/zip."

Directory Indexing

Directory indexing is a powerful Web server feature that enables the server to function somewhat like an FTP server. When the server receives a document request containing only a directory name, it can automatically generate a hypertext list of all files in the specified directory, complete with dates, sizes, descriptions, and icons. Figure 5.1 shows a directory index produced by the WebQuest server. You can also include information about the directory listing above.

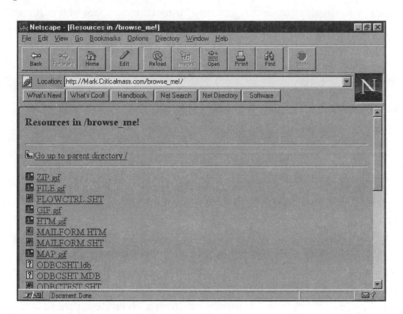

Fig. 5.1
Directory Index returned by the WebQuest Server.

Types of Directory Indexes

A simple directory index contains only the names of files in the requested directory. You can create more detailed indexes by turning on *fancy indexing*, in which file size and date information is displayed along with file names. In Windows, you turn on fancy indexing with the `FancyIndexing` directive.

FancyIndexing

Usage: `FancyIndexing {on¦off}`

Example: `FancyIndexing on`

Default: `on`

The `FancyIndexing` directive controls whether automatically generated directory indexes contain icons, file size and date information, and descriptions as well as file names. If `FancyIndexing` is off, only file names are listed.

> **Note**
>
> In automatically generated directory indexes, files are listed alphabetically. Unfortunately, there is no way to list files by size or date.

It is also possible (and in many instances preferable) to control individual elements of a fancy index using the directives in the next three sections.

In addition to displaying server-generated directory indexes, you can configure most servers to display a prewritten index. A *prewritten index* can be any Web document having the name specified in the DirectoryIndex directive. If a prewritten index file is present in a directory, it is displayed instead of a server-generated index.

DirectoryIndex

Usage: DirectoryIndex *file*

Example: DirectoryIndex index

Default: index.html

The `DirectoryIndex` directive specifies a file name to look for when a client sends a directory URL to the server. This is usually an HTML file, but does not have to be. `DirectoryIndex` provides a convenient way to establish a standard for locating top-level descriptions of Web documents. For example, suppose a company has assigned directories to various departments on an internal Web server. If each department creates a home page with the name specified by `DirectoryIndex`, information from a given department is easy to find. Only one `DirectoryIndex` directive is permitted in the server resource map.

Including Directory Information

It is often useful to include general information about a directory along with the list of files generated by the server. Most servers support this by including the contents of a README file in a directory index, if one is present. The name of the README file is defined in the `ReadmeName` directive.

ReadmeName

Usage: ReadmeName *file*

Example: ReadmeName readme

Default: none

If a file having the name defined by the `ReadmeName` directive is present in a directory, it is included as a footer to the directory listing. The file can either be plain text or HTML, depending on the extension. In this example, if the server found a file named "readme," it would display the file as plain text at the bottom of the index. If it found a file named "readme.html," it would display it as HTML. Only one ReadmeName directive is allowed.

It is also possible to include information before the directory listing. This is possible using the HeaderName directive.

HeaderName

>   Usage: HeaderName *file*
>
>   Example: HeaderName header
>
>   Default: none

The HeaderName directive works just like ReadmeName, except that the included file is displayed before, rather than after, the directory index. Only one HeaderName directive is allowed.

Adding Icons and File Descriptions

Icons in front of the file names make indexes more attractive and allow file types to be identified quickly. To add icons to a directory index, you can specify a default icon and any number of additional icons. You can define the default icon with the DefaultIcon directive.

DefaultIcon

>   Usage: DefaultIcon *virtual_path*
>
>   Example: DefaultIcon /icons/default.gif
>
>   Default: none

Only one default icon is permitted in the server resource map.

> **Tip**
>
> The default icon should be the same size as all other icons used in the directory to achieve a consistent appearance for all files.

You can define icons in three ways: for all files having a certain extension or extensions, for all files having a certain name, or for exactly on file matching a specified path. Add icons with the AddIcon directive.

AddIcon

>   Usage: AddIcon *virtual_path* {*.extension*¦*file*¦*physical_path*}...
>
>   Example: AddIcon /icons/image.gif .gif .jpg .bmp .pcx
>
>   Default: none

The file type specified in the AddIcon directive can either be an extension, a file name, or the full path to a file. You can add icons to directories using the special keyword ^^DIRECTORY^^. In addition, you should specify a blank icon for the keyword ^^BLANKICON^^. The blank icon appears as a placeholder at the beginning of the line containing column labels and should be the same size as the other icons to preserve correct column alignment. You can define multiple icons in the server resource map.

> **Note**
>
> Unlike the other directives that use file extensions (AddType and AddEncoding, for example), AddIcon requires a leading dot (.) before the extension.

Often you can specify an additional element in the AddIcon directive. This element specifies text to appear in place of an icon on nongraphical browsers. In place of the virtual path to the icon file, you can use an expression in the form (ALT, *virtual path*), where ALT is any three-letter text abbreviation for the icon.

Another consideration is that file icons can be considered informational only or can actually be part of the hypertext links to the files. To make icons part of the hypertext links, use the IconsAreLinks directive.

IconsAreLinks

    Usage: IconsAreLinks {on¦off}

    Example: IconsAreLinks on

    Default: off

If IconsAreLinks is on, the user can click either on the file name or its icon.

Besides icons, files listed in a directory index can contain descriptions. You can add descriptions for files of any name or type with the AddDescription directive.

AddDescription

    Usage: AddDescription "*description*" {*extension*¦*file*¦
                      physical_path}

    Example: AddDescription "Microsoft Word document" doc

    Default: HTML title

By default, most servers use a document's title (as specified by the HTML <TITLE>...</TITLE> construct) as its description. Some servers only do this if ScanHTMLTitles is included in IndexOptions. You can specify multiple descriptions in the server resource map.

Excluding Files from Indexes

By default, a directory index displays all files in the directory. However, in many cases it is not desirable to provide a link to the parent directory (..) or to any configuration files in the directory. You can exclude these from the directory index with the `IndexIgnore` directive.

IndexIgnore

> Usage: `IndexIgnore {extension¦file}`
>
> Example: `IndexIgnore CNF #HACCESS #README #README.HTM`
>
> Default: . (the symbol for the current directory)

You can specify a file to be ignored by extension or file name. In this example, all configuration (CNF), access configuration (#HTACCESS), and #README files are to be ignored, along with the parent directory (..).

Tip

It is useful to ignore access configuration files to prevent unauthorized users from learning about your access control mechanisms. Ignoring files specified by the ReadmeName directive prevents redundancy, because these files are displayed as the index footer.

Tip

Be sure to exclude local access configuration files from automatic directory indexes to prevent possible security problems. Do this with the `IndexIgnore` directive.

Access Control

Access configuration files (ACFs) allow or deny permission to use various server features based on Internet address or password security. For example, a whole server can be locked out to all Internet addresses, allowing only internal use. A subscription Internet service can allow access from only paying customers by allowing requests only from their IP addresses. A sensitive document or script can be password-protected so that only authorized users have access.

In addition to providing security, you can use access configuration files to modify features in the server resource map on a per directory basis. This is possible because there are actually two types of access configuration files: the global access configuration file and per directory (local) access configuration file. The next section covers the global access configuration file and its capabilities. The section "Local Directory ACFs" at the end of the chapter explains local directory ACFs.

The Global Access Configuration File

The global access configuration file is the master file. It determines the permissions and features allowed in each directory. The global file also determines the permissions and features that local directory ACFs can override. By default, the global ACF is located in C:\HTTPD\CONF\ACCESS.CNF.

The global file is broken up into sections for each directory in question. By default, all permissions are wide open. If this is not your intended configuration, you must describe the permissions for each controlled directory tree in a separate section of the global ACF.

Each section of the global ACF can contain directives that enable or disable various security features. These security features include the ability to disable potentially dangerous server features, restrict requests based on IP address, require user authorization, and disallow per directory overrides. In addition, the global ACF can contain directives that allow certain document and index capabilities defined in the server resource map to be implemented on a per directory basis.

Sectioning

The global ACF uses a *sectioning directive* named `Directory` to break up the file into one section for each controlled directory.

Directory

Usage: `<Directory physical_path>...options...</Directory>`

Example: `<Directory c:\httpd\htdocs>`
          `Options None`
          `</Directory>`

Default: none

A pair of `Directory` tags designates a section of the ACF. All directives contained between the `Directory` tags apply to the specified directory and all subdirectories. Every `<Directory>` tag must be accompanied by a corresponding `</Directory>` tag, and nested sections are not permitted.

> **Caution**
>
> Every controlled directory hierarchy must be called out specifically in the global ACF. A common oversight is to protect the document root directory, but to overlook directories accessible via aliases and script aliases. These are not protected under the auspices of the document root directory because the global ACF is based on the real paths, not virtual paths.

Disabling Potentially Dangerous Server Features

Many Web Server "Features" open the door to potentially dangerous operations that can be controlled by the global access file. These include using server side includes, implementing automatic directory indexing, executing CGI scripts, and following symbolic links.

Automatic directory indexing is potentially dangerous because people can use this feature to search directories for files you really don't want them to see. If this feature is disabled, they have to guess the names of any files not specifically mentioned in accessible HTML files.

Server side includes allow the server to automatically insert certain elements such as date and time in HTML documents each time the document is requested. One server side include option, exec, is particularly dangerous because it can run any program accessible from the server.

Executing CGI scripts is as dangerous as using server side includes because, like the exec function, scripts can execute any program accessible to the server.

You can control each of these potentially dangerous operations with the Options directive, which you can place in each section of the global ACF.

▶ See Chapter 15, "CGI Scripts, Server Side Includes, and Server APIs," p. 415.

Options

Usage: Options {None¦Indexes¦All}

Example: Options Indexes FollowSymLinks IncludesNoExec

Default: All

Under some basic servers, only the Indexes option is available. Table 5.3 lists many of the elements your server may support. If Indexes is turned off, automatic directory indexes are disabled. However, prewritten index files specified by DirectoryIndex are always allowed.

Table 5.3 Options Available Under NCSA	
Name	**Description**
None	Disallow all options
All	Allow all options
Indexes	Allow server-generated directory indexes
Includes	Allow all server side include functions
IncludesNoExec	Allow server side includes except exec
ExecCGI	Allow CGI scripts to execute
FollowSymLinks	Follow all symbolic links
SymLinksIfOwnerMatch	Follow links only if the destination file has the same owner as the link itself

Restricting Access by IP Address

In many cases, it is necessary to restrict access to a directory or perhaps an entire server to only certain IP addresses. You can do this with the `Limit` directive, which uses a paired tag format similar to `Directory`.

Limit

Usage: `<Limit {GET¦PUT¦POST} ...>...options...</Limit>`

Default: Open to all addresses, no passwords required

The `Limit` directive occurs inside a pair of `Directory` tags and limits access to files in the specified directory tree. The first `Limit` tag specifies what kind of access is restricted. `GET` access is the most commonly used and includes all document requests from the directory. `PUT` access is not yet implemented in the NCSA servers. `POST` access means posting form data to the server for script processing. Limit supports four options inside the pair of `Limit` tags: `Order`, `Deny`, `Allow`, and `Require`. `Order`, `Deny`, and `Allow` are discussed here, and `Require` is discussed under user authorization.

Deny

Usage: `Deny from {host(s)¦all}`

Default: No hosts are denied

The `Deny` directive refuses the type of access specified in the `Limit` directive to the specified host(s). A *host* can be a full or partial host name or IP address or the keyword all.

Examples:

```
Deny from 127.0.0.1
Deny from 127.0
Deny from racecar.ncsa,uiuc.edu
Deny from .uiuc.edu
Deny from all
```

Allow

Usage:	Allow from {*host(s)*¦all}
Default:	All hosts are allowed

The Allow directive allows the type of access specified in the Limit directive to the specified host(s). A host can be a full or partial host name of IP address or the keyword all.

Examples:

```
Allow from 142.167.100.115
Allow from 142.
Allow from 142.167
Allow from monkey.zoo.stlouis.com
Allow from all
Allow from.stlouis.com
```

Order

Usage:	Order {deny,allow¦allow,deny}
Default:	deny,allow

The Order directive specifies in what order Deny and Allow directives are evaluated. This is very important when a host occurs in both Allow and Deny directives because of wild cards. By default, the order is deny, and then allow.

> **Caution**
>
> The order in which Deny and Allow directives appear in a Limit section has no bearing on the order of evaluation. This is determined strictly by the Order directive.

Examples:

```
<Limit GET>
Order deny, allow
Allow from 167.142.
Deny from all
</Limit>
```

In this example, only host addresses beginning with 167.142 are allowed. All others are denied.

```
<Limit GET>
Order allow, deny
Allow from 167.142.
Deny from all
</Limit>
```

In this example, GET access is denied to all hosts, even though 167.142. is specified in an Allow directive. Why? Because the Allow directive is evaluated first, but then all hosts are denied!

Requiring Authorization

Besides restricting access by IP address, directories can be password-protected by requiring a valid user name and password combination. If a directory is protected, users need authorization to access any files in that directory. Access can only be restricted on a per directory (not per file) basis.

The following directives apply to user authorization:

AuthType

AuthName

AuthUserFile

AuthGroupFile

Require (in a Limit section)

In order for password protection to be enforced, an access configuration file must contain all of the above directives except AuthGroupFile, which is only necessary when allowing access to a group of individuals.

The AuthType directive specifies the kind of authorization in effect for the directory. Currently, only the Basic type is implemented.

AuthType

Usage:	AuthType Basic
Default:	none

The `AuthName` directive specifies the reason for requiring access. The name is displayed on the user's browser when the user is asked for a user name and password, and gives some indication as to why authorization is necessary. Of course, if you want to keep unauthorized users totally in the dark, you can specify `AuthName Secret` or something equally unclear to potential users. The specified name may contain spaces, as in the example.

AuthName

Usage:	AuthName *name*
Example:	AuthName Policy Working Group
Default:	none

In order to enforce password security, the Web server needs a list of acceptable user names and passwords. These are contained in a password file, or authorized user file, specified by the `AuthUserFile` directive.

AuthUserFile

Usage:	AuthUserFile *file*
Example:	AuthUserFile /webaccess/working_group/passwd
Default:	None

The `AuthUserFile` specifies a physical path to a user authorization file containing user names and passwords of authorized users.

User authorization files are created with the htpasswd utility included in the Web server support directory. To create a new password file, type **htpasswd -c file username**, where *file* is the name of the file to create and *user* is the password. To add a user to an existing file or to change a user's password, simply omit the -c option.

Caution

Passwords created with `htpasswd` are totally unrelated to network login and system passwords. They are stored in encrypted format on the server; someone reading the `AuthUserFile` cannot obtain passwords. However, when passwords are transmitted from client to server they are only UUEncoded. Users can employ programs called *sniffers* to detect certain types of traffic on the Internet. It is unlikely, but not impossible, for someone to capture your password by sniffing password traffic and UUDecoding it. Consequently, you should choose a password for Web authorization that is unrelated to any other password you may have.

In addition to requiring a single user name and password, standard servers can require membership in a group of authorized users. To implement group security, you must create a user authorization file as usual containing names and passwords. This can be a new file or an existing one. In addition, you must create a group authorization file as defined by the `AuthGroupFile` directive.

AuthGroupFile

Usage: AuthGroupFile *file*

Example: AuthGroupFile c:\webauth\working_group.pwd

Default: none

The `AuthGroupFile` directive defines groups of users whose user names and passwords are stored in a user authorization file. Group files are plain text files that have the following format on each line:

    Group:user1 user2 user3 user4 ...

You can define multiple groups in one group file.

The previous directives have merely set up the locations of files to be used in password protection. The directive that actually enforces this protection is the `Require` directive, which occurs in a `Limit` section and requires that all accesses to files in the restricted directory must be accompanied by a valid user name and password.

Require (in a `Limit` section)

Usage: Require {user¦group} *name*

The `Require` directive pulls together all the other authorization directives to enforce user authorization. If an individual is specified, `Require` looks for that user's information in the `AuthUserFile` specified for the directory. If membership in a group is required, `Require` checks to see that the user is in the specified group as listed in `AuthGroupFile`.

Examples:

```
<Directory c:\httpd\htdocs\secrets>
AuthType Basic
AuthName Secrets
AuthUserFile c:\auth\user\user.auth
AuthGroupFile c:\auth\user\group.auth
<LimitGET>
Require user Dickens
</Limit>
</Directory>
```

In this example, any user attempting to access a file in the Secrets directory is asked to provide authorization for Secrets. If the user enters user name Dickens and the correct password in `AuthUserFile`, access is granted.

```
<Directory c:\httpd\htdocs\more_secrets>
AuthType Basic
AuthName More Secrets
AuthUserFile c:\auth\user\user.auth
AuthGroupFile c:\auth\user\group.auth
<Limit GET>
Order deny, allow
Deny from all
Allow from .hp.com
Require group Wise
</Limit>
</Directory>
```

In this example, a user attempting to access a file in the `more_secrets` directory would be asked to provide authorization for `More Secrets`. In order for access to be granted, the user's user name must appear in group `Wise` in `AuthGroupFile` and the user name and password must be valid in `AuthUserFile`. In addition, the user's IP address must end in "hp.com" or else access is denied.

Local Directory ACFs

Local directory ACFs allow most Web server features to be applied to individual directory trees. This includes features pertaining to MIME types, directory indexing, and security. The name of the Access Configuration File in each directory is given by the `AccessFileName` directive in the server resource map.

Local ACFs can use all the same directives as the global file with the exception of `Directory` and `AllowOverride`.

Security Features

Local ACFs provide a more convenient way to edit security and document features on a per directory basis than editing the global access configuration file. In addition, through the use of the AllowOverride directive, the administrator who maintains the global ACF can grant permission in the global ACF to use some or all of the features of local ACFs. This way, you can preserve essential security, but control less dangerous features such as indexing in each directory.

> **Note**
>
> Directives appearing in access configuration files, whether the global ACF or per directory ACFs, apply recursively to all subdirectories.

Document and Indexing Features

You can specify many of the directives in the server resource map in the global and local directory ACFs. This allows you to modify various document and indexing options for each directory. The server resource map directives that you can include in ACFs are listed below:

```
DefaultType

AddType

AddEncoding

ReadmeName

DefaultIcon

AddIcon

AddDescription (Directory ACFs only)

IndexIgnore
```

Disabling Local Directory ACFs

The administrator of the global ACF can selectively disable features in the local directory ACFs using the `AllowOverride` directive in each directory section. This directive can only appear in the global ACF.

AllowOverride

Usage: AllowOverride *options*

Example: AllowOverride FileInfo options

Default: All

The `AllowOverride` directive allows local directory ACFs to override some or all of the settings in the global ACF. You can specify any of the following options:

```
None

All

Options (indexes, includes, and so on)

FileInfo (AddType, AddEncoding)

AuthConfig (AuthType, AuthName, AuthUserFile, AuthGroupFile)

Limit (Order, Deny, Allow, Require)
```

> **Note**
>
> In order to give authors of documents on your server the capability to password protect their document directories, you must allow both the AuthConfig and Limit directives in local ACFs. Be aware, however, that this also gives document authors the capability to use the access control provisions of the Limit directive to restrict or unrestrict access from Internet addresses.

Configuring Windows NT

The Windows NT Web servers depend on the configuration of the underlying operating system to varying degrees. This section examines all of the necessary steps for configuring Windows NT to maximize the performance and security of your site.

This chapter assumes that you have already successfully installed Windows NT on your system and that you have a NIC (Network Interface Card) installed.

> **Tip**
>
> You can stay up-to-date on Windows NT Server through the Windows NT Server home page at **http://www.microsoft.com/NTServer/**. The Windows Workstation home page is located at: **http://www.microsoft.com/NTWorkstation/**.

Windows NT Versions

There are two versions of Windows NT: NT Server and NT Workstation. The major differences between the two pertain to networking which is an important issue for you to consider. With the standard NT operating system you get peer-to-peer networking, server networking, remote access services, and all the administration tools typically needed to maintain and manage a network server.

Both versions are built around the same Core NT kernel and both feature C2-level security. NT Workstation is meant to be utilized as an individual computing environment or as a small workgroup server. NT Server is meant to be used as an enterprise-wide server platform. The NT server feature set includes a greater degree of fault tolerance and greater network capabilities. Remote administration is a particularly salient benefit for the busy Webmaster coordinating among remote sites.

> **Note**
>
> Although NT Server and NT Workstation use the same basic kernel, NT Server is optimized to be a file and print server, and NT Workstation is optimized as a single user operating system.

If you are a serious Web publisher, you should run NT Server rather than NT Workstation. Also note that some Web servers including the Microsoft IIS server will not run on NT Workstation, only NT Server.

> **Note**
>
> Microsoft publishes upgrades and enhancements to the NT operating systems through distributions known as Service Paks. Be sure to stay current with service pack distributions as they often solve numerous common problems. Many of the Web servers for NT will not operate without the latest service paks installed.

> **Note**
>
> There has been much confusion over whether users of Internet services were considered clients and therefore needed licenses. Recently Microsoft has clarified its position and stated that, essentially, users connecting to your Web server do not need to be licensed.

Basic Concepts

The essentials of setting up and maintaining Windows NT for your Web server revolve around the following concepts:

- Network Setup
- Security
- Administration
- Trouble Shooting

Windows NT Network Setup

The Internet is a worldwide collection of individual Transmission Control Protocol/Internet Protocol (TCP/IP) networks. Each computer on the Internet has a unique address (IP address). Information is transmitted on the Internet in data packets. Each packet is addressed to a specific computer's IP address, such as 10.212.57.189.

Because IP addresses are difficult to use and remember, the Domain Name System (DNS) was created to pair a specific IP address, such as 205.182.161.5, with a friendly domain name, such as **www.Criticalmass.com** (shameless plug for my own Web server!). When a user browses the Internet by using a domain name, the browser first must contact a DNS server to resolve the domain name to an IP address, and then contact the computer with that address.

This has three implications for your Web Server:

■ You must install TCP/IP on your server.

■ You must have a permanent IP address assigned to your server on the Internet.

■ You should register a domain name in the DNS for your permanent IP address. Without a domain name, your users will need to access your site by remembering your IP Address. Ugh!

> **Note**
>
> Your ISP will generally provide your IP addresses and may also register your domain names. Contact the Internet Network Information Center (InterNIC) at **http://rs.internic.net** or your ISP for more information about DNS registration.

Setting Up TCP/IP

Because the language of the Internet is TCP/IP, it is necessary for you to install and bind the TCP/IP protocol to your network adapter.

Like most other networking software for Windows NT, TCP/IP is installed through the network applet in the control panel. Before beginning installation you will need to gather some information:

▶ See "Building the Perfect Server," p. 67, for information regarding network adapter recommendations.

■ The IP address(es) to be assigned to your network card

■ The IP address of your default gateway

■ The IP address of the DNS servers you will use

■ Your Domain name

If you are building an intranet based system you may also need:

■ Your primary and secondary WINS server IP addresses (if any)

■ The LMHOST file for your network (if any)

To install TCP/IP:

1. Open the network applet in the control panel and click on the add software button. See figure 5.2.

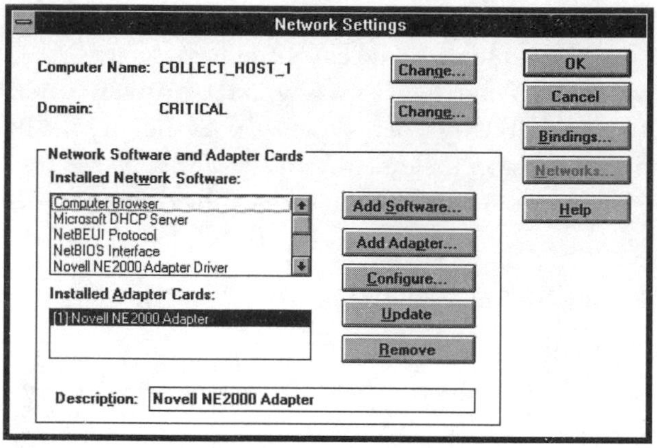

Fig. 5.2
Windows NT
Network Settings
dialog box.

2. Select TCP/IP Protocol and Related Components and the dialog box in figure 5.3 will appear. Select any additional components you desire. Click on Continue and you will be prompted for the location of the files (most likely the CD-ROM distribution disk if your NT software).

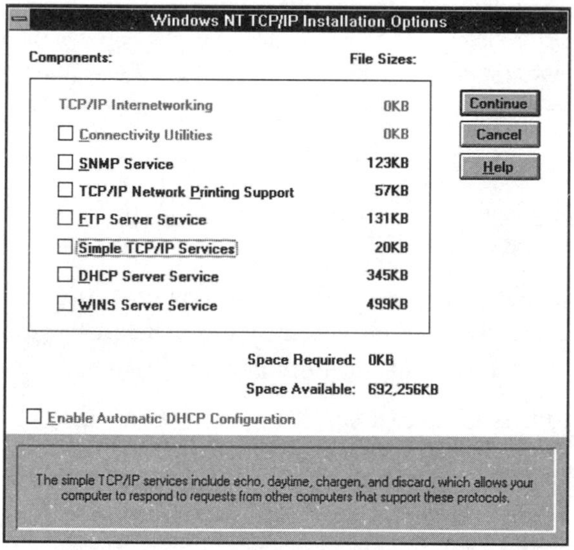

Fig. 5.3
Windows NT TCP/
IP Installation
dialog box.

3. Upon exiting the network configuration applet you will be prompted by the SNMP configuration dialog box. Unless you are familiar with SNMP and understand the settings that you need, simply select the OK button.

4. You will be prompted to set up any additional services (such as FTP) that you selected in the TCP/IP dialog box.

> **Caution**
>
> If you are installing the Microsoft IIS server, do *not* install the FTP service that comes with Windows NT Server. They will conflict and neither FTP service will work.

5. After you have configured the TCP/IP services you will be shown the TCP/IP dialog box shown in figure 5.4.

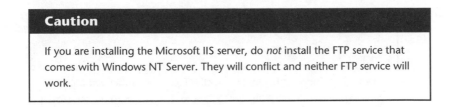

Fig. 5.4
IP Address Configuration dialog box. Make sure these numbers are correct!

6. If you're using DHCP to assign an IP address (this is highly unlikely unless you are on a corporate NT based LAN or WAN), check the Enable Automatic DHCP configuration check box. Otherwise, Enter the TCP/IP address for the network card shown in the adapter field. If you don't know the TCP/IP address, contact your Internet Service Provider or corporate network manager. Your TCP/IP address must be unique. Do not enter in a random TCP/IP address, it will cause unpredictable behavior.

> **Note**
>
> If you intend to host multiple Webs on this host that are accessed via separate domain names, you will need to attach multiple IP addresses to your network adapter(s). This is partly how the concept of "virtual Web servers" is implemented. Each IP address will be matched up with a domain name and during Webserver configuration we will specify which files are to be "served" for each domain.

Caution

You can attach up to 256 IP addresses per network adapter, but the TCP/IP dialog box will only configure 5 per adapter. To go beyond this requires you to edit the Windows NT registry directly. This is recommended only if you have experience editing the registry! Improper changes to the registry can cause your system to fail.

Adding More Than Five IP Addresses to a Network Card

Now that we've properly warned you, here's how to add more than five IP addresses to a network card:

You must use Regedt32.exe to assign more than five IP addresses to a network adapter card. You need to know the network adapter card name and card number used in the Registry. You can get the name from the manufacturer of your network adapter card. For example, the first Intel EtherExpress PRO card installed in a computer running Windows NT uses the name EPRO1.

To configure more than five IP addresses on a network card:

1. Start Regedt32.exe and open:

   HKEY_LOCAL_MACHINE\SYSTEM\CurrentControlSet\Services\<net card name><card number>

   \Parameters\Tcpip

2. Double-click the IPAddress value.

3. Type every IP address you want assigned to the network adapter card. Each address must be separated by a space or carriage return.

4. If applicable, double-click the SubnetMask value.

5. Type subnet masks for the IP addresses added in step 3. Pair the subnet masks to an IP address by entering the subnet masks in the same order as the IP addresses.

Caution

Many users have reported that using more than 15 or 16 IP addresses per network adapter has resulted in unstable system behavior. Others have reported using hundreds with no ill side effects. Be warned, your mileage may vary!

7. Enter your subnet mask into the appropriate field. You will get the mask from the same entity that provided your TCP/IP address. The most common scenario is that you will be using a class C address. The subnet mask will then be 255.255.255.0

8. In the default gateway field enter in the TCP/IP address of the router or computer that connects your Web host to the Internet.

9. If you are using WINS to assign NetBIOS names (again, unlikely if you are not on a corporate LAN / WAN) enter the IP addresses of the WINS servers as appropriate.

10. If you have access to a Domain Name Server (if you are on the Internet you will need this) click on the DNS button to configure the DNS addresses. See figure 5.5.

> **Tip**
>
> You will want to use the DNS servers that are as few network hops away as possible. Don't pick a DNS server that a friend happens to be using in Duluth. Ask your ISP or your network administrator for the closest DNS server. Your computer may communicate with the DNS server frequently, so you are wise to minimize the amount of time this takes.

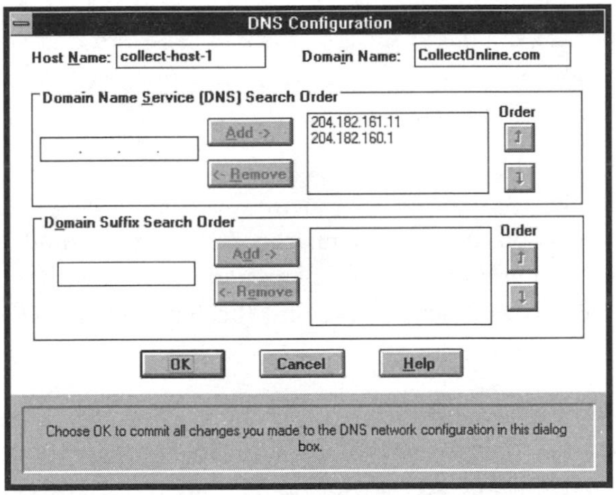

Fig. 5.5
Domain Name Service Configuration.

DNS Configuration

Host Name: collect-host-1   Domain Name: CollectOnline.com

Domain Name Service (DNS) Search Order
Add ->
<- Remove
204.182.161.11
204.182.160.1
Order

Domain Suffix Search Order
Add ->
<- Remove
Order

OK   Cancel   Help

Choose OK to commit all changes you made to the DNS network configuration in this dialog box.

11. Enter a name for your system in the Host Name field. If you have not been assigned one, simply put in a descriptive name such as "Webhost".

12. In the domain name field enter in the name of the DNS domain that this host will be part of. Be careful not to confuse this with an NT server domain, which is entirely different.

II

Setting Up a Web Server

13. In the Domain Name Service (DNS) Search Order box, enter the IP addresses of the domain servers on your network. Place the DNS server closest to this station on the network (or Internet) to speed up name resolution.

14. Click OK and reboot the NT operating system for these changes to take effect.

Securely Configuring Windows NT Server

The Internet is often depicted as a cyber-frontier, wilder and woolier than even the wild, wild west of yesteryear. This may be somewhat overblown by slanted media coverage, but it is a serious topic for all Webmasters. Windows NT provides user-account security and Windows NT File System (NTFS) file-system security. You can use the topics below as a checklist to ensure you have effectively used User Accounts and NTFS to secure Windows NT Server. Additionally, you can prevent security breaches by properly configuring the services running on your computer.

Preventing Intrusion by Setting Up User Accounts

Windows NT security helps you protect your computer and its resources by requiring assigned user accounts. You can control access to all computer resources by limiting the user rights of these accounts.

Every operation on a computer running Windows NT identifies who is doing the operation. For example, the user name and password that you use to log on to Windows NT identifies who you are and defines what you are authorized to do on that computer.

What a user is authorized to do on a computer is configured in User Manager by setting User Rights in the Policies menu. User rights authorize a user to perform certain actions on the system. Your Web service should be logged on "locally" utilizing a user name that is restricted to access only what is necessary to provide services. Create an account (I call mine WEBLOGON) specifically for this purpose.

Choose Difficult Passwords

The easiest way for someone to gain unauthorized access to your system is with a stolen or easily guessed password. Make sure that all passwords used on the system, especially those with administrative rights, have difficult-to-guess passwords. In particular make sure to select a good administrator password (a long, mixed-case, alphanumeric password is best) and set the appropriate account policies. Passwords can be set by using the User Manager utility, or at the system logon prompt.

Maintain Strict Account Policies

The User Manager utility provides a way for the system administrator to specify how quickly account passwords expire (which forces users to regularly change passwords), and other policies, such as how many bad logon attempts will be tolerated before locking a user out. Use these policies to manage your accounts, particularly those with administrative access, to prevent exhaustive or random password attacks.

Limit the Membership of the Administrator Group

By limiting the members of the Administrator group, you limit the number of users who might choose bad passwords and expose your system.

NTFS File Security

In addition to user accounts, you should place your data files on an NTFS partition. NTFS provides security and access control for your data files. You can limit access to portions of your file system for specific users and services by using NTFS. In particular, it's a good idea to apply Access Control Lists (ACLs) to your data files for any Internet publishing service.

The NTFS file system gives you very granular control on files by specifying users and groups that are permitted access and what type of access they may have for specific files and directories. For example, some users may have Read-only access, while others may have Read, Change, and Write access. You should ensure that the WEBLogon account or authenticated accounts are granted or denied appropriate access to specific resources.

> **Note**
>
> You should note that the group Everyone contains all users and groups. By default, the group Everyone has full control of all files created on an NTFS drive. You will want to change this to suit your needs.

You should review the security settings for content and CGI directories and adjust them appropriately. Generally you should use the settings in the following table:

Directory Type	Suggested Access
content	Read access
programs	Read and Execute access
databases	Read and Write access

II

Setting Up a Web Server

Enable Auditing

You can enable auditing of NTFS files and directories on Windows NT Server through the File Manager. You can review the audit records periodically to ensure that no one has gained unauthorized access to sensitive files.

Running Other Network Services

You should review all of the network services that you are using on any computer connected to the Internet. When reviewing consider two things:

- Is this service necessary?
- Does it create any security holes?
- Is it running under an account name with appropriate security?

Caution

Run only the services that you need! The fewer services you are running on your system, the less likely a mistake will be made in administration that could be exploited. Use the Services applet in the Windows NT Control Panel to disable any services not absolutely necessary on your Internet server.

Tip

Unbind unnecessary services from your Internet adapter cards to improve performance and security.

Use the Bindings feature in the Network applet in the Windows NT Control Panel to unbind any unnecessary services from any network adapter cards connected to the Internet. For example, you might use the Server service to copy new images and documents from computers in your internal network, but you might not want remote users to have direct access to the Server service from the Internet. If you need to use the Server service on your private network, the Server service binding to any network adapter cards connected to the Internet should be disabled. You can use the Windows NT Server service over the Internet; however, you should fully understand the security implications and licensing issues.

Tip

The FTP Server service included with Windows NT should also be disabled (this is required if the Microsoft Internet Information Server FTP service will be installed) or configured to ensure adequate security.

Check Permissions on Network Shares

If you *are* running the Server service on your Internet adapter cards, be sure to double-check the permissions set on the shares you have created on the system. It is also wise to double-check the permissions set on the files contained in the shares' directories to ensure that you have set them correctly.

NT Management Tools

NT ships with two management tools that will come in extremely handy during the day-to-day management of your Web server. These are the Event Log and the performance monitor. Take the time to understand the information these services can report back to you and you will go a long way towards gaining complete control of your system.

Tracking Problems with Event Viewer

Event Viewer, in the Administrative Tools program group can notify administrators of critical events by displaying pop-up messages, or by simply adding event information to log files. The information allows you to better understand the sequence and types of events that led up to a particular state or situation. You can use Event Viewer to view and manage three separate types of logs:

- System
- Security
- Application

The System log reports information regarding system level issues events. These include system startup and shutdown. See figure 5.6.

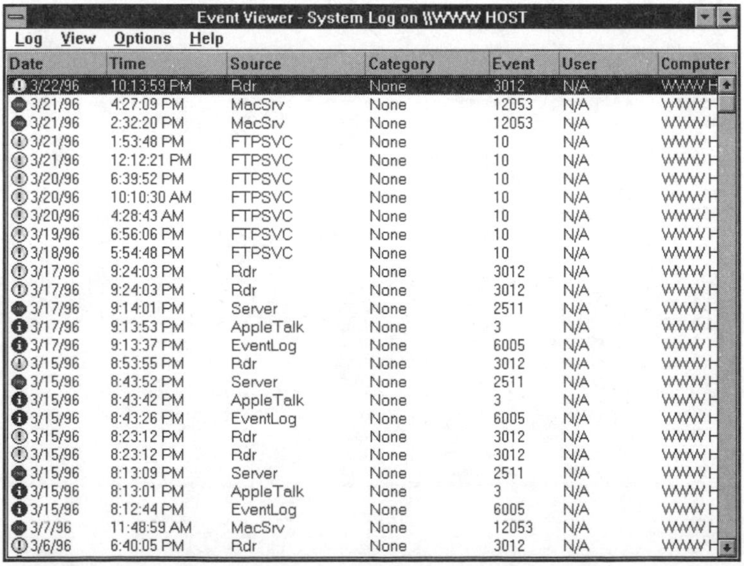

Date	Time	Source	Category	Event	User	Computer
3/22/96	10:13:59 PM	Rdr	None	3012	N/A	WWW H
3/21/96	4:27:09 PM	MacSrv	None	12053	N/A	WWW H
3/21/96	2:32:20 PM	MacSrv	None	12053	N/A	WWW H
3/21/96	1:53:48 PM	FTPSVC	None	10	N/A	WWW H
3/21/96	12:12:21 PM	FTPSVC	None	10	N/A	WWW H
3/20/96	6:39:52 PM	FTPSVC	None	10	N/A	WWW H
3/20/96	10:10:30 AM	FTPSVC	None	10	N/A	WWW H
3/20/96	4:28:43 AM	FTPSVC	None	10	N/A	WWW H
3/19/96	6:56:06 PM	FTPSVC	None	10	N/A	WWW H
3/18/96	5:54:48 PM	FTPSVC	None	10	N/A	WWW H
3/17/96	9:24:03 PM	Rdr	None	3012	N/A	WWW H
3/17/96	9:24:03 PM	Rdr	None	3012	N/A	WWW H
3/17/96	9:14:01 PM	Server	None	2511	N/A	WWW H
3/17/96	9:13:53 PM	AppleTalk	None	3	N/A	WWW H
3/17/96	9:13:37 PM	EventLog	None	6005	N/A	WWW H
3/15/96	8:53:55 PM	Rdr	None	3012	N/A	WWW H
3/15/96	8:43:52 PM	Server	None	2511	N/A	WWW H
3/15/96	8:43:42 PM	AppleTalk	None	3	N/A	WWW H
3/15/96	8:43:26 PM	EventLog	None	6005	N/A	WWW H
3/15/96	8:23:12 PM	Rdr	None	3012	N/A	WWW H
3/15/96	8:23:12 PM	Rdr	None	3012	N/A	WWW H
3/15/96	8:13:09 PM	Server	None	2511	N/A	WWW H
3/15/96	8:13:01 PM	AppleTalk	None	3	N/A	WWW H
3/15/96	8:12:44 PM	EventLog	None	6005	N/A	WWW H
3/7/96	11:48:59 AM	MacSrv	None	12053	N/A	WWW H
3/6/96	6:40:05 PM	Rdr	None	3012	N/A	WWW H

Fig. 5.6
The System Log.

The Security log can be used to monitor all logons to your server. This is a critical log for you to monitor if your server is on the Internet. See figure 5.7.

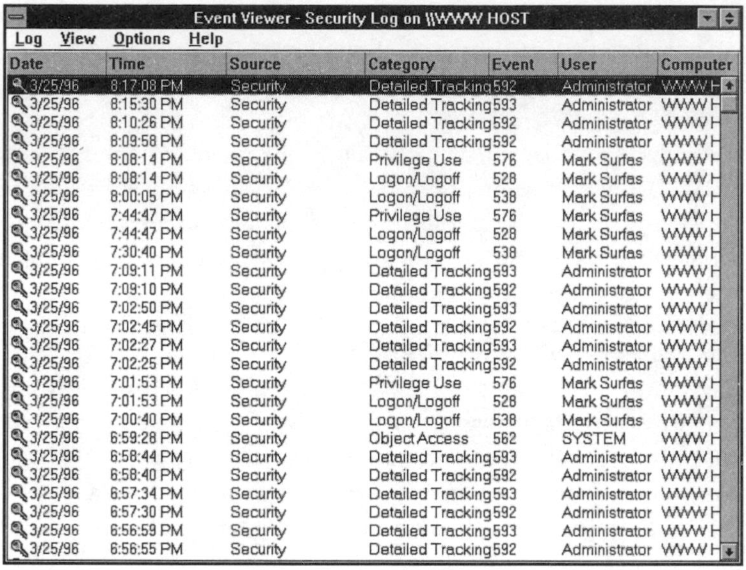

Date	Time	Source	Category	Event	User	Computer
3/25/96	8:17:08 PM	Security	Detailed Tracking	592	Administrator	WWW H
3/25/96	8:15:30 PM	Security	Detailed Tracking	593	Administrator	WWW H
3/25/96	8:10:26 PM	Security	Detailed Tracking	592	Administrator	WWW H
3/25/96	8:09:58 PM	Security	Detailed Tracking	592	Administrator	WWW H
3/25/96	8:08:14 PM	Security	Privilege Use	576	Mark Surfas	WWW H
3/25/96	8:08:14 PM	Security	Logon/Logoff	528	Mark Surfas	WWW H
3/25/96	8:00:05 PM	Security	Logon/Logoff	538	Mark Surfas	WWW H
3/25/96	7:44:47 PM	Security	Privilege Use	576	Mark Surfas	WWW H
3/25/96	7:44:47 PM	Security	Logon/Logoff	528	Mark Surfas	WWW H
3/25/96	7:30:40 PM	Security	Logon/Logoff	538	Mark Surfas	WWW H
3/25/96	7:09:11 PM	Security	Detailed Tracking	593	Administrator	WWW H
3/25/96	7:09:10 PM	Security	Detailed Tracking	592	Administrator	WWW H
3/25/96	7:02:50 PM	Security	Detailed Tracking	593	Administrator	WWW H
3/25/96	7:02:45 PM	Security	Detailed Tracking	592	Administrator	WWW H
3/25/96	7:02:27 PM	Security	Detailed Tracking	593	Administrator	WWW H
3/25/96	7:02:25 PM	Security	Detailed Tracking	592	Administrator	WWW H
3/25/96	7:01:53 PM	Security	Privilege Use	576	Mark Surfas	WWW H
3/25/96	7:01:53 PM	Security	Logon/Logoff	528	Mark Surfas	WWW H
3/25/96	7:00:40 PM	Security	Logon/Logoff	538	Mark Surfas	WWW H
3/25/96	6:59:28 PM	Security	Object Access	562	SYSTEM	WWW H
3/25/96	6:58:44 PM	Security	Detailed Tracking	593	Administrator	WWW H
3/25/96	6:58:40 PM	Security	Detailed Tracking	592	Administrator	WWW H
3/25/96	6:57:34 PM	Security	Detailed Tracking	593	Administrator	WWW H
3/25/96	6:57:30 PM	Security	Detailed Tracking	592	Administrator	WWW H
3/25/96	6:56:59 PM	Security	Detailed Tracking	593	Administrator	WWW H
3/25/96	6:56:55 PM	Security	Detailed Tracking	592	Administrator	WWW H

Fig. 5.7
The Security Log.

The Application log is used by programs running on the server to report information. Your Web server will probably report startups and shutdowns, as well as statistics and errors. See figure 5.8.

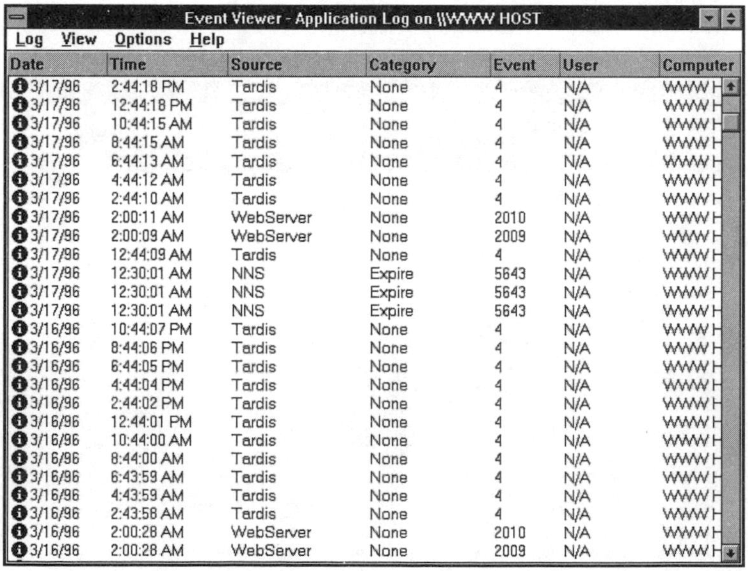

Date	Time	Source	Category	Event	User	Computer
3/17/96	2:44:18 PM	Tardis	None	4	N/A	WWW H
3/17/96	12:44:18 PM	Tardis	None	4	N/A	WWW H
3/17/96	10:44:15 AM	Tardis	None	4	N/A	WWW H
3/17/96	8:44:15 AM	Tardis	None	4	N/A	WWW H
3/17/96	6:44:13 AM	Tardis	None	4	N/A	WWW H
3/17/96	4:44:12 AM	Tardis	None	4	N/A	WWW H
3/17/96	2:44:10 AM	Tardis	None	4	N/A	WWW H
3/17/96	2:00:11 AM	WebServer	None	2010	N/A	WWW H
3/17/96	2:00:09 AM	WebServer	None	2009	N/A	WWW H
3/17/96	12:44:09 AM	Tardis	None	4	N/A	WWW H
3/17/96	12:30:01 AM	NNS	Expire	5643	N/A	WWW H
3/17/96	12:30:01 AM	NNS	Expire	5643	N/A	WWW H
3/17/96	12:30:01 AM	NNS	Expire	5643	N/A	WWW H
3/16/96	10:44:07 PM	Tardis	None	4	N/A	WWW H
3/16/96	8:44:06 PM	Tardis	None	4	N/A	WWW H
3/16/96	6:44:05 PM	Tardis	None	4	N/A	WWW H
3/16/96	4:44:04 PM	Tardis	None	4	N/A	WWW H
3/16/96	2:44:02 PM	Tardis	None	4	N/A	WWW H
3/16/96	12:44:01 PM	Tardis	None	4	N/A	WWW H
3/16/96	10:44:00 AM	Tardis	None	4	N/A	WWW H
3/16/96	8:44:00 AM	Tardis	None	4	N/A	WWW H
3/16/96	6:43:59 AM	Tardis	None	4	N/A	WWW H
3/16/96	4:43:59 AM	Tardis	None	4	N/A	WWW H
3/16/96	2:43:58 AM	Tardis	None	4	N/A	WWW H
3/16/96	2:00:28 AM	WebServer	None	2010	N/A	WWW H
3/16/96	2:00:28 AM	WebServer	None	2009	N/A	WWW H

Fig. 5.8
The Application Log.

Monitoring Your Server with Performance Monitor

The Performance Monitor, also found in the Administrative Tools program group, provides a way of measuring and monitoring system performance. Many NT based servers and services automatically install Windows NT Performance Monitor counters. With these counters you can use the Windows NT Performance Monitor for real-time measurement of your Internet service use. See figure 5.9.

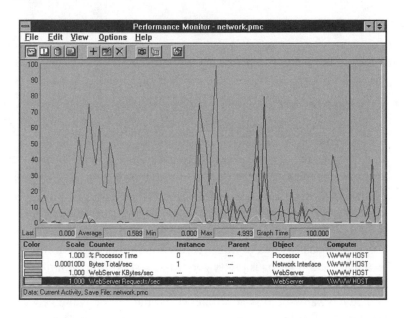

Fig. 5.9
Performance Monitor for a busy server!

An excellent example of this is the Web service included in the Microsoft IIS package. This server provides counters to monitor a vast array of performance elements. These include:

Bytes Sent/sec	Files Sent
Bytes Total/sec	Files Total
CGI Requests	Get Requests
Connection Attempts	Head Requests
Connections/sec	Logon Attempts
Current Anonymous Users	Maximum Anonymous Users
Current ISAPI Requests	Maximum ISAPI Requests
Current CGI Requests	Maximum CGI Requests
Current Connections	Maximum Connections
Current Nonanonymous Users	Maximum Nonanonymous Users
Files Received	Not Found Errors

Other Request Methods   Total Anonymous Users

Post Requests   Total Nonanonymous Users

While running your server, you should get to know the performance monitor and establish benchmarks for standard behavior. When these performance benchmarks are deviated from, you can decide whether action is warranted. Key areas to monitor are CPU usage and disk requests.

Optimizing Windows NT Performance

One of the advantages of Windows NT is that much of the work to optimize is done for you automatically by the system. A few of the most common methods for boosting performance are covered briefly below.

- *RAM*   Most NT GURU's will tell you that the easiest way to boost system performance is to add RAM. You should have a minimum of 16 MB to run Windows NT and 32 is recommended. If you are running a highly active server that uses CGI programming you will likely see nice performance increases with each addition of RAM. Many of the popular NT Web sites use 128 MB of RAM, and sometimes more.

- *Hard Disk*   A Web site lives and dies by its hard disk. The first rule in hard disks today is to get a hard drive with a fast access rating. Drive speeds are usually rated in milliseconds and in today's environment a 5 to 9 millisecond rating is pretty good. The second rule in hard drives is to connect it to your system through a 32-bit interface. Your server should have a 32-bit disk controller either built in or available via a 32-bit slot. The third rule is to defragment your hard drive. This can greatly speed up file access by placing your files in contiguous blocks on the hard drive. Unfortunately there are only a few defragmenters on the market for Windows NT, and all of them are expensive.

> **Tip**
>
> Many experts will tell you that increasing the performance of NT is simply a function of adding RAM. My experience has shown me that RAM is definitely your best value when speeding up your system.

- *CPU*   Serving Web is generally not much of a strain on the microprocessor. The CPU is only likely to become a factor as you start running sophisticated CGI type applications. If you plan on a busy Web site, utilize a fast Pentium and consider the Pentium Pro.

■ *Virtual Memory*   Windows NT utilizes a virtual memory system. This means that when necessary, NT utilizes hard disk space as RAM allowing more and larger applications to run. NT uses a paging file on each logical drive for virtual memory. The size and location of these files is configurable through the system applet on the control panel. Be sure that you have plenty of available hard disk space available. If you notice that your NT system is constantly accessing the hard drive during normal activity, this is an indication that you need more RAM.

Tip

Run only 32-bit applications. Windows NT is a 32-bit operating system that is backwards compatible to allow you to run 16-bit applications. 16-bit applications cause NT to run a sub-system for compatibility. This will slow down all of the applications that are currently executing on your system.

Configuring Windows 95

Configuring Windows 95 to run a Web server is relatively simple when compared to Windows NT. The fact is that as a server platform Windows 95 is adequate for only smaller and simpler Web sites. That doesn't mean that you can't create a Web site that's perfect for your individual needs, just scale your expectations accordingly.

This chapter assumes that Windows 95 has been successfully installed on your PC. This chapter also assumes that you have a NIC (Network Interface Card) installed on a LAN connected to the Internet.

Note

It is also feasible to connect your server to the Internet via dial-up modem. This is done in many low volume cases due to the low cost relative to a permanent circuit. Most of the steps here are similar to those required for a modem connection. If you have a modem installed you will see it referred to as a Dial-up Adapter in the network configuration (see figure 5.10). Simply substitute *Dial-up Adapter* where you see *NIC*. We recommend that you eliminate most or all graphics from your site if serving via dial-up.

We will configure Windows 95 to run the WebQuest server included on the Webmaster CD.

WebmasterCD

The configuration steps this section covers are:

- Network Setup
- Security

These configuration needs are the same as those covered previously in the section on Windows NT. In fact we will often refer you there for the background material already covered.

Network Setup

▶ See "Windows NT Network Setup," p. 130.

The Internet uses the TCP/IP network protocols to establish and maintain communications between computers. You can review our discussion of this earlier in this chapter.

Installing TCP/IP

To install TCP/IP:

1. Open the network applet in the Windows 95 control panel and click on the Add Software button.

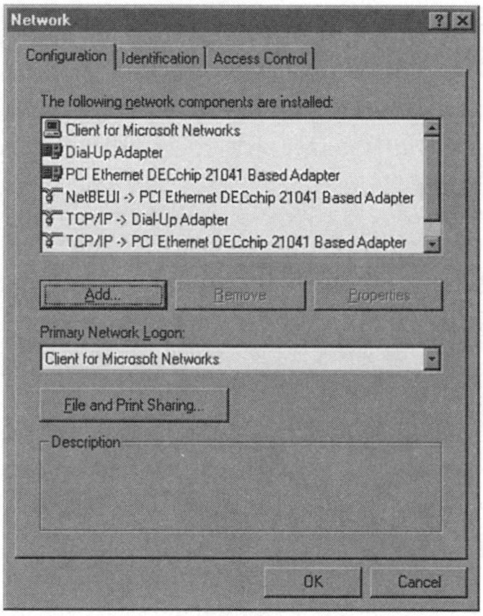

Fig. 5.10
Windows 95
Network Configuration applet.

2. Single click to highlight your NIC (Network Interface Card) and then click on the Add button. See figure 5.11.

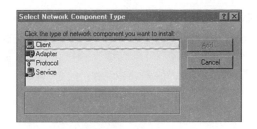

Fig. 5.11
Windows 95
Network Compo-
nent dialog box.

3. Select Protocol and click the Add button.

This will bring up the dialog box in figure 5.12. This is a list of network protocols that come with Windows 95, ordered by the manufacturer. In most cases you will want to use the native Microsoft TCP/IP compo-nent. In a corporate environment, you will need to verify this with your network administrator.

Fig. 5.12
Windows 95
Network Protocol
dialog box.

4. Select Microsoft in the left-hand list box as shown in figure 5.12. Click on TCP/IP in the Network Protocols box on the right. Click the OK button.

Windows will now automatically bind the TCP/IP network protocol to your NIC. You will see a new entry in the Network Configuration dialog that begins with TCP/IP ->.

5. Highlight the new TCP/IP binding and click on the Properties button. This will bring up the TCP/IP properties dialog box.

The initial configuration page is the TCP/IP address page.

> **Note**
>
> Unlike Windows NT you can only bind one TCP/IP address per Network Inter-face card. This makes Windows 95 a poor choice to serve Virtual Webs.

II

Setting Up a Web Server

6. Enter the TCP/IP Address assigned to this PC and the appropriate Subnet Mask. If you don't know this information contact your ISP or network administrator.

7. Select the Tab titled Gateway as shown in figure 5.13. Enter the TCP/IP address of the remote gateway. This information should be obtained from your network administrator or ISP.

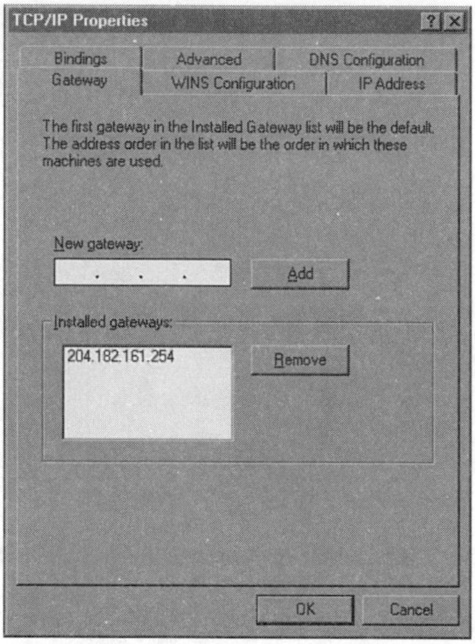

Fig. 5.13
TCP/IP Gateway
dialog box.

8. Select the Tab titled DNS Configuration as shown in figure 5.14 and enter in the DNS Server IP addresses as given to you by your ISP or network administrator.

9. In the host and domain boxes of the DNS Configuration dialog enter the name of your PC and the TCP/IP domain you belong to. If you don't have a name assigned to you from your network administrator simply enter any name you wish. This name is public and will be received by remote machines under certain circumstances so be prudent.

10. Click the OK button and return to the Network Configuration dialog. You have finished configuring the physical network access for your web server. Select the OK button and reboot your PC. You are now ready to install your Web server software.

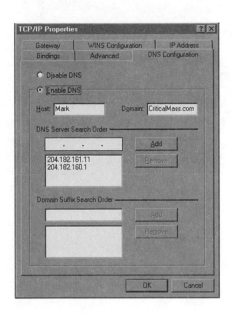

Fig. 5.14
DNS configuration
dialog box.

Security

Setting up network security for your Web site is accomplished from the same
Network Configuration applet that you used for the physical network
configuration. ❖

▶ See "Access
Controls on a
Windows 95
System,"
p. 207.

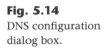

II

Setting Up a Web Server

## CHAPTER 6

Configuring and Managing the Microsoft Internet Information Server

Like something you'd hear in a bad TV advertisement, the Microsoft IIS is more than just a Web server—it's three, yes, three servers in one:

- World Wide Web (WWW)
- File Transfer Protocol (FTP)
- Gopher

You will run across the FTP and Gopher servers during the operations used in this chapter, but this chapter focuses on the specifics of configuring the Web server component of the Microsoft IIS.

Now that you've completed setup and tested your installation, you can use Microsoft Internet Service Manager and other tools to configure the more advanced features of the Internet Information Server services. This chapter tells you how to:

- Configure access permissions for remote clients
- Establish logon requirements for remote clients
- Specify home directories and other virtual directories
- Create multiple virtual servers on a single computer
- Require content encryption
- Configure logging options
- Specify other default settings

The Microsoft Internet Service Manager

The IIS configuration is implemented via the Internet Service Manager, a simple yet powerful tool. One of the strengths of this tool is that it functions as both a local and a remote administrator. See figure 6.1.

Fig. 6.1
The Internet
Server Program
Group.

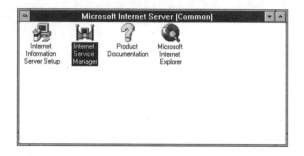

The Internet Service Manager is the tool that you will use to configure and monitor your IIS. You can use the Service Manager to administer both locally running services and remote servers elsewhere on your network.

Three views are available in Internet Service Manager: Reports, Servers, and Services.

Report View

Report view as shown in figure 6.2 is the default view. This view alphabetically lists the selected computers, with each installed service shown on a separate line. Click the column headings to alphabetically sort the entire list. Report view is probably most useful for sites with only one or two computers running Internet Information Server.

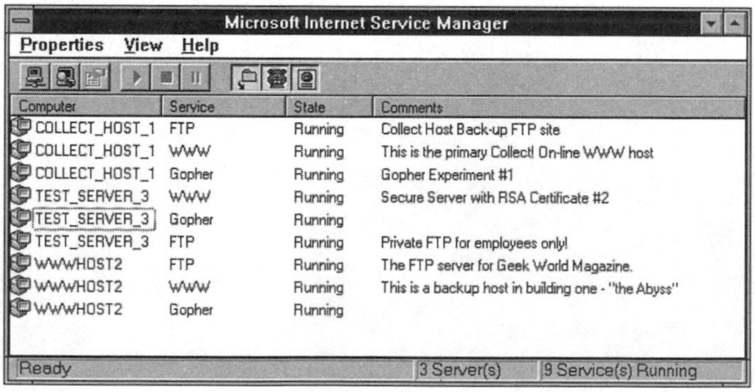

Fig. 6.2
The Internet
Service Manager
Report View.

Servers View

The Servers view in figure 6.3 displays services running on network servers by computer name. Click the plus symbol (+) next to a server name to see the status of the services that server is running. Double-click a service name to see its property sheets. The Servers view is most useful for sites running a large number of servers when you need to know the status of the services installed on a specific computer.

Fig. 6.3
The Internet Service Manager Server View.

Services View

The Services view shown in figure 6.4 lists the services on every selected computer grouped by service name. Click the plus symbol next to a service name to see the servers running that service. Double-click the computer name under a service to see the property sheets for the service running on that computer. Services view is most useful for sites with widely distributed servers when you need to know which computers are running a particular service.

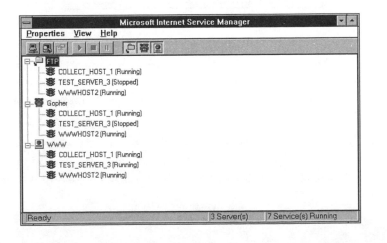

Fig. 6.4
The Internet Service Manager Services View.

II

Setting Up a Web Server

Property Sheets

Double-clicking on the service icons will launch the property sheets associated with that service instance. The Internet Service Manager property sheets are used to configure and manage the WWW and other services. There are four property sheets for the WWW server:

- Service
- Directories
- Logging
- Advanced

Service Property Sheet

The Service page is used to control high-level access to your server, including the user account that nonauthenticated browsers will use. See figure 6.5.

Fig. 6.5

Service property sheet for the IIS WWW Server.

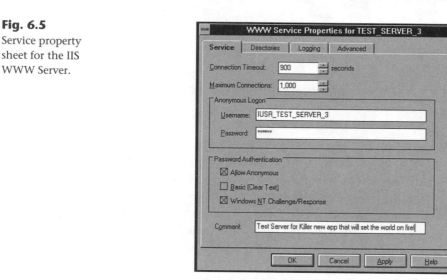

The IIS utilizes the native NT security permissions to control access to your WWW server. This is a nice benefit if you have an existing NT server setup that you will now use to serve Web. No access control files are needed; you will use the existing NT user manager and file manager to implement your security.

You use the Service property sheet to control who can use your server and to specify the account used for anonymous client requests to log on to the computer. If your site is like most, you will allow some (or many!) anonymous connections. If you allow anonymous logons, all user permissions for the user, such as permission to access information, will use the IUSR_*computername* account. To use a different default user from your current security system to control information access, change the anonymous logon account to an existing account on your network.

The IUSR_*computername* Account

The IUSR_*computername* account is created during Microsoft Internet Information Server setup. For example, if the computer name is marketing1, then the anonymous access account name is IUSR_marketing1.

By default, all Microsoft Internet Information Server client requests use this account. In other words, information server clients are logged on to the computer using the IUSR_*computername* account. The IUSR_*computername* account is permitted only to log on locally. No network rights are granted that could allow an unauthorized user to damage your server or its files.

> **Note**
>
> The IUSR_*computername* account is also added to the group Guests. If you have changed the settings for the Guests group, those changes also apply to the IUSR_*computername* account. Review the settings for the Guests group to ensure that they are appropriate for the IUSR_*computername* account.

If you allow remote access only by the IUSR_*computername* account, remote users do not provide a user name and password, and have only the permissions assigned to that account. This prevents hackers from attempting to gain access to sensitive information with fraudulent or illegally obtained passwords. For some situations this can provide the best security.

Password Authentication

You can require users to logon and become "authenticated" clients by specifying that users must supply valid Windows NT user names and passwords. This all happens through the native NT tools that you already know and love. The File manager will dictate which areas are secured and the NT User manager will become your WWW user manager!

Allow Anonymous

Anonymous browsing is the *modus operandi* for most Web surfing. You click, you connect, you surf. For most purposes, this works fine. Many Web sites are a combination of anonymous access and secured access. If this is the case for you, select Allow Anonymous to allow anonymous access via the IUSR_*computername* account.

Basic Authentication

Basic authentication is supported by all modern browsers. When a document or directory is accessed that isn't accessible via the anonymous account, the user must log in and authenticate the session.

Basic authentication does not encrypt your user name and password before transmission. Basic authentication is encoded only by using UUencode, and can be decoded easily by anyone with access to your network, or to a segment of the Internet that transfers your packets.

> **Caution**
>
> With only basic authentication, you will send your Windows NT user name and password unencrypted over public networks. Intruders can easily learn user names and passwords.

Windows NT Challenge/Response

The WWW service also supports the Windows NT Challenge/Response encrypted password transmission. This method encrypts the user name and password, providing secure transmission of user names and passwords over the Internet. Unfortunately Windows NT authentication is currently supported only by the Microsoft Internet Explorer.

With both basic authentication and Windows NT authentication, no access is permitted unless a valid user name and password is supplied. Password authentication is useful if you want only authorized individuals to use your server or specific portions controlled by NTFS. You can have IUSR_*computername* access and authenticated access enabled at the same time.

Directories Property Sheet

The Directories property sheet shown in figure 6.6 gives you a straightforward means of defining Webs and their directories.

Directories

You will start with one initial Web space and directory defined. All the immediate directories within this directory are accessible to the Web browser (security permitting). To add additional directories from the outside of this immediate directory tree to this Web structure, click the Add button (see fig. 6.7).

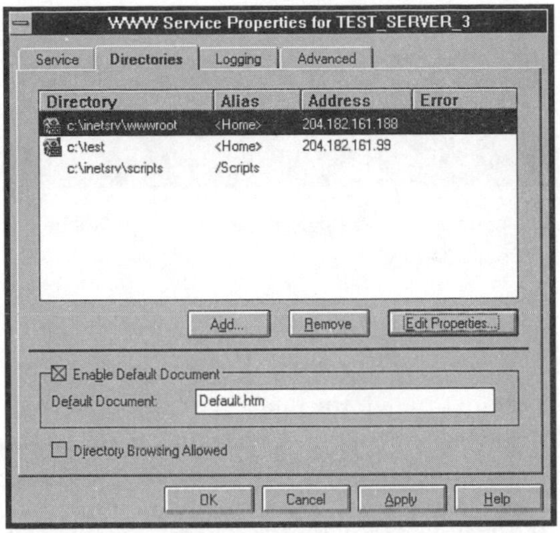

Fig. 6.6
Directory property
sheet for the IIS
WWW Server.

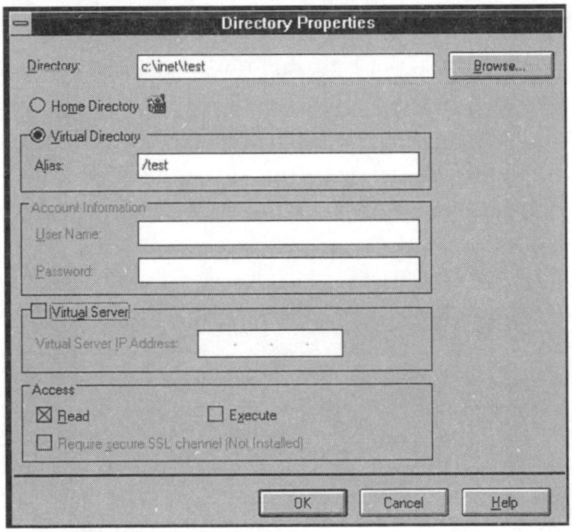

Fig. 6.7
Add/Edit a
directory.

II

Setting Up a Web Server

In the directory box, indicate the directory to add to this Web space. Remember that the security for this directory will be dictated by NTFS, and set it accordingly.

Each directory must be given an alias. The directory alias allows you to mask long directory names with a simple concise name. This alias will be called by the browser immediately after the computer domain name. In this example the c:\inet\test\excitement directory will be accessible by the URL **http://www.scoop.com/coolthing/**.

If the physical location of the directory is on a remote network drive, use the Account Information box to provide a valid user name and password to logon to that network drive.

Caution

If you connect to a remote network drive, all security access will be governed by the logon name you supply. Be careful!

Virtual Servers

Virtual serves are set up through the same Add button you use to set up additional directories for your Web space. Setting up a virtual server is a similar process with a few differences.

Enter the name of the directory that will be the home, or default, directory. If you specify a directory on a remote server you will need to enter a valid user name and password to log on.

Select the Home Directory radio button, and the Alias radio button and text box will gray-out. Because this will be the default directory, no alias is needed. You will need to select the Virtual Server check box to let IIS know that this is not just another directory, but a distinct Web space. The IP address box will become available for the IP address that will access this Web space. See figure 6.8.

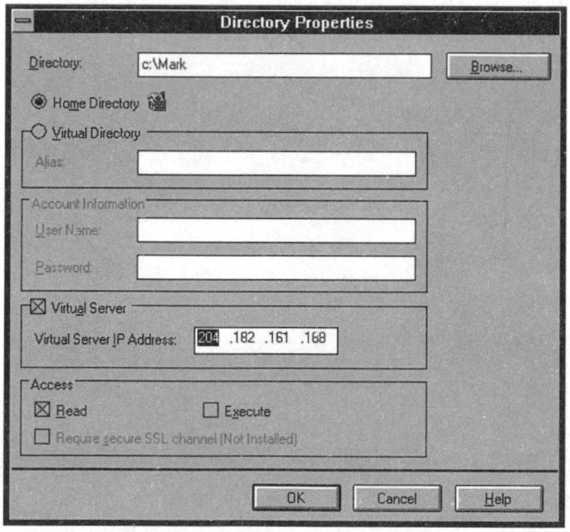

Fig. 6.8
Each virtual server requires a unique IP address.

Directory Properties

Directory: c:\Mark   Browse...

◉ Home Directory
○ Virtual Directory
Alias:

Account Information
User Name:
Password:

☒ Virtual Server
Virtual Server IP Address: 204 .182 .161 .168

Access
☒ Read   ☐ Execute
☐ Require secure SSL channel (Not Installed)

OK   Cancel   Help

> **Note**
>
> If you've assigned multiple IP addresses to your Network Interface Card, you will likely want to specify which IP address has access to each directory you create. If no IP address is specified, the directory becomes available to all virtual servers—which could come in handy in some cases.

> **Note**
>
> The default Web space will operate for all TCP/IP addresses defined on your network Interface card unless you begin to specify additional virtual Webs.

Default Directory Behavior

In the bottom half of the directories page, you can specify the default document name. This is the document the server will look for when a URL is specified that does not contain a specific document name. This is a nice way to keep your URLs short and your users out of trouble.

If a URL is called without a specific document and a default document does not exist, the server checks to see if directory browsing is allowed. If it is allowed, a hypertext listing of directories and files will be presented to the browser. Directory browsing (sometimes referred to as Automatic Directory Indexing) can only be allowed or disallowed for all directories and Webs on the server. You cannot allow it for some and not for others. If you turn on directory browsing, be sure that you have a default document in the directories in which you don't want browsing to occur.

Logging Property Sheet

The IIS server shines when it comes to control over logging. Perhaps this is a result of the corporate nature of Microsoft software—Microsoft understands that businesses love to analyze!

You can send log files to either a text file or to an ODBC connected database. One really neat feature here is that multiple servers can log activity to a single file or database anywhere on the network. This has powerful implications for popular sites and for Web service providers that bill according to usage levels (see fig. 6.9).

II

Setting Up a Web Server

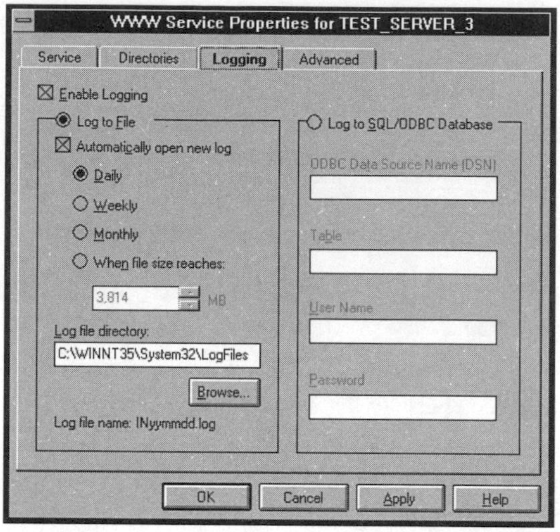

Fig. 6.9
Logging Property
sheet for the IIS
WWW Server.

Log to File

When logging to a file, you can specify how often the server should close the file and create a new one. This is usually referred to as *log file cycling*. IIS lets you cycle your logs according to a periodic schedule—Daily, Weekly, or Monthly, as well as when the log file reaches a certain size. This feature is rare among NT Web servers.

If you fail to specify a log cycle event, the log file will grow indefinitely.

> **Note**
>
> Try not to let your log files grow too large. Most of the statistical report generators today refuse to give up the goods when confronted with a 100 megabyte log file.

SQL/ODBC Logging

You can use any ODBC-supported database to log server activity. Logging to a database can allow you to direct the logging of all Internet Information Server services to a single source. This also means that you can use any ODBC-compliant application to view the log data in your database. In addition, you can use the Internet Database Connector to view log data in a Web browser.

Converting Log File Formats

The Microsoft Internet Log Converter converts Microsoft Internet Server log files to either European Microsoft Windows NT Academic Centre (EMWAC) log file format or the Common Log File format. Convlog.exe is located by default in the \Inetsrv\Admin directory. At the command prompt, type **convlog** without parameters to see syntax and examples, or see Help.

Advanced Property Sheet

The Advanced property sheet is used to throttle access to your server based on IP addresses and transfer rates (see fig. 6.10). IP address restriction is used as a security measure while transfer rate restriction preserves the quality of service by reducing the consequences of overloading.

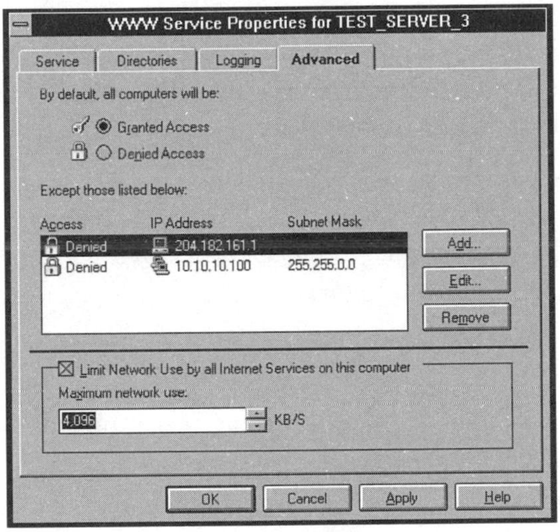

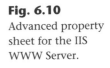

Fig. 6.10
Advanced property sheet for the IIS WWW Server.

II

Setting Up a Web Server

IP Access Control

You can control access to the IIS Web service by specifying the IP address of the computers to be granted or denied access.

If you choose to grant access to all users by default, you can then specify the computers to be denied access. For example, if you have a form on your WWW server and a particular user on the Internet is entering multiple forms with fictitious information, you can prevent the computer at that IP address from connecting to your site. Conversely, if you choose to deny access to all users by default, you can then specify which computers are allowed access.

Limiting Network Use

You can lessen the drain on your network and server bandwidth by limiting the network bandwidth available to the server. While this feature has some value, it would be a fantastic feature for a Web service provider if it could be configured by individual Web space.

The FTP and Gopher Services

The FTP and Gopher services are essentially "Last Generation" or legacy services. They are from an era that predates the Web; they've largely been superseded. They do offer some functionality that the Web does not.

The FTP Service

FTP (File Transfer Protocol) is a method of transferring files between Client and Server. The key advantage of FTP is that *clients can send files to the server*. At this time, HTTP lacks this extremely useful capability.

Files made available through FTP can be in any format, such as document files, multimedia files, or application files. If your remote clients are using configurable browsers, the clients can specify whether to copy a file or to start a helper application to immediately display or play the file.

FTP servers offer you a nice way to allow your users to browse file directories and to download what they need, with no configuration required on your part. While this is similar to the automatic directory indexing that most Web servers offer, there are a few advantages:

- Any FTP client can connect to your server (including most Web browsers).
- FTP clients are optimized for file management and make it extremely easy to move files between client PC and the server.
- FTP servers can set a longer time-out period to ensure that file transfer can be successfully completed by users using slow Internet links.

You will find that the FTP server portion of the IIS is setup in the same fashion as the WWW server. The directory security is managed by the File Manager, and logon access is restricted to valid user names from the User Manager. Once you have set up the WWW Server, the FTP Server should take only a few minutes to configure.

The Gopher Service

The Gopher Server is a hybrid of sorts between FTP and HTTP. The Gopher service allows you to create links to other computers or services, to annotate your files and directories, and to create custom menus. In some ways it's best described as a searchable hypertext interface to an FTP server.

While gopher is entirely text-based, it remains a powerful way to deliver information to client browsers. Like FTP, Gopher is an easy way to serve directories of existing files. Although more elegant than its FTP cousin, Gopher falls short in presentation compared to the WWW. Most WWW browsers today will also connect to a Gopher server.

Setting up a Gopher site is as simple as copying your files to the \Inetsrv\Gophroot directory. Clients can then browse the Gopher directories as easily as using File Manager. To enhance your site, you can create tag files that enable links to other computers or services, annotate your files and directories, and create custom menus. See the IIS help files for more information on tag files and on the Gopher Server. ❖

II

Setting Up a Web Server

## CHAPTER 7

Configuring Your Questar WebQuest Server

This chapter covers in detail the steps necessary to configure the WebQuest servers included on WebmasterCD. The basic steps of installation were covered in Chapter 6, and we continue here with WebMeister—the Multi Domain Manager. The makers of WebQuest, Questar Microsystems, maintain a Web presence at **http://www.questar.com**. Be sure to check it for software updates, news, and additional tools for managing your WebQuest server.

The configuration of WebQuestNT is essentially the same for WebQuest95; WebQuest 95 lacks some of the features of WebQuestNT.

Note

WebQuest NT must be configured through WebMeister before any Web serving can take place. WebQuest 95, however, can begin serving Web immediately after installation.

Getting Started with WebMeister, the Multi Domain Manager

One of the great features of the WebQuest servers is WebMeister, a GUI administration tool. You will use WebMeister to initially configure your Web spaces and then to administer security and update MIME types.

WebMeister is organized around the concept of the Virtual Web Server or multi-homing. This is where many Web spaces are actually hosted by a single Web server.

> ### Tip
>
> The Virtual Server is quickly becoming a standard feature for Web server software, but there are still servers that don't support this feature. Without Virtual Server capabilities, your Web server is limited to a single domain name. This is often unacceptable to companies that want to put up multiple Web spaces. If you're planning to provide Web support to multiple organizations, you will need this feature.

This is an important feature and, in essence, this means for each Web space you will need to define two essentials:

- TCP/IP Address
- File Directory

When the Web server receives a request by a client browser, it matches the IP address of the request with the proper file directory. The proper files are served and the single server appears to be many servers.

Double-click on the WebMeister icon in the WebQuest program group to launch WebMeister.

WebMeister is divided into nine different areas, each has a border around it; Web Spaces, Web Space, SSI+ Control, Callback Handler DLL, Log File Directory, Log Database (ODBC), Load Sensor, Service Parameters, and the button bar. See figure 7.1.

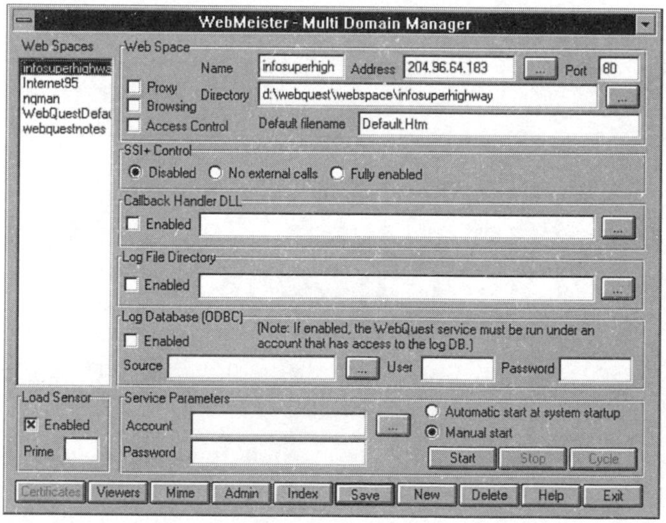

Fig. 7.1
The WebMeister—
Multi Domain
Manager window.

Creating a Web Space with WebMeister

When WebQuest NT installs, it creates a default Web space using the system IP address as the IP address of the Web space. This default Web space contains a number of reference files that further describes the abilities of WebQuest NT.

To create a new Web space, click the New button located at the bottom of the WebMeister window. This will reset all the fields giving you a blank form. The following are the steps you will need to go through in order to create a Web space:

1. *Web Space Name*   This is an internal name for you to identify your Web. Enter the domain name for the Web space or one associated with the mission of this Web space.

2. *Address*   Enter a TCP/IP address to access this Web through. If you don't have a TCP/IP address setup yet for this Web space, you can click on the Ellipsis button and open the address administration dialog. See figure 7.2.

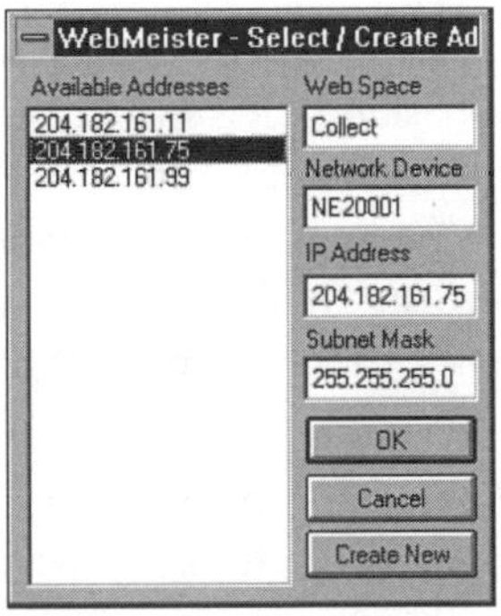

Fig. 7.2
Select/Create Address dialog box.

Type in the new TCP/IP address in the TCP/IP address box and then click on Create New.

This will bind this new TCP/IP address to your network adapter. This is another nice feature of WebMeister, an entire set of network configuration steps has been reduced to two simple entries.

Now that we have an IP address, select OK and return to the Main WebMeister window. Note that this address will not actually take effect until you restart Windows NT.

II

Setting Up a Web Server

> **Note**
>
> An alternative way of assigning new IP addresses to your server is through Control Panel...Network by selecting the TCP/IP Protocol under Installed Network Software and clicking on Configure. Go to Advanced and from there you can add an IP to that server from the pool of your assigned IP addresses.

> **Tip**
>
> Using the Network control panel applet, you can enter a maximum of five IP addresses for each network interface card. Use the WebQuest Domain Manager to get around this limitation. With other Web servers you will be forced to enter the TCP/IP information into the system registry.

3. *Directory*   Specify the directory location of the files of this Web space. Clicking on the Ellipsis button allows you to browse to help you find the appropriate directory.

4. *Default Filename*   If a user accesses this Web space by Domain Name or TCP/IP address without asking for a specific file, this file will be served to the client. The default is Default.htm, but you can configure it to your Web space. This is particularly useful when you are importing an existing Web space from another server with links that are already in place for a different home page. The default file is the same as the home page file.

▶ See table 5.2, "Commonly Used Internet Ports," p. 105, to see a listing of standard ports.

5. *Port*   Each TCP/IP service that runs on your server is tuned to listen to a particular port for requests. Each service must have its own port—it can't share that port with other services. This is actually how multiple services coexist on one machine. When a request comes in from the Internet, the server looks at what port is requested and forwards the request to the appropriate service for processing. The standard HTTP port is 80.

   If you specify a port other than 80, the client will have to request that port specifically for the request to be answered. Don't change the port number from 80 unless you need to.

6. *Proxy*   Select this box if you wish for this Web to act as a proxy server. If you are setting up a proxy, you will want to use a port number other than 80. Proxy services are used as part of an overall network security implementation that is beyond the scope of this chapter.

If you wish to learn more about proxy services, check out the firewall FAQ at **http://www.cis.ohio-state.edu/hypertext/faq/usenet/ firewalls-faq/faq.html**.

7. *Browsing*   This check box determines whether directories in this Web space are browseable. If browsing is allowed, any directory in this Web space that does not contain a file with the default page name (see item number 4) will return a list of files in the directory when accessed without a file name. This list of files will contain an Icon next to each name and will be a hypertext link. Double-clicking on the file name will cause the file to be retrieved. This is a valuable feature for easily creating lists of files and requires virtually no maintenance. To update the directory, simply add or delete the files as appropriate!

   If you select directory browsing, be aware that this is a potential security hole. A user is free to look at all files in a directory that don't include the default file name.

8. *Access Control*   When Access Control is checked, file and directory-specific security is activated. The specifics of your security implementation will be defined in the Admin function, Directory display. This access control enhances the NT file manager-based security. The users and passwords are unrelated to the User Manager database. You can create users and passwords by clicking on the Meister button and adding users. See the Meister section later in this chapter. Access control is an extra layer of overhead and is, therefore, a performance inhibitor. Only select access control if you need it. From the Administration window, you specify the users and passwords that are granted access.

9. *SSI+ Control*   The selections of Disabled, No External calls, and Fully Enabled allow you to control whether a Web space can run an executable or make program calls out of the server. Disabled means that no CGI or SSI+ functions are allowed on the pages. No External calls prevents the use of DLLs from a Web page but allows the use of the SSI+ tags.

10. *Callback Handler DLL*   When the Callback Handler is enabled, integration of a Callback DLL is allowed within a Web space. This Callback DLL allows a programmer to implement almost any kind of protocol within the client/server relationship. This is a very technical discussion and is addressed in the file wqsdk.htm included with WebQuest. The Ellipsis button allows the selection of the specific callback DLL that is enabled for the Web space. The Ellipsis button allows you to browse to find the DLL you want.

11. *Log File Directory*   If you activate file logging, each "hit" or request on your server will be recorded in a text file. This is often valuable information if you need to keep statistics on your Web space or in times of troubleshooting.

12. *Log Database (ODBC)*   Instead of logging hits to a text file, you can log access, error, and request events to an ODBC database. Click the Ellipsis button next to Source, and WebMeister will present a list of available ODBC data sources. See figure 7.3.

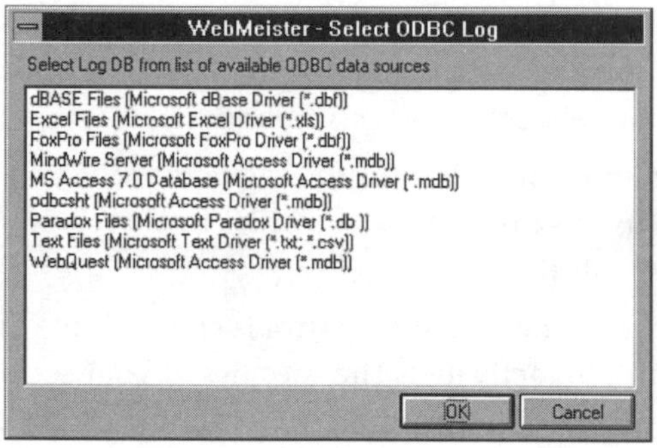

Fig. 7.3
The WebMeister—
Select ODBC Log
dialog box.

During the installation process, WebQuest set up a Microsoft Access database and a properly configured ODBC driver titled WebQuest. You may select this database or configure another database and ODBC driver to use. If you configure another data source, be sure to utilize the same format as the database provided with WebQuest.

> **Caution**
>
> The amount of data captured in the ODBC data logs is significantly greater than that captured into the text log. This is a trade-off against the additional overhead required by the server to access the database. Additionally, the data bases will grow much larger, much faster than the text log. It is possible to crash your server if your database consumes all the available hard drive space.

In the User and Password dialogs you must enter an account with sufficient rights under Windows NT to access the database.

13. *Load Sensor*   This is another special feature of WebQuest. Load Sensor allows the server to tune itself and respond to changing conditions. When usage goes up, WebQuest allocates additional resources to keep performance at an optimum level. Select the Enabled box to activate

Load sensor and set prime to the minimum number of threads that WebQuest will maintain. For my medium load server, a prime of 5 seems to work well.

14. *Service Parameters*   This is a control that is global for all the Web spaces maintained on your server. The account and password are used to determine the security permissions of the WebQuest server. You can use this to ensure that a hacker does not gain access to your system resources beyond what the Web server is intended to offer. If you select the Ellipsis button (dotted dialog box) next to the Account field, you will be presented with a recommended account choice.

    In this dialog box, see figure 7.4, the recommendation is the Administrator account. I will instead use the WEBLOGON account that I have created. This account has sufficient rights to allow access to the ODBC data sources and the file directories, but no more. This way I can be sure that any security holes in my scripts will do limited damage.

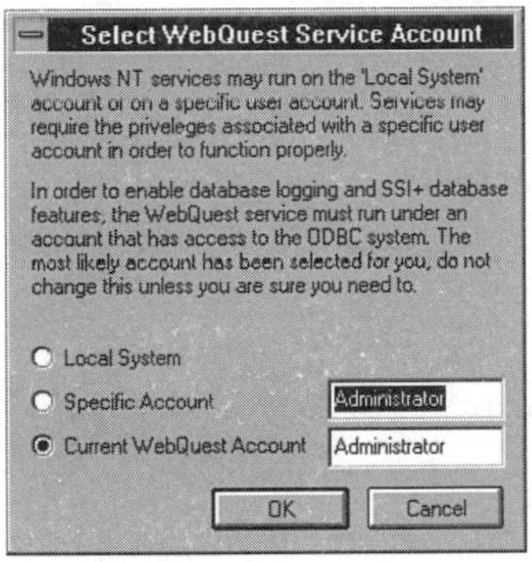

Fig. 7.4
Select WebQuest Service Account dialog box.

15. *Startup*   WebQuest runs as an NT service and can be set up to start automatically when the Windows NT is booted. Select automatic if you'd like WebQuest to start up immediately should Windows NT restart. Selecting Manual means you will have to log on and start WebQuest from either WebMeister or the Services Control Panel.

16. *Save*   Click to save this new Web space! If you created new IP addresses for your server, you will need to shut down and restart your server.

17. *Start, Stop, Cycle*   Use these buttons to start, stop, and cycle WebQuest. Most changes and additions to WebQuest made from WebMeister will require that WebQuest be restarted. Cycle is a combined Stop and Start for quick updating of your Web services (see fig. 7.5).

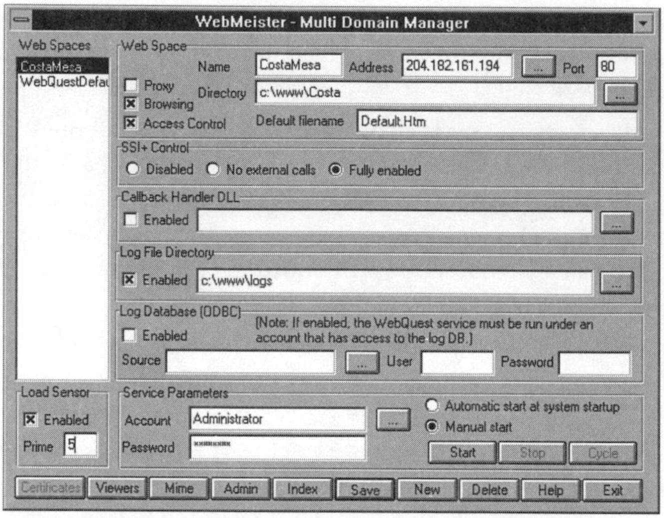

Fig. 7.5
The Service
buttons.

> **Note**
>
> Changes made (with the exception of adding or deleting access control and users) with WebMeister will take effect the next time the WebQuest service is started.

Administration of Your Web Space

The Admin button on the bottom button bar of WebMeister opens the Access Control Administrator (see fig. 7.6). The Administrator performs two functions: Access control and link validation.

Encryption

This feature is disabled in this version of WebQuest NT.

Access Control

The access control administrator controls access to both documents and directories. This way you can either set security for all files in a particular directory or just a few. To set an access control for a document or directory, first select it in the list box. Select Enabled and then type in the user name and password required to retrieve the contents of the document or to gain access to the directory. For access control to work, it must be enabled in the Web spaces section of WebMeister. See figure 7.7.

Directory access may be based on AND or OR.

Fig. 7.6
The WebMeister—
Administrator
window in Default
Directory Mode.

II

Setting Up a Web Server

AND access specifies that a user must be granted access to both the directory and the document. OR access specifies that the user may access a document if granted access to the directory or the document.

Note that a stoplight icon appears next to all documents and directories for which access control is enabled.

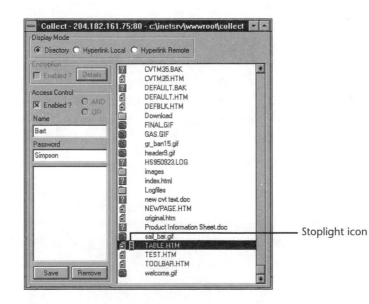

Stoplight icon

Fig. 7.7
The WebMeister—
Administrator
window showing
Access Controls.

Hyperlink Validation

The Admin portion of WebMeister is also used to maintain the Web space documents and directories. From here you view the layout of your Web and both edit and delete documents.

Directory Display

The right-hand side of the Administrator window is the Web space list box presenting an alphabetized listing of the Web space files by document type. Each document is identified and graphically represented with an icon. See figure 7.8.

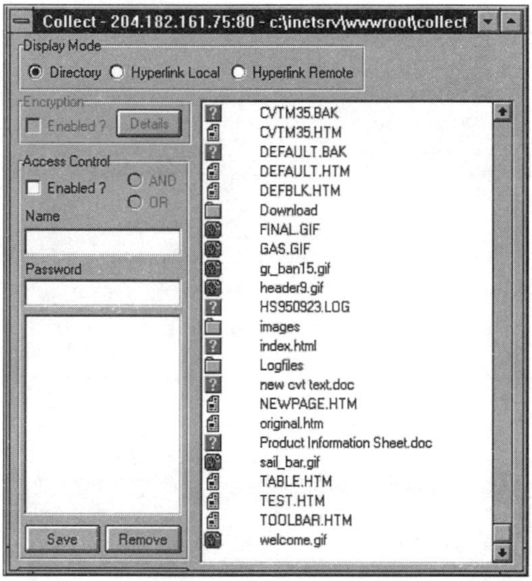

Fig. 7.8

The WebMeister—Administrator window in Default Directory Mode.

You can either double-click on a document to open into the viewer configured for that file type or you may right-click on a document and a pop-up menu will appear giving you the choice of edit, delete, or launch a viewer.

If you double-click on a directory, it will open the directory and display the files in it.

The exact format of how documents are displayed and acted upon depends on the selection of the display mode radio buttons. One of three views may be selected: Directory, Local Hyperlink, and Remote Hyperlink. See figure 7.9.

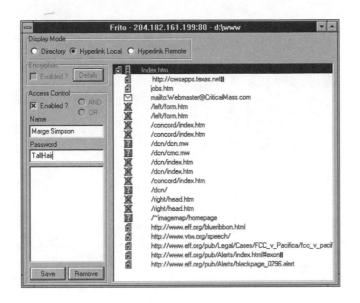

Fig. 7.9
The WebMeister—
Administrator
window in
Hyperlink Local
Mode.

Hyperlink Local Display

The hyperlink local view displays the hierarchy of your Web space as defined by the hyperlinks in your HTML documents. All hyperlinks to files local to your machine are evaluated when you open the Web space for administration. Remote hyperlinks are left unvalidated. You may double-click on a document to open and display the hyperlinks on the document, which may in turn be opened, viewed, or edited. If a hyperlink refers to a document on the local server, the Web Space Administrator will try to validate its existence. If the document cannot be located, a red X is superimposed over the document's icon.

Hyperlink Remote Display

The hyperlink remote view displays the hierarchy of your Web space as defined by the hyperlinks on your HTML documents. All local and remote hyperlinks are validated in real-time. WebQuest creates a thread for each remote link and resolves all links simultaneously. This results in extremely fast validation of very large numbers of remote hyperlinks. If you right-click on a LOCAL document, a pop-up menu will appear giving you the choice to edit or view. If you double-click on a LOCAL document, the document will be opened displaying the hyperlinks within that document, which may in turn be opened, viewed, and edited. See figure 7.10.

Fig. 7.10
The WebMeister—
Administrator
window in
Hyperlink Remote
Mode.

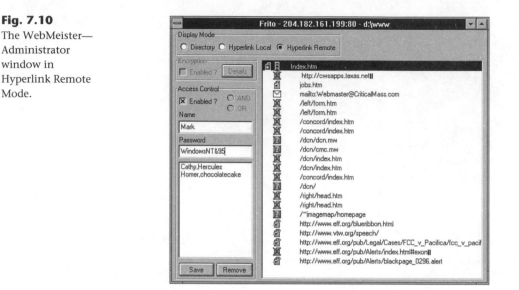

If a hyperlink refers to a document on another server, Web Space Administrator attempts to contact that document.

If the document is located, a green check will be superimposed over the document's icon. Note the document blueribbon.html in figure 7.10.

If the remote server does not respond, or if the document cannot be located on the remote server, a red X is superimposed over the document's icon. This is the case with link cwsapps.texas.net.

Additional WebMeister Functions

The button bar located at the bottom of the WebMeister window gives you access to all of the control panels you will use to configure your server. See figure 7.11.

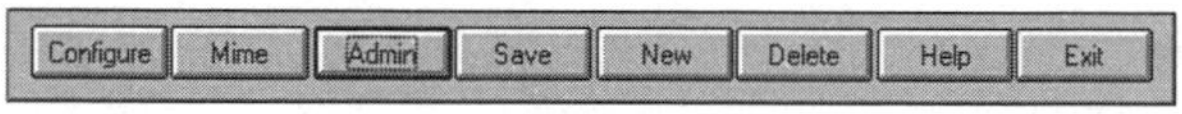

Fig. 7.11
The WebMeister
button bar.

| Configure | Mime | Admin | Save | New | Delete | Help | Exit |

Certificates

This feature is disabled in this version. This feature would allow the use of RSA certificates and SSL transactions.

Viewer and Editor Configuration

Select the Viewer button from the button bar to configure the viewers and editors you use to manipulate Web space files from within the Administrator. By right-clicking on a document in the Administrator, you are offered a menu where you may manipulate the document depending on the Display mode. See figure 7.12.

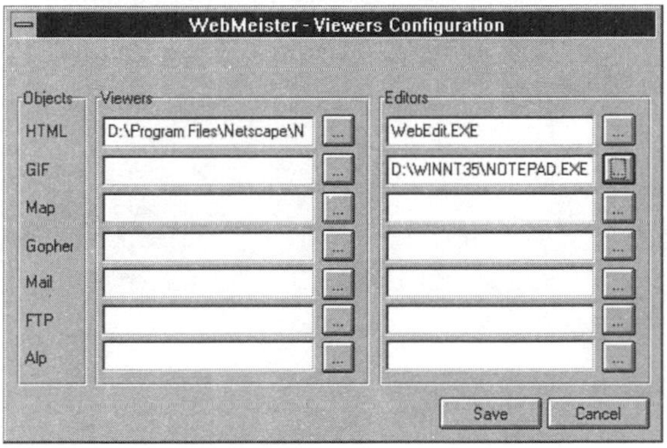

Fig. 7.12
The WebMeister—Viewers Configuration.

After selecting Viewers, the Viewers and Editors dialog box will appear. Click on the Ellipsis button to browse for the editors and viewers of your choice.

MIME Type Configuration

Click the Mime button to display the Mime Types dialog box, see figure 7.13. You may add and delete mime types here. MIME type changes are applied across all Web spaces defined on the server. Do not delete any existing MIME types unless you are sure you know what you are doing.

▶ See "MIME Types," p. 107, for more information.

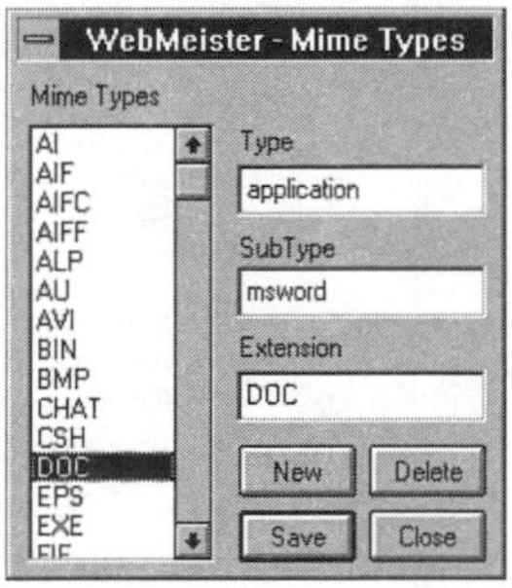

Fig. 7.13
The WebMeister—Mime Types.

II

Setting Up a Web Server

Index

The Index button creates a WAIS-based index of the highlighted Web space. Clicking on the button brings up the Web Space Index Configuration dialog box. From here you can create, edit, update, and delete an index. More than one index can be created for a Web space. See figure 7.14.

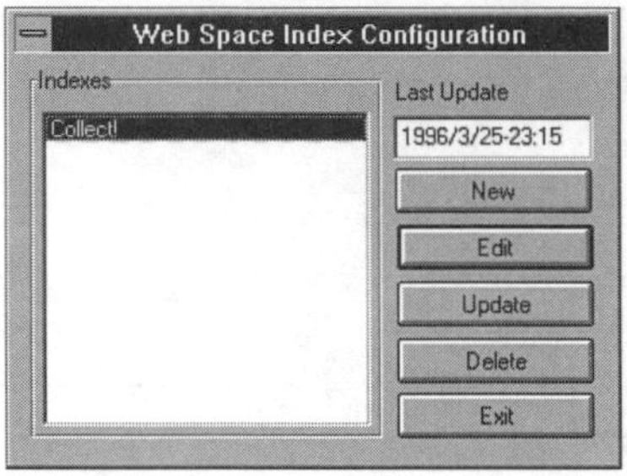

Fig. 7.14
Web Space Index
Configuration.

Creating an Index

To create an index click on New, and type in the name of the index. The content of the index is based on the file or files selected in the Edit Index window. See figure 7.15.

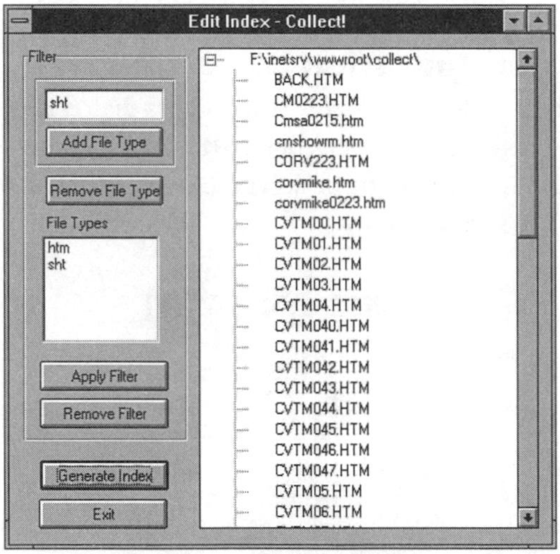

Fig. 7.15
Edit Index
window.

On the right side of the screen is a graphical display of the files in the Web space. Double-clicking on a file or directory selects it and adds it to the list of files to be indexed. A green check mark is placed next to the file or directory after it is selected. After you have selected the file or files to index, click on Generate Index. While the index is being generated the buttons are grayed out; when the index has been created the buttons are available again.

Now that the index is created, you need to assign it to a Web space. Exit out of the Index mode and open up the Administrator window in Directory mode. Notice the index you created is now listed in the Index list. Highlight the HTML file that you set up as the WAIS search page.

▶ See "WAIS," p. 470, to learn how to set up a WAIS search page using <ISINDEX>.

Customizing an Index

When creating or updating an index, you can use the filtering features in the Edit Index window. The filter changes the display on the right side of the window. The default setting is to display all files with an SHT or HTM extension. Adding or deleting file types and clicking the Apply filter changes the display. Clicking on remove filter returns the display back to the default settings.

Editing an Existing Web Space

To edit a Web space, select the Web space (domain) from the list box by left-clicking on it, then simply edit the information that you want to update. After saving the update, you will need to Cycle WebQuest for the changes to be updated.

Deleting an Existing Web Space

To delete an existing Web space you will select the Web from the list box and click the Delete button. All references to the Web space will be deleted but note that all directories and documents of the Web space will remain intact. You must cycle WebQuest for the deletion to be updated.

Logs

WebQuest supports three different types of logging: File Logs, ODBC Database Logs, and NT Event Logs.

File Logs

File Logs are simple ASCII text files that are added to incrementally every time the server receives a "hit." This is the standard way of recording server activity. Most Webmasters then take these logs and run them through statistical generation programs to create reports.

▶ See "Understanding Usage Logs," p. 498, for more information about using logs to create reports.

File Log Structure

WebQuest logs all requests to files specified in the Logfile Directory box. Each day at midnight a new log file is created. The format of the log file name is WM<yy><mm><dd>.LOG where <yy> is the year, <mm> is the month, and <dd> is the day of the month. The log file follows the standard EMWAC format. The following details are logged:

Date

Time

Server IP

Client IP

HTTP method

URL

HTTP version

The following is an example line from a WebQuest log file:

```
Mon May 17 15:34:25 1996 204.96.64.171 204.96.64.51 GET
/default.htm HTTP/1.0
```

Enabling this log file generates a small amount of overhead, but it is an important capability. If you don't care about the contents of the logs, don't enable the log file. However, the log files do also contain useful information for tracking down the cause of a server crash. Using the log file you can identify which site was hit last, from there you may identify a problem with the page/site.

Note

Bear in mind that logs keep track of the number of requests made of each element in a Web space. Each page can have more than one element that needs to be requested in order to send the whole page to the client. Therefore, this log is not an accurate representation of the number of hits a site has received. You will often hear outrageous claims of "millions of hits per day." When evaluating the popularity of a site listen for the count of unique clients and unique pages.

WebQuest ODBC database logging is a way to record in greater detail what is transpiring with your site. This is invaluable information for any serious Webmaster. As noted earlier, this comes with a significant performance penalty. For each element that is accessed on one of your pages a record is inserted in a database.

ODBC Database Layout

The sample database structure contains three tables: Access, operations, and errors.

Operations. The operations table lists requests from clients and certain internal operations. The following details are logged:

Detail	Definition
Operation	The type of call made to the server—the same as the HTTP method discussed previously.
PeerIP	The IP address of the client.
URL	The URL for every item in every page requested by the client.
Year	The current year (1996).
Month	The current month (1 - 12).
Day	The day of the month (1 - 31).
Hour	The hour of the request made by the client of the server (24-hour format).
Minute	The minute of the request made by the client (0 - 59).
Second	The second of the request made by the client (0 - 59).
Index	A unique identifier (a counter) used as a key field.

The following is an example from an Operations log file:

```
Operation  PeerIp        URL         Year   Month  Day Hour Minute  Second  Index
GET        204.96.64.101 /studioe3/  1996   5      11  13  5       55      7
GET        204.96.64.101 /           1996   5      11  13  9       5       8
```

Each complete line written into the log file represents one request made of the server by a client.

Errors. The errors table lists errors that have occurred during the processing of requests. Errors may occur in many different phases of processing a request; the subsystem involved in the error is indicated in the log. Examples of subsystems are: HTTP, E-Mail, and ODBC.

Access. The access table lists authorization details for access controlled documents.

NT Event Logs

WebQuest logs startup and critical events to the NT Application Event Log. This feature is not configurable, but this information is valuable to the system administrator for daily management and troubleshooting. ❖

II

Setting Up a Web Server

CHAPTER 8

Managing an Internet Web Server

Operating a public Web server is a fun and exciting endeavor. It is absolutely true that whatever your imagination can conceive, you can deliver. This chapter helps you get started on the way to harnessing the power of the Web to fulfill your goals and create a dynamic and rewarding site. This chapter also includes tips on avoiding some of the potential pitfalls of running a public Web server.

Many of the topics addressed in the next chapter ("Creating and Managing an Intranet Web Server") are also applicable to running an Internet server. These include managing server content and many security topics. To get a thorough understanding of running either an Internet or Internal Web server, you should read both chapters. This is especially important where security is concerned because many companies run both an internal and Internet Web server and need to keep the data separate.

In this chapter, you learn:

- How to plan your Web strategy
- The best ways to use hypertext and graphics effectively
- How to make your site accessible to all browsers
- Popular and useful server features
- How to make your site accessible to users not on the Internet
- How to protect your image and data
- Popular ways to draw attention and keep readers coming back for more
- How to advertise your server

The Planning Process: Putting the Web To Work for You

Many newcomers to the Web are tempted to take existing literature and marketing materials and simply translate it to HTML to create Web pages. There is nothing wrong with getting your feet wet through this approach, but it doesn't take full advantage of the possibilities of HTML for turning large amounts of information into a fun and interactive journey. The following sections teach you how to make the most of your server's capabilities.

Plan Your Journey!

You wouldn't dream of attempting to efficiently drive a car from Los Angeles to New York without first plotting your course, would you? If you would, be prepared for the worst! You will travel far longer than you ever thought possible, all the while you are seemingly driving in circles—and you haven't even left the driveway yet! Developing a Web site is a creative journey, and it is a journey that is rarely complete. By utilizing proper planning techniques you will always have a site that is well "in hand" and always presentable.

Planning Concepts

Designing the Web site starts with understanding the goals that have moved you or your organization to undertake this venture. A mission statement is the anchor for any sound business plan, and it is the same with your Web site. Define your mission!

Some sample mission statements:

- This Web site will be a shopping mall that is both fun for the user and easily provides access to the purchase of goods and services.

- Our Web site is an internal Web server that serves the entire corporate community of XYZ industries, from the President to the stock room. It is *the* source of corporate information.

- This Web site is a ground-breaking experiment in online publishing, aimed squarely at the 25 to 29 post college demographic.

Audience Considerations

Acknowledgment of your intended audience is a must during the planning process. Who is the Web site for? Who are the likely users? Consider the answer to these questions against the goals you have set for your site. Do you need to broaden your approach to attract a larger audience? Is the Web site plan strong enough to attract the core audience you desire?

Resources

Take stock of the resources that you have available to you. Whether you're working with an in-house team or hiring a consultant, realistically approach the project. A Web site conceived on a grand scale but only partially completed has much less impact and utility than a properly planned site.

Designing Your Web Masterpiece

Your mission, if you decide to accept it, is to create a framework for your Web space that is optimal for the mission of the site. You will shape this site by balancing the many needs that all the interested parties have, and in this way you will find success. There are many factors in judging the overall user satisfaction of a Web site. Your balancing act will include many trade-offs—The trade-off of rich graphics against users running across slow links; the trade-off of less than the most advanced formatting so that older browsers will still be able to access your site. The list goes on. Essentially, your design must balance user needs against performance, visual design, and usability. Because all users have different tastes, and many different browsers are in use, it is impossible to please everyone all the time. However, by keeping your mission statement firmly in mind and with a good knowledge of the strengths and weaknesses of Web media you can create a solid plan.

Concepts

The design of the Web site is essentially a coordination of the "look and feel" and the organizational structure of the information. As you become more fluent in Web design, you will build a set of techniques for providing the visual cues that are a Web site's strength. The nature of the Web demands attention to the layout of the graphics, information, and visual cueing that is a Web layout. Follow this set of general design principles:

- *Build meaning through association.*   Use the power of hypertext to link related pages and information.
- *Focus on the user.*   Don't make your Web site a showcase for your latest cool design tool. Your Web site should serve the audience for which it is designed. Meeting the users' needs is the highest priority of your Web site. Use your mission statement to help stay focused.
- *Create context everywhere.*   Your users may link into your site at any point. Always lay a clear path to the important traffic centers of your Web.

■ *Create a consistent look and feel.*   The best laid Web uses a cohesive design strategy to provide a pleasing visual context. In other words, the design should be consistent and each page should include visual clues as to its purpose and importance.

Web Design Methodology

There are many, many ways to weave your Web! A simple browse of the **Comp.Infosystems.WWW.Author** newsgroup will yield a rich treasure trove of concepts, methods, and ideology. A few are listed in this section.

Top Down

Use Top Down when you have an extremely strong idea of what the content areas of the site are, but don't have all the information in hand. Consider the typical management organizational chart, the upside-down tree. Lay out the home page and the top levels, and put in placeholder pages when the information is not yet available. These placeholder pages can be predesigned templates that hold the visual theme of the site, and can be filled in when ready. This allows you to develop a theme for your site, and carry it down through pages as it grows.

Bottom Up

Often the content drives the creation of a site. When a site is being created without an in-place visual context, the form usually follows the function. Design your pages so that they best fit the information and activity and use intermediate pages to collect these pages. When a visual theme is deployed later, you can go back and make common adjustments throughout the site.

The Creeping Web

Often a Web is deployed without an overall design in place. There is not enough time or resources, and the Web must be implemented. As time goes on, more pages are grafted onto the original site. You've seen these sites more than once, haven't you?

Web Design Techniques

The essential theory of Web design rides on the concept of "keep the user in mind." Consider the users' experience as they surf your Web for the first time. Does it make sense? Is it easy to find your way around? Are the links easily accessible? How long does it take to download each page?

Web Chunks!

Your Web pages will often repeat the same information across many pages. Common information is often included in page headings and particularly page footers. This content can be thought of as a Web chunk—a piece of HTML that does not vary from page-to-page and is reusable.

Database-driven Web systems and systems that use server-side includes can make great use of Web chunks. Let's say that we create a common footer across all pages, in this case a simple copyright notice:

> *All Pages and Images Copyright © 1995 & 1996 Critical Mass Communications, Unless Otherwise Noted.*

This is a discrete chunk that does not vary from page-to-page, and when it needs to be updated, it needs to be updated everywhere. If you make use of WebQuest Server Side Includes, this chunk can be accessed from a separate HTML file and joined with the requested page on-the-fly. If you don't use SSI, you still can use chunks to create a library of HTML chunks that you use each time you create a particular type of page.

Universal Layout

You can give your Web a cohesive look and feel by developing an initial layout template, and then sticking to it whenever possible. A layout in essence is a set of general rules for the dimensions and elements of the page, and their spatial relationships.

To implement this layout, create a diagram and indicate where the header sits, what repeated elements follow through the site, and the approximate dimensions of the page.

Beware the Browser!

As a Web designer you must remain aware of the universe of browsers that currently exists at all times. There was a great example of this in the Dilbert cartoon strip recently where a rat dances on a keyboard hoping to destroy information only to discover that he has authored a Web browser.

Understand that the latest extensions are *not* universally implemented, and that standard HTML is often interpreted differently from browser to browser. We keep ten or so browsers available in addition to utilizing the built-in browsers for the major online services, AOL, CompuServe, and Prodigy. The major online services represent a challenge: often they have the weakest browsers, but by far the most users. Many client log analyses show that the vast majority of their hits are from AOL!

Test your site often and understand the trade-offs you must make to utilize that hot new Netscape extension.

Links and Icons

A great technique for creating a coherent look and feel is to use repeated icons across all pages to maintain a sense of context. A popular implementation of this is to create an icon strip across the top, bottom, or side of the page, and differentiate the icon whose context the user is currently in by shading or depressing it.

Repeated icons are a great way to implement consistency and they keep the byte count of a page transfer low. After the browser has loaded the icon, it will be cached for the remainder of the session.

The Friendly Page

A common malady for Web designers is that of page overloading. The size of a page (or as we say around here *byte count*) is a problem for the majority of Web surfers. Too often a user surfs to a promising page only to lose patience as a 150K graphic downloads through the 14.4K modem.

When you are designing a Web page, you are probably in one of two modes: local use or network use. *Local use* means that you are editing pages on your local PC and browsing them directly. *Network use* indicates that you are on a high-speed network attached to the Web server. Both of these scenarios give rise to inflated byte counts that the poor 14.4K user simply can't tolerate. Be sure to continually connect to your Web in the same mode that you expect your surfers to. If your client demographic is the 14.4K modem user, build accordingly!

One rule of thumb is that it should take no more than 15 seconds to download a page. At maximum throughput this would mean that text and graphics included would equal less than 27K.

Content Concepts

A successful Web site delivers content that is focused on the intended audience. You are a publisher and you must begin to think like one! Demographics, layout, frequency of exposure—these concepts all deserve consideration. Understand what your audience is looking for. Cater to it.

Popular and Useful Features

Here are some ideas for things to include at your Web site. Many of these are already commonplace on the Web, and others are hybrid ideas based on several different related concepts. This is not a how-to section—just ideas. However, references to how-to information are presented where possible.

Press Releases and News

Many Web sites offer press releases about the company or organization. They are usually presented in a hypertext, chronological index. Currently, many of these are plain text files in standard press release format. While this is useful for people who want to find out what's going on in your organization, the possibilities with HTML are even greater. You can include graphics, links to related releases, sound clips, video, and more. You also can provide a search facility for finding things in old releases.

Many media organizations insist on electronic releases rather than hard copy—they don't have to retype everything. In a sense, a Web site is a press organization, using the Web as a convenient way to get that information. Of course, the media still has to make the effort to come get information on your Web server, whereas press releases are usually unsolicited. How can you meet both goals?

If you intend to distribute press releases automatically, consider using e-mail. By constructing an address list of the intended news organizations, you can drastically reduce time spent copying and addressing envelopes by sending releases via e-mail. Your e-mail releases can then point to your Web server for additional information.

▶ See "Hypermail," p. 491.

To take it a step further, if several people in your organization need to send releases to the same list of places, you can set up a list server software. This software retransmits all mail received at the list server address to all the recipients. Many list server packages also allow new recipients to add themselves to the list by e-mailing a special message to a subscription address. By advertising this capability on your Web server, you can pick up new recipients of your news automatically. You can use this same technology to send out newsletters to your interested customers. Mailing lists are commonly used on the Internet to form discussion groups where all mail sent to the list is sent to all recipients.

▶ Chapter 10, "Basic HTML: Understanding Hypertext," contains more information on the news: URL. See p. 237.

An alternative way of providing news that may require less maintenance of HTML files is simply to set up an Internet news server and create a new newsgroup at your site solely for press releases and news. The advantage of a news server is that after you post news, newsreaders (Web browsers) automatically handle the formatting and presentation of the articles in chronological order. You simply include a link on your Web page to your press release newsgroup and Web browsers can read all the articles in the group.

▶ Chapter 17, "Search Engines and Annotation Systems," discusses the relative merits of using mail or news for distributing information. See p. 469.

II

Setting Up a Web Server

What's New (and What's Old)

A What's New list of some kind is a must on every server to enable users to quickly find new information without having to search their entire server. Perhaps equally important, however, is a What's Old feature, which enables users to discover what's on their server in a logical or fun manner. This might be a hypertext tour or overview of what's on their server, or a game that takes users to a new place every time.

The idea of discovering the Web via game was pioneered by the University of Kansas Campus Internet Association (KUCIA) with the creation of URouLette at **http://kufacts.cc.ukans.edu/cwis/organizations/kucia/ uroulette/uroulette.html**. Every time you spin the wheel, you're taken to a random site anywhere on the World Wide Web. Because of the Web's immensity, this is a fun and semipractical way to discover what's on the Web. The same thing can be applied locally on your server.

Product Selection Guide

If your company offers many closely related products, it may be useful to offer a product selection flowchart or configuration guide. This can simply be a graphical flowchart or a series of questions in a form. For example, an industrial control firm might use a form to determine the proper type of controller to recommend to a customer.

If HTML-form capability is too limited for your applications, you can distribute a small program written in the language of your choice for several different operation systems. Users simply download the program, run it, and then use the results to make purchasing decisions. Using a macro language, you can even have your custom program command a browser to download an updated data file from your server.

Forms to E-mail Processing

Using forms or the mailto: URL, you can allow Web users to send e-mail directly from their browser. This way, users do not have to remember, type in, or even copy an e-mail address. You might use this capability to allow users to submit feedback or request further information from sales. By specifying different addresses, mail can be routed automatically to the right people inside your company. Some older browsers don't support the mailto: URL, so you may consider using forms to reach the widest audience.

Accommodating Users Who Don't Have Internet Access

Although full Internet services are common in the workplace, many smaller businesses and home users have e-mail-only connections to the Internet through an online service. Ideally, you want these people to have access to your Web site so you don't have to duplicate information on another system, such as a dial-up BBS. You can provide dial-up access to your Web server that behaves just like a dial-up SLIP/PPP connection to the Internet. Users without Internet access can then dial up via modem, run TCP/IP software and a Web browser (both of which are free), and use your Web site.

Windows NT offers a nice solution for doing just this: RAS. Remote Access Server is a dial-up network solution that many ISPs (Internet Service Providers) are now discovering. Setting up RAS is beyond the scope of this book, but you can learn more at: **http://www.microsoft.com/ntserver/ras.htm**.

Caution

Operating a RAS server can give any dial-up user full access to the Internet, not just to your Web server. This can make your site very popular in a hurry, but nobody would be looking at your Web server. To prevent this, you need to configure the RAS server, or your network routers and a proxy server, to disallow all Internet traffic from the dial-up address except to your Web server. In addition, configure your routers or a firewall to prevent the dial-up users from getting access to your internal network.

▶ See "Protecting Your Data," p. 205.

Protecting Your Data and Your Image

This section deals with two different aspects of protecting your Web server: protecting your graphics and files from being copied, and protecting your server from hostile or accidental damage.

Copyrights and the Internet

After you invest considerable time developing a unique atmosphere at your Web site, make sure no one can copy your efforts. The problems of stolen software and plagiarism are magnified many times on the Internet because of the ease with which materials can be copied electronically. Unfortunately, there isn't an easy answer.

The Internet was built with the intent to make information freely available. Indeed, thousands of programmers and document authors give selflessly of their time to write programs and utilities, read newsgroups, and publish frequently asked question lists (FAQs) for everyone to read and freely copy. Huge volumes of material on the Internet are not copyrighted, or they have notices placing them in the public domain.

Because of the Internet's origins, many people assume that everything on the Internet is in the public domain. This is not true. However, you can't technically keep people from copying documents that are copyrighted—just as it's impossible to keep people from running to the copier. Anything you can view on a Web page can be copied. For graphics, even with the most clever protection schemes, all it takes is a screen capture program to make a local copy. If you are really worried about protecting your look and feel, including graphics, layout, and so on, you must seek competent legal counsel.

Your Server Can Be Used Against You

There are plenty of things you can do technically to keep people from misusing or abusing your Web server. Some of the common pitfalls are covered in this section.

Hide Your Logs and Configuration Files

If any directories or capabilities on your server are restricted to certain users or IP addresses, make sure you don't allow public access to your configuration files. To see your access configuration files, a user just has to guess a few popular names or look at a directory index—if you didn't use the IndexIgnore directive to keep these files from being displayed. Seeing the configuration files does not necessarily mean that a user can "break in" to unauthorized areas of your server, but it can certainly provide clues. And a user smarter than you are might look at your configuration files and see holes immediately. If you intend your server to be a public server, of course, you don't need to worry about unauthorized use.

▶ See "Server Configuration," p. 101, for more information on establishing document directories.

It is important to hide your access and error logs if other machines on your network access the public Web server. Hiding your logs is easy—just don't place them in any publicly accessible document directory. Every access shows up in the logs; mischievous people can use the information in the logs to find out the names and/or addresses of machines on your network. When they have those addresses, they can wreak havoc on your systems. Even if you don't access your own Web server internally, it's good to hide your logs so other people's organizations are not exposed. To illustrate this, go to a popular Web search site, such as WebCrawler, and search for the last part of your own Internet address (company.com or a1.company.com). If you were using the Internet a lot, your address shows up in several access logs around the world. These are public and therefore indexed by the Web search engines. This happens most often not with the raw logs themselves, but in usage statistics.

A Note About E-mail

If you allow users to send e-mail through their Web browsers to obtain feedback or request information, make sure they can only send mail to predefined addresses rather than specifying an address of their choosing. Why? If you use forms and some form of the sendmail program to send the mail, the mail will arrive at its destination showing that the author is your Web server (such as webserver@www.company.com) instead of the Web user who actually wrote the message. This may confuse, annoy, or shock the reader, depending on what your Web user wrote.

In reality, there are dozens of easy ways to "forge" e-mail, so don't be too concerned about this one. However, abusing form-based e-mail is probably one of the most obvious ways to the casual user. In general, you should never trust the origins of e-mail, anyway. It's really no different than writing someone else's return address on any envelope you send. There is no security required or enforced in either system. Thankfully, people don't go around writing other people's return addresses on envelopes all the time. There's no reason they couldn't, but they just don't. It's the same with e-mail.

Data Validation

If your site uses scripts for forms processing, be sure to check for loopholes in your scripts that might cause unusual results. This is just an application of good programming practice. You can have a script, for example, that enables a user to type a value between 1 and 100. What happens if the user enters 200? Does your script make the user try again, does it just die quietly, or does it use the erroneous input in a system command that then impairs some aspect of your system?

Scripts are the most dangerous aspect of running a Web server. For example, it's quite possible to embed system commands in a form's text field by using the proper syntax. In the course of processing the form data, the script executes the embedded commands. In general, it isn't a good idea to allow the public to execute programs on your machine. To protect against this, screen user input for embedded commands before performing any operation on the input, or simply remove any potentially dangerous commands from the server. This might be an unlikely scenario, but it isn't impossible.

One final note on scripts and data validation. Form data is sent to the server just like any other document request (URL). A user who knows a little about how scripts and forms work can easily edit a URL to make it look as though it was generated by a form, but actually wasn't. In essence, the user can take your intended form, change anything in it, and post data based on the re-

▶ See "CGI Scripting," p. 430, before you implement any scripts on an Internet Web server.

▶ See "Passing Form Data," p. 409.

II

Setting Up a Web Server

vised form to your script rather than data based on the original. This just means that you can't rely on forms for data validation. The validation must occur in the script itself.

Note

Don't leave old Web pages on your server if you don't want them to be seen! Just because you aren't linking to them doesn't mean that no one else is. You will be surprised at the pages on your site that get linked to from external sites. Many Webmasters have been embarrassed to find that old discarded pages are still being viewed around the globe!

Promoting Your Web Site

After you've built your Web server, how do you draw attention to it? People won't start coming automatically; this section discusses publicity pointers. First, you need to know what things on your server will draw attention. Second, you need to know how to actively promote your server.

Give Back to the Net

In any business, word-of-mouth advertising and networking play a large role in overall exposure. When you offer a superior product or service, people pass the word quickly to their friends and neighbors, coworkers and so on. The same thing happens on the Net, only word spreads even faster through e-mail in Internet newsgroups.

What kind of Web site generates enthusiasm that spreads itself all over the world? Basically, any site that has something free to offer as well as advertising. An excellent example is on the author's Web server. I offer a searchable archive of all the World Wide Web and related newsgroups. This is a terrific resource for anyone involved in creating, managing, or surfing the Web. Check it out at **http://www.CriticalMass.com/concord/**.

This Internet was built on freebies and cooperation. The amount of perfectly legal free software on the Internet is unbelievable. Similarly, why individuals would volunteer their time and expertise to answer thousands of questions on Internet newsgroups is equally amazing. But that's part of Internet culture. If you want to receive the benefits of Internet exposure, you have to give something back to the Net. Here are some popular offerings.

Free Software

Free software is an excellent way for your site to get noticed. General-purpose software certainly draws attention. But better yet is software related to your field. If your company sells astronomical supplies, for example, you can offer an astronomy screen saver containing planet photos. If your company offers financial services, you can offer a program to assist in simple home financial decisions. If your company is an engineering or scientific organization, there are probably already dozens of free programs distributed around the Internet to do various types of calculations related to your field. Collect them and make your site the clearinghouse for these kinds of programs, and you will have a steady stream of visitors as the word gets around.

A Free Service or Database

In addition to free software, people will come to your site for information they can't find anywhere else (or have to pay for elsewhere). For example, a stockbroker might offer a stock charting service or mutual fund database. Why would you want to give away this data? Simply put, if you don't, someone else will—and they'll get all the credit. A single benevolent company or institution can dry up the demand for certain kinds of information services overnight by offering the same data for free on the Web! To use this particular example, some students at MIT have already created a decent set of Web pages to track popular stock offerings. Had a commercial company done that, they could have received a lot of good publicity that could have led to enormous sales of related products, such as the actual stocks.

Tutorials and How-To Information

Another popular type of free offering on the Net is information on new technologies, topics of public interest, or general information related to your product or service. For example, Rockwell Network Systems (**http:// www.rns.com/**), which makes networking hardware, has some great white papers on the Internet, connecting to the Internet, and LAN remote access. This type of information demonstrates that your company or organization is knowledgeable in your field and that you stay on top of developments. In short, it positions your company as an industry leader.

Fun Stuff

As mentioned earlier, a good sense of humor is always a drawing card for the Internet community. Include a "purely-for-fun" link somewhere in your Web site with pointers to interesting and humorous activities you discovered on the Web. People always appreciate finding something they didn't know was there. If you update your fun stuff daily, people are more inclined to frequently connect to your site to see what's new. Fun stuff doesn't have to be related to your work, either. Maybe you're a small business owner and you're interested in gardening. Include links to your favorite gardening sites on the Web. Perhaps only a few of your customers will be interested in gardening, but they will be glad to know that you are, too, and will frequent your business more often. The Web is often as toy-like as it is business-like, so go ahead and have some fun.

Actively Promoting Your Server

While your Web site's intrinsic qualities are certainly important in garnering interest on the Internet, you must also expend some small effort to let people know about your site. Several different methods of making your server well-known are included here.

Complementing Traditional Advertising

For starters, you should put your Web address on all of your standard literature and advertising right along with your phone number and e-mail address. If you already enjoy a widespread market reputation, this is the quickest way to garner interest among those who already read your ads.

Name Recognition on the Web

A simple way to draw in people without even advertising is to choose a name for your Web server that is easy to find and remember. The most popular naming convention is www.company-name.com. Anyone wondering if Microsoft is on the Web would only need to try **www.microsoft.com** to find that they are indeed. If your company name is already well-known, this is an excellent technique. Universities follow a similar convention, such as **www.iastate.edu** (Iowa State) or **www.uiowa.edu** (University of Iowa).

Internet Shopping Malls

Many Internet providers offer a shopping mall concept. When you buy Internet service or Web space through these providers, your storefront is listed prominently in the mall. Your site immediately benefits from the publicity the mall receives, and customers who visit other stores in the mall can see your store, also.

The What's New List

NCSA, Netscape Communications Corporation, and O'Reilly and Associates Global Network Navigator got together to offer a single What's New page for the entire World Wide Web. Entries are currently pouring in at the rate of four hundred per week, so there's a two-week delay before publication. You can view the What's New list, as well as add your own entry, at **http://www.ncsa.uiuc.edu/SDG/Software/Mosaic/Docs/whats-new.html**.

UseNet

An easy way to advertise your Web site is to post it to relevant Internet newsgroups. However, be very careful here. Advertising on newsgroups is generally unwanted, and has been abused in the past. You should only post to immediately relevant groups, and only if your site can offer some value to the newsgroup (not just the other way around). Some newsgroups were created just for this purpose, such as **comp.infosystems.announce**. It's appropriate to announce all new Web sites here.

Internet Directories

There are many directories of Internet servers, some more complete than others. There is an excellent directory of directories at **http://Home.netscape.com/home/internet-directory.html**. Some of the more popular directories are listed here, as well. One of the most comprehensive directories of Web servers is Yahoo at **http://www.yahoo.com**. Yahoo is organized by subject, is fully searchable, and contains many tens of thousands of entries. It's a very popular Internet resource.

Search Engines

Somewhat similar to Internet directories, Internet search engines enable you to search for any subject matter on the Web. However, search engines are unique because they automatically roam the Web day and night, reading and indexing several thousand documents per day. Many search engines not only search for document titles, but also for works inside documents. The idea of a full-text index of the World Wide Web is almost unimaginable, but it is being done.

In many cases, search engines can find you even if you don't tell them where you are. This happens when a site that is currently known to the search engine contains a link to your site. Of course, the best way to make sure you're noticed is to tell the search engine that your site exists. Most search engines can add new sites.

A very popular and thorough engine is Lycos at **http://lycos.cs.cmu.edu/**. An excellent list of other search engines is available at **http://home.netscape.com/home/internet-search.html**. The best approach is to make your server known to all engines.

> **Tip**
>
> Because many search engines sort by number of occurrences of the search word, pick a few keywords describing your site and make sure they appear frequently on one page.

Final Pointers for Success

If you apply the principles in this chapter, you will soon have a thriving site on the Web. To put on the finishing touches, follow these last few pointers.

Don't Release Unfinished Pages

Due to the relative novelty of the Web, it's still common to see pages with sections marked "Coming Soon" or "Under Construction." This may be acceptable in moderation, but large numbers of these can create the appearance that your site is not finished, so people won't bother coming back. If you plan to add lots of new features, wait until they're ready, and then tell the world about them.

Make It Look Like You're Home

The Web thrives on novelty. Update your site frequently to keep people coming back for new information. This takes a lot of work, but can be very rewarding. Let people know that you're really committed to using what the Web has to offer.

Have Fun!

This has already appeared twice in this chapter for good reason. The Internet has become what it is because people have had fun doing it. Programmers, who spend countless hours working on code to give it away on the Net, do it because they enjoy it. Home users who had to struggle with the Internet before *The Complete Idiot's Guide to the Internet* did so because they enjoyed it. And people will continue to use the Web because it's fun. So sit back and think of the craziest thing you can offer to the world of the Web. One all-time favorite is the Amazing Fish Cam at **http://home.netscape.com/ fishcam/**, where the programmers at Netscape Communications Corporation point a camera at their fish tank and publish the resulting images on the Net every minute or so. Who says you can't have a fish tank in your office? ❖

## CHAPTER 9

Creating and Managing an Intranet Web Server

This chapter discusses some of the many aspects of running an Internet Web server for internal use within your organization. While a Web server can be a fantastic information resource, like any computing resource, it must be configured properly to work reliably and securely.

The first part of this chapter examines some concepts behind a Web server and presents some ideas for the uses of your own internal Web server. The second part discusses some of the technical issues when your Web server is on a network connected to the Internet.

In this chapter, you learn:

- Why Web servers are useful as information resources within an organization
- Some possible applications for your Web server
- Important issues regarding network security
- An overview of security options and techniques
- How to create a "private" network between two remote sites using the public Internet

Overview

An internal Web server can be the central information clearinghouse for your department or company. Other systems may give you the capability to access data, but Web-based systems make data access *easy*.

The Strengths of Hypermedia

Hypermedia is one of the strongest methods ever devised to make information easy to find. Users don't need to enter complex commands or fight their way through unfamiliar applications to find the information they need; all they have to do is click on a highlighted word or phrase. Since Web browsers are fully multimedia capable, you can distribute graphical data (such as charts, diagrams, or artwork) as easily as text.

Web hypermedia also enables you to use other existing technologies, such as e-mail, with the same easy-to-learn, easy-to-use interface.

Useful Features

The most useful feature of Web-based hypermedia in a company setting is cross-platform compatibility. Users in different departments frequently have different systems. For example, the business office may run Windows, graphics and publications may use Macintosh systems, and other divisions may even use UNIX systems; but they can all access the same data files using the common medium of the Web.

A browser-based information clearinghouse has many other advantages over traditional database systems.

- You don't need to pay expensive software-license or vendor-support fees for an exotic database system; all you need is one Web server and a Web browser for each user (and browsers are available today for almost every conceivable hardware platform, either free or at a very low cost).

- You don't have to spend programmer time (and funds) designing new views whenever you expand your database; the browser automatically presents all information using a consistent, unified system.

- You don't need to custom-design applications for different hardware platforms or worry about translating file or data formats between PCs and other systems. HTML, the language that makes the magic of the Web possible, is easy to learn and provides a convenient platform-independent document format. Macintosh, UNIX, VMS, and PC—all use HTML and users on all these platforms can exchange files freely and contribute equally to the information storehouse.

▶ See "HTML Editors," p. 328.

- You don't need expensive authoring tools to develop your data files. Most HTML editors are either free over the Internet or very reasonably priced (or, if your users know how to write HTML, you can get away with just a text editor).

▶ See Chapter 14, "HTML Forms," p. 393.

- And, finally, Web browsers are so easy to use, training time is extremely low—all you need to learn is how to point and click. Web browsers' form capabilities provide a very easy interface for searches or data entry. Users don't need to learn complex applications or data-search systems; just fill in the form and click Submit.

The Company Information Center

In an age where communication is the key to success, a Web server can be a fantastic clearinghouse for information of all kinds. And the good news is that you can create a company information center with just simple HTML files. Once your server is operational and your HTML files created, you'll be ready to go.

Many companies are finding a competitive advantage by making interoffice communications and documents freely available to anyone within the offices. With a little training and a simple HTML editor, anyone can create and update files available. Managers can post the status of their projects; Inventory controllers can post inventory counts for the sales department. Information that used to require considerable restructuring can be displayed quickly.

The company information center is simply the collected functions and Web based applications that you or your company has developed. The following are some examples.

Information Publishing

The Web server can be easily used to display announcements company-wide. Vacation schedules, press releases, upcoming deadlines, letters from customers (both good and bad)—anything that is of general interest can reside on the Web server. For example, by editing the home page, a "message of the day" can be distributed to all users whenever they check the server for the latest news.

Even more importantly, the Web server can be integrated into a database for dynamic information retrieval, online inventories, employee documentation, or phone list. Any ODBC-compliant database can be used with a Web server.

Using one of many HTML editors, you can quickly transform a document or text file into an HTML file. Once the files are created, you can go back through them and link them together.

A WorkGroup Tool

The hypertext system that eventually became the World Wide Web was first designed as a workgroup tool. When used as a workgroup tool, the Web server can be the central source for information for a department or project. Here are just a few ideas.

Schedules

Keep other project members apprised of changing schedules by keeping the master schedule in HTML on the server. As priorities or dates change, it's a small matter to change the central schedule—and since HTML documents

II

Setting Up a Web Server

can be updated with any text editor, you don't need to license multiple copies of expensive or hard-to-use project management software. The easiest way to maintain a master schedule is to integrate it with a database. A schedule integrated with a database allows easy form-based entry of information by the users. The kind of scheduling information tracked by the database can be as simple as a "When I will be out of the office" to integrating the schedules with other members of the workgroup. Figure 9.1 is an example of a form that a user could fill out to post schedule information.

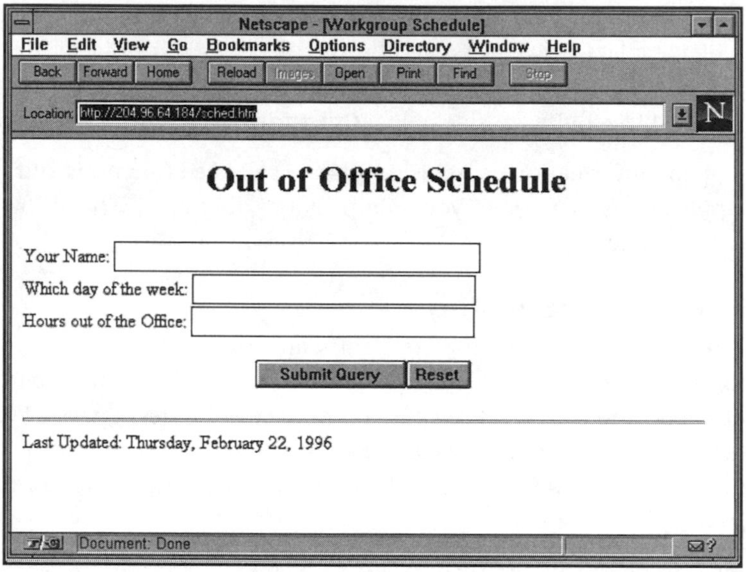

Fig. 9.1
HTML form-based schedule page.

▶ See "Editing and Updating Data within an Existing Database," p. 535.

This form sends the information to the database through a SHT file. That same SHT file could then display the information in a table or some other format. A more involved scenario would allow multiple users to display and update their "Out of Office" schedules. This application would require a minimum of three pages/files. The first page allows the user to choose what information to add or update; the second page allows the user to input that information; and the third page displays the changes.

Specifications

▶ See "Hypertext and Hypergraphics," p. 265, to review how to use links.

Workers involved with different parts of a project can resolve questions by referring to the master specification on the Web server. In the early stages of a project, comments can be added to the specification document and shared between all project members as the work evolves. This example is the easiest to produce. This involves taking existing specification pages, determining what relationship exists between the pages, and then simply using links to create a simple way for the viewer to navigate from page to page.

Suppose a company has a set of specifications about a construction project. The cover sheet becomes the main page, with links to each of the outline items. There could be an Index, displaying links to any part of each of the pages. A link at the bottom of each page to the front page and the Index provide a complete and thorough navigation structure between the pages. Comments to any or a specific page can be produced a couple of different ways. Simply opening the page and editing the HTML is the simplest for some users. Create a simple text file that is included on the page using the SSI+ tag <!—#include file="comments.txt" —>. Place the include tag where you want the file inserted in the document. The most complicated and easiest way for the user requires building a database, connecting to the database, updating and retrieving information from it, and then displaying that information on the page. This last way is the most flexible and most powerful.

Time Cards and Project-Based Billing

Employees can have individual time clock pages that when used automatically generate a time card by sending the information to an Excel spreadsheet (see fig. 9.2).

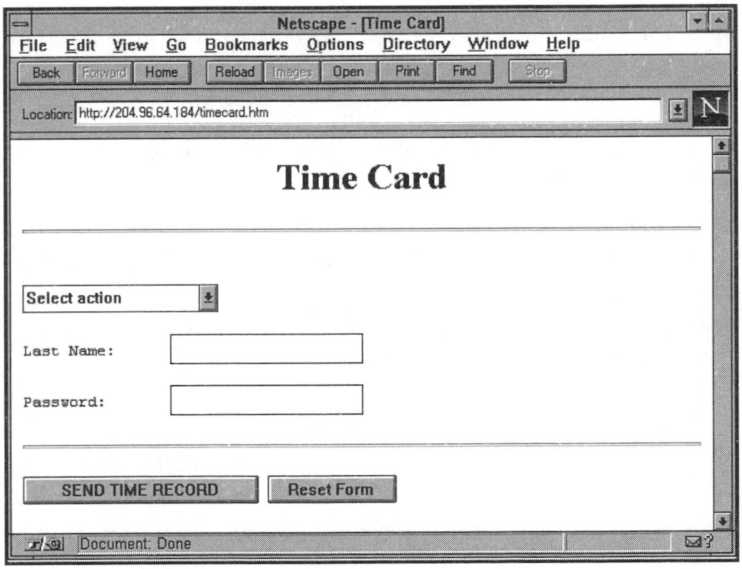

Fig. 9.2
HTML form time card.

This is a simple example that stamps the time and associates that time with an action, like Start of Day or End of Break. A time card is generated and is viewable through Excel. It would be possible to create an HTML page that retrieves the information from the Excel spreadsheet and displays it for the user. The calculation abilities of Excel can be used in this way. For example, the spreadsheet could be set up to track the amount of overtime accumulated and display that information. Another Web page could be created that would query each individual's time sheet and would display how much overtime each employee has accumulated.

To-Do Lists

The project leader can track workers' progress in a common To-Do list, or by observing each other's progress, team members may find new areas of cooperation and task sharing. Perhaps the easiest way of creating this To-Do list is to create a simple database table with the name of the project, action or to-do, status, and priority fields. The first page would query the database table for all the information in it and display that information for the user. The user could then pick which "to-do" to update, click it, and be presented with a form to fill out. Clicking on Submit would update the database and then display the updated information for the user.

Maintaining the Workgroup Information Center

Someone in the workgroup will need to be assigned to maintain the files that are the Workgroup Information Center. This person need not be the System Administrator, but needs to be someone who deals with the following:

1. Plans the information to provide. Decides whether the workgroup files has a central maintainer, or whether workgroup members can edit the files.

2. Creates the HTML pages that contain the information your workgroup tool is to provide.

3. Stores the HTML pages in a directory on your server where authorized workgroup members can *modify* the HTML files. Windows NT enables you to establish directory sharing permissions which you can use to allow specific users access to the workgroup directory; Windows NT security is discussed in greater detail later in this chapter.

Interdepartmental Information

The Web server can be a great asset to departments, such as Human Resources, whose concerns are company-wide. This is especially useful in organizations where not every employee's hours coincide with a "nine to five" HR department.

Policies

The company employee handbook can be published in HTML on the server; so can important documents like vacation or sick-leave policies, employee review schedules, or details of fringe benefits. HTML also affords quick and easy indexing, or hypertext links to important sections.

Using forms, employees can query an ODBC database for vacation or sick days unused, status of their 401K plan, health-plan policy numbers, or even something as simple as the company phone directory.

Technical Resources

The Web server can be a source of technical information for anyone from "help desk" operators to salesmen fielding questions from potential customers. Putting information on a Web server saves printing costs and easily distributes material to anyone who needs it.

Setting Up a Web-Based Information Center: A Quick Overview

This section will give you some guidelines regarding the general steps to plan and develop your Web information center. Since each site's information and requirements are unique, these are only general guidelines. Once you've created your first few HTML pages, you'll see your site taking shape in no time.

▶ See Part III, "Doing HTML," p. 235, for more information about setting up links and creating a Web page.

To set up a central information system on your internal Web server:

1. Decide what kind of information you want to present on your server. (This might seem to go without saying, but it can't be stressed enough that a little bit of initial planning will save a lot time in the long run.) A good place to start is by collecting all the printed information that exists with regard to the information you want to present. In many cases, the information is not "new," it already exists and is in use. The kind of information you want to present will also suggest a way to structure the links between HTML documents.

   > **Tip**
   >
   > Brainstorming your Web site on paper, rather than on the computer, is often a good way to start these projects; it enables you to plan not only the information, but also the links between pages.

2. Plan your access control scheme. First, you must decide who will have write access to the Web data files themselves (HTML documents, graphics, CGI scripts, and so on). For example, if you are using the Web server as a workgroup tool, members of the group may need to edit certain files; if you are using the Web server as a central information clearinghouse, you may want to be the only user with access to the Web files, while providing a storage place for others to place their files until you post the files for them. Use access control within

Windows NT to grant users permissions to files. Generally, only administrators need full control access, people updating and modifying HTML files need change control.

Next, you must plan any access controls you want to implement through the server—that is, who will be allowed to view the server files using a browser (a separate issue from who can edit the data files). You can use the access control included in WebQuest and some other servers to require passwords to specific files or subdirectories. Are there areas you want to restrict to certain users or groups? Or to prevent certain users or groups from reading?

There are several ways to approach access control issues; these are discussed later in this chapter.

3. Create a separate HTML document for each subject you want to cover. Keep in mind the size of the screen, generally people only look at the first screen of information. If your document is a couple pages, consider creating multiple smaller documents. For example, make one page for the vacation schedule, another for the intercom or telephone list, and another for product price lists.

If you have many files that are related, you can consider grouping them under other HTML files or indexes. For example, if you have thirty press releases, create another HTML file that indexes them by day or topic. If you have a separate HTML file describing each product, create an HTML file that indexes them by product line or by name. Another option is to build a database of your press releases with one of the fields as a link to the actual document, or with a product listing create a database and create various queries to retrieve the information.

If you want your server to provide form-based data retrieval, you must write the necessary CGI applications and HTML forms. You also have other options. WebQuest, for example, makes creating a database back end to any form both simple and quick, through the use of SSI+ tags.

4. Create the server's home page. The home page and the default pages generally are the same file. There can be multiple home pages per server, one for each subcategory, but only one default page per domain name. The main function of this page is to act as a central starting point for your Web site. Be sure that these links clearly describe the information to which they are connected. Remember to reserve an area of the home page for the "message of the day" or other important information.

5. Once the server is operational, internal users should configure their browsers to display the internal server's home page whenever they start their browser. This will display your "message of the day" and enable them to immediately access the information you've provided.

Protecting Your Data

Whether you are running an Intranet server, a public Internet server, or a private server accessible through the public Internet, you need to protect your server from accidental or malicious tampering. Network security can be extremely complex and technical, and this section will not answer all of your security questions: however, it will give you a good overview of the basic issues and the choices you will need to make.

Understanding the Risks

A computer on a network is part of a computing community. Some communities are small (for example, a mini-net of your computer, your partner's computer, and a shared printer). If your system is in anyway connected to the Internet, you are a member of a community of several million users. Within almost any community (especially within the larger ones), there are some who have less respect for privacy or property than others. Computer criminals range from the curious who enjoy cracking security systems for the challenge but cause no damage, to vandals who destroy the systems they invade; business owners have the additional concern of industrial espionage. "Computer crime" is not just a danger of the Internet; even as an Intranet Webmaster, you must concern yourself with securing your server against internal tampering (and more so if your server provides access to confidential information).

There are two kinds of risk involved with a Web server. First, and most obvious, is that unauthorized users can access the information the server provides. Second, and far more insidious, is that improper configuration can enable malicious users to exploit security inadequacies to invade or destroy not only your server, but the rest of your network systems through their connection to that server. If the server executes scripts, configuration becomes an even more important concern; incorrectly written scripts running on improperly configured systems are a sure recipe for disaster.

The safeguards on your Web server are like the safeguards on your home—the locks and the doors that keep your property inside and intruders outside. A string across a doorway with a "Do Not Enter" sign is enough to keep out most reasonable people, but it doesn't provide any protection to someone armed only with determination. A solid oak door with a chain and deadbolt sends the same message, but requires a great deal more resolve to penetrate. Network security works much the same way—you select a technique appropriate to the amount of protection you want to provide. The sad truth is that no security system (computer-based or otherwise) can be completely secured against someone with the proper tools, talent, information, and determination. But by taking the proper steps, you will be able to provide sturdy, reasonable security against all but the best-equipped intruders.

There are different challenges in protecting Intra- and Internet Web sites. Intranet Webs on networks with Internet connections provide the greatest challenges of all. For example, a very simple way to protect your Intranet server from Internet-based attacks is simply not to connect it or its network to the Internet. Unfortunately, this solution also prevents everyone else on the server's network from connecting to the Internet. Whether you are tasked with protecting your server from several dozen people or several million, the basic challenge is the same: how you permit certain kinds of access and prevent all other kinds of access.

Planning Your Security Needs

When beginning the design of your security plan, you must ask yourself one simple question: What is the *worst* thing that could happen—what *real, tangible* damage would result—if unauthorized users had access to the Web server? If your answer is "Not much," then your task is easy—by shutting off most network services and taking a few simple steps further, you will secure your server against all casual intruders and a great number of more persistent ones. The thought of unauthorized users snooping through your files is certainly distasteful, but if such prying won't cause you $10,000 worth of damage, you may decide not to spend $10,000 in extra security hardware to protect against it.

If, on the other hand, compromising your security would cause you or your organization serious trouble, serious security measures are called for— measures sturdy enough to turn back even the most determined attacks. If you need that much protection for your internal Web server, you certainly need it for your site in general.

Let's take a look at the steps you can take to increase your server's security, starting with the simplest (and least expensive) and proceeding to the most complex.

Internal Security

No matter how large the network to which your server is connected, the first thing you should do to protect the server's data is to make the best use of all available *internal* access controls. These measures will increase the general security of your system and its data, protecting against accidental (or malicious) tampering from within a local network; and, if your system is connected to the Internet, it will stand as the last line of defense against external attacks.

- Your server should always be behind a locked door, where only authorized users can get at it.

- Use the system's keylock. A stolen password is no good if the keyboard is locked.

- You may wish to designate a "Webmaster" through whom all Web pages are channeled, or allow a number of users to edit their own departmental Web pages; but no matter the organization, the *number* of users who have access to the data files should be small, and those who can access the server program itself and its configuration files should be very few indeed.

- If your server is on a network, such as a Microsoft or Novell network, be sure that the server files are not publicly accessible via that network. This would obviate any access control that the Web server could provide, and could act as a "back door" for anyone trying to attack your system.

- Back up your server religiously, but store the backups in a secure location; attackers could gather valuable information about your installation by examining the backups.

Access Controls on a Windows 95 System

Windows 95 is designed primarily as a single-user desktop system. Although Windows 95 supports file and printer sharing, it does not have nearly the level of configurable security features that Windows NT supports. There are, however, some good basic access controls you can impose to improve the security of your Windows 95 system.

The Most Secure Option: Turn Off File Sharing

File sharing is an option you can enable to allow other users to access a computer's files using Microsoft's own network protocol (called NETBEUI in Windows 95 network setup screens). If you turn off file sharing, users can edit the server's files only by using the server computer itself. Normally, this option is turned *off*. Follow these steps to be sure that file sharing is disabled.

1. Open the Control Panel and double-click the Network icon. Figure 9.3 shows a typical network configuration.

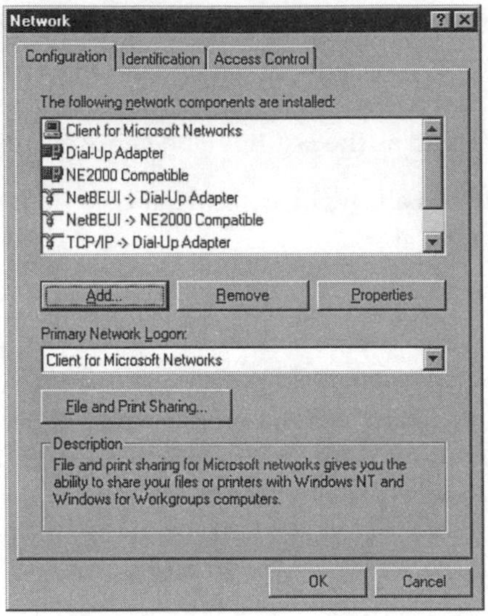

Fig. 9.3
Configuring
Windows 95 file
and print sharing.

2. Look through the configuration list for the service File and Printer Sharing for Microsoft Networks. If you *do not* see this service in the configuration list, file and printer sharing is already disabled; click Cancel to exit without making any changes.

3. If you *do* see that the File and Printer Sharing for Microsoft Networks service is installed, the File and Print Sharing button will be enabled. Click File and Print Sharing.

4. The File and Print Sharing dialog box displays. Clear the I Want To Be Able To Give Others Access To My Files check box.

5. Click OK. You will return to the Network configuration screen; click OK to exit.

6. You will be prompted to restart the computer; click Yes to reboot the computer.

Password-Protect the Document Directory
If you do not wish to turn off file sharing entirely (for example, to enable authorized users to edit files over the network), you can assign *share permissions* to specific directories. For example, you can allow authorized users write access to the document directory, while protecting all other directories on the system.

These steps will show you how to password-protect a shared directory. Windows 95 will also allow you to specify a list of authorized users, but your network must be set up to support this feature (and not all networks are so configured). See your network administrator and the Windows 95 online help for further assistance.

Caution

Windows 95's file and print sharing has been known to wreak havoc on installations that use non-Microsoft protocols (such as some versions of Novell NetWare). Check with your network manager before you enable file and print sharing under Windows 95. As a general rule, however, users can access files shared under Windows NT without adversely affecting other network services.

To assign share permissions, you must first set up and configure the Microsoft network. Then, you can apply share permissions to individual directories. If you already have the Microsoft network options installed and configured, skip ahead to the next section; otherwise, follow these steps. You will need to have your Windows 95 CD or floppy disks handy.

1. First, you need to enable file sharing. Open the Control Panel and select the Network icon.

2. The Network configuration screen displays. Check the configuration list; if you already have the service File and Printer Sharing for Microsoft Networks, skip ahead to step 11.

3. If you do not have the service File and Printer Sharing for Microsoft Networks installed, you must install it. Click Add.

4. The Select Network Component Type dialog box displays. Double-click Service, or select Service and click Add.

5. The Select Network Service dialog box displays, as shown in figure 9.4.

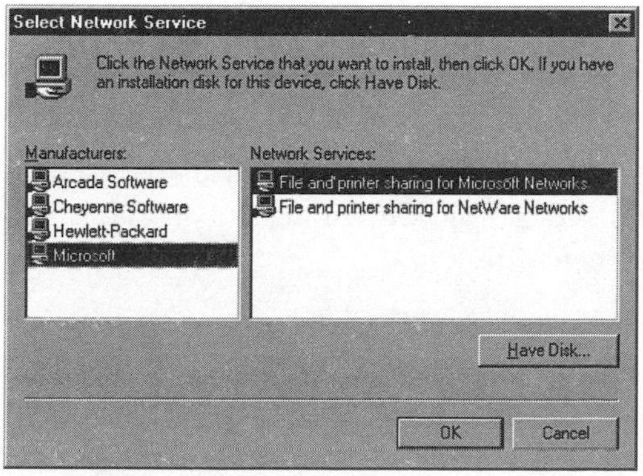

Fig. 9.4
Selecting the File and Printer Sharing service.

In the Manufacturers list, select Microsoft. Then, from the Network Services list, select File and Printer Sharing for Microsoft Networks.

6. Click OK. You will return to the Network configuration dialog box.

7. You also need the NetBEUI protocol (required for file and printer sharing over Microsoft networks). Click Add.

8. The Select Network Component Type dialog displays. Double-click Protocol, or select Protocol and click Add.

9. The Select Network Protocol dialog box displays. From the Manufacturers list, select Microsoft. Then, from the Network Protocols list, select NetBEUI.

10. Click OK. You will return to the Network configuration dialog box.

11. Next, you need to define a name and a workgroup for the server. Click the Identification tab.

12. The Identification tab displays. You need to fill out this tab so that other users will be able to contact this system via the network. In the Computer Name box, enter the system's name (something simple like "Web server" should do nicely). Next, in the Workgroup box, enter the name of the server's workgroup (again, something simple like "ServerAdmin"). Finally, enter a description for this system (such as "Internal Web server").

13. The last few steps are just to double-check that some default options have been set correctly. Click the Access Control tab. When this tab displays, be sure the Share-level Access Control option is selected (it should already be selected).

14. Now, make sure that file sharing is enabled over Microsoft Networks. Click File and Print Sharing.

15. Check I Want To Be Able To Give Others Access to My Files, and then click OK.

16. Click OK to exit the configuration dialog box. You will be prompted to insert the Windows 95 CD or floppy disks. Follow the on-screen directions.

17. Finally, you will be prompted to reboot your system. Select Yes.

Once you have the Microsoft network installed and configured, you can apply share permissions. Follow these steps to define a share permission for the server's document directory.

1. From the desktop, open My Computer.

2. Double-click on the drive that contains your Web server.

3. The folders contained on the selected drive will display. Navigate to the directory \Program Files\Questar\WebQuest95 (or to whichever directory you installed your server).

4. By default, the server's data files are stored in the WebSpace directory. Right-click on the WebSpace folder.

5. The Properties menu displays. Select Sharing.

6. The WebSpace Properties dialog box displays. Select the Sharing tab (see fig. 9.5).

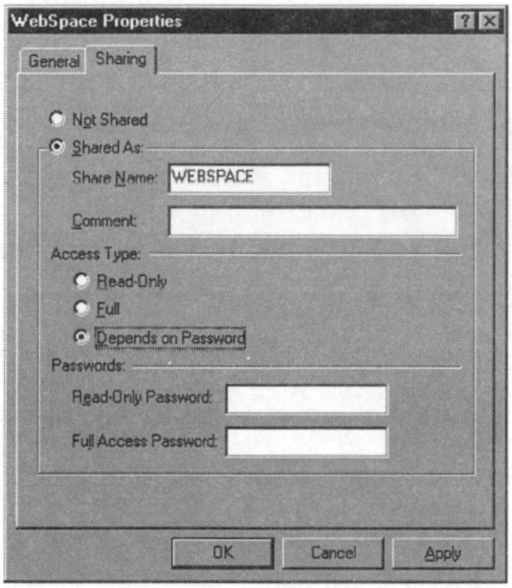

Fig. 9.5
Adding Share permissions.

Select Shared As. When you select this option, most of the other options on the tab will be activated.

7. The Share Name box lists WEBSPACE as the *share name*, or the name by which users on the network will request this directory. You can leave that unchanged. Optionally, you can add a comment (such as "Web server data directory").

8. Next, in the Access Type group, select Full Access. This will enable users to edit files within the directory.

9. In the Full Access Password box, enter the password for the directory. When you type the password, only asterisks (***) will display in the dialog box.

10. Click OK to apply the changes and exit the dialog box. You will be prompted to re-type the password to be sure it is correct; do so and press Enter or click OK.

Users can now access this directory over the network by using the Explorer's Map Network Directory option. Before they are allowed to connect to the directory, they will need to supply the password you specified.

Questions and Answers about File Sharing and Share Permissions

This seems rather complicated. Do I have to do this to make my Web server work?

No; this procedure is entirely optional, and has nothing to do with how the Web server provides files to other users. This procedure enables you to allow "trusted" users to edit HTML documents remotely. ("Trusted" means that you trust them to behave as responsibly as you would when working on the Web system.) Remote editing enables users—including you—to make changes to the web files without logging in to the server system itself. This can be a great convenience for you if the Web server isn't physically located at your work-station, and enables trusted users to edit files on their own, without requiring you to implement the changes for them. If you find that configuring or using remote access is troublesome, or for some reason you can't use file sharing on your network, no problem—you'll just need to edit the server's document files directly on the server system (or copy them from floppy or other media), and users who want changes made to their files will need to make the changes themselves, or to mail the changes (or the updated files) to you.

What does the Microsoft network, NetBEUI, and workgroups have to do with IP addresses?

Nothing; they are completely separate systems. You can think of these net-work protocols like AM and FM radio signals; one radio can receive both kinds of signals without getting them confused.

These instructions show how to share the HTML data directory. Can I share the server root directory as well?

Yes, but this will enable users to access the server configuration utility and the server program itself. Server administrators generally regard this as a very bad idea: be *very careful* when allowing this kind of access.

Can I share more than one directory?

Yes. For example, you can set one password for the server root directory, and a separate password for the data directory, so that different sets of users can access the administrative functions and the HTML documents.

I saw that I can set up "read only" share access as well. Must I make share the server files as "read only" so users can read them with their browsers?

No; in fact, you can shut off sharing entirely and not affect browsers in any way. These "share permissions" don't affect browser/server transactions.

Access Controls for Windows NT

Windows NT features an extremely sophisticated security system; if your server is running under Windows NT, you have an excellent opportunity to vastly increase the security of your system.

Use Separate Disks or Disk Partitions

Put the server and its data files on a separate partition, or even on a physically separate disk. Isolating the server from the rest of the system helps preserve general system security; if security on the server's file system is compromised, the rest of the system is still safe.

Unfortunately, whenever you repartition a disk, you lose whatever information is currently stored on that disk. Repartitioning is best done when you first install Windows NT, or when you first install a new disk.

To repartition a disk, follow these general steps:

1. Log in to Windows NT as an Administrator (either with the ADMIN account or in an account with Administrator privileges).

2. Open the Administrative Tools group and start the Disk Administrator.

3. You will see a message if this is the first time you have run the Disk Administrator. The Disk Administrator will display a status bar as it starts. Occasionally, the Disk Administrator does not immediately display in front of other open applications. If this happens, just press ALT+TAB to cycle through the open applications and select the Disk Administrator. Figure 9.6 shows a typical system with three physical disks, and one disk with a logical disk partition.

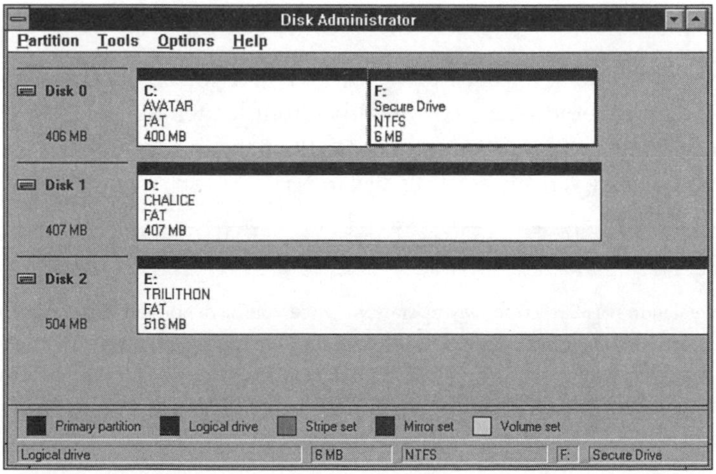

Fig. 9.6
Use the Disk Administrator to repartition a drive.

4. If you are partitioning a new disk, skip to step 6.

If you are partitioning an existing disk, you must first delete the current partition. Click on the partition you want to delete. A black box will display around the selected partition.

5. Choose Partition, Delete. You will be warned that you are about to delete any existing data; click Yes to confirm and delete the partition.

6. An unpartitioned area of the disk will display with gray diagonal stripes. Click on the unpartitioned area to select it.

7. Choose Partition, Create. A dialog box will prompt you for the size of the new partition. If you are partitioning a large disk into smaller logical disks, be sure to make each partition large enough for its intended use.

8. Repeat steps 6 and 7 for as many logical drives as you want to create.

9. Choose Partition, Exit. You will be asked whether to implement the changes you have made (because partitioning is irreversible, the Disk Administrator asks for extra confirmation before doing the partitioning); click Yes.

Once you have repartitioned a disk, you must format it. We recommend you consider formatting the disk with NTFS (described in the next section).

Use NTFS

NTFS (the Windows NT File System) affords a further level of protection beyond system- and share-level security. When a disk is formatted as NTFS, you can assign a range of file and directory permissions based on user or group name.

If you want to use user- or group-level security controls, you *must* use NTFS.

There are two ways to format a drive with NTFS. If you are formatting a new drive or want to reformat an existing drive from scratch, you can use the Disk Administrator. Or, if you want to preserve the data on your current disk drive, you can convert the existing disk to NTFS.

> **Note**
>
> Conversion to NTFS is a one-way operation. Once you have converted a disk to NTFS, you can change it back to DOS format (FAT) only through a very involved process, using a Microsoft utility called FDISK. Reformatting the disk will not allow you to change the format back to FAT.

To format a new drive with NTFS, follow these steps:

1. Log in to Windows NT as an Administrator (either with the administrator account or in an account with Administrator privileges).

2. Open the Administrative Tools group and start the Disk Administrator.

3. You will see a message if this is the first time you have run the Disk Administrator. The Disk Administrator will display a status bar as it starts. Occasionally, the Disk Administrator does not immediately display in front of other open applications. If this happens, just press ALT+TAB to cycle through the open applications and select the Disk Administrator.

4. Select the drive you want to format. A black box will display around the selected drive.

5. Choose Tools, Format. A new dialog box will display, as shown in figure 9.7.

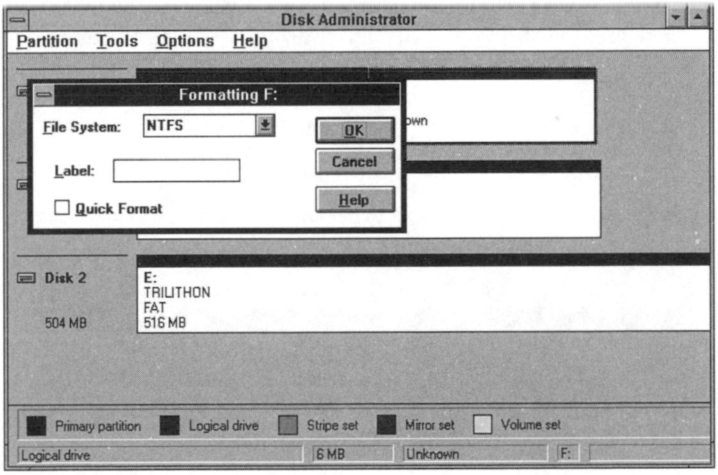

Fig. 9.7
Formatting a drive with the Disk Manager.

6. Select the NTFS file system. If you like, you can add a volume label. Then, click OK.

7. You will be asked to confirm whether to format the disk; click Yes.

8. The Disk Administrator will format the drive. Click OK when the disk space message displays.

9. Choose Partition, Exit to exit the Disk Administrator.

If you have an existing disk whose data you wish to preserve but that you want to convert to NTFS, follow these steps:

1. Open the Main group and select MS-DOS Prompt to open a DOS command-prompt window.

2. At the DOS prompt, type **CONVERT x: /FS:NTFS** (where **x:** is the letter of the drive you wish to convert). Note: You cannot convert the currently connected drive.

3. After the drive has been converted, type **EXIT** to close the DOS window.

Create Accounts and Groups for Web Server Access

If your Web server system is used for any other purposes, such as a desktop system or as a file server, and users other than yourself or other administrators will be working on the Web project, you should create a special group just for Web server access. This will ensure that the Web maintainers get the access they require, but without requiring Administrator privileges.

After you have created the Web maintainer groups, you can use NTFS security to grant those groups access to the Web server files.

To create a "Webmaster" group, follow these steps:

1. Log in to Windows NT as an Administrator.

2. Open the Administrative Tools group and double-click the User Manager icon. The User Manager will display (see fig. 9.8).

Fig. 9.8
The User Manager creates accounts and groups.

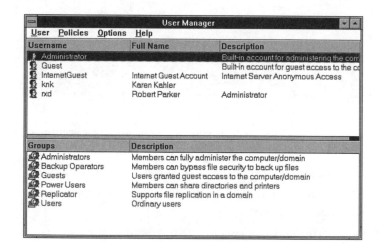

3. To create a new group, choose User, New Local Group.

4. The New Local Group dialog box displays. In the Group Name box, enter the name of the new group: **Webmasters**.

5. In the Description box, enter **Web server administrators.**

6. If accounts already exist for users who will be members of this group, you can add those users to the group now. (See the next section for instructions on creating new user accounts.) To add users to the group, click Add.

7. The Add Users and Groups dialog box displays, as shown in figure 9.9.

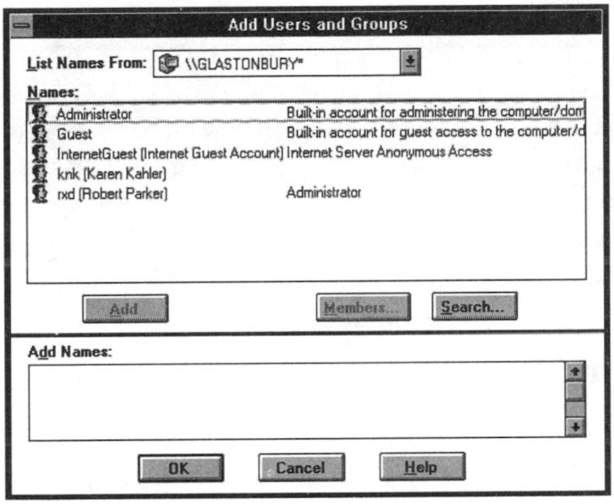

Fig. 9.9
Adding users to the Webmaster group.

8. From the Names list, select the user you want to add to the Webmaster group, and then click Add. Repeat for as many users as you need to add to the Webmaster group.

9. When you have finished adding users to the Webmaster group, click OK.

10. You will return to the New Local Group dialog box. Click OK to close this dialog box and return to the User Manager.

11. To exit the User Manager, choose User, Exit.

To create a new user account as a member of the Webmaster group, follow these steps:

1. Log in to Windows NT as an Administrator.

2. Open the Administrative Tools group and double-click the User Manager icon. The User Manager will display.

3. To create a new account, choose User, New User.

4. The New User dialog box will display, as shown in figure 9.10.

II

Setting Up a Web Server

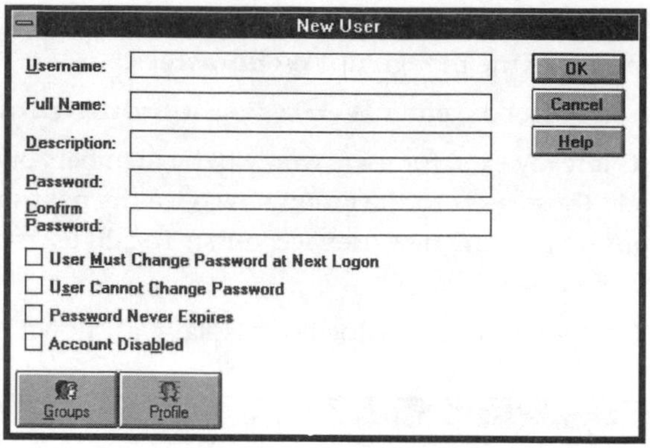

Fig. 9.10
Creating a new
login account.

5. Enter the account information. In the Username box, enter the name of the login account (such as "karen" or "jsmith"). In the Full Name box, enter the user's full name. Use the Description box for optional comments (such as "Web access only").

   When you enter data into Password and Confirm Password, the boxes will only display asterisks (***).

6. Click Groups. The Group Membership dialog box will display. The new user will already be a member of the "Users" group and no other. (By default, all users are members of the "Users" group. This enables you to create a system-wide access scheme for all users at once.)

7. In the Not Member Of list, select Webmasters, and then click Add. Webmasters will be added to the user's Member list.

8. Click OK to close the Group Membership dialog box. When you return to the New User dialog box, click OK.

10. To exit the User Manager, choose User, Exit.

Use NTFS Security To Control Access to Server Files

You can use NTFS security controls to ensure that only authorized users have access to Web server files. You can apply these controls to individual users, or to a "Webmaster" group.

To restrict access to server files to the Webmaster group, follow these steps:

1. Log in to Windows NT as an Administrator.

2. Start the File Manager, and select the NTFS directory you want to protect. To protect an entire NTFS drive, select its root directory.

3. Click the key button at the far right of the toolbar, or choose Security, Permissions. The Directory Permissions dialog box will display.

4. The default security permission is to allow anyone full control to the directory; we'll remove that first. Click Remove to remove this global permission.

5. Next, we'll add the Webmaster permission. Click Add.

6. The Add Users and Groups dialog box will display (refer to figure 9.9). From the list in the Names box, select Webmasters (you may need to use the scroll bars to scroll to the bottom of the list).

7. At the bottom of the dialog box, from the Type of Access list, select Full Control.

8. Repeat steps 6 and 7 to add full control to the Administrators group.

9. Click OK. You will return to the Directory Permissions dialog box.

10. To apply these new permissions to all subdirectories of the selected directory, select the Replace Permissions on Subdirectories check box.

11. Click OK to close the Directory Permissions dialog box. You will be asked whether you want to replace the existing permissions on all subdirectories; click Yes.

You can also use this procedure to assign permissions to individual users. In step 6 of the instructions above, click Show Users, and then select the user rather than the group from the Names list.

Questions and Answers about Users, Groups, and NTFS

Can I create just one "Webmaster" user with appropriate access, and give several people the password?

You could; it all depends on how you prefer to manage your site's security. Some administrators prefer to give each user a unique account; if you need to track logins or other transactions on your server, this is the preferable system. Some administrators feel that the more accounts one creates, the more potential security holes one opens; if you think fewer accounts are better, use a single "Webmaster" account.

Why can't the Webmaster be an administrator?

Again, it depends on your installation. If you are working in a trusted and secure environment—that is, you trust the other users to act responsibly, and you are safe from outside attacks—there's no reason not to run almost any account as an Administrator. If, however, your site is connected to the Internet, or you work in an environment where it's important to protect your system from either accidental or malicious change, it's mandatory that you guard Administrator privileges very carefully.

Use Restrictive Share Permissions

If you use Microsoft's NetBEUI network protocol, TCP/IP or IPX, other users can share your system's drives and printers. While this is often desirable (or necessary, in the case of network file servers), you want to make sure to disable or restrict this feature on the drive or directory tree that contains the Web server.

To set share permissions, follow these steps:

1. Log in to Windows NT as an Administrator.

2. Open the File Manager, and select the directory for which you want to set share permissions. To set the permission for an entire drive, select its root directory.

3. Select Disk, Share As. The New Share dialog box will display, as shown in figure 9.11.

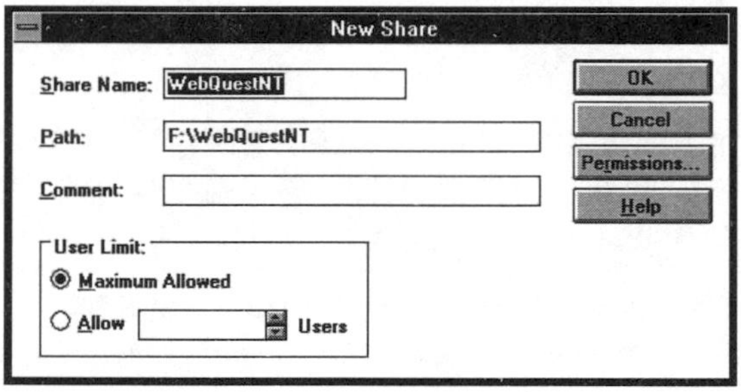

Fig. 9.11
Setting share permissions.

4. In the Share Name box, enter the name by which other users will access this directory.

5. Click Permissions. The Access Through Share Permissions dialog box will display (except for its title, this dialog box is identical to the one shown in figure 9.11).

6. The default share permission allows anyone to access this directory; this must be removed. Click Remove.

7. Next, add the permission that allows the Webmaster group (or user) to access this directory. Click Add.

8. The Add Users and Groups dialog box displays (refer to figure 9.9). From the Name list, select the Webmasters group, or click Show Users to include the users in the name list and select the appropriate user.

9. At the bottom of the dialog box, from the Type of Access list, select Full control, and then click Add.

10. Repeat steps 8 and 9 to add any other users and groups to the share list.

11. Click OK.

12. When the previous dialog box redisplays, click OK.

13. Finally, click OK to exit the New Share dialog box. (Note: if you used a share name longer than eight characters, you will be informed that some DOS systems won't be able to access the directory; click Yes if you want to accept that limitation.)

Unbind Internal Network Protocols from Network Adapter

This procedure is rather technical, but it very important on NT systems that serve both the Internet and an internal network.

First, a brief explanation is in order. Under Windows NT, various protocols are "bound" to the network card to enable the network card to use those protocols. For example, if the TCP/IP protocol (the one that Web servers use) is bound to the network card, the network card can send and receive data using TCP/IP—and thus, the Web server can communicate with uses on the network.

By unbinding protocols such as IPX or NetBEUI, you prevent the network card from communicating using those protocols; thus, you prevent external users from using those protocols to contact your server. For example, NetBEUI enables users to map your server's drives; without NetBEUI, that's impossible. Therefore, by unbinding NetBEUI, users can't map your server's drives—and that's good news for the safety of your server.

> **Caution**
>
> If you have any questions about this procedure, don't attempt it without assistance from your network administrator or other network expert. You can easily cut off all network access, including the access you want to permit, by doing this procedure incorrectly.

To unbind network protocols, follow these steps:

1. Log in to Windows NT as an Administrator.

2. Open the Control Panel and double-click Network.

3. Make a note of the name of the adapter card that is connected to the Internet, or to another network from which you want to block all but TCP/IP access (especially if you have more than one adapter card).

4. The Network dialog box displays. Click Bindings. The Network Bindings dialog box displays, as shown in figure 9.12.

Fig. 9.12
Unbinding
network protocols.

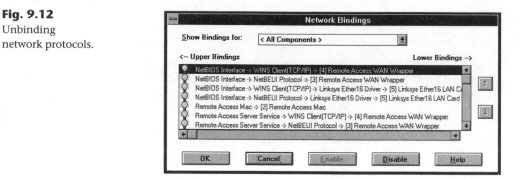

5. Select any bindings that connect services you do not want to support (for example, NetBEUI) to your network card, and click Disable to disable them.

6. Click OK to exit the Network Bindings dialog box, and then click OK again to exit the Network Settings dialog box. You may be prompted to restart your computer; do so.

Other Windows NT Security Resources and Suggestions

As you can see from the preceding sections, Windows NT security is a very sophisticated system that can be made quite respectably secure. The previous sections have discussed some of the basic security procedures; here's a short list of other security options and suggestions for your consideration.

■ Windows NT has an auditing system with which you can track login or other access attempts. A security log that shows a long list of unsuccessful access attempts is a sure sign that someone is trying to break into your system. Audits are controlled in the User Manager; select Policies, Audit, and then click Help for more information.

■ You can further restrict system access by user or group name, even to controlling what groups may log in to the system locally. These additional restrictions are also controlled by the User Manager; select Policies, User Rights, and then click Help for more information.

■ This chapter contained instructions on how to use NTFS to permit only Webmasters to access the Web server files. You can continue the process to protect *all* the files on the computer against any user except Administrators (of course, you should probably allow access to programs like Notepad or the File Manager). This is an especially good idea for Windows NT systems connected to the Internet.

■ You must have at least one account with Administrator privileges, but it does not need to be named "ADMIN." Delete the ADMIN and GUEST accounts—they are prime targets for break-in attempts. For the best security, give your Administrator account a nonsense name, like "zw8icop."

■ Run the Web server as a service, rather than as a desktop application. This has two benefits: the server will restart automatically if the system reboots for any reason, and unauthorized users who log in to the server system will be unable to affect the server process. WebQuest runs as a service; you cannot run it as a desktop application.

■ In general, do not run the Web server itself as Administrator; create a special user (perhaps called "Web") with exactly enough privilege to read the server files and *nothing else*. This way, if your Web account is compromised, the rest of your system will be safe.

> ### Caution
>
> WebQuest, as well as some other servers, *must* run as administrator. Creating an account for the server to run with a special user can drastically affect WebQuest.

■ All login accounts on any system with direct connection to the Internet must—*must*—have strong, uncrackable passwords. (A password "cracker" is a program that tries to log in by "guessing" passwords—some password crackers can go through 20,000 passwords per *minute*.) Weak passwords are the single most common, and potentially most devastating, security leak. There are many discussions of password security on the Internet, and Windows NT has several helpful pass-word-related features; they merit serious investigation.

■ To implement a very serious password policy, you can force users to change their passwords regularly, prevent users from repeating previous passwords, or lock out accounts after a certain number of failures. Pass-word policies can be implemented through the User Manager; choose Policies, Account, and then click Help for more information.

> ### Caution
>
> Through most literature on security, there runs a single theme: "The door only locks if you remember to turn the key." Incorrect or inadequate configuration of available resources is possibly the single most common cause of all security breaches. Before you add an additional level of security, be absolutely sure that the current level is as strong as possible.

Run Your Server on a Non-Standard Port

► For more information about the Port directive that selects the port your server uses, see Chapter 5, "Server Configuration," p. 101.

Ports are internal addresses that provide a means to direct network traffic to the appropriate services. By default, Web servers use port 80, and URLs include requests for that port by default. If you run your server on a non-standard port, requests for service on the standard port will go unanswered. For example, if you run your server on port 2056, users would need to request **http://yourserver:2056/**. Users who omit the port number and request just **http://yourserver/** will only receive an error message. Do not do this unless you are configuring the Web server to run as a proxy. Be careful not to choose a port that is the default for any other Internet protocol.

Port numbers range from 0 to 65,535. You can use any port number you like, but many numbers under 1024 are reserved for other network services (such as Gopher, mail, or FTP). It is suggested you avoid those port numbers to prevent conflicts with other network services.

Managing Web-Based Search Engines

If your Web server is on the Internet and you are concerned about whether a Web-based search engine has found or will find your site, you can put a unique string of words between the <TITLE> tags. We recommend something that accurately reflects the contents of that specific page like "Welcome to my Sheetmetal company home page." You can perform a search based on that line to see if your site has been found by a search engine. Note that it can take from a couple of days to a couple of weeks before your site could be examined by a search engine, and that users (whether authorized to do so or not) can add sites to many major search engines using online forms.

Restricting Access through Software

► For more information about implementing all these systems, see Chapter 5, "Server Configuration," p. 101.

The next level of protection comes from the server itself. Whether you decide to "hide" your server or not, you can use the server's own access control systems to protect your data.

IP Address Restrictions

One way to keep your data private is to instruct the server not to release your data to any requests from IP addresses that are not on an "approved" list. When a browser sends a request to a server, part of the request includes the browser's IP address. You can instruct the server to check these IP addresses, and to fulfill requests from only certain addresses (for example, only users whose IP addresses indicate that they are on your internal network). Some Internet access providers use this technique to create "subscribers only" areas on their public Web pages.

IP address restrictions do not stop *people* from viewing data—they stop *browsers* from displaying data, based on their IP addresses. An unauthorized user, using a system with an authorized address, can still view your data.

As secure as it may seem, this access control can be circumvented by a technique called *IP spoofing*, where a remote computer in effect "lies" about its IP address. To protect against this kind of sophisticated attack, you need to go to the next higher level of security (described in the next section).

User Authentication

Another time-honored way to keep prying eyes away from data is to require a user name and password to view the data. You can instruct the server to require users to supply a name and password before they can display a requested page. This "user name," by the way, has nothing to do with login names on your server, and doesn't grant login privileges to Web browsers— and so much the better, since it means you can assign totally different user names and passwords used to access the Web pages. Accesses to password-protected pages are tracked in the server log by user name; you can use these log entries as an audit trail in the event of a suspected security breach.

▶ See Chapter 6, "Configuring and Managing the Microsoft Internet Information Server," p. 149, to learn how to set access control and user authentication with WebQuest.

> **Tip**
>
> Never use a single password more than once and never issue the same combination of user name and password. A classic break-in technique is to reuse a discovered user name/password combination on other systems (for example, if Bill's password on one account is "sally," a cracker will try to log in as Bill using the password "sally" on every system he can contact).

Again, this seemingly straightforward solution has its drawbacks as well, since data is sent over the Internet in *clear* (unscrambled), anyone with the proper equipment can read the user name and password as it is being sent to the server. You can protect against this kind of attack using a server that supports a *secure transport layer*, which scrambles the data so that anyone eavesdropping will not understand any data he intercepts. Any server that supports enough security to send credit card information over the Internet has this feature, as does other specialized network hardware.

Preventing Access Using Routers

Routers are the first level of security beyond the server itself. Routers are separate devices that regulate the flow of information between networks. You can think of a router as a combination receptionist and security guard. When data is sent from the first network to the second network, the router compares the data against a list of rules that determine what data is allowed in and what data is rejected. For example, you can use a router to allow incoming e-mail, but to reject all other data, including requests for your internal Web server.

Fig. 9.13
Routers filter incoming network traffic.

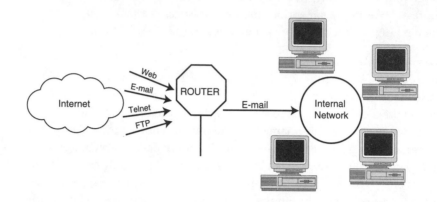

Routers are an excellent first line of defense between your network and the Internet, and properly configured routers can turn aside even sophisticated attacks like address spoofing. When combined with other systems, like firewalls or proxy servers, they help create a substantial security barrier. For more information, see the section "Advanced Security Topics."

Router installation and configuration is a good deal more complex than setting up the Web server's security system. If you think you need the kind of security routers provide, you should strongly consider obtaining professional assistance to install it. Most router vendors offer a package deal for the hardware plus installation.

Protecting Multiple Internal Servers

Web servers are so useful and so easy to set up, you could put a Web server on every desk of your company. If you can trust your users not to sabotage each other's systems and these "mini-servers" supply nonconfidential documents like conference room schedules, interoffice volleyball scores, or recipes for home-brewed beer, you can safely assign each server's owner the risk and responsibility for maintaining his own system's security. However, if your site is connected to the Internet, you must be certain that each little server isn't a security risk just waiting to be discovered. The best way to protect multiple internal servers—and your entire network, for that matter—is to provide a single gateway to the Internet, and to guard that gate securely using routers and firewalls.

Advanced Security Topics

As you saw in the last section, network security can be applied in layers, beginning with the server itself and proceeding outward. This section will discuss how network security can be implemented for some typical server applications.

Running Both Internal and External Servers

Many sites may want to use Web servers to distribute information both internally and externally. There are several ways to run both internal and external servers; again, the method you choose depends on how secure you want to make your internal server.

Separate Systems

The simplest method to support internal and external servers is to run them on physically separated systems. The safest way to connect them is, of course, not to connect them at all—put the external server on the Internet and the internal server on an entirely separate network that is not connected to the Internet. Computer experts often call the connection between such systems *sneakernet*, meaning that to move files between systems, you put the data on a disk and walk from one system to the next.

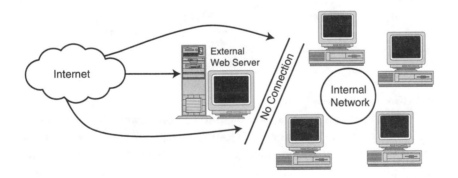

Fig. 9.14
No connection is sure protection, but the trade-off is convenience.

As mentioned earlier, this has the disadvantage of keeping everyone on the internal network off the Internet. If that doesn't matter, this is certainly the cheapest method to use. Be sure that your external server has *absolutely nothing* on it besides the Web files and whatever version of Windows that runs it.

> ## The Sacrificial Lamb Concept
>
> Internet security experts sometimes call an external server isolated from the internal network a *sacrificial lamb,* the idea being that Internet vandals will spend their energy compromising an inconsequential system, rather than destroying your far more valuable internal network. While not exactly a cheery thought, it does have a certain grim logic. Be sure to keep current backups of your external server, just in case.

A Single External Server with a Protected "Internal Use Only" Area

This method relies on the server's access control systems to keep out unwanted users. For example, some schools put class schedules or syllabus information on areas the server will only release to requests from in-school IP addresses. This technique will block casual inquiries, but won't keep out more sophisticated intruders. Remember the question "How bad will it be if the data is discovered?" Use this technique only if the "internal" area doesn't contain particularly sensitive information.

> ## Tip
>
> You can improve the security of "internal use only" areas by *not* putting any links to that area in any externally-accessible page. Internal browsers can request the internal home page manually; the server's address restrictions will then act as backup, rather than as primary security. By not advertising the link to the internal site, you reduce the chance that someone undesirable will try to use it.

Multi-Homed Systems

A *multi-homed* server is one that provides services on separate IP addresses. Some servers running on Windows NT can serve separate trees of Web documents at different IP addresses. Some servers can serve separate trees only at different port addresses, which gives each server its own URL, but not its own host name or address.

Proper configuration becomes extremely important in multi-homed servers. The greatest danger in running both servers on a single system is that a compromise on the public side will leave an opening through the private side to your internal network. Whether your internal and external trees have different port numbers or different IP addresses, make sure you use the following safeguards:

- Keep the internal and external server files in completely separate directories; if possible, on separate disks or disk partitions. Under *no* circumstances store the internal files in a subdirectory of the external files' directory tree.

- Apply the same security considerations to each server as you would for a single server. Be sure that each server, and *especially* the external server, has the best protection possible. See the section above on internal security for more information.

- Use "layered" security on the internal server; for example, give it an unusual host name *and* use the server's IP address restriction to block external requests.

- Do not create any HTML links between the documents in the internal and external directory trees, or share any files (even inconsequential files like graphic bullets) between them. Set up the external server as if the internal server does not exist. (Computer experts call this "security through obscurity"—if the bad guys don't know it's there, they won't try to break into it.)

- If you are running Windows NT, use two network cards, one for the internal network, and one for the external. Unbind the internal networks protocols from the external network card. This will prevent users on the external network from using the protocols that might enable them to access the internal network (see the section earlier in this chapter for more information). (Be advised, however, that heavy traffic on one of the networks will slow response on the second, and if the system goes down, you will lose *both* servers.)

Firewall Implementation

If your site needs protection against even the most serious attacks, you also need a *firewall*, the generic name for systems that control the flow of data between networks, not just by applying filters like a router, but by performing more sophisticated processing on the network data itself.

There are many ways to implement firewalls within a network security system. In one of the most common, a combination of filters and routers direct all traffic between the Internet and the internal network through the firewall system. Running on the firewall is a program called a *proxy*, so called because it acts as an intermediary between your internal and external network.

When the proxy intercepts a request from the internal network (for example, for a remote Web page), it forwards the request to the Internet under the *proxy's* name and IP address, and not under the requester's address. When the remote server returns the response to the proxy, the proxy returns it to the original requester. This way, the remote site never communicates with the protected internal network—just with the proxy. While "brokering" Web transactions, the proxy can also refuse transactions you want to prohibit (for example, form transactions that carry information about the systems on the protected network).

Fig. 9.15
Proxies protect your internal network by "brokering" network requests.

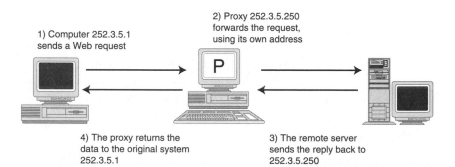

1) Computer 252.3.5.1 sends a Web request

2) Proxy 252.3.5.250 forwards the request, using its own address

4) The proxy returns the data to the original system 252.3.5.1

3) The remote server sends the reply back to 252.3.5.250

Firewalls can work with other services besides Web servers and browsers. For example, the firewall can filter services such as e-mail and news. Firewalls, with other security hardware, can be used in many different configurations. Figure 9.17 illustrates just one possibility (for the sake of clarity, other services such as e-mail are not included in this diagram). Figure 9.17 illustrates three-layered security:

- A router is the first line of defense, filtering incoming network data and allowing only requests for the external Web server and responses to requests from the firewall/proxy system.

- A proxy firewall mediates between the internal and external networks, and acts as a second defensive layer.

- An internal Web server provides information for the protected internal network. The internal Web server uses address restrictions, declining service to all but its internal network (a third line of defense).

Is all this necessary—extra computers, extra software, extra time, and the expense to configure it? The definitive answer is...it depends; it depends on the complexity of your system and the amount of security you need. Simple solutions often suffice for simple installations; the more complex your network and the more protection you require, the more complex your security solutions.

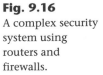

Fig. 9.16
A complex security system using routers and firewalls.

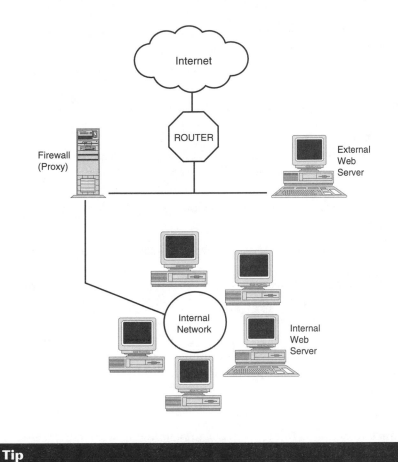

II

Setting Up a Web Server

Tip

Computer security is a hot topic on the Internet. Many security-hardware vendors and consultants manage pages on the Web, which are often superb sources of information.

Running a Private Web Server

An interesting hybrid of the public server and the internal server is the private Web server on the public Internet—a server that only authorized users can access using the World Wide Web. For example, you may want your sales force to be able to receive messages or view schedules, make product demonstrations available remotely, or you just may want to exchange "not ready for prime time" draft documents.

Setting up a private server requires the same techniques used to protect an internal Web server, which are discussed earlier in this chapter. In summary:

- Use address restrictions to allow only users from authorized IP addresses to access the server.

- Require a user name or password to access the server's private home page.

- "Hide" the server using any appropriate technique.

Data Encryption

One further concern that is extremely important in operating truly private servers on the public Internet is *data encryption*, a mathematical system for scrambling and unscrambling network transmissions so that anyone eavesdropping on the network connection won't be able to understand what they intercept.

If you have a commercial server, such as the Netscape Commerce Server, designed to enable users to safely send credit card information over the Internet, you can safely use any browser that supports secure transactions and feel safe about the security of your network transmissions. There are also routers that support *hardware encryption*, a scrambling system built right in to the router hardware. If you do not have a secure server or other scrambling hardware, you might consider using an intermediary system such as PGP (for Pretty Good Privacy, a very popular encryption program) to encode your data before sending it.

Other Options

A simple workaround to the challenge of maintaining a private server on the Internet is to use Windows NT's Remote Access Services (or RAS). Using RAS, you can dial in to a Windows NT system; then, you can access whatever files your login account allows. RAS offers greatly improved security (for example, since you are using regular phone lines, you don't need to worry about Internet eavesdropping), but at the cost of the flexibility that true Web access provides (for example, although you can still view files with the browser's "local mode," you will not be able to run scripts). You may be willing to make the compromise if your security needs demand it.

Connecting Divisional Web Servers via the Internet

Many organizations are beginning to use the Internet as an extension of their own networks. Rather than pay the cost of leased lines or ISDN lines, you can use the Internet to carry inter-site traffic.

Of course, the greatest challenge is in maintaining security across an unregulated medium such as the Internet. You already know many techniques you can use to connect two sites via the Internet. Routers can be used to direct traffic between Web servers, accepting only data from the authorized IP address of the remote site; address restrictions on the server act as a backup to the protection provided by the router. Again, you must be concerned about sending unencrypted data over the Internet, but encrypting routers are available that will encode and decode data as it is sent and received.

> **Caution**
>
> With this technique, you rely on the security of two separate sites to keep your internal network secure; misconfiguration at either site could open a security breach into both sites.

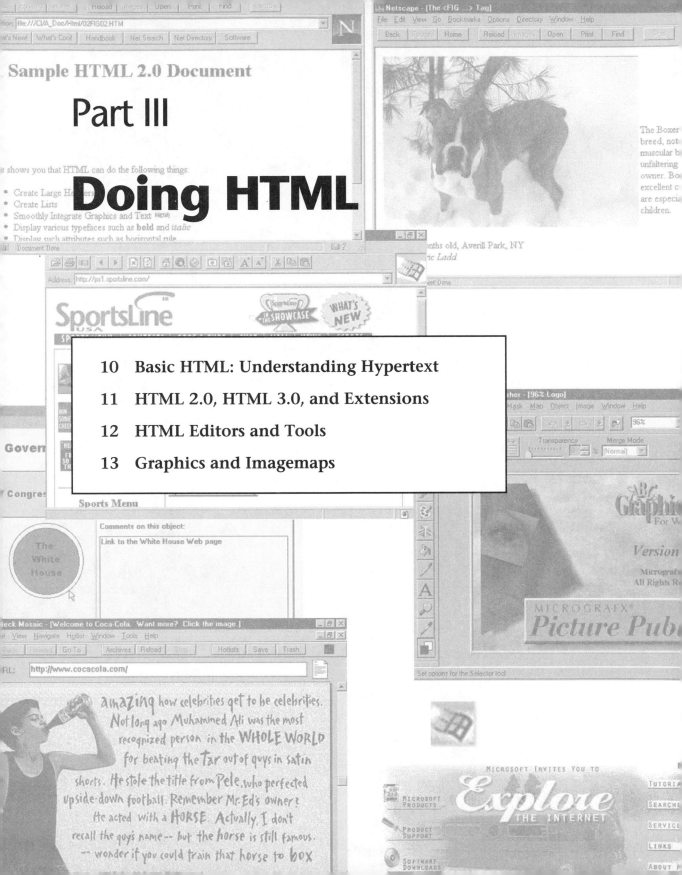

Part III

Doing HTML

CHAPTER 10

Basic HTML: Understanding Hypertext

The whole point of setting up a Web site is so that users can access the information you place on the site. Publishing documents on the Web requires them to be prepared in *HyperText Markup Language (HTML)*, a page description language with provisions for linking related documents together. It's a simple, text-based language that you can view in a variety of fonts on any platform. You can use it with text-only clients, such as Lynx, on a VT220 terminal or with fully graphical clients, such as Mosaic, on advanced graphical workstations.

The present version of HTML, otherwise known as *HTML 2.0,* is the most commonly used version. Most clients support HTML 2.0, but a few, such as Netscape Navigator and Microsoft Internet Explorer, support additional features, such as blinking text or background sounds, that are not in any HTML specification. Most of this chapter covers standard HTML. *HTML 3.0* (formerly called HTML+), which is near the final stages of its formulation, includes more formatting features, such as style sheets, tables, figures, and mathematical characters. HTML 3.0 promises to make strides toward a universal document format that is both compact and rich in formatting.

In this chapter, you learn the basics of HTML, including:

- The basic structure of an HTML document
- How to format text into headings, paragraphs, and lists
- The difference between physical and logical styles and how to apply these styles in your documents
- The GIF and JPEG graphical formats
- How to place inline images in a document
- How to set up hypertext and hypergraphic links to other documents

HTML Fundamentals

Before charging right into the HTML tutorial, it's helpful to review some introductory remarks on HTML to give you a sense of what it is, where it came from, and where it's heading.

History of HTML

HTML is an application of the Standard Generalized Markup Language (SGML). SGML arose out of the international standards community to meet the need for standards in electronic publishing. Content creators can specify sets of rules called *document type definitions* (*DTDs*) for applying SGML to marked-up documents. HTML is one of many SGML DTDs in use today.

> **Note**
>
> For a complete discussion of SGML, consult Que's *Special Edition Using SGML*.

The first version of HTML, HTML 0, was developed at CERN in 1990 and is largely out of use today. HTML 1.0 incorporated inline images and text styles (highlighting) and was the version of HTML used by most of the initial Web browsers. HTML 2.0 is the current standard. HTML 3.0 will incorporate tables, figures, mathematical characters, and other more advanced formatting features.

HTML Is ASCII-Based

An HTML document is simply the informational text of the document with formatting instructions embedded in the text. These instructions are in the form of *tags,* character sequences that begin with a less-than sign (<) and end with a greater-than sign (>). Tags can be used to, among other things, apply a style to text, insert a line break, or place an image in the document. The idea is similar to older word processors and page layout systems that require insertion of formatting tags to specify bold, underlined, or italicized type. Newer word processors use the same premise, but usually hide these tags from the user. Some word processors, however, allow you to display the formatting tags—WordPerfect, for example, provides you with the Reveal Codes menu option.

For a look at some HTML, first consult figure 10.1, which shows the World Wide Web (W3) Consortium's home page (**http://www.w3.org/**). Choose the Document Source option from Netscape Navigator's View menu to activate a window with the HTML source loaded. The HTML source corresponding to figure 10.1 is shown in figure 10.2.

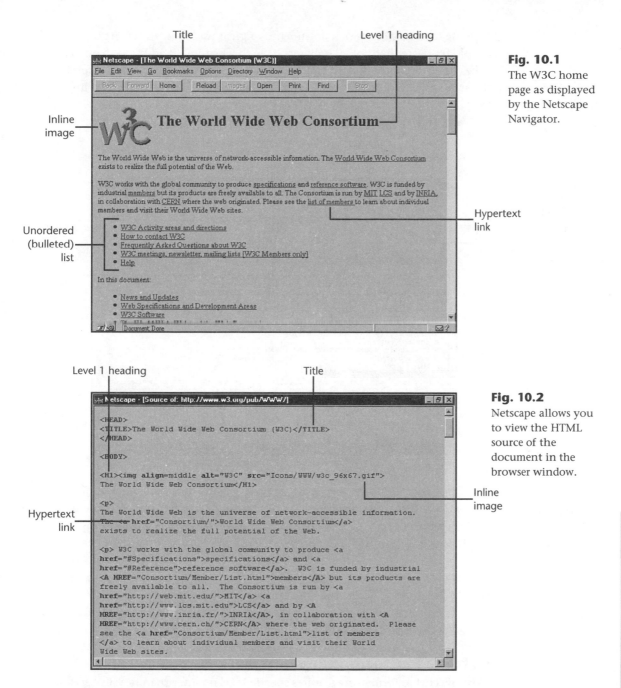

Fig. 10.1
The W3C home page as displayed by the Netscape Navigator.

Fig. 10.2
Netscape allows you to view the HTML source of the document in the browser window.

Viewing the source code of a document is a great way to learn HTML, but you should be aware that not all browsers have this feature. In addition to differences in features, you should also know that different browsers often display the same page in different ways. Figure 10.3 shows the W3C home page in Lynx, a text-only browser. Notice how the elements pointed out in figures 10.1 and 10.2 are rendered differently in Lynx.

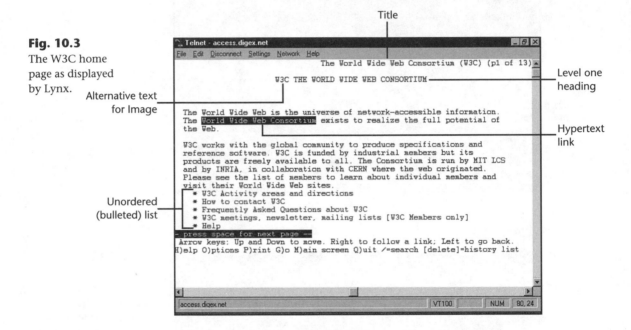

Fig. 10.3
The W3C home page as displayed by Lynx.

The differences in browser rendering are not a significant problem with the basic HTML formatting tags, but they can be an issue when your documents contain more advanced HTML, particularly those tags that are extensions to HTML supported by only a few browsers. This points to an important challenge in creating Web documents: how to incorporate the advanced features while not breaking browsers that can't render those features. As you read this chapter and the next, note the suggestions for writing browser-friendly HTML. Following these suggestions will make your documents accessible to the largest audience possible.

► See "Netscape Extensions," p. 289, to learn more about extensions to HTML supported by the Netscape Navigator.

HTML Is Platform-Independent

Most of HTML's formatting features specify logical rather than physical styles. For example, the heading tags, which normally indicate larger font sizes, do not specify which size to use. Instead, a browser chooses a size for the heading that is larger than its default text size. This allows Macs to view files written on PCs and served by UNIX boxes. The disadvantage to this approach is that it is impossible to control the exact formatting of any HTML document because users can configure the fonts and physical styles to go with each HTML logical style.

Three Basic Rules of HTML Parsing

In spite of the differences between them, Web browsers do consistently follow three rules when parsing HTML. These are:

- White space is ignored
- Formatting tags are not case-sensitive
- Most formatting tags occur in pairs

White Space Is Ignored

The fact that browsers ignore white space is often a source of frustration for the beginning HTML author. Consider the following HTML:

```
<TITLE>Our Mailing Address</TITLE>
Que Corporation
201 West 103rd Street
Indianapolis, IN  46290-1097
```

The address looks fine on the page, but notice how Netscape renders it in figure 10.4.

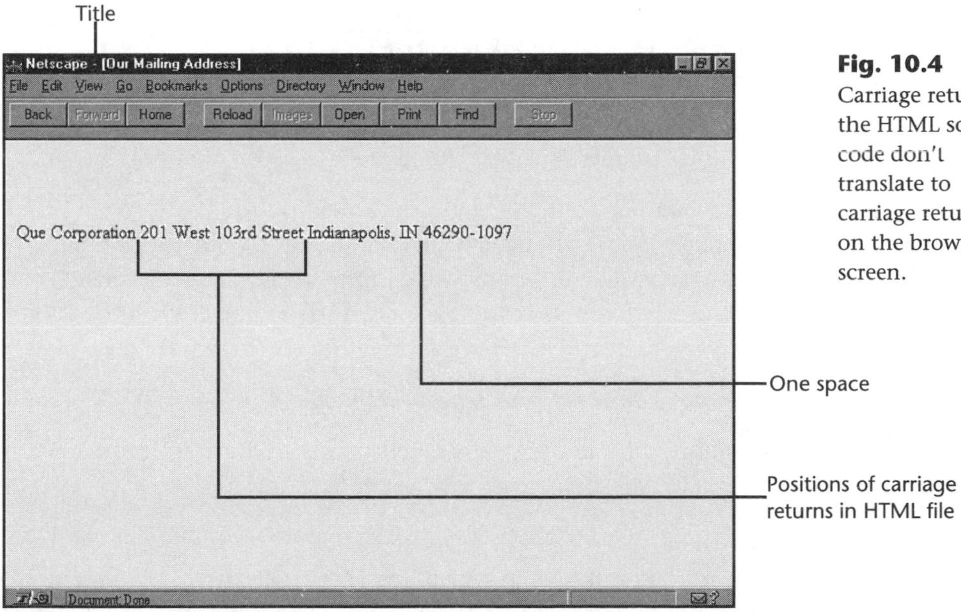

Fig. 10.4
Carriage returns in the HTML source code don't translate to carriage returns on the browser screen.

Title

One space

Positions of carriage returns in HTML file

III

Doing HTML

Netscape tries to display the address all on one line! The carriage returns in the file, which make the address look fine in an editor or on a printout, are ignored by the browser. The same is true of other white space characters like tabs and extra spaces. In the HTML above, there are two spaces between IN and 46290-1097, but only one space between them in the browser window. The second space character is ignored.

Formatting Tags Are Not Case-Sensitive

You can write all HTML formatting tags in upper-, lower-, or mixed case. For example, browsers interpret <TITLE>, <title>, and <Title> the same way.

Most Formatting Tags Occur in Pairs

With only a few exceptions, HTML formatting tags occur in pairs in which the beginning tag activates an effect and the ending tag turns off the effect. Tag pairs are often called *container tags,* since the effects they turn on and off are applied to the text they contain. For example, to specify that a line of text appears in bold, you write:

```
<B>This text will appear in bold.</B>
```

The ending tag in the pair is always preceded by a slash. Among the basic HTML tags, those that do not have a companion ending tag include: <BASE> (base information),
 (line break), <HR> (horizontal rule), and <IMG> (image).

Uniform Resource Locators (URLs)

While not directly related to HTML, *Uniform Resource Locators* (*URLs*) are an important part of HTML documents used in many different tags. For this reason, a quick primer on URLs is in order.

A URL is basically the address of a document on the World Wide Web. The URL scheme is a way of compactly identifying any document on any type of Web-compatible server anywhere in the world. The URL consists of four parts: a protocol, Internet address, port, and file name. With the exception of the News protocol, the general format for a URL is as follows:

▶ See "URL Encoding," p. 410, for more information on attaching query data to a URL.

protocol://internet_address:port/file_name

In addition, you can optionally specify search or query information after the *file_name* when sending data to a search or script.

Protocol

The *protocol* indicates what type of Internet application is requested. In order to use a given protocol, both the client (browser) and Internet server must be able to speak that protocol. The most common protocol in Web documents is "http" (HyperText Transfer Protocol), which is spoken by all Web servers and clients. In addition, almost all browsers support FTP, Gopher, Telnet, and News. Some also support WAIS. Some examples of URLs using these protocols follow:

http://webwise.walcoff.com/frontier/pick.html

ftp://ftp.fedworld.gov/pub/irs-pdf/form1040.pdf

gopher://gopher.government.gov/reports/census.txt

telnet://loc.gov

news:sci.psychology.clinical

mailto:info@netscape.com

> **Note**
>
> The news URL is substantially different than the others because it does not specify an Internet address or file name. Instead, it simply names a newsgroup. The name of the news server must be made known to the browser when you initially configure the browser.

> **Where To Get News**
>
> To read Internet news through a Web browser, you have to be able to connect to a news server, which continually receives messages over the Internet and stores them locally for a short time (usually about two weeks). Newsfeeds cost money, and for this reason, no news servers are publicly available on the Internet. If your site wishes to take full advantage of Internet news, you must obtain a newsfeed from your Internet service provider or obtain authorization to connect to your provider's news server.

The mailto: URL allows you to send electronic mail to the specified address directly from your browser. The mailto: URL is supported by Netscape, Lynx, and others, but it isn't supported by all browsers.

Address

The address portion of a URL is simply the name or IP (Internet Protocol) number of an Internet server. This address can be either the familiar named dot notation (like **ftp.ncsa.uiuc.edu**) or a number sequence (like **127.0.0.1**).

Port

The port is an optional URL element. If the port is omitted, the default port for the specified protocol is assumed.

File Name

The document path, or *file name,* is the same as that used by DOS and UNIX systems alike, although the slash is forward (/) rather than backward (\) for DOS users. Each slash goes down to the next subdirectory having the specified name, and the path ends in a file name with an extension (such as TXT or HTML). It is also possible to specify a path to an entire directory simply by ending with the directory name and a trailing slash (/). For example, to see the contents of the fruits directory on an FTP server, you can use:

ftp://ftp.healthy.com/fruits/

A URL that specifies a protocol, Internet address, and file name is said to be *absolute* or *fully qualified.* In some cases, it is also possible to specify one URL relative to another, resulting in a *relative* or *partially qualified* URL. For example, suppose your base URL is http://www.healthy.com/fruits/citrus/ tarty_fruits.html and you need to specify the URL of the file intro.html located in the fruits directory (one directory level up from citrus). You can do this with the absolute URL http://www.healthy.com/fruits/intro.html, but it can also be appropriate to give the URL relative to the base URL. In this case, the relative URL would be ../intro.html. The two dots followed by a forward slash (../) are an indicator to move up one directory level. If you need to specify the URL of the file lemonade.html in the lemons directory (a subdirectory of the citrus directory), you can use the relative URL lemons/ lemonade.html.

> **Note**
>
> The base URL for a document is specified in the <BASE HREF="*base_url*"> tag. This tag is discussed in the Document Structure portion of the next section.

General HTML Style

While you are generally free to write HTML any way you want, there are a few issues of style to keep in mind. If you're just starting out, take these style issues to heart and develop good authoring habits from the onset. If you've been writing HTML for a while and have perhaps "forgotten" about some of the aspects of good style, this is a great time to remind yourself of them and work them back into your documents.

Uppercase Tags

While it is true that HTML tags are not case-sensitive, it is a good idea to always make them all uppercase. Remember that tags are embedded in other text and this can make them difficult to read when writing or editing HTML. Tags that are all uppercase stand out much better in a sea of text.

Note

Unlike HTML tags, URLs are case-sensitive. Be sure to pay attention to uppercase and lowercase letters in your URLs.

Document Structure

It used to be that a discussion of HTML document structure would be right at the beginning of an HTML tutorial. However, since most browsers can still parse an HTML file without the structure-defining tags, many authors have fallen out of the habit of including these tags in their documents and their inclusion becomes an issue of style. Good HTML style suggests that you always include tags to define the major parts of your documents. The three major parts are:

- The HTML declaration
- The document head
- The document body

The HTML Declaration

The HTML declaration is simply accomplished by making the <HTML> tag the first thing in your file and making the </HTML> tag the last thing in your file. These container tags say "Everything between us is HTML code."

The Document Head

The document head should immediately follow the <HTML> tag and is contained in the <HEAD> ... </HEAD> tag pair. The document head contains information about the document that is typically transparent to the user. While many informational items can be specified in the document head, the two that you should always include are the title and the base URL of the document.

The document's title is designated with the <TITLE> ... </TITLE> tag pair. You should make your titles descriptive, while still keeping them fairly short. A forty character title is a good rule of thumb. Document titles typically appear at the top of the browser window (refer to fig. 10.1). They are also used in bookmark files.

> **Tip**
>
> In the absence of a specified title, the URL of the document is displayed at the top of the browser window and in bookmark files. URLs aren't as descriptive to users as titles are, so always be courteous to your users and include a title.

The base URL of the document is given in the <BASE HREF="*base_url*"> tag. The base URL of the document should be set equal to the document's absolute URL. With this done, you are free to specify other URLs relative to this one.

The Document Body

The document body immediately follows the head and is enclosed in the <BODY> and </BODY> tags. The body contains all of the information that will be presented to the user and the tags used to format that information.

Putting these three parts of the document together, you have the following basic template for an HTML document:

```
<HTML>
<HEAD>
<TITLE>Document Title</TITLE>
<BASE HREF="absolute_url_of_document">
</HEAD>
<BODY>
Information and formatting commands
</BODY>
</HTML>
```

Many HTML editing programs make this basic template available to you when you create a new document. If you're using a word processor or a simple text editor to write HTML, you can probably create and store this template easily. In either case, there's no reason not to include the structure-defining tags.

Getting Started

To start writing HTML, all you really need is an editor that allows you to save files in ASCII format and a browser to test your documents. If you plan to include images in your documents, you'll need a graphics program as well.

Editor

In Windows, an accessory program like Notepad is sufficient for writing HTML files. You can use word processing programs, saving as ASCII, as well. Many such programs have plug-in libraries designed to help make HTML authoring easier. If you'll be writing a lot of HTML code, you may want to consider a program specifically created for HTML authoring.

▶ See "Word Processing Programs" p. 314 and "HTML Editors," p. 328, to learn more about word processor macro libraries and stand-alone editing programs.

Browser

You only really need one browser for testing your documents, but it's a good idea to look at your HTML files in two or three browsers to make sure your code is as browser-friendly as possible. It's easy to get a copy of the popular browsers. NCSA Mosaic 2.0 and beta versions of Netscape Navigator 2.0 are available for public download on Mosaic and Netscape's Web sites. Windows 95 users will find Microsoft Internet Explorer packaged with their operating system.

> **Note**
>
> You can download Mosaic from **http://www.ncsa.uiuc.edu/SDG/Software/ WinMosaic/HomePage.html** and Netscape Navigator from **http:/home. netscape.com/comprod/mirror/index.html**.

Graphics Program

To create images for your pages, you'll need a graphics program that can save in the GIF or JPEG graphics formats. You can use an accessory program like Microsoft Paint or a shareware program like Lview Pro for this purpose. For more advanced graphical effects, a package like Adobe Photoshop may be in order.

▶ To learn more about several different graphics programs, see "Graphics Tools," p. 367.

HTML Tutorial

With the preliminaries covered, you're now ready to learn the basic HTML tags. All of the tags discussed in this section are found in the document body (between the <BODY> and </BODY> tags) and fall into several categories:

- Comments
- Paragraphs and line breaks
- Heading styles
- Physical styles

III

Doing HTML

- Logical styles
- Lists
- Special characters
- Horizontal lines
- Images
- Hypertext and hypergraphics

Comments

It is possible to include comment lines in HTML that do not show up in browsers. You should consider placing comments in documents that you and others will be working on together. Many stand-alone HTML editors provide templates that include a comment area for information like the author's name and the date the document was last changed. The format for a comment is as follows:

```
<!-- Everything in here is part of the comment. -->
```

▶ See "Server Side Includes with WebQuest," p. 433, to learn more about server side includes.

> **Note**
>
> Server side includes commands embedded in HTML use the same character sequence as comments. This is so that the server side includes commands do not show up even when a server does not support server side includes. Documents utilizing server side includes must have the extension SHTML; this distinguishes them from documents containing normal comments.

Paragraphs and Line Breaks

The <P> tag is used to indicate the start of a new paragraph. Ending a paragraph with the </P> tag is currently optional, but you may want to get into the habit of using it. HTML 3.0 calls for the introduction of style sheets whereby an author can specify attributes—like alignment, indentation, and font size—right inside the <P> tag. Since the browser will need to know when to stop using the prescribed style, use of the </P> tag will most likely be necessary under HTML 3.0. Paragraphs are separated by a blank line. To start a new paragraph without the extra line of separation or to just move to the next line, use the <BR> tag (line break). Line breaks were needed back in figure 10.4 to render an address properly. Figure 10.5 shows the difference between paragraphs and line breaks. The corresponding HTML follows:

```
<P>Que is the premiere publisher of Internet-related books.
Be sure to visit our Web site at http://www.mcp.com/que/
for more information.
<P>Our mailing address is:
<P>Que Corporation<BR>
201 West 103rd Street<BR>
Indianapolis, IN  46290-1097
```

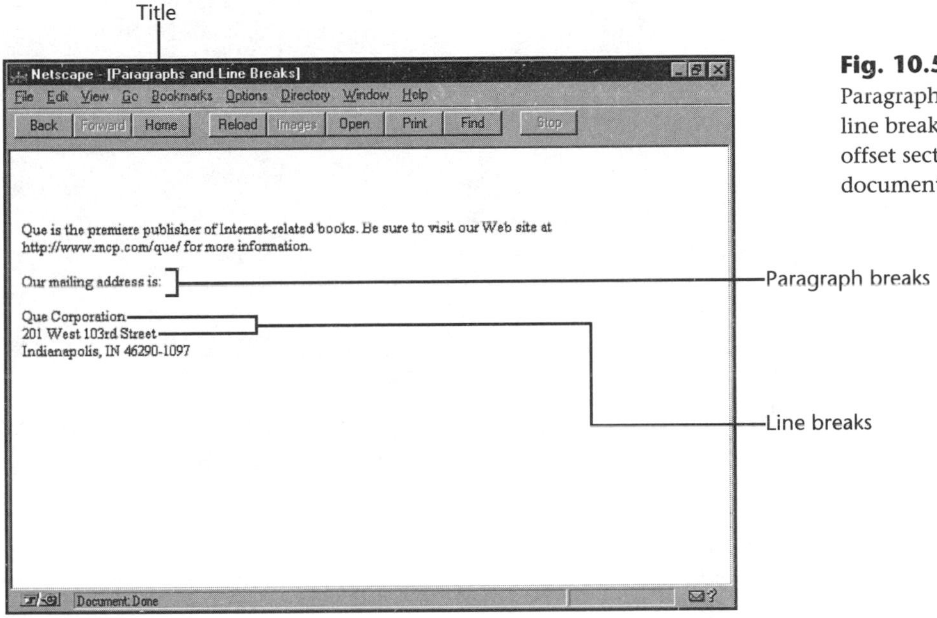

Title

Fig. 10.5
Paragraphs and
line breaks help to
offset sections of a
document.

Heading Styles

HTML supports six heading styles, which are used to make text stand out by
varying degrees. These are numbered one through six, with one being the
largest. To format text in a heading style, enclose it in the <H*n*> and </H*n*>
tags, where *n* is the number of the heading style you want to apply. Figure
10.6 shows how the six heading styles are rendered in Microsoft Internet
Explorer by default. The corresponding HTML is:

```
<H6>Heading Style 6</H6>
<H5>Heading Style 5</H5>
<H4>Heading Style 4</H4>
<H3>Heading Style 3</H3>
<H2>Heading Style 2</H2>
<H1>Heading Style 1</H1>
```

III

Doing HTML

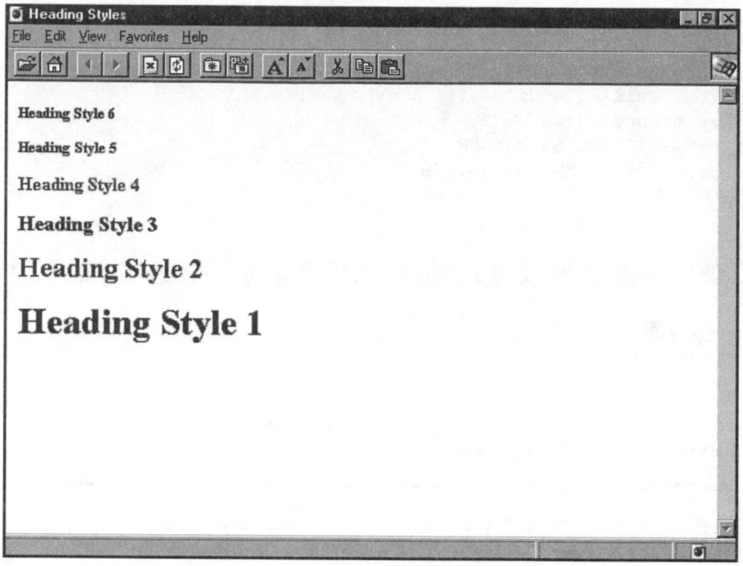

Fig. 10.6
Headings are used to name and separate sections of a document.

> **Note**
>
> In addition to changing the size of the text and making it boldface, applying a heading style adds some white space above and below the line containing the heading.

Physical Styles

Physical styles are actual attributes of a font, such as bold or italic. HTML supports the four physical styles shown in table 10.1. To apply a physical style, simply place the text to be formatted between the appropriate tag pair shown in the table.

Table 10.1 Physical Styles in HTML

Name	Tag
Bold	`<B>. . .</B>`
Italics	`<I>. . .</I>`
Underline	`<U>. . .</U>`
Typewriter (fixed-width)	`<TT>. . .</TT>`

> **Note**
>
> According to the HTML specification, browsers are not required to support any text styles. Do not assume that any given style is available in all browsers. In many browsers, for example, the underline style is reserved for displaying hyperlinks. These browsers will ignore the <U> and </U> tags, as shown in figure 10.7.

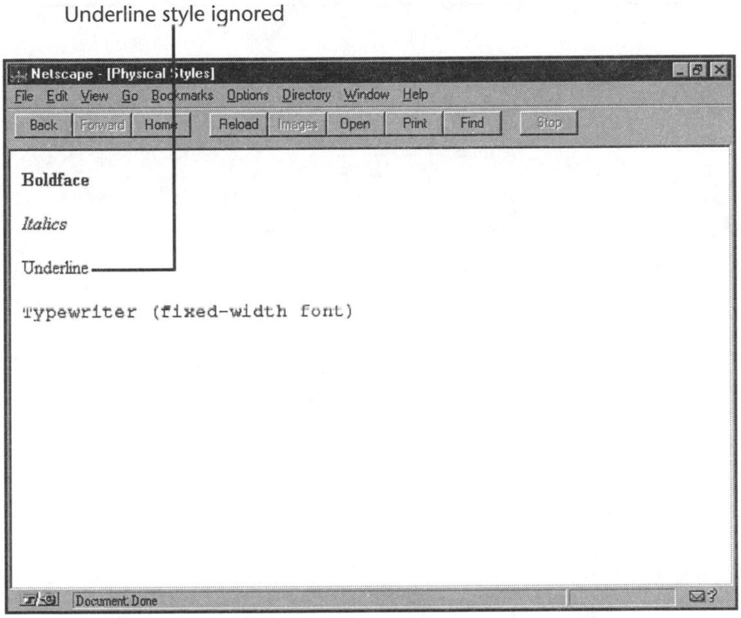

Underline style ignored

Fig. 10.7
Physical styles are used to render text in boldface, italics, or a fixed width. The underline style is frequently not supported.

> **Note**
>
> The HTML specification allows nesting of physical text styles, though not all browsers support this. For example, <B><I>bold italics</I></B> (italics nested inside boldface) is valid HTML.

Logical Styles

Logical styles indicate the meaning of the text they mark in the context of the document. Since they are not related to font attributes, logical styles can be rendered differently on different browsers. Table 10.2 lists the common logical styles and their meanings and typical renderings. Closing tags are required for all logical styles, but have been omitted in the table to save space. To create a closing tag, just add a slash before the tag name, like </ADDRESS>.

Table 10.2 Logical Styles in HTML		
Style Name	**Tag**	**Typical Rendering**
Address	<ADDRESS>	Italics
Block quote	<BLOCKQUOTE>	Left and right indent
Citation	<CITE>	Italics
Code	<CODE>	Fixed-width font
Definition	<DFN>	Bold or bold italics
Emphasis	<EM>	Italics
Keyboard	<KBD>	Fixed-width font
Sample	<SAMP>	Fixed-width font
Strong	<STRONG>	Bold
Variable	<VAR>	Italics

Figure 10.8 shows how Netscape renders many of the logical styles. The corresponding HTML is:

```
<H1>Logical Styles</H1>
According to <CITE>Corporate Manual of Style</CITE>,
you <EM>must</EM> include your
<VAR>e-mail address</VAR> below the signature block
of your business letters. Specifically:
<BLOCKQUOTE>Employees with electronic mail addresses
<STRONG>must</STRONG> include them in the signature block.
For example:<BR>
Mary Simpson<BR>
Account Representative<BR>
<ADDRESS>msimpson@abc_corp.com</ADDRESS>
</BLOCKQUOTE>
```

Note

While some browsers allow it, nesting logical styles often does not make sense. For example, why would you ever put a block quote inside keyboard input?

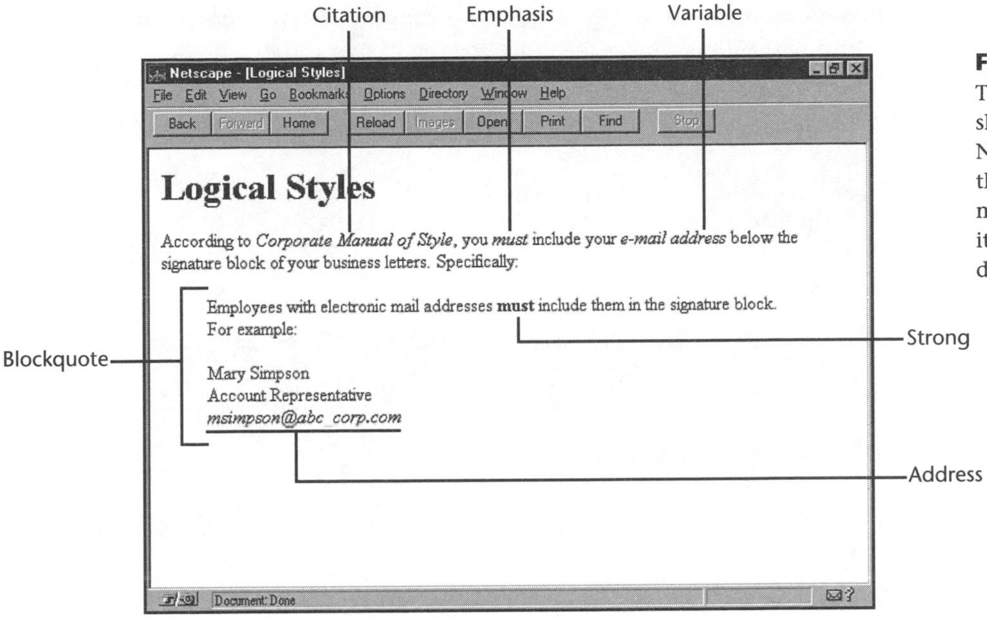

Citation   Emphasis   Variable

Blockquote

Strong

Address

Fig. 10.8
The logical styles,
shown here in
Netscape, describe
the meaning of
marked-up text as
it relates to the
document.

Physical versus Logical Styles

As you look at the typical renderings in table 10.3, you probably noticed that you can accomplish almost all of them by using the physical styles. If you did notice, you're likely asking "Why should I use the logical styles?" An "official" answer is: to give a contextual meaning to the text that you're marking up. Formatting doesn't really matter with the logical styles; it's the meaning they impart that is important. Such an official answer would come from a person who subscribes to the school of thought that HTML is a page-description language only.

Authors who use HTML as a design tool are likely to cast aside such official responses and just use the physical styles to get the same effect. After all, it is easier to type <I>info@abc_corp.com</I> than it is to type <ADDRESS>info@abc_corp.com</ADDRESS>.

The decision to use physical styles, logical styles, or both ultimately rests with each author, based on his or her take on whether HTML is for page description or page design.

Preformatted Text

Text tagged with the <PRE> and </PRE> tags is treated as *preformatted text* and rendered in a fixed-width font. Since each character in a fixed-width font has

III

Doing HTML

the same width, it is easy to line up text into columns and produce a table. The following HTML produces the table you see in figure 10.9.

```
<H1>Preformatted Text</H1>
<PRE>
User Name                 Login ID        Disk Space
---------------           --------        ----------
Terri Johnson             tjohnson          15 MB
Fred Hansen               fredh             15 MB
Pat Norton                pnorton           20 MB
</PRE>
```

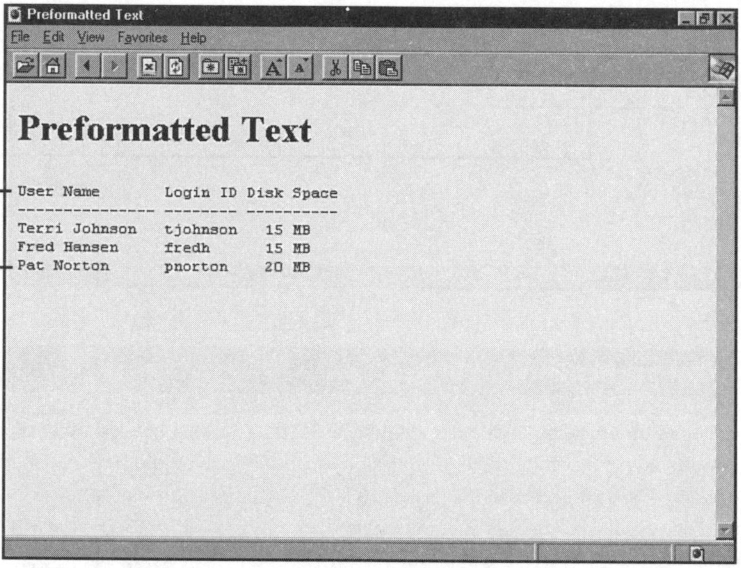

Fig. 10.9
Preformatted text is rendered in a fixed-width font and includes extra white space characters, making it easy to create tables.

Preformatted text

Note

Extra spaces, tabs, and carriage returns inside the <PRE> and </PRE> tags are *not* ignored.

Tip

Before you make all of your tables with preformatted text, you should look into the table tags proposed in the HTML 3.0 specification. Many browsers, such as Netscape and Mosaic, already support these tags.

▶ See "Tables," p. 280, for more information about the HTML table tags.

Lists

HTML lists provide an easy and attractive way to present information in your documents. All lists require a pair of tags for the type of list and for each list item. Table 10.3 lists the five types of formatted lists.

Table 10.3 Formatted Lists in HTML		
Type	**List Tag**	**Item Tag(s)**
Ordered	<OL>...</OL>	<LI>...</LI>
Unordered	<UL>...</UL>	<LI>...</LI>
Description	<DL>...</DL>	<DD>...</DD>,<DT>...</DT>
Menu	<MENU>...</MENU>	<LI>...</LI>
Directory	<DIR>...</DIR>	<LI>...</LI>

Items in an ordered list are automatically numbered by the browser, starting with the number one. The automatic numbering is convenient, because it spares you from having to do it if you rearrange list items. Unordered list items are bulleted rather than numbered. Description lists allow you to present a term, followed by a description below and indented under the term. Not all browsers support menu and directory lists, which are similar to unordered lists, but are generally assumed to have short list items.

Note

Description lists are sometimes called *definition lists* since they are useful in presenting the term/definition structure of a glossary.

List items in all five list types are indented from the left margin, making it easy to distinguish them from the rest of the body text.

Tip

You can use list tags to trick your browser into indenting for you. For example, a <UL> tag in your document will create an indent from the left margin. If text following the <UL> tag doesn't contain an <LI> tag, the browser won't render anything as a list item and the text is presented as indented. When you want to go back to the normal left margin, use a </UL> tag to turn off the indenting.

III

Doing HTML

Figure 10.10 shows examples of unordered, ordered, and description lists as produced by the following HTML:

```
<H2>Unordered Lists</H2>
<UL>
<LI>Bulleted list items</LI>
<LI>List items are indented</LI>
</UL>
<H2>Ordered Lists</H2>
<OL>
<LI>Numbered list items</LI>
<LI>List items are indented</LI>
</OL>
<H2>Description Lists</H2>
<DL>
<DT>First term</DT>
<DD>Description of first term</DD>
<DT>Second term</DT>
<DD>Description of second term</DD>
</DL>
```

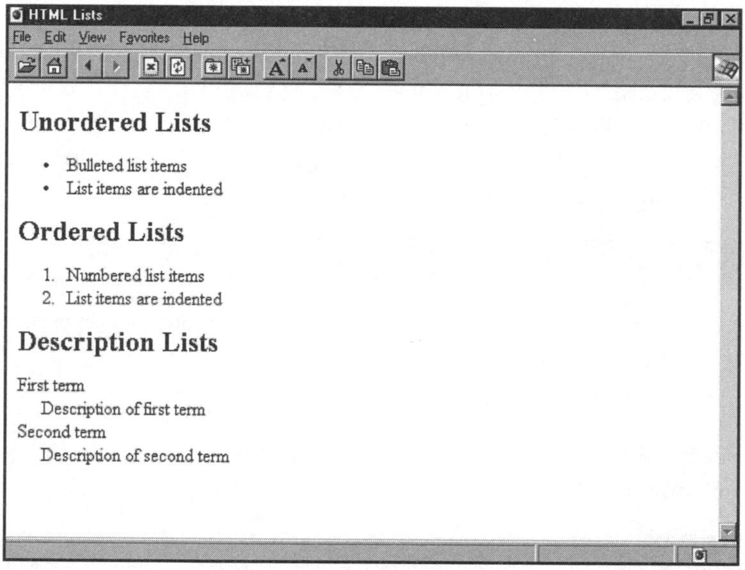

Fig. 10.10
Unordered, ordered, and description lists provide an easy way to break up information.

Caution

Many browsers will "forgive" you if you leave off the </LI> tag at the end of a list item. The next <LI> tag is enough to tell the browser to end the current list item and start a new one. However, browsers *won't* forgive you if you leave off a </DT> or a </DD> tag, so don't forget them.

You can nest lists inside of other lists, as shown in figure 10.11. The HTML to produce this figure is:

```
<H1>Nested Lists</H1>
<UL>
<LI>Basic HTML</LI>
<OL>
<LI>Text formatting</LI>
<LI>Graphics</LI>
<LI>Hyperlinks</LI>
</OL>
<LI>Advanced HTML</LI>
<OL>
<LI>HTML 2.0</LI>
<LI>HTML 3.0</LI>
<LI>Netscape Extensions</LI>
</OL>
</UL>
```

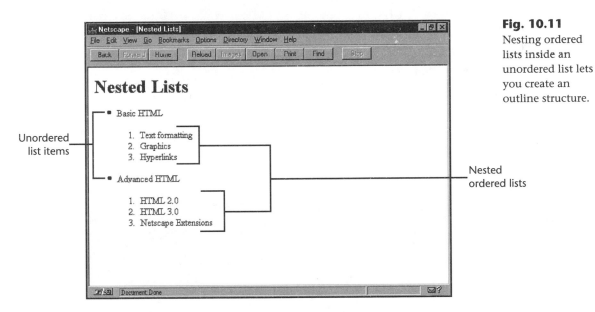

Fig. 10.11
Nesting ordered lists inside an unordered list lets you create an outline structure.

Unordered list items

Nested ordered lists

Special Characters

Because many characters have special meanings in HTML, it is necessary to use special character sequences when you want special characters to show up as themselves. You can also use special character sequences to produce foreign language characters and symbols.

Reserved Characters

Because the less than (<), greater than (>), and quotation mark (") characters are used in HTML formatting tags, the characters themselves must be represented by special character sequences. The ampersand (&) is used in these special sequences, so it also must be represented differently. Table 10.4 lists all the special character sequences in HTML. The semicolon (;) is necessary to indicate where the character description ends and normal text resumes.

Table 10.4   Special Character Sequences for HTML-Reserved Characters

Sequence	Appearance	Meaning
<	<	Less than
>	>	Greater than
&	&	Ampersand
"	"	Quotation mark

If you're writing HTML code to produce HTML code on a browser screen, you will use the sequences in table 10.4 frequently. For example, to produce a list of the physical style tags, you would need to use the following HTML:

```
<H2>HTML Physical Style Tags</H2>
<UL>
<LI>&lt;B&gt. . .&lt;/B&gt;</LI>
<LI>&lt;I&gt. . .&lt;/I&gt;</LI>
<LI>&lt;U&gt. . .&lt;/U&gt;</LI>
<LI>&lt;TT&gt. . .&lt;/TT&gt;</LI>
</UL>
```

The resulting screen is shown in figure 10.12.

Fig. 10.12
Writing HTML to produce on-screen HTML requires the use of special character sequences.

Less than (<) and greater than (>) signs produced by special character sequences

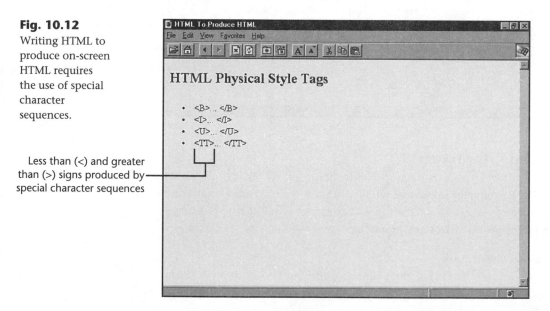

Foreign Language Characters

HTML uses the ISO-Latin1 character set, which includes foreign language characters for all Latin-based languages. Since these characters are not on most keyboards, you need to use special character sequences to place them in your documents. Like the other special character sequences in HTML, these sequences begin with an ampersand (&) followed by a written-out description of the character and a semicolon (;). Table 10.5 lists all the foreign-language sequences available.

Table 10.5   Foreign Language Characters in HTML

Character	Sequence
Æ,æ	&Aelig;,æ
Á,á	Á,á
Â,â	Â,â
À,à	À,à
Å,å	Å,å
Ã,ã	Ã,ã
Ä,ä	Ä,ä
Ç,ç	Ç,ç
Ð,ð	Ð,ð
É,é	É,é
Ê,ê	Ê,ê
È,è	È,è
Ë,ë	Ë,ë
Í,í	Í,í
Î,î	Î,î
Ì,ì	Ì,ì
Ï,ï	Ï,ï
Ñ,ñ	Ñ,ñ
Ó,ó	Ó,ó
Ô,ô	Ô,ô
Ò,ò	Ò,ò
Ø,ø	Ø,ø
Õ,õ	Õ,õ
Ö,ö	Ö,ö

(continues)

Table 10.5	Continued
Character	**Sequence**
ß	&szlig;
Þ,þ	Þ,þ
Ú,ú	Ú,ú
Û,û	Û,û
Ù,ù	Ù,ù
Ü,ü	Ü,ü
Ý,ý	Ý,ý
ÿ	&yuml;

Characters by ASCII Number

You can reference any ASCII character in an HTML document by including the ampersand (&) and pound sign (#) followed by the character number in decimal and a semicolon (;). For example, to include the copyright symbol (©) in an HTML document, you write:

```
Copyright &#169;, 1996
```

Tip

Windows users can use the Character Map program that comes with Windows to see the codes for all ASCII characters.

Note

Netscape supports the special character sequences © for the copyright symbol (©) and ® for the registered trademark (®) symbol.

Nonbreaking Space

You can prevent a browser from breaking a line between two words by inserting a non-breaking space between the words. Non-breaking spaces are represented by the special character sequence .

Tip

Non-breaking space characters can also be used to put in extra white space where you need it. A browser ignores the last two spaces in a sequence of three space characters, but it does print three spaces if you use   .

Horizontal Lines

Horizontal lines are a great way to break up sections of text-intensive documents. Placing a horizontal line is easy: just put an <HR> (horizontal rule) tag in where you want the line to go. No closing tag is required.

Images

Without the visual appeal of inline images, it is doubtful that the World Wide Web would have become as popular as it has so rapidly. Graphical Web browsers such as Netscape Navigator, Mosaic, and Microsoft Internet Explorer can automatically display images in both the GIF and JPEG formats inside documents.

Note

The HTML standard only requires graphical browsers to support GIFs, though more and more browsers are beginning to support JPEG as well.

Graphics Formats: GIF and JPEG

GIF (Graphics Interchange Format) was originally developed for users of CompuServe as a standard for storing image files. Graphics stored as GIFs are limited to 256 colors.

GIFs support two desirable Web page effects. The first is *interlacing,* in which non-adjacent parts of the image are stored together. As a browser reads in an interlaced GIF, the image appears to "fade in" over several passes. The other effect supported by GIFs is *transparency*. In a transparent GIF, one of the colors is designated as transparent, allowing the background of the document to show through.

III

Doing HTML

Transparent GIFs

A frequently asked question on the World Wide Web newsgroups is: "How can I create transparent GIFs?" On the PC, LView Pro is one program that can create transparent GIFs. PhotoGIF is a plug-in to Photoshop that allows you to create both transparent and interlaced GIFs. Both UNIX and Windows users can use a program called *Giftrans* to create transparent GIFs from existing images.

JPEG (Joint Picture Experts Group) refers to a set of formats that supports full-color images and stores them in a compressed form. Most popular graphical browsers currently display JPEG images, though previously these images had to be viewed in a separate program. The *progressive JPEG* format, which has recently emerged, gives the effect of an image fading in just as an interlaced GIF would. Transparency is not possible with JPEG images because the compression tends to make small changes to the image data. If a pixel originally colored with the transparent color is given another color, or if a nontransparent pixel is assigned the transparency color, the on-screen results would be dreadful.

Tip

As a general rule, you should use JPEG for color photos so you can harness its full-color capabilities. Other graphics and illustrations should be stored as GIFs.

The <IMG ...> Tag

You must save images as separate files even though they are referenced and displayed inside an HTML document. To place an inline image on a page, you use the <IMG. . .> tag.

Syntax: <IMG SRC="*URL*">

Inline images always aligned flush left, although future versions of HTML may allow centering and flush right alignment. For example, to place the World Wide Web Consortium's logo next to its name on its home page (refer to fig. 10.2), the HTML looked like:

```
<H1><IMG ALIGN=MIDDLE ALT="W3C" SRC="Icons/WWW/w3c_96x67.gif">The
World Wide Web Consortium</H1>
```

The SRC attribute, which is mandatory, specifies the URL of the image file. Because URLs can point anywhere, you can reference images on remote servers as well as your local server. Browsers can load images from a server running any protocol supported by the browser, including FTP and Gopher. You can modify the <IMG. . .> tag by several other attributes as well (see table 10.6).

> **Note**
>
> Because browsers can load images from any server on the Internet, browsers establish separate server connections for each image in a document, even if all images are on the same server. For small images, it takes more time to establish the connection than to transfer the image data. Therefore, avoid numerous small images.

Table 10.6   IMG Tag Attributes

Attribute	Description
ALIGN={TOP¦MIDDLE¦BOTTOM}	Location of text next to image
ALT="*text*"	Text to show instead of image
ISMAP	Used to make imagemaps

The ALIGN attribute controls the location of text that follows the image. By default, text appears at the bottom of an inline image. Figure 10.13 shows how you can use the ALIGN attribute to change the text to be aligned with the middle or top of the image. Specifically, ALIGN=MIDDLE aligns the baseline of the text with the middle of the image and ALIGN=TOP aligns the top of the text with the top of the image. The HTML for this figure follows.

```
<IMG SRC="/images/w3c.gif" ALIGN="MIDDLE">
The World Wide Web (W3) Consortium
<HR>
<IMG SRC="/images/w3c.gif" ALIGN="TOP">
The World Wide Web (W3) Consortium
```

The ALT attribute specifies alternate text to be shown in place of an image in text-only browsers. Including the ALT attribute tag is a courtesy to dial-up and dumb terminal users; don't overlook this courtesy. Also, graphical browsers sometimes fail to load an image, in which case they use the text specified by ALT instead. For example, to include text-only support in the previous example, the line would look like this:

```
<IMG SRC="/images/w3c.gif" ALIGN="TOP" ALT="W3C Logo">
The World Wide Web (W3) Consortium
```

III

Doing HTML

Fig. 10.13
The ALIGN attribute lets you align text with the middle and top of an image.

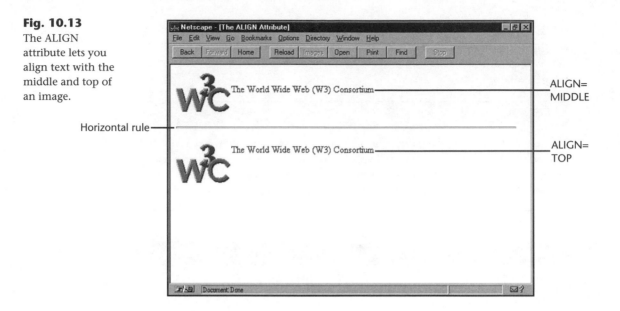

In Lynx, this line would appear as:

```
[W3C Logo]The World Wide Web (W3) Consortium
```

▶ To learn how to implement both server side and client side imagemaps, see "Implementing Imagemaps," p. 374.

ISMAP is a stand-alone attribute that signifies that the image is to be used as an imagemap.

Note

Two Netscape extensions to the <IMG ...> tag that bear an early introduction are WIDTH and HEIGHT. These attributes are set equal to the width and height of the image in pixels. The advantage of doing this is that it allows the browser to leave an appropriately-sized space for the image as it lays out the page. Thus, page layout is finished quickly, without having to wait for the image to load completely so that the browser can determine its size.

The HTML Graphics Format

Support for inline images as single files allows convenient reuse of graphics on your server because you can set up a common graphics library, or directory, for all documents on the server. On the other hand, the fact that graphics must be separate files, and GIF files at that, is one of the most difficult aspects of converting documents from any other format into HTML because of the time and effort required to separate all the graphics.

Hypertext and Hypergraphics

Now to the other half of the HyperText Markup Language—the hypertext part. A hypertext reference is very simple. It consists of only two parts: an anchor and a URL. The *anchor* is the text or graphic that the user clicks to go somewhere. The URL points to the document that the browser will load when the user clicks on the anchor.

In HTML, an anchor can be either text or a graphic. Text anchors usually appear underlined and in a different color than normal text on graphical browsers and in bold on text-only browsers such as Lynx. Graphic anchors (hypergraphics) usually have a colored border around them to distinguish them from plain graphics.

Creating Hypertext Anchors

Any text can be a hypertext anchor in HTML, regardless of size or formatting. An anchor can consist of a few letters, words, or even lines of text. The format for an anchor-address pair is simple:

```
<A HREF="URL">text of the anchor</A>
```

The letter A in the <A HREF> tag stands for "anchor." HREF stands for "hypertext reference." Everything between the <A HREF="*URL*"> and </A> tags is the text of the anchor, which appears underlined or bold, depending on the browser.

> **Note**
>
> Other formatting codes can be used in conjunction with hypertext anchors. For example, to create a text anchor that appears in the level 3 heading style, you write:
>
> ```
> <A HREF="URL"><H3>text of the anchor</H3></A>
> ```
>
> The order of nesting formatting codes is not important. It's also possible to write:
>
> ```
> <H3><A HREF="URL">text of the anchor</A></H3>.
> ```

Creating Hypergraphics

You can use hypergraphics to create button-like effects and provide a nice alternative to clicking plain text. The format for a graphic anchor is the same as a text anchor. However, instead of putting text between the <A HREF> and </A> tags, you reference an inline image. Figure 10.14 shows a hypergraphic.

```
<A HREF="http://www.w3.org/"><IMG SRC="images/w3c.gif">
</A>Visit the World Wide Web (W3) Consortium's Home Page
```

III

Doing HTML

Fig. 10.14
Hypergraphics
create button-like
objects.

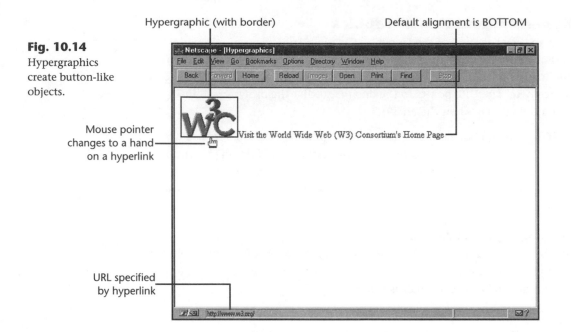

In this example, when the user clicks the W3C logo, the browser jumps to the W3C home page.

> **Tip**
>
> If text or images used in hypertext anchors don't seem to be working right, check to see that the URL in the <A...> tag is completely enclosed in quotes. Omitting the final quotation mark is a common and easy mistake.

Linking to a Named Anchor

When you link to another document, the browser shows information starting from the top of the linked document. This is fine, unless the document is long and the information you really want displayed isn't near the top. In this case, users have to scroll through the document to find the information you want them to see. An alternative to inflicting this on your users is to set up *named anchors* in longer documents and then have your hyperlink references point directly to the named anchors.

As an example, suppose you have a ten part document stored in a single file longdoc.html and that each section has its own heading. You can set up

named anchors on each of the headings using the <A
NAME="anchor_name"> and </A> tags as follows:

```
<A NAME="one"><H1>Part One</H1></A>
```

With all of the anchors established, you can instruct a browser to link to a
specific anchor by including a pound sign (#) and the anchor's name at the
end of the long document's URL:

```
View <A HREF="longdoc.html#seven">Part Seven</A>.
```

When users click on the hypertext "Part Seven," they are taken directly to
part seven in the document, rather than to the top of the document from
which they would have to scroll all the way down to part seven (see fig.
10.15).

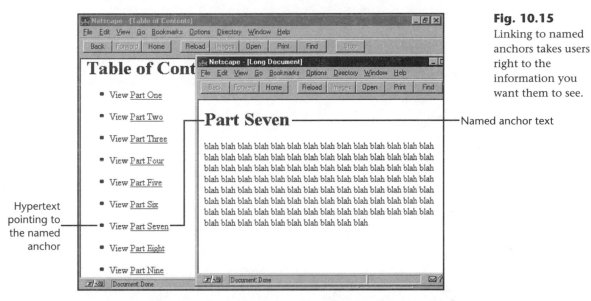

Hypertext
pointing to
the named
anchor

Fig. 10.15
Linking to named
anchors takes users
right to the
information you
want them to see.

Named anchor text

III

Doing HTML

Tip

Named anchors let you set up a miniature "Table of Contents" at the top of long
documents with links pointing to the different sections of the manuscript. Users
appreciate this courtesy because it spares them from excessive scrolling and searching through the document.

## CHAPTER 11

HTML 2.0, HTML 3.0, and Extensions

In the last chapter, you learned enough HTML tags to start authoring your own pages. Additionally, because these tags are known to almost every Web client program, the documents you write with them should not cause errors on anyone's browser.

If you're like most Web authors, you'll soon find yourself wanting finer control over your documents. When you reach this point, you're ready to expand your command of HTML to include more advanced tags and tag attributes. Control comes with a price: many of these advanced HTML entities are not understood by all browsers. Indeed, some of them can only be parsed by one browser! As you include more advanced features, you increase the chances of alienating visitors from your site.

This chapter examines advanced HTML tags from three sources: the HTML 2.0 spec, which attempts to outline the currently accepted HTML standard; the proposed HTML 3.0 spec, which promises greater capacity for mathematical expressions and general layout control; and the Netscape Navigator and Microsoft Internet Explorer extensions to HTML, which can only be properly rendered by those browsers. In particular, you learn how to implement:

- The elements of HTML 2.0 beyond those discussed in Chapter 10
- New elements proposed under HTML 3.0, including tags for banners, figures, footnotes, admonishments, mathematical characters, and text styles
- Tables as proposed in the HTML 3.0 spec
- Netscape extensions to HTML that control image characteristics, produce rule and list effects, and enhance table spacing
- Frames as proposed by Netscape

- Microsoft Internet Explorer extensions to HTML that control background sounds, inline video clips, and scrolling marquees
- Simple Virtual Reality Modeling Language (VRML) and how to find tools that support VRML creation and viewing

The Evolving Standard

HTML was developed in 1990 at CERN, Europe's major research laboratory for high-energy physics. CERN's intent behind developing the World Wide Web and HTML was to facilitate a global exchange of research information among physicists. This was during a time when the Internet was still used largely for military, research, and academic purposes. The scientists at CERN probably did not anticipate that the Web would evolve into the popular application that it is today.

The evolution of the Web drove the evolution of HTML. For example, the National Center for Supercomputing Applications (NCSA) at the University of Illinois released Mosaic, the first graphical Web client, in 1993, creating the need for tags to handle images. Design became a greater issue as more people, desiring better looking pages, started using the Web. This shifted HTML's evolution in the direction of being a design language instead of just a way to mark up documents.

Last year, the HTML 2.0 specification was compiled and released as a Request for Comment (RFC) by the World Wide Web Consortium (W3C). The 2.0 spec sought to summarize the de facto HTML standard and describe how people should be using the HTML that was out there. Since then, the W3C and the Internet Engineering Task Force (IETF) have been considering proposals for HTML 3.0. The proposed HTML 3.0 spec is nearing completion and should be available by the time you read this.

What you are about to read is merely a summary of one instant in HTML's short but dynamic history. HTML will continue to evolve with the Web. The increasing popularity of Java and JavaScript have brought about the need for tags to build applets (Java "mini-applications") and script code right into HTML documents. Browser plug-in programs, like Macromedia's Shockwave, will drive the need for tags to embed other program items into Web pages. No doubt, in another year, the tags you are about to learn will be commonplace and newer tags will have taken their place on these pages.

> **Note**
>
> For the latest information on the HTML specs, visit W3C's Web site at **http://www.w3.org/pub/WWW/MarkUp/**.

HTML 2.0

As noted earlier, the HTML 2.0 spec was written to describe how HTML was being used at the time. The majority of the tags in this spec are covered in Chapter 10. Tags in the spec that are not covered in Chapter 10 are presented in the next three sections. These tags are "new" in the sense that this is the first place in the book that discusses them. They were not necessarily newly introduced as part of the HTML 2.0 spec.

> **Note**
>
> To read the September 22, 1995 release of the HTML 2.0 spec, direct your browser to **http://www.w3.org/pub/WWW/Markup/html-spec/html-spec_toc.html**.

Document Type Definitions (DTD)

If you've looked at many HTML files, you've probably seen a tag at the very beginning of the file that looks like:

```
<!DOCTYPE HTML PUBLIC "-//IETF//DTD HTML//EN">
```

Such a tag is a *Document Type Definition (DTD)*. DTDs are used to specify the set of rules that apply SGML to the markup tags in the text. Most DTDs you'll see are like the one above, though there are others specific to HTML 2.0, HTML 3.0, Netscape extensions to HTML, and HTML that contains Java or JavaScript.

> **Tip**
>
> You can check your documents' conformance to established DTDs by submitting them to the HTML validation service at **http://www.webtechs.com/html-val-svc/**. The site also provides information on each of the DTDs you can check against.

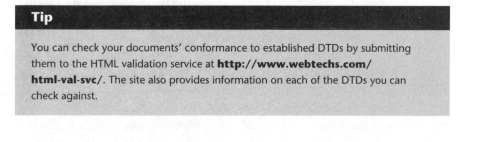

III

Doing HTML

New Elements in the Document Head

The 2.0 spec includes a number of tags beyond <BASE ...> and <TITLE> for the document head. Probably the most useful of these is the <META ...> tag, which is intended to contain document meta-information. <META ...> requires a name/content pair that can be specified by combinations of three attributes: HTTP-EQUIV, CONTENT, and NAME. HTTP-EQUIV is used to "simulate" an HTTP header right in the HTML document. If you don't use HTTP-EQUIV, then you should use the NAME attribute to give the meta-information a unique name. CONTENT is set equal to the meta-information itself.

An emerging application of the <META ...> tag is for bulletins—messages that Web authors can put on their sites to notify users of changes. Some <META ...> tags that set up a bulletin might look like:

```
<HEAD>
<META HTTP-EQUIV="Bulletin-Text" CONTENT="You can now order
from our new online catalog!">
<META HTTP-EQUIV="Bulletin-Date" CONTENT="Tues, 05-Mar-96
00:00:00">
</HEAD>
```

The tags above would post a bulletin about the new online catalog at midnight on Tuesday, March 5, 1996. Web users who have bookmark management software that can receive bulletins would be notified of the new catalog by their programs.

The <META ...> tag can also be used to specify document keywords, expiration dates, and reply-to e-mail addresses. You can have as many <META ...> tags in the document head as you need.

Two other document head tags in the 2.0 spec are <NEXTID=*n*> and <LINK ...>. In the past, <NEXTID=*n*> was used to assign a unique numerical identifier (*n*) to a document. Nowadays it is rarely used and the spec discourages authors from including <NEXTID=*n*> tags in their HTML. The <LINK ...> tag takes the HREF attribute and specifies links to related documents. Related documents might include author information, indexes, glossaries, and earlier versions of the document. Just as with the <META ...> tag, you can put as many <LINK ...> tags in a document head as you like.

New Elements in the Document Body

A handy attribute for ordered, unordered, and description lists is the COMPACT attribute, which compels a browser to render a list in the most space-efficient form that it can. To make a list compact, you simply include the COMPACT attribute in the list's starting tag. Figure 11.1 shows two versions of the same list. The first list is rendered normally and the second is compacted. The HTML to produce the second list is:

```
<UL COMPACT>
<LI>HTML 2.0</LI>
<LI>HTML 3.0</LI>
<LI>VRML</LI>
</UL>
```

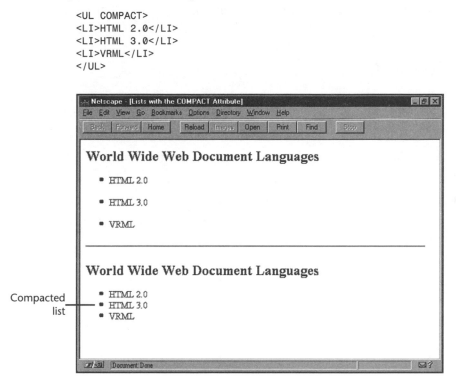

Compacted
list

Fig. 11.1
The COMPACT attribute forces your browser to squeeze a list into the smallest amount of space possible.

The <A ...> tag picks up a few interesting, though infrequently used, attributes in the HTML 2.0 spec. The TITLE attribute is meant to suggest a title for the hyperlinked resource. REL and REV are attributes that describe a document's relationship to documents it links to or to documents that link to it, respectively.

The spec also mentions two sets of container tags: <XMP> ... </XMP> for marking up an example to illustrate a concept and <LISTING> ... </LISTING> for tagging a list of items. These tag pairs were originally intended to work like <PRE> and </PRE> in that text between them was taken to contain no markup. However, not all browsers implement this intent consistently, so the spec discourages the use of these tags. You should stick with <PRE> and </PRE> instead.

Forms

The HTML 2.0 spec includes a set of tags used to produce online forms. Forms were an important step in the evolution of Web pages; they were the first means of user interactivity. Today forms are used to set up complicated

▶ See "Creating Forms," p. 395, to learn how to construct HTML forms.

III

Doing HTML

database queries, conduct market research, take product orders, and collect user feedback. Once entered, form data is packaged and sent to a server for processing by a *script*. Scripts typically compose and return an HTML page as output.

HTML 3.0

The HTML 3.0 specification is in the final stages of its development and contains some exciting proposals for expanding HTML's ability to well-formatted documents including:

- A <RANGE ...> tag for the document head to facilitate searching
- New tags and attributes to give you finer control over page layout
- Several new physical and logical styles
- A <DIV ...> tag for marking specific divisions of a document (such as the abstract or an appendix)
- Support for footnotes
- A <NOTE ...> tag for including admonishments in your document
- New tags and entities for rendering mathematical characters
- A <FIG ...> tag with several useful attributes to support wrapping of text around figures and placement of captions and overlays
- Tags for creating tables without using preformatted text

The next several sections introduce many of these proposals.

The <RANGE ...> Tag

Placing a <RANGE ...> tag in the document head allows you to set up a range in the document for searching. <RANGE ...> takes the CLASS attribute, which is set equal to SEARCH to set up a search range, and the FROM and UNTIL attributes, which designate the beginning and end of the search range. A sample <RANGE ...> tag might look like:

```
<RANGE CLASS=SEARCH FROM="startspot" UNTIL="endspot">
```

The "startspot" and "endspot" markers are set up in the body of the document using the <SPOT ID="startspot"> and <SPOT ID="endspot"> tags at the points where you want the search range to begin and end, respectively.

Finer Layout Control

A number of HTML 3.0 proposals give authors greater control over page layout. One interesting proposal calls for the addition of <TAB ...> tag, which would allow you to set up your own tab stops in a document. To use a tab stop, you need to first define it using the ID attribute:

```
My first tab stop is <TAB ID="first">here, followed by some other
text.
```

The HTML above sets up the first tab stop in front of the letter "h" in the word "here." To use the tab stop, you use the <TAB ...> tag with the TO attribute:

```
<TAB TO="first">This sentence starts below the word "here."
```

On the browser screen, the "T" in the word "This" will be aligned directly below the "h" in the word "here."

Other enhancements to layout control come in the form of new attributes to existing tags. For example, under HTML 3.0, you can center headings and paragraphs using the ALIGN=CENTER attribute in your <H1> through <H6> and <P> tags. Additionally, the CLEAR attribute will be available on many tags, giving you the ability to clear one or both margins or to leave a specific amount of space between page items.

Note

When specifying a quantity of spacing, the units of the CLEAR attribute can be in pixels, en spaces, or em spaces; for example, CLEAR="5 en" or CLEAR="40 pixels."

Physical and Logical Text Styles

Several new physical and logical styles are proposed in the 3.0 spec. Tables 11.1 and 11.2 summarize these additions. Closing tags are left out of the tables in the interest of space.

Table 11.1   New Physical Styles Proposed in HTML 3.0

Style Name	Tag	Rendering
Strikethrough	<S>	Text is struck through with a slash (/)
Big	<BIG>	Makes text bigger than its current size
Small	<SMALL>	Makes text smaller than its current size
Subscript	<SUB>	Makes text a subscript
Superscript	<SUP>	Makes text a superscript

III

Doing HTML

Note

The HTML 3.0 spec says that <SUB> and <SUP> tags are only appropriate inside the and container tags (discussed below), but the Netscape Navigator browser recognizes these tags outside of a mathematical context.

Table 11.2 New Logical Styles Proposed in HTML 3.0

Style Name	Tag
Abbreviation	<ABBREV>
Acronym	<ACRONYM>
Author name	<AU>
Deleted text	<DEL>
Inserted text	<INS>
Language context	<LANG>
Person's name	<PERSON>
Short quotation	<Q>

Note

Recall that logical styles are often rendered differently on different browsers. You'll need to experiment to see how your HTML 3.0 compatible browser renders these new styles.

Most of the new physical and logical styles are self-explanatory. Text marked with the <Q> style will appear in quotation marks appropriate to the document's language context. The <INS> and <DEL> styles are expected to be useful in the context of legal documents. The <PERSON> style marks a person's name for easier extraction by indexing programs.

The <DIV ...> Tag

The <DIV ...> and </DIV> tags work similarly to the <P> and </P> tags, except that <DIV ...> and </DIV> denote a special division of the document. The <DIV ...> tag takes the CLASS attribute, which describes the type of division being defined. Division types include abstracts, chapters, sections, and appendixes. The <DIV ...> tag can also take the attributes shown in table 11.3, allowing greater control over how that division is formatted. A sample <DIV ...> ... </DIV> container pair might look like:

```
<DIV CLASS=CHAPTER ALIGN=JUSTIFY CLEAR=ALL>
... the text of the chapter goes here ...
</DIV>
```

The above HTML produces a chapter that starts with clear left and right margins and that has justified text throughout.

Table 11.3 Attributes of the <DIV ...> Tag	
Attribute	**Purpose**
CLASS	Specifies the type of document division being marked
ALIGN=LEFT ¦ RIGHT ¦ CENTER ¦ JUSTIFY	Sets the alignment for the entire division
NOWRAP	Turns off auto-wrapping of text. Text lines are broken explicitly with tags.
CLEAR=LEFT ¦ RIGHT ¦ ALL	Starts the division clear of left, right, or both margins

Note

You also can use the CLEAR attribute to specify spacing between the division and any page items around it. For example, CLEAR="2 em" leaves two em spaces between the division and the item it wraps around.

Footnotes

One HTML 3.0 proposal calls for an <FN ...> tag to define footnotes. To set up a footnote, you use the <FN ...> tag together with its ID attribute:

```
<FN ID="footnote1">HTML = HyperText Markup Language</FN>
```

Then, you must tag the footnoted text with an <A ...> ... </A> tag pair that includes an HREF pointing to the footnote. For "footnote1," you could tag every instance of the acronym "HTML" with:

```
<A HREF="#footnote1">HTML</A>
```

When users clicks on "HTML," they should see the footnote telling them what HTML stands for. The spec calls for footnotes to be displayed in pop-up windows, though it isn't clear that all browsers will be able to support this.

Admonishments

The <NOTE ...> tag lets you set up admonishments like notes, warnings, and cautions on your pages. The text of the admonishment appears between the

III

Doing HTML

<NOTE ...> and </NOTE> tags. Additionally, you can include an image with your admonishment using the SRC attribute of the <NOTE ...> tag. SRC and other attributes of <NOTE ...> are summarized in table 11.4.

Table 11.4 Attributes of the <NOTE ...> Tag	
Attribute	**Purpose**
CLASS=NOTE ¦ CAUTION ¦ WARNING	Specifies the type of admonishment
SRC="*url*"	Provides the URL of an image to precede the admonishment text
CLEAR=LEFT ¦ RIGHT ¦ ALL	Starts the admonishment clear of left, right, or both margins

As with the <DIV ...> tag, you can also use the CLEAR attribute to compel browsers to leave a certain amount of space between the admonishment and surrounding page items. A sample admonishment might look like:

```
<NOTE CLASS=WARNING SRC="images/stopsign.gif" CLEAR=ALL>WARNING!
You are about to provide your credit card number to a non-secure
server!</NOTE>
```

Mathematical Symbols

If you've ever tried to prepare a document with mathematical content for the Web, you've probably ended up with a substantial headache. Prior to HTML 3.0, mathematical symbols like Greek letters, integral signs, and vector notations had to be read in and placed *as separate images* in the document. Just imagine the number of <IMG ...> tags required, to say nothing about the effort it would take to align them properly! The HTML 3.0 spec calls for tags and entities to make the preparation of mathematical documents much less agonizing.

Under the proposal, all mathematical tags and entities need to be contained inside the and tags. Greek letters are to be drawn from the Symbol font and are incorporated into documents with their entity names. For example, ψ would produce a lowercase psi (ψ) and Ψ would produce an uppercase psi (Ψ). Other variables, notations, and operator symbols are built in through a *large* number of special tags and entities. For a complete rundown on the proposals for these new tags and entities, direct your browser to **http://www.hp.co.uk/people/dsr/html3/maths.html**.

> **Tip**
>
> If you're familiar with the LaTex language for mathematical typesetting, you should have little trouble with HTML math formatting; the two use very similar approaches. If you don't have experience with LaTex and you will be preparing documents with mathematical content for the Web, you can get a jump on things by reading up on LaTex before the HTML math tags and entities become widely supported.

The <FIG ...> Tag

The <FIG ...> tag has been proposed as an alternative to the <IMG ...> tag for larger graphics. As you might expect, <FIG ...> requires the SRC attribute to specify the URL of the image file to be loaded. <FIG ...> can also take the attributes shown in table 11.5. The BLEEDLEFT and BLEEDRIGHT values of the ALIGN attribute align the figure all the way to the left and right edges of the browser window, respectively.

Table 11.5   Attributes of the <FIG ...> Tag

Attribute	Purpose
SRC="*url*"	Gives the URL of the image file to load
NOFLOW	Disables the flow of text around the figure
ALIGN=LEFT ¦ RIGHT ¦ CENTER ¦ JUSTIFY ¦ BLEEDLEFT ¦ BLEEDRIGHT	Specifies an alignment for the figure
UNITS=*unit_of_measure*	Specifies a unit of measure for the WIDTH and HEIGHT attributes (default is pixels)
WIDTH=*width*	Specifies the width of the image in units designated by the UNITS attribute
HEIGHT=*height*	Specifies the height of the image in units designated by the UNITS attribute
IMAGEMAP	Denotes the figure as an imagemap

The <FIG ...> tag is different from the <IMG ...> tag in that it has a companion </FIG> tag. Together, <FIG ...> and </FIG> can contain text, including captions and photo credits, that should be rendered with the figure. Captions are enclosed with the <CAPTION> and </CAPTION> tags and photo credits are enclosed with the <CREDIT> and </CREDIT> tags. Regular text found between the <FIG ...> and </FIG> tags will wrap around the figure unless the NOWRAP attribute is specified.

III

Doing HTML

Figure 11.2 shows an example of a photo with a caption, photo credit, and surrounding text. The HTML to produce the figure follows:

```
<FIG SRC="drew.jpg" WIDTH=422 HEIGHT=284 ALIGN=LEFT>
    <CAPTION>Drew - 5 months old, Averill Park, NY</CAPTION>
    <P><P><P>The Boxer is a handsome breed, noted for its
    broad, muscular build and unfaltering devotion to its owner.
    Boxers make excellent companions and are especially good with
    children. </P>
    <CREDIT>Photo by Eric Ladd</CREDIT>
</FIG>
```

Fig. 11.2

The <FIG ...> and </FIG> tag pair can be used to contain captions, credits, and text to wrap around the figure.

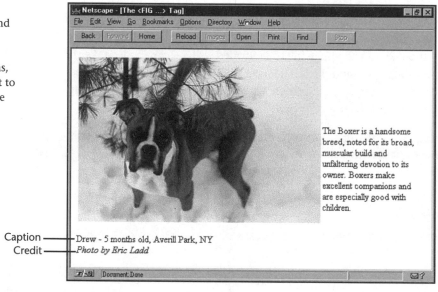

Caption ——— Drew - 5 months old, Averill Park, NY
Credit ——— *Photo by Eric Ladd*

▶ See "Client-Side Image-maps with the <FIG ...> and </FIG> Tag Pair," p. 379, to learn how to implement client-side imagemaps with the <FIG ...> tag.

Another feature proposed for the <FIG ...> and </FIG> tag pair is the ability to overlay two images. This is accomplished with the <OVERLAY ...> tag, which specifies a second image to overlay the image given in the <FIG ...> tag. HTML to produce an overlay might look like:

```
<FIG SRC="main_image.gif" WIDTH=250 HEIGHT=186 ALIGN=LEFT>
    <OVERLAY SRC="overlay.gif">
    <P>The image to the left is actually two images,
    one on top of the other.
</FIG>
```

The <FIG ...> tag also plays a critical role in the implementation of client-side imagemaps.

Tables

Until now, the only means for creating tables has been to use preformatted text . HTML 3.0 calls for several table tags that make it possible to build tables on Web pages without having to convert everything to a fixed-width font. Many browsers have already implemented these tags in anticipation of the table tag proposals being accepted into the 3.0 standard.

▶ To learn how to make tables with preformatted text, see "Preformatted Text," p. 253.

To understand the table tags better, it helps to take a moment to consider how HTML tables are structured. Tables are made out of one or more rows. These rows, in turn, are made up of cells, which can contain a data element of the table or a heading for a column of data. If you can keep this breakdown in mind as you read the next few paragraphs, the syntax of the table tags will make much more sense to you.

Table Basics

To start a table, you need to use the <TABLE ...> tag. <TABLE ...> has a companion closing tag </TABLE>. Together these tags contain all of the tags that go into creating a table. The <TABLE ...> tag can take the BORDER attribute, which places a border around the table. By default, a table has no borders.

To put a caption on your table, enclose the caption text in the <CAPTION ...> and </CAPTION> tags. Captions appear centered over the table. The text may be broken to match the table's width. If you prefer your caption below the table, you can include the ALIGN=BOTTOM attribute in the <CAPTION ...> tag.

Tip

Put your caption immediately after the <TABLE ...> tag or immediately before the </TABLE> tag to prevent your caption from unintentionally being made part of a table row or cell.

Because tables are built out of rows, you need to know how to define a row. The <TR> ...> and </TR> tags contain the tags that comprise a row of the table. The <TR ...> tag can take the ALIGN and VALIGN attributes. ALIGN controls the horizontal alignment of cell contents in the row and can be set to LEFT, RIGHT, or CENTER. VALIGN controls the vertical alignment and be set to TOP, BOTTOM, or MIDDLE. Values of ALIGN or VALIGN given in a <TR ...> tag apply to each cell in the row and will override all default alignments.

With a row defined, you're ready to put in the cells that make up the row. If a cell contains a table data element, you create the cell with the <TD ...> and </TD> tag pair. The text between <TD ...> and </TD> is what appears in the cell. Similarly, you use <TH ...> and </TH> to create a header. Header cells are exactly like data cells, except that header cell contents are automatically rendered in boldface type and are aligned in the center.

III

Doing HTML

There are default horizontal and vertical alignments associated with each type of cell. Both types of cells have a default vertical alignment of MIDDLE. Data cells have a default horizontal alignment of LEFT, while header cells have the aforementioned CENTER alignment. You can override any of these defaults *and* any alignments specified in a <TR ...> tag by including the desired ALIGN or VALIGN attribute in a <TD ...> or <TH ...> tag. Thus, in the following one row table:

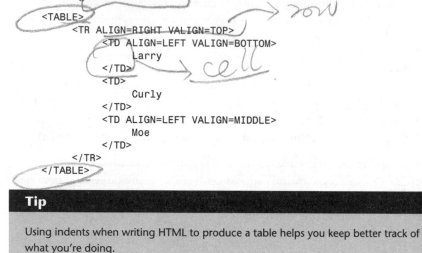

```
<TABLE>
        <TR ALIGN=RIGHT VALIGN=TOP>
            <TD ALIGN=LEFT VALIGN=BOTTOM>
                Larry
            </TD>
            <TD>
                Curly
            </TD>
            <TD ALIGN=LEFT VALIGN=MIDDLE>
                Moe
            </TD>
        </TR>
</TABLE>
```

> **Tip**
>
> Using indents when writing HTML to produce a table helps you keep better track of what you're doing.

The data element "Larry" is horizontally aligned along the left edge of the cell (ALIGN=LEFT overrides the ALIGN=RIGHT in the <TR ...> tag) and vertically aligned along the bottom of the cell (VALIGN=BOTTOM overrides the VALIGN=TOP in the <TR ...> tag). In the second cell, "Curly" is aligned according to the alignments given in the <TR ...> tag, since there are no alignments specified in the second <TD ...> tag. Finally, "Moe" is horizontally aligned left (again ALIGN=LEFT overrides the ALIGN=RIGHT in the <TR ...> tag) and vertically aligned in the middle (VALIGN=MIDDLE overrides VALIGN=BOTTOM in the <TR ...> tag). Note that Moe's alignment is the same as the default alignment for any data cell, but we had to undo the alignments set forth in the <TR ...> tag to get back to the defaults.

Aligning data elements and headers in your tables may seem a bit confusing, but if you keep the following hierarchy in mind, you can master table alignment quickly:

- Alignments specified in <TD ...> or <TH ...> tags override all other alignments, but apply only to the cell being defined.

■ Alignments specified in a <TR ...> tag override default alignments and apply to all cells in a row, unless overridden by an alignment specification in a <TD ...> or <TH ...> tag.

■ In the absence of alignment specifications in <TR ...>, <TD ...>, or <TH ...> tags, default alignments are used.

With what you've read so far, you can construct the following table template (see listing 11.1). The template is a good starting point for building any HTML table.

Listing 11.1   Table Template

```
<TABLE>
    <CAPTION>Caption Text</CAPTION>
    <TR>                    <!-- Row 1 -->
        <TD> ... </TD>
        <TD> ... </TD>
        ...
        <TD> ... </TD>
    </TR>
    <TR>                    <!-- Row 2 -->
        <TD> ... </TD>
        <TD> ... </TD>
        ...
        <TD> ... </TD>
    </TR>
    ...
    <TR>                    <!-- Row m -->
        <TD> ... </TD>
        <TD> ... </TD>
        ...
        <TD> ... </TD>
    </TR>
</TABLE>
```

The template above gives you a skeleton for a table with *m* rows that has a caption over the top and no borders. You can adjust this structure however you like by adding or deleting the appropriate tags and attributes.

Other Table Tag Attributes

For greater control over the appearance of your tables, there are other attributes of the <TD ...> and <TH ...> tags to help you. Either tag can take the NOWRAP attribute, which disables the breaking of data elements and headers onto a new line.

Caution

Use NOWRAP with care! It can produce cells that are inordinately wide if the cell contents aren't kept short.

By default, a cell spans one row and one column of a table. You can alter this default by using the ROWSPAN and COLSPAN attributes in a <TD ...> or <TH ...> tag. ROWSPAN and COLSPAN are set equal to the number of rows and columns, respectively, a cell is to span. If you try to extend the contents of a cell into rows that don't exist on the table, the contents of the cell are truncated to fit the number of rows available.

Sample Tables

To illustrate the utility of HTML tables, this section presents some examples of how to use them. The primary intent of the table tags is to give you a means of presenting tabular data without having to resort to preformatted text. Most tables that do this can be constructed from the template given in listing 11.1. For example, the table in figure 11.3 was produced by the HTML in listing 11.2.

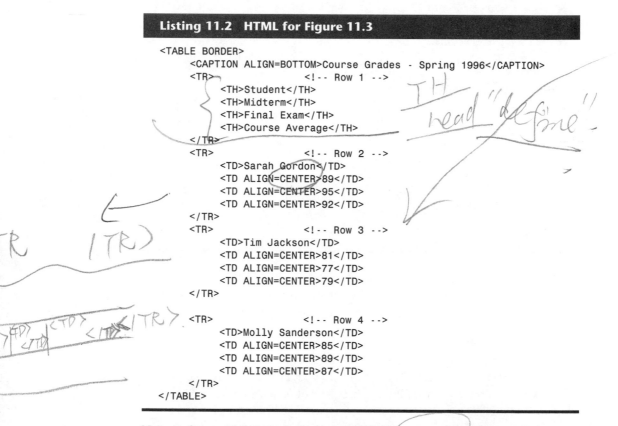

Listing 11.2   HTML for Figure 11.3

```
<TABLE BORDER>
    <CAPTION ALIGN=BOTTOM>Course Grades - Spring 1996</CAPTION>
    <TR>                    <!-- Row 1 -->
        <TH>Student</TH>
        <TH>Midterm</TH>
        <TH>Final Exam</TH>
        <TH>Course Average</TH>
    </TR>
    <TR>                    <!-- Row 2 -->
        <TD>Sarah Gordon</TD>
        <TD ALIGN=CENTER>89</TD>
        <TD ALIGN=CENTER>95</TD>
        <TD ALIGN=CENTER>92</TD>
    </TR>
    <TR>                    <!-- Row 3 -->
        <TD>Tim Jackson</TD>
        <TD ALIGN=CENTER>81</TD>
        <TD ALIGN=CENTER>77</TD>
        <TD ALIGN=CENTER>79</TD>
    </TR>
    <TR>                    <!-- Row 4 -->
        <TD>Molly Sanderson</TD>
        <TD ALIGN=CENTER>85</TD>
        <TD ALIGN=CENTER>89</TD>
        <TD ALIGN=CENTER>87</TD>
    </TR>
</TABLE>
```

Note in figure 11.3 that all grades in the table are centered below their respective column headings. This was accomplished by the ALIGN=CENTER attribute in each of the <TD ...> tags that creates a cell containing a grade. The ALIGN=BOTTOM in the <CAPTION ...> tag placed the caption below the table instead of above it.

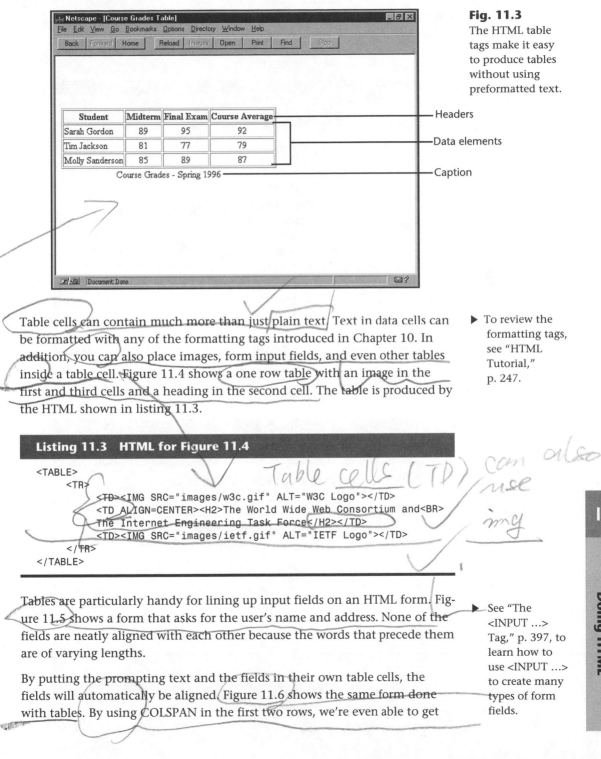

▶ To review the formatting tags, see "HTML Tutorial," p. 247.

Fig. 11.3
The HTML table tags make it easy to produce tables without using preformatted text.

Table cells can contain much more than just plain text. Text in data cells can be formatted with any of the formatting tags introduced in Chapter 10. In addition, you can also place images, form input fields, and even other tables inside a table cell. Figure 11.4 shows a one row table with an image in the first and third cells and a heading in the second cell. The table is produced by the HTML shown in listing 11.3.

Listing 11.3   HTML for Figure 11.4

```
<TABLE>
    <TR>
        <TD><IMG SRC="images/w3c.gif" ALT="W3C Logo"></TD>
        <TD ALIGN=CENTER><H2>The World Wide Web Consortium and<BR>
        The Internet Engineering Task Force</H2></TD>
        <TD><IMG SRC="images/ietf.gif" ALT="IETF Logo"></TD>
    </TR>
</TABLE>
```

Tables are particularly handy for lining up input fields on an HTML form. Figure 11.5 shows a form that asks for the user's name and address. None of the fields are neatly aligned with each other because the words that precede them are of varying lengths.

By putting the prompting text and the fields in their own table cells, the fields will automatically be aligned. Figure 11.6 shows the same form done with tables. By using COLSPAN in the first two rows, we're even able to get

▶ See "The <INPUT ...> Tag," p. 397, to learn how to use <INPUT ...> to create many types of form fields.

III

Doing HTML

the "City," "State," and "Zip" fields to fit across the same width as the fields above them. Listing 11.4 shows the HTML to produce figure 11.6. The <INPUT ...> tags shown there are used to create form input fields.

Fig. 11.4
Table cells may contain inline images in addition to text.

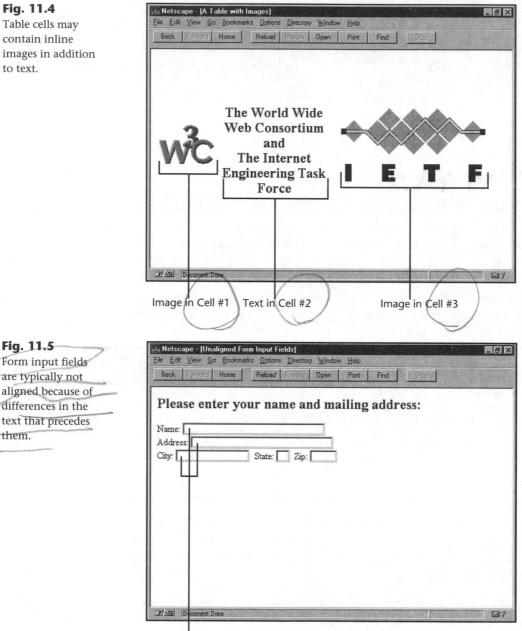

Image in Cell #1   Text in Cell #2   Image in Cell #3

Fig. 11.5
Form input fields are typically not aligned because of differences in the text that precedes them.

Unaligned input fields

Important

X

Listing 11.4   HTML for Figure 11.6

```
<TABLE>
    <TR>
        <TD>Name:</TD>
        <TD COLSPAN=5><INPUT NAME="name" TYPE="text" SIZE=30></TD>
    </TR>
    <TR>
        <TD>Address:</TD>
        <TD COLSPAN=5><INPUT NAME="address" TYPE="text" SIZE=30></TD>
    </TR>
    <TR>
        <TD>City:</TD>
        <TD><INPUT NAME="city" TYPE="text" SIZE=11></TD>
        <TD>State:</TD>
        <TD><INPUT NAME="state" TYPE="text" SIZE=2></TD>
        <TD>Zip:</TD>
        <TD><INPUT NAME="zip" TYPE="text" SIZE=5></TD>
    </TR>
</TABLE>
```

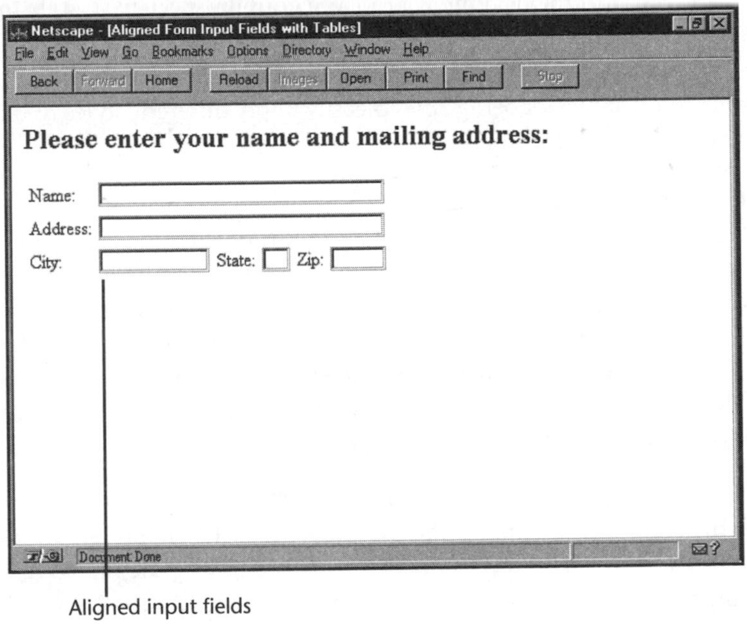

Fig. 11.6
Placing form input
fields in table cells
is an easy way to
get them to align
properly.

Netscape - [Aligned Form Input Fields with Tables]

File Edit View Go Bookmarks Options Directory Window Help

Back Forward Home   Reload Images Open Print Find   Stop

Please enter your name and mailing address:

Name:

Address:

City: State: Zip:

Document: Done

Aligned input fields

Coming Soon!

Even after it is released, the HTML 3.0 spec will continue to evolve. Two
items you should look for in the spec in the not-too-distant future are
stylesheets and *client-side imagemaps*.

III

Doing HTML

HTML Stylesheets

HTML stylesheets contain information on how a document or a portion of a document should be formatted, including text size, font and color, indenting, and other layout instructions. Using stylesheets will help eliminate the need to keep adding new formatting tags to HTML since any new formatting instructions can be placed in the stylesheets and not in the HTML file.

There are different proposals as to how stylesheets should be attached to HTML files. One proposal calls for using the <LINK ...> tag in the document head. By using the many attributes of <LINK ...>, you could attach the stylesheet with the HTML:

```
<LINK TITLE="General Purpose Style Sheet" REL="stylesheet"
HREF="styles/general.style" TYPE="text/css">
```

HREF points to the file containing the stylesheet information and TYPE specifies the MIME type of the stylesheet ("css" stands for "cascading stylesheet").

A second proposal introduces the <STYLE> and </STYLE> container tags. These tags also go in the document head and contain specialized style information that overrides any styles brought in through the <LINK ...> tag. Yet another proposal suggests placing style information into <P> and <DIV> tags. This has the advantage of being able to easily apply different styles to different parts of the same document.

Client-Side Imagemaps

Another interesting proposal calls for the support of client-side imagemaps. Imagemaps are multiply linked images that take users to different URLs depending on where they click on the image. Imagemap clicks are processed by sending the coordinates of the click to the server. The server then checks a file that defines the linked regions of the map to determine what URL the client (browser) should load. Once this determination is made, the client receives the URL and loads it for presentation to the user.

There is nothing special about the computations that the server does to determine which region of the image the user clicked on. The main reason for having the server do this work is because the file defining the linked regions of the map lives there. Other than that, the client could do the computations just as easily.

The main premise behind client-side imagemaps, is that the client can do the computations as long as it has the information defining the linked regions of the map. Having the client do the work eliminates the need to open another connection to the server (making imagemap processing much faster) and it reduces the load on the server.

The trick to implementing client-side imagemaps is to find a way to store the information that defines the linked regions in your HTML code. This is under consideration for HTML 3.0.

▶ See "Client-Side Imagemaps," p. 379, to learn more about client-side imagemapping techniques.

> **Note**
>
> Both Netscape Navigator 2.0 and Microsoft Internet Explorer 1.0 support client-side imagemaps.

Netscape Extensions

As noted at the start of the chapter, some software companies program their browsers to understand tags that are not part of standard HTML. Such tags are called *HTML extensions,* and they are usually associated with the name of the company that devised them.

A leader in developing HTML extensions is Netscape Communications Corporation. The Netscape Navigator browser is widely used, so the extensions that Netscape introduces are usually embraced very quickly by the Web community. Most, if not all, of the Netscape extensions are submitted to W3C and the IETF as candidates for inclusion in upcoming HTML specifications.

The next few sections review the Netscape extensions to HTML, including:

- Extensions to tags in the document head
- Extensions to HTML 2.0 tags
- Entirely new HTML tags
- Extensions to the HTML table tags
- Tags to create frames in the Netscape browser window

Extensions to Tags in the Document Head

Netscape has extended the <META ...> tag in the document head to include a value of "Refresh" for the HTTP-EQUIV attribute. Refresh instructs the browser to reload the same document or a different document after a specified number of seconds. The time delay and the URL of the next document, if applicable, are stored in the CONTENT attribute. The syntax for the <META ...> tag in this situation is:

```
<META HTTP-EQUIV="Refresh" CONTENT="n; url">
```

where *n* is the number of seconds to wait and *url* is the URL of the next document to load. If you want to reload the same document, just use CONTENT="*n*" with no URL specified.

III

Doing HTML

> **Caution**
>
> URLs in the CONTENT attribute should be fully qualified.

This dynamic reloading of documents is called *client pull*. The name is appropriate because the client automatically pulls in the next document with no prompting from the user. The client pull technique has already been used on Web pages to produce simple animations and to automatically load and play sounds.

▶ See "A One-Field Form: The <ISINDEX> Tag," p. 408, to learn how to use <ISINDEX> to create a searchable document.

Another extended tag in the document head is the <ISINDEX> tag. The <ISINDEX> tag designates a document as searchable and gives the user an input field into which search criteria is entered. The default prompting text in front of this search field is This is a searchable index. Enter search keywords:. The PROMPT attribute is a Netscape extension of the <ISINDEX> tag that lets you change the default prompting text to whatever you like. For example listing 11.5 produces the search field shown in figure 11.7.

Listing 11.5   HTML for Figure 11.7

```
<HEAD>
<TITLE>An Application of the PROMPT Attribute</TITLE>
<ISINDEX PROMPT="Please enter the keyword you wish to search on:">
</HEAD>
```

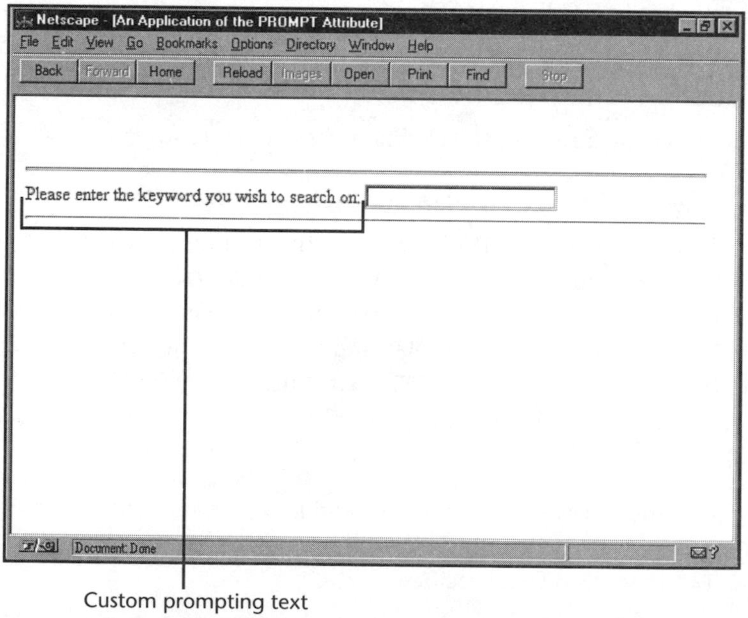

Fig. 11.7
The PROMPT attribute of the <ISINDEX> tag gives you control over the search field prompting text.

Custom prompting text

Extensions to HTML 2.0

Many of the tags you learned back in Chapter 10 have been extended by
Netscape, including:

- The list tags (<UL>, <OL>, and <LI>)
- The <HR> tag
- The <IMG ...> tag
- The <BR> tag

The additional attributes to these tags are introduced in the next four
sections.

The List Tags

Unordered list items are preceded by bullets. If you nest unordered lists,
Netscape automatically changes bullet characters for each new list. The
default bullet progression is from solid circle (disc) to open circle (circle) to
square (square). The new TYPE attribute of the <UL> tag gives you control
over which bullet character to use in nested lists. By setting TYPE equal to
DISC, CIRCLE, or SQUARE, you can override the default progression and
make Netscape use the bullet you want. This is illustrated in figure 11.8. The
nested list in the figure uses solid circles as bullets just as the initial list does.
Listing 11.6 shows the corresponding HTML.

Listing 11.6   HTML for Figure 11.8

```
<UL>
     <LI>HTML 2.0</LI>
     <LI>HTML 3.0</LI>
     <UL TYPE=DISC>
          <LI>Mathematical symbols</LI>
          <LI>Tables</LI>
          <LI>Style sheets</LI>
     </UL>
     <LI>Netscape extensions to HTML</LI>
</UL>
```

The <OL> tag also picks up the TYPE attribute, but in this case, TYPE changes
the numbering scheme used in the ordered list. By default, ordered list item
are numbered with consecutive integers starting with "1." By setting TYPE
equal to "A," "a," "I," or "i," you can change the scheme to be uppercase
letters, lowercase letters, uppercase Roman numerals, or lowercase Roman
numerals, respectively. Having these five numbering schemes makes it easy
to replicate the standard outline format using ordered lists. Figure 11.9 illustrates this point. The HTML to produce the figure is shown in listing 11.7.

III

Doing HTML

Listing 11.7   HTML for Figure 11.9

```
<OL TYPE="I">
    <LI>Introduction</LI>
    <OL TYPE="A">
        <LI>Problem statement</LI>
        <LI>Results of previous research</LI>
    </OL>
    <LI>Approach</LI>
    <OL TYPE="A">
        <LI>Research objectives</LI>
        <LI>Equipment</LI>
        <OL>
            <LI>Lab equipment</LI>
            <LI>Computing equipment</LI>
        </OL>
        <LI>Techniques</LI>
    </OL>
    ...
</OL>
```

Fig. 11.8
You can control the bullet character in unordered lists using the TYPE attribute of the <UL> tag.

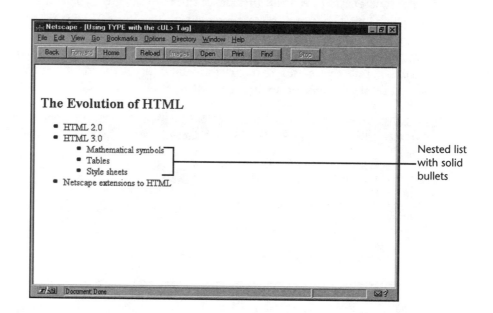

Nested list with solid bullets

Another Netscape extension to the <OL> tag is the START attribute, which lets you change the starting value of the list item numbering. START=1 by default, but you can change it to any number you choose. If you're using a TYPE different from the default numbering scheme, you can still specify a different starting value using numbers. Netscape automatically converts the new starting value to the chosen numbering scheme for you. Thus, the HTML in listing 11.8 produces the list seen in figure 11.10.

Listing 11.8   HTML for Figure 11.10

```
<P>Users' favorite Internet applications
after e-mail and the World Wide Web were:
<OL TYPE="i" START=3>
<LI>Usenet newsgroups</LI>
<LI>FTP</LI>
<LI>Telnet</LI>
<LI>Internet Relay Chat (IRC)</LI>
</OL>
```

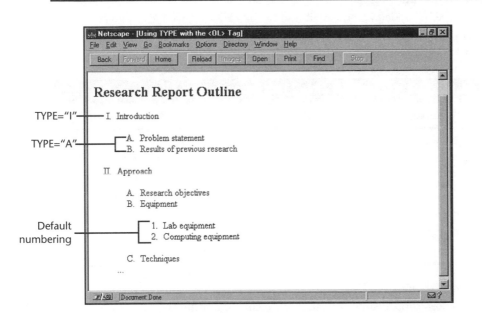

Fig. 11.9
Creating outlines in HTML is simple with the TYPE attribute of the <OL> tag.

TYPE="I"

TYPE="A"

Default numbering

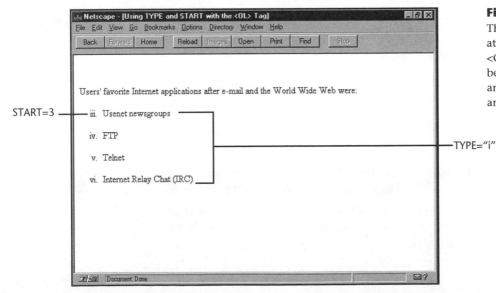

Fig. 11.10
The START attribute of the <OL> tag lets you begin numbering an ordered list at any value.

START=3

TYPE="i"

III

Doing HTML

Finally, Netscape extends list type control all the way down to the list item level by adding the TYPE attribute to the <LI> tag. In an unordered list, using TYPE in an <LI> tag lets you change the bullet character for that list item and all subsequent items. For ordered lists, a TYPE attribute in an <LI> tag changes the numbering scheme for that list item and each one after it. The <LI> tag can also take the VALUE attribute in an ordered list. VALUE lets you change the numbering count to any other number you choose.

The <HR> Tag

Netscape has added several attributes to the <HR> tag that give you control over the width, thickness, alignment, and shading characteristics of rule. The new attributes are summarized in table 11.6.

Table 11.6   Attributes of the <HR> Tag (Netscape Extensions)

Attribute	Purpose
WIDTH=pixels ¦ percent	Allows you to change the width of the rule to a set number of pixels or to a percentage of the browser screen width
ALIGN=LEFT ¦ RIGHT ¦ CENTER	Sets the alignment of a piece of rule (default is CENTER)
SIZE=*n*	Controls the thickness of the rule (default is 1)
NOSHADE	Disables the shading Netscape uses when rendering rule, producing a solid bar

Figure 11.11 illustrates some of the new types of rules you can produce with these extensions. Listing 11.9 shows the corresponding HTML.

Listing 11.9   HTML for Figure 11.11

```
<HR>
Normal rule<P>
<HR SIZE=8 WIDTH=40% ALIGN=RIGHT>
Size 8, 40% width, flush right alignment<P>
<HR SIZE=12 NOSHADE>
Size 12, no shading<P>
<HR SIZE=16 NOSHADE WIDTH=80% ALIGN=LEFT>
Size 16, no shading, 80% width, flush left alignment<P>
```

Tip

Since you can't know how many pixels wide every user's browser screen is, you should always specify WIDTH in terms of a percentage rather than in terms of a set number of pixels.

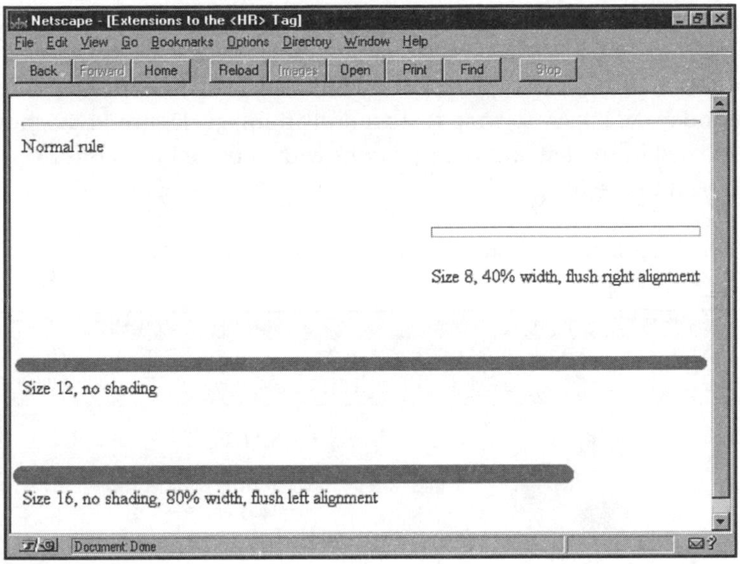

Fig. 11.11
Netscape extensions to the <HR> tag let you specify width, thickness, alignment, and shading of your horizontal rule.

Normal rule

Size 8, 40% width, flush right alignment

Size 12, no shading

Size 16, no shading, 80% width, flush left alignment

The <IMG ...> Tag

The ALIGN attribute of the <IMG ...> tag has been greatly extended by Netscape. The Netscape Navigator understands the values of ALIGN shown in table 11.7.

Table 11.7 Values of the ALIGN Attribute of the <IMG ...> Tag (Netscape Extensions)

Value	Effect
TOP	Aligns text following the image with the top of the image
MIDDLE	Aligns the baseline of text following the image with the center of the image
BOTTOM,BASELINE	Aligns the baseline of text following the image with the bottom of the image
TEXTTOP	Aligns the top of the tallest text following the image with the top of the image
ABSMIDDLE	Aligns the middle of the text following the image with the middle of the image
ABSBOTTOM	Aligns the lowest text following the image with the bottom of the image
LEFT	Floats the image in the left margin, allowing text to wrap around the right side of the image
RIGHT	Floats the image in the right margin, allowing text to wrap around the left side of the image

III

Doing HTML

▶ See "The
<IMG...> Tag,"
p. 262, to
review the
TOP, MIDDLE,
and BOTTOM
values of
ALIGN.

TEXTTOP, ABSMIDDLE, ABSBOTTOM, and BASELINE are small modifications to the TOP, MIDDLE, and BOTTOM values of ALIGN. What's new and interesting are the LEFT and RIGHT values of ALIGN, which produce *floating images* and make it easy to wrap text around an image. Figure 11.12 shows an image floated in the left and right margins with centered text in the open margin next to the image.

Fig. 11.12
Using ALIGN=LEFT
or ALIGN=RIGHT
lets you float images
in the left or right
margins.

Floating image in the left margin   Text wraps to the right of the image

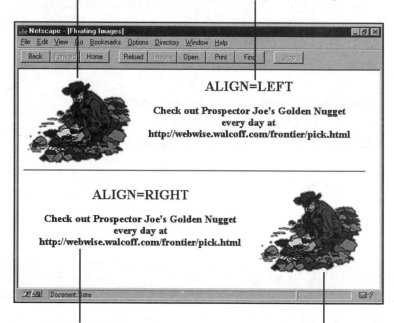

Text wraps to the left of the image   Floating image in the right margin

Beyond the new values for the ALIGN attribute, Netscape also adds three other attributes to the <IMG ...> tag. The BORDER=n attribute lets you specify the thickness of the border around your images. The default value of n is 1, but you can change it to any value you choose, including zero. Setting BORDER to zero is useful with transparent GIFs because it eliminates the rectangular box that would otherwise surround the image.

Caution

Setting BORDER=0 on a hyperlinked image will remove the colored border and users may not be able to tell that the image is linked.

Because it's possible to wrap text around a floating image, it becomes necessary to have a way to put some additional space around the image so that wrapping text doesn't bump right up against it. The HSPACE=n attribute lets you insert *n* pixels of white space to the left and right of the floating image. VSPACE=*n* works similarly to put white space above and below the image.

> **Note**
>
> Don't forget the HEIGHT and WIDTH attributes introduced in Chapter 10. Technically, these attributes are Netscape extensions to the <IMG ...> tag, but their function is important enough to earn them an early introduction.

The
 Tag

The availability of floating images also makes it necessary to be able to break to the next line that is clear of a floating image. To address this, Netscape added the CLEAR attribute to the <BR> tag. CLEAR can be set to LEFT, to move to the first line whose left margin is clear of floating images; RIGHT, to move to the first line whose right margin is clear of floating images; or ALL, to move to the first line that is completely free of floating images.

Additions to HTML

In addition to new attributes for many existing tags, Netscape has also introduced some entirely new tags to HTML. These new tags apply in the areas of word breaking and text effects.

Word Breaks

Text contained in the <NOBR> and </NOBR> tags will not have any line breaks in it. The tags are meant to prevent breaks at places where it is absolutely necessary to avoid them. You should keep the amount of text between these tags short, as long unbroken strings of text look awful on-screen.

The <WBR> tag can be used two ways. One way is to specify *exactly* where you want a line break inside the <NOBR> and </NOBR> tags. The other way is to indicate a preferred location for text breaks to the browser. <WBR> does not actually create the line break; it just says "It's okay to break the line here."

Text Effects

The <FONT ...> and </FONT> container tags give you control over the size and color of the text they contain. To modify the size of the text, you use the SIZE attribute in the <FONT ...> tag. SIZE can be set to any number between 1 and 7. The default text size is 3. You can also specify SIZE relative to the base font size by indicating how many sizes above (+) or below (-) the base font size you want the text to be.

With a base font size of 3, the following two lines of HTML do the same thing:

```
<FONT SIZE=5>This text is big!</FONT>
<FONT SIZE=+2>This text is big!</FONT>
```

Similarly, to go two sizes below 3, you could use either of the following:

```
<FONT SIZE=1>This text is small!</FONT>
<FONT SIZE=-2>This text is big!</FONT>
```

The base font size is always 3, unless you change it with the <BASEFONT SIZE=*n*> tag. *n* can be any number between 1 and 7.

A popular effect you can create with the SIZE attribute is "small caps." With small caps, each letter in a word is in uppercase, but the first letter of each word is bigger than the others. Figure 11.13 shows some text in small caps as produced by the following HTML:

```
<FONT SIZE=+2>I</FONT> <FONT SIZE=+2>L</FONT>IKE
<FONT SIZE=+2>S</FONT>MALL <FONT SIZE=+2>C</FONT>APS!
```

Fig. 11.13

You can create text in small caps using the SIZE attribute of the <FONT ...> tag.

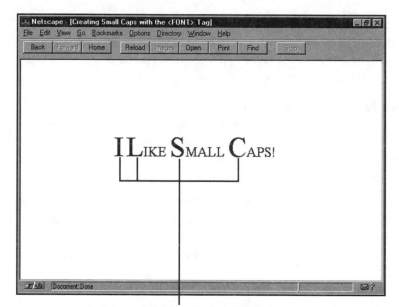

Letters made larger with the <FONT> tag

You can also change the color of text between <FONT ...> and </FONT> by using the COLOR attribute of the <FONT ...> tag. COLOR is set equal to the RGB (Red/Green/Blue) hexadecimal triplet of the color you want. Thus, the HTML:

```
Here is some <FONT COLOR="#FF0000">red text.</FONT>
```

instructs Netscape to render the words "red text." in red.

Tip

To determine the RGB hexadecimal triplet of a desired color, first find that color in Netscape's custom color palette. You can access the palette by choosing the General Preferences option under the Options menu and then by selecting the Colors tab in the dialog box. Point your mouse to the color you want and click on it. After clicking, the decimal Red, Green, and Blue values should be displayed near the bottom right of the dialog box. Use the Windows calculator in Scientific mode to convert these decimal values to hexadecimal. Then write these three two-digit hex numbers in sequence to produce your color triplet.

Setting Other Colors in Netscape

You can also change the colors of browser window background, body text, unvisited hyperlinks, visited hyperlinks, and active (clicked on) links in Netscape. The BGCOLOR, TEXT, LINK, VLINK, and ALINK attributes of the <BODY> tag can be set equal to an RGB hexadecimal triplet to change their colors from the default values.

Two other Netscape extensions for creating text effects are the <CENTER> ... </CENTER> and <BLINK> ...</BLINK> tag pairs. Text, headings, and images contained between the <CENTER> and </CENTER> tags are centered on the browser screen. Enclosing text in the <BLINK> and </BLINK> tags instructs Netscape to make the text blink.

Extensions to the Table Tags

The Netscape Navigator understands four attributes of the <TABLE ...> tag that are not part of the original HTML 3.0 proposal for tables. These extended attributes are listed in table 11.8

Table 11.8 Attributes of the <TABLE ...> Tag (Netscape Extensions)	
Attribute	**Purpose**
WIDTH=pixels ¦ percent	Sets the width of the table to a specific number of pixels or to a percentage of the browser window width
BORDER=n	Allows the use of borders of varying size
CELLSPACING=n	Controls the amount of space between cells (default value is 2)
CELLPADDING=n	Controls the amount of space between the edges of a cell and its contents (default value is 1)

III

Doing HTML

The WIDTH attribute is useful in creating tables of varying width, but the same advice that applied to the WIDTH attribute of the <HR> tag applies here: always set your WIDTH to be a percentage of the browser screen width. That way, users with browser screens of any size will all see the same, albeit scaled, effect. However, you may need to see the width to a certain number of pixels if you're placing an image in your table.

Control over the border size is desirable when nesting tables. You can use the BORDER=n attribute to give your main table a wide border and your nested tables smaller borders. If space is at a premium, you can set BORDER=0 to recapture the space that is typically reserved for a border.

Caution

Remember that other browsers treat BORDER as a Boolean attribute: if they see BORDER in the <TABLE ...> tag, they put a border on the table. Otherwise, they don't. This can be a problem when setting BORDER=0. Netscape understands BORDER=0 to mean "Don't include a border and give me back the space you re-served for a border." Other browsers will look at BORDER=0 and, seeing the word BORDER in the tag, put a border around the table—the complete opposite of what you intended!

CELLSPACING and CELLPADDING are useful in two ways. Setting them to values higher than their default opens a table up and lets the cells "breathe" with more white space. If space is tight, you can set them both to zero to get the most compact table possible.

Note

In a table with CELLPADDING=0, the contents of the cell will be able to touch the edges of the cell. If this is undesirable, change your CELLPADDING to a non-zero value.

Frames

Version 2.0 of the Netscape Navigator supports an exciting new concept called *frames*. Using the frame tags, you can break up the browser window into separate areas that can each load its own HTML document. This is a valuable feature because it lets you put static items, like tables of contents and navigation aids, in small, yet permanent windows while still leaving a considerable amount of space for changing material. Thus, users can look at different documents in the largest frame and always have the useful static items available in smaller frames.

Creating the Frames: The <FRAMESET ...> and </FRAMESET> Tag Pair

The first step in creating a framed document is to split up the Netscape screen into the frames that you want. You accomplish this with an HTML file that uses the <FRAMESET ...> and </FRAMESET> container tags instead of the <BODY> and </BODY> tags. <FRAMESET ...> and </FRAMESET> are not just container tags though. Attributes of the <FRAMESET ...> tag are instrumental in defining the frame regions.

The <FRAMESET ...> tag can take one of two attributes: ROWS, to split the screen up into multiple rows, or COLS, to split the screen up into multiple columns. Each attribute is set equal to a list of values that tells Netscape how big to make each row. The values can be a number of pixels, a percentage of a browser window dimension, or an asterisk (*), which acts as a wildcard character and tells the browser to use whatever space it has left. For example, the HTML:

```
<FRAMESET COLS="40%,20%,30%,10%">
...
</FRAMESET>
```

breaks the browser window into four columns. The first column has a width equal to 40% of the browser screen width, the second column 20%, the third column 30%, and the fourth column 10%. Similarly, the following HTML:

```
<FRAMESET ROWS="100,150,2*,*">
...
</FRAMESET>
```

splits the window into four rows. The first row is 100 pixels deep and the second is 150 pixels deep. The remaining space is divided between the third and fourth rows with the third row being twice as big (2*) as the fourth (*).

To produce really interesting layouts, you can nest <FRAMESET ...> and </FRAMESET> tags. Suppose you want to split the browser window into eight equal regions. You can first split the screen into four equal rows with the HTML:

```
<FRAMESET ROWS="25%,25%,25%,25%">
...
</FRAMESET>
```

This produces the screen shown in figure 11.14.

Next you need to divide each row in half. To do this, you need a <FRAMESET ...> ... </FRAMESET> pair for each row that splits the row into two equal columns. The HTML <FRAMESET COLS="50%,50%"> ... </FRAMESET> will do the trick. Nesting these tags in the HTML above produces listing 11.10.

III

Doing HTML

Fig. 11.14
The Netscape
Navigator window
split into four
equal rows.

Window broken into
four equal rows

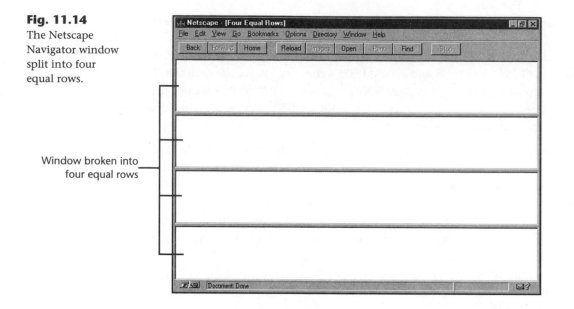

Listing 11.10   HTML for Figure 11.15

```
<FRAMESET ROWS="25%,25%,25%,25%">
    <FRAMESET COLS="50%,50%"> <!-- Break Row 1 into 2 columns -->
        ...
    </FRAMESET>
    <FRAMESET COLS="50%,50%"> <!-- Break Row 2 into 2 columns -->
        ...
    </FRAMESET>
    <FRAMESET COLS="50%,50%"> <!-- Break Row 3 into 2 columns -->
        ...
    </FRAMESET>
    <FRAMESET COLS="50%,50%"> <!-- Break Row 4 into 2 columns -->
        ...
    </FRAMESET>
</FRAMESET>
```

Listing 11.10 completes the task of splitting the window into eight equal regions. The resulting screen is shown in figure 11.15.

Tip

Not sure whether to do a <FRAMESET ...> with ROWS or COLS first? Make a pencil and paper sketch of what you want the browser window to look like. If you have unbroken horizontal lines that go from one edge of the window to the other, do your ROWS first. If you have unbroken vertical lines that go from the top of the window to the bottom, do your COLS first. If you have both unbroken horizontal and vertical lines, it doesn't matter which one you do first.

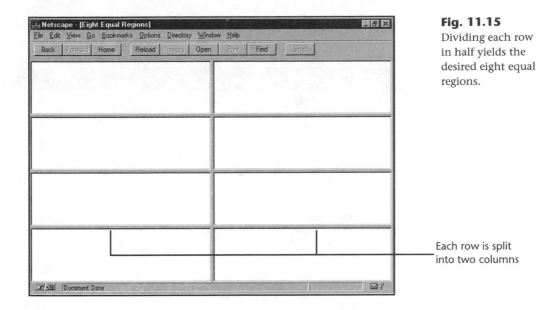

Fig. 11.15
Dividing each row
in half yields the
desired eight equal
regions.

Each row is split
into two columns

Placing Content in Frames: The <FRAME ...> Tag

With your frames all set up, you're ready to place content in each one with
the <FRAME ...> tag. The most important attribute of the <FRAME ...> tag is
SRC, which tells Netscape the URL of the document you want to load into
the frame. The <FRAME ...> tag can take the attributes summarized in table
11.9 as well. If you use the NAME attribute, the name you give the frame
must begin with an alphanumeric character. The default value of SCROLL-
ING is AUTO, which means Netscape will automatically put scrollbars in if
they are needed. SCROLLING=YES means Netscape should always put
scrollbars in and SCROLLING=NO means there should be no scrollbars.

Table 11.9   Attributes of the <FRAME ...> Tag

Attribute	Purpose
MARGINHEIGHT=*n*	Specifies the amount of white space to be left at the top and bottom of the frame
MARGINWIDTH=*n*	Specifies the amount of white space to be left along the sides of the frame
NAME="*name*"	Gives the frame a unique name so it can be targeted by other documents
NORESIZE	Disables the user's ability to resize the frame
SCROLLING=YES|NO|AUTO	Controls the appearance of horizontal and vertical scrollbars in the frame
SRC="*url*"	Specifies the URL of the document to load into the frame

III

Doing HTML

To place content in each of the eight equal regions you created earlier, you can use listing 11.11. The resulting screen appears in figure 11.16.

Listing 11.11   HTML for Figure 11.16

```
<FRAMESET ROWS="25%,25%,25%,25%">
    <FRAMESET COLS="50%,50%"> <!-- Break Row 1 into 2 columns -->
        <FRAME SRC="one.html">
        <FRAME SRC="two.html">
    </FRAMESET>
    <FRAMESET COLS="50%,50%"> <!-- Break Row 2 into 2 columns -->
        <FRAME SRC="three.html">
        <FRAME SRC="four.html">
    </FRAMESET>
    <FRAMESET COLS="50%,50%"> <!-- Break Row 3 into 2 columns -->
        <FRAME SRC="five.html">
        <FRAME SRC="six.html">
    </FRAMESET>
    <FRAMESET COLS="50%,50%"> <!-- Break Row 4 into 2 columns -->
        <FRAME SRC="seven.html">
        <FRAME SRC="eight.html">
    </FRAMESET>
</FRAMESET>
```

Fig. 11.16
The <FRAME ...> tag lets you place a different HTML document into each frame.

Content is placed in a frame using the <FRAME...> tag

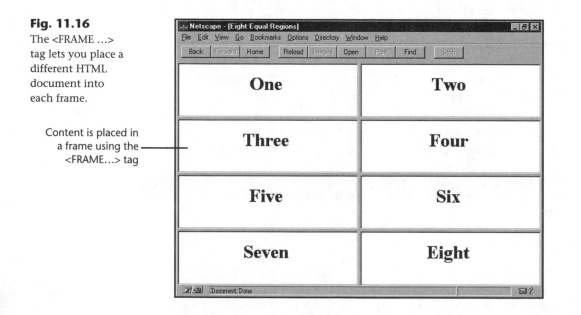

Respecting "Frames-Challenged" Browsers

If you create a document with frames, people who are using a browser other than Netscape 2.0 will not be able to see the content you want them to see because their browsers don't understand the <FRAMESET ...>, </FRAMESET>, and <FRAME ...> tags. As a courtesy to users with "frames-challenged" browsers, you can place alternative HTML code between the <NOFRAMES> and </NOFRAMES> container tags. Any HTML between these two tags will be understood and rendered by other browsers. Netscape, on the other hand, ignores anything between these tags and just works with the frame-related HTML.

Caution

The <NOFRAMES> and </NOFRAMES> tags must occur after the initial <FRAMESET ...> tag, but before any nested <FRAMESET ...> tags.

Microsoft Internet Explorer Extensions

Now that it's producing its own browser, Microsoft has also gotten into the act of extending HTML. The following HTML tags and attributes can only be properly parsed by Microsoft Internet Explorer.

Extensions to Existing Tags

Like many of Netscape's extensions, several of the Internet Explorer extensions to HTML take the form of new attributes of existing HTML tags.

Extensions to the <BODY ...> Tag

If you use the BACKGROUND attribute of the <BODY ...> tag to tile a graphic as your document background, the background scrolls as you scroll through the document. Internet Explorer gives you greater control over scrolling by supporting a BGPROPERTIES attribute. If you set BGPROPERTIES to FIXED, the background image will not scroll as you move through the document, creating a "watermark" effect.

Internet Explorer also supports LEFTMARGIN and TOPMARGIN attributes of the <BODY ...> tag. You can set either one to the number of pixels of white space you want Internet Explorer to leave along the left and top edges of the browser window.

Extensions to the <FONT ...> Tag

You can use the FACE attribute of the <FONT ...> tag to specify a typeface that Internet Explorer should use when rendering text. You can even set FACE to a list of typefaces, giving the browser other options if the most desirable face is not available. For example, the HTML:

```
<FONT FACE="Palatino,Times,Helvetica">Custom Typefaces!</FONT>
```

would instruct Internet Explorer to render the text "Custom Typefaces!" in Palatino if that typeface were available. If Palatino weren't available, Internet Explorer would then try to use Times, followed by Helvetica.

Extensions to the <IMG ...> Tag

Microsoft has greatly extended the <IMG ...> tag to provide exceptional support of inline video clips and VRML worlds stored in the Audio Video Interleave (AVI) format. The extended attributes are shown in Table 11.10

Table 11.10 Internet Explorer Extensions to the <IMG ...> Tag	
Attribute	**Purpose**
DYNSRC="*url*"	Specifies the URL of the AVI file containing the video clip
CONTROLS	Places a control panel in the browser window so the user can control the playing of the clip
START=FILEOPEN¦MOUSEOVER	Specifies when to start the video clip
LOOP=*n*¦INFINITE	Controls how many times the clip is repeated
LOOPDELAY=*n*	Specifies how many milliseconds to wait before repeating the clip

For example, the HTML tag:

```
<IMG DYNSRC="ballgame.avi" CONTROLS START=FILEOPEN LOOP=2>
```

instructs Internet Explorer to play the clip stored in ballgame.avi two times when the file is opened. A control panel will be present while the clip is playing so that the user may stop, rewind, or fast-forward.

> **Tip**
>
> You can set START to both FILEOPEN and MOUSEOVER together (START=FILEOPEN,MOUSEOVER). This configuration will play the clip once when the file is opened and then once each time the mouse is moved over the clip window.

Extensions to Table Tags

In the <TABLE ...> tag, you can specify the BORDERCOLOR attribute to control what color Internet Explorer uses when rendering table borders. BORDERCOLOR should be set equal to the hexadecimal RGB triplet that describes the desired color.

You can also use the BGCOLOR attribute in a <TD ...> tag to change the background color of a table cell. Just like when you use it in the <BODY ...> tag, you set BGCOLOR to a hexadecimal RGB triplet.

Additions to HTML

Beyond the extensions to existing tags noted in the previous section, Microsoft Internet Explorer also supports two entirely new HTML tags: <BGSOUND ...> and <MARQUEE ...> ... </MARQUEE>.

The <BGSOUND ...> Tag

You can have a background sound play while your Web pages are open by using the <BGSOUND ...> tag in your document. <BGSOUND ...> takes the SRC attribute, which is set equal to the URL of a file containing the sound. The file can be in .wav, .au, or .mid (MIDI) format.

<BGSOUND ...> also takes the LOOP attribute which lets you specify how many times to play the sound. LOOP can be set to a number of times to repeat the sound or to INFINITE to play the sound as long as the page is open.

> **Caution**
>
> Keep your sound files small. Large sound files can take a long time to download and users may be off a page before your sound is done downloading.

The <MARQUEE ...> and </MARQUEE> Tag Pair

The <MARQUEE ...> and </MARQUEE> tag pair places a scrolling text marquee on your Web page. The text that scrolls is the text found between the two tags.

The <MARQUEE ...> tag can take a number of attributes that give you very fine control over the appearance and behavior of the marquee. These attributes are summarized in Table 11.11.

Table 11.11 Attributes of the <MARQUEE ...> Tag	
Attribute	**Effect**
BGCOLOR="*RGB triplet*"	Specifies the background color of the marquee window
BEHAVIOR=SCROLL¦SLIDE¦ALTERNATE	Specifies how the text should move in the marquee window
DIRECTION=LEFT¦RIGHT	Controls the direction in which the marquee text moves

(continues)

III

Doing HTML

Table 11.11   Continued

Attribute	Effect
SCROLLAMOUNT=*n*	Sets the number of pixels of space between successive presentations of marquee text
SCROLLDELAY=*n*	Sets the number of milliseconds to wait before repeating the marquee text
HEIGHT=*pixels ¦ percent*	Specifies the height of the marquee window in either pixels or a percentage of the browser window height
WIDTH=*pixels ¦ percent*	Specifies the width of the marquee window in either pixels or a percentage of the browser window width
HSPACE=*n*	Specifies how many pixels to make the left and right margins of the marquee window
VSPACE=*n*	Specifies how many pixels to make the top and bottom margins of the marquee window
LOOP=*n* ¦ INFINITE	Controls how many times the marquee text should scroll
ALIGN=TOP ¦ MIDDLE ¦ BOTTOM	Specifies how text outside of the marquee window should be aligned with the window

While the purposes of most of these attributes are straightforward, the BEHAVIOR attribute values require some explanation. Setting BEHAVIOR to SCROLL make the marquee text scroll on and then off the marquee window in the direction specified by the DIRECTION attribute. If BEHAVIOR equals SLIDE, the text will slide into the window and stay there. If BEHAVIOR is set to ALTERNATE, the text will bounce back and forth in the window.

Virtual Reality Modeling Language (VRML)

By now, you've probably heard some of the hype surrounding Virtual Reality Modeling Language, or VRML. VRML is a three-dimensional equivalent of HTML that allows you to render interactive 3-D environments in real time over the Web.

The VRML 1.0 spec was written by Mark Pesce, Tony Parisi, and Gavin Bell in late 1994. Since then, VRML has been updated and extended very much as HTML has. VRML 1.1 cleared up a few loose ends from the 1.0 spec. Sony has created its own extensions to VRML just as Netscape has created HTML extensions. The VRML 2.0 spec, which is nearing completion, has a special focus on action and interaction.

> **Note**
>
> For up-to-date information on the evolving VRML 2.0 standard, consult the VRML FAQ at **http://www.oki.com/vrml/VRML_FAQ.html** or Mesh Mart at **http://cedar.cic.net/~rtillman/mm/vrml.html**. An excellent text reference on VRML is Que's *Special Edition Using VRML*.

Concepts

VRML is objected-oriented. You create VRML objects and place them in a 3-D environment. VRML browsers let you not only see this environment, but move around in it as well. As you move, the browser must perform many complex calculations to move, scale, rotate, and shade the objects in the environment so that the rendering continues to appear three-dimensional and realistic. This is why early VRML was done on high-powered computing platforms. As algorithms have become more efficient and high-powered computers have become more readily available, VRML has worked its way out of labs and universities and into people's homes and places of work.

Implementation

To view VRML documents, you need a VRML browser or a browser with a VRML plug-in. There are a few good options available to you that run on the Windows NT platform. GLView is a combination VRML browser and object format converter that is available as shareware. You can check out GLView at **http://www.inx.de/~hg/**. VRealm is a relatively new VRML browser that you can find at **http://www.ids-net.com/ids/instruct.html**. If you use Netscape 2.0, check out the VREAM VRML plug-in for Netscape at **http://www.vream.com/**.

If you want to create your own VRML site, you'll need a few extra tools. The first is a VRML editor that lets you create VRML objects. GWEB for NT is worth investigating. You can find it at **http://www.demon.co.uk/presence/gweb.html**. If you have 3-D graphics stored in formats that existed before VRML, you may wish to convert them to VRML objects using a format converter. The GLView browser mentioned above also acts as a format converter. Once you have your objects created, you can place them in a 3-D environment using a scene assembler. Scene assemblers let you position and scale objects to create the 3-D effect.

Most Web servers can serve VRML documents by using the MIME type x-world/x-vrml, but there are VRML servers available that specialize in serving VRML pages. VRServer, included on the CD-ROM with this book, can act as both a stand-alone Web server or as a VRML-capable add-on to an existing Web server. VRServer lets you create 3-D worlds from local files and files on local or remote Web sites. You can use one of VRServer's ten professionally done themes for your virtual world, customizing each one down to the room or object level.

> **Note**
>
> To run VRServer, you need Windows NT version 3.51 or higher, a TCP/IP stack, a regular Web browser and a VRML-capable browser. You can license your copy of VRServer from WebMaster, Inc. for $249.00.

## CHAPTER 12

HTML Editors and Tools

It's easy to write an HTML document. After all, the main document is nothing but ASCII text, most of which is the plain-language text that you're trying to communicate on the page. The tricky part is getting the proper tags in the right place to make your text and images look like you want them to. Browser programs are very literal in the way that they interpret HTML, so errors in your HTML syntax make your page look very unusual. You need to take extra care to ensure that your page comes out looking like you planned.

Because HTML documents are all ASCII code, originally Web documents were written with simple text editors, such as the Windows Notepad. As people began writing longer and more complex documents, many turned to their favorite word processing programs (which can save documents in plain ASCII text) and wrote macros and tools to help them.

As the Web expanded, dedicated HTML editing programs (similar to word processing programs, but designed to produce results for the screen and not the printed page) began to appear. These programs allow Web page creators to more quickly format their text into proper HTML format by allowing authors to have codes placed automatically around text at the click of a toolbar button. Stand-alone HTML editors have since evolved into very advanced HTML authoring systems that provide end-to-end support for the Web page creation process.

In addition to editors and authoring systems, special filters and utilities that convert existing documents to HTML format have cropped up. These applications save authors an immense amount of time; they take information formatted for other programs and mark it up with HTML to produce the same formatting on a Web page.

As you can see, there are many ways you can write your HTML documents; you can use your favorite line editor, a word processor, or a dedicated HTML tool. The choice of which system to use depends on personal preference and your confidence in your use of HTML.

This chapter looks at five types of applications that are useful in developing HTML documents:

- Plain text editors and word processors
- Stand-alone HTML editing tools
- Advanced HTML authoring systems
- Converters and filters for importing other types of documents into HTML
- Analyzers and other tools that check the syntax of your HTML documents

Plain Text Editors

You can use any ASCII editor to write HTML pages. The tags necessary to indicate special effects that a Web browser should show are only combinations of ASCII characters (such as <B> at the beginning of text that's supposed to be bold and </B> at the end). In contrast, most word processing programs embed special binary codes in the text to indicate changes in font styles or the location and format of graphics. Because hypertext authors know the HTML codes, they can write in various formatting effects as easily as they can enter sections of text.

This simplicity can be extremely useful. Many veteran HTML authors rely on a simple plain-text editor as they tweak specific points on any given page. Plain-text editors have the advantage of taking up less memory, which allows experienced authors to open multiple Web browser programs simultaneously to see how their page looks in each format. (Although a code for something to be bold is read by Internet Explorer, Mosaic, and Netscape as bold, the way bolded text appears may vary slightly with each browser.)

The major annoyance with plain-text editors is that HTML codes are not treated as complete units. You have to edit each keystroke in the HTML code, whereas many editor programs treat the code as an entire entity. In a plain-text editor, getting rid of the tag pair <B> and </B> around text requires deleting each keystroke. Some of the dedicated editors recognize the combination and eliminate the whole tag (and even delete its companion tag on the other side of the text).

Nevertheless, you will probably need to use a simple editor some time; become familiar with at least one, even if it's not what you usually use to compose your HTML files. You will undoubtedly use one someday to quickly edit your HTML.

MS-DOS Editor

You might not have used it in a very long time, but the MS-DOS Editor is a perfectly good tool for composing or making quick changes to an HTML document. The Editor provides menu options for all of the basic editing operations like cut, copy, and paste. It also has find and replace options to make it fairly easy to make global changes to your documents. The Editor automatically saves documents in ASCII format; there's no need to do any special conversions.

The big drawback, of course, is that you have to open an MS-DOS window to get to the Editor. If you're not adverse to this, you can open up a window and type **edit** at the DOS prompt to fire up the Editor.

Windows Notepad

If you can't bring yourself to leave the Windows environment, you can use the Windows Notepad. Notepad is a fine way to edit HTML documents, as long as the documents are not too long. Notepad has a file size limit of 64K; any particularly complex HTML document probably exceeds this file size.

Like the MS-DOS Editor, Notepad saves files in ASCII format. It also provides menu options to cut, copy, paste, and find text, but it does not have a find-and-replace feature.

Caution

Be careful when saving from Notepad that you don't save in the Unicode format. This is an encoded format and you won't be able to see your files with a browser.

Notepad proves most useful if you just need to make a quick tweak on a document that's already mostly edited. You may be able to open the HTML document in Notepad and make the minor adjustment without having to go through the hassle of opening your word processor and activating the proper template.

III

Doing HTML

Tip

If you use Notepad to edit HTML, activate the WordWrap option under the Edit menu. Otherwise, your HTML code can run off the edge of the window and you'll have to scroll to see parts of it.

Windows WordPad

If the document you want to edit is too big for Notepad, Windows will give you the option to open the document in WordPad—a document editor that falls somewhere between a simple editor like Notepad and a full-featured word processor like Microsoft Word.

WordPad offers full editing support through menu options to cut, copy, paste, and find and replace. When saving a document in WordPad, you have a choice of several formats. Be sure to choose the Text Document option.

Tip

You'll need to turn word wrapping on in WordPad as well when you work with plain text documents. You can do this by selecting Options under the View menu. The word wrap radio buttons are on the Text tab of the Options dialog box.

Note

No plain text editor will check the syntax of your HTML for you. If you do most of your HTML authoring in a plain text editor, it's a good idea to check the HTML syntax in your documents before putting them on your server. See the "Analyzers" section at the end of this chapter for programs that will check HTML syntax.

Word Processing Programs

Because many people are already familiar with the editing features of their favorite word processor, a number of HTML authors have turned to creating specialized macros and tools that take advantage of the properties of the word processing programs to make editing HTML easier. Now, even developers are getting into the act, and producing programs designed explicitly as add-ons for commercial word processors.

For whatever reason, be it the strong use of Styles or an easy, powerful macro language, Microsoft's Word seems to be the word processor of choice for those writing HTML editing tools; the vast majority of these types of tools are written expressly for Word for Macintosh or Windows. The first two discussed in this section are simple shareware templates that add helpful toolbars and HTML-specific pull-down menu options to those already available in Word. Quarterdeck's WebAuthor 2.0 is a commercial package that not only provides assistance for HTML authoring, but for syntax checking as well. And, naturally, Microsoft has an offering to enhance Word: Microsoft Internet Assistant turns Word into a fully functional Web browser, in addition to adding support for HTML editing.

CU_HTML

CU_HTML, named after the Chinese University of Hong Kong where it was created by Kenneth Wong and Anton Lam, is a template-based add-on for Word 2 and Word 6.

> **Note**
>
> The information in this section is based on CU_HTML.DOT, version 1.5.3. You can acquire the template and its related files by directing your browser to **http://www.cuhk.hk/csc/cu_html/cu_html.htm**. This document provides information on the current release of CU_HTML and provides a link to the file cu_html.zip, which is the file you want to download.

CU_HTML comes with installation instructions in an HTML format. Use your browser to open the file CU_HTML.HTM. If your browser isn't working, just open the Word document CU_HTML.DOC. After you install CU_HTML's files, you can select the CU_HTML template when you open a new document in Word.

If you choose this template, several new styles equivalent to HTML tags are loaded. From the Style option of the Format menu, you can apply formatting to produce the six heading levels, addresses, preformatted text, ordered and unordered lists, and horizontal rule. You can apply bold, italic, and underline styles using Word's usual formatting toolbar. When you instruct CU_HTML to write your final HTML document, it will convert these formats into the appropriate HTML tags.

There's also an extra pull-down menu, called HTML, and a new toolbar (see fig. 12.1). The HTML menu provides you with some options for tagging text, mostly for linking text in the document to other files (such as graphics or other hypertext links). Buttons on the toolbar replicate the choices found under the HTML menu, giving you quick access to these functions.

III

Doing HTML

> **Tip**
>
> If you don't see the CU_HTML toolbar, place your mouse pointer over any toolbar button, right-click the mouse, and select HTML from the list you see to activate the toolbar.

Fig. 12.1
Loading the CU_HTML template gives you an HTML pull-down menu and extra toolbar to assist you in your editing.

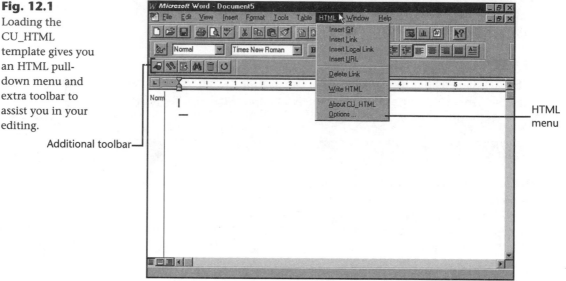

Additional toolbar

HTML menu

After you open a new document, you should save it. CU_HTML requires that you save a copy of the file before formatting text, placing graphics, and writing the final HTML file.

Once you've entered text, you can use the options under the HTML menu to format links to other files. You can link to a graphics file with the Insert Gif option, or another locally stored HTML file with Insert Link. You can create a link to another section of your Web document with Insert Local Link, or link to another document on the Web with Insert URL. The Delete Link option lets you remove any type of link you've inserted.

Like most of the templates for Word, CU_HTML creates files in Word format. You must be sure to save the completed document in HTML format before you try to use it on the Web. To do this using CU_HTML, open the HTML menu and choose Write HTML. This instructs CU_HTML to create an ASCII file in which all Word formatting codes are converted to HTML. The file will have the same name as your Word document, but it will end with the HTM extension.

GT_HTML

GT_HTML is a template add-on for Word developed at Georgia Tech. It is as easy to install as CU_HTML, but it supports many more editing features.

> **Note**
>
> The following section is based on GT_HTML, version 6.0d. You can download GT_HTML by pointing your browser to **http://www.gatech.edu/word_html/**. Look for the download link to the file GT_HTML.ZIP.

Installation of GT_HTML is simple; just copy the template file GT_HMTL.DOT into your templates subdirectory for Word. If you activate the template when you open a new document in Word, you have the ability to add the two new toolbars shown in figure 12.2. To activate the toolbars, open the View menu and choose Toolbars. In the Toolbars dialog box, select the Toolbar 1 (Gt_html) and Toolbar 2 (Gt_html) check boxes.

GT_HTML toolbars

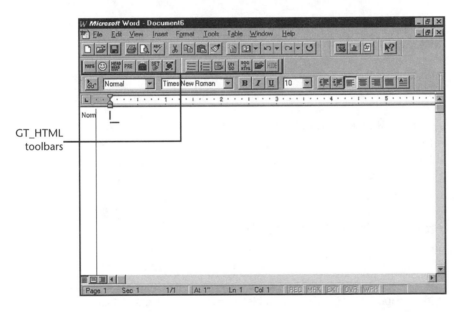

Fig. 12.2
When you install GT_HTML, you have the option of turning on two toolbars to help you edit HTML.

In addition to the two toolbars, GT_HTML adds HTML-related options to most of Word's pull-down menus. The new options appear at the bottom of each pull-down menu and start with the word "HTML." Since GT_HTML doesn't load a lot of styles into Word like CU_HTML does, most of your special formatting will be done using the new menu options.

III

Doing HTML

One of the more helpful menu options is the HTML Browser option under the File menu. Selecting this option opens the browser you want to work with GT_HTML. Having quick access to a browser while you edit makes it easier to test your documents as you develop them.

▶ See "Creating Forms," p. 395, to learn about the HTML tags used to create forms.

Another helpful menu option is the HTML Toolbox under the Tools menu. You can quickly insert tags for rules, titles, comments, centering and blinking text, and line breaks using selections from the Toolbox. The Toolbox also gives you a way to launch GT_HTML's handy HTML Form Creator and HTML Table Converter. The Forms Creator launches a second dialog box in which you can configure your form input fields, while the Table Converter will convert a simple Word table (no cell in the table spans more than one row or one column) to HTML format. Toolbox items are shown in figure 12.3.

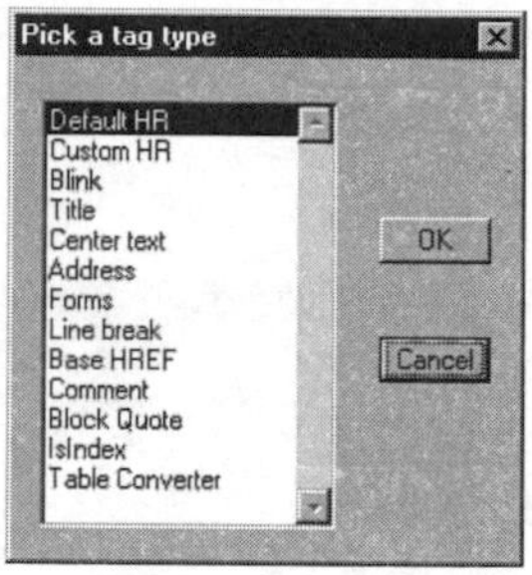

Fig. 12.3
GT_HTML's HTML Toolbox makes it easy to insert many types of HTML tags.

The Format menu includes options for formatting highlighted text as a heading, preformatted text, or a numbered or bulleted list. To apply bold, italics, and underline styles, you can use Word's normal formatting toolbar. GT_HTML converts these formats to HTML tags when it saves the HTML version of your document.

Quarterdeck WebAuthor 2.0

Quarterdeck recently released version 2.0 of its HTML editing plug-in for Word 6.0 called WebAuthor. WebAuthor 2.0 offers a number of enhancements over earlier versions, including new toolbars for text and paragraph formatting, support for HTML 3.0 and Netscape extensions, and faster importing and exporting of documents.

Note

Windows 95 and NT users should note that the current release of WebAuthor only works with Word 6.0 (a 16-bit application). Quarterdeck anticipates releasing a 32-bit version of WebAuthor 2.0 in early 1996. Consult the Quarterdeck Web site at **http://www.qdeck.com/** for the status of this release.

> **Note**
>
> The information in this section is based on the trialware version of WebAuthor 2.0. You can download the self-extracting archive containing the trialware files from Quarterdeck's Web site at **http://www.qdeck.com/**. You may evaluate the trialware version of WebAuthor 2.0 for 30 days, after which time the features that convert and save files to HTML will disable. If you choose to purchase the full WebAuthor package after the evaluation period, you will also get WebImage, a useful image editor and converter, and the Quarterdeck Mosaic browser. For current pricing information, consult Quarterdeck's Web site or contact their sales department at (800) 354-3222.

Getting Started

It's easy to install WebAuthor once you've downloaded the archive file. A standard install program will walk you through the installation steps and set up the Windows program group. Once WebAuthor is installed, you'll find an extra option under the Microsoft Word Tools menu (see fig. 12.4).

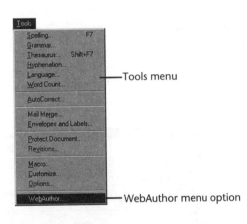

Tools menu

WebAuthor menu option

Fig. 12.4
Installing
WebAuthor 2.0
adds an HTML
Authoring option
to the Word Tools
menu.

III

Doing HTML

> **Note**
>
> WebAuthor places GIF images in your Windows document by converting the images to the Windows BMP format. When you access WebAuthor through the Tools menu, it checks to see if this converter has been installed. If you get a warning message telling you that your GIF graphics converter has not been installed, you'll need to run your Word Setup program to install it. The filter you want to install is the CompuServe GIF filter.

You activate WebAuthor's capabilities by selecting this new menu option. When you do, you're presented with a dialog box that gives you four options on how to proceed (see fig.12.5). You can Create a New HTML Document if you have yet to write any or you can Open/Import Existing Documents for Editing. Additionally, you can choose to Convert Existing Documents to HTML or Set/Change Options for Document Conversion to HTML.

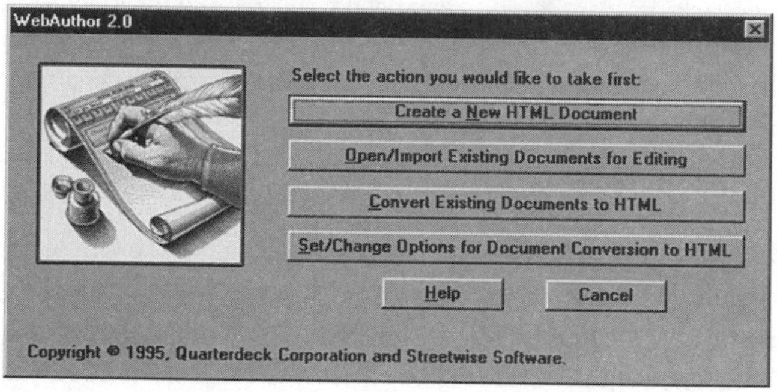

Fig. 12.5

WebAuthor gives you four different options when you activate it from the Word Tools menu.

Starting a New Document

If you choose to start a new document, WebAuthor immediately presents you with a dialog box where you can enter the document's title. If you want to specify other options in the document head, you can choose the Switch to Advanced dialog option. The resulting Document Parameters (Advanced) dialog box is shown in figure 12.6.

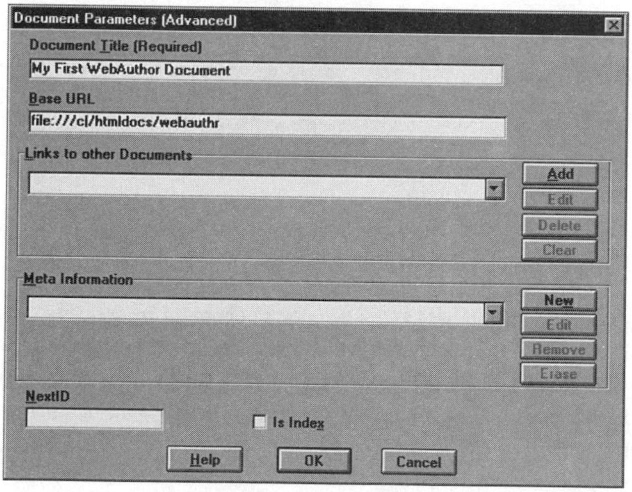

Fig. 12.6

When starting a new document, you can set any document head option in the Document Parameters (Advanced) dialog box.

Once you specify a title and other document head information, you'll see a screen like the one in figure 12.7. Note that WebAuthor adds an extra toolbar to your Word window. Buttons on this toolbar let you create new documents (Word and HTML), open files (with or without converting), save files (in Word and HTML formats), toggle to the Edit view where you can make changes to your document, format characters and lists, or activate one of WebAuthor's special function managers. The three buttons on the end of the toolbar, labeled "Char," "Para," and "Form," toggle additional toolbars on and off. Figure 12.7 shows the new toolbar with the additional three turned on.

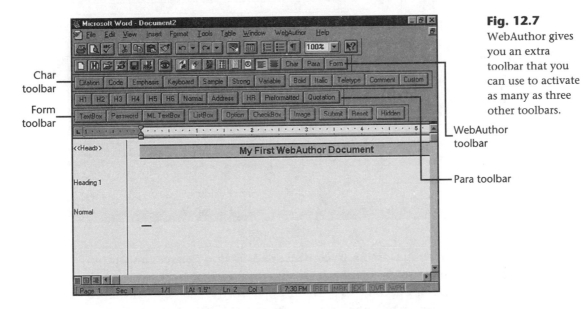

Char toolbar

Form toolbar

Fig. 12.7
WebAuthor gives you an extra toolbar that you can use to activate as many as three other toolbars.

WebAuthor toolbar

Para toolbar

The document view you see in figure 12.7 is called the Edit view. While in this view, you can make additions or changes to your document. The Toggle Document View button in the main WebAuthor toolbar switches you to a near-WYSIWYG view that gives you a sense of how your document might look on a browser screen. You can't make edits while you're in the near-WYSIWYG view, so be sure to toggle back to the Edit view to make changes.

Opening or Converting an Existing Document

If you choose to open or import an exiting HTML file, WebAuthor will look for documents that have the DOC, HTM, or RTF (Rich Text Format) extensions. Find the document you want and click on OK to load it. Figure 12.8 shows a previously created HTML document loaded into Word by WebAuthor.

III

Doing HTML

> **Tip**
>
> After you load a document, you may find that WebAuthor has placed a blank toolbar in your toolbar area. If so, find the Hide Blank Toolbar button at the left edge of the empty space and click it to recapture the space for your editing window.

Fig. 12.8
You can load existing Word, HTML, or Rich Text Format documents with WebAuthor.

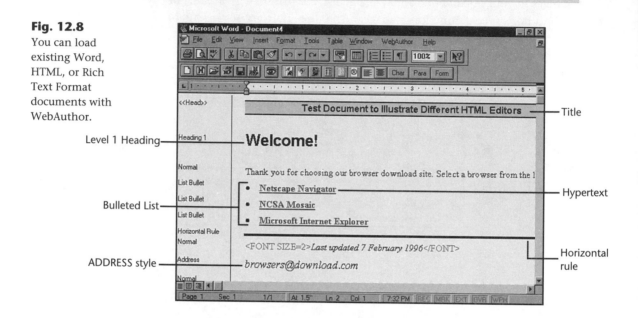

Converting Existing Documents and Setting Conversion Options

Another two choices you get when activating WebAuthor pertain to converting existing documents to HTML format. If you choose to convert an existing document, WebAuthor lets you select a Word (DOC) or Rich Text Format (RTF). Once you select the file, WebAuthor loads it into Word and then performs the conversion to HTML according to a set of customizable conversion options.

If you choose to set conversion options, you'll activate the Options File Editor. Selections under the Options menu in this program let you specify conversion parameters for logical and heading styles (Styles), physical styles (Direct Formatting), document head information (Document Information), hyperlinks (File Links), and tables (Tables). The Options File Editor with the File Links dialog box, which you activate through the Options File Editor, is shown in figure 12.9.

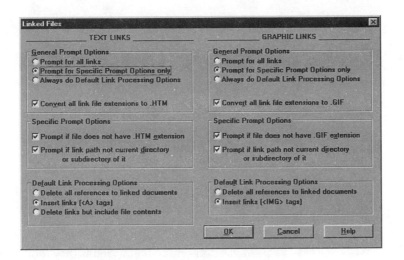

Fig. 12.9
The Options File Editor utility program lets you specify how WebAuthor should perform conversions to HTML from Word or RTF formats.

Editing Features of WebAuthor 2.0

Once you have started a new document or have loaded a new one, it's fairly easy to make edits using WebAuthor's many editing features. The extra "Char" and "Para" toolbars make it very easy to apply logical, physical, and heading styles to highlighted text. Buttons on the "Form" toolbar can be used to drop form elements wherever your cursor is positioned.

WebAuthor also gives you three different "managers" to assist you with placement of more complicated items. The Anchor Manager lets you specify an internal or external anchor to which a hypertext link can point. The Image Manager dialog box, shown in figure 12.10, prompts you for a GIF or JPEG file, the size of the image, how it should be aligned, and what alternative text should be used if the image is unavailable. The Form Manager walks you through a set of dialog boxes in which you indicate: what input fields should be used to build the form; the URL of the processing script; and how the form data should be sent to the script. Each of WebAuthor's special managers is accessible by a button on the main WebAuthor toolbar.

The List button on the main WebAuthor toolbar lets you create any one of the five types of HTML list. The Insert Symbol buttons gives you a dialog box full of special characters like copyright and trademark symbols and characters with diacritical marks.

III

Doing HTML

Fig. 12.10
WebAuthor's
Image Manager
prompts you for
the basic informa-
tion needed to
place an inline
image into your
document.

New Graphic Image	
Image Path	Select Graphic Image
file:///c|/images/logo.gif	
Height 365	Width 222
Alignment	Spacing from Text
left	Vertically 5
	Horizontally 5
Alternate Text	
Our Logo	
Help	OK	Cancel

Saving Documents in HTML Format

To save a document in HTML format, choose Save to HTML under the File menu or click the Save to HTML button on the main WebAuthor toolbar. If you save using an option other than these two, your document will be saved in Word format and it will not be suitable for transfer to your server.

Microsoft Internet Assistant for Word

Given the surge of HTML authoring add-ons for Word, it's no surprise that Microsoft itself has produced one. Internet Assistant for Word is a no-cost add-on that turns Word into a Web browser. It includes styles, toolbars, and tools for authoring HTML. Microsoft is also releasing Internet Assistant add ons for each of the Microsoft Office products. Currently, only Excel has been released, but by the time this book comes out others should be available. Look for the Assistants at Microsoft's Office Web site **http://www.microsoft.com/msoffice/**.

> **Note**
>
> The information in this section is based on beta release 4 of Internet Assistant version 2.0z. This beta was written to work with Word 7.0 in Windows 95 or with Word 6.0 in Windows NT. For the latest release and links to the downloadable file, direct your browser to **http://www.microsoft.com/msoffice/freestuf/msword/download/ia/default.htm**. Microsoft will also ship a copy on floppy disk to registered owners of Word for a shipping and handling charge of $5. Call (800) 426-9400.

After downloading the file, the installation of Internet Assistant is fairly easy. If you have installed a Microsoft program yourself, this process should be familiar. During the installation, you're given the option to make Internet Assistant your default HTML browser. If you choose to do this, the Internet Assistant add-on will be placed in your Word Startup directory. This causes Internet Assistant's functionality to be loaded each time you start Word.

> **Caution**
>
> Be sure to close all open Windows applications, especially Word, before you install
> Internet Assistant. This minimizes the risk of crashing your computer.

The Internet Assistant Web Browser

When you start Word with Internet Assistant installed, the only difference
you'll notice at first is the addition of the Switch to Web Browse View button
(see fig. 12.11). Clicking on this button takes you to the browser side of Word
that Internet Assistant creates. As you can see in figure 12.12, the Word
browser has most of the usual features found in other popular browsers including forward and backward navigation buttons, reload and stop buttons,
and the ability to store the URLs of your favorite sites (Favorites). To return to
the Word editing window, you can click on the Switch to Edit View button.

Switch to
Web Browse
View button

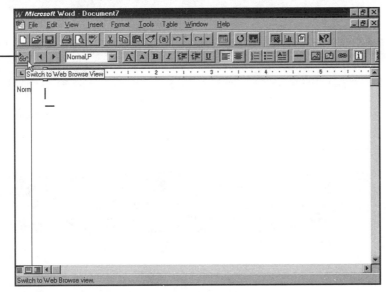

Fig. 12.11
The Switch to Web
Browse View
button activates
the Web browser
features included
as part of Internet
Assistant.

III

Doing HTML

Loading and Editing Documents

When you start a new document, you will find that you have access to a new
template called HTML.DOT. This template provides an extensive set of HTML
styles and additional menu options and toolbars to support HTML authoring.
Figure 12.13 illustrates the modified toolbars. If you want to edit an existing
HTML document, Word will automatically open the HTML template when
you select a document with an HTM extension.

Fig. 12.12
The Word Web browser supports most popular browser features for navigation and bookmarking.

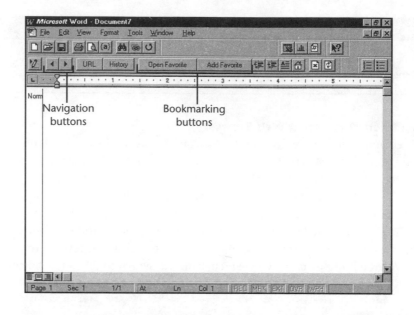

Note

In the figure, both the Standard and Formatting toolbars are open. Keep in mind that you can customize these toolbars, like all of the toolbars in Word. You can add buttons and rearrange their order; your toolbars may look different, therefore, than those shown in figure 12.13.

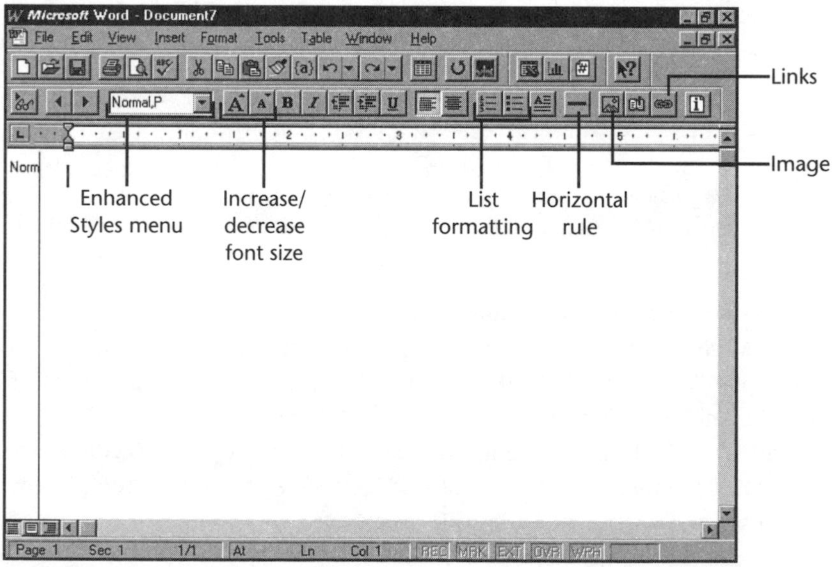

Fig. 12.13
Starting a new document with Internet Assistant's HTML template modifies Word's Standard and Formatting toolbars.

As you type in the text of your Web page, you can mark it for specific text effects, such as bold or italic, using the standard Word tools. Word automatically translates those effects into HTML tags. You can also format text in HTML modes, such as Strong or Preformatted, by using the styles available under the HTML template. You can select a style using the Styles tool in the formatting toolbar, or you can open the Format menu and choose either Style or Style Gallery.

Internet Assistant also provides a way to place special codes such as diacritical marks, copyright and trademark symbols, or other special punctuation. To access these special characters, open the Insert menu and choose the Symbol option. A dialog box with listings of special characters appears. Double-clicking a specific character places it in the text where the I-beam cursor is located.

Handling HTML Codes Not Supported by Internet Assistant

There are also several HTML tags and effects that Internet Assistant does not accommodate through styles or tools. To enter these additional tags (or any extra HTML code), open the Insert Menu and choose HTML Markup. A dialog box with a large window for entering direct HTML code appears (see fig. 12.14). The entered text is handled and displayed as HTML code without ever being translated into Word format. This feature is nice because it lets you include newly introduced HTML tags in your document, although you do have to type out the tags yourself.

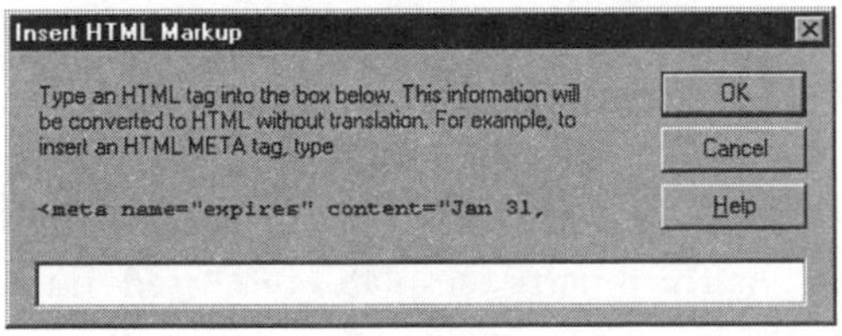

Fig. 12.14
Internet Assistant's Insert HTML Markup dialog box lets you enter unsupported HTML tags.

Creating Forms Using Internet Assistant

Internet Assistant has some fairly extensive features for creating HTML forms. You can begin a form by opening the Insert menu and choosing the Form Field option. This causes Internet Assistant to enter the HTML tags that surround a form. The Form Field dialog box and Forms floating tool palette are shown in figure 12.15.

▶ To learn about the tags used to produce HTML forms, see "Creating Forms," p. 395.

III

Doing HTML

Fig. 12.15
Internet Assistant
provides extensive
support for
creating HTML
forms.

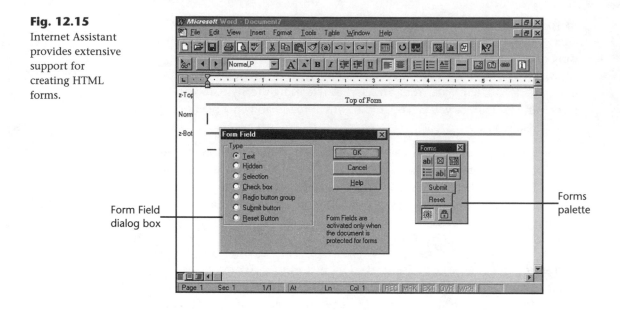

Form Field
dialog box

Forms
palette

If you've created forms in Microsoft Access, you may recognize the look of some of these form tools. The Forms tool palette gives you point-and-click access to creating check boxes, pull-down list boxes, radio buttons, and text boxes. This palette also provides standard Submit and Reset buttons. When you place a field in the form area, additional dialog boxes open to help you create the necessary choices for a pull-down list box or other controls to help make the form work.

Saving Documents in HTML Format

Internet Assistant for Word saves documents in HTML format by default. The resulting document is then ready to be used on your Web server. This is a contrast to many of the third-party templates discussed in this chapter, which require a special File menu option to save your document in ASCII format.

HTML Editors

Beyond the templates for word processors, some stand-alone editors are designed completely for the purpose of authoring HTML documents. Many of the initial versions of these products have been re-released in "professional" versions that offer souped-up editing capabilities for people who do large amounts of commercial HTML editing. This section covers some of the more popular stand-alone HTML editors available.

Netscape Navigator Gold

After setting the standard for browser software, Netscape has taken its browser a step further by adding document editing features. Packaged under the name Netscape Navigator Gold, the browser/editor combination provides a What-You-See-Is-What-You-Get (WYSIWYG) editing environment. What's more, with Navigator Gold, you can create a Web document *without ever seeing an HTML tag!*

> **Note**
>
> The following information on Netscape Navigator Gold is based on the first public beta release of the software. When the final version of the software is released, a license will cost $79.00. For the most recent information on Navigator Gold, visit Netscape's Web site at **http://home.netscape.com/**.

Getting Started

There are two ways to get started editing a document in Navigator Gold. The first is to load a document into the browser and then switch to the editor. What you see in the editor window will look exactly like what's in the browser window, except that you can make changes to the version in the editor window. Figures 12.16 and 12.17 show the same document in the browser and editor windows, respectively. Notice how little difference there is between them.

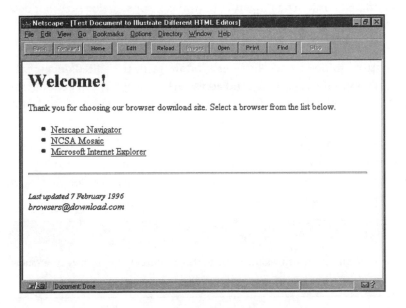

Fig. 12.16
A sample document loaded into the Navigator Gold browser.

III

Doing HTML

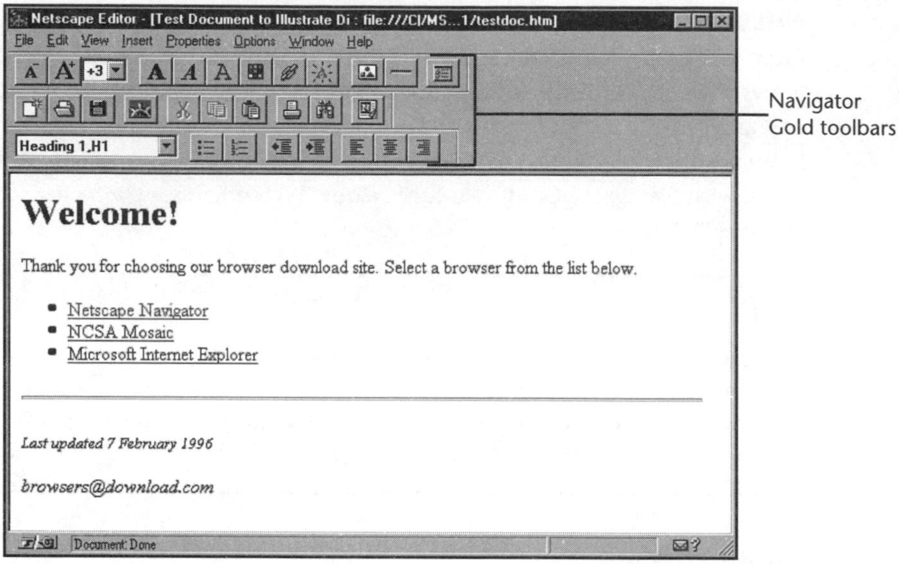

Fig. 12.17
The same sample
document loaded
into the Navigator
Gold editor.

Navigator
Gold toolbars

Navigator Gold Toolbars

One thing that is fundamentally different in the editor window is the presence of three toolbars to assist you with your authoring tasks. Most of the buttons in the top toolbar are for formatting text at the font level. You can increase or decrease font size, set the font color, and apply bold, italic, and fixed-width styles. Other buttons let you set up links, place an image, or insert a horizontal rule. The Properties button calls up a dialog box that details the attributes of a selected item and lets you change them if needed.

The middle toolbar handles common file and editing operations. It also provides buttons to open a new browser window, print the edited document, search for a specific text string, and access the Netscape Web Page Starter—a new feature on Netscape's Web site with links to several HTML authoring resources.

Items on the bottom toolbar are for the purpose of formatting text. A pull-down menu lists several styles you can apply to highlighted text. Other buttons let you format ordered and unordered lists, increase or decrease indent levels, and specify left, right, and center alignments.

Note

Depending on your screen width, Navigator Gold's toolbar buttons may be arranged differently from how you see them in figure 12.17.

Opening and Editing a Document

Once you've opened a document by either loading what's in your browser window into the editor or by starting a new one, editing the document becomes almost like using a word processor. Applying a style is just a matter of highlighting the text to be formatted and choosing a style from the pull-down menu or from a toolbar button. You can move images, links, and rules around by simply clicking and holding them, dragging them to where you want them to be, and then releasing your mouse button. This drag-and-drop feature of Navigator Gold makes it easy to place these items exactly where you want them.

Along with the toolbars in the editor window, you also pick up two new menus in your menu bar. The Insert menu lets you place new links, images, rules, line breaks, and non-breaking spaces into your document. Many of these options call up a dialog box in which you can specify the different attributes of the item you're placing. Figure 12.18 shows the dialog box for inserting an image. Note how the information you're asked for in the dialog box directly corresponds to the different attributes of the <IMG ...> tag.

Fig. 12.18
When inserting a new image into a Navigator Gold document, you can specify the attributes of the image in this dialog box.

The other new menu is the Properties menu. The different options under Properties let you review and change properties at the font, character, list, paragraph, and document levels.

Perhaps the most curious thing about the Navigator Gold editor is that there is no sign of any HTML tags. You don't see them on-screen and there are no menu options or toolbar buttons that explicitly refer to them. As you read

III

Doing HTML

about other HTML editors, you'll see that many of them make explicit mention of tags. Because they do this, the people who use them have to know at least *some* HTML. With Navigator Gold, you could theoretically *not know a single HTML tag* and still be able to author a Web document! The upshot of this is that Navigator Gold will make Web publishing accessible to a much larger group of people. Whether this is beneficial or not remains to be seen.

Publishing Your Documents

In the shipping version of Navigator Gold, you'll be able to publish your finished document right to a Web server with the press of a single button. Navigator Gold will write the HTML file and then transfer it and any necessary image files to the destination server. This saves you from having to save and FTP all of the files by yourself.

HoTMetaL 2.0

WebmasterCD

If your objective is to write nearly perfect HTML on the first try, you should look into HoTMetaL 2.0 from SoftQuad. There are two versions of HoTMetaL 2.0 available. HoTMetaL FREE 2.0 is intended for use in academe and for internal business purposes. Commercial users are required to purchase HoTMetaL PRO 2.0. When you pay for a license, you also get technical support and some features that are not active in the freeware version, including a spell checker, thesaurus, and user-defined macro capability.

> **Note**
>
> This review of HoTMetaL 2.0 is based on HoTMetaL FREE 2.0, which you can download by visiting **http://www.sq.com/products/hotmetal/hm_ftp.htm**. The features discussed here are also available in the PRO version, along with the added functionality noted above.

Getting Started

When you open a new document in HoTMetaL, you see the window shown in figure 12.19. The figure shows HoTMetaL's standard document template which is stored in the file TUTOR.HTM. Notice that the tags in the template are easy to pick out, with starting and ending tags both pointing inward toward the text they contain. Also notice that the template is very complete. All of the tags that are technically required are present, including <HTML>, <HEAD>, <TITLE>, <BODY>, and their corresponding closing tags.

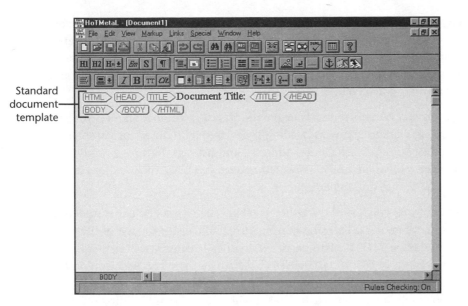

Standard
document
template

Fig. 12.19
HoTMetaL's
standard document
template is in
proper HTML form
and encourages
you to title your
document
immediately.

The completeness of HoTMetaL's default template points to one of the
program's strengths: it forces you to use good HTML. HoTMetaL's Rules
Checking feature makes it almost impossible to insert an inappropriate tag
into your document. When Rules Checking is on, the tag insert features of
HoTMetaL are context-sensitive and you are limited to inserting only those
tags that are legal at the current cursor position. For example, if you were inside the <DL> and </DL> tags, you could only insert <DT> and </DT> tags or
<DD> and </DD> tags. HoTMetaL prevents you from inserting other tags by
graying them out or by just not presenting them.

> **Tip**
>
> Rules Checking can be annoying if you're a seasoned pro who has developed a par-
> ticular authoring style. You can turn Rules Checking off or on by pressing Ctrl+K.

In addition to Rules Checking, HoTMetaL also comes with an SGML validator
that tests your document for conformance to the rules of proper HTML.
These features make HoTMetaL a great choice for the HTML beginner since
they encourage good authoring habits right from the start.

The HoTMetaL Toolbars

HoTMetaL provides three toolbars to assist with typical editing tasks. The
Standard Toolbar is at the top and provides buttons for frequently used file

(New, Open, Save) and editing (Cut, Copy, Paste) operations. Other buttons support searching the document (Find, Find Next), showing, hiding, inserting, and removing HTML tags, and activating the SGML validator. In the freeware version of HoTMetaL, the buttons to activate the Spell Checker and Thesaurus are grayed out.

The Common HTML Toolbar is below the Standard Toolbar and lets you quickly tag markup text with heading styles, frequently used logical styles (Emphasis, Strong, Block Quote, Address), and list tags. Buttons toward the end of the toolbar are not style-related and let you place images, horizontal rules, line breaks, and hyperlinks.

At the bottom, you'll find the Other Toolbar. The Other Toolbar is something of a concession on HoTMetaL's part because it allows for the use of the extensions to standard HTML. This becomes significant when you consider that earlier versions of HoTMetaL refused to recognize these tags and wouldn't even *open* documents that contained them! The HTML extensions are accessible on a pull-down menu that you see when clicking and holding on the HTML Extensions button. Other such pull-down menus give you quick access to tags for the document head, computer-related logical styles (Code, Keyboard, Variable, Sample), compact list tags, and form tags. You can also mark up text with physical styles using buttons in the Other Toolbar. Pressing the Special Characters button produces the floating palette you see in figure 12.20. This palette is handy when coding multilingual pages as it lets you place special characters by pointing to and clicking on them, rather than having to remember the escape sequence of the character. To close the special characters palette, just double-click the button at the upper left-hand corner of the palette.

Note

You can suppress the display of any of the HoTMetaL toolbars by choosing the Toolbars option under the View menu.

Opening and Editing a Document

Figure 12.21 shows part of an HTML document open in the HoTMetaL window. Note how *all* tags—even tags such as <HR> and <BR>, which ordinarily occur by themselves—have a closing tag. You can also get a greater sense of HoTMetaL's tolerance for non-standard HTML tags since it let us load a document that contained <FONT SIZE=-2> and </FONT> tags.

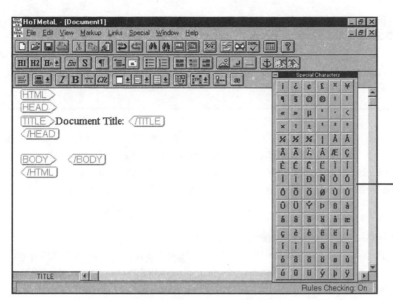

Fig. 12.20
The floating Special Characters palette makes placing foreign language characters as easy as pointing and clicking.

Special Characters palette

Fig. 12.21
Unlike its predecessors, HoTMetaL 2.0 lets you load documents with non-standard HTML tags.

As you edit the document, you'll notice that HoTMetaL treats tag pairs as a single unit. If you delete one tag in the pair, its companion tag and all of the text between them is deleted as well. This is helpful in that it saves you some keystrokes and provides an almost iron-clad guarantee that there will be no stray tags floating around in your document.

> **Caution**
>
> When you delete a tag pair, you also delete all text that appears between the two tags. Make sure you cut and paste this text to another position in your document if you don't want to lose it.

When it's time to insert a tag, choose the Insert Element option under the Markup menu. You can then choose the tag you want to insert from the dialog box that appears. Remember that if Rules Checking is on, you'll be restricted to inserting only those tags that are legal at that point in the document.

Publishing Your Documents

The Publish option under the Links menu is handy if you've developed the pages for a site with all hyperlinks pointing to files on your local hard drive and you need to change those URLs once you place the documents on your server. Once you've validated and saved your documents, you can use the Publish option to prepare your documents for life on the Web server. The Publish dialog box lets you do a search for all URLs that start with the file: protocol and replace them with URLs that start with http:. This dialog box is shown in figure 12.22.

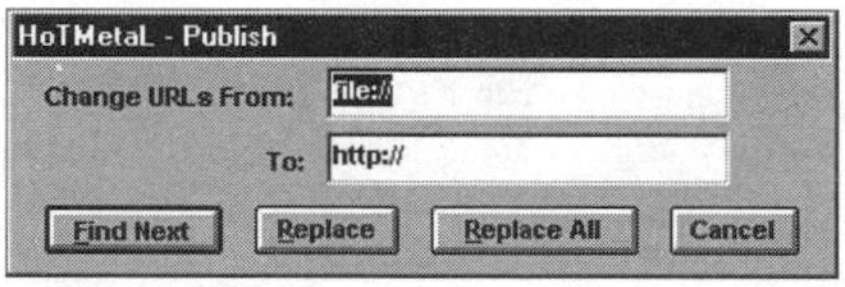

Fig. 12.22
The Publish feature allows you to convert URLs in documents to URLs appropriate for a Web server.

HTMLEd Pro

Hailing from Canada, HTMLEd Pro is the commercial version of the HTMLEd editor that has been around for a few years. Both programs are produced by Internet Software Technologies.

> **Note**
>
> The information about HTMLEd Pro presented here is based on the demo copy of version 1.1. You can download the most recent version from Internet Software Technologies by visiting **http://www.ist.ca/htmledpro/index.html**. If you choose to buy HTMLEd Pro, the license will set you back US$99.95 plus US$10 for shipping and handling.

Getting Started

Just starting up HTMLEd Pro leaves you with an empty editing window. You need to start a new document to activate most of the program's toolbars (which HTMLEd Pro calls *speedbars*) and menu options. When you choose the New option under the File menu, you are presented with a dialog box that lets you set up a basic template for your new document. Check boxes in the dialog box let you include <HTML>, <HEAD>, <BODY>, and corresponding closing tags. You can also specify your document's title and include comments to indicate that you wrote the document and the date you started it. Once you've filled in the dialog box and clicked OK, you'll see a screen much like the one in figure 12.23. Notice that once the new document is open, HTMLEd Pro's speedbars are no longer grayed out and many new items appear in the menu bar.

> **Note**
>
> You can also choose to create a new document with a custom template of your own design. Just select the New with Document Template option under the File menu.

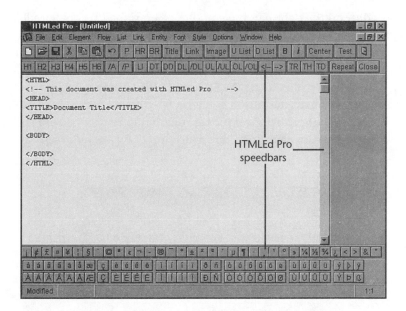

Fig. 12.23
Starting a new document in HTMLEd Pro activates the program's speedbars and menu options.

HTMLEd Pro Speedbars

One of the first things you notice about HTMLEd Pro is all of its speedbars. There are five across the width of the screen and you can even put one down the right-hand side! You can toggle the display of each speedbar on or off under the Options menu.

III

Doing HTML

When all speedbars are displayed, the topmost one is the Standard Speedbar. Buttons on this speedbar handle the most frequently used options like file and editing operations, paragraph and line breaks, horizontal rules, placing images, setting up hyperlinks, formatting unordered and definition lists, centering text, and applying bold and italics styles.

Just below the Standards Speedbar is the Common Tags Speedbar. Here you'll find many of the tags you use most, like heading styles, list and table tags, and tags for creating comments. The closing tags of many popular tag pairs are also available.

The first of the three speedbars at the bottom of the window is the Extended Characters speedbar. Placing any of the characters in this speedbar is as easy as clicking its button. This relieves you from having to remember or look up the escape sequences to produce these characters.

The other two speedbars along the bottom are the Special Characters speedbars. The two are essentially identical with the upper bar supporting the lowercase versions of characters in the lower bar. If you're editing other-than-English language HTML, you'll want to have these two speedbars active.

The speedbar on the right-hand side of the screen is the Custom Speedbar. Each button in this bar is custom-designed by you. To place a button on the bar, right-click your mouse while it is pointing to an empty spot on the bar and choose New Button. Once you've placed the button, you can right-click again and choose Modify to get the Custom Button dialog box (see fig. 12.24). Next, highlight the button you wish to edit, and then select the Edit button. Custom buttons are great for tag combinations, such as bold and italics, that would otherwise require the application of two or more separate styles.

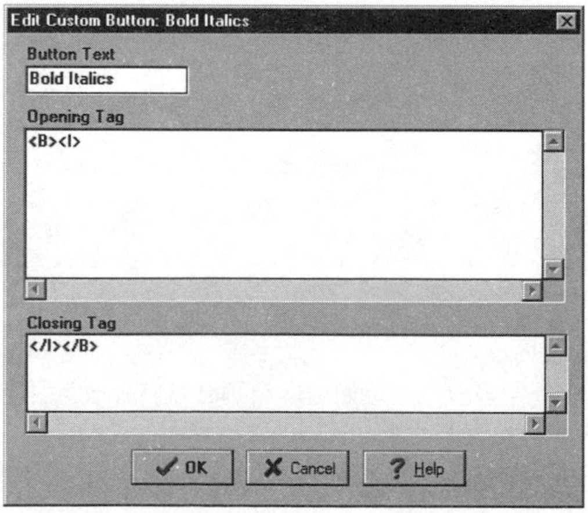

Fig. 12.24

You can customize buttons on HTMLEd Pro's Custom speedbar.

Opening and Editing Documents

Once you have a document open, HTMLEd Pro provides extensive support for inserting tags and marking up text through a large number of pull-down menus. HTMLEd Pro supports all of the tags proposed in HTML 3.0 and many of the Netscape extensions to HTML.

Most of the text formatting styles are found under the Font or Style menus. Specifically, the Font menu lets you apply any of the physical text styles and gives you access to the <FONT ...> and <BASEFONT ...> tags. The Style menu is home to the heading styles and the logical text styles.

Under the Element menu, you'll find options to activate HTMLEd Pro's Table Designer and Form Designer. The Table Designer makes it easy to set up a simple table of any number of rows or columns and to place headers and data in each of the table's cells. The Form Designer, shown in figure 12.25, is particularly nice because it lets you drag-and-drop form elements around on a blank worksheet. Click OK when you're done to place the appropriate HTML in your document.

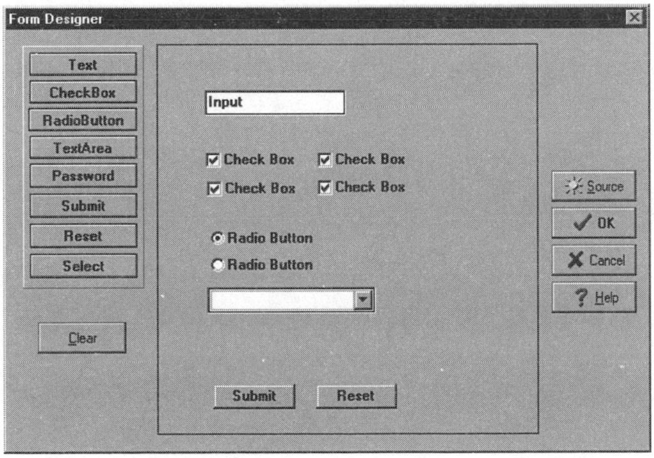

Fig. 12.25
HTMLEd Pro's Form Designer lets you drag-and-drop form elements on a blank page.

If you or a friend needs to get a home page up quickly, the HTML Page Builder under the Options menu is probably the way to go. The Page Builder "interviews" you over a series of several dialog boxes and composes a home page based on your responses. One of the Page Builder's dialog boxes appears in figure 12.26.

You can further customize the editing environment by defining your own Quick Keys under the Quick Keys tab of the Preferences dialog box located under the Options menu. Rather than typing the same text in over and over, you can store frequently repeated text under one of the Quick Keys and save your fingers the extra effort.

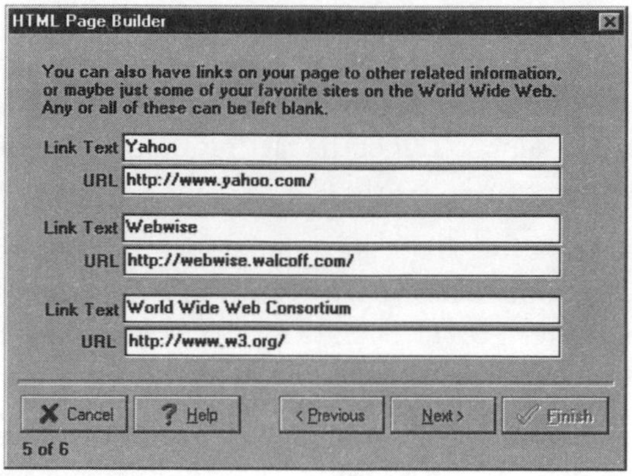

Fig. 12.26
The HTMLEd Pro HTML Page Builder "interviews" you and creates a personal home page based on your responses.

Publishing Your Documents

When you save your documents, you can choose a DOS or UNIX (no carriage returns) file format. If your documents need to end up on a remote server, you can choose the Save Remote option under the File menu to save directly to that server using the FTP protocol.

You can also save a document without HTML tags. This option is useful when you've downloaded an HTML file and just want the plain-text content of the document. By saving the document without the HTML tags, you automatically strip out the HTML, leaving just a text file.

HotDog Pro

HotDog Pro is a popular new HTML editor from Sausage Software in Australia. You have to pay to license the commercial version, but there is a freeware version (just called HotDog) available as well.

> **Note**
>
> The following information on HotDog Pro is based on the fully functional demo that you can find bundled with the WebQuest software. You can also download it from Sausage Software's Web site at **http://www.sausage.com/**. You have 30 days to review the demo. After that, you can pay US$99.95 to license HotDog Pro or let the demo expire. If you choose to pay for a license, Sausage Software will send you a registration number by e-mail, saving you shipping and handling charges.

Getting Started

When you first start HotDog Pro, you see the screen shown in figure 12.27. Note that HotDog Pro gives you a standard document template, complete with <HTML>, <HEAD>, <TITLE>, and <BODY> tags, without having to start a new document. You can create and save your own custom templates in HotDog Pro, but you'll need to choose the New option under the File menu to load them.

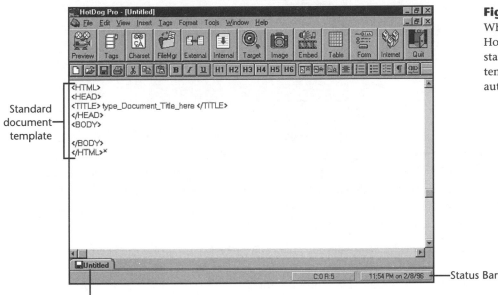

Standard document template

Documents Bar

Status Bar

HotDog Pro Toolbars

HotDog Pro has two toolbars at the top of the editing window and two informational bars at the bottom of the window. The topmost toolbar, shown in figure 12.27 with buttons containing both text and icons, is called the Button Bar. The buttons on the Button Bar are preconfigured to perform the tasks you will probably do most often when editing HTML. However, it is very easy to customize the Button Bar to your own editing habits. Choose the Customize Button Bar option under the Tools menu to open the dialog box shown in figure 12.28. In the dialog box, you can remove buttons from the bar by dragging them to the trash or add a new button to the bar by specifying the text label, icon, tool tip, and function of the new button.

Tip

You can reduce the amount of space the Button Bar takes up by changing them to "text only" buttons. This is done on the Display tab of the Options dialog box. You can shut off the Button Bar, as well as any other toolbar or informational bar, under the View menu.

III

Doing HTML

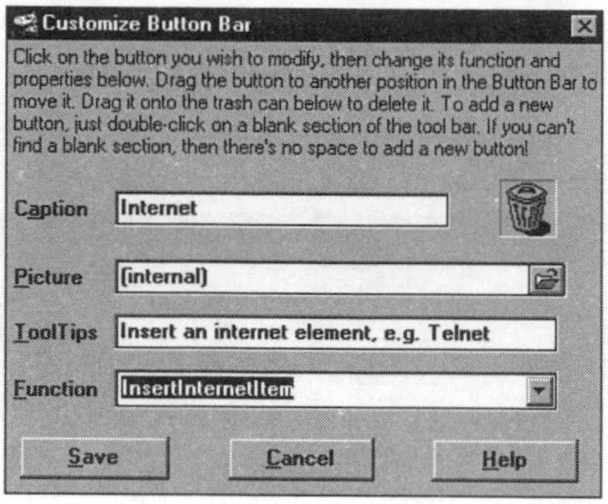

Fig. 12.28
You can remove buttons from the Button Bar or add your own custom buttons.

Immediately below the Button Bar is the Elements Bar. This toolbar has significantly smaller buttons than the Button Bar, but it provides you with single-click access to a large number of program options. Buttons on the Elements bar let you do common file and editing operations, apply physical or heading styles, align text after an image, create a list, insert a paragraph or line break, or place a horizontal rule very quickly.

The first informational bar is immediately below the horizontal scrollbar in figure 12.27. This bar is called the Documents Bar. A different tab, much like the tabs you see at the bottom of an Excel workspace to denote the different spreadsheets in the space, shows up on the bar for each document you have open. HotDog Pro lets you save multiple files together in what's called a *project*. Opening or saving a project opens or save each file contained in the project. This is a handy feature because the sites you develop are not likely to be comprised of just one page. You'll author many pages in creating a site and HotDog Pro's project capability is a great way to keep track of them all. The Project Manager, accessible under the File menu, lets you perform different tests on documents in a project and prints a report for you when the tests are complete.

Directly below the Documents Bar is the Status Bar. The Status Bar lets you know what the program is doing at any point and provides time and date information as well.

Opening and Editing Documents

You open documents in HotDog Pro with the Open option of the File menu. A new twist is that you can open multiple files at once from the Open File dialog box.

Once you're editing, HotDog Pro supplies you with lots of helpful editing tools. The Tags and Entity palettes are shown in figure 12.29. You can select and insert just about any piece of HTML markup you'll ever need from these two palettes. If a palette with the complete list of HTML tags is too much to scroll through, you can use options under the Tags menu to call up smaller versions of the palette that have similar tags grouped together. For example, the Graphics palette contains the <IMG ...> and <FIG ...> tags, along with standard and extended attributes for each. The Entity palette is useful when you have a lot of special characters in your document.

> ### Tip
>
> You can activate the Tags or Entity palettes quickly by pressing the F6 or F7 keys, respectively.

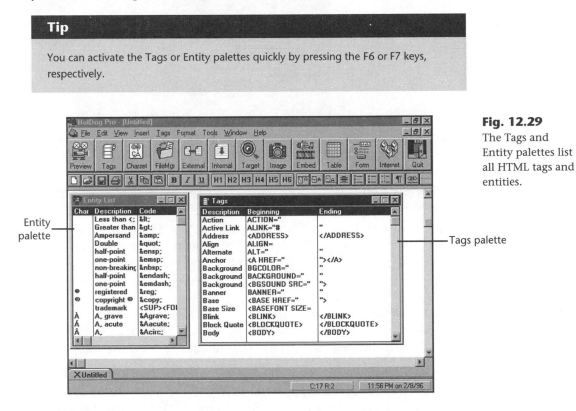

Entity palette

Tags palette

Fig. 12.29
The Tags and Entity palettes list all HTML tags and entities.

Options under the Insert menu use easy-to-follow dialog boxes to guide you through the insertion of complicated tags and tag sequences. The Insert List dialog box is shown in figure 12.30. Notice the options to create unordered, ordered, definition, and plain lists, as well as fields for entering a heading, specifying the bullet character, and making the list compact. Other options under the Insert menu let you insert embedded program items and marquees (a Microsoft Internet Explorer extension to HTML).

If you find you're performing a certain operation frequently and there is no shortcut key for that operation, you can define your own shortcut key in the Shortcut Keys dialog box (choose Tools, Shortcut Keys).

III

Doing HTML

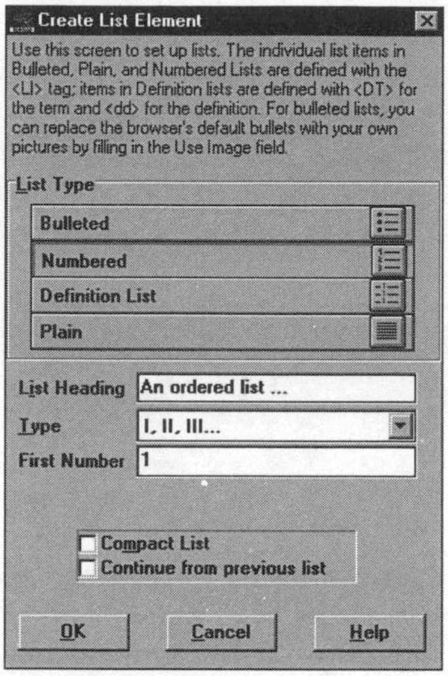

Fig. 12.30
Dialog boxes accessible from the Insert menu guide you through the placement of complex HTML tags.

Caution

If you define a shortcut key that HotDog Pro assigns to another operation at startup, your definition will override the startup definition. However, the shortcut key will continue to appear next to the operation to which it was originally assigned.

Publishing Your Documents

Once you're done editing, you should spell check your document and validate the HTML. HotDog Pro can do both with options under the Tools menu.

After you make these checks on your document, you'll want to look at them in a browser to see how they appear on-screen. If you don't want to open a separate browser program to do this, you can try HotDog Pro's Real-time Output ViewER (ROVER) to test your document. Figure 12.31 shows the HotDog Pro editing window with a ROVER window open below it. The ROVER window provides a near-WYSIWYG display of how your document will look.

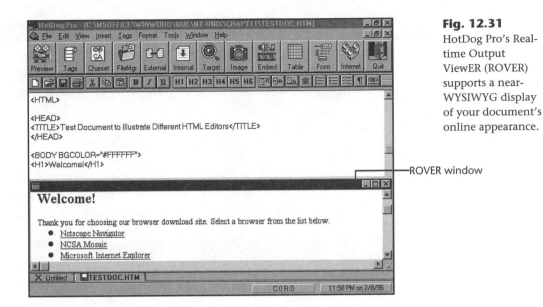

Fig. 12.31
HotDog Pro's Real-time Output ViewER (ROVER) supports a near-WYSIWYG display of your document's online appearance.

ROVER window

Kenn Nesbitt's WebEdit

WebEdit is another Windows-based text editor designed to ease the editing of HTML documents. Specifically, WebEdit includes support for every feature of every version of the HTML specification, from HTML 1.0 through the current draft specification for HTML 3.0, including optional features and special non-standard extensions supported by browsers such as Netscape. The latest version also includes the new HTML extensions defined by Netscape 2.0 and Microsoft's Internet Explorer 2.0. Moreover, WebEdit makes all of these features available in a consistent, well-organized fashion, with a minimum number of keystrokes, allowing you to create HTML documents rapidly.

WebmasterCD

> **Note**
>
> This section on WebEdit is based on the shareware version of WebEdit 1.4b that is included on the CD-ROM or that you can download from Nesbitt Software's Web site. The URL is **http://www.nesbitt.com/**. You have 30 days to use the software. After that, the commercial license is US$79.95 and the educational license is US$39.95. When you pay for the license, Nesbitt Software will send you a registration number by e-mail, saving you shipping and handling charges. Some of the advanced features are disabled in the demo version and are only available in the "unlocked" version.

III

Doing HTML

Caution

The 16-bit version of WebEdit can only handle files the size of 64K or less. Windows 95 and Windows NT users will be pleased to know that a 32-bit version of WebEdit is scheduled for release on April 1, 1996. The 32-bit version will be able to handle files of any size.

Getting Started

When WebEdit starts, it creates a new HTML file without any HTML tags. To add all the basic structural HTML tags simply click on the + (plus sign) and they are added to the blank file. The resulting screen is shown in figure 12.32.

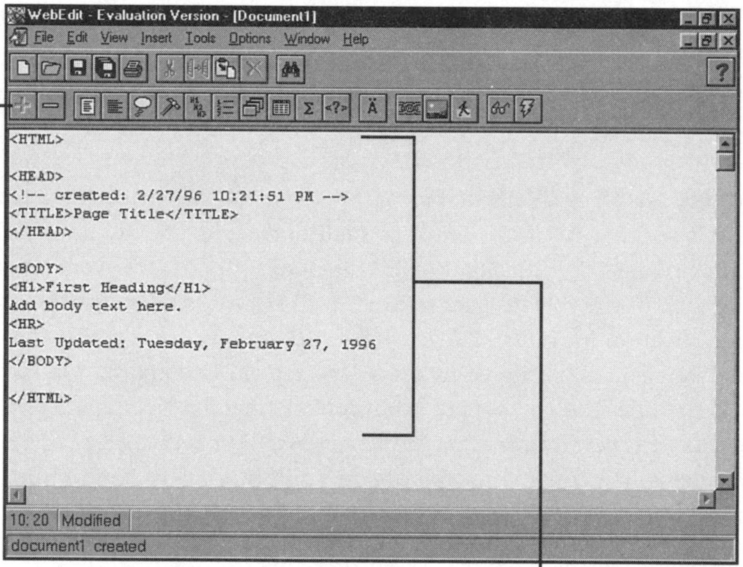

Fig. 12.32
The Plus (+) button on the WebEdit toolbar automatically places document structure tags into a blank file.

Plus button

Template created by clicking the Plus (+) button

If this is your first time creating a page, WebEdit includes a Home Page Wizard. The Home Page Wizard allows you to create a simple home page with colored or textured backgrounds, inline images, a paragraph of text, links to other sites and pages, and contact information. Figure 12.33 shows one of the Home Page Wizard's dialog boxes.

WebEdit Toolbars

Figure 12.33 also shows the two toolbars WebEdit provides for quick access to frequently used program functions. Buttons on the top toolbar are primarily for common file (New, Open, Save, Save All, Print) and editing (Cut, Copy, Paste, Delete, Find) operations.

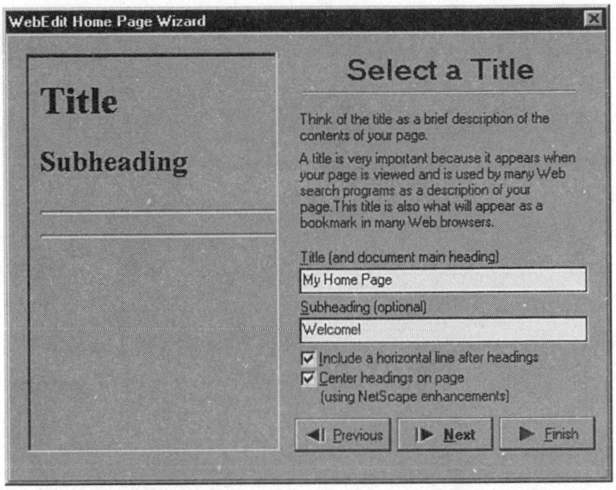

Fig. 12.33
WebEdit's Home Page Wizard authors a custom home page for you based on information it collects over a series of dialog boxes.

Buttons on the lower toolbar are for more HTML specific functions. You've already seen how the Plus button works to place document structure tags into a document. The corresponding Minus (-) button removes all HTML tags from a highlighted portion of the file. Following the Plus and Minus buttons are ten buttons that give you access to practically any HTML tag you might need. Clicking any of the first nine of these buttons produces a drop-down list with the tags available under that button. Figure 12.34 shows the tags available under the List and Misc Tags button. Other buttons play host to document structure, block style, logical style, physical style, heading style, form, table, and math tags.

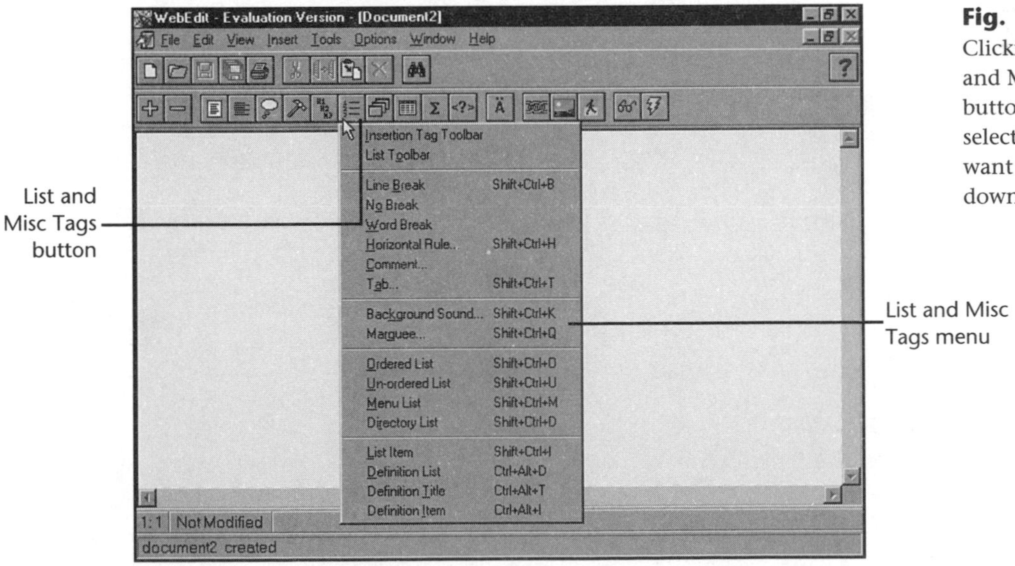

Fig. 12.34
Clicking the List and Misc Tags button lets you select the tag you want from a drop-down list.

List and Misc Tags button

List and Misc Tags menu

Doing HTML

> **Caution**
>
> WebEdit has floating toolbars corresponding to each of the drop-down boxes. However, these toolbars are locked until you enter your registration code, so don't try to activate them until after you have entered your code.

The remaining buttons on the lower toolbar allow you to define custom tags, to gain access to a special characters sets, and to place hyperlinks, images, and figures into your documents. The two buttons on the end each provide a different way to look at the documents you have under development. The View Document with Browser button fires up whatever browser you've selected to work with WebEdit and the Quick Preview button activates WebEdit's Quick Preview feature (see fig. 12.35). Quick Preview splits the screen in half and allows you to see the HTML source code on the left-hand side and what the document might look like on a browser on the right-hand side.

> **Note**
>
> WebEdit's Quick Preview feature can only handle HTML tags up through those in the HTML 2.0 specification, even though the program provides full support for HTML tags from the HTML 3.0 and Netscape and Microsoft extensions to HTML.

Fig. 12.35
WebEdit's Quick Preview gives you a quasi-WYSIWYG display of your documents.

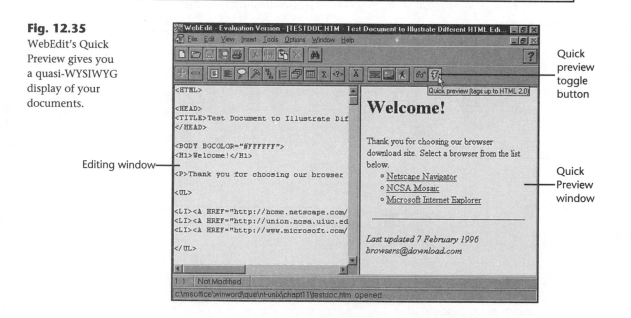

Editing window

Quick preview toggle button

Quick Preview window

WebEdit Editing Features

Apart from its very thorough support of most HTML tags, WebEdit offers other features that make HTML authoring easier. WebEdit uses extensive dialog boxes to walk you through the placement of links, images, figures, forms, and tables in your documents. Input fields in these dialog boxes let you specify any or all of the attributes you might put into the HTML tags that place these items. WebEdit also features a near-WYSIWYG Table Builder that lets you compose a table right on-screen. The Table Builder dialog box is shown in figure 12.36.

Fig. 12.36
The WebEdit Table Builder allows you to create a table right in the dialog box.

If you're putting imagemaps on your pages, you can use WebEdit's Map Builder to define the hot regions and their associated URLs. To activate the Map Builder, click the Use Mapping check box you see in the Image dialog box and then click the Map Builder button. The Map Builder supports both server-side and client-side imagemaps.

If you like to use color in your Web pages, you probably know the frustration of having to find out the Red/Green/Blue (RGB) codes for the color and then having to convert those numbers to hexadecimal (base 16) so you can specify the color in your HTML code. Using the Hexadecimal Color Value option under the Insert menu, you can choose the color you want from either a preconfigured or custom color palette. Once you choose the color and click on OK, WebEdit converts the decimal RGB values to hexadecimal and places the hexadecimal triplet for the color right into your document.

III

Doing HTML

Publishing Your Documents

Once you have created your document, you should proofread them. WebEdit helps with this process by including spellcheckers for multiple languages.

Note

The spellcheck feature is locked until you purchase your license and enter your registration code.

Once your documents are spellchecked, you can save them individually (Save) or all at once (Save All). The Export option under the File menu lets you export the files in either UNIX or Macintosh formats, making cross-platform development much easier.

Advanced Editing Systems

The job of maintaining a Web site goes well beyond the creation of HTML pages. Just by looking at the Table of Contents of this book, you can see that there are other tasks involved. You need to plan your site and configure your server according to the plan. You may need to write scripts to process data collected by online forms. Or you may need to develop a database interface or provide support for real-time interactivity. Whatever the purpose of your site, you will most certainly find yourself doing more than just HTML.

The programs you've read about thus far can only assist you with the HTML authoring component of your job as a site administrator. However, some forward-thinking companies are releasing software to assist you with all aspects of site administration including document authoring and management, script authoring, and controlling access to the server. The next two sections point out the highlights of two such software packages: Netscape's LiveWire Pro and Microsoft's FrontPage.

Netscape LiveWire Pro

Netscape unveiled LiveWire Pro at the March 1996 Netscape Developer's Conference in San Francisco. The LiveWire Pro package comes with:

- Netscape Navigator Gold 2.0
- LiveWire Site Manager
- LiveWire Server Extensions
- A Java-compatible scripting language
- LiveWire Server Front Panel

■ Native support for several databases

■ A developer version of Informix

You have already read about Navigator Gold 2.0 and how it can support you in creating Web pages. The LiveWire Site Manager gives you a graphical depiction of your site and lets you restructure the site using drag-and-drop operations. A page that is dragged and dropped to a new location will automatically have all links pointing to it reassigned to its new URL. The Site Manager also checks the validity of external links, supplies several Web page templates and page creation wizards, converts documents prepared in other programs (like Microsoft Word or Novell WordPerfect) to HTML form, and converts many types of images to a Web-compatible format.

The LiveWire Server Extensions are meant to plug into the Netscape Application Programming Interface (NSAPI) and become an integral part of the server's operations. Server Extensions let you interpret and run scripts, install, remove and update applications created in LiveWire, and make local or remote additions and updates to pages.

Using Java is sometimes overkill in the case of small programs that perform relatively simple tasks. Netscape's Java-based scripting language gives programmers an easy-to-learn way of creating scripts to take care of these tasks. Scripts written in the Netscape scripting language can run on both the Netscape Navigator and Netscape server software. You can even compile the code to produce executable versions of your scripts.

The LiveWire Server Front Panel gives you a Web-like interface to operations of your server. The Front Panel lets you install, remove, and update applications running on your Netscape server. It also monitors these applications and provides you with an almost real-time display of performance information.

If you're building a database into your site, you'll want to make use of LiveWire's easy connectivity to many popular Structured Query Language (SQL) databases including those from Oracle, Informix, Sybase, and Microsoft. You can also use LiveWire to create the applications that allow users to query, browse, or update these databases.

> **Note**
>
> The beta release of LiveWire Pro is due out during the second quarter of 1996—right around the time this book is being published. For the most up-to-date information on LiveWire's specifications and pricing, consult Netscape's Web site at **http://home.netscape.com/**.

III

Doing HTML

Microsoft FrontPage

When it bought out Vermeer Technologies, Inc., Microsoft acquired the rights to Vermeer's FrontPage software package for Web site content creation and management. Now released under the name Microsoft FrontPage, the software has been made compatible with the Microsoft Office suite so that corporate users can easily create Intranet or Internet documents right on their desktops. The client portion of Microsoft FrontPage includes:

- FrontPage Explorer
- FrontPage Editor
- Templates for entire Web sites and individual Web pages
- Wizards for creating different sites and pages
- WebBots that support common Web server functions
- Personal Web Server software

The server side of FrontPage is called Server Extensions. Server Extensions are CGI-based applications that are compatible with Netscape and Microsoft Web server software.

The FrontPage Explorer gives you several ways to look at your entire site. The Outline View presents documents in a hierarchical format much like the way files are presented in File Manager (Windows 3.1 or 3.11) or in Windows Explorer (Windows 95). You can expand an element of the hierarchy to see the documents below it or collapse an element to see a more compressed view. The Link View shows how the pages of your site link to one another and the Summary View gives you a sortable list of the pages on the site and their properties. Additionally, FrontPage Explorer lets you restructure the site by dragging and dropping documents. Any link changes required after dragging and dropping are done automatically. FrontPage Explorer also validates internal and external links, gives you access to FrontPage's many templates and wizards, lets you control access to pages on your site, and makes it simple to port your site to another server.

The FrontPage Editor supports you in HTML authoring tasks. The Editor lets you easily create basic HTML constructs like headings and lists, as well as more complicated constructs like forms. You can convert images that aren't in GIF or JPEG format using the Editor's image conversion facility. The Editor also converts RTF and text files to HTML format. You can even create imagemaps (clickable images) right in the Editor.

FrontPage's templates and wizards guide you in creating individual Web pages or your entire Web site. Web templates include a Normal Web, Personal Web, Project Web, and Customer Support Web. The Corporate Presence

Web and Discussion Web Wizards walk you through the creation of a site according to your specifications in wizard dialog boxes. FrontPage has ready-made templates for many types of pages commonly found on a site including Frequently Asked Questions (FAQ), Feedback, Guest Book, Press Release, Table of Contents, and What's New pages. The Personal Home Page and Forms Page Wizards let you custom-design a personal page and online forms.

FrontPage WebBots handle common Web site functions without you having to program them yourself. You can use WebBots to implement searches, feedback forms, threaded discussion groups, user registration, and tables of contents.

So that you can get a server up and running right away, FrontPage also includes an NCSA-based Personal Web Server that fully supports HTTP and CGI standards.

> **Note**
>
> For the latest price information on Microsoft FrontPage, consult Microsoft's Web site at **http://www.microsoft.com/**.

> **Note**
>
> Web site administrators with higher-end site management needs should keep their eyes open for Microsoft's Internet Studio. Internet Studio was originally designed only for use with the Microsoft Network, but Microsoft decided in February 1996 to forego the MSN-only version and develop its first release based on Internet standards. Keep watching Microsoft's Web site for information on Internet Studio pricing and release date.

Document Conversion Tools

HTML filters are useful tools that let you convert a document produced with any kind of editor (including ASCII text editors) to HTML. Filters are useful when you work in an editor that has its own proprietary format, such as Word, WordPerfect, or Rich Text Format (RTF).

HTML filters are attractive if you want a utility to convert your document with tags to HTML as you continue to work in your favorite editor. Filters tend to be fast and easy to work with, because they take a file name as input and generate an HTML output file.

III

Doing HTML

> **Note**
>
> The World Wide Web Consortium maintains a good list of HTML filters and converters. Check it out at **http://www.w3.org/hypertext/WWW/Tools/Filters.html**.

Converting Word Documents

Word for Windows and Word for DOS documents can be converted to HTML using the CU_HTML and GT_HTML add-ons mentioned earlier. A few stand-alone conversion utilities have also begun to appear. Because Word can read other word processor formats (including WordPerfect and RTF), you can use these filters when error checking is required or when a dedicated filter for your word processor is not available.

> **Note**
>
> You can find many other filters by visiting **http://www.w3.org/hypertext/WWW/Tools/Word_proc_filters.html**.

Converting WordPerfect

WebmasterCD

The utility WPTOHTML converts WordPerfect documents to HTML. WPTOHTML is a set of macros for WordPerfect versions 5.1 and 6.0. You can also use the WordPerfect filter with other word processor formats that WordPerfect can import.

> **Note**
>
> A link to download WPTOHTML can be found at **http://www.w3.org/hypertext/WWW/Tools/Word_proc_filters.html**.

If the documents you need to convert were created in WordPerfect 6.1, you can use Novell's Internet Publisher to do the conversion.

> **Note**
>
> Internet Publisher is available free-of-charge from Novell at **http://wp.novell.com/elecpub/intpub.htm**.

Converting FrameMaker

FrameMaker release 5 includes a filter to translate FrameMaker documents to HTML. This release also lets you export your document in RTF format, in which case you can use the RTF converter RTFTOHTM discussed next.

> **Note**
>
> To learn more about FrameMaker 5, consult the Adobe site **http://www.frame.com/PRODUCTS/fm5.html**.

Converting Rich Text Format (RTF)

RTFTOHTML is a common utility that converts RTF documents to HTML. While most versions are available for UNIX and Macintosh systems, there is a version for DOS as well.

> **Note**
>
> The DOS binary file for RTFTOHTML can be downloaded from **http://www.georgetown.edu/acc/software/rtftohtm.zip**. Note the name is abbreviated because of DOS's eight-character limit on file names.

Because many word processors handle RTF formats, you can import an RTF document into your favorite word processor, and then run one of the word processor specific filters. However, RTFTOHTML seems to be faster at performing this conversion.

Converting TeX and LaTeX

If you're using Windows NT, your best bet here is to convert TeX and LaTeX files to RTF with TEX2RTF. You can convert the file to HTML from RTF using one of the other tools that have already been mentioned.

> **Note**
>
> TEX2RTF is available in a 32-bit version for Windows NT by anonymous FTP at **ftp://ftp.aiai.ed.ac.uk/pub/packages/text2rtf/tex2rtf1.52_win32.zip**.

III

Doing HTML

Converting PageMaker

EDCO produces the PM2HTML converter in both freeware and production versions. The production version costs $49.00 and can handle a greater number of conversions.

Note

The freeware version of PM2HTML is available by anonymous FTP at **ftp://ftp.gate.net/pub/users/edco/**. This is a busy site and it may take you a while to access it.

The World Wide Web Consortium's list of filters reports that Adobe has released an HTML authoring plug-in for PageMaker 6.0, but a search of Adobe's Web and FTP sites yielded no information about this add-on.

Converting Excel Spreadsheets

There are a couple of good options for converting Excel spreadsheets into HTML table format. Microsoft has created a simple Internet Assistant that is available from the Microsoft Web site. Also, XL2HTML.XLS contains a Visual Basic macro for Excel 5.0 that allows you to specify a range of cells and then generate the HTML that converts data in the cells to table form. XTML is an add-on for Excel 5.0 that can do this conversion as well.

Note

You can learn more about XL2HTML.XLS at **http://www710.gsfc.nasa.gov/704/dgd/xl2html.html**. XTML lives under Ken Sayward's directory at **http://users.aol.com/ksayward/xtml/**.

Converting Lotus Notes

Lotus Notes users can now convert their documents to HTML format with Lotus InterNotes Web Publisher. Lotus Notes databases can be converted to HTML by using the program TILE from Walter Shelby Group, Ltd.

Note

Lotus has online information about Lotus InterNotes Web Publisher at **http://www.lotus.com/inotes/**. You can get information on how to order TILE at **http://tile.net/info/about.html**.

Converting Interleaf

Interleaf users can use Cyberleaf 2.0 to not only convert Interleaf documents to HTML, but Framemaker, RTF, WordPerfect, and ASCII documents as well. Additionally, Cyberleaf converts graphics to either GIF or PostScript formats and it converts tables to GIF images, PostScript files, or HTML 3.0 markup.

> **Note**
>
> Cyberleaf 2.0 for Windows NT is due for release in early 1996. For the latest information, consult Interleaf's Web site at **http://www.ileaf.com/ip.html**.

HTML Analyzers

If the editing tool you use doesn't have a syntax checker, you might encounter problems once your documents are up on the Web. Mismatched or incorrect tags can produce on-screen results that detract from the content you're presenting. Another problem is that as HTML documents age, links may point to files or servers that no longer exist (either because the locations or documents have changed). It is, therefore, good practice to validate the hyperlinks in a document on a regular basis.

Several HTML analyzers exist to help you avoid these problems. These handy utility programs are often Web-based and using them is a matter of pointing your browser to the appropriate page and letting the utility know the URL of the document to analyze. Others live on your hard drive and process the HTML files right on your machine.

> **Caution**
>
> Make sure Access Control is not enabled or Web-based HTML checkers will not have access to your files.

Doctor HTML

Doctor HTML is a Web-based HTML analyzer that lets you perform several different tests on your documents, including:

- Spell checking
- An analysis of the document structure that looks for unclosed or extraneous tags

- An image analysis that loads each image and measures how much bandwidth each consumes
- An image syntax check that makes sure you've used WIDTH, HEIGHT, and ALT attributes in your <IMG ...> tags
- Proper table and form structure tests
- A check on hyperlinks that reports all links that timeout after 10 seconds
- A command hierarchy analysis that displays all HTML commands in the document

The command hierarchy analysis also indents nested tags, making them easier to read. The hierarchy test is best used in combination with one or more of the other tests.

> **Note**
>
> To check your documents with Doctor HTML, direct your browser to **http://imageware.com/RxHTML.cgi**. The form-based interface lets you specify which tests you want done and the URL of the document to test.

HTML Check Toolkit

The HTML Check Toolkit measures how well your documents conform to the rules of standard HTML. You can choose Strict, HTML 2.0, HTML 3.0, Mozilla (recognizes Netscape extensions to HTML), and HotJava (recognizes HTML used to embed Java applets) conformance tests. The report you get back can include a display of the input, the parser output, and the formatted output. In addition to being able to supply a URL to test, you can also submit a smaller chunk of HTML code for testing.

> **Note**
>
> You can open the HTML Check Toolkit at **http://www.webtechs.com/html-val-svc/**.

WWWeblint

WWWeblint "picks the lint" off your HTML documents by performing an extensive number of tests. Some highlights of WWWeblint's analysis include checking for:

- Proper document structure
- Unknown tags or attributes
- Overlapping tags
- The presence of a title in the document head
- The use of ALT in <IMG ...> tags
- Inappropriate nesting of tags
- Unmatched quotation marks
- Existence of local anchors

WWWeblint supports elements proposed in HTML 3.0, including table and math tags. You can ask WWWeblint to check a URL or you can supply a chunk of code for it to test.

Note

You can clean the lint off your documents by checking out **http://www.unipress.com/weblint/**.

HTML_ANALYZER

A popular hyperlink analyzer is HTML_ANALYZER. It examines each hyperlink and the contents of the hyperlink to ensure that they are consistent. HTML_ANALYZER functions by examining all of a document's links, and then creating a text file that has a list of the links in it. HTML_ANALYZER uses the text files to compare the actual link content to what it should be.

HTML_ANALYZER actually does three tests. It validates the availability of the documents pointed to by hyperlinks (called *validation*). It looks for hyperlink contents that occur in the database but are not, themselves, hyperlinks (called *completeness*). And it looks for a one-to-one relation between hyperlinks and the contents of the hyperlink (called *consistency*). Any deviations are listed for the user.

Note

You can download the compressed archive that contains the HTML_ANALYZER files from **http://www.gatech.edu/pitkow/html_analyzer/README.html**.

Note

Because new HTML authoring tools become available all the time, you should check one of the following Web sites for the most up-to-date information. The World Wide Web Consortium maintains a list of HTML editing tools at **http://www.w3.org/hypertext/WWW/Tools/**. You can read Mag's Big List of HTML Editors by pointing your browser to **http://union.ncsa.uiuc.edu/HyperNews/get/www/html/editors.html**. And of course, Yahoo provides an extensive list of editing tools at **http://www.yahoo.com/Computers_and_Internet/Internet/World_Wide_Web/HTML_Editors**.

Server-Based Hyperlink Checking

Many Web servers, like the WebQuest server included on the CD-ROM with this book, will validate local and remote hyperlinks. Refer to your server's documentation for how to perform the check.

CHAPTER 13

Graphics and Imagemaps

One of the strongest draws to the World Wide Web is graphics. In the early 1990s, inline graphics became part of Web pages and made them much more interesting than plain-text documents. Now, just a handful of years later, it's possible to animate the graphics on a Web page by using server push techniques (for the Netscape Navigator) or by using Java, the newest trend in Web programming languages. While these applications are compelling, they are, unfortunately, outside the scope of an introductory chapter on graphics.

Web graphics basically come in two flavors: GIF (for Graphics Interchange Format), a format developed by CompuServe, and JPEG (for Joint Picture Experts Group). Each format has its merits and drawbacks. You'll want to choose one or the other based on how you're using images on your pages. If you have designers at your disposal to produce your graphics, all you need to do is take the hand-off from them and put the files where they belong on your server. Otherwise, you'll need to develop some expertise in a graphics program so you can create your own.

In Chapter 10, you learned how to use the <IMG ...> tag to place an inline image in your documents. You later saw that sandwiching an <IMG ...> tag between the <A ...> and </A> tags set up a linked graphic, or hypergraphic, that users can click on to jump to another document. An extension of this idea is the *imagemap*. Imagemaps are graphics that have been divided into special sections called *hot regions*. Clicking on different hot regions instructs the browser to load different URLs. You've probably seen imagemaps on the main pages of many Web sites, where they provide a popular point-and-click interface to the rest of the site. The first implementation of imagemaps placed the burden of figuring out which URL to load squarely on the server (*server-side imagemaps*), but the current trend is to shift this burden to the client (*client-side imagemaps*).

▶ See "Images,"
p. 261, to re-
view how to
place images
in HTML
documents.

In this chapter, you learn about:

■ The basics of the GIF and JPEG graphics formats

■ Several different graphics programs and what features they have to assist with the development of Web page graphics

■ Server-side and client-side imagemaps

■ Tools to help you create and test imagemaps

Note
If you're familiar with graphic storage formats and graphics software, you may wish to skip ahead to "Implementing Imagemaps."

Graphics Standards

There are a large number of graphics storage formats in the world, but only two are used in the Web graphics realm: GIF and JPEG. GIF is the format originally put forward in HTML standards, but more and more browsers are able to display JPEG images as well.

Note
It is often possible to configure a browser to use a helper application to display images stored in formats other than GIF or JPEG. For example, you can instruct the browser to run a TIFF format viewer if it encounters an image file that has a TIF extension.

The next few sections look at some of the specifics of the GIF and JPEG formats.

GIF

The GIF format was originally developed by CompuServe as a standard for storing and transmitting images. GIF is an 8-bit format, meaning that GIF images are limited to 256 colors. The current GIF specification, released by CompuServe in 1990, is GIF89a.

How GIF Works

Image data in GIF format is organized into related blocks and sub-blocks that can be used to reproduce the graphic. When transmitting a GIF, a program called an *encoder* is used to produce a GIF data stream of control and data blocks that are sent along to the destination machine. There, a program called a *decoder* parses the data stream and assembles the image.

GIF employs a compression scheme called *LZW compression* to reduce the amount of data it needs to send to completely describe the image. LZW compression works best on simple images like line drawings or graphics with a only a few distinct colors. For more color-rich images, LZW is less efficient, producing compression ratios around 2:1 or less.

Interlaced GIFs

When you place an inline GIF on a Web page, the browser reads it in over the course of one pass over the area the image is to occupy. During the pass, each pixel is set to exactly what it has to be to produce the image. The problem with this approach is that it can take a while for the entire image to be read in. One way to reduce this time and still give the user an idea of what the whole image looks like is to use *interlaced* GIFs.

An interlaced GIF file contains the same image data as a regular GIF file, but it is organized differently. As a browser decodes an interlaced GIF, it receives *incomplete* information about the *entire* image. As it presents this information on-screen, an incomplete version of the whole image shows up. Because it is incomplete, the quality of the image will not be very good, but it is usually good enough to impart a sense of what the final image will look like. As it continues to read more data, the approximation to the actual image is improved, producing a "fade in" effect. When the browser reaches the end of the file, it has all of the image data and it makes the last few changes to the approximate image to reproduce the original. The advantage to this approach is that the user can quickly get a sense of the what the entire image looks like without having to wait for the whole thing to load.

Transparent GIFs

Another attractive feature of the GIF format is *transparency*. In a transparent GIF, one color is designated as transparent. When the image is displayed, all pixels colored with the transparent color are instead set to the color of the background. This gives the effect of the background color "showing through" the image in certain places. Figure 13.1 shows images with and without a transparent background. Note how the oval in the image with the transparent background appears to just be sitting on the background, whereas the oval on the non-transparent background appears to be sitting on a rectangular box that is sitting on the background.

Fig. 13.1
Transparent GIFs
have one color
that is always
changed to the
background color,
allowing the
background to
show through.

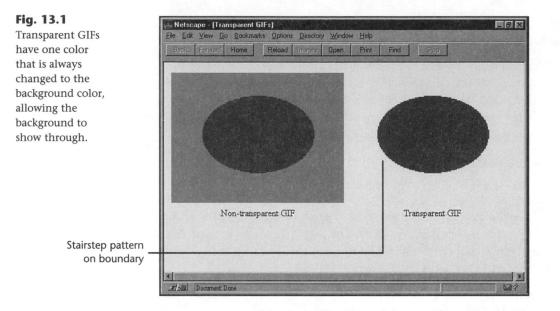

Stairstep pattern
on boundary

When you knock out the background behind an object in an image, you tend to get a "stairstep" pattern along the boundary, rather than a smooth curve. You can see this with the oval on the right in figure 13.1. To alleviate the stairstep pattern, you can use *anti-aliasing.* By anti-aliasing the image, you change the color of pixels on the boundary to a color halfway between the color inside the boundary and the color outside the boundary. By being colored with this middle-ground color, the boundary appears less jagged.

> **Note**
>
> A number of the programs discussed in "Graphics Programs" can create interlaced and transparent GIFs.

Animation

You can create simple animations using GIF files. The GIF89a standard allows you to store the images that make up the animation in the same file. When a decoder detects a file with multiple images, it decodes and presents them in sequence to produce the animation.

Not all browsers have decoders that are sophisticated enough to properly present an animation. Version 2.0 of the Netscape Navigator does though. If you're using Netscape 2.0, you can check out the URL **http:// members.aol.com/royalef/gifanim.htm** to see some sample GIF animations and to learn how to create them.

JPEG

The JPEG format refers to a set of standards for compressing full-color or gray-scale still images. JPEG's ability to work with full-color (16.7 million colors, 24 bits per pixel) images make it preferable to the GIF format (256 colors, 8 bits per pixel) for working with photographs and nature-related art where the entire color spectrum is in play.

How JPEG Works

JPEG can handle so many colors in a relatively small file because it *compresses* the image data. You can control how big or small the image file ultimately is by adjusting the parameters of the compression. A highly compressed file can be very small, but the quality of the image on-screen will suffer for it.

When you decompress a JPEG image, there is always some amount of *loss,* meaning the image will not look exactly the way it did originally. Fortunately, JPEG's compression/decompression scheme is such that the lost image data is in the higher color frequencies where it is harder for the human eye to detect the differences. In spite of this loss, you can still use JPEG to achieve compression levels of about 10:1 or 20:1 without appreciable change in the image. This means you've changed from storing 24 bits per pixel to 1 or 2 bits per pixel—a very impressive savings! As noted above, you can take the compression ratios even higher, but as you do, the loss becomes more and more detectable.

Progressive JPEGs

One attractive feature of the GIF format was the ability to interlace images. Interlacing reorganizes the image data so that as the file is read in, the image "fades in" over several passes, rather than just being read in from top to bottom. The analogous effect on the JPEG side is produced with *progressive JPEG* or *p-JPEG*. A machine displaying a p-JPEG presents a lower-quality approximation to the entire image after the first pass, followed by improvements in quality during subsequent passes. Thus, the user gets to see a rough version of the image right away and doesn't have to wait for the whole thing to display from top to bottom. The drawback of p-JPEG is that each pass over the image requires as much computational effort as the first, so the later passes are not necessarily faster.

In a Windows environment, you have a few options for converting to p-JPEG. The Independent JPEG Group (IJG) offers a series of command line programs for working with JPEG and p-JPEG files. You can download the source code from **ftp://ftp.coast.net/SimTel/msdos/graphics/jpegsrc6.zip**. Version 1.C of LView Pro (described later in this chapter) can also handle p-JPEGs.

III

Doing HTML

> **Note**
>
> There is no analogy for transparency in the JPEG format. The approach to transparency requires the selection of one color to be transparent. Because there can be data loss in JPEG compression/decompression, it's possible that a pixel colored with the transparent color may change to a slightly different color during the compression/decompression computations. Similarly, a pixel colored with a non-transparent color could become transparent and disappear. Either situation would undo the transparency effect you want to achieve.

Growing Acceptance

More and more browsers are warming up to the JEPG format and are able to display JPEG images without launching a helper application. Browsers that can fully support JPEGs and p-JPEGs include:

- Netscape Navigator 2.0
- Microsoft Internet Explorer 2.0 (under Windows 95)
- Spyglass Enhanced Mosaic 2.1
- UdiWWW 1.0.010
- Java 1.0

> **Note**
>
> An extensive list of frequently asked questions about the JPEG format can be found at **http://www.cis.ohio-state.edu/hypertext/faq/usenet/jpeg-faq/top.html**.

When Should I Use JPEG over GIF?

There are a number of situations in which you might choose the JPEG format over the GIF format. If preservation of more than 256 colors is important, you want to use JPEG. If you try to store a full-color image as a GIF, the first thing that happens is that it gets knocked down to 256 colors. You can imagine how much different this might look when you consider that full, 24-bit color supports over 16 million colors!

Another factor is speed. A well-compressed JPEG version of an image is likely to be much smaller than a GIF of the same image. Smaller file size means faster transmission time over the Internet. In some cases, once the file arrives at the browser or image decoder, you can further speed things up by configuring the decompression process to use reduced accuracy in doing the necessary calculations. However, this will increase data loss and reduce image quality.

A third reason is portability. With GIFs, you're locked into 256 colors. JPEGs make no predetermination of how many colors to use, so it is more useful for transferring images among systems with different display hardware.

On the flip side, you'll want to use GIFs for images with a few distinct colors, for black-and-white art like line drawings, and for images with sharp color changes. Most logos and icons found on Web pages fall into this category. Also, if you need an image with a transparent background, you have to use the GIF format because there is no way to achieve transparency with JPEGs.

Graphics Tools

Some Web authors work in conjunction with graphics people who design and develop all of the images that go into a Web site. Other authors have to create the graphics themselves. If you ever find yourself in the latter situation, you'll need to know how to use one of the many graphics programs on the market. This section gives an overview of five such programs with emphasis on how they can help you create graphics for the Web.

> **Note**
>
> For a lot of good information on graphics programs and utilities, consult the FAQ at
> **http://www.public.iastate.edu/~stark/gutil_sv.html**.

Microsoft Paint

Windows users have a basic graphics program right at their disposal in Microsoft Paint. Paint's main window is shown in figure 13.2.

Paint's tool palette lets you select one of many tools you can use to create and color graphical items and text. The lower four tools let you create rectangles with square or rounded corners, polygons, and ellipses. You can color the regions you create with the Pencil, Brush, Airbrush, or Fill tools.

> **Tip**
>
> To create circles in Paint, use the Ellipse tool while holding down the Shift key.

The Text tool enables you create pieces of text in various sizes and fonts. Be sure to turn on the Text Toolbar under the View menu when placing text as this will make changing text attributes easy.

Fig. 13.2
Microsoft Paint is a basic graphics program that comes bundled with Windows.

Tool palette —

Color palette —

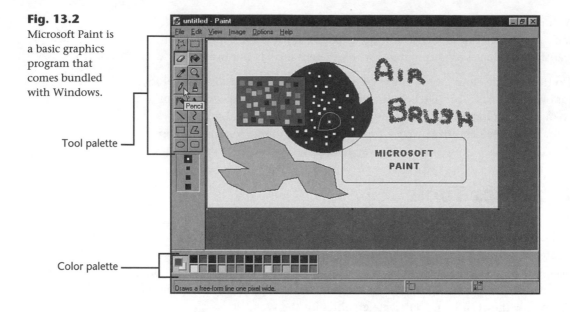

The rest of Paint's tools are equally handy. If you just need a simple line or curve, the Line and Curve tools (found just above the Rectangle and Polygon tools, respectively) provide an easy way to produce one. The Magnify tool increases the magnification of the image so you can do detailed work on small parts of it. The Erase tool can erase anything you've drawn by moving the tool over the image and holding down the left mouse button.

At the bottom left of the Paint window, you'll find the color palette. Left-clicking on a color sets the foreground color to that color. Right-clicking a color does the same thing for the background. The default foreground/background combination is black on white.

Most of Paint's menu options are fairly standard or self-explanatory. The Image menu gives you options to flip, rotate, stretch, or skew your image and to modify its size and colors.

One useful feature that you find in Paint and most other graphics programs is a readout of the x and y coordinates of the pointer or cursor as you move it over the graphic. When you learn about imagemaps later in the chapter, you'll see that knowing certain coordinates on the image is critical to defining the hot regions on an imagemap.

For all of its features, Paint has one major drawback in the context of creating Web graphics: it can't save images in the GIF or JPEG formats. If you want to use a Paint graphic on the Web, you need to convert it from a Windows bitmap to a GIF or a JPEG using a format converter or a different graphics program.

LView Pro

LView Pro is a great little shareware program you can use to edit existing graphics or to convert them to GIF or JPEG format. It offers most of the same image-manipulation features—such as flip and rotate—that Paint does, plus several other options that give you very fine control over image appearance.

> **Note**
>
> The information on LView Pro presented here is based on the evaluation copy of version 1.C/32. You can download the latest version of LView Pro by pointing your browser to **http://www.std.com/~mmedia/lviewp.html**. A license costs US$30.00 plus US$5.00 for shipping and handling.

Figure 13.3 shows the LView Pro window along with its extensive tool palette. Almost every tool in the palette corresponds directly to one of LView Pro's menu options.

Fig. 13.3
LView Pro's tool palette enables you to make modifications to most aspects of an image.

—— Tool palette

One nice feature is that LView Pro will let you open multiple images. This makes it easy to cut, copy, and paste objects from one image file to another. When you save an image, you can use LView Pro as a format converter and choose a format different from the original.

Notice that LView Pro doesn't have tools to create rectangles, polygons, and ellipses like Paint does. Indeed, the only LView Pro tool for creating anything is the Add Text tool. It stands to reason then that you'll probably have to use a different program to create your graphics. But what LView Pro lacks in ability to create, it makes up for with its ability to make very particular changes to an image.

LView Pro lets you change just about any facet of the image you could ever want. Tools on the palette call up dialog boxes to modify quantities like:

- Image brightness and contrast
- Red, Green, and Blue (RGB) color components
- Hue, Saturation, and Value (HSV) values
- Luminance and Chrominance (YCbCr) values
- Transformation maps and filters for RGB color components

Other tools let you convert the entire image from color to grayscale or to its photographic negative.

Used in conjunction with a program that has more graphics creation capabilities, LView Pro is powerful editing tool that you can use to fine-tune the images you make for your Web pages.

Paint Shop Pro

WebmasterCD

Another good shareware program for graphics work is Paint Shop Pro from JASC, Inc. Paint Shop Pro handles many types of image storage formats, lets you do the most common image manipulations, and even comes with a screen capture facility.

> **Note**
>
> The following information on Paint Shop Pro is based on the Shareware 3.11 version of the program. You can download this version from **ftp://ftp.the.net/mirrors/ ftp.winsite.com/pc/win95/desktop/psp311.zip**. A license costs US$69.00 plus US$5.00 for shipping and handling.

Figure 13.4 shows an image loaded into Paint Shop Pro along with the many available tool panels that give you single-click access to Paint Shop Pro's functions. The Zoom panel lets you zoom in to magnifications as high as 16:1 and out to magnifications as low as 1:16. Tools on the Select panel sample colors, move the image around in the window, define a custom area of the image to clone or resize, and change the foreground and background colors. The Paint

panel is a welcome addition to Paint Shop Pro that was not available in earlier versions. It supports 22 different tools that you can use to make your
own graphics. These tools let you create brush, pen, pencil, marker and chalk
effects; draw lines, rectangles and circles; fill a closed region with color; add
text; and sharpen or soften part of an image. The Histogram window gives
you a graphic representation of the luminance of all colors in the image,
measured with respect to the brightest color.

> **Tip**
>
> You can toggle any of the tool panels on or off by using options found under the
> View menu.

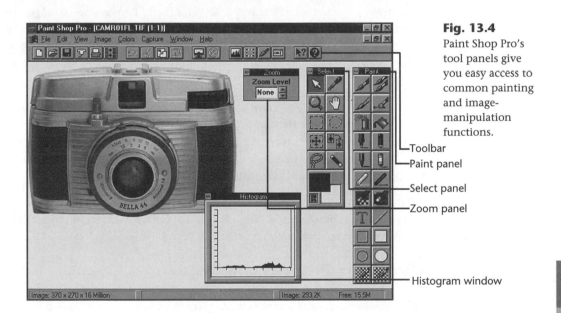

Fig. 13.4
Paint Shop Pro's
tool panels give
you easy access to
common painting
and image-
manipulation
functions.

Toolbar
Paint panel

Select panel
Zoom panel

Histogram window

Paint Shop Pro is a versatile program that can open images stored in 25 raster
(pixel-based) formats, including GIF and JPEG, and 9 meta/vector (image
components stored as geometric shapes that combine to produce the entire
image) formats, including CorelDRAW!, Micrografx, and Ventura. However, it
can only save in one of the raster formats. Nevertheless, Paint Shop Pro is still
handy for converting to pixel-based formats. The Batch Conversion option
under the File menu lets you select any number of files to convert to a new
storage format.

TWAIN refers to a set of industry standards that allow graphics programs
to work with image-acquisition hardware such as scanners. If you have a

III

Doing HTML

TWAIN-compliant scanner attached to your computer, you can use the File|Acquire option to scan in a new image. The Select Source option, also under the File menu, lets you choose what device you want to use for the acquisition.

Under the Image menu, you'll find options to do many of the standard manipulations such as flipping the image upside down, creating a mirror image of an image, and rotating the images. The Image|Resample option allows you to change the size an image with the jagged edges you get by standard resizing. You'll also find several effect filters under the Image menu that let you add or remove noise, enhance darker or lighter colors, and blur, sharpen, or soften the image. You can even define effect filters of your own.

The Colors menu is host to many standard functions such as adjustment of brightness, gamma correction and RGB values, and conversion to grayscale or photographic negative versions of an image. You can also load, modify, and save color palettes from the Colors menu. The Increase and Decrease Color Depth options allow you to change the number of colors being used to render the image.

One very useful feature of Paint Shop Pro is its screen and window capture facility. Options under the Capture menu let you capture the whole screen, a single window on the screen, the client area inside a window, or a user-define area. You can also choose whether the mouse pointer should be included in the capture and which hotkey will activate the capture.

Paint Shop Pro alone is a very capable image editing program, but you can also purchase it bundled with Kai's Power Tools SE for added functionality. To order this combination package, contact JASC sales at 1-800-622-2793.

Micrografx Picture Publisher 6.0

Micrografx Picture Publisher 6.0 is an image creation and editing program that comes as part of Micrografx's ABC Graphics Suite. The Picture Publisher main window is shown in figure 13.5.

To completely describe all of Picture Publisher's many features would fill several chapters, so the discussion here is limited to those features related to creating Web graphics. In addition to image painting capabilities that exceed those of Microsoft Paint and editing capabilities that at least match those of LView Pro, Picture Publisher supports the creation of Web graphics with features such as:

- Transparent and interlaced GIF creation
- Effect filters to sharpen or smooth image edges or to lighten or darken an image

Fig. 13.5
Micrografx Picture
Publisher 6.0 is a
feature-rich image
creation and
editing program.

■ Layers that act like sheets of acetate; you can place image objects on separate layers and then overlay them to produce the entire image.

■ Anti-aliasing of object edges

■ Easy-to-create 3-D effects like drop shadows

■ Support for creating custom textures like wood grain or brushed steel

■ Filters that let you export your image in one of over 30 formats, including GIF and JPEG

■ A highly customizable editing environment that lets you create your own "toolboxes" of tools, commands, and macros

The other programs that come bundled with Picture Publisher 6.0 add value to the entire ABC Graphics package. ABC FlowCharter makes it easy to create diagrams and charts. Micrografx Designer is a useful graphics illustrator program and the ABC Media Manager puts over 30,000 clipart images, photos, and diagramming symbols at your fingertips.

For all you get, you'd probably expect that the Micrografx ABC Graphics Suite isn't shareware—and you'd be correct. However, a license for the entire package costs substantially less than what other stand-alone graphics programs might. Since software prices can change rapidly, you should consult your software dealer or Micrografx (1-800-671-0144) for the most up-to-date price information.

III

Doing HTML

> **Note**
>
> To learn more about the complete Micrografx product line, check out their newly redesigned Web site at **http://www.micrografx.com/**.

Adobe Photoshop

Adobe Photoshop sets the industry standards for both high-end imaging and importing other graphics. Additionally, there are versions of Photoshop that run on Macintosh, Windows, Silicon Graphics, and Sun platforms, making it the most powerful, cross-platform graphics application discussed in this chapter.

Just as with Micrografx Picture Painter, a full description of all of Photoshop's features would fill volumes. Photoshop supports many of the useful features noted for Picture Publisher like transparent and interlaced GIFs, layers, anti-aliasing, drop shadows, and broad graphics file support, plus several others including:

- Numerous plug-in programs that support custom effect filters and emerging image formats like progressive JPEG
- Many options for dithering to lower color depths and different color palettes
- Highly efficient memory management
- A flawless interface with other Adobe products such as Illustrator and PageMaker

Because it is so powerful, Photoshop doesn't come cheap. Depending on what platform you want to run Photoshop on, a single license can set you back almost $1,000. Check with your software retailer or Adobe for current pricing.

> **Note**
>
> For more information about Photoshop and other Adobe products, visit their Web site at **http://www.adobe.com/**.

Implementing Imagemaps

As noted at the start of the chapter, there are two kinds of imagemaps. The original kind is the server-side imagemap, in which the server does the work to determine what hot region the user clicked on. The newer variety is the client-side imagemap, in which the client makes this determination.

The major difference between the two approaches is where you find the information that defines the map hot regions and the URLs associated with those regions. For a server-side imagemap, the information is found in a *map file* that resides on the server. With client-side imagemaps, the information is embedded in the HTML code that produces the page the imagemap is on.

Server-Side Imagemaps

When a reader clicks on an image that is part of a server-side imagemap, the mouse coordinates relative to the upper-left corner of the image are sent to the server for processing by an *imagemap script.* The script looks at a map file to decide which hyperlink to follow based on the mouse coordinates.

In order for a server-side imagemap to work, several configuration steps are necessary. First, depending on what server software you use, certain imagemap support files must be present on your server. Second, you must create the graphic and determine the coordinates that define the various hot regions. These coordinates, along with the URLs associated with each hot region, are used to make up the map file. Finally, you need to set up the <IMG ...> tag that places the image so that the client knows it's dealing with an imagemap and what the name of the map file is.

Configuring Your Server for Server-Side Imagemaps

The NCSA, CERN, Netscape, and Windows httpds feature imagemap support, although there are differences among them. Important differences are noted as the section progresses. NCSA httpd requires two files for imagemap support. The first is a script called *imagemap,* which must be compiled for your machine and placed in the cgi-bin directory. CERN httpd requires a similar file. With Netscape and Windows httpds, the imagemap script is pre-installed and ready to go.

Second, for NCSA and CERN httpds, you need write permission to the imagemap.conf file in the server's conf directory. This file maps image names, which you create, to their associated map files. You have to add a line to this file for each new imagemap you create. The format of the imagemap.conf file is simple:

```
image_name : physical_path
```

The path to the map file is not a URL. It's the physical path on your system. A sample imagemap.conf is included below.

```
homepage : /maps/homepage.map
```

III

Doing HTML

```
buttonbar : /maps/buttons.map
usmap : /maps/countries/us.map
```

The Netscape and Windows httpds do not require an imagemap.conf file.

Creating a Graphic and Defining Hot Regions

Standard HTML requires that the image you use for an imagemap be in the GIF format. You can use any of the image editing programs discussed earlier in the chapter, possibly with a GIF conversion tool, to make the GIF file itself. The most difficult part of making an imagemap is mapping image coordinates to corresponding actions.

Imagemap scripts can process hot regions that are rectangles, circles, and polygons. Lines in a map file define these regions using the minimum number of (x,y) coordinates required to completely describe the region. Rectangles are defined by the coordinates of the upper-left and lower-right corners, circles by the coordinates of its center and a point along the circle itself, and polygons by the coordinates of its vertices. Coordinates are measured with respect to the upper-left corner of the image, which is taken to have the coordinates (0,0). The x-coordinate increases as you move to the right along the image and the y-coordinate increases as you move down the image.

Each line in a map file defines one hot region and specifies the URL associated with the hot region. For example:

```
rect URL upper_left(x,y) lower_right(x,y)
circle URL center(x,y) edge_point(x,y)
poly URL vertex1(x,y) vertex2(x,y) vertex3(x,y) …
```

> **Caution**
>
> All URLs in the map file should be *fully qualified*.

> **Note**
>
> The CERN imagemap facility uses the keywords *rectangle*, *circle*, and *polygon* instead of NCSA's and Netscape's *rect*, *circle*, and *poly*. In addition, the format of the map file is slightly different.
>
> Netscape's imagemap script recognizes the keyword *point* in a map file as well. It is followed by the URL and the coordinates of the point.

You can also include a line in the map file beginning with the keyword *default*, which specifies what action to take if the coordinates of the mouse click are outside any hot region.

Caution

If you're doing imagemaps on a Netscape server, avoid using point and default lines in the same map file. If one or more point lines is specified, a click outside of a hot region is taken to be a click at the nearest hot point. This means that any default URL is disregarded.

Figure 13.6 shows a GIF file to be set up with links to several government sites. The image contains a rectangle, a circle, and a pentagon (5-sided polygon) whose defining coordinates and associated URLs are shown in table 13.1.

Fig. 13.6
A GIF file to be linked to three different government sites.

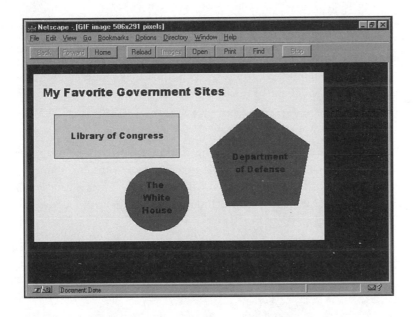

III

Doing HTML

Table 13.1   Defining Coordinates and URLs for Sample Imagemap

Shape	Coordinates	URL
Rectangle	(36,70),(252,146)	http://www.loc.gov/
Circle	(214,219),(269,221)	http://www.whitehouse.gov/
Polygon	(389,61),(480,125),(459,231),(334,230),(305,131)	http://www.dtic.dla.mil/defenselink/

> **Note**
>
> At this stage, your only option for finding the necessary coordinates is to use the pointer in your graphics program and to read the coordinates from the program window. Later in this chapter, you'll learn about imagemap tools that let you create a map file without knowing the coordinates. These tools let you trace over shapes on your graphic and it figures out the coordinates for you.

Using the coordinates and URLs in table 13.1, you can write the map for the imagemap. In this case, the file would be:

```
rect http://www.loc.gov/ 36,70 252,146
circle http://www.whitehouse.gov/ 214,219 269,221
poly http://www.dtic.dla.mil/defenselink/
389,61 480,125 459,231 334,230 305,131
```

Linking to the Imagemap (NCSA and CERN httpd)

After you create a map file for an image, you must make it an anchor to include it in an HTML file, like this:

```
<A HREF="/cgi-bin/imagemap/govtsites">
<IMG SRC="images/govtsites.gif" ISMAP></A>
```

The hypertext reference must contain the URL to the imagemap script followed by a slash (/) and the name of the map defined in the imagemap.conf file. The actual picture is then included with the <IMG ...> tag. The <IMG ...> tag also includes the ISMAP attribute, indicating that the image placed by the tag is to be an imagemap.

For this example to work, there must also be a line in the imagemap.conf file pointing to a map file for the imagemap "govtsites." That line might look like this:

```
govtsites :/maps/govtsites.map
```

> **Note**
>
> The CERN httpd includes a slightly different version of the imagemap script, called *htimage,* that eliminates the need for the imagemap.conf file. Instead, htimage allows you to specify a URL to the map file directly. Using htimage instead of imagemap in the previous example, you would write:
>
> ```
> <A HREF="/cgi-bin/htimage/maps/govtsites.map">
> <IMG SRC="images/govtsites.gif" ISMAP></A>
> ```

> **Tip**
>
> You can use CERN's htimage script even if you run the NCSA httpd.

Linking to the Imagemap (Netscape and Windows httpd)

Linking to the imagemap script on the server is somewhat easier under Netscape and Windows httpd. For these servers, you just use:

```
<A HREF="/maps/govtsites.map"><IMG SRC="images/govtsites.gif"
ISMAP></A>
```

These servers don't require the imagemap.conf file, so you can "eliminate the middle man" and point directly to the map file.

Client-Side Imagemaps

Having the server do the work to find out where the user clicked and where to send the user based on the click involves a lot of wasted resources. The client has to open another http connection to the server to pass the coordinates and get the response back regarding what URL to load next. The computations the server has to do to find out what hot region the user clicked on are straightforward and there's no reason they couldn't be done by the client. Slow transmission times between client and server means that users may have to wait quite a while from the time they click the mouse to the time the new URL is loaded.

Until recently, the compelling reason for having the server do the imagemap computations was because the map file data resided on the server. If there were a way to get this information to the client, the client could do the computations and the imagemap process would become much more efficient. This is the spirit behind client-side imagemaps.

Currently, there are two proposals for implementing client-side imagemaps. Both provide a way to get the map file data to the client, but specifics of each approach are different. One proposal suggests the use of the <FIG ...> ... </FIG> tag pair with map file data contained in <A ...> tags between them. The other proposes a new tag pair—<MAP ...> and </MAP>—with <AREA ...> tags between them to contain the map file data.

Client-Side Imagemaps with the <FIG ...> and </FIG> Tag Pair

The key to using the <FIG ...> and </FIG> tags for a client-side imagemap is that these tags can contain text that acts as an alternative to the image being placed by them. Thus, any text between the <FIG ...> and </FIG> tags is much like text assigned to the ALT attribute of the <IMG ...> tag.

For example, the HTML:

```
<IMG SRC="logo.gif" ALT="Company Logo" WIDTH=120 HEIGHT=80>
```

and

```
<FIG SRC="logo.gif" WIDTH=120 HEIGHT=80>
Company Logo
</FIG>
```

essentially do the same thing.

To implement the government sites map as a client-side imagemap with the <FIG ...> and </FIG> tags, you need to place the information previously found in the map file between these tags. This is done with the <A ...> tag as follows:

```
<FIG SRC="images/govtsites.gif" WIDTH=530 HEIGHT=300>
<B>Select a government site to visit:</B>
<UL>
<LI><A HREF="http://www.loc.gov/" SHAPE="rect 36,70,252,146">
Library of Congress</A></LI>
<LI><A HREF="http://www.whitehouse.gov/" SHAPE="circle
214,219,269,221">
The White House</A></LI>
<LI><A HREF="http://www.dtic.dla.mil/defenselink" SHAPE="polygon
389,61,480,125,459,231,334,230,305,131"></A></LI>
</UL>
</FIG>
```

The HREF attribute in each <A ...> tag contains the URL to load when the user clicks on a hot region and the SHAPE attribute contains the information needed to define each hot region. SHAPE is assigned to the shape of the hot region, followed by a space, and then followed by the coordinates that specify the region. Each number in the coordinate list is separated by a comma.

SHAPE also has a secondary function in this setting. If the image file specified in the SRC attribute of the <FIG ...> tag is placed on the page, the browser ignores any HTML between the <FIG ...> and </FIG> tags, unless it is an <A ...> tag with a SHAPE attribute specified.

On the other hand, if the image is not placed, the browser renders the HTML between the two tags. The result for the HTML above is a bulleted list of links that can act as a text alternative for your imagemap. This is an important feature of client-side imagemaps done with the <FIG ...> and </FIG> tags: they degrade into a text alternative for nongraphical browsers, browsers with image loading turned off, browsers that don't support the <FIG ...> and </FIG> tags, or when the desired image file can't be loaded.

Tip

Make sure that the alternative text between the <FIG ...> and </FIG> tags is format-ted nicely into something like a list or a table. Users will appreciate this extra effort.

Note

For the full scoop on the <FIG ...> ... </FIG> tag pair proposed for HTML 3.0, visit **http://www.w3.org/pub/WWW/MarkUp/html3/figures.html**.

Client-Side Imagemaps with the <MAP ...> and </MAP> Tag Pair

While working on a version of Mosaic that could read from CD-ROM, people at Spyglass had an immediate need for client-side imagemaps. Their solution was to introduce a <MAP ...> and </MAP> tag pair to contain the hot region information previously found in map files. Each map defined by these tags is given a unique name so that it can be referenced from the <IMG ...> tag used to place the graphic for the imagemap.

To define a map for the government sites map above, you would use the HTML:

```
<MAP NAME="govtsites">
<AREA SHAPE="RECT" COORDS="36,70,252,146" HREF="http://www.loc.gov/">
<AREA SHAPE="CIRCLE" COORDS="214,219,269,221"
HREF="http://www.whitehouse.gov/">
<AREA SHAPE="POLYGON"
COORDS="389,61,480,125,459,231,334,230,305,131" HREF="http://
www.dtic.dla.mil/defenselink/">
</MAP>
```

The NAME attribute of the <MAP ...> tag gives the map information a unique identifier. The <AREA ...> tags between the <MAP ...> and </MAP> tags are used to define the hot regions and the URLs to which they link. You can have as many <AREA ...> tags as you like. If the hot regions defined by two <AREA ...> tags overlap, the <AREA ...> tag that is listed first gets precedence.

The <AREA ...> tag can also take a NOHREF tag, which tells the browser to do nothing if the user clicks on the hot region. Any part of the image that is not defined as a hot region is a NOHREF region, so if users click outside of a hot region, they won't go anywhere by default. This means you don't have to set up an <AREA SHAPE="DEFAULT" ... NOHREF> tag for all of your maps.

The HTML used to define a map region can reside in the same file in which the <IMG ...> tag for the graphic lives or in an entirely different file. If the map definition is in the same file, you reference the map with the HTML:

```
<IMG SRC="images/govtsites.gif" WIDTH=530 HEIGHT=300
USEMAP="#govtsites">
```

The USEMAP attribute in the <IMG ...> tag tells the browser it's dealing with a client-side imagemap and what the name of the map is. If you store all of your map information in a separate HTML file, the tag to link to the map would be:

```
<IMG SRC="images/govtsites.gif" WIDTH=530 HEIGHT=300
USEMAP="maps.html#govtsites">
```

Storing all of your maps in a single file is a good idea if you're placing the same imagemap on several pages. This is frequently the case with navigational button bars.

Note

To read the Spyglass proposal for client-side imagemaps, visit the URL
**http://www.ics.uci.edu/pub/ietf/html/
draft-seidman-clientsideimagemap-01.txt**.

Using Client-Side and Server-Side Imagemaps Together

Client-side imagemaps are a great idea because they permit faster imagemap processing and enhance the portability of your HTML documents. Unfortunately, not all browsers support even one of the client-side imagemap approaches just described. Since you want to write HTML that is friendly to as many browsers as possible, you should consider combining server-side and client-side imagemaps whenever possible.

To combine a Netscape- or Windows-style server-side imagemap with the <FIG ...> and </FIG> tag approach to client-side imagemaps, you can modify the earlier example to be:

```
<FIG SRC="images/govtsites.gif" WIDTH=530 HEIGHT=300>
<A HREF="maps/govtsites.map"><IMG SRC="images/govtsites.gif"
WIDTH=530 HEIGHT=300 ISMAP></A>
<B>Select a government site to visit:</B>
<UL>
<LI><A HREF="http://www.loc.gov/" SHAPE="rect 36,70,252,146">
Library of Congress</A></LI>
<LI><A HREF="http://www.whitehouse.gov/" SHAPE="circle
214,219,269,221">The White House</A></LI>
<LI><A HREF="http://www.dtic.dla.mil/defenselink" SHAPE="polygon
```

```
389,61,480,125,459,231,334,230,305,131"></A></LI>
</UL>
</FIG>
```

The second line in the HTML above is new. It places the same map graphic on the page and links it to the map file govtsites.map on the server. If the browser recognizes the <FIG ...> tag and places the image it specifies, the additional line of HTML is ignored.

To combine a Netscape- or Windows-style server-side imagemap with the <MAP ...> and </MAP> tag approach, you can modify the earlier HTML to be:

```
<A HREF="maps/govtsites.map">
<IMG SRC="images/govtsites.gif" WIDTH=530 HEIGHT=300
USEMAP="#govtsites" ISMAP>
</A>
```

Flanking the <IMG ...> tag with <A ...> and </A> tags makes it point to the govtsites.map map file on the server. You need to include the ISMAP attribute in the <IMG ...> tag to let the browser know that the image is linked as a server-side imagemap as well.

Note

You can also link NCSA- and CERN-style server-side imagemaps to client-side imagemaps. Instead of the HREF in the <A ...> tag pointing directly to the map file, you need to make it point to the imagemap script.

Imagemap Tools

Whether you're creating a server-side or client-side imagemap, it can be cumbersome to determine and type in all of the coordinates of the points you need to define hot regions. Luckily, there are programs to help you through this process that will let you load your imagemap image, trace out the hot regions right on the screen, and then write the appropriate map file or HTML file to implement the imagemap. The next few sections describe some of these programs and tell you how to get them.

MapEdit

MapEdit 2.1 is a shareware imagemap tool produced by Boutell.Com, Inc. This version of MapEdit supports client-side images and images in the JPEG format, and cleans up a number of small bugs in the 2.0 release.

III

Doing HTML

Using MapEdit is easy. To begin, select the Open/Create option under the File menu. The dialog box you see prompts you for several things. First, you need to specify if you are doing a server-side or client-side imagemap. If you choose server-side, you then need to select either NCSA or CERN formats and specify a name for the map file. If you choose client-side, you need to tell MapEdit the name of the file to which it should write the HTML code. Finally, you tell MapEdit the file containing image for the imagemap. When you click OK, the image file is loaded into the MapEdit window and you're ready to start defining hot regions.

You can choose Rectangle, Circle, or Polygon tools under the MapEdit Tools menu. Each tool lets you trace out a hot region shaped like the name of the tool. To use the Rectangle tool, point your mouse to the upper-left corner of the rectangular hot region and click the left mouse button. Next, move your mouse pointer to the lower-right corner of the region. As you do so, a black rectangular outline is dragged along with the pointer, eventually opening up to enclose your hot region (see fig. 13.7).

Fig. 13.7
MapEdit lets you trace out a hot region using your mouse.

Hot region trace—

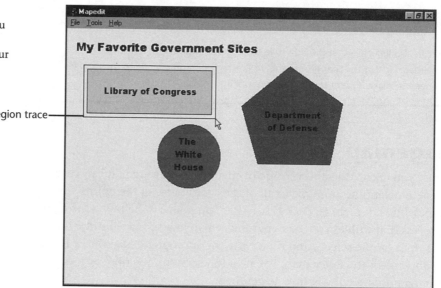

With the mouse pointer pointing at the lower-right corner, left-click the mouse again. When you do, you see a dialog box like the one shown in figure 13.8. Type the URL that is associated with the hot region you're defining into the dialog box, along with any comments you want to include, and click OK. MapEdit puts this information into the file it's building and is then ready to define another hot region or to save the file and exit.

Note

Comments in a server-side imagemap map file are offset with a pound sign (#).

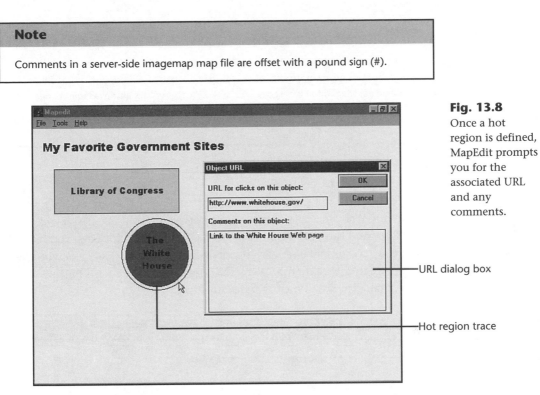

Fig. 13.8
Once a hot
region is defined,
MapEdit prompts
you for the
associated URL
and any
comments.

URL dialog box

Hot region trace

Mapedit's Circle and Polygon tools work similarly. With the Circle tool, you
place your mouse pointer at the center of the circular region (this is sometimes difficult to estimate!) and left-click. Then move the pointer to a point
on the edge of the circular region and left click again to define the region and
call up the dialog box. To use the Polygon tool, simply left-click on the vertices of the polygon in sequence. When you hit the last unique vertex (i.e., the
next vertex in the sequence is the first one you clicked), do a right-click
instead to define the region and reveal the dialog box.

Tip

If you're ever unhappy with how your trace is coming out, just press the Esc key to
erase your trace and start over.

Other MapEdit Tool menu options let you move an entire hot region, add or
remove points from a polygon, and test the imagemap file as it currently
stands. The Edit Default URL option under the File menu lets you specify a
default URL to go to if a user clicks on something other than a hot region.

III

Doing HTML

> **Note**
>
> You can download MapEdit 2.1 by directing your browser to **http://www.boutell.com/mapedit**. After a 30-day evaluation period, you must license your copy of MapEdit at a cost of US$25.00. Site licenses are also available. Educational and nonprofit users do not have to pay for a license, but they should register their copies of MapEdit.

Web Hotspots

Web Hotspots 2.0 is a shareware imagemap tool developed by Keith Doty at 1Automata. Web Hotspots supports both server-side and client-side imagemaps and can load graphics in both GIF and JPEG formats. Figure 13.9 shows the government sites graphic loaded into the Web Hotspots window. You can see in the figure that Web Hotspots provides you with buttons that let you change between tracing tools quickly.

Fig. 13.9
You can access Web Hotspots tools quickly using buttons in the main window.

Hot region tool buttons

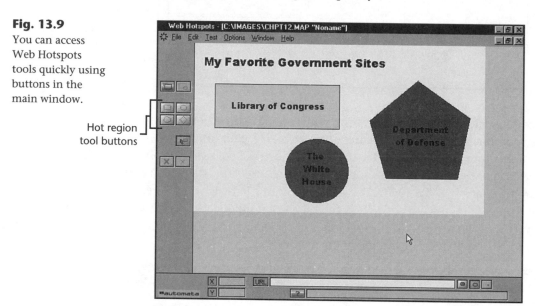

In addition to the usual rectangle, circle and polygon tools, you also get a freeform region tool that lets you define unusually-shaped hot regions. As you define a region, Web Hotspots shades it for you, making it easy to see in relation to objects in the graphic. The shading feature is illustrated in figure 13.10.

> **Note**
>
> Web Hotspots converts a freeform region into a many-sided polygon, so the line for the freeform region in the map file or <AREA ...> tag in the HTML file will start with the keyword polygon. You can see all of the vertices in the many-sided polygon that describes the freeform region in figure 13.10.

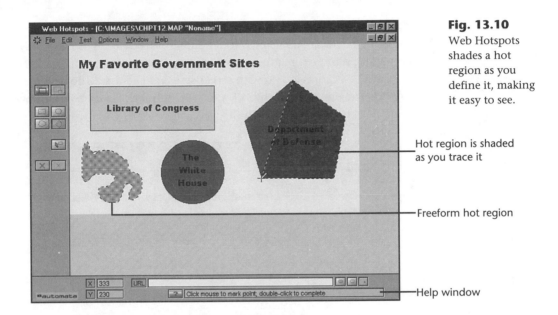

Fig. 13.10
Web Hotspots shades a hot region as you define it, making it easy to see.

Hot region is shaded as you trace it

Freeform hot region

Help window

Once a hot region is defined, you can type in the associated URL into the URL edit box near the bottom of the window.

Web Hotspots offers a number of other useful features beyond its basic functionality including:

- A context-sensitive help box
- A zoom feature that lets you increase or decrease the size of the image
- A testing mode that supports live testing over the Internet (you need to have WinSock installed to do this)
- Image rescale and rotate options
- The capability to move a hot region to the front of the map file or HTML file, giving it precedence over the other regions

III

Doing HTML

> **Note**
>
> You can download an evaluation of Web Hotspots 2.0 from **http://www.cris.com/~automata/hotspots.shtml**. After 30 days, you can remit US$49.00 plus US$5.00 shipping and handling to purchase a license. The US$49.00 price is valid through May 1, 1996.

Map THIS!

WebmasterCD

Map THIS! is a freeware imagemap tool written by Todd C. Wilson. It only runs on 32-bit Windows platforms, but that's about the extent of its limitations. Map THIS! can help you with server-side and client-side imagemaps and can load images in both the GIF and JPEG formats. Figure 13.11 shows the Map THIS! main window with the government sites graphic loaded.

Fig. 13.11
Map THIS! is a
freeware
imagemap tool
that supports
server-side and
client-side
imagemaps on
graphics in both
GIF and JPEG
format.

Hot region
tool buttons

Area list box

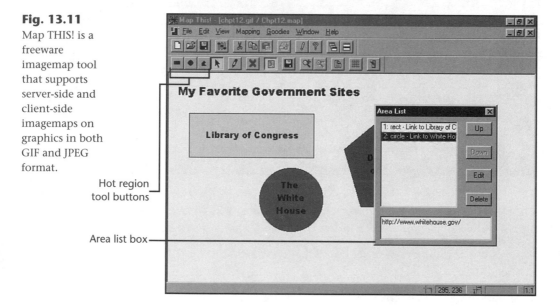

Most of Map THIS!'s features are accessible through buttons in the main window. The rectangle, circle, and polygon tools occupy the first three buttons in the second row. The circle tool is particularly nice because you drag out the circle from one point on the circle to the point that is diametrically opposite it, rather than trying to start on the exact center of the circle. As you use one of the tools, you get instructions on what to do next in a box at the lower left of the window. You can enable the shading feature to make the hot regions you define easier to see.

The Area List, shown in figure 13.11, is a floating box that you can activate to show the regions you've defined and what URLs they're linked to. You can also turn on a grid pattern to help you measure out hot regions with greater accuracy.

Map THIS! lets you work on multiple images. You have the choice of cascading or tiling the windows that contain the images. When it's time to save your work, you can save in CERN or NCSA format for server-side imagemap map files or in HTML format for client-side imagemaps. Other useful features of Map THIS! include:

- Adding points to or deleting points from polygons
- Color support all the way up to 24-bit color
- Zoom in and out
- A Preferences window in which you can set the map type and color choices for outlining and shading hot regions
- A Mapfile Information window in which you can specify a default URL, the map title, your name, and other descriptive comments
- Context-sensitive menus accessible by right-clicking the mouse

> **Note**
>
> To download the latest version of Map THIS!, point your browser to **http://www.ecaetc.ohio-state.edu/tc/**.

Testing

A great feature of the imagemap tool programs is that you can use them to test your imagemaps. MapEdit's test mode presents the imagemap graphic to you and lets you click on it. If you click on a hot region, the URL dialog box opens and displays the URL associated with the region on which you clicked. Web Hotspots' test mode allows you to test your imagemap right on the Internet. As long as you have an active WinSock layer, Web Hotspots will fetch the URL that goes with the hot region on which you clicked. The Map THIS! testing mode opens up a completely separate window (see fig. 13.12). As you move your mouse pointer over a hot region, its corresponding URL shows up in the box at the bottom of the screen.

III

Doing HTML

Fig. 13.12
As you move your mouse over a hot region in the Map THIS! test window, the URL you'd jump to shows up at the lower left.

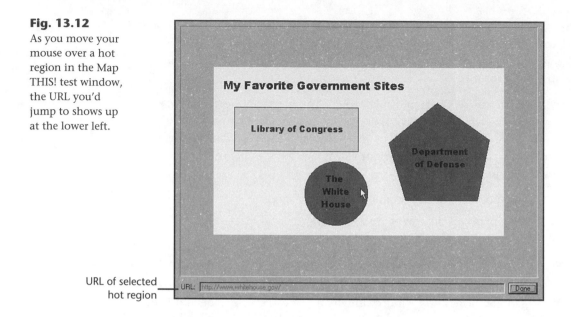

URL of selected hot region

If none of these programs are available to you, you'll have to put your map or HTML files on your server and test them with a browser. You can make small changes to these files using a simple text editor.

Tip

If you're testing a client-side imagemap with a browser, make sure the browser can implement the approach (<FIG ...> or <MAP ...>) that you used.

Part IV

Forms and Scripting

## CHAPTER 14

HTML Forms

Static Web pages are fine for presenting information, but they don't harness the full capabilities of Web technology. The Web community's craving for interactivity has led to the incorporation of animation, audio, video clips, and other multimedia items into Web pages. One of the earliest types of interactivity on Web pages were HTML *forms*—sets of clickable buttons and boxes, text fields, and menus into which the user enters data. The browser then passes the data to a *script* on a server that processes the data and sends a response back to the browser.

This powerful form of interactivity initially allowed for querying of databases and for soliciting feedback from Web users. As encryption technology improved, forms became a common part of electronic commerce sites where they gave Internet shoppers a secure interface for entering their orders, shipping addresses, and credit card numbers. Recent innovative applications of HTML forms include real-time chat and conducting online research.

On the client side of HTML forms are a few basic, yet versatile, tags that make it easy to create familiar graphical elements for data input and to specify where and how to send the form data.

In this chapter, you learn:

- The basics of form data flow
- How to create HTML forms
- The two methods clients use to pass form data to a server
- How to query a script without filling out a form

Overview of Form Data Flow

Before learning about the HTML tags used to create forms, it is helpful to have a perspective on the "path" that form data takes as it moves from the browser to the processing script. Once a user enters the data, the browser *encodes* it and makes a call to the server where the processing script resides. One part of this call indicates which script the server should run and the other part passes the form data.

Once the server has the data and knows which script to run, it starts the script and passes the form data to the script by the *Common Gateway Interface (CGI)*—a set of specifications that allows clients to make calls to server scripts, regardless of platform. The script processes the data and creates a response to be sent back to the client. Typically this response is an HTML file, but it can also take the form of things like a plain text file or a URL. The response is (in most cases) handed back to the server, which then passes it on to the browser for display to the user.

> **Note**
>
> When a script produces an HTML document, it is sometimes referred to as generating HTML "on-the-fly."

Form Support in HTML

Like other elements of HTML, forms have a similar appearance in different browsers, but the appearance is not identical. The appearance of a form always matches the graphical environment in which the form is displayed. For example, Windows pull-down menus and check boxes look significantly different than they do in X-Windows. This platform portability is part of the power of forms. Authors of HTML forms don't need to worry about the details of interacting with the user's graphical operating system—the browser handles all the details. This is what allows you to use the same HTML form under Windows, Mac, OS/2, X-Windows, and even in text-mode with Lynx.

HTML's form support is very simple, and yet surprisingly complete. A handful of HTML tags can create the most popular elements of modern graphical interfaces, including text windows, check boxes and radio buttons, pull-down menus, and push buttons. In fact, using HTML forms in conjunction with server scripts is arguably the fastest and simplest way to create cross-platform graphical applications! The only programming required is the script itself, and the programmer can choose the language.

Creating Forms

Composing HTML forms might sound like a complex task, but there are re-markably few tags that you need to master to do it. All form-related tags oc-cur between the <FORM ...> and </FORM> container tags. If you have more than one form in an HTML document, the closing </FORM> tag is essential for distinguishing between the multiple forms.

Each HTML form has three main components: the *form header,* one or more *named input fields,* and one or more *action buttons.*

The Form Header

The form header is really just the <FORM ...> tag and the attributes it con-tains. The first of these is the ACTION attribute. You set ACTION equal to the URL of the processing script so that the client knows where to send the form data once it is entered. ACTION is a mandatory attribute of the <FORM ...> tag. Without it, the browser has no idea where the form data should go.

The ACTION URL can also contain extra path information at the end of it. The extra path information is passed on to the script so that it can correctly process the data. It's not found anywhere on the form and is, therefore, trans-parent to the user. To allow for the possibility of extra path information, an ACTION URL has the form:

```
protocol://server/path/script_file/extra_path_info
```

You can use the extra path information to pass an additional file name or di-rectory information to a script. For example, on some servers, the imagemap facility uses extra path information to specify the name of the map file. The name of the map file follows the path to the imagemap script. A sample URL might be:

```
http://cgi-bin/imagemap/homepage
```

The name of the script is imagemap, and homepage is the name of the map file used by imagemap.

Note

On many CGI capable servers, you will find the script executable files in the cgi-bin directory. Having a special directory for the executable files helps the server adminis-trator keep ill-intentioned users from getting to portions of the server where they might do serious harm.

The second attribute found in the <FORM ...> tag is the METHOD attribute. METHOD specifies the HTTP method to use when passing the data to the script and can be set to values of GET or POST. When using the GET method, the browser will append the form data to the end of the URL of the processing script. The POST method sends the form data to the server in a separate HTTP transaction. More specific information about the differences between these two methods can be found in the "HTTP Methods" section later in this chapter.

METHOD is not a mandatory attribute of the <FORM ...> tag. In the absence of a specified method, the browser will use the GET method.

Caution

Some servers have operating environment limitations that prevent them from processing a URL that exceeds one kilobyte of information. This can be a problem when using the GET method to pass a large amount of form data. Since the GET method appends the data to the end of the processing script URL, you run a greater risk of passing a URL that's too big for the server to handle. If this is a concern on your server, you should use the POST method to pass form data.

In summary, a form header follows the syntax:

```
<FORM ACTION="URL" METHOD={GET¦POST}>
```

Following the form header are the tags to create named input fields and action buttons. These tags are discussed next.

Named Input Fields

The named input fields typically comprise the bulk of a form. The fields appear as standard GUI controls such as text boxes, check boxes, radio buttons, and menus. You assign each field a unique name that eventually becomes the variable name used in the processing script.

Tip

If you aren't coding your own processing scripts, be sure to sit down with your programmer to agree on variable names. The names used in the form should exactly match those used in coding the script.

You can use several different GUI controls to enter information into forms. The controls for named input fields appear in table 14.1. The TYPE="FILE" control allows you to create forms that ask for files as input. This control is a Netscape extension to standard HTML and is only supported by the Netscape Navigator browser.

Table 14.1 Types of Named Input Fields

Field Type	HTML Tag
Text Box	<INPUT TYPE="TEXT" ...>
Password Box	<INPUT TYPE="PASSWORD" ...>
Check box	<INPUT TYPE="CHECKBOX" ...>
Radio Button	<INPUT TYPE="RADIO" ...>
Hidden Field	<INPUT TYPE="HIDDEN" ...>
File	<INPUT TYPE="FILE" ...>
Text Window	<TEXTAREA ...> ... </TEXTAREA>
Menu	<SELECT ...> ... <OPTION> ... </SELECT>

Note

Even though it is a text-only browser, Lynx emulates GUI elements to achieve complete support for forms.

The <INPUT ...> Tag

You may have noticed in table 14.1 that the versatile <INPUT ...> tag, together with the appropriate TYPE attribute, is used to produce most of the named input fields available to form designers. The following sections discuss each of the different possible TYPE attributes in greater detail.

Text and Password Fields

Text and password fields are simple data entry fields. The only difference between them is that text typed into a password field appears on-screen as asterisks (*).

Caution

Using a password field may protect users' passwords from the people looking over their shoulders, but *it does not protect the password as it travels over the Internet.* To protect password data as it moves from browser to server, you need to use some type of encryption or similar security measure.

▶ To learn more about encryption and other security issues, see Chapter 9, "Creating and Managing an Intranet Web Server," p. 197.

The most general text or password field is produced by the HTML (attributes in square brackets are optional):

```
<INPUT TYPE="{TEXT¦PASSWORD}" NAME="Name" [VALUE="default_text"]
[SIZE="width"] [MAXLENGTH="width"]>
```

The NAME attribute is mandatory as it provides a unique identifier for the data entered into the field. The optional VALUE attribute allows you to place some default text in the field, rather than having it initially appear blank. This is useful if there is a certain text string that the majority of users will enter into the field. In such cases, you can use VALUE to put the text into the field, thereby saving most users the effort of typing it. The optional SIZE attribute gives you control over how many characters wide the field should be. The default SIZE is 20 characters. MAXLENGTH, which is also optional, allows you to specify the maximum number of characters that can be entered into the field.

Note

Previously, the SIZE attribute used to take the form SIZE="width,height," where setting a height other than 1 produced a multiline field. With the advent of the <TEXTAREA ...> ... </TEXTAREA> tag pair for creating multiline text windows, height has become something of a vestige and is ignored by most browsers.

A simple application of text and password fields would be to provide a user login interface. For example, the HTML shown in listing 14.1 produces the screen shown in figure 14.1.

Listing 14.1   HTML Providing a User Login Interface

```
<HTML>
<HEAD>
<TITLE>XYZ Corporation Login Screen</TITLE>
</HEAD>
<BODY>
<H1>Welcome to XYZ's Computer System!</H1>
<HR><P>
Please enter your ID and password.<P>
<FORM ACTION="http://www.xyz.com/cgi-bin/login.cgi" METHOD="POST">
ID:   <INPUT TYPE="TEXT" NAME="Username" SIZE="10" MAXLENGTH="10"><P>
Password:   <INPUT TYPE="PASSWORD" NAME="Password" SIZE="10"
MAXLENGTH="10"><P>
<INPUT TYPE="SUBMIT" VALUE="Log On">
</FORM>
</BODY>
</HTML>
```

The "Log On" button you see is an *action button.* See the "Action Buttons," section later in this chapter.

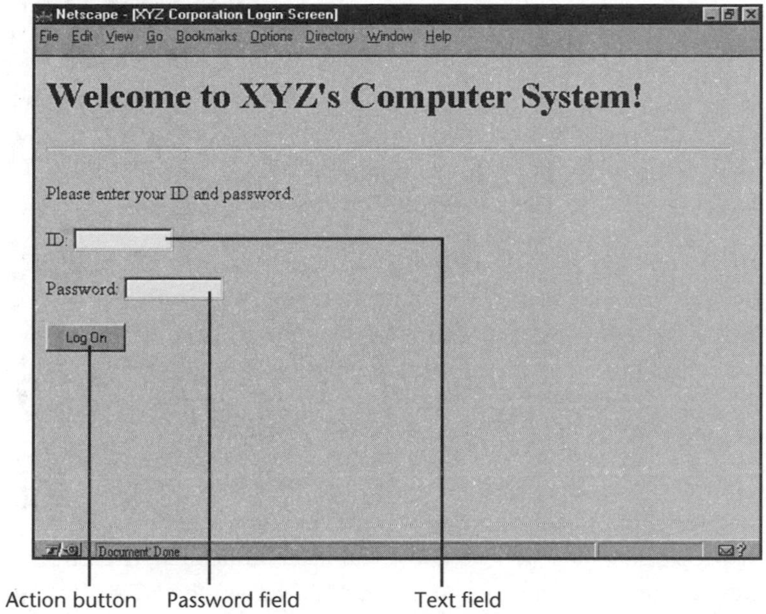

Fig. 14.1
You can use text and password fields to produce a login facility like this one.

Action button   Password field   Text field

Note

The <INPUT ...> tag and other tags that produce named input fields just create the fields themselves. It's up to you as the form designer to include some descriptive text next to each field so that users know what information to enter.

Tip

Because browsers ignore white space, it's difficult to line up the left edges of text input boxes on multiple lines because the text to the left of the boxes are of different lengths. One solution is to put label text to the right of input boxes. Another solution is to set up the text labels and input fields as cells in the same row of an HTML table.

Check Boxes

You can use check boxes to provide users with several choices, from which they may select as many of them as they want. An <INPUT ...> tag to produce a check box option has the syntax:

```
<INPUT TYPE="CHECKBOX" NAME="Name" VALUE="Value" [CHECKED]>
```

Each check box option is created by its own <INPUT ...> tag and must have its own unique NAME. If you give multiple check box options the same NAME, there will be no way for the script to determine which choices the user actually made.

Check boxes only show up in the form data sent to the server if they are selected. Check boxes that are not selected do not appear. For check boxes that are selected, the VALUE attribute specifies what data is sent to the server. This information is transparent to the user. The optional CHECKED attribute will preselect a commonly selected check box when the form is rendered on the browser screen.

Figure 14.2 shows an expanded version of the login screen in figure 14.1. The expanded screen has several options that the user can specify at login time. Because people generally want to check their electronic mail, the Check for New Messages option is preselected. Listing 14.2 shows the HTML needed to produce the check box options in figure 14.2.

Listing 14.2   HTML That Produces Check Box Options

```
<B>Login Options -</B> Select any, all or none of the following:<P>
<INPUT TYPE="CHECKBOX" NAME="Suppress" VALUE="Yes">Suppress greeting
screen<P>
<INPUT TYPE="CHECKBOX" NAME="Email" VALUE="Yes" CHECKED>Check for new
messages<P>
<INPUT TYPE="CHECKBOX" NAME="Schedule" VALUE="Yes">Display today's
schedule<P>
```

Radio Buttons

Radio buttons are used to present users with several options *from which they may select one and only one option.* When you set up options in a radio button format, make sure that the options are mutually exclusive so that a user won't try to select more than one.

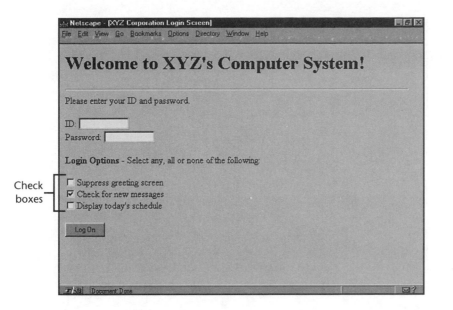

Check boxes

Fig. 14.2
Check boxes give users many options from which they can choose as many as they like.

The HTML to produce a set of three radio button options is shown below in listing 14.3.

Listing 14.3   HTML for Three Radio Button Options

```
<INPUT TYPE="RADIO" NAME="Name" VALUE="VALUE1" [CHECKED]>Option 1<P>
<INPUT TYPE="RADIO" NAME="Name" VALUE="VALUE2">Option 2<P>
<INPUT TYPE="RADIO" NAME="Name" VALUE="VALUE3">Option 3<P>
```

The VALUE and CHECKED attributes work exactly the same as they do for check boxes, though you should only have one preselected radio button option. A fundamental difference with a set of radio button options is that *they all have the same NAME.* This is permissible because the user can only select one of the options.

Figure 14.3 shows one more extension to our login screen, giving the user the choice of a UNIX shell or to load X-Windows at login. Listing 14.4 shows the HTML used to produce these radio buttons.

Listing 14.4   HTML for Radio Buttons in Figure 14.3

```
<INPUT TYPE="RADIO" NAME="X_WIN" VALUE="NO" CHECKED>UNIX
Shell  
<INPUT TYPE="RADIO" NAME="X_WIN" VALUE="YES">Start X-Windows<P>
```

Fig. 14.3
Radio buttons
present users with
multiple options
from which they
may select one
and only one
option.

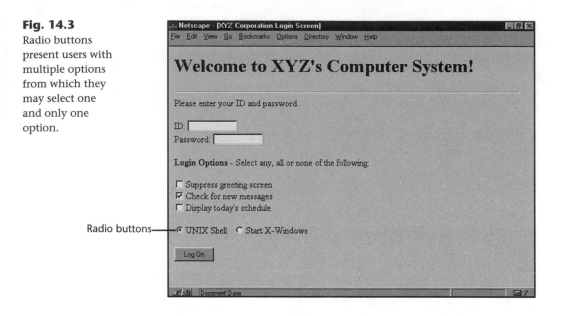

Note that the two radio button options are side-by-side in figure 14.3, separated by nonbreaking space. This is fine for radio button or check box options described with a small amount of text.

Hidden Fields

Technically, hidden fields are not meant for data input. However, you can send information to the server about a form without displaying that information anywhere on the form itself. The general format for including hidden fields is:

```
<INPUT TYPE="HIDDEN" NAME="name" VALUE="value">
```

One possible use of hidden fields is to allow a single general script to process data from several different forms. The script needs to know which form is sending the data, and a hidden field can provide this information without requiring anything on the part of the user. For example, all forms processed by the script can have a hidden name of FormID and hidden values of Sales, Order, Followup, NewUser, and so on.

A closely related use of hidden fields is to use a generic script to process several forms that vary only in one or two fields. For example, a generic script to send comments via e-mail might use a hidden field to specify the e-mail address. This way, the user doesn't have to type an address or even know where the mail is going, but because the form contains the address information in a hidden field, a single script can still be used to send automated feedback to several different e-mail addresses.

> **Note**
>
> In general, anything you can do with hidden fields, you can do by specifying extra path information in the form's ACTION attribute. However, hidden fields appear as regular data items in a form and may, therefore, be easier to process, especially if there are multiple hidden items.

A third possible use of hidden fields is to embed information into forms generated on-the-fly. For example, a form that is generated in response to a previous form can contain the original contents of the first form in a hidden field. This way, when the data from the second form is sent, the data from the first form is sent, too, and the processing script has a complete history of the necessary information. This can be useful in a search for returning preliminary results to the user while still maintaining a record of the original query.

Files

Netscape Navigator supports an extension to the <INPUT ...> tag that allows a file to be specified as input. To accomplish this, you need to do two things. The first is to add the ENCTYPE attribute to the form header to let the browser know that it will be sending a file. The modified form header looks like:

```
<FORM ACTION="URL" METHOD="POST" ENCTYPE="multipart/form-data">
```

The second change is to set the TYPE attribute in the <INPUT ...> tag to FILE:

```
Enter file name:<INPUT TYPE="FILE" NAME="filename">
```

> **Note**
>
> Because the browser will be transferring an entire file as part of the form data, use the POST method for this type of form so that you don't run the risk of creating too large a URL for the server to process.

The <TEXTAREA ...> and </TEXTAREA> Tag Pair

Text and password boxes are used for simple, one-line input fields. You can create multiline text windows that function in much the same way by using the <TEXTAREA ...> and </TEXTAREA> container tags. Listing 14.5 shows the HTML syntax for a text window.

Listing 14.5 HTML for a Text Window

```
<TEXTAREA NAME="Name" [ROWS="rows"] [COLS="columns"]>
Default_window_text
</TEXTAREA>
```

The NAME attribute gives the text window a unique identifier, just as it did with the variations on the <INPUT ...> tag. The optional ROWS and COLS attributes allow you to specify the dimensions of the text window as it appears on the browser screen. The default number of rows and columns varies by browser. In Netscape Navigator the defaults are 1 row and 20 columns, while in Microsoft Internet Explorer they are 3 rows and 30 columns.

Multiline text windows are ideal for entering of long pieces of text, such as feedback comments or e-mail messages. Figure 14.4 shows a text window being used as an online suggestion box. Listing 14.6 shows the corresponding HTML.

Listing 14.6 HTML That Produces the Text Window in Figure 14.4

```
<HTML>
<HEAD>
<TITLE>XYZ Corporation Suggestion Box</TITLE>
</HEAD>
<BODY>
<H1>XYZ Corporation Suggestion Box</H1>
<HR><P>
<FORM ACTION="http://www.xyz.com/cgi-bin/suggest.cgi" METHOD="POST">
<TEXTAREA NAME="Suggest" ROWS="10" COLS="60">
Enter your suggestions here.
</TEXTAREA>
<P>
<INPUT TYPE="SUBMIT" VALUE="Submit Suggestion">
</FORM>
</BODY>
</HTML>
```

The <SELECT ...> and </SELECT> Tag Pair

The final technique for creating a named input field is to use the <SELECT ...> and </SELECT> container tags to produce a pull-down or scrollable menu of options. Listing 14.7 shows the HTML used to create a general menu.

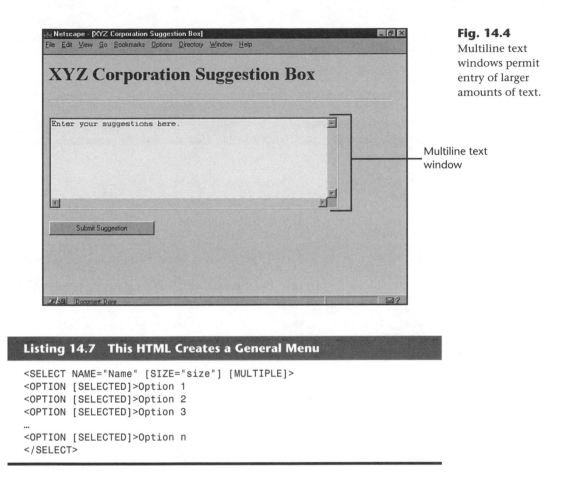

Fig. 14.4
Multiline text
windows permit
entry of larger
amounts of text.

Multiline text
window

Listing 14.7   This HTML Creates a General Menu

```
<SELECT NAME="Name" [SIZE="size"] [MULTIPLE]>
<OPTION [SELECTED]>Option 1
<OPTION [SELECTED]>Option 2
<OPTION [SELECTED]>Option 3
...
<OPTION [SELECTED]>Option n
</SELECT>
```

In the <SELECT ...> tag, the NAME attribute again gives the input field a
unique identifier. The optional SIZE attribute lets you specify how many options should be displayed when the menu is rendered on the browser screen.
If there are more options than there is space for displaying them, they will be
available either by a pull-down window or by scrolling through the window
with scrollbars. The default SIZE is 1. If you want to let users choose more
than one menu option, you can include the MULTIPLE attribute. When
MULTIPLE is specified, users can choose multiple options by holding down
the Control key and using the mouse to click on the options they want.

Note

If you specify the MULTIPLE attribute and SIZE=1, a one-line scrollable list box is
displayed instead of a drop-down list box. This is because you can only select one
item (not multiple items) in a drop-down list box.

Each option in the menu is specified with its own <OPTION ...> tag. If you want an option to be preselected, you can include the SELECTED attribute in the appropriate <OPTION ...> tag.

The HTML code in listing 14.8 produces figure 14.5.

Listing 14.8   This HTML Produces a Scrollable Menu Box

```
<HTML>
<HEAD>
<TITLE>XYZ Corporation Report Generator</TITLE>
</HEAD>
<BODY>
<H1>XYZ Corporation Report Generator</H1>
<HR><P>
Select the reports you want to generate.<P>
To select multiple options, hold down the Control key while clicking
the mouse.<P>
<FORM ACTION="http://www.xyz.com/cgi-bin/reports.cgi" METHOD="POST">
<SELECT NAME="Reports" SIZE="4" MULTIPLE>
<OPTION SELECTED>Bi-weekly Payroll
<OPTION>Accounts Payable
<OPTION>Accounts Receivable   ₣
<OPTION>YTD Revenue
<OPTION>YTD Expense
<OPTION>YTD Profit and Loss
<OPTION>Balance Sheet
</SELECT>
<P><INPUT TYPE="SUBMIT" VALUE="Submit Report Request">
</FORM>
</BODY>
</HTML>
```

Fig. 14.5
Scrollable menu boxes allow you to pack several options into a compact space.

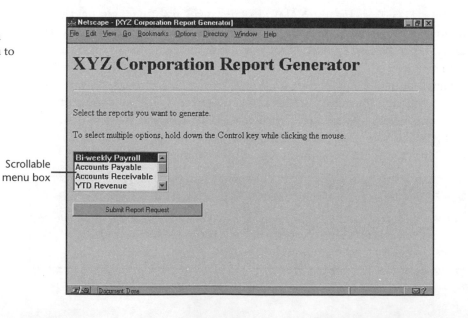

You may have noticed that there are no VALUE attributes for the <SELECT ...> or <OPTION ...> tags. This is because the values passed to the server are the text items that appear after each <OPTION ...> tag.

> **Tip**
>
> You can replace radio buttons with pull-down menus to save space on-screen. Including the MULTIPLE option in a <SELECT ...> tag allows menus to replace check boxes, as well.

Action Buttons

The handy <INPUT ...> tag returns to provide any easy way of creating the form action buttons you have seen in the preceding figures. Buttons may be of two types: submit and reset. Pressing a submit button instructs the browser to package the form data and send it to the server. Pressing a reset button clears out any data entered into the form and sets all the named input fields back to their default values.

Any form you compose should have a submit button so that users can submit the data they enter. The one exception to this rule is a form containing only one input field. For such a form, pressing Enter automatically submits the data. Reset buttons are technically not necessary, but are usually provided as a user courtesy.

To create submit or reset buttons, you use the <INPUT ...> tags:

```
<INPUT TYPE="SUBMIT" VALUE="Submit Data">
<INPUT TYPE="RESET" VALUE="Clear Data">
```

The VALUE attribute is used to specify the text that appears on the button. You should set VALUE to a text string that concisely describes the function of the button. If VALUE is not specified, the button text will read "Submit Query" for submit buttons and "Reset" for reset buttons.

> **Note**
>
> Normally, forms include only one submit button. In some cases, however, you may want to include multiple buttons that take different actions. You can achieve this by naming submit buttons with a NAME attribute so that the NAME and VALUE of the button pressed show up in the query string. However, this capability is not yet part of standard HTML and is not supported by many browsers.

A One-Field Form: The <ISINDEX> Tag

There is an exception to the rule about forms having headers, input fields, and action buttons. You can use the <ISINDEX> tag to create a single field form. No other tags are required. <ISINDEX> fields are used to allow a user to enter search criteria for queries against Gopher servers or database scripts. For example, you may be maintaining a directory of employees where you work that is searchable by a person's last name. You can use an <ISINDEX> field as a front-end to search the directory. Figure 14.6 shows such a field. The user would enter the last name to search on and press Enter to initiate the search.

Fig. 14.6
The <ISINDEX> tag creates a single field form that can be used for entry of search criteria

ISINDEX Field

You may be wondering where the data entered into an <ISINDEX> field goes. After all, there's no <FORM ...> tag with an ACTION specified. How does the client know which URL to send the data to? The answer is that it sends the data to the URL of the page containing the <ISINDEX> field. This requires one of two things: (1) that the page be created by some sort of a script, since a static HTML page could not receive and process the data or (2) that the <ISINDEX> field be part of a Gopher document, since Gopher servers are configured to process such queries.

▶ See Chapter 15, "CGI Scripts, Server Side Includes, and Server APIs," p. 415, which contains more details on how to create scripts that return HTML documents.

Note in figure 14.6 that the <ISINDEX> field is preceded by the default text This is a searchable index. Enter search keywords:. Netscape Navigator supports a PROMPT attribute of the <ISINDEX> tag that allows you to alter this default and make the text in front of the field more descriptive. For example, listing 14.9 shows the HTML that produces the page shown in figure 14.7.

Listing 14.9   The PROMPT Attribute

```
<BODY>
<H1> XYZ Company Employee Directory</H1>
<ISINDEX PROMPT="Enter the last name to search by:">
</BODY>
```

Fig. 14.7
Netscape lets you customize the text in front of an <ISINDEX> field.

ISINDEX field with customized prompt

Passing Form Data

Once the user clicks the submit button after filling out a form or presses Enter after specifying an <ISINDEX> query value, the form data or query is packaged by the browser for transmission to the server. There are two key aspects to this transmission: the *HTTP method* used to transmit the data and the *URL encoding* used to format the data. All form data or query information gets encoded, regardless of which HTTP method is used. Once you understand how the encoding works, it becomes easy to make calls to the same script with the same data later on.

HTTP Methods

In the earlier discussion of form headers, you learned that there are two HTTP methods by which form data can be passed to the server. The GET method attaches form or query data onto the end of the URL of the processing script. The POST method sends form data to the server in a separate transaction. If you don't specify the METHOD attribute in the <FORM ...> tag, the client will use the GET method by default.

> **Note**
>
> Query data entered into an <ISINDEX> field is always sent by the GET method.

The GET Method

The default GET method appends data onto the end of the URL specified in the ACTION attribute in the case of forms, and onto the end of the URL of the page containing the <ISINDEX> field in the case of an <ISINDEX> query. A URL created by the GET method has the form:

```
protocol://server/path/filename/extra_path_info?query_string
```

where the query string is the form data or <ISINDEX> query data formatted as described in the following section, "URL Encoding."

Caution

If your form contains several input fields, it's possible that your query string will grow too large for the server to process (more than one kilobyte of data). If this is a concern, use the POST method.

Since <ISINDEX> query information is generally short, use of the GET method is not a problem.

The POST Method

The POST method sends the form data to the server in a separate HTTP transaction, passing it to the standard input device on the server's operating system. By sending the data separately, you no longer need to be concerned about a URL becoming too long for the server to process. Even though it is sent separately, the data is still encoded in the same way as data sent by the GET method.

Note

The HTTP protocol supports the ability to POST data files of any type from browser to server, even outside of a script context. However, this capability is not yet widely supported by browsers or servers. Form data is of MIME type x-www/url-encoded.

URL Encoding

The browser must somehow convert all data represented graphically in a form to a string of text it can send to the server. This involves both packaging the form data and formatting it for proper transmission to the server.

Packaging Form Data

The form designer assigns each field, or graphical control, a unique name using the NAME attribute, except for submit and reset buttons. This naming provides a way for the server to associate data with where it came from.

The browser translates the entire contents of a form into a single text string using the following format:

```
name1=value1&name2=value2&name3=value3...
```

where name1 is the name of the first form variable and value1 is the value of that variable as entered by the user. For example, the URL from a form that adds names and phone numbers to the employee directory described earlier might look like this:

```
http://www.xyz.com/cgi-bin/
add.cgi?name=Beth+Roberts&number=2025551234
```

Because you give each field in a form a unique name, the processing script can figure out what each form entry represents. The type of graphical control in which a user enters a value is not specified directly in the information sent to the server. This lack of specification is okay, though, because the processing script can use each field's unique name to figure out the control type if necessary.

> **Note**
>
> Query data entered into an <ISINDEX> field is simply added onto the end of the URL. For example, a query to the employee phone directory might take the form:
>
> ```
> http://www.xyz.com./cgi-bin/lookup.cgi?Adams
> ```
>
> Since there is only one input field, it is impossible to confuse the meaning of the query data and there is no need to use a name=value packaging approach.

Formatting Rules

Most operating environments interpret spaces in character strings as some type of delimiter indicating the start of a new field, a new parameter, and so on. Consequently, you must remove spaces from all form data and queries in order to ensure that the data is successfully received by the processing script. By convention, all spaces become plus signs (+).

This replacement presents a minor problem. What if a query itself contains a plus sign? Or what if form data contains an equals sign or ampersand, both of which are used to package the form data? There must be some way to distinguish between those characters inside form data versus those characters used to package the data. Consequently, when these characters appear in the form data itself, they are *escaped* by converting them into their hexadecimal ASCII representations, beginning with a percent sign (%). For example, the string "#$%" is converted to "%23%24%25." In hexadecimal ASCII, 23 represents the pound sign (#), 24 represents the dollar sign ($), and 25 represents the percent sign. For programming convenience, most nonalphanumeric characters are represented in hexadecimal ASCII notation.

> **Note**
>
> The exact range of characters represented in hexadecimal ASCII is not important because the decoding operation converts all character sequences beginning with a percent sign to their hexadecimal ASCII equivalent. Even if letters and numbers in a query string were encoded this way, they would still be decoded properly.

In summary, for both form data and <ISINDEX> queries, any data inside the form or query itself is converted according to the following rules:

- All spaces in the data are converted to plus signs (+).
- Nonalphanumeric characters are represented by their hexadecimal ASCII equivalents.

Storing Encoded URLs

As you have seen in the previous discussion of URL encoding, packaging form or query data into a single text string follows a few simple formatting rules. Consequently, it is possible to "fake" a script into believing that it is receiving form or query data without using a form. To do this, you simply send the URL that would be constructed if a form were used. This may be useful if you frequently run a script with the same data set.

For example, suppose you frequently search the Web index Yahoo for new documents related to the scripting language JavaScript. If you are interested in checking for new documents several times a day, you could fill out the Yahoo search query each time. A more efficient way, however, is to store the query URL in your browser's hotlist or bookmark list. Each time you select that item on the hotlist, a new query is generated as if you had filled out the form. The query URL stored in the hotlist would look like:

```
http://search.yahoo.com/bin/search?p=JavaScript
```

Innovative Uses of Forms

Forms have come a long way from just being front-ends for search facilities and directory updates. Currently, forms are used to conduct electronic commerce, to conduct research on who is using the Web, and to have fun! Here are some examples:

Electronic Commerce: The Nashville Country Store

The Nashville Country Store at **http://www.countrystore.com/** is an example of doing business over the Web or electronic commerce. As technology to keep Internet transactions secure has emerged, Web users have developed more confidence in buying merchandise online. Figure 14.8 shows a screen from the Country Store that uses check boxes, text fields, and pull-down menus to create a shopping interface for visitors. Hidden fields are used to keep track of shoppers' purchases as they browse through the store.

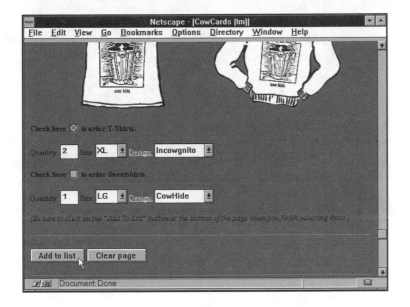

Fig. 14.8
HTML forms support electronic commerce by providing users with an interface to facilitate their shopping.

Research: Georgia Tech GVU Web Surveys

The Graphics, Visualization, and Usability Center at Georgia Tech has conducted four World Wide Web user surveys since January 1994. Online forms collect data on user demographics and the results are made publicly available on the Web. The last survey occurred in October 1995, with the next one planned for April 1996. You can visit the GVU Center's Web site at **http:// www.cc.gatech.edu/gvu/user_surveys/**.

Fun: The Dreaded Matching Question '95

In a play on the popular testing format, a faculty member at Tulane University has put a 26-item matching question online. The question tests knowledge of popular culture and is taken from actual exams given in the course Management of Promotion. Figure 14.9 shows the first few items in the question. The boxes next to the numbered items in the first column are text boxes into which you type the letters of the matching item from the second column. You can take the test at **http://129.81.234.19/courses/ dmq95.htm**.

Fig. 14.9
HTML forms
allowed one
faculty member
to replicate a
matching question
online.

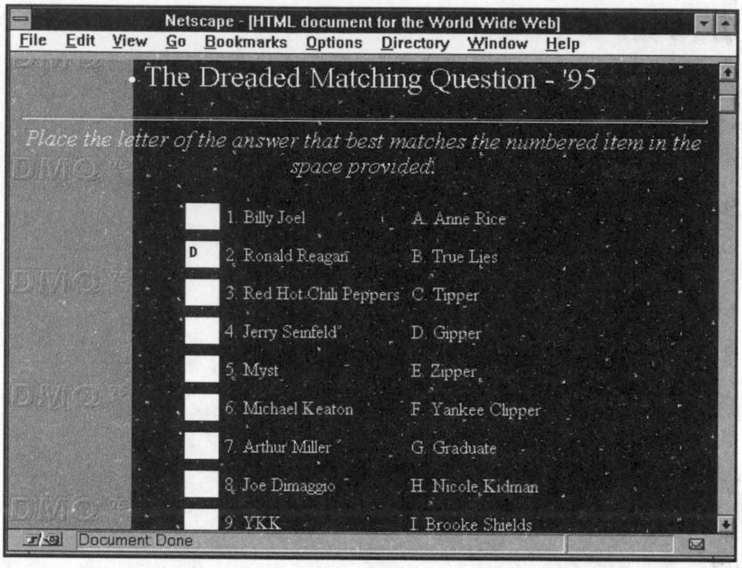

## CHAPTER 15

CGI Scripts, Server Side Includes, and Server APIs

By now, you know enough to get your server up and running. You can create and publish HTML documents and display images. You can sit and watch people from around the world log onto your server but you still seem to have this nagging feeling that there's something missing. Maybe your server should be doing...something. You know, something like searching documents or even displaying one of those cute little access counters that tell how many people have linked to your page. Your server just seems a little reactive and not interactive.

It's time to talk about creating dynamic documents on your server. One of the earliest means of creating documents on-the-fly is through the use of the *Common Gateway Interface* (CGI). Using CGI scripts, your server can interact with third-party applications that can execute document searches, query databases, or return a dynamically-created HTML page. These types of services give a professional feel to your server.

There are other means of creating interactive services on your Web servers. *Server Side Includes* are customized capabilities offered by Web server applications that allow you to produce dynamic documents but without the resource overhead of CGI script processing. In addition, some servers offer access to dynamically-linked code libraries known as *Application Programming Interfaces* (APIs).

This chapter covers the following topics:

- An introduction to the CGI standard and CGI scripting
- Use of Server Side Includes with the WebQuest server
- Use of Web server APIs

Introduction to CGI

▶ See Que's *Special Edition Using CGI* for more discussion regarding CGI script development.

Normally, Web servers respond to requests from Web browsers in the form of HTML documents and images. The browser sends a URL to the server and the server sends the file, whether it's an HTML document, GIF or JPEG graphic, sound file, or movie, to the browser via an HTTP connection. Sometimes, the browser sends a URL that does not point to a document but instead points to an application. The server activates this application which then responds to the browser with the requisite information. This application is a CGI script. This section covers how this script interacts with the Web server and browser.

One important feature of HTML 2.0 is the capability for Web designers to use the language to create interactive forms. These forms collect data entered by the user; the Web browser processes this data and sends it via an HTTP request to a Web server. Usually, the Web server will receive requests for HTML documents or graphic images. However, the HTML form implies that a specific action is requested of the server. With this type of request, the server knows to ignore the content of the form data and redirect the information to a CGI script specified in the HTML form page.

The CGI script is actually a third-party application developed in a language such as C, C++, Perl, Visual Basic or really any language supported by the operating system in which the server is running. However, some languages lend themselves to CGI scripting more than others and we'll discuss those later in this chapter. See "CGI Scripting," in this chapter, for more discussion on different CGI scripting languages.

How the CGI Works

The process through which the Common Gateway Interface works is quite simple.

1. The browser accumulates data from an HTML form and prepares it for transmission to the server.

2. The server reads the URL enclosed in the browser request and activates the application.

3. The server relays the information from the HTML form to the CGI application.

4. The CGI script processes the form data and prepares a response. This processing can include a database query, a numerical calculation, or an imagemap request. The response is usually in the form of an HTML document. However, the response is cleverly phrased by the CGI application to convince the Web browser that it originated from the server.

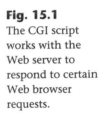

5. The CGI application passes the response to the server which immediately redirects it to the Web client. The server does not process the response in any way.

This process is outlined in figure 15.1. Note that the server merely passes information to the script. The script receives the data from the Web server through some mechanism unique to the language in which the script was developed. As long as this mechanism is in place, you can use any programming language to implement a CGI script.

Client-Server HTTP Header Formats

Web browsers communicate with Web servers via the HTTP protocol. Not only does this protocol specify the physical packet structure of the protocol, but it also defines the manner in which the server and browser exchange information. For example, a Netscape Navigator client might send the text shown in listing 15.1 to a Web server for a simple file request.

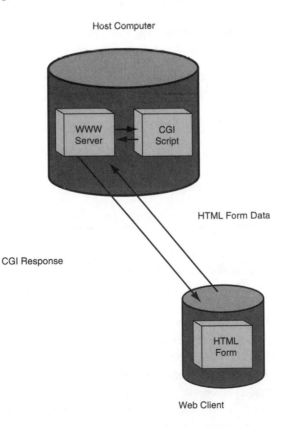

Host Computer

WWW
Server

CGI
Script

HTML Form Data

CGI Response

HTML
Form

Web Client

Fig. 15.1
The CGI script works with the Web server to respond to certain Web browser requests.

Listing 15.1   Making a Simple File Request

```
GET /article1.html HTTP/1.0
Accept: www/source
Accept: text/html
Accept: image/gif
Accept: image/jpeg
User-Agent: Mozilla/2.0b5 (Windows; I; 32bit)
 ...a blank line...
```

▶ See Chapter 6,
p. 149, for
more discus-
sion on MIME.

This message header informs the server that the browser is looking for the file article1.html and intends to use version 1.0 of the HTTP specification. The browser then informs the server as to which file formats it can interpret. In the above message, this list is truncated from what browsers usually express, but the server is informed that the client can interpret several text and graphics MIME types. The browser then informs the server as to its brand of client; in this example, the browser is defined as Netscape Navigator. Finally, the browser passes a blank line to complete the request.

The server will respond with a message generally like that shown in listing 15.2.

Listing 15.2   The Server's Response

```
HTTP/1.0 200 OK
Date: Thursday, 01-Feb-96 19:15:32 GMT
Server: WebQuest 1.0
MIME-version: 1.0
Last-modified: Friday, 15-Dec-95 17:54:01 GMT
Content-type: text/html
Content-length: 7562
 ...a blank line...
<HTML><HEAD><TITLE>Article....
```

In this response, the server provides enough information to allow the browser to process the requested data. The server denotes that it too is providing data using the HTTP v.1.0 protocol. Furthermore, it returns an HTTP code of 200 OK which tells the browser to relax and that the requested file was not only found but is being returned in this message. The date and server type are described in the header. The server type is included as the browser may interpret certain features not described in other servers. The server tells the Web client which version of MIME encoding is being used so that the browser can reprocess the data. The browser is also informed as to the MIME type of the data and the size of the file; this last datum is important because it allows the browser to inform the user as to the progress of the data transfer. Before including the file data the server inserts a blank line informing the browser (HTML is used in the example above).

The server needs to be flexible enough to provide the file in a format that is accessible to the client. For example, the server would need to provide a GIF file if a browser, which could only process GIF files, requests a file that is offered in JPEG.

> **Tip**
>
> The client and server header formats are defined in RFC 822. The Internet Engineering Task Force maintains an archive of all active Request for Comment (RFC) documents at **http://ds.internic.net/ds/dspg2intdoc.html**.

As mentioned previously, the HTTP server doesn't process output from a CGI application; the response is merely funneled through the server back at the browser. The message, however, must be configured so as to conform to the HTTP message header specifications.

Later in the section "The CGI Data File," we will discuss ways that you can program your CGI script to insert an HTTP header at the beginning of your response to ensure correct processing by a Web browser.

HTML Forms and CGI

By using an HTML form page, you can allow users to enter data that is processed by a CGI script. You can enter text and specify options using forms developed with HTML. The types of data input options are as follows:

- Multiline text entry fields
- Pop-up selection menus
- Radio buttons
- Check boxes

Figure 15.2 shows an example of an HTML form that you can use to transfer data to a CGI application. Note that this sample page contains text, check boxes, and radio buttons. The HTML code for this page is shown in listing 15.3.

Listing 15.3   HTML Code for the Sample Page Shown in Figure 15.2

```
<HTML>
<HEAD>
<TITLE>
Forms Test
</TITLE>
</HEAD>
<BODY>
```

(continues)

Listing 15.3 Continued

```
<FORM ACTION="http://hoohoo.ncsa.uiuc.edu/cgi-bin/
post-query" METHOD=POST>
A normal text field:
<TEXTAREA NAME="comments1"></TEXTAREA><p>
<HR>
<DL>Please indicate your favorite holiday:
<DD>
<INPUT TYPE="radio" NAME="holiday" VALUE="Christmas">Christmas
<DD>
<INPUT TYPE="radio" NAME="holiday" VALUE="Thanksgiving">Thanksgiving
<DD>
<INPUT TYPE="radio" NAME="holiday" VALUE="Easter">Easter
<DD>
<INPUT TYPE="radio" NAME="holiday" VALUE="NYDay">New Year's Day
</DL>
<DL>Please put a check next to the applications you own:
<DD>
<INPUT TYPE="checkbox" NAME="msword" VALUE="No" CHECKED>Microsoft
Word
<DD>
<INPUT TYPE="checkbox" NAME="photoshop" VALUE="No">Adobe Photoshop
<DD>
<INPUT TYPE="checkbox" NAME="netscape" VALUE="No">Netscape
<DD>
<INPUT TYPE="checkbox" NAME="excel" VALUE="No">Microsoft Excel
</DL>
<INPUT TYPE="submit" VALUE="Submit This Form">
</FORM>
</BODY>
</HTML>
```

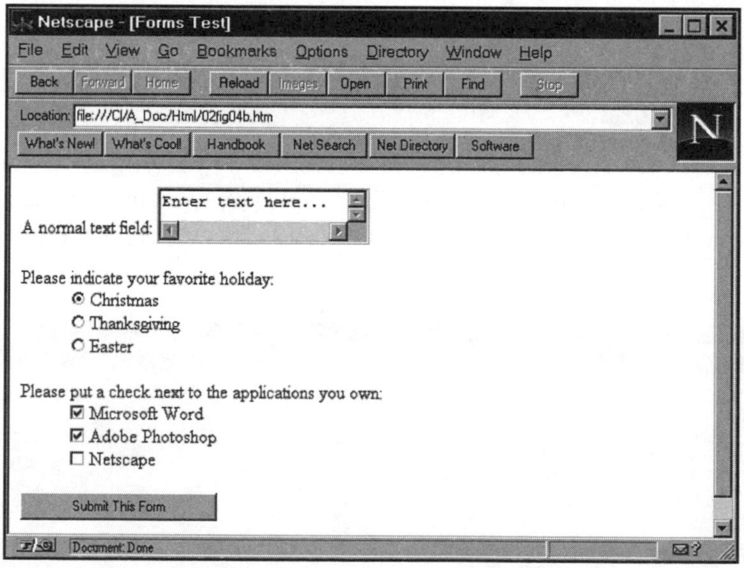

Fig. 15.2

You can use several types of HTML forms to retrieve information from Web users.

Note that all of the form elements in the above code use the NAME attribute. The idea is that the user enters text in a field or checks a radio button; this data is assigned a variable corresponding to the value of the NAME attribute. The CGI script uses these data by referencing the corresponding variable name. For example, the response from a post-query script to listing 15.3 is shown in figure 15.3.

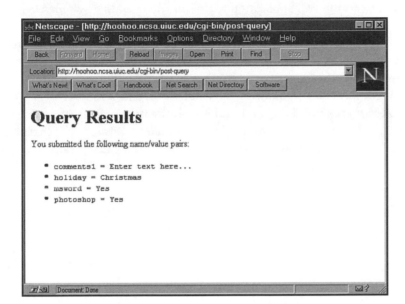

Fig. 15.3
A post-query script is useful for displaying the values of an HTML form.

Note

A *post-query script* is a generic term for any script that merely echoes back the results of an HTML form submission. In the nominal NCSA httpd software distribution, a simple CGI script entitled post-query reflects the values of the entered text data. Post-query scripts are one of the simplest implementations of CGI scripting and are useful for debugging HTML form pages.

Two alternative methods of transferring form data to a CGI script are POST and GET. These are the possible values of the METHOD attribute in the opening <FORM> tag. The GET method of transferring data is somewhat antiquated and dates back to the old Gopher days. You're limited in the amount of data you can pass back to the server using GET. POST, however, allows you to transfer much greater amounts of data. This results from the fact that a request made through the GET method concatenates all the HTML form variables into a single string; this string is appended to the URL in the HTTP message that identifies the CGI script. Requests made through the POST method combine all the form parameters into an internal variable that is passed to the script.

The CGI Data File

In order to get the CGI application to run on any operating system, there needs to be some mechanism to convey the form data from the HTTP server to the CGI application. With UNIX, this is done through the use of environment variables, standard input and output. With Web servers running under the MacOS, AppleEvents are used to convey data to and from the CGI script and Web server. With Windows 3.1, Windows 95, and Windows NT, CGI variables are exchanged using a Windows private profile file in key-value format. The CGI script can then use standard Windows APIs for differentiating and retrieving the key-value pairs from the file. This file is separated into several parts the contents of which will be discussed in this section.

CGI Variables

The variables described in this section are passed from the browser to the server; they pertain to information about the browser. Your CGI application can use these variables to display information about the server, the user, the user's browser, or the user's connection to the server. The DOS CGI environment variable is included in parentheses where applicable.

- Server Software (SERVER_SOFTWARE)

  The name and software version of the Web server answering the request and launching the CGI application.

  Example: WebQuest/V1.0

- Server Name (SERVER_NAME)

  The server's host name or IP address.

  Example: www.mcp.com

- Server Port (SERVER_PORT)

  The port number that received the request.

  Example: 80

- CGI Version (GATEWAY_INTERFACE)

  The version of the CGI standard to which the server replies.

  Example: CGI/1.2 Win

- Request Protocol (SERVER_PROTOCOL)

  The name and version of the protocol used by the client for this request.

  Example: HTTP/1.0

- Request Method (REQUEST_METHOD)

  The HTTP method specified in the request.

  Examples: GET, HEAD, POST

- Referrer (REFERRER)

  The URL of the document from which the CGI script was referred.

  Example: http://www.anywhere.com/cgi-test.html

- From (FROM)

  The e-mail address of the Web browser user.

> **Note**
>
> The From variable is not used by every browser because of privacy concerns although it is included in the HTTP specification.

- User Agent (HTTP_USER_AGENT)

  This variable contains the description of the browser software. This is useful, although not used by all browsers, for using CGI specific to various browsers.

  Example: Mozilla/2.0b6 (Windows; I; 32bit)

- Logical Path (PATH_INFO)

  Sometimes, a request may specify a logical path to a needed resource. This path may be in a logical path name. This variable can be used as an alternative to repeatedly referring to an excessively long path name.

> **Tip**
>
> As of this writing, the WebQuest server does not support the Logical Path variable.

  Example: Instead of http://myweb/cgi-bin/myscript/homepage, use "homepage"

- Physical Path (PATH_TRANSLATED)

  If a logical path is specified in the client message, that path can be referenced to a physical location on the WWW server.

Example: http://myweb/cgi-bin/myscript/homepage is equivalent to "C:\WEBQUEST\USER\HOME"

■ Executable Path (SCRIPT_NAME)

The logical path of the CGI script specified by the request. This is referenced to the server URL.

Example: cgi-dos/test-cgi.bat

■ Query String (QUERY_STRING)

The encoded version of the query data. This data follows the ? in the URL and is usually the result of a query from an HTML form.

Example: Joe%20Smith+5551321

■ Remote Host (REMOTE_HOST)

The IP host name of the Web browser making the request.

Example: s115.slipper.net

■ Remote Address (REMOTE_ADDRESS)

The IP address of the Web browser making the request.

Example: 167.142.100.115

■ Authentication Method (AUTH_TYPE)

The protocol-specific method of authentication used to validate the user if the document is protected and the server supports authentication.

> **Note**
>
> This corresponds to the AuthType directive in NCSA's HTTPd.

■ Authenticated User Name (REMOTE_USER)

The name of the authenticated user if the document is protected and the server supports authentication.

> **Note**
>
> This corresponds to the AuthUser directive in NCSA's HTTPd.

■ Authentication Realm

The authentication realm used if the document is protected and the server supports authentication. The list of members of a particular realm are checked upon requested access of a particular document.

- Authenticated Username

    The authenticated username if the document is protected and the server supports authentication.

- Content Type (CONTENT_TYPE)

    The MIME type/subtype of the HTML form data contained in a PUT or POST request.

    Example: text/plain

- Content Length (CONTENT_LENGTH)

    The number of bytes of data contained in a PUT or POST request. This allows the browser to display the progress of a lengthy transmission to the user.

    Example: 42

- Content File

    The path to the server-created temporary file that contains the content (query string) sent by the client in a PUT or POST request. This is used when a file is included in the HTTP request.

The Accept Section

This section contains the MIME types that can be processed by the Web client making the connection.

- Accept (HTTP_ACCEPT)

- The list of MIME types accepted by the client. You can pass parameters for some of the MIME type/subtype combinations.

- Example: text/plain, text/html, image/gif

The System Section

This section contains information relevant only to the Windows implementation of CGI.

- Output File (OUTPUT_FILE)

    The full name and location of the file from which the server is told to look for the CGI script output. The server sets this variable and makes it available to the script.

    Example: C:\DOS\HS063D62.ACC

- GMT Offset (DATE_GMT)

    The number of seconds to be added to Greenwich Mean Time (GMT) to reach local time. Note that this value changes if your server resides in an area of the US that uses Daylight Savings Time.

■ Debug Mode

This variable can be used to provide conditional tracing within the CGI program.

Example: Yes|No

The Extra Headers Section

This section contains additional headers that were included in the request. These headers must be implemented in the key=value format in the browser request. The server needs to parse the key/value pair before writing them to the CGI data file.

The Form Literal Section

If the Web browser request is made using the POST method from an HTML form, the server will decode the data and put it in the Form Literal section of the CGI data file. If the MIME type of the encoded data is application/x-www-form-urlencoded, the input will be in the form of `key=value&key=value&`... with the latter parts of the pair in URL-encoded format. The server processes this input by differentiating between the different pairs and then again by key and value. The key and decoded value are installed in key/value pairs in this section. If the encoded data is of MIME multipart format (MIME type is multipart/form-data), the input is delivered to the server in a MIME-style multipart format with separated fields. The server extracts this information and installs it in key/value pairs in this section.

Several HTML form types (check boxes, radio buttons, and pop-up menus) allow the user to select multiple options. In this case, there will be multiple occurrences of the identical key value passed to the server. In this instance, the server generates a key/value pair for the first selection and appends a sequence number for the following occurrences.

The Form External Section

This section contains the path name of a temporary file written by the server when a decoded value string is longer than a certain amount (usually 254 characters). This temporary file is also written if the string contains special characters such as double-quotes or nonstandard ASCII characters. The server writes the decoded string to a temporary file and inserts the path name and length of the string in this section.

The Form Huge Section

In instances where a value string is longer than a large amount, usually 65,535 bytes, it is not decoded but instead stored in a temporary file. The server notes the size of the file and its offset position in the content file in this section. A value string this large usually is not a string but a binary file sent with the browser request; for this reason, the CGI application stores the data in a separate file.

The Form File Section

If the browser request is transmitted using the multipart/form-data format, the browser request consists of several file uploads. In this case, each file upload is stored in an external file. The server takes note of the location of the uploaded file, the transfer MIME type, and the original name of the uploaded file and stores this information in this section.

Sample CGI Data File

Listing 15.4 details part of a hypothetical CGI data file. Note that in the Form Literal section, the results of a multiple selection are displayed with the field name followed by a sequence number. Also note the expression of a large field and a field with quote characters in the Form Large section. A file is stored in a temporary file and its location and size are denotes in the Form Huge section.

Note

Note that the CGI data file sections are denoted with left and right brackets ([]). These aid in processing by the CGI script.

Listing 15.4   Part of a Hypothetical CGI File

```
[CGI]
Request Protocol: HTTP/1.0
Request Method: Post
...
[Accept]
Accept: text/html
Accept: image/gif
Accept: image/jpeg
[Form Literal]
streetaddress=234 Elm St
phonenumber_1=5552323
phonenumber_2=5553434
phonenumber_3=5551234
[Form External]
largefield=C:\TEMP\FG18AF6C.000 300
fieldwithquotes=C:\TEMP\FG18AF6C.001 56
[Form Huge]
hugefield=C:\TEMP\ FG18AF6C.002 30345
```

Choosing a CGI Platform

Now that we have a good idea of how CGI applications work, we can talk about the environment in which to develop your scripts. Your main options are DOS and Windows. This section examines the strengths and weaknesses of each system as a platform for developing CGI applications. There are several tasks that you will want your script to perform.

> **Note**
>
> In reality, you can utilize CGI applications that reside on different computers. Your NT server can access a CGI application that resides on a UNIX computer or even a Macintosh Web server. The Web server will communicate with a remote script with only a nominal communication delay. This technique is advisable if the script you want to execute is sizable and the remote computer is a faster machine than the one on which your NT server resides.

Text Manipulation and Searching

You will find text-processing CGI scripts written in DOS provide superior performance to those written in Windows. One reason for this is that DOS provides a native file search command (FIND) and other file redirection utilities. Windows supports no command-line interface, so all operations must be scripted requiring a significant amount of overhead for these operations.

Binary Data Manipulation

There may be instances where you will want to access information stored in spreadsheets or databases. In these instances, it may be more advantageous to work with Windows CGI scripts. You will be able to take advantage of OLE and DDE to exchange data between your scripts and sophisticated applications such as Microsoft Excel or Oracle databases. Furthermore, you will find it much easier and faster to open these applications within Windows than from a DOS batch file.

Many of the sophisticated Windows applications also maintain powerful macro languages. You can utilize these macros within a Windows script file to further customize your CGI application. Using these macros in conjunction with the powerful OLE and DDE capabilities of a language such as Visual Basic affords you many scripting opportunities.

> **Tip**
>
> Although launching Windows applications such as word processors and spreadsheets as scripts is possible, the time required to load these programs for each request is significant. A better way is to run the desired applications continually in the background and to communicate with them via small Visual Basic executables that utilize DDE or OLE.

Miscellaneous Trade-offs

Running a DOS CGI under Windows NT will, in most instances, provide slower performance than a script written entirely with NT applications. There is a great deal of overhead involved in launching a DOS script within Windows NT because the DOS session much be launched as well. Furthermore, the DOS CGI environment is designed for 16-bit DOS programs so you will be able to inherit neither standard input and output handles nor the environment variables from a 32-bit NT server. Instead, the DOS CGI interface stores these variables in a BAT file containing SET statements for all of the environment variables and explicit command line redirection for the input and output files.

> **Note**
>
> The latest version of DOS (version 7.0) uses a 32-bit architecture but has not been extensively tested as a CGI interface as of this writing.

> **Tip**
>
> Examination of DOS CGI files provides an excellent means of debugging your scripts. All of the environment variables, input, and output files are available for your perusal. Using the WebSite server, you can easily swap your CGI applications from the Windows to the DOS interface by moving the executable from the \cgi-shl\ directory to the \cgi-dos\ directory. Simply change the URL in the HTML document and you have an effective means of debugging your scripts.

Except for very simple scripts, such as text searches or simple HTML document creation, you will want to develop your CGI scripts using the Windows interface. While there is sufficient overhead in developing and utilizing a Windows CGI script, the exchange protocols inherent in the 32-bit operating system make it a powerful scripting environment.

CGI Scripting

Under Windows NT, you have several environments to choose from in developing your CGI scripts. Just as certain operating systems lend themselves to certain tasks, certain scripting languages are better suited for various CGI applications. There is nothing requiring you to develop all of your CGI applications in only one language. You can develop text-processing CGIs in DOS batch files, search CGIs in PERL, and spreadsheet and database manipulation scripts using Visual Basic or Delphi. In this section, we will look at the various languages and scripting environments at your disposal.

Security

CGI scripts are potentially dangerous in that they do so much with so little code and with so much compliance from the HTTP server. With this in mind, you will need to shield your server from attacks by users seeking to gain unauthorized access. For example, as a value in an HTML form, a user could insert a high-level command that would initiate a process that would give him access to your machine. Keep in mind also that forms are not the only way to convey data to your CGI scripts. Users can telnet to your HTTP port and send data through a manually-constructed URL. The directory containing your CGI scripts needs to be protected at all costs; the damage that a bogus script entered on your server could do is difficult to imagine. The best rule-of-thumb is "that which is not expressly permitted is expressly prohibited."

DOS Shell Scripts

You can take advantage of the DOS CGI interface using the default MS-DOS shell, COMMAND.COM. This shell environment allows you to create rudimentary scripts that return files and simple text. The biggest disadvantage of this shell is that the left and right brackets (<>) used to develop HTML formatting tags imply special file redirection commands. To get around this shortcoming, you can insert files containing preformatted HTML commands. As an alternative to the MS-DOS shell, you can use more robust DOS environments such as those offered by Norton Utilities' NDOS, IBM's PC-DOS, or DR-DOS. Except for scripts that perform the most rudimentary functions, you should avoid developing scripts using DOS shell commands.

C/C++

Many people write CGI applications using C or C++ under all major operating systems. Compiled 32-bit code will run extremely quickly; it would be difficult to see a script run more quickly using a different application environment. However, C is extremely difficult to learn and C++ is slightly less so.

Furthermore, there is no freeware/shareware C/C++ compiler; you have to acquire a compiler from a commercial vendor such as Borland or Microsoft.

Many CGI programmers find it difficult to work with C and C++. Even so, there are many libraries of CGI scripts based on these languages; the chances are good that you can find a C/C++ script that suits your needs. CGIs written in these languages will provide superior performance for complicated text processing. However, if you wish to develop a script that works with other NT applications, these languages may not be for you. Such an interface would be clumsy and complicated.

Visual Basic

Microsoft's Visual Basic (VB) is a visually-oriented programming tool designed to aid you in creating applications under the Windows environment. Using VB, you can develop CGI applications that read and interpret the CGI data file and process the key/value pairs. Visual Basic scripts execute considerably faster than DOS shell scripts. Furthermore, the language has seen a rise in popularity as a CGI platform; there are many libraries of VB CGI applications available on the Internet.

> **Note**
>
> If you're looking for a good reference for Visual Basic uses with OLE and DDE, you can find thorough coverage of Visual Basic along with OLE and DDE in Que's *Using Visual Basic for Applications Excel Edition.*

Delphi

Similar to Visual Basic and PowerBuilder, Borland's Delphi is an extremely popular programming language that uses a compiler optimized to create very fast applications. Like these other languages, Delphi applications are self-contained and do not need to run with dynamically-linked libraries as is the case with Visual Basic. Delphi incorporates the Borland Database Engine (BDE), providing direct access to data stored in dBASE, Paradox, and the Local InterBase Server, and to other data formats via ODBC. Therefore, Delphi is a platform that provides an easy means of developing very nimble CGI applications that work with external databases.

PERL

The Practical Extraction and Report Language (PERL) is a popular text-processing language with origins in the UNIX operating system. PERL offers much of the utility of C and C++ but with easier syntax rules. As a result,

PERL is wildly popular as a CGI platform in the UNIX environment and has been ported to the major OS platforms such as OS/2, MacOS, DOS, and Windows NT.

PERL is a compiled language and sports one of the fastest compilers of any high-level language. However, PERL scripts are compiled at run-time; using PERL scripts as CGI applications will give them that interpreted "feel." The ubiquity of PERL throughout the major operating systems ensures that you will find a vast resource of CGI scripts available for your perusal. With minor modifications, you can incorporate these PERL scripts into your server.

PERL has been ported to the 32-bit Windows environments. This version of PERL for Win32 is available at Hip Communication's WWW site (**http://www.perl.hip.com**). Binaries are available for the MIPS, Alpha, PowerPC, and Intel architectures. You will need a copy of WinZip, rather than pkzip, to decrypt the file because PERL for Win32 uses long file names.

When unzipping the distribution, make sure that you preserve directory structure. This will prevent errors when you compile the source code. In order to compile the source code, you will also need a Win32 compiler such as MSVC2.0 or the Win32 Software Developer Kit). The makefiles require the utility nmake to build the tree.

While the hooks are in PERL for Win32 to access applications like databases through OLE Automation extensions, you will not be able to interact with other Windows 32-bit applications with the ease offered by Visual Basic or Delphi CGI scripts. For this reason, you will want to use PERL for Win32 to develop large scripts that do not require sophisticated interaction between Windows applications. Examples of scripting applications useful for PERL are guestbooks, document access counters, and mail forwarding.

Java

Java ranks slightly below Windows 95 as one of the most hyped developments in the computer world. Many landmark developments, such as the Web and Netscape itself, have stealthily crept on the Internet community whereas few developments have been anticipated as intensely as Java. Developed by Sun Microsystems, Java is an object-oriented programming language in the pattern of C++. Originally developed as a means of controlling consumer electronics devices, Java is garnering a lot of attention for its coordination with the Netscape browser. Your Web pages, when incorporated with Java applications or *applets*, can be greatly customized beyond the limited capabilities of the HTML language.

> **Note**
>
> See Que's *Special Edition Using Java* for more about using Java to extend the capabilities of your Web server.

Java is an *interpreted language,* meaning that Java applets are converted into executable code each time the applets are run. This is in contrast to *compiled languages*; an application constructed using a compiled language is created only one time and is executed many times. Applications created using interpreted languages generally run more slowly than executable code developed by compiled languages. The advantage is that by being interpreted, Java applets can run on any platform. Therefore, Java applets can be downloaded with any HTML page and executed under any operating system, making Java a truly cross-platform tool.

Currently, Java is used to extend the functionality of Web pages without employing the standard CGI interface. As of this writing, Netscape Navigator, soon to be followed by Microsoft's Internet Explorer, processes Java applets in conjunction with standard HTML documents. The applets are loaded with the page and then disappear when the page is cleared or when the browser is closed. Java applets can create animations, process form data without referring back to the server, perform mathematical calculations, or any of a variety of tasks.

The degree to which Java, and its derivative scripting language JavaScript, will supplant conventional CGI scripting remains to be seen. CGI scripts can perform complicated tasks, such as database queries, very quickly using compiled executable code. For less intensive tasks, Java may well become a preferred means of extended standard HTML.

Server Side Includes with WebQuest

You may have portions of your Web site that are actually documents within documents. For example, you may want to include on your home page a "news of the day" file that you edit separately from your HTML document. One way that you can do this is to create a CGI script that creates your home page by creating an HTML document and processing the updated file. However, the disadvantage of this is that your home page, which is no doubt accessed frequently, will now be a script instead of a simple HTML file. Regardless of your scripting language and your skills as a programmer, your server will always execute the script more slowly than it will display the HTML file.

Another alternative is to use Server Side Includes (SSIs) to display the file within your HTML document. An SSI allows you to server a file on-the-fly without the use of CGI scripting. Some possible uses of SSIs include:

- Send e-mail via HTML form input
- Include output from a CGI script
- Display current date and time
- Display file modification dates
- Conditional execution of external applications

Questar has developed an extension to the SSI concept known as SSI+ for use with the WebQuest server. You can still run SSIs and CGI scripts as with other servers. However, with SSI+, you can add additional functionality to your server. See "SSI+ Specifications," later in this chapter, for more information on SSI+.

How SSIs Work

When a Web server responds to a document request from a Web browser, it sends the file as it's stored in the file system. When the document contains SSI commands, the server scans the file looking for the commands to instruct it to include various files. The server knows that a file contains SSI information by the extension; normal HTML documents contain HTML suffices, but documents containing SSI commands have suffices of SHTML. The MIME type for these documents is text/x-server-parsed-html.

> **Note**
>
> You are not required to assign a special suffix for HTML files. You could assign the MIME type text/x-server-parsed-html to files with the HTML suffix. However, this would significantly degrade performance because the server would have to read every file before sending, even those without SSI commands,.

SSI Specifications

SSI statements in HTML documents have the general format:

```
<!--#command tag1="value1" tag2="value2" -->
```

Note that SSI statements begin with the same formatting characters as HTML comments. This is so that browsers will ignore include statements as if they were comments. Normally, the server replaces the include statements with the items to be included, but if SSI support were turned off on the server, the statements are passed along intact. This also allows you to port your code, with minimal impact, if you're forced to move your documents to a server that doesn't support SSI statements.

Including Files

To include another file in an HTML document, the format is:

```
<!--#include virtual="virtual_path"-->
```

or

```
<!--#include file="relative_path"-->
```

The `virtual` option specifies a URL-style virtual path to any document on your server. This virtual path is referenced to the server URL. The `file` option specifies a path relative to the current directory.

Any normal document, or even a document containing SSI commands, can be included using the `include` command.

Including CGI and SSI Variables

The `echo` command can be used to display the contents of any DOS CGI environment variable (discussed earlier in this chapter in the section "The CGI Data File") or one of the special variables defined for include statements. The general format is:

```
<!--#echo var="variable_name"-->
```

Besides the DOS CGI environment variables, `variable_name` can be one of the several SSI variables.

Variable	Definition
DOCUMENT_NAME	The document file name
DOCUMENT_URI	The virtual path to the document
DATE_LOCAL	The current date and time in the local time zone
DATE_GMT	The current Greenwich Mean Time
LAST_MODIFIED	The last modification date of the document
QUERY_STRING_UNESCAPED	The text of any query string sent by the client

Including Information About Other Files

Two commands can be used to include information about files other than the current document. These are `fsize`, which prints the size of any file, and `flastmod`, which prints the last modification date of any file.

The format for these commands is:

```
<!--#fsize file_spec-->
```

and

```
<!--#flastmod file_spec-->
```

The *file_spec* is either *file*="*relative_path*" or *virtual*="*virtual_path*" as in the include command.

Including Script and Command Output

You can include the output of any command or CGI script in a parsed document. The general format for this is:

```
<!--#exec cmd="command_string"-->
```

or

```
<!--#exec cgi="virtual_path"-->
```

where *command_string* denotes a DOS command file and *virtual_path* denotes a path to a CGI executable relative to the base directory of the Web server.

> **Caution**
>
> The *exec* option is the most dangerous Server Side Include command because it can be used to run any command or program on the server. Among other things, this could rapidly crash your server if a particularly large program were executed every time a certain document was accessed.

Customizing Output

The config command is used to control the output format of other include commands. The format is:

```
<!--#config [errmsg="error_message"] [sizefmt="{bytes¦abbrev}"]
➥[timefmt="format_string"]-->
```

The following tags are used with the *config* command:

Tag	Function
errmsg	Specifies error message to be sent to client if error occurs during document parsing
sizefmt	Specifies whether file size information will appear in bytes (251,335) or in abbreviated format (251K)
timefmt	Specifies the format to be used for all time and date information

SSI+ Specifications

SSI+ extends the functionality of SSI by adding such capabilities as database access, comparison statements, e-mail, and other capabilities. Furthermore, you can use DLL and ODBC calls to run in the code space of your server which is much more efficient than using external CGI scripts. Furthermore, the SSI+ specifications, as defined by Questar, call for an interface to the new CScript language; CScript is a C-like programming language with object-oriented extensions customized for HTTP service. CScript allows you to develop applications that integrate seamlessly with your server.

Output Configuration

In the SSI+ specification, the config statement is further extended with the following options:

Option	Function
cmdecho=[ON¦OFF]	When a command is executed using exec, this tag determines whether any output is issued with the HTML document. The default is OFF.
cmdprefix="string"	Determines "string" that is used to prefix any command output.
cmdpostfix="string"	Determines "string" that is used to postfix any command output.
onerr=<action>	Performs some action upon error. The action is equivalent to the action described in the *if* command below.

Updating ODBC Databases

The obdc command is used to query and update ODBC databases. The syntax for the command is similar to the SSI commands discussed above. There are four types of obdc tags listed below.

Tag	Function
debug	Turns on advanced diagnostic messages to be used during application development
connect	Defines data source name, user name, and password
format	Defines format and appearance of query result
statement	Describes the SQL statement to be performed

Listing 15.5 shows an example using the obdc tags.

Listing 15.5   HTML Showing Use of the *obdc* Tags

```
<HTML>
<HEAD>
<TITLE>Database Example</TITLE>
</HEAD>
<BODY>
<H1>Database Output</H1>
<!--#obdc connect="obdb,tobin,jump!"-->
<!--#obdc format="<P>Total sales for fiscal year %s amount to $ %s"--
>
<!--#obdc statement="SELECT YEAR, SALES FROM SALES REPORT GY 2,1"-->
</BODY>
</HTML>
```

Sending E-mail

When included in an HTML file accessed by the server, the `email` command sends a message via SMTP according to certain parameters. These parameters are listed in the following minitable.

Parameter	Function
debug	Enables advanced diagnostics for use during application development
fromaddress	Defines the e-mail From field
toaddress	Defines the e-mail address to which the message will be directed
message	Defines the content of the mail message
subject	Describes the subject of the message
sender	Defines a sender e-mail address
replyto	Describes the e-mail address to which replies should be sent
cc	Defines the carbon copy address
inreplyto	Contains the in-reply-to field of the message
id	Defines the ID field of the message

The variables `fromhost`, `tohost`, `fromaddress`, and `toaddress` are the only required fields. An example using the `email` tag is given in listing 15.6. The variables in double ampersands (&&) come from HTML form entries.

Listing 15.6   Use of the *email* Tag

```
<HTML>
<HEAD>
<TITLE>E-Mail Example</TITLE>
</HEAD>
<BODY>
<H1>E-Mail Output</H1>
<!--#email debug="ON" fromhost="anywhere.com" tohost=
"mail.somewhere.net" message="First-&&First&&, Last-
&&Last&&,Message=&&Message&&,fromaddress="&&Email&&" toaddress=
"joe@mail.somewhere.net"-->
<P> Your e-mail has been sent.
</BODY>
</HTML>
```

Conditional Statements

Using the if command, you can execute conditional statements in your HTML documents. With this statement, you can evaluate numerical, alphabetic, or CGI or SSI+ variable conditions. For example, you may wish to display a certain message if your browser is using a non-Netscape Web client warning them that there are Netscape extensions used in the page.

```
<!--if {logical expression #1}{operator}{logical expression #2}
{action}-->
```

The expressions, *logical expression #1* and *logical expression #2* are evaluated using the logical *operator*. The operator consists of one of the following:

Operator	Function
==	Equal
!=	Not Equal
<	Less Than
>	Greater Than
!<	Not Less Than
!>	Not Greater Than
hasstring	Returns *true* if string in *logical operator #1* contains *logical operator #2*.

If the if statement is evaluated as *false*, nothing happens. If the comparison is evaluated as *true*, then one of the following operations can take place as defined in the action tag.

Operation	Function
goto "label"	Causes a jump to a pre-defined SSI label.
print "string"	Prints "string" to the HTML document.
error	Prints the error message defined in *config*.
break	Terminates HTML transmission to the client.
errorbreak	Prints the *config* error message, then suspends the HTML transmission.
printbreak "string"	Prints "string", and then suspends the HTML transmission.

For example, you may wish to notify non-Netscape users that your page contains Netscape HTML extensions. This could be done with the script shown in listing 15.7.

Listing 15.7   Notifying Non-Netscape Users of HTML Extensions

```
<!--#if"&&HTTP_USER_AGENT&&" hasstring "Mozilla" goto nscplabel-->
<P>You will need Netscape Navigator to view the features on this
page.
<!--#break-->
<!--#label="nscplabel"-->
...next SSI commands
```

Note

The DOS CGI environment variable was accessed by enveloping it with double ampersands (&&). All environment and HTML form variables are accessed in SSI+ scripts in this manner.

Be Careful with SSIs

Use Server-Side Includes sparingly. Users can imbed SSI statements into CGI script requests that could download sensitive data such as password files. Make sure that your SSIs don't have access to your script directories. Some server administrators even disable the exec command to prevent users from bogging the system down with execution of large files.

Summary

The advantages of Server Side Includes is that they offer a sophisticated means of processing data without the overhead or complication of developing CGI scripts. These commands are built into the server architecture and the server performs the processing. The disadvantage is that your Web pages are no longer portable and must be served by the WebQuest server or some server that supports SSI or SSI+. As the Web is a very volatile environment, you can't say for sure that you will be using a server application 12 months from now or even 6 months from now. While SSI+ offers many sophisticated capabilities, it is still not widely supported by Windows NT servers other than WebQuest at this time. You will need to evaluate your commitment to WebQuest or other servers before making extensive use of SSI.

Other Scripting Additions

Besides the CGI and SSI specifications, there are other means with which you can add functionality to your server. The two methods discussed in this section pertain to the Netscape browser and server but may be eventually extended to other servers as well.

The Netscape Server API

The Netscape Server API (NSAPI) is an extension that allows you to customize the capabilities of the Netscape server. Using the NSAPI, you can provide a scalable and high-performance mechanism for building interfaces between the server and external applications.

Your external applications are executed as if they were part of the HTTP server application itself. The applications are stored as code libraries to which the Netscape server can dynamically link. You will need to spend time adjusting your applications to take advantage of the NSAPI and you will also need to modify the server configuration files to include your software libraries. This means that you will need to use higher-level languages such as C/C++ or Delphi over simpler scripting environments such as Perl or DOS Shell. However, data will transfer much more quickly because the applications will be linked into the server as if they were part of the Netscape server application.

> **Note**
>
> The NSAPI specification is available at **http://www.netscape.com/newsref/std/ server_api.html**

Using HTTP Cookies

Cookies are a new CGI add-on mechanism proposed by Netscape Communications, but as of this writing, cookies are also supported by the Microsoft Internet Explorer. Cookies are designed to communicate information to the browser from the server. This is in contrast to the standard HTTP process where server information outside of the HTTP response is not communicated to the browser.

When a browser accesses a CGI script containing a cookie header, that cookie type is transferred back to the browser along with the CGI response. Each time the browser accesses that CGI script, it will send the cookie value in the environment variable HTTP_COOKIE. Possible applications include client preferences, such as user accounts and personal information, for online shopping services.

The syntax for a cookie header is as follows:

```
Set-Cookie: name=Value; expires=Date;
path=Path; domain=Domain_Name; secure
```

The cookie name is the only required attribute and identifies the cookie. You can set an expiration date with the expires tag; after that date, the cookie becomes invalid. The domain keyword is used by the server to validate the cookie; while searching the cookie list for valid entries, the domain keyword is matched against the domain of the requesting host. This enables the server to match the cookie from many other browsers making similar requests. Similarly, the path keyword is used to validate the cookie request. The cookie is transferred if the path defined by the requesting browser matches the cookie path attribute. The secure keyword alerts the server to transfer the cookie only if the connection is made using the Secure Sockets Layer protocol.

> **Note**
>
> The Cookie specifications are available at **http://www.netscape.com/newsref/std/cookie_spec.html**. As of this writing, the implementation of the cookie mechanism has not been finalized; consult the specifications before attempting to utilize cookies.

## CHAPTER 16

More Scripting Options

As the World Wide Web has expanded and included more and more information, users have clamored for more interactivity beyond "point-and-surf." Especially with the advent of online information requests and product ordering, a need has developed for efficient data gathering and validation without the time-consuming and cumbersome process of developing CGI scripts and the inherent slow transmission of information across phone lines.

Enter the new world of scripting, with JavaScript and Visual Basic Script. With a compatible browser or add-on software components, much of the necessary interactive work is accomplished on the client machine without the need for exchanging information back and forth with the server.

In this chapter, you learn about:

- What functionality scripts add to HTML documents
- The basics of Netscape's JavaScript
- What is possible with Microsoft's Visual Basic Script
- New options for linking outside applications with ActiveX and Network Loadable Objects

Concepts

Scripts are small sections of code embedded in HTML tags or stand-alone sections of commands that are triggered by specific events in the document.

Normal HTML tags define static page appearances (headings and graphics), user interfaces (forms and links), and other features in addition to the text that appears on-screen. Scripts add interactivity to normal HTML tags by looking for events such as mouse clicks, mouse movements, and entering and leaving form fields.

For example, the tag <input type="button" value="Click Me, Please" onClick="sayHowdy()"> is the normal definition of a button up to the "onClick" statement. This addition to the tag calls a function called "sayHowdy" when the button is pushed.

Functions are defined using HTML script tags. If the browser does not recognize the script tag, the actual tag is ignored and any subsequent text is handled like any other text on the page.

Note

Using script tags with HTML documents requires the following format:

```
<SCRIPT>
Statements...
</SCRIPT>
```

The optional, but recommended, attribute "language" specifies which scripting commands are being used:

```
<SCRIPT LANGUAGE="JavaScript">
JavaScript statements...
</SCRIPT>
```

The language specification for Visual Basic Script is "VBS." There is no limit to the number statements enclosed by script tags, or the number of occurrences of scripts in an HTML document.

JavaScript and Visual Basic Script, while similar in purpose and function, are implemented in different ways. JavaScript capability is included as part of the browser, notably Netscape 2.0. No additional files or programs are needed to add JavaScript capability, just an HTML document embedded with a valid script.

At the moment, Visual Basic Script is an add-on application that requires a set of VBS files on the client machine in order to function; Internet Explorer 3.0 includes VB Script. When the browser finds the <script> command denoting VB Script, it will invoke the VB compiler add-on to handle the text denoted by the tags.

Because VB Script is a subset of Microsoft's Visual Basic programming language, it is likely that it will remain a separate application from the browser, although the two will be closely linked.

Both script languages discussed in this chapter allow Web authors and administrators to add interactivity to Web pages, including functions to respond to queries, ask questions, validate data, calculate expressions, and link to external controls and applications.

Checking for Helper Applications

How do I know if a user has the proper "helper application" or right browser to view my page? In two words, you don't. Unless you have control over the types of browsers end-users have on their computers, it's a good idea to identify pages that require compatibility with a script language.

Tip

To prevent your script from appearing on-screen with an incompatible browser, it's also a good idea to encompass the material between the "<script>" and "</script>" tags with comment HTML tags "<!--" and "-->". This will prevent your script from cluttering an otherwise attractive page.

When planning which scripting language to use, keep in mind that not all browsers support all scripts, if any. At publication, Microsoft announced support for JavaScript in its Internet Explorer, while Netscape has not yet reciprocated for VB Script. Other scripting possibilities are also on the horizon based on other popular Web languages, including Tcl, Python, and Caml.

JavaScript

JavaScript is a set of commands that are included in HTML documents to add additional interactivity and functionality to Web pages. It began its life as LiveScript until collaboration with Sun Microsystems and its object-oriented language called Java caused a name change. Although JavaScript is not directly derived from Java, it is very similar in its form and construction. The primary difference between the two is that JavaScript is interpreted while Java is compiled.

Interpreted versus Compiled

Interpreted languages are evaluated line by line at run-time. Compiled languages are passed through a compiler, where it is converted into a form readily usable by the computer. Interpreted languages are easier to work with in areas like HTML page design, but they sacrifice a lot in speed. A compiled program runs very fast since the interpretation of commands was done "ahead of time."

For example, a JavaScript function can verify that users enter valid information into a form requesting a ZIP code. Without any network transmission, an HTML page with embedded JavaScript interprets the text and alerts the user with a message for invalid input. Or, you can use JavaScript to perform an action (such as play an audio file, execute an applet, or communicate with a plug-in) in response to the user opening or exiting a page.

With an effective script, it is possible to respond without any network transmission to user-initiated events, such as mouse clicks and form entries.

JavaScript Isn't Java

An important distinction to make is the difference between JavaScript and Java, which has caused confusion for a great number of folks. Java is a full-fledged object-oriented programming language. It makes use of a compiler to create stand-alone applications and browser applets. Applets are separate files downloaded to the client computer that can add special effects to HTML pages (scrolling banners are the current rage), but the code still resides in a separate file from the browser.

JavaScript, although related to Java, was developed by Netscape and does not require compiling. JavaScript exists as a set of commands supporting interactive levels above and beyond HTML without the need for server-based CGI programs.

JavaScript's vocabulary is much smaller than Java's, and is easily understandable by authors currently working with HTML. Java is a full-blown programming language, and benefits from knowledge of C and C++. Programming in Java requires a set of development tools, including a compiler and class library. All that is needed to take advantage of JavaScript is a text editor or HTML authoring application and a compatible browser, such as Netscape Navigator 2.0.

Note

For the most up-to-date information, check out Netscape's home page at **http://home.netscape.com**. It includes access to online documentation for JavaScript and links to pages exploiting JavaScript.

JavaScript Basics

In order to understand what is happening inside a section of JavaScript code and how to use it on your pages, it is necessary to understand a few key ideas of how JavaScript is constructed.

Objects and Properties

An object is similar to a noun. Cars, people, buildings, dogs, pencils, and coffee cups can all be considered objects. They're tangible things we can touch and feel. Properties help define the object. They can be variables or other objects.

IV

Forms and Scripting

Let's create an object called `libraryBook` with the properties of title, author, and dueDate. In JavaScript, we can define the object like this:

```
libraryBook = new checkOutBook("Return of the Native",
➥"Thomas Hardy", "04/15/96")
```

This line calls a function which results in a creation of a new object with the following values:

```
libraryBook.title = "Return of the Native"
libraryBook.author = "Thomas Hardy"
libraryBook.dueDate = "04/15/96"
```

Writing a function to create an object is covered later in this section.

Tip

JavaScript is case-sensitive, which can lead to confusion when creating objects and errors at run-time. For example, libraryBook and LibraryBook would be two different objects in JavaScript. It is important to strictly adhere to one style for naming items in JavaScript — your sanity depends on it.

Now, include another object called `libraryInfo` with the properties of branch, address, phone, which contains the following values:

```
libraryInfo.branch = "Downtown"
libraryInfo.address = "111 Higgins St."
libraryInfo.phone = 4065551212
```

To add more information to our `libraryBook` example, add the `libraryInfo`:

```
libraryBook.publicLibrary = libraryInfo
```

Here's what just happened. A new property named `publicLibrary` was added to `libraryBook`. This new property was assigned the value from the `libraryInfo` object. The properties for `libraryBook` are listed in table 16.1.

Table 16.1 Values of *libraryBook* Object

Object/Property Name	Value
libraryBook.title	"Thomas Hardy"
libraryBook.author	"Return of the Native"
libraryBook.dueDate	"04/15/96"
libraryBook.publicLibrary.branch	"Downtown"
libraryBook.publicLibrary.address	"111 Higgins St."
libraryBook.publicLibrary.phone	4065551212

JavaScript assigns values by adding properties to objects. If an object is added as a property, then the parent object (librarybook) inherits the properties of the child (publicLibrary).

Methods and Functions

Methods and functions are the verbs of JavaScript. These are the items that "do" something. JavaScript includes a set of predefined methods and functions, in addition to allowing users to create their own special-purpose items.

Functions and methods begin with the function declaration:

```
function printTextAndLine (string) {
document.write(string + "<HR>")
}
```

First, function lets the browser know that this is the definition of a process. Until the end of the function declaration is reached, no statements are executed. The function must be called somewhere else in the document before anything happens.

The name of the function follows. The name is used to invoke the function later on. The last item is an argument list surrounded by parentheses. In our example, there is only one argument called string.

The body of the function is enclosed in curly brackets ({ }). When the closing bracket is reached, the function definition is completed.

> **Tip**
>
> JavaScript text is treated like any other HTML text. Extra spaces and carriage returns are ignored, but should be used to make the code more readable. Normally in coding, a carriage return is used to delineate the start of a new command or line. In JavaScript, command lines are separated with a semicolon.

When a function is added to an object, it is called a method.

Continuing with the librarybook example, let's define a new function called printCheckout:

```
function printCheckout() {
document.write("Your book: " + this.title + "<BR>");
document.write("  Due on: " + this.dueDate + "<P>");
}
```

This function is added to the object the same as another object:

```
libraryBook.printInfo = printCheckout
```

To invoke the method requires a single statement:

```
libraryBook.printInfo().
```

> **Tip**
>
> There are two ways of formatting text inside JavaScript. The first uses standard HTML tags generated by the document.write function. In order for these to work, they must be sent to the screen encapsulated in quotation marks like any other text.
>
> The second is with JavaScript codes, which are included in the string expression NOT enclosed in quotation marks. JavaScript formatting codes are listed in table 16.2.
>
> The following two statements would yield the same results, a break at the end of the line:
>
> ```
> document.write("Something<BR>another line")
> document.write("Something  \n another line")
> ```

Table 16.2 JavaScript Text Formatting Codes

Code	Purpose
\b	backspace
\f	form feed
\n	new line
\r	carriage return
\t	tab character

JavaScript can use an additional set of codes to format text displayed with document.write. These codes are included in the string with a plus sign (+) and no quotation marks.

Creating Objects

Creating objects is a two-step process.

1. Create a function which defines the object.

2. Assign a variable to the function using new.

Going back once again to the libraryBook, a function to create a book object could look something like this:

```
function book(title, author, dueDate) {
this.title = title;
this.author = author;
this.dueDate = dueDate;
}
```

Our library book is defined with the following statement:

```
libraryBook = new book("Return of the Native","Thomas Hardy","04/15/96")
```

Tip

JavaScript supports a special object called `this`. In general, this refers to the calling object. It is especially useful for validating form information.

For example, the tag `<input type="text" name= "ssn" width="9" onChange="validId(this)>` will call the function `validId` with the information entered by the user in the ssn text box.

In turn, we can create other objects using the same definition:

```
libraryBook2 = new book("Life Among the Savages","Shirley
➥Jackson","03/18/96")
collegeLibraryBook = new book("Red Shirt, Green Shirt","Sandra
➥Boynton","05/01/96")
```

Variables

Unlike Java, JavaScript does not enforce explicit data types.

Note

An explicit data type can only handle a specific type of data, such as integers, floating point decimals, or strings. Implicit data types are defined on-the-fly as a value is assigned to the variable. For example, a variable called `weekDay` is assigned a number representing the day of the week, 3 for Wednesday. When it's time to print the text, the variable can change type by a simple expression such as, "if weekDay = 3 : weekDay = "Wednesday".

JavaScript supports four basic kinds of variables: object, numeric, string, and date. As discussed earlier, JavaScript is based on objects. While similar to other variables, it is different in a key behavior. The "value" of objects are changed by adding properties, methods, and other objects. So, while a variable can be a property of an object, an object is never a property of a variable.

The next two variables, numeric and string, are straightforward. Numeric is any number, integer or floating-point decimal. A string is any collection of characters, included letters, numbers, and special characters.

Note

JavaScript has a feature called *automatic type conversion*. This feature will convert a string variable to numeric and vice versa, depending on its use.

For example, the variable x is assigned to 10, and the variable increment is assigned to "3." The statement "x = x + increment" evaluates to 13. The first type encountered by JavaScript is numeric, so the second variable is also converted to a numeric value. If increment was assigned to "Bob," the statement would return an error, since numeric conversion is impossible for "Bob."

Using implicit typing, JavaScript has eliminated the need for commands found in other languages, such as val and str, used to convert strings to numeric values and vice versa. It also places more responsibility on the person writing the code to manage variables to ensure that inconsistent data types are not brought together in a 3 + "Bob" situation.

Dates

The date data type does not contain a "date" the way we normally think of a date. JavaScript calculates the date and time based on the number of milliseconds since midnight on January 1, 1970. It sounds a little complicated, but it is a fairly standard form of calculating dates and times with computers.

Where it starts to get complicated is assigning a new date variable. The date is entered "yy,mm-1,dd,hh,mm,ss". Translated, this means entering the year, the month minus one, the day, hours, minutes, and seconds. For example:

```
docFirstDay = new Date(96,0,13,6,15,00)
```

This creates a variable called docFirstDay with a value of January 11, 1996 at 6:15 am.

Accessing the current date requires creating a new variable, usually called today, the same way docFirstDay was created. Then, each component is accessed through separate methods:

```
today.getMonth()
today.getDate()
today.getYear()
today.getHours()
today.getMinutes()
today.getSeconds()
```

Tip

Don't forget to add 1 to the month. JavaScript begins its year with January equal to 0.

You can add and subtract the values from date methods. For example, using the onLoad event handler, you could check the current date against the date the document was modified and inform the user if the information they're going to read is out of date.

> **Note**
>
> The date on the client's computer is used for all date calculations. So, if your date is based on the correct date and time, and the client computer is set to 1/1/85, any calculation based on the current time will be inaccurate.

Adding JavaScript to HTML

As seen in some of the previous examples, adding JavaScript to HTML is a fairly simple matter. There are a couple of points to keep in mind when deciding where to place the scripts.

- When an HTML document is called by a browser, the page is loaded into memory before its tags are evaluated and displayed. For this reason, it's best to place all function definitions inside the <head> tags at the beginning of the document, where they are loaded into memory before the user has a chance to initiate any events. The exception is JavaScript code that is executed with the rest of the page. It should be included inside the <body> tags so it is processed at the proper time.

- Browsers incompatible with script languages will display any text inside the <script> tags as text, so it's best to use comment tags to hide it. Hiding the script will not interfere with a compatible browser's ability to load and run it.

With this ability in mind, JavaScript can reside in two places inside an HTML document.

- As statements and functions using <script> tags.
- As event handlers using HTML tags.

Scripts

Now that some of the basic building blocks are in place for creating JavaScript procedures, it's time to try some examples.

Listing 16.1 illustrates a simple script to display text on a page.

Listing 16.1 A Simple HTML Document with JavaScript

```
<html>
<head>
This is an HTML page.
</head>
<body>
```

```
This begins the body of an HTML page.
<script language="JavaScript">
<!-- Hide text from old browsers
document.write("<hr>Hello from JavaScript.<hr>")
alert("You have entered a JavaScript-powered page")
//finish hiding script -->
</script>
That's all, folks.
</body>
</html>
```

Examining the code line by line reveals what is happening. First, under HTML commands, a simple text line is displayed on the screen. Then, the script flag is encountered, letting the browser know that the following lines will need to be interpreted as JavaScript commands.

The two JavaScript lines, *alert* and *document.write*, are both methods for displaying information on the screen. The alert function beeps and displays a dialog box with a message, which can then be cleared by the user. The next line displays text on the screen like normal HTML text. Since JavaScript commands are interpreted separate from the browser, any formatting needs to be inserted into the string before it is sent to the page. In this example, the <hr> tag inserts a horizontal line above and below the JavaScript text to separate it from the HTML text on the screen.

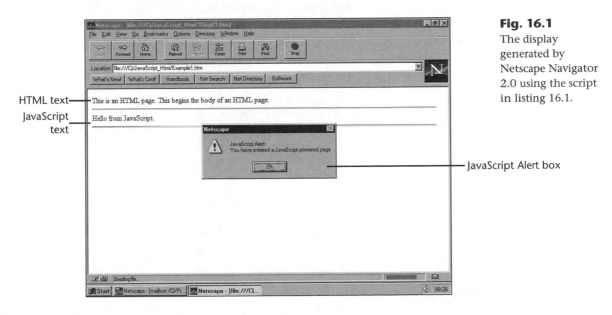

Fig. 16.1
The display generated by Netscape Navigator 2.0 using the script in listing 16.1.

HTML text

JavaScript text

JavaScript Alert box

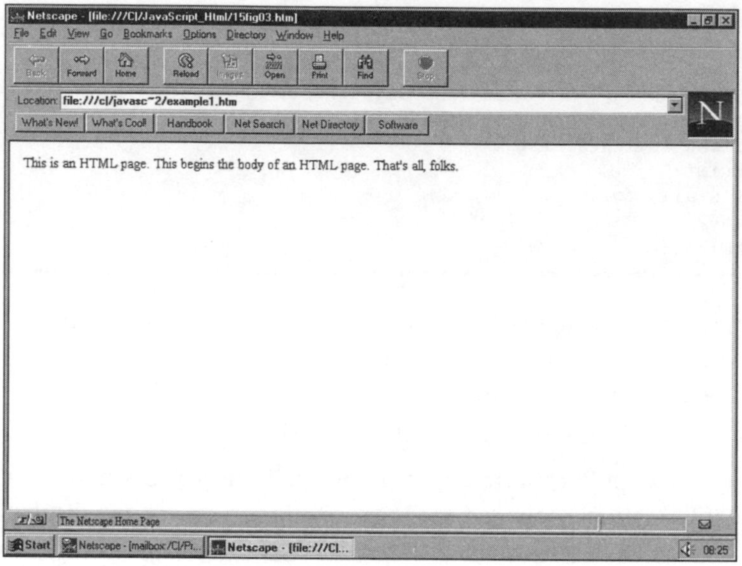

Fig. 16.2
The display generated by a noncompatible browser only shows HTML text. The script commands are ignored and hidden by comment tags.

Listing 16.2 illustrates the placement of functions and events that trigger them. This code produces figure 16.3.

Listing 16.2   A Simple JavaScript Event-Handling Function

```
<html>
<head>
This is an HTML page.
<script language="JavaScript">
<!-- Hide text from old browsers
function outTheWindow() {
newWin =open("","DisplayWindow","toolbar=no,directories=no,menubar=no");
newWin.document.write("<HEAD><TITLE>HTML On The Fly!</TITLE><HEAD>");
newWin.document.write("<H1>Now is the time to make HTML work.</H1>");
}
//finish hiding script -->
</script>
</head>
<body>
This begins the body of your average HTML page.
<form>
<input type="button" name="button" value="Press Here For Results"
➥onClick="outTheWindow()">
</form>
</body>
</html>
```

When the document is loaded, the outTheWindow function is defined for future use. A button is drawn on the screen inside a form. Clicking the button is detected by the onClick event handler, which triggers the function.

The function itself is the basis for some intriguing possibilities with script languages. JavaScript opens a new window in the browser and begins to generate HTML code. The initial value that is left blank can also contain a URL to another file on your server, or any other address on the Web.

Event Handlers

Event handlers, coupled with the basic programming functions, allow Web developers to implement client-based interactivity. JavaScript includes a basic set of event handlers that provide the capability to deal with most things a user will do with a form or the mouse pointer (see table 16.3).

Table 16.3 JavaScript Event Handlers		
Name	**User Event**	**Example**
click	Click on form element or link	onClick
mouseover	Mouse pointer moved over a link or anchor	onMouseOver
blur	Remove input focus from form element	onBlur
focus	Form element selected for input	onFocus
select	Form element's input field selected	onSelect
change	Changed value of text, textarea, or select element	onChange
load	Navigator loads page	onLoad
unload	User exits the page	onUnload
submit	Form is submitted	onSubmit

The following script shows how additional information can be provided for links to other items by using the onMouseOver event to place a custom message in the status bar.

```
<html>
<body>
If you need more information about JavaScript, check out
<a href="http://home.netscape.com/" onMouseOver="window.status=
↪'The Netscape Home Page'; return true"> Netscape.</a>
</body>
</html>
```

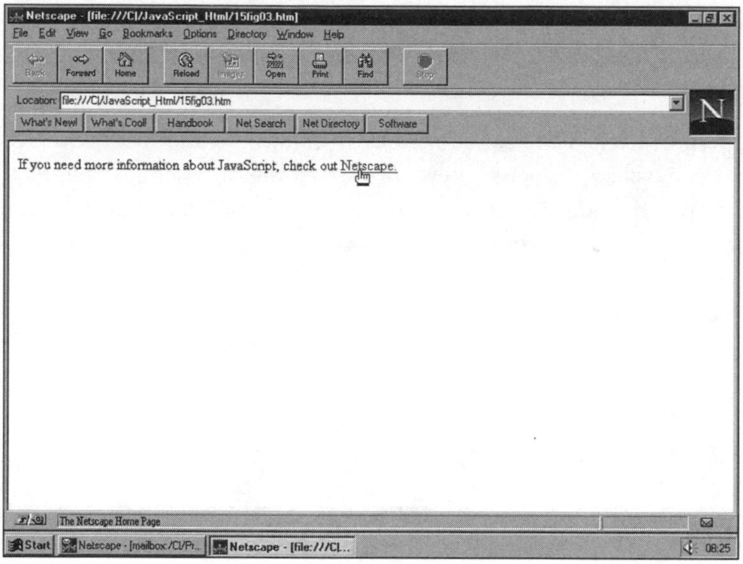

Fig. 16.3

The display generated by listing 16.2. Note the status bar at the bottom of the screen, where the link's URL is replaced by text from the event handler tag.

The real power of event handlers is evident in validating user information (see listing 16.3).

Listing 16.3   A Script To Validate User-Entered Information

```
<html>
<head>
<script language="JavaScript">
<!-- Hide script from old browsers
function checkPassword(string) {
if (string="password") {
newWin = open("download/safezone/index.html","DisplayWindow",
➥"toolbar=no,directories=no,menubar=no");
}
else {alert("Invalid password.")
}
// end script hiding -->
</script>
<body>
Please type your name in the box:
<form>
<input type="password" name="name" size=8
➥onBlur="checkPassword(this.value)" value="">
</form>
</body>
</html>
```

After entering a password in the form box, it is checked against the generic password. If "password" is entered, then a new window is opened with a different HTML document.

Obviously, this is not a secure way to deal with passwords, but you get the idea of the kind of validation and entry-checking possible without accessing the server.

The Future of JavaScript

As of publication, JavaScript is implemented as part of Netscape 2.0 and 2.01. This is not the end of its development, however, as Netscape has reserved words for future properties and methods. Proposed HTML specifications will limit script actions to events generated within form tags, but currently, JavaScript capabilities extend beyond the defined limits. Two examples are the OnLoad and OnUnLoad events, triggered when a page is entered and exited, which are possible to include within body tags.

Netscape also has plans to support JavaScript from the server through a compiled form of the language. When a Web page containing server-side JavaScript is encountered, it will only perform the code locally. This type of application can be used to track the current browser connection and other information from the user. In this form, JavaScript could be pressed into CGI service without dealing with PERL or C. Future plans call for JavaScript-related applications to provide access to standard database products.

JavaScript can also interact with the exposed properties and methods of Java applets and plug-ins. Once the object is declared on the page, JavaScript can get and set properties and call methods within scripts by using its standard object hierarchy, beginning with the class or plug-in name as the object name.

Visual Basic Script

Visual Basic Script, also known as VB Script, is a new scripting language packaged with Microsoft's Internet Explorer 3.0. VB Scripts are connected to events, defined by attaching "On" handlers to HTML tags. The event triggers the script, which interacts with its environment through a set of objects representing HTML page element, history list, plug-in applications, object files, and applets.

The syntax of VB Script is based on Visual Basic, although VB Script offers a much smaller and simpler set of commands to work with. It is used to validate form data, create new Web pages on-the-fly, and perform other operations with user input.

While VB Script resembles the object-oriented JavaScript, it is not necessary to understand object-oriented programming.

Visual Basic Script Isn't Visual Basic

VB Script is described by Microsoft as a "fast, lightweight" subset of Visual Basic designed for use inside HTML pages. While requiring a compiler on the host machine, VB Script has no ability to create user interfaces. Every item manipulated by VB Script must first exist in the HTML page. The files required to integrate VB Script with a browser take approximately 200K of disk space.

Microsoft Visual Basic is a programming language geared towards developing applications for Windows. It includes editors, debuggers, and compilers for the creation of independent applications. It consumes approximately 1 MB of disk space for the basic set of tools.

Note

Updates on Microsoft's development and support of Visual Basic Script can be found through Microsoft's Web site at **http://www.microsoft.com/intdev/vbs/**.

Visual Basic Tools

Since VB Script is a subset of Visual Basic, it is upwardly compatible to Visual Basic for Applications which is upwardly compatible with Visual Basic. For Web managers and developers already familiar with Visual Basic, the trip to productivity and interactivity will be a short one.

Note

Browsers often employ "helper applications" to extend the capabilities of HTML documents. Some of these applications are built-in or generally included as part of the software package (some sound and graphics), while others are added later by the user (animation and compressed files).

If a browser sees an item tag it doesn't recognize, it checks its list of helper applications and calls the matching program to handle the information between the tags.

Data and Variable Types

VB Script's only data type is called a *variant*. A variant can contain different types of information depending on how it's assigned or used. Since it's the only data type in VB Script, all functions return it.

Since different types of information may be passed to the variant, the command **VarType** is used to return information about what kind of data is stored within. At a simple level, variants contain string or numeric data. If it is used in a mathematical equation, it is treated as a number; if used in a string, it behaves like a string.

Since the basic types of data come in many varieties, the variant is equipped with subtypes to help further define its use. Subtypes include boolean, integer, single, and double (floating point numbers), date and string. Information can be translated from one subtype to another using the conversion functions included with VB Script.

Variables are declared using the `Dim` statement. For example:

```
Dim TotalBill
```

creates a variable called `TotalBill`, which is a variant. Its subtype is empty, since no value has been assigned yet. Variables can also be declared implicitly by using a valid name somewhere within your script. For example:

```
ItemCharge = 10.50
```

creates a variable named `ItemCharge`, which is a variant of subtype single, since it has been assigned a floating point value.

Standard Naming Rules

Variable names follow a simple set of standard rules which also apply to all other user-defined items.

- Names must begin with an alphabetic character.
- It can't contain an embedded period.
- Length is restricted to 255 characters.
- Must be a unique name within the scope it's used.

When a variable is declared within a procedure, only commands and statements within that procedure can access or change the value of the variable. This is called local scope. If a variable needs to have a scope that extends to all procedures within a script, it should be declared outside of a procedure definition. It has script-level scope.

Local scope variables retain their value only while the procedure is running. Once the procedure returns control to the script, the variable is lost until created again by calling the procedure again. A script-level variable will maintain its value until the script is completed.

VB Script also supports arrays. The only difference in declaration is the addition of parentheses with the number of elements.

```
Dim ExecutiveBoard(12)
```

Since all arrays include a 0 element, the previous example contains 13 elements. Arrays can contain up to 60 dimensions.

Tip

To create a dynamic array, whose size can change during run-time, use the ReDim statement.

```
ReDim ItemsOrdered()
```

Note the difference with the parentheses. A dynamic array does not use a size value.

To increase or decrease the size of the array, use ReDim with a value. Changing the number of elements will clear existing values in the array unless the Preserve statement is used.

```
ReDim ItemsOrdered(6)
...
ReDim Preserve ItemsOrdered(7)
```

Procedures

Procedures come in two varieties with VB Script, Sub and Function.

A Sub procedure can accept parameters and perform actions, but does not return a value when it is completed. If it doesn't accept parameters, it is declared with a set of empty parentheses.

```
Sub AddNumbers(First,Second)
    NumSum = First + Second
    MsgBox "The sum of " & First & " and " & " Second " is " &
    ➥NumSum & "."
End Sub
```

A Function is similar to a Sub, but it can return a value. This is accomplished by assigning a value to the function name.

```
Function AddNumbers(First,Second)
    AddNumbers = First + Second
End Function
```

Tip

Like functions in JavaScript, Subs and Functions should be declared in the <head> portion of an HTML page. This ensures the procedures are loaded and ready by the time the user sees the page and has a chance to act.

Working with Forms

One of VB Script's most powerful uses is for data validation without server interaction. This makes it possible to ensure users submit information that your server is expecting, preventing unexpected error messages.

Values from forms are referenced using their names. For example, a text box named "SSN" is accessed using SSN.value in a calling function.

Using Objects

In order for VB Script to get and set object properties from OLE controls or Java classes, it is first necessary to define the object using the <object> declaration with the "ID" parameter to identify it.

Once it is inserted, its properties and methods are invoked by using the appropriate syntax.

For properties and values, use the name and a dot:

```
PictureButton.Caption = "Display Image"
```

For event handlers, use an underscore:

```
Sub PictureButton_Click ()
...
End Sub
```

Embedded Objects

One key item that is included with Microsoft's entry into scripting is control of Object Linking and Embedding (OLE) controls, expanded and renamed as ActiveX.

Getting ActiveX

An ActiveX software development kit (sdk) is available for download from Microsoft's Internet Developer Web site at **http://www.microsoft.com/intdev/sdk/ sdkdownl.htm**. It includes ActiveX development tools and a copy of Internet Explorer 3.0. This is a very large download (12 MB), which is also available in 2 MB or 1 MB chunks if your modem is slower or your Internet connection is less-than-reliable.

OLE controls, also called OCXs, are graphical objects with well-defined external interfaces which may be manipulated by Visual Basic and other Microsoft-related tools.

These controls are embedded in HTML documents in formats similar to Netscape's plug-ins, although the formal standard is still under development.

ActiveX expands the capabilities of OCX controls by adding additional tools for embedding a wide variety of software components directly into a Web page, including graphics viewers, animation sequences, credit card transaction objects, or spread sheet applets. For example, the ActiveMovie API released by Microsoft is an ActiveX control that plays video sequences within the browser.

ActiveX controls can be included as part of VB Script or JavaScript applications to extend interactivity and functionality of Web pages. It will also extend beyond Microsoft's browser to Netscape with a plug-in module co-developed by Microsoft and nCompass Labs. By implementing multiple-browser support, ActiveX could become a very popular way of including live objects in HTML documents.

The new object controls also allow authors and developers easier access to client-server communications, including WinSock TCP, FTP Client, HTTP, HTML, POP, SMTP, and NNTP.

Note

For the most recent W3 Consortium proposal regarding HTML embedded objects, check out the W3 Web site at **http://www.w3.org/pub/WWW/TR/ WD-insert9512221.html**. This site also includes other HTML and Web standards information useful for Web administrators and authors.

Two important properties planned for Internet-aware OCXs are known as `ReadyState` and `OnReadyStateChange`. This will allow specific OCXs to declare their current state and trigger actions based on changes to that state. This could lead to interesting developments in OCX planning, as it allows an OCX to progressively load itself while supporting greater levels of functionality and responsibility for actions.

For example, a button could be active as soon as the button state code is loaded, even though graphics display is not fully rendered or active.

But, Microsoft is not alone in its pursuit of easy-to-use embedded objects. Oracle has developed Network Loadable Objects (NLOs) for its PowerBrowser software. NLOS are programs and program modules that load and run on the client machine, and are similar in function to a CGI application on the server. NLOs offer the developer access to the user interface and client network access facilities, which are especially useful for long-term operations which must maintain states across network access.

One of the first ready-made NLO programs being offered by Oracle supports integrating a Netscape plug-in interface, so HTML pages with this type of content can be loaded and displayed correctly by PowerBrowser.

NLOs are similar to Visual Basic controls in the sense that they are third-party applications that can be plugged into the browser to implement new functions. However, this also means they share a common drawback. NLO programs are binary objects, which makes it easier to insert viruses or Trojan horses into the code. One recommendation is to distribute NLOs in combination with their source code so they can be inspected and compiled by the user. However, because NLOs are similar to other plug-in modules, they can also be downloaded and scanned for corruption before you run them on your system.

CScript

CScript is an extension of the Server Sides Includes specification. It is implemented as a part of SSI+. CScript is an enhanced subset of the C programming language. With CScript you are able to include complete C-like programs within an HTML page without needing to compile the program. CScript is the natural complement to JavaScript; while JavaScript is client-based, CScript is server-based. Like JavaScript, CScript follows the C syntax conventions. Anyone familiar with C will be able to use CScript. CScript is native to WebQuest NT 2.0, and currently is only available with WebQuest NT 2.0.

> **Note**
>
> More information about CScript is provided with WebQuest NT 2.0 files, including SSIPLUS.HTM. Also, information is available at Questar's Web site, **http://www.questar.com/**.

Features

CScript is a complete programming language. Most of the features of C are available within CScript. Like C, CScript includes variables, flow control, operators, string manipulation, type casting, assignment, and outputting. Also, CScript has some unique features relevant to the World Wide Web like ODBC, Cookies, and SMTP mail. The following is a quick overview of some of the elements of CScript.

CScript Basics

The CScript tag allows you to embed C-like code directly into a HTML file. All the semantics and features of a high-level object-oriented language like C are available without a compiler or the limitations of CGI. CScript is added to a HTML file using the opening <!--#cscript tag and the closing --> tag.

Listing 16.4 shows a simple CScript that calls a DLL called WQODBC.DLL. This DLL connects to the nwind datasource, queries the datasource and returns data in the specified format.

Listing 16.4   ODBC Manipulation Using CScript

```
<!--#cscript
WQODBC,Connect("nwind",NULL,NULL,FALSE,LOCAL_SOCKET);
WQODBC,Query("nwind","SELECT Freight,Freight,Freight,Freight
➥FROM Orders","String: %s<BR>Currency(10.2f): $%10.2f<BR>
➥Currency Left Aligned(-10.2f): $%-10.2f<BR>Percent:
%%%.2f<P>",TRUE,LOCAL_SOCKET);
WQODBC,Disconnect("nwind",FALSE,LOCAL_SOCKET);
-->
```

In listing 16.5, flow control and logical operators are used to find out if the variable USER_NAME matches the name on a hard coded list. If the name matches, the second message is displayed. If the name does not match the first message, "You are not on the list" is displayed.

Listing 16.5   Flow Control and Comparison Using CScript

```
<!--#CScript
if( !strstr( "Kevin Alan Sue", USER_NAME )
{
print( "<p>You are not on the list" );
exit(0);
}
else
print( "<p>Yes,  you are on the list" );
-->
```

Variables

All variables are represented as self-allocating objects, and are available in the following formats:

- Form objects, like standard SSI environment variables
- Ordinals, standard C data types: int, float, and char
- Nonstandard data types: text, logic, and dword

- Strings, text objects
- Structures, user defined data types
- Arrays, sequential list of CScript data types and structures.

Flow Control

A complete implementation of flow control is available with CScript using standard operands.

- if, else, switch
- for, while, goto
- break, exit

Operators

Mathematical, logical, and comparison operators are implemented as in C.

- Math: +, −, *, /, ^
- Logic: &, |, !
- Comparison: ==, >, <, >=, <=, !=, !>, !<

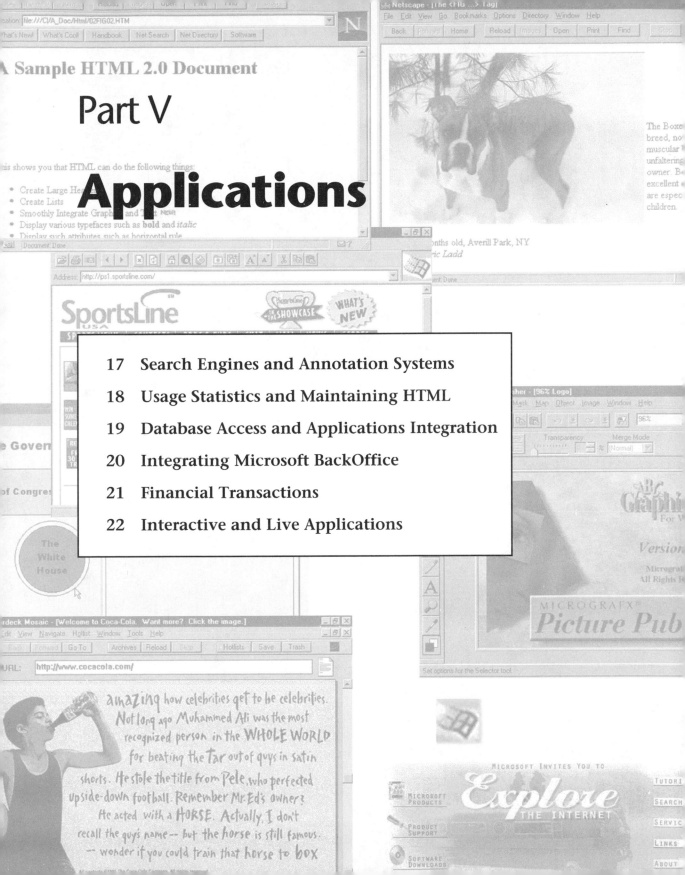

Part V

Applications

## CHAPTER 17

Search Engines and Annotation Systems

The previous chapters covered the basics of setting up a Web server, writing HTML, and creating forms and scripts. The last chapters in this book use the tools discussed in the first part of the book to build or explain several useful applications that can be built with Web servers.

This chapter starts off with an introduction to search engines—a mechanism to search through simple databases—and more sophisticated indexing and retrieving software that search through an entire Web space and present the resulting list in a hypertext document in accordance with the tradition of the Web. Specifically, we look at two popular freeware Web search engines, namely, ICE and WAIS.

This is the age of information sharing. The data is of little use that cannot be shared and shared alike. The second part of this chapter presents techniques for using the Web technology as a workgroup tool for information sharing. Several vehicles for conducting workgroup discussion are presented, including list servers, newsgroups, and Web conferencing systems. Methods of creating annotation capabilities are also discussed.

In this chapter, you learn:

- How to build simple search and retrieval scripts for simple databases
- How to set up and use an advanced search engine to search an entire Web server
- How to use Web technology as a workgroup tool, including document annotation capabilities and Web conferencing systems

Searching Simple Databases

In the last chapter, you saw how to write a simple script to search an online phone book for names and numbers. Although this can be considered a simple database application, it differs from what is normally thought of as a database because users can view but not enter information. Creating Web database applications that can modify, add, and delete from databases is covered in Chapter 19, "Database Access and Applications Integration"; this chapter is more concerned with search and retrieve applications that are used as guide maps around the vast Web, providing a simple form-query-result paradigm to navigate the Web.

Even though many types of data in an organization are maintained centrally, they often still need to be made available to hundreds or even thousands of users, either internally or externally. Examples of this type of data include a company phone and address book, a product catalog that maps product numbers to titles, or a list of regional sales offices and contacts. All of these types of information can be stored in a relational database, but there's really no need for anything more than a text file, if the goal is to quickly and easily make information available. A simple Web search routine can achieve the desired result without requiring the maintenance of a relational database.

WAIS

Yet another popular freeware search utility for Web and Gopher servers running on Windows NT is the European Microsoft Windows NT Academic Centre's (EMWAC) Wide Area Information Server (WAIS). It is included on the WebmasterCD.

WAIS Architecture

WAIS is comprised of three basic components:

- WAISSERV—a protocol handler and search engine
- WAISINDEX—the indexing utility
- WAISLOOK—the search utility

The WAIS Search engine implements features like Boolean (AND, OR, NOT) searches and synonym files.

WAIS and WebQuestNT

In Chapter 7, "Configuring the Questar WebQuest Server," you reviewed the steps needed to create a WAIS index using the built-in Indexing of WebQuest NT. Incorporating the index into an HTML page is very simple.

The methodology for creating and setting up a WAIS index is to

1. Create the index.
2. Create the HTML index page.
3. Bind the index to the page.

Before you begin, make sure you have created the index for the Web space. Included with WebQuest is a group of HTML files. The following examples use an index of all of those files. Create the index by clicking on the Index button, and then New. Type the name of the index; for this example use **index**. Now the Edit Index window opens allowing you to select the files to index. Select them all and click on Generate Index. Now you need to bind the index to an HTML document. Listing 17.1 is sufficient code to create an HTML index page.

Listing 17.1   HTML for Creating an Index Page

```
<HTML>
<HEAD><TITLE>INDEX PAGE</TITLE>
<ISINDEX>
</HEAD>
<BODY>
<H1>MY INDEX PAGE</H1>
</BODY>
</HTML>
```

Create an HTML file called INDEX.HTM identical to the one shown above and save it in the default Web space. Open up WebMeister and click on the Admin button. In the right window you will see a list of files and one of them is INDEX.HTM. Highlight it by clicking on it once. On the left side of the window is a list of indexes that have been created for this Web space. Double-click on the index you want to bind to the index page; in this example double-click on "index." Notice the NOT INDEXED listing; double-clicking on this will unbind an index from an index page. What distinguishes the example index page from a normal HTML file is the <ISINDEX> tag located in the header. This tag tells the server to put a data entry field on the page where the tag is located (see fig. 17.1).

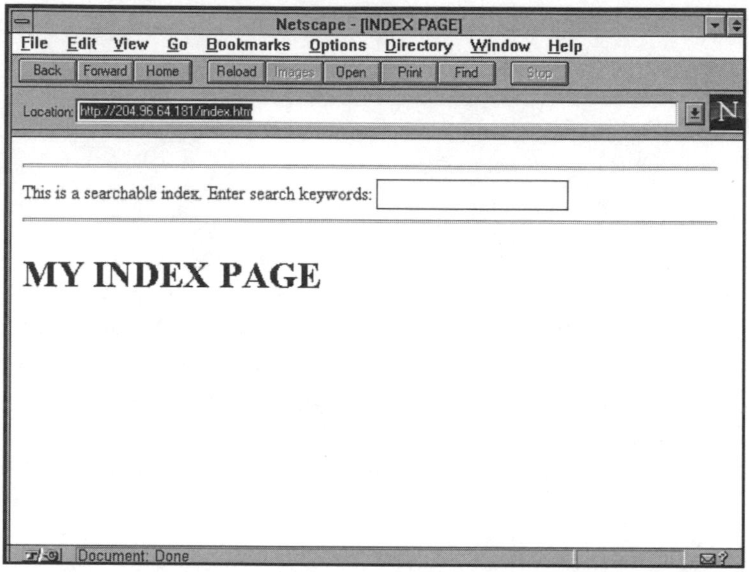

Fig. 17.1
Sample Index
HTML page.

The WAIS search engine built in to WebQuest will take any query entered into the datafield and search for it, weigh it, and return the information to the client. Notice that the results are returned as links (see fig. 17.2).

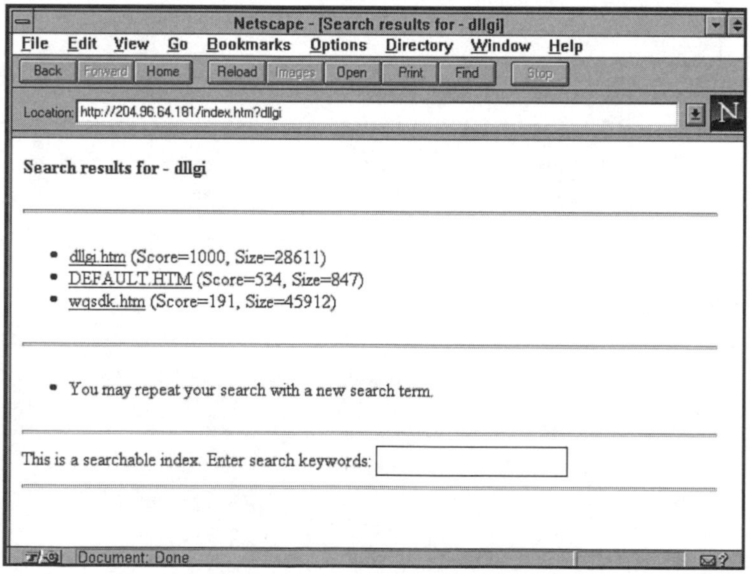

Fig. 17.2
Results of Query
from Sample
Index HTML page.

The index created by WebMeister consists of nine files. You will need to leave them intact to use WebQuest's built-in WAIS engine. A word of caution: the index is the sum of the words of the selected files. The index files can get very large. One of the few disadvantages of using WAIS is the preprogrammed formatting. For example, the results of a search can't be returned into a table. WAIS is a very simple robust way of searching a Web space. Included with WebQuest, WAIS becomes the easiest, quickest way of creating a search engine for your Web space.

WAIS Operation

Operation of WAIS is similar to that of ICE. It involves creation and periodic updating of the index files.

> **Note**
>
> The configuration information of WAIS is set up using the WAIS Control Panel Applet. See figure 17.3.

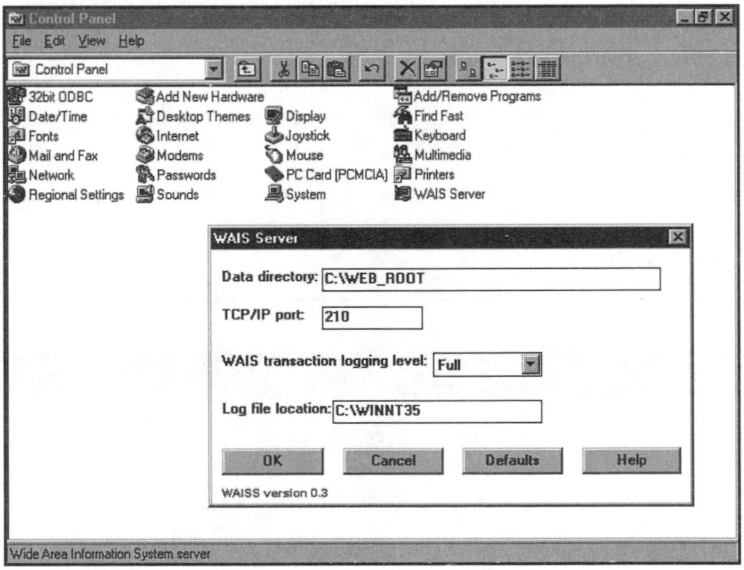

Fig. 17.3
The WAIS Control Panel applet.

Once the configuration information has been set up, the index can then be created using the WAISINDX program. The WAISINDX program can be used to create indexes that are intended to be used internally, within the site, or it can be used with the -export option, which allows us to register it with the database of databases, thus opening our database to public use. To register, send the index.src file to the following e-mail addresses:

wais-directory-of-servers@cnidr.org

wais-directory-of-servers@quake.think.com

> **Note**
>
> To export a WAIS database and register it with the WAIS database of databases, check the information in index.src, making sure it contains an IP address and a DNS name, as well as the TCP/IP port under which the WAIS Server is running.

Grepping for Data

In the previous chapter, the phone book example demonstrated how to search a text file containing names and phone numbers. At the heart of the search is the grep command, which simply looks for pattern matches in a file. One of the benefits of this approach is that the text file need not be in any certain format. Grep just reads each line of the file for a match; it doesn't care how many columns there are or what characters are used to separate fields. Consequently, the phone book script from the previous chapter can be used to search any text file database. That script has been generalized from the phone book example and is reprinted in listing 17.2. Figure 17.4 shows the resulting search form.

> **Note**
>
> Grep is a command native to UNIX. There is a command line that is grep-executable (grep.exe) included with the Windows NT resource kit. You will need the executable to run these examples.

> **Tip**
>
> You can make searches case-sensitive by removing the -i option from the grep command.

Listing 17.2   A Simple Search Program To Sift Through a Phone List

```perl
# search.pl

# Define the location of the database
$DATABASE="\\web_root\\cgi-bin\\phone.txt";

# Define the path to cgiparse
$CGIPATH="\\web_root\\cgi-bin";
# Convert form data to variables
eval '$CGIPATH\\test\\cgiparse -form -prefix $';

# Determine the age of the database
$mod_date=int(-M $DATABASE);

#Display the age of the database and generate the search form
print <<EOM;
Content-type: text/html

<TITLE>Database Search</TITLE>
<BODY>
<H1>Database Search</H1>
The database was updated $mod_date days ago.<p>
<FORM ACTION="/cgi-bin/search.pl" METHOD="POST">
Search for: <INPUT TYPE="TEXT" NAME="QUERY">
<INPUT TYPE="SUBMIT" VALUE="SEARCH">
</FORM>
<p><hr><p>
EOM

# Do the search only if a query was entered
if (length($query)>0) {
  print <<EOM;
Search for <B>$query</B> yields these entries:
<PRE>
EOM

#Inform user if search is unsuccessful
$answer = 'grep -i $query $DATABASE';
if (!$answer) { print "Search was unsuccessful\n" ;}
else { print $answer\n" ; }

print <<EOM;
</PRE>
</BODY>
EOM
}
```

To use the script for data other than the phone book, simply change the name and location of the text file containing the desired information. Because the script uses the generic grep command, it can be used with almost any text file for any purpose.

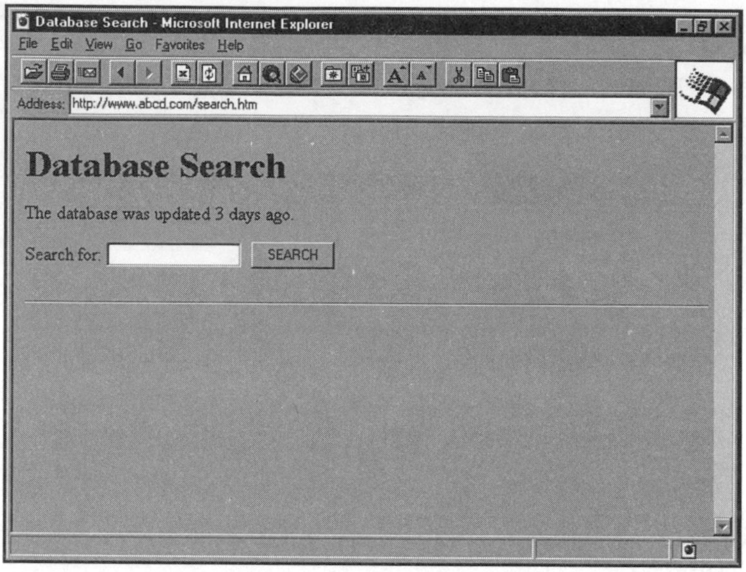

Fig. 17.4
This generalized database search form is used with the search script in listing 17.2 to search any text file database.

Generating Text Files from Databases

To take advantage of the simple search routine in listing 17.2, you must have some text file data to start with. If your data is currently in another format, such as a proprietary database, you must first convert it to an ASCII text file. You can easily create the necessary text file by exporting the data from the native format to ASCII text. Almost all databases include the capability to export to text files.

> **Tip**
>
> For easiest use of the search script, export data so that there is exactly one record per line. This produces the neatest output from the script.

After the text file has been created, you simply need to specify its path in the search script.

Choosing between Several Databases

With a few simple modifications, you can use the script generically to search one of many databases that all have different paths. This can be done most efficiently in one of two ways. You can allow the database to be chosen by selecting one of several hyperlinks, in which case extra path information in the URL can be used to specify the database. Or, you can allow the user to choose which database to search in a fill-in form.

Choosing via Hyperlinks

Suppose you want users to be able to choose between several different divisional phone books. One way to do this is to include a pre-search page on which the user selects the database by clicking the appropriate hyperlink. Each link calls the same database search script, but each includes extra path information containing the path to the database. The following HTML demonstrates how the hyperlinks are constructed.

```
<H2>Company Phonebooks</H2>
<A HREF="/cgi-bin/search.pl/db/IAphone.txt">Iowa Locations</A>
<A HREF="/cgi-bin/search.pl/db/CAphone.txt">California Locations</A>
<A HREF="/cgi-bin/search.pl/db/KSphone.txt">Kansas Locations</A>
```

The name of the search script in this example is /cgi-bin/search.pl and the databases are named /db/IAphone.txt, and so on. The search script itself needs to be modified to use the extra path information.

First, the name of the database to search is now specified in the extra path information rather than hard-coded into the script. Therefore, the line at the top of the script that specifies the path to the data needs to read the extra path information. This is done by reading the PATH_INFO environment variable. In PERL, the syntax for this is:

```
$DATABASE=$ENV{"PATH_INFO"};
```

Second, the ACTION attribute of the form, which is generated inside the script, needs to specify the path to the database, as well. This way, after the user performs the initial query, the correct database will still be in use. This is done by changing the <FORM ACTION...> line to:

```
<FORM ACTION="/cgi-bin/search.pl$DATABASE">
```

> **Note**
>
> No slash (/) is necessary to separate the script name (/cgi-bin/search) from the extra path information because $DATABASE already begins with a slash.

These are the two modifications necessary to implement choosing a database via hyperlinks. The hyperlinks to other databases are now included in the search form also. The resulting form is shown in figure 17.5. The complete modified script code is included in listing 17.3. Only new or changed lines have been commented.

V

Applications

Listing 17.3 Choosing Databases Using URLs

```perl
# search2.pl

# Get database name from extra path info.
$DATABASE=$ENV{"PATH_INFO"};

$CGIPATH="\\web_root\\cgi-bin";
eval '$CGIPATH\\test\\cgiparse -form -prefix $';

$mod_date=int(-M $DATABASE);

# Show the current database and list other available databases.
# The <FORM ACTION ...> line now includes the database name as extra
# path info.
print <<EOM;
Content-type: text/html

<TITLE>Database Search</TITLE>
<BODY>
<H1>Database Search</H1>
Current database is $DATABASE.           Show the current database
It was updated $mod_date days ago.<P>
You can change to one of the following databases at any time:<P>
<A HREF="/cgi-bin/search/db/IAphone.txt">Iowa Location</A><BR>
<A HREF="/cgi-bin/search/db/CAphone.txt">California Locations</A><BR>
<A HREF="/cgi-bin/search/db/KSphone.txt">Kansas Locations</A><P>
<FORM ACTION="/cgi-bin/search2.pl$DATABASE" METHOD="POST">
Search for: <INPUT TYPE="TEXT" NAME="QUERY">
<INPUT TYPE="SUBMIT" VALUE=" Search ">
</FORM>
<p><hr><p>
EOM

if (length($query)>0) {
  print <<EOM;
Search for <B>$query</B> yields these entries:
<PRE>
EOM

$answer = 'grep -i $query $DATABASE';
if (!$answer) { print "Search was unsuccessful\n" ;}
else { print $answer\n" ; }

print <<EOM;
</PRE>
</BODY>
EOM
}
```

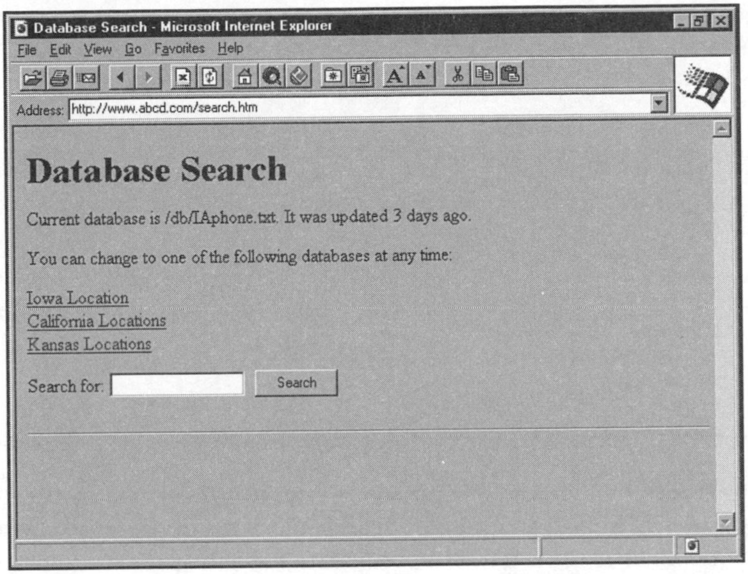

Fig. 17.5
This method uses hyperlinks to select a new search database.

Choosing via a Form

Depending on the application, it may be more convenient for users to choose their database via a form rather than via hyperlinks. The initial form uses radio buttons to choose the desired database, and after that the chosen database is active for all searches. Figure 17.6 shows the initial form used to select the database. The form code is included in listing 17.4.

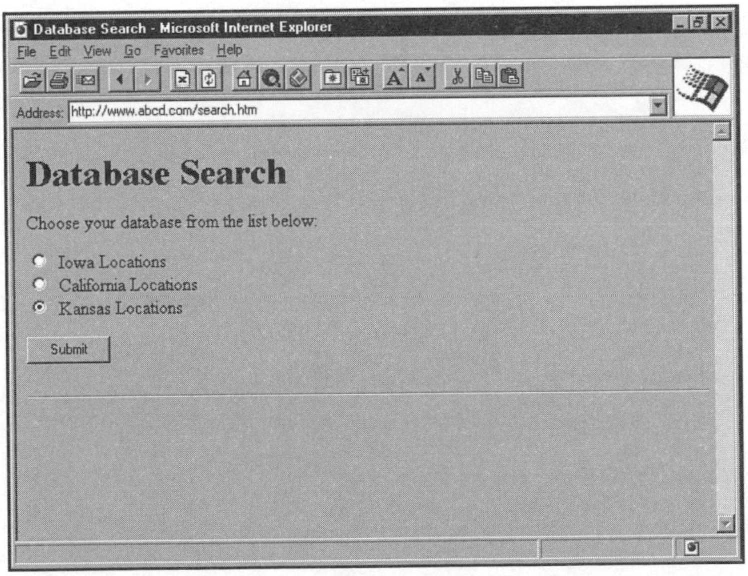

Fig. 17.6
In this form, you select the search database and then proceed to the search form.

Listing 17.4   Choosing Search Database via a Form

```
<TITLE>Database Search</TITLE>
<BODY>
<H1>Database Search</H1>
Choose your database from the list below:<P>
<FORM ACTION="/cgi-bin/search3.pl" METHOD="POST">
<INPUT TYPE="RADIO" NAME="DATABASE" VALUE="/db/IAphone.txt"
CHECKED>Iowa Locations<BR>
<INPUT TYPE="RADIO" NAME="DATABASE" VALUE="/db/
CAphone.txt">California Locations<BR>
<INPUT TYPE="RADIO" NAME="DATABASE" VALUE="/db/KSphone.txt">Kansas
Locations<P>
<INPUT TYPE="SUBMIT" VALUE=" Submit ">
</FORM>
<p><hr><p>
```

The initial selection form passes the path of the chosen database in the input field named "DATABASE", so only two modifications are necessary to the original search script that receives this information. First, the path to the database is now read from the initial selection form, so a separate line defining $DATABASE is no longer necessary. Second, the search form must have a way to keep track of the current database. This is conveniently accomplished by including a hidden input field in the search form named "DATABASE". This way, whether the search form is called from itself or from the initial selection form, it always knows the path to the correct database. The code for the search script is included in listing 17.5. Only the new or changed lines are commented. The resulting search form appears in figure 17.7.

Listing 17.5   Passing Database Name via Hidden Form Fields

```
# search3.pl

$CGIPATH="\\web_root\\cgi-bin";
eval '$CGIPATH\\test\\cgiparse -form -prefix $';
# $DATABASE is now defined as a form variable

$mod_date=int(-M $DATABASE);

# A hidden field <INPUT TYPE="HIDDEN" NAME="DATABASE" ...> stores the
# database path.
print <<EOM;
Content-type: text/html

<TITLE>Database Search</TITLE>
<BODY>
<H1>Database Search</H1>
The current database is $DATABASE.
The database was updated $mod_date days ago.<p>
```

```
<FORM ACTION="/cgi-bin/search3.pl" METHOD="POST">
<INPUT TYPE="HIDDEN" NAME="DATABASE" VALUE="$DATABASE">
Search for: <INPUT TYPE="TEXT" NAME="QUERY">
<INPUT TYPE="SUBMIT" VALUE=" Search ">
</FORM>
<p><hr><p>
EOM

if (length($query)>0) {
  print <<EOM;
Search for <B>$query</B> yields these entries:
<PRE>
EOM

$answer = 'grep -i $query $DATABASE';
if (!$answer) { print "Search was unsuccessful\n" ;}
else { print $answer\n" ; }

print <<EOM;
</PRE>
</BODY>
EOM
}
```

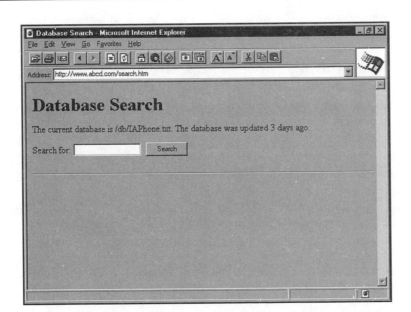

Fig. 17.7
Once the search
database is selected
in a separate form,
this form is used
to perform the
search.

Searching Multiple Files and Directories

The previous examples searched only one file at a time. However, grep is
flexible enough to search multiple files and directories simultaneously.

Searching Multiple Files

In the previous example, the user was allowed to choose between several different phone directories. However, it's also possible to search several files at the same time. The script is easily modified to do this because the grep command can search multiple files simultaneously. Instead of specifying one file in the $DATABASE environment variable, specify a path to the directory containing the phone text files (\db). So, the line beginning $DATABASE= in the original script (search.pl) changes to:

```
$DATABASE="\\db\\*.txt";
```

The grep command now searches all files in the \db directory that correspond to the wildcrd pattern specified for the desired information.

Searching Multiple Directories

Taking it a step further, the grep command can also accept multiple files in different directories. For example, you can specify the following database files:

```
$DATABASE="\\db\\phone*.txt \\db2\\address*.txt"
```

Now, the grep command searches all TXT files in the \db directory beginning with phone and all TXT files in the \db2 directory beginning with address.

Accommodating Formless Browsers

Although most Web browsers today have forms capability, not all do. To allow these browsers to search for information, it's common to offer an alphabetical or numerical index of data as an alternative to entering a form-based query. Typically, you create a hyperlink for each letter of the alphabet and specify a URL for each hyperlink that performs the appropriate search. For example, in a phone book listing where last names are listed first, you could search for capital Cs at the beginning of a line to get a listing of all last names beginning with C. To create a hypertext index that can submit this type of search automatically, write the code shown in listing 17.6.

Listing 17.6 Breaking Down Databases Alphabetically

```
<H1>Phone Book Index</H1>
Click on a letter to see last names beginning with that letter.<P>
<A HREF="/cgi-bin/search?A">%26A</A>
<A HREF="/cgi-bin/search?B">%21b</C>
...
<A HREF="/cgi-bin/search?Z">%26Z</Z>
```

> **Note**
>
> The queries in this example begin with the caret (%26 = ^) to force grep to look for the specified character at the beginning of a line.

Searching an Entire Web Server

So far, we have only looked at searching collections of simple text files. However, one of the most useful utilities on any Web server is the capability to search for words anywhere on the server, including plain text and HTML files. It's theoretically possible to simply grep all HTML and TXT files under the document root (and other aliased directories), but this can be very time-consuming if more than a handful of documents are present.

The solution to the problem of searching a large Web server is similar to that used by other types of databases. We maintain a compact index that summarizes the information present in the Web server's content area. As data is added to the database, we just keep updating the index file. The usual method of maintaining the integrity of the index file is to run a nightly (or more frequent) indexing program that generates a full-text index of the entire server in a more compact format than the data itself.

Indexing with ICE

A popular indexing and searching solution on the Web is ICE, written in PERL by Christian Neuss in Germany. It's freely available on the Internet from **http://www.informatik.th-darmstadt.de/~neuss/** and is included on the WebmasterCD. In the discussion that follows, we cover ICE, how it works, and how it can be modified to include even more features. By default, ICE includes the following features:

- Whole-word searching using Boolean operators (AND and OR)
- Case-sensitive or case-insensitive searching
- Hypertext presentation of scored results
- The ability to look for similarly spelled words in a dictionary
- The ability to find related words and topics in a thesaurus
- The ability to limit searches to a specified directory tree

ICE presents results in a convenient hypertext format. Results are displayed using both document titles (as specified by HTML <TITLE> tags) and physical file names. Search results are scored, or weighted, based on the number of occurrences of the search word or words inside documents.

The ICE Index Builder

The heart of ICE is a PERL program which reads every file on the Web server and constructs a full-text index. The index builder, `ice-idx.pl` in the default distribution, has a simple method of operation. The server administrator specifies the locations and extensions (TXT, HTML, etc.) of files to be indexed. When we run `ice-idx.pl`, it reads every file in the specified directories and stores the index information in one large index file (by default, `index.idx`). The words in each file are alphabetized and counted for use in scoring the search results when a search is made. The format of the index file is simple (see listing 17.7).

Listing 17.7   Format of ICE Index File

```
@ffilename
@ttitle
word1 count1
word2 count2
word3 count3
...
@ffilename
@ttitle
word1 count1
...
```

Running the Index Builder

The index builder is typically run nightly, or at some other regular interval, so that search results will always be based on updated information. Normally, ICE will index the entire contents of directories specified by the administrator, but it can be modified to index only new or modified files, as determined by the last modification dates on files. This saves a little time, although ICE zips right along as it is.

Windows NT users can use the native `at` command to schedule the indexing utility.

Tip

It's often a good idea to schedule `at` jobs at odd times because many other jobs run on the hour by necessity or convention. Running jobs on the hour that don't have to be run this way unnecessarily increases the load on the machine.

> **Note**
>
> The Windows NT "scheduler" service has to be running in order to schedule jobs using the at command

Space Considerations

Searching an index file is much faster than searching an entire Web server using grep or a similar utility; however, there is a definite space/performance tradeoff. Because ICE stores the contents of every document in the index file, the index file could theoretically grow as large as the sum of all the files indexed! The actual "compression" ratio is closer to 2:1 for HTML because ICE ignores IITML formatting tags, numbers, and special characters. In addition, typical documents use many words multiple times, but ICE stores them only once, along with a word count.

> **Note**
>
> When planning your Web server, be sure to include enough space for index files if you plan to offer full-featured searching.

The Search Engine

The HTML which produces the ICE search form is actually generated from within a script (ice-form.pl), but calls the main search engine (ice.pl) to do most of the search work. The search simply reads the index file previously generated by the index builder. As the search engine reads consecutively through the file, it simply outputs the names and titles of all documents containing the search word or words. The search form itself and the search engine can be modified to produce output in any format desired by editing the PERL code.

Tips and Tricks

The ICE search engine is powerful and useful by itself. However, there's always room for improvement. This section discusses several modifications you can make to ICE to implement various additional useful features.

Directory Context

A very useful feature of ICE is the ability to specify an optional directory context in the search form. This way, you can use the same ICE code to conduct both local and global searches. For example, suppose you're running an internal server that contains several policy manuals and you want each of them to be searchable individually as well as together. You could simply require that users of the system enter the optional directory context themselves; however, a more convenient way is to replace the optional directory context box with radio buttons that can be used to select the desired manual.

A more programming-intensive method is to provide a link to the search page on the index page of each manual. The URL in the link can already include the optional directory context so that users don't have to enter this themselves. This way, when a user clicks the link to the search page from within a given manual section, the search form automatically includes the correct directory context. For example, you can tell the ICE search to look only in the /benefits directory by including the following hyperlink on the Benefits page:

```
<A HREF="/cgi-bin/ice-form.pl?context=%2Fbenefits>Search this
manual</A>
```

> **Note**
>
> The slash (/) in front of benefits must be encoded in its ASCII representation (%2F) for the link to work properly.

In order for this to work, you'll need to make the following necessary modifications to ice-form.pl:

- Set the variable $CONTEXT at the beginning of the script (using cgiparse or your favorite parsing utility) based on what was passed in from the search URL.

- Automatically display the value of $CONTEXT in the optional directory context box (<INPUT TYPE="TEXT" NAME="CONTEXT" VALUE="$CONTEXT">).

Speed Enhancements

If the size of your index file grows larger than two or three megabytes, searches will take several seconds to complete due to the time required to read through the entire index file during each search. A simple way to improve this situation is to build several smaller index files, say, one for each major directory on your server, rather than one large one. However, this means you can no longer conduct a single, global search of your server.

A more attractive way to break up the large index file is to split it up into several smaller ones, where each small index file still contains an index for every file searched, but only those words beginning with certain letters. For example, `ice-a.idx` contains all words beginning with "a," and `ice-b.idx` contains all words beginning with "b." This way, when a query is entered, the search engine is able to narrow down the search immediately based on the first letter of the query.

Note

In the event that your server outgrows the first-letter indexing scheme, the same technique can be used to further break up files by using unique combinations of the first two letters of a query, and so on.

In order to break up the large index file alphabetically, you need to modify the ICE index builder (`ice-idx.pl`) to write to multiple index files while building the code. The search engine (`ice.pl`) also needs to be modified to auto-select the index file based on the first letter of the query.

Searching for Words Near Each Other

Although ICE allows the use of AND and OR operators to modify searches, it only looks for words meeting these requirements anywhere in the same document. It would be nice to be able to specify how close to each other the words must appear, as well. The difficulty with this kind of a search is that the ICE index doesn't specify how close to each other words are in a document. There are two ways to overcome this.

First, you can modify the index builder to store word position information, as well as word count. For example, if the words "bad" and "dog" each occur three times in a file, their index entries might look like this:

```
bad 3 26 42 66
dog 3 4 9 27
```

In this case, 3 is the number of occurrences, and the remaining numbers indicate that "dog" is the 4th, 9th, and 27th word in the file. When a search for "bad dog" is entered, the search engine first checks if both "bad" and "dog" are in any documents, and then whether any of the word positions for "bad" are exactly one less than any of those for "dog." In this case, that is true, as "bad" occurs in position 26 and "dog" occurs in position 27.

There's another way to search for words near each other. After a search is entered and files containing both words are found, those files can simply be read by the search program word-by-word, looking for the target words near each other. Using this method, the index builder itself doesn't have to be modified. However, the first method usually results in faster searches because the extra work is done primarily by the index builder rather than by the search engine in real-time.

Other Web Search Solutions

The Net seems vastly endless in its repertoire of solutions to choose from. You should thoroughly study the feature sets of the various search systems to decide on one that would best suit your Web site with respect to operating system, Web server, volume and value of content, and security. The following list should serve as a basic checklist of things to consider before deciding on any one of the solutions:

- Compatibility with Operating System
- Compatibility with Web Server
- Boolean Searches (AND, OR, NOT operators)
- Synonym searches
- Plural searches (a search for "woman" also returns all documents with reference to "women")
- Weighted results
- Ease of installation and integration
- Amount of programming involved

The following table shows a list of available commercial, shareware, and freeware Search systems that may be used on a Web site. It is important to note that this list is, by no means, exhaustive.

Product	Company	Address
Excite	Architext Software	**www.excite.com**
Livelink Search	OpenText Corp.	**www.opentext.com**
Verity	Verity Inc.	**www.verity.com**
CompasSearch	CompasWare Development Inc.	**www.compasware.com**
NetAnswer	Dataware Technologies Inc.	**www.dataware.com**
Fulcrum Search Server	Fulcrum Technologies Inc.	**www.fultech.com**

Including Content

A very desirable enhancement to a search system would be to include some sort of summary of each document presented in the search results. The Lycos

Web searcher does exactly this by displaying the first couple of sentences of each document on its search results page. This allows users to quickly find the documents most relevant to their topic of interest.

> **Tip**
>
> The Lycos Web searcher is located at **http://lycos.cs.cmu.edu/**.

To include summary content, store the first 50-100 words in every document in the index file created by the index builder. Doing this, however, requires yet more storage space for the index file, and therefore, may not be desirable.

Web Conferencing: Discussion and Annotation Systems

The World Wide Web was originally developed as a medium for scientific and technical exchange. One of the important elements of that exchange is the sharing of ideas about other people's work. This has been common on UseNet news for many years now, but articles are limited largely to plain ASCII text. The Web, with its superior hypertext presentation, presents opportunities for richer exchange, but has developed as a remarkably one-sided communications medium thus far. This is unfortunate for those who would like to take advantage of the Web's superior document capabilities along with the flexibility and interactivity of UseNet.

Why Is the Web One-Way?

In spite of various techniques such as CGI scripting, the World Wide Web is still primarily a one-way medium, with the client issuing requests and the server serving requested documents. However, these limitations are not fundamental to either the HTTP protocol or HTML. The ingredients necessary for worldwide annotation of Web documents and posting new documents to servers are already in place, but these have not yet been implemented. There are, however, a few exceptions, which are discussed in the following section.

Group Annotations

The most notable exception is NCSA Mosaic, which supported a feature called *group annotations* in the first few versions. This feature allows users to post text-only annotations to documents by sending annotations to a group annotation server, which NCSA provided with earlier versions of its Web server. Group annotations, however, have been abandoned in later versions of Mosaic in favor of the HTTP 1.0 protocol, which supports group annotations in a different manner.

CGI and HTTP POST

The second exception is CGI scripting, which allows data to be received rather than sent by a server. The data is usually simple text, such as a query or form information, but it can also be an entire document, such as an HTML file, spreadsheet, or even an executable program. The ability to post documents to CGI scripts, however, is not particularly useful, as of yet, because Web clients don't support it. What would be useful is an introduction of a <FILE> element to forms, which, when selected, would ask the user to specify the name of a local file to be sent to the server when the form is submitted. This would be a convenient way to upload documents to a Web server in the same way that documents are uploaded to CompuServe or bulletin board systems.

Because HTTP and HTML already support most (if not all) of the ingredients necessary for a more interactive Web, it's probably only a matter of time before these will be incorporated into browsers and servers alike. In the meantime, however, prototypes of what the future holds have been constructed using news, e-mail, and CGI scripts.

News and the Web

UseNet news makes available today in plain ASCII text some of what the Web will do tomorrow in HTML. News can effectively be used as both a private or public tool for information exchange. Public newsgroups are the most familiar, with worldwide distribution and the ability for anyone to post articles to these groups. By running your own news server, you can also create entirely private newsgroups (as for an internal bulletin board system) or semiprivate groups, which the public can read but not post to. The ability to control who can read news and who can post to a local server makes news a useful tool for workgroup discussion.

Tip

Many Web browsers can both read and post news. This simplifies the use of both news and hypertext in an organizational context by providing a common interface for viewing both kinds of documents.

While news is an excellent medium for conducting entirely private (inside a corporate network) or entirely public conversations (UseNet), it's not as well suited for allowing discussions between a select group of individuals located all over the world. It's possible to create a special news server for this purpose and use password security to ensure that only the intended group of people can read and/or post news to the server. However, users of the system would be inconvenienced because most news readers expect to connect to one news server only. If users were already connecting to another news server to receive public news, they would have to change the configuration information in their news reader in order to connect to the special server. Fortunately, there are other answers to this problem.

Hypermail

E-mail is a more flexible method of having semiprivate discussions among people all around the world. Using a mailing list server (list server), it is possible to create a single Internet e-mail address for a whole group of people. When an item is sent to the mailing list address, it's forwarded to all members of the list. This approach has several advantages over running a news server, in addition to the previously mentioned convenience issue.

First, e-mail is the most widely accessible of all Internet services. Individuals are more likely to have e-mail access than any other Internet service. Secondly, e-mail is something that users typically check regularly for new messages. Consequently, there is less effort involved in receiving "news" or discussion items from a mailing list than in checking for news in a separate news reader. The same applies to posting news, which tends to encourage use of the system.

> **Tip**
>
> Through various e-mail gateways, it's possible to do almost anything by e-mail that can be done on FTP, Gopher, news, or the Web, only slower.

A very nice complement to a mailing list is a *mailing list archive*, which stores past items on the mailing list. Public mailing list archives are frequently found on FTP sites, but they can also be stored on the Web. A really powerful tool called *hypermail* converts a mailing list archive into a hypertext list of messages, neatly organized to show message threads. Mail archives converted with hypermail can be sorted by author, subject, or date.

> **Tip**
>
> A commercial mail server for Windows NT which integrates other features such as List Server, Hypermail, etc. is NTMail. Information on NTMail is available at **http://www.mortimer.com/ntmail/default.htm**.

V

Applications

Annotation Systems

While e-mail and news are both valuable tools for workgroup discussion, they still lack an important feature: the ability to make comments on a document in the document itself. In the paper world, this is accomplished with the infamous red pen. However, the equivalent of the editor's pen in the world of hypertext markup is just beginning to manifest. The ultimate in annotation would be the ability to attach comments, or even files of any type, anywhere inside an HTML document. For now, however, it's at least possible to add comments to the end of an HTML page. Several people are working on annotation systems using existing Web technology. The following sections take a brief look at a few of them.

HyperNews

Not to be confused with hypermail, HyperNews does not actually use the UseNet news protocol, but it allows a similar discussion format and is patterned after UseNet. You can see examples of HyperNews and find out more about it at **http://union.ncsa.uiuc.edu/HyperNews/get/ hypernews.html**. Figure 17.8 shows a sample screen of a browser's access to a HyperNews server.

Fig. 17.8
A HyperNews
server.

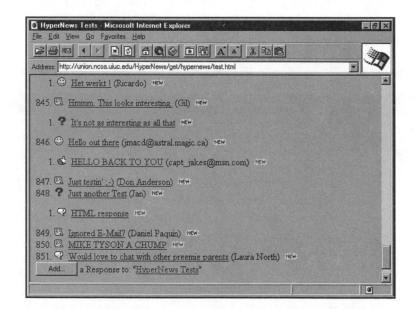

W3 Interactive Talk (WIT)

A similar system originating at CERN allows new *proposals*, or comments, to be submitted in response to a given document. This is a practical way for a group of engineers, for example, to discuss a document. Some degree of security is possible by requiring users to have a valid user name and password before they can post comments. This can be combined with user authorization procedures to control who can see documents, as well. More information on W3 Interactive Talk is available at **http://www.w3.org/hypertext/WWW/WIT/User/Overview.html**.

Web Conferencing Systems

The glaring deficiency of the Web, namely, that it has been a one-way drive, has not gone unnoticed, however. There are quite a few systems available that employ the traditional client-server architecture to implement Web conferencing systems.

One commercially available Web conferencing product is WebNotes for Windows NT, a product of OS TECHnologies Corporation. WebNotes is a client-server solution where the "client" is any HTML-capable Web browser (Mosaic, Netscape, etc.). The WebNotes server software maintains discussion threads of topics of discussion, remembers "already-seen" messages by users, and allows users to post discussion material either as text, or as HTML documents with inline graphics. It also employs a text search engine that facilitates retrieving discussions based on the result of a search query. Figures 17.9 and 17.10 show sample screens of discussion threads and the general navigation concepts.

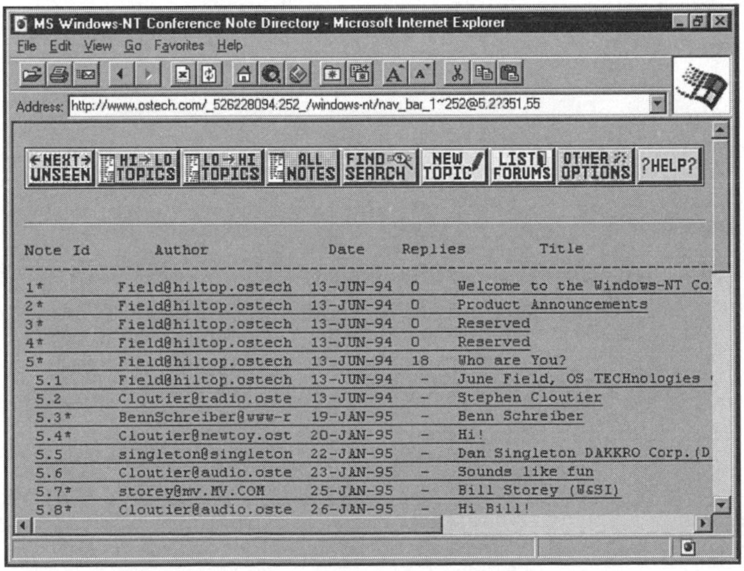

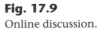

Fig. 17.9
Online discussion.

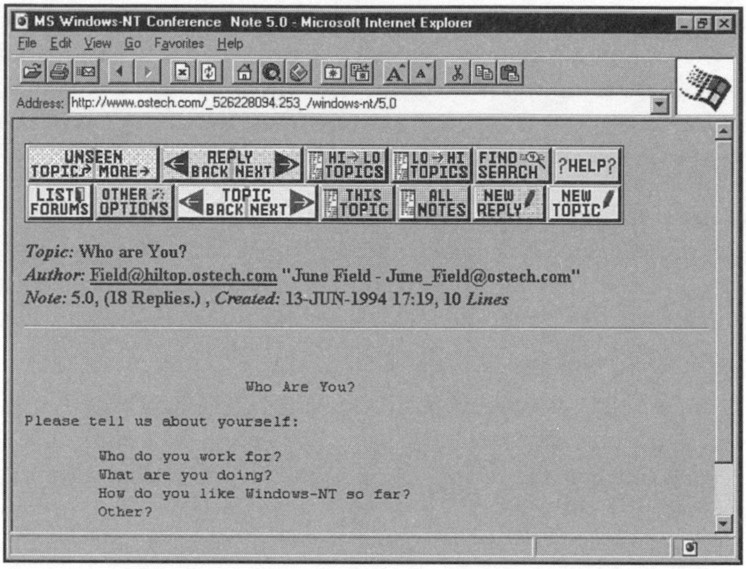

Fig. 17.10
Notice the navigation buttons at the top of this figure.

Note

You can find more information and a live demonstration of WebNotes on OS TECHnologies' home page at **http://www.ostech.com**.

Other Web conferencing systems that you can find on the Net include, but are not limited to:

- Agora Web Conferencing System—**http://www.ontrac.yorku.ca/agora**
- WebBoard from O'Reilly and associates—**http://webboard.ora.com/**
- Futplex system—**http://gewis.win.tue.nl/applications/futplex/index.html**
- Cold Fusion Forums from Allaire—**http://www.allaire.com/**
- InterNotes from Lotus—**http://www.lotus.com/inotes**

Some of these systems also facilitate users in uploading files to the server, thereby allowing them to upload picture binaries to inline their message content with graphics.

Academic Annotation Systems

Many of the annotation-like systems on the Web today are academic in nature. At Cornell, a test case involving a computer science class allows students to share thoughts and questions about the class via the Web. Documentation on the Cornell system is available from **http://dri.cornell.edu/pub/davis/annotation.html**. The Cornell site also has useful links to related work on the Web. Some of the related systems that have been developed use custom clients to talk to an annotation database separate from the Web server itself, much like the early versions of Mosaic. This architecture may well be the future of annotations and the Web.

On the lighter side, take a peek at MIT's Discuss->WWW Gateway to get a behind-the-scenes look into an American hall of higher education. For a particularly novel and entertaining use of the Web, take a peek at the Professor's Quote Board at **http://www.mit.edu:8008/bloom-picayune.mit.edu/pqb/**.

Summary

In this chapter, you saw how to write a simple query system to search a textual database and to publish the result on the Web. You also took a look at how to use existing search engines to implement search functionality on a Web server and search through the entire Web server's HTML content. The later sections of the chapter gave you an overview of the future applications of the World Wide Web (Web conferencing systems and annotation systems). These sections also encouraged you to see the Web not as a one-way street, but as a totally interactive solution over the Internet. It will not be too long before the Web browser takes on the role of the universal client and act as a front-end to access all kinds of servers such as Web, news, Mail, FTP, bulletin boards, databases, and other client-server applications, even operating systems. ❖

## CHAPTER 18

Usage Statistics and Maintaining HTML

Setting up your server is literally just the start of your work. Administering, maintaining, and monitoring usage are important tasks that will keep you busy after your server is operational. The rapid growth of Internet usage and the growing interest in analyzing that usage means that there is a lot of work. Among your tasks will be monitoring usage statistics and monitoring and presenting those statistics.

Your customers, those people who put up the content of the WWW site and expect it to provide some return on investment, need to know if other people are coming to the site and what they do when they are there. Fortunately, with some effort, you can provide that information. A tremendous amount of information about the client systems and activities of the WWW site is captured and available for analysis.

Information such as how often your server is being accessed, what files are being accessed most often, what client is accessing your server, and how often they visit. You can convert any or all this information into graphical summaries quite easily using programs designed to collate server usage statistics.

When the amount of information on your server becomes large, checking that all intended files have been properly linked becomes more and more difficult. As the number of related documents grows, the only practical way to do this is to use automated programs that check your documents for you. Some of these programs are described below.

In this chapter, you learn:

- How to extract and interpret information from the server access and error logs
- What tools are available for analyzing and graphing usage statistics

- What tools are available for ensuring the integrity of your HTML files
- How to automatically find new and changed files on your server

Understanding Usage Logs

When your Web server is running, every document or file request is logged as a separate entry in the server's log files. The names and directory for these files can be administrator defined during server setup. For example, the access log file can be named "access.log" and placed in a logs directory under the computer's root directory. Errors are logged separately in "logs/error.log." The access and error logs are very similar but are discussed separately for clarity. The log files should *not* be located in a subdirectory of the Web documents directory! This makes this information too easily accessible to the world and you most likely will not want to share it.

The Log Formats

All major Web servers produce logs in one of two common formats, either CERN or EMWAC. This means you must use utilities written for the correct log format to analyze logs on your server. The formats include a lot of useful information about every document request except how long the transfer took.

The Access Log

The access log file records every single connection made to your server by other computers. These accesses are written in real-time and include a lot of information on the connection. Most server programs either have a default directory for storing log files or allow you to configure the server program to set where the log files should be kept. On NT computers, the default is in the system's "LogFiles" subdirectory usually on the C drive. However, most servers allow you to not only specify another directory but even a different name for the files. If you are trying to keep this information inaccessible to others or even if it will be easier for you to have a different name, you should change the defaults.

Information in the access log can include, depending on the server:

- The IP address of the client that requested the document
- The country code
- The domain type, i.e. EDU, COM, GOV, and ORG
- The domain name
- The precise date and time the transfer took place

- The day of the week and month
- The hour, minute, and second of the day
- The HTTP method and protocol used for the connection or transfer
- The virtual path to the document served
- The status of the transfer, whether it was successful or not
- How many bytes were transferred in both directions
- The browser used by the client
- The URL of the location the browser was at before it came to your server
- The login name if any authentication is in effect

If the information is not captured in the log file, it still is accessible from an environmental array passed by the client browser application to the server. If this is the case, you will have to write some code to parse the environmental array. Listing 18.1 is a short PERL script that returns all the values passed by a browser.

Listing 18.1   PERL Script Returning All Values Passed by a Browser

```
#!/usr/bin/perl
print "Content-type: text/html\n\n<HEAD>\n";
print "<PRE>\n";
printf ("%-24.24s %-80.80s\n", "Variable", "Value");
foreach (sort keys %ENV) {
    printf ("%-24.24s %-80.80s\n", $_, $ENV{$_});
}
print "<?PRE>\n";
```

The following is an excerpt from an access log generated by NCSA HTTPD for Windows, this log is in the CERN format:

```
s115.infonet.net - - [20/Oct/1994:20:53:17 -0500]
➥"GET / HTTP/1.0" 200 418
s115.infonet.net - - [20/Oct/1994:20:53:37 -0500]
➥"GET /httpddoc/overview.htm HTTP/1.0" 200 3572
s115.infonet.net - - [20/Oct/1994:20:54:00 -0500]
➥"GET /httpddoc/setup/admin/Overview.htm HTTP/1.0" 200 1165
s115.infonet.net - - [20/Oct/1994:20:54:17 -0500]
➥"GET /httpddoc/setup/Configure.html HTTP/1.0" 200 2500
s115.infonet.net - - [20/Oct/1994:20:54:27 -0500]
➥"GET /httpddoc/setup/httpd/Overview.html HTTP/1.0" 200 1121
```

The first item in each log entry is the address of the system that requested the document, followed by the date and time, the HTTP method (GET in this example), the virtual path to the file requested, the HTTP protocol level (1.0 in this example), status information (200 means OK), and the number of bytes transferred.

V

Applications

The following is an excerpt from an access log generated by WebQuest NT, this log is in the EMWAC format:

```
Tue Mar 05 11:29:45 1996 204.96.64.103 205.23.164.13 GET / HTTP/1.0
Tue Mar 05 11:29:54 1996 204.96.64.103 205.23.164.13 GET /
➥ssiecho.sht HTTP/1.0
Tue Mar 05 11:30:04 1996 204.96.64.103 205.23.164.13 GET /
➥flowctrl.sht HTTP/1.0
Tue Mar 05 11:30:20 1996 204.96.64.103 205.23.164.13 GET /
➥ssiplus.htm HTTP/1.0
Tue Mar 05 11:30:53 1996 204.96.64.103 205.23.164.13 GET /
➥odbctest.sht HTTP/1.0
Tue Mar 05 11:30:56 1996 204.96.64.103 205.23.164.13 GET /
➥mailform.htm HTTP/1.0
Tue Mar 05 11:31:04 1996 204.96.64.103 205.23.164.13 GET /
➥odbcupdt.htm HTTP/1.0
```

The first item in each log entry is the date and time of the request, followed by the IP address of the web space/virtual server, then the IP of the client, the request method, the element requested and the protocol.

The following is an excerpt from an access log generated by Microsoft IIS:

```
205.242.205.145, -, 3/5/96, 16:15:46, W3SVC, REDBACK, 204.96.64.10,
➥2203, 198, 3193, 200, 0, GET, /Default.htm, -,
205.242.205.145, -, 3/5/96, 16:15:51, W3SVC, REDBACK, 204.96.64.10,
➥4997, 211, 440, 200, 0, GET, /pix/cupid.gif, -,
205.242.205.145, -, 3/5/96, 16:15:57, W3SVC, REDBACK, 204.96.64.10,
➥5558, 213, 3066, 200, 0, GET, /pix/jm_logo.gif, -,
205.242.205.145, -, 3/5/96, 16:16:22, W3SVC, REDBACK, 204.96.64.10,
➥36603, 212, 21089, 200, 0, GET, /pix/butbar.gif, -,
205.242.205.145, -, 3/5/96, 16:16:32, W3SVC, REDBACK, 204.96.64.10,
➥41220, 220, 300, 200, 0, GET, /butbar.map, 456,61,
```

The first item in each log entry is the client's IP address, followed by their user name or a hyphen if the username is unavailible. Next is the date and time of the request followed by the services that responded to the request, either WWW (W3SVC), FTP (MSFTPSVC), or Gopher (GopherSVC). Next is the computer name of the server and its IP address, followed by the processing time, bytes received, and bytes sent. Next is the service code status, Windows NT status code, type of operation, and the element of the operation. The MS IIS logs can be converted into the CERN or EMWAC format using utilities that come with MS IIS.

> **Note**
>
> The address of the requesting client is usually in a name format, such as **s115.infonet.net** in this example, but can also be numerical if the server is unable to look up the name corresponding to the client's numerical IP address.

From these files and arrays, it is possible to put together a wide variety of statistics on your server usage, including

- Which documents are accessed most frequently
- Which hours of the day, days of the month, and so on are the busiest
- Which computers and domains (GOV, EDU, COM, and so on) access your server most
- The total volume of byte traffic (and percentage of your connection bandwidth) for any given time period
- Any error trends that may be occurring

Because every document access is recorded, log files can grow very quickly. This is compounded by the fact that inline GIF files are processed as separate requests, so, for example, a request for a document with three in-line GIFs actually shows up as four separate requests—one for the document and three for the GIFs. On even a moderately busy server, the access logs can grow to many megabytes each month.

With most servers, you can specify that new log files be generated every week or even daily. With the Microsoft IIS, the default is to create log files daily. In almost every circumstance, it is recommended that you set the server to generate daily logs. You can always combine them if needed. If you want to save historical log data, it is a good idea to periodically compress the log files and move them to an archive. You might want to do this automatically at the beginning of each month. The log files are plain text files viewable at any time by your favorite editor. Therefore you can keep track of usage on a real-time basis if you desire.

The Access Log of the Microsoft's Internet Information Server

Log entries recorded by Microsoft's Internet Information Server (IIS) service have the following items in this order:

1. Client IP address
2. Client User name (if known)
3. Date
4. Time
5. Service
6. Computer name
7. IP address of server
8. Processing time (ms)

V

Applications

9. How many bytes received

10. How many bytes sent

11. Service status code

12. Windows NT status code

13. Type of operation

14. Target of operation

If no information is available, the server inserts a dash (-) into the log file. For example, the Microsoft IIS generates access listings such as:

```
154.73.22.8, -, 12/28/96, 13:45:07, W3SVC, INETSRVR2, 157.55.84.1,
➥220, 250, 2593, 200, 0, GET, /Intro/tour/netshow.htm, -,
```

This means that an unidentified user from a computer with an IP address of 154.73.22.8 connected on December 28, 1996 seven seconds after 1:45 P.M. The user requested to GET and was served the file NETSHOW.HTM from the Intro/tour/ subdirectory. The request was all of 250 bytes and took 220 milliseconds to execute (without error) and resulted in a data return of 2593 bytes.

Literally every file requested is recorded in this fashion. GIFs and other files referenced from an HTML file are recorded as separate accesses. This is why an access log file can get big pretty fast!

The Access Log of the WebQuest Server

The WebQuest server records accesses in the following format:

```
Tue Dec 19 06:40:12 1995 204.96.64.11 137.175.2.66 GET /ict05.gif
➥HTTP/1.0
```

This indicates the date and time, the IP addresses of the server and the client computers, the operation performed (in this case a GET), the file requested, and the protocol.

The Access Log of Other Servers

Other servers generate slightly different listings. The Microsoft IIS provides a log conversion utility to convert a log from the default format to NCSA Common Log File or EMWAC format as well as perform reverse-DNS-lookup replacing all IP addresses with domain names.

The EMWAC's log file provides less information. A typical listing for the EMWAC access log looks like this:

```
Sun Mar 17 00:28:44 1996 inetsrvr.business.com 236.29.10.128 GET /
➥images/sept.gif HTTP/1.0
```

This listing only includes the date and time, the name of the server, the IP address of the client and the operation and file requested. This example shows a GIF file, even though the file was an image that was part of an HTML file.

The following is an example from an access log generated by NCSA HTTPD for Windows:

```
guest.info.net - - [20/Oct/1995:20:53:17 -0500] "GET /index.html
➡HTTP/1.0" 200 418
```

The first item in the log entry is the address of the system that requested the document, followed by the date and time, the HTTP method (GET in this example), the virtual path to the file requested, the HTTP protocol level (1.0 in this example), status information (200 means OK), and the number of bytes transferred (418).

> **Note**
>
> The address of the requesting client is usually written as the numerical IP address. It is more useful if the address is converted to a name format, such as **guest.info.net** as in the example above. However, log analysis software, like the products described below can take the numerical IP address and look up the name corresponding to the client's computer. Therefore, how the access log records the client is not a critical consideration. However, the more the access log does directly record is an advantage.

> **Note**
>
> If you want to see document requests as they happen rather than after the fact, the log files are accessible any time through your favorite text editor, even Notepad.

The Error Log with HTTPD

The format of the error log is very similar to that of the access log. Instead of reporting the number of bytes transferred, however, the error log reports the reason for the error. The following is an excerpt for an error log generated by NCSA HTTPD for Windows; this log is in the CERN format:

```
[20/Oct/1994:21:02:20 -0500] httpd: access to
➡c:/httpd/htdocs/httpddoc/setup/admin/AccessingFiles.html failed
➡for s115.infonet.net, reason: client denied by server configuration
[20/Oct/1994:21:07:53 -0500] httpd: access to c:/httpd/htdocs/docs
➡failed for s115.infonet.net, reason: file does not exist
```

```
[20/Oct/1994:21:08:13 -0500] httpd: access to c:/httpd/htdocs/
➥failed for s115.infonet.net, reason: client denied by server
➥configuration
```

The format of the file is pretty self-evident. The first part of the line indicates the date and time of the error. The second part of the log entry indicates what the client was trying to access when the error occurred. The third part of the log entry explains why the error occurred.

Error logs are valuable for showing attempted access to controlled documents by unauthorized users and reporting server problems. If error logs are monitored frequently, they may be your first clue that a hyperlink is "broken" because a document is missing or has moved. If you see several failed connection attempts to the same document, and the document does not exist, you could find the broken hyperlink (missing link?) by looking in the access log during the same time frame to see where the client was linking from.

Hopefully, your error log doesn't grow nearly as quickly as your access log, so archiving it is not as important for conserving space. However, if there are secure documents on your server, it may not be a bad idea to keep the error log in case it's needed to track down security problems discovered later.

The Error Logging with WebQuest

Error logging within WebQuest has been disabled. The logging was part of the ODBC-enhanced logging that is an option from WebMeister. Very few people use the ODBC-based logging given the added workload for the server. By default, Error and Access logging are disabled with WebQuest. Contact Questar if you need to have these features enabled.

Sifting Usage Data

The access file is a great record of your server's activity, but it's pretty tough to get anything meaningful out of the raw data. You need to sift and sort the log files and turn them into valuable demographics that illustrate the usage of the Web site. This will justify the investment in the successful pages and assist in understanding how to improve the less successful pages. This information can be used to support the quality of the server or justify the need to upgrade.

There are a wealth of tools and products available for sifting and analyzing the access log file. They range from simple operating system commands to sophisticated relational databases.

Quick and Dirty Analysis in DOS

Although there are a number of programs available to analyze access logs, the following are easy-to-do steps for finding answers quickly. Using some simple searches, however, you can find many items you need without having to write a line of code. For starters, look at the basic search tools available under DOS.

Searching in DOS

The DOS FIND command is the easiest way to perform a search of a text file. To search for all instances of nasa.gov in the access log, enter

```
FIND "NASA.GOV" ACCESS.LOG
```

> **Note**
>
> With FIND, all search strings must be enclosed in quotes, regardless of whether they contain special characters.

Although the DOS FIND command does not have as many options as grep, it has enough for simple log-file searching, including

- ■ /v   Displays all lines not containing the search string
- ■ /c   Returns only a count of all matching lines
- ■ /n   Displays the line number with each matching line
- ■ /i   Performs a case-insensitive search

Because the log files are just ASCII text, you can also open your logs in a word processor and use the search features that are part of that particular program. You can also write macros to search for particular strings of text, such as certain error codes, to help you scan through your logs faster.

Useful Search Patterns

Now it's time to put FIND to work looking for useful data in the access log. Without writing a line of programming code, you can see

- ■ A history or count of all accesses from an address or class of addresses
- ■ A history or count of all accesses to any file or directory
- ■ The number of total accesses to your server, excluding inline GIFs
- ■ A history or count of all accesses during a given time period

Sifting by Address

Suppose you get a couple of calls one day from users wanting to know why they can't get to the weather map anymore. You ask for their addresses and discover that they never should have had access in the first place. What do you do now? To verify their claims and assess the damage, you can start by simply searching for their addresses in the log file. Suppose the unauthorized users are from **iam.illegal.com** and **ur.illegal.com**. To see what they've looked at besides the weather map, you can simply search for **illegal.com**. With trepidation, you enter

```
FIND "illegal.com" access.log
```

The result is a fascinating chronicle of unauthorized activity. If there are too many lines to count, use FIND /C to do the dirty work for you, and e-mail the results to your boss on a good day.

This scenario is not all that unlikely, by the way. Basic Web server security itself is good but only as good as the rules that are made for it. More often than not, problems arise when people make assumptions or generalizations that turn out to be false. You may think, for example, that all addresses in a certain subnet (beginning with 127.34.26, for example) are located on your network, only to find out later that the first 20 addresses belonged to another company. The trick here is just to be aware of what you're doing when you're doing it. Taking the "easy way out" can sometimes open up more of a hole in your security than you're really intending.

If you're running a restricted-access Web server, you might want to check now and then to make sure that no one has gotten in from the outside. You can do this easily by looking for all accesses not from your site:

```
FIND /V "widgets.com" ACCESS.LOG
```

In this case, anything returned by the search indicates a possible security breach.

Sifting by File or Directory

Perhaps you've recently added a new feature to your Web site and want to see how much attention it's getting. Just search your logs for the directory or file name and you're in business. To see how many times your What's New page has been read in the current logging period, you simply enter

```
FIND "whatsnew.htm" ACCESS.LOG
```

Or if you've added a whole new directory of stuff (called "/stuff"), try

```
FIND "/stuff" ACCESS.LOG
```

> **Note**
>
> The correct URL to get an automatic directory index is the directory name followed by a slash (/). Some servers, like NCSA's HTTPD for Windows, return an error if the trailing slash is omitted. Most others, however, generate a Redirect URL (status code 302) and then a second request containing the proper URL, causing the document request to show up twice, and thus distorting true usage figures.

> **Tip**
>
> The ease with which simple searches can find all accesses to a given directory is a strong argument for maintaining a close relationship between the hyperlink structure of documents and the physical directory structure.

Computing Total Accesses

One measure of your Web server's utilization or exposure is the number of total document requests. This is not necessarily a measure of effectiveness because many people who visit your site may spend but a few seconds there and travel on. This is especially true now because of the Web's notoriety. In fact, the ratio of tourists to seriously interested patrons of the Web may even be lower than the percentage of sales resulting from direct-mail campaigns. Fortunately, Web space is a lot cheaper. Nonetheless, the number of documents requested or "hits" is of major interest.

If nothing else, measuring your server's growth in utilization can give you a good indication of when you'll have to buy more powerful hardware. Without running a more advanced usage statistics program, you can get a good feel for you server's growth simply by counting the number of total document accesses. In general, you want to exclude GIF files, however, because in-line GIFs show up as separate document requests, hence distorting the true number of HTML pages accessed. Of course, if providing images is a major part of your site, you may not want to exclude them in the count. But for example, to find out many HTML pages have been accessed on your server, less the GIF files, you enter

```
FIND /C /V ".gif" ACCESS.LOG
```

To see how many accesses occur during some specified time period, simply run this command every six hours and compute the difference between each run. For more regular time periods, however, such as days and hours, you can use the next technique.

Computing Accesses During a Given Period

The access log turns out to be in a very convenient format for finding out how many document requests have been processed in most common time periods. For example, if you wanted to find out how many documents were transferred between 3:00 and 4:00 p.m. on October 25, 1994, use

```
FIND /C "25/Oct/1994:15" ACCESS.LOG
```

Using this technique, you can look at total accesses in a given hour, day, month, or year. By piping the output of one FIND command into another, you can obtain even more detailed information. For example, to find all accesses from **red.widgets.com** in the month of October, use

```
FIND "red.widgets.com" ACCESS.LOG ¦ FIND "/Oct/"
```

The first FIND command finds all occurrences of red.widgets.com, while the second FIND looks only in that data for occurrences of /Oct/. (Of course, if you haven't cleaned up your log files for a while, you end up with data from this and all previous Octobers since you last purged or archived your file.)

Usage Utilities

Now for the really neat stuff. What has been described above gives you a lot of answers about your site and its usage. But they require separate actions and still give you raw output. There are numerous products, some free, some commercial that take all the grunt work out of collating and totaling usage statistics. They range from freeware that still requires some programming effort on your part to commercial packages that provide easy to use graphical user interfaces to set up and customize. They all take the raw data in your log files and create reports and graphs customized to your specifications.

> **Note**
>
> These utilities don't work with all Web servers. Contact the respective software company to find out if a utility works with your server. URLs are provided in the following sections.

Amongst the freeware offering, one of the nicest is *wwwstat*, available from **http://www.ics.uci.edu/WebSoft/wwwstat/**. Wwwstat is nice because it produces thorough and nicely-formatted output and can be used with *gwstat,* which turns the output of wwwstat into attractive usage graphs (in GIF format, of course). Gwstat is available from **ftp://dis.cs.umass.edu/ pub/gwstat.tar.gz**, and both wwwstat and gwstat are available on the WebmasterCD.

wwwstat

Wwwstat is a PERL script that reads the standard access-log file format and produces usage summaries in several categories. Wwwstat produces summary information for each calendar month and can be run for past months as well as the current month.

Summary categories include

- Monthly Summary Statistics
- Daily Transmission Statistics
- Hourly Transmission Statistics
- Total Transfers by Client Domain (EDU, GOV, and so on and country codes)
- Total Transfers by Reversed Subdomain (the address of every computer that accessed the server)
- Total Transfers from each Archive Section (the number of accesses to each file on the server)

Figure 18.1 shows an example of Daily Transmission Statistics generated by wwwstat.

NCSA Mosaic - World-Wide Web Access Statistics
File Edit Options Navigate Annotate Personal Help
file:///C|/PROWIN/DNLOAD/WWWSTAT.HTM

Last updated: Thu, 12 Jan 1995 23:40:03 (GMT -0600)

- Daily Transmission Statistics
- Hourly Transmission Statistics
- Total Transfers by Client Domain
- Total Transfers by Reversed Subdomain
- Total Transfers from each Archive Section

Totals for Summary Period: Jan 1 1995 to Jan 12 1995

Files Transmitted During Summary Period	62607
Bytes Transmitted During Summary Period	247583105
Average Files Transmitted Daily	5217
Average Bytes Transmitted Daily	20631925

Daily Transmission Statistics

%Reqs	%Byte	Bytes Sent	Requests	Date
5.52	4.55	11258710	3457	Jan 1 1995
6.21	5.50	13619057	3885	Jan 2 1995
8.27	8.89	21999541	5180	Jan 3 1995
8.69	9.10	22520857	5441	Jan 4 1995
7.30	6.37	15769198	4571	Jan 5 1995
9.10	8.35	20672292	5700	Jan 6 1995
7.91	6.61	16361285	4953	Jan 7 1995
7.12	7.34	18167570	4456	Jan 8 1995
9.97	10.64	26343489	6244	Jan 9 1995

Fig. 18.1
Wwwstat generated these Daily Transmission Statistics.

Figure 18.2 shows wwwstat's summary of statistics by client domain, which brings home the truly global nature of the Internet. Part of the wwwstat distribution is a file containing all the country codes in use on the Internet.

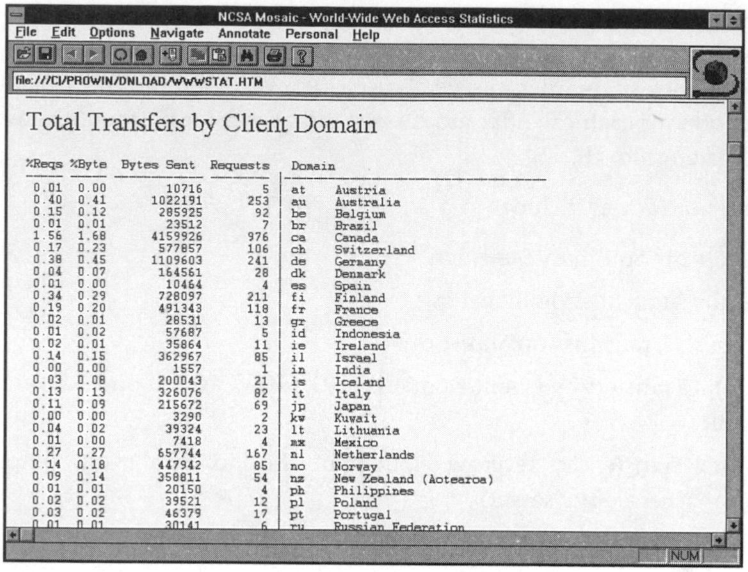

Fig. 18.2

Wwwstat's output of country codes and names.

Because wwwstat is a PERL program, you can port it to other platforms, although no one has, as yet, done that publicly.

statbot

Another popular WWW log analyzer is Statbot. It works by "snooping" on the log files generated by most WWW servers and creating a database that contains information about the server. This database is then used to create a statistics page and GIF charts that can be "linked to" by other WWW resources.

Because Statbot "snoops" on the server log files, it does not require the use of the server's cgi-bin capability. It simply runs from the user's own directory, automatically updating statistics. Statbot uses a text-based configuration file for setup, so it is very easy to install and operate, even for people with no programming experience.

You can find Statbot at **http://www.xmission.com/~dtubbs/club/cs.html**.

AccessWatch

A third freeware product is AccessWatch, a PERL script from Bucknell University. It converts the analyzed data into an HTML file. Figure 18.3 is an example of AccessWatch output. It was generated for a subdirectory of HTML files about creating an online newspaper, called *CReAte*.

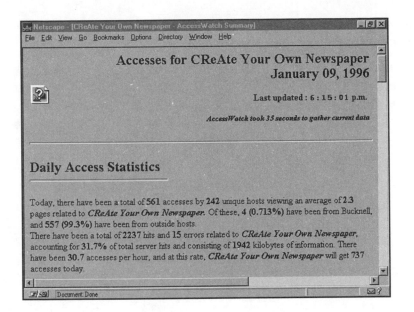

Fig. 18.3
Example of
AccessWatch.

It then adds detailed data in HTML tabular form. The full page can be viewed at **http://www.eg.bucknell.edu/~dmaher/accesswatch/ crayon/**.

AccessWatch is available from **http://www.eg.bucknell.edu/~dmaher/ accesswatch/getAccessWatch.html**.

You can find a long list of other analysis tools in the Yahoo directory **http://www.yahoo.com/Computers_and_Internet/Internet/ World_Wide_Web/HTTP/Servers/Log_Analysis_Tools/**.

Commercial Products

Commercial products will be proliferating soon. Two early offerings are *WebTrends* and *net.Analysis*. *WebTrends* is a mid-range product that functions more in a batch processing mode and *net.Analysis* is a high-end product complete with an *Informix* database and real-time capability. Both offer great flexibility in customizing reports.

Reports generated by *WebTrends* include statistical information as well as colorful graphs that show trends, usage, market share, and much more. Reports are generated as HTML files that can be viewed by a browser on your local system or remotely from anywhere on the Internet if you want. *WebTrends* claims it can read the log files of all available servers. You are able to download an evaluation copy from **http://www.webtrends.com/** and try it out with your server. It is highly recommended that you try out any software for an evaluation period before you purchase it.

Figures 18.4 through 18.11 show are some examples of *WebTrends* output available from its Web site. These are representative of the kinds of output possible from all of the packages.

Fig. 18.4
This graph illustrates what Internet domains connected and the number of user sessions over a sample day.

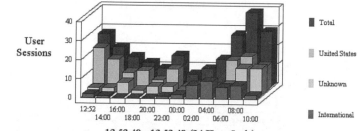

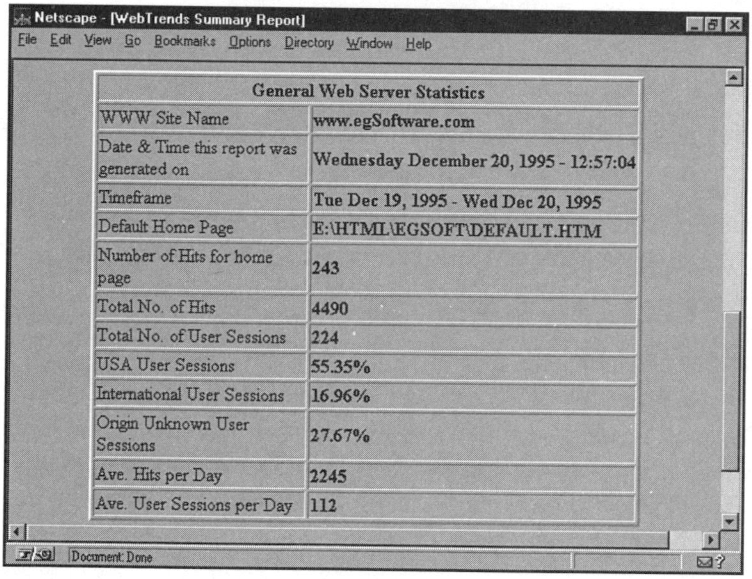

Fig. 18.5
This table includes additional information such as total and average hits per day.

General Web Server Statistics	
WWW Site Name	www.egSoftware.com
Date & Time this report was generated on	Wednesday December 20, 1995 - 12:57:04
Timeframe	Tue Dec 19, 1995 - Wed Dec 20, 1995
Default Home Page	E:\HTML\EGSOFT\DEFAULT.HTM
Number of Hits for home page	243
Total No. of Hits	4490
Total No. of User Sessions	224
USA User Sessions	55.35%
International User Sessions	16.96%
Origin Unknown User Sessions	27.67%
Ave. Hits per Day	2245
Ave. User Sessions per Day	112

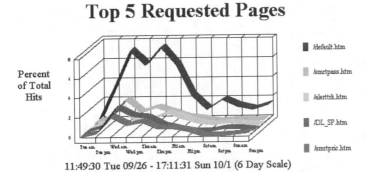

Top 5 Requested Pages

Percent of Total Hits

- /default.htm
- /smrtpass.htm
- /alerttrk.htm
- /DL_SP.htm
- /smrtpric.htm

11:49:30 Tue 09/26 - 17:11:31 Sun 10/1 (6 Day Scale)

Fig. 18.6
This graph illustrates the hits to the pages over a set period of days.

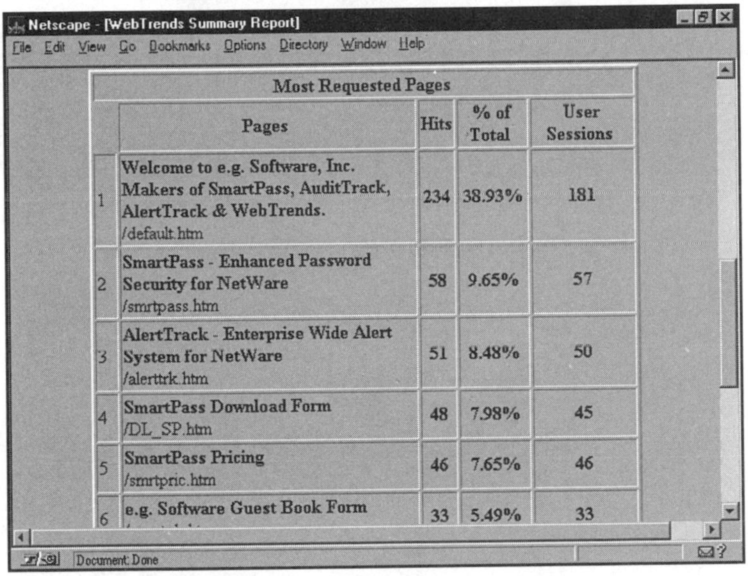

Fig. 18.7
This table includes additional information such as total number of hits and user sessions.

Netscape - [WebTrends Summary Report]

File Edit View Go Bookmarks Options Directory Window Help

Most Requested Pages

	Pages	Hits	% of Total	User Sessions
1	Welcome to e.g. Software, Inc. Makers of SmartPass, AuditTrack, AlertTrack & WebTrends. /default.htm	234	38.93%	181
2	SmartPass - Enhanced Password Security for NetWare /smrtpass.htm	58	9.65%	57
3	AlertTrack - Enterprise Wide Alert System for NetWare /alerttrk.htm	51	8.48%	50
4	SmartPass Download Form /DL_SP.htm	48	7.98%	45
5	SmartPass Pricing /smrtpric.htm	46	7.65%	46
6	e.g. Software Guest Book Form	33	5.49%	33

Document: Done

V

Applications

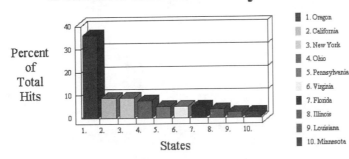

Domestic Breakdown by States

Percent of Total Hits

States

- 1. Oregon
- 2. California
- 3. New York
- 4. Ohio
- 5. Pennsylvania
- 6. Virginia
- 7. Florida
- 8. Illinois
- 9. Louisiana
- 10. Minnesota

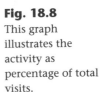

Fig. 18.8
This graph illustrates the activity as percentage of total visits.

Fig. 18.9
This table includes additional information such as the number of user sessions per state.

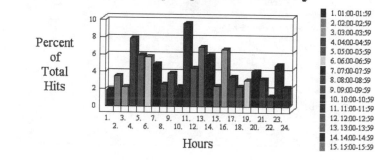

Netscape - [WebTrends Summary Report]

File Edit View Go Bookmarks Options Directory Window Help

Domestic USA Organization Activity by State		
	State	User Sessions
1	Oregon	29
2	California	7
3	New York	7
4	Ohio	6
5	Pennsylvania	4
6	Virginia	4
7	Florida	4
8	Illinois	3
9	Louisiana	2
10	Minnesota	2
	Total	**68**

Document: Done

Fig. 18.10
This graph illustrates the activity over a 24-hour period as percentage of total visits.

Activity By Hour of Day

Percent of Total Hits

Hours

1. 01:00-01:59
2. 02:00-02:59
3. 03:00-03:59
4. 04:00-04:59
5. 05:00-05:59
6. 06:00-06:59
7. 07:00-07:59
8. 08:00-08:59
9. 09:00-09:59
10. 10:00-10:59
11. 11:00-11:59
12. 12:00-12:59
13. 13:00-13:59
14. 14:00-14:59
15. 15:00-15:59

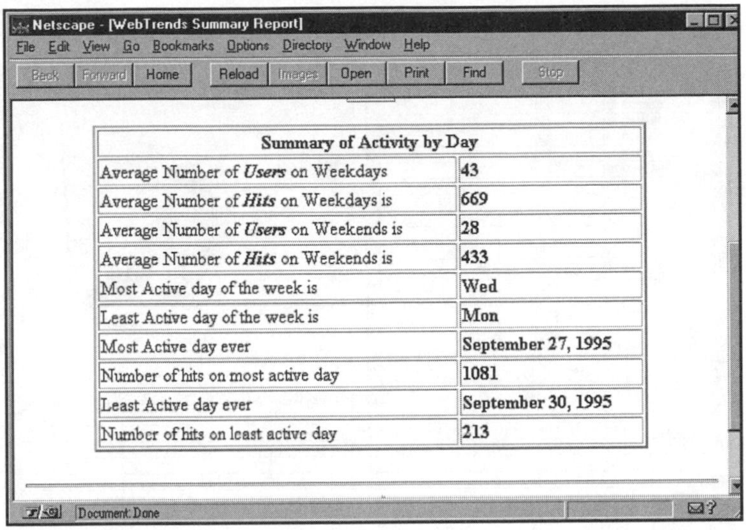

Summary of Activity by Day	
Average Number of ***Users*** on Weekdays	43
Average Number of ***Hits*** on Weekdays is	669
Average Number of ***Users*** on Weekends is	28
Average Number of ***Hits*** on Weekends is	433
Most Active day of the week is	Wed
Least Active day of the week is	Mon
Most Active day ever	September 27, 1995
Number of hits on most active day	1081
Least Active day ever	September 30, 1995
Number of hits on least active day	213

Fig. 18.11
This table includes additional information that contrasts the weekdays and weekends as well as indicates the busiest and slowest times.

net.Analysis

net.Analysis is a product designed for complex real-time log analysis. It places the log into an Informix database and runs a host of customizable queries to present as complete an analysis as is possible. Figures 18.12 and 18.13 are two examples of the results generated by net.Analysis.

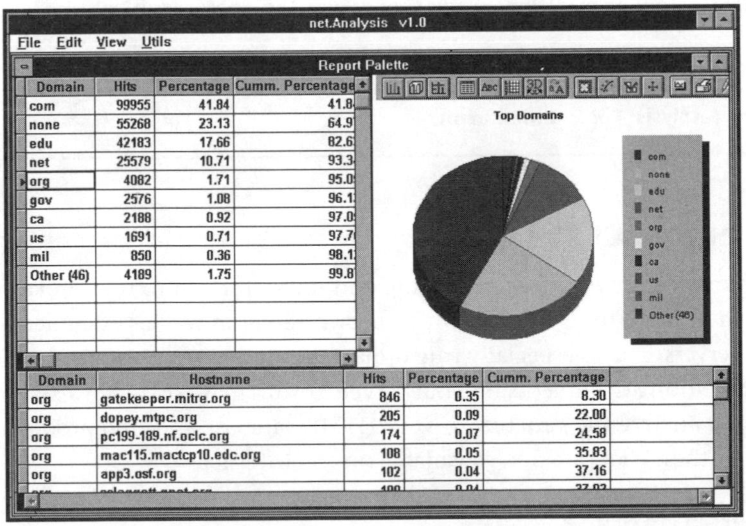

Domain	Hits	Percentage	Cumm. Percentage
com	99955	41.84	41.8
none	55268	23.13	64.9
edu	42183	17.66	82.6
net	25579	10.71	93.3
org	4082	1.71	95.0
gov	2576	1.08	96.1
ca	2188	0.92	97.0
us	1691	0.71	97.7
mil	850	0.36	98.1
Other (46)	4189	1.75	99.8

Domain	Hostname	Hits	Percentage	Cumm. Percentage
org	gatekeeper.mitre.org	846	0.35	8.30
org	dopey.mtpc.org	205	0.09	22.00
org	pc199-189.nf.oclc.org	174	0.07	24.58
org	mac115.mactcp10.edc.org	108	0.05	35.83
org	app3.osf.org	102	0.04	37.16

Fig. 18.12
You can customize net.Analysis to present data in pie-chart form.

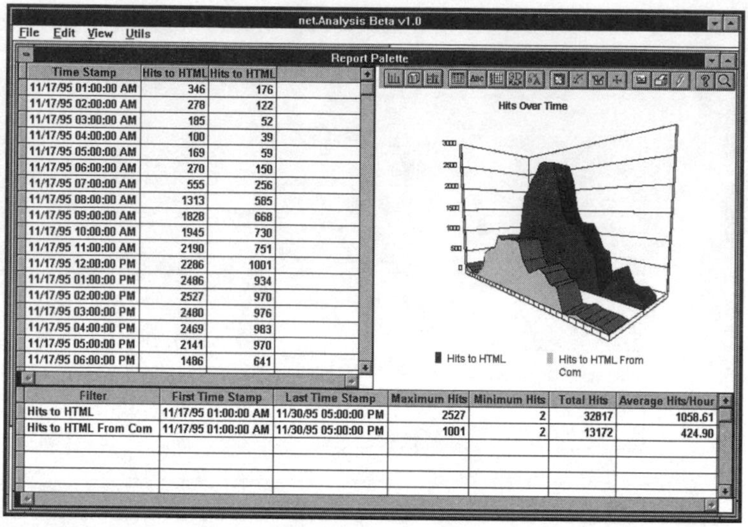

Fig. 18.13
net.Analysis is
available from:
http://
www.netgen.com/

Note

These examples are not meant as an endorsement of any particular products. There
are literally new products and updates daily. You should check what is currently
available, download evaluation copies, and decide for yourself what you want.

A list of other programs to analyze log files is available from **http://
union.ncsa.uiuc.edu/HyperNews/get/www/log-analyzers.html**.

Also there is a list at the Yahoo directory at **http://www.yahoo.com/
Computers_and_Internet/Internet/World_Wide_Web/HTTP/Servers/
Log_Analysis_Tools/index.html**

Checking HTML

As your server grows, it becomes more and more difficult to find broken
hyperlinks, both to documents on your own server as well as documents on
other servers. This is especially true if many people are responsible for creating and editing documents on your server. Fortunately, there are also tools to
help you analyze the structure of your HTML database and find problems.
Some of these tools are freely available on the Internet.

HTML Analyzer

HTML Analyzer is a C program that both finds broken links and attempts to
ensure that the HTML database is well-organized and makes sense to users.
It is available in various forms from

**http://wsk.eit.com/wsk/dist/doc/admin/webtest/
verify_links.html**

ftp.cc.gatech.edu/pub/gvu/www/pitkow/html_analyzer

ftp://ftp.ncsa.uiuc.edu/Web/Mosaic/Contrib/

The file name will be something like "html_analyzer-0.30.tar.gz." The documentation for HTML Analyzer is contained in the program's distribution.

The basic philosophy of HTML Analyzer is that the text of any given hyperlink should always point to the same place and that no other text should point to that same place. This is necessary in order for users to get a clear picture of the organization of the HTML database. HTML Analyzer performs three checks on a database of HTML files—validity, completeness, and consistency.

Checking for Validity

The first check performed by HTML Analyzer is for link validity. This ensures that all hyperlinks point to valid locations (that is, no server errors are returned). Empty hyperlinks (such as, HREF=""), local links (such as HREF="#intro"), and links to interactive services (Telnet and rlogin) are not checked. Even without running the other two checks, validity checking helps to ensure that users of your site won't be frustrated by broken links.

Checking for Completeness

The completeness check ensures that each anchor's contents always occur as a hyperlink. If a hyperlink contained the text Beginner's Guide, for example, and the same text occurred as regular text (not a hyperlink) elsewhere, this is reported. The intent of the completeness check is to improve user-convenience by expecting a hyperlink everywhere there can be, and also to prevent user confusion because the same text sometimes occurs in a hyperlink but not in others.

Checking for Consistency

The final check ensures that every occurrence of a hyperlink anchor points to the same address and that every occurrence of that address is pointed to by the same hyperlink anchor. In other words, HTML Analyzer checks to see that there is a one-to-one correspondence between hyperlink anchors and their respective addresses.

Listing 18.2 is an example of the results of HTML_Analyzer. In this example, there is no file: /u/CIMS/Demo_Description.html located on the server named nsidc1.colorado.edu, a HTTPD server listening on port 1729. The first series of tests discovered this and notified the user as such. It also discovers an incomplete link and an inconsistent link.

Listing 18.2   Sample Results of HTML_Analyzer

```
+++++++++++++++++++++++++++++++++++++++++++++++++++
VERIFYING LINKS...
WWW Alert:  HTTP server at nsidc1.colorado.edu:1729 replies:
HTTP/1.0 500 Unable to access document.
WWW Alert:  Unable to access document.
WARNING:  Failed in checking:
 http://nsidc1.colorado.edu:1729/u/CIMS/Demo_Description.html
   With content of:  Description of this demo
   In local file: ./temp/example.html

VERIFYING COMPLETENESS...
WARNING: These filenames contain the content:
   Description of this demo
 Without a link to:
   http://nsidc1.colorado.edu:1729/u/CIMS/Demo_Description.html
example.html

 VERIFYING CONSISTENCY OF LINKS...
WARNING: Link used inconsistently.
  HREF: http://nsidc1.colorado.edu:1729/u/CIMS/More_info.html
  occurs 1 time with content:
Free Text Frame
  as in file: ./temp/example.html, but also
  occurs 1 time with content:
More Info Frame
  as in file: ./temp/example.html

VERIFYING CONSISTENCY OF CONTENTS...
WARNING: Content used inconsistently.
  CONTENT:
Free Text Frame
  occurs 1 time with href: http://nsidc1.colorado.edu:1729/u/CIMS/
Even_more_info .html
  as in file: ./temp/example.html, but also
  occurs 1 time with href: http://nsidc1.colorado.edu:1729/u/CIMS/
More_info.html
  as in file: ./temp/example.html

+++++++++++++++++++++++++++++++++++++++++++++++++++
```

MOMspider

MOMspider is a PERL program originally written as a class project in distributed information systems at the University of California. MOMspider stands for Multi-Owner Maintenance Spider and is similar to other spiders and robots that traverse the World Wide Web looking for information. MOMspider is available from **http://www.ics.uci.edu/WebSoft/MOMspider/** and requires *libwww-perl,* a library of PERL code for the World Wide Web available from the same site.

Because MOMspider is designed to follow hyperlinks anywhere on the Web, it has many features for controlling the depth of searches and is respectful of other sites' wishes not to be visited by automated robots like MOMspider. MOMspider also has an interesting feature that can build a diagram of the structure of the documents it finds. In addition, MOMspider can avoid sites that are known to cause problems for Web-roaming robots. Examples of these kinds of sites are those that use scripts to generate all output rather than static HTML documents.

WebQuest's Webmeister

The WebQuest Server comes with a utility called *Hyperlink Mode* that shows you the hierarchical structure of your Web space based on the hyperlinks in your HTML documents. It starts with the default document of your Web space and then displays all the links. To see all hyperlinks in a particular document, double-click on the document's name.

Each hyperlink is then validated with a network call (see fig. 18.14). Valid links on the local server appear white, invalid links on the local server appear white with a red X superimposed. Valid links to remote servers appear yellow with a green check, invalid links to remote servers appear yellow with a red X.

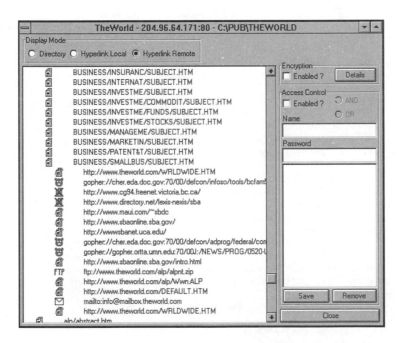

Fig. 18.14
Here you can learn the status of each link in a document.

V

Applications

Finding What's New

When your Web site is being maintained by many people independently, such as an internal server might be in a large organization, it becomes impractical, if not impossible, to require that HTML authors tell you every time they create or modify a page on your server. However, it is highly desirable that server administrators be able to quickly and easily find out what new items have been added each day in order to spot potential problems before they spread too far.

In addition to administrative concerns, information about new or modified documents on the server is helpful for users, who can look on the What's New page and see that the server is continually being updated with valuable information.

By including a FIND command in a shell or PERL script, you can easily generate a list of the What's New page, as in the following PERL example (see listing 18.3).

Listing 18.3   PERL Script That Generates a What's New Page

```perl
#!/usr/bin/perl

# whatsnew.pl—David M. Chandler—January 13, 1995
# This program finds all files underneath the search directory which
have been
# created or modified within the last day. The output is an HTML
What's New
# page with hyperlinks to the new pages.

# Invoke the script and redirect the output to your What's New page
# whatsnew.pl >whatsnew.html

#Put your server's document root here
$SEARCHDIR="/httpd/htdocs";

#Create header for What's New document
print "<TITLE>What's New<TITLE>\n";
print "<H1>What's New!</H1>\n";
print "The following documents were created or modified
➥yesterday:<P>\n";
print "<DL>\n";

#Find all new/modified HTML files in the past day
for each $file (`find $SEARCHDIR -type f -mtime 1 -name '*.html'`)
{
  #Construct the URL from the filename by removing the
# directory path
  if ($file =~ m%$SEARCHDIR/(.*)%) {
  $url = $1; }
```

```
    #Find the document title
    chop($title = `grep '<TITLE>' $file`;
    if ($title =~ m%<TITLE>(.*)</TITLE>%i) {
      $anchor = $1; }

    #Create the What's New listing
    print "<DD><A HREF=\"$url\">$anchor</A>\n";
  }
    print "</DL>\n";
```

Windows for Workgroups users can accomplish this task easily in File Manager by using the Date Sort tool, which lists all files in chronological order. Likewise, many Windows-based shells, such as Norton Desktop or PC Tools for Windows have similar features in their file management utilities. DOS users aren't fortunate enough to have the -mtime option available to list only those files modified recently; however, it is possible to see a directory listing sorted by date so that a quick scan reveals any new or modified files. To list a directory with the most recently created or modified files last, use

```
    DIR /OD directory_name
```

To list a directory with the most recently created or modified files listed first, use

```
    DIR /O-D directory_name
```

Summary

This chapter will set you well on the way to managing the usage of your Web site. You will be able to furnish the content managers with detailed and organized data on the accesses to the site and its pages. You will also be able to check the HTML pages that get placed on the server to see if they are linked properly. This will help to make your site more professional and productive. ❖

## CHAPTER 19

Database Access and Applications Integration

The explosion of the Internet is being discussed within the business community almost as much as it is in general. Companies are struggling with the meaning of the Internet, and how it may be exploited. New external and internal threats may arise as a consequence of their exploitation of it. One thing is certain, the Internet has fundamentally and irreversibly altered the rules for constructing and delivering business information systems.

This and the following chapter explore these issues and provide some insight regarding the construction of business systems that extend a company's reach through the use of the Internet and World Wide Web technology.

In this chapter, you learn about:

- Business applications and their match with Web technology
- The kinds of information you should store in a relational database rather than as HTML documents in the file system
- Business transactions that work well and ones that don't

Traditional Wide Area Networks (WAN)

Traditionally, only very large corporations had the resources to develop and deploy online business systems that reached beyond a campus. Generally, available solutions for wide area communications infrastructure did not exist. Companies were limited to in-house design, construction, and administration of private networks. The cost to these solutions was prohibitively high for all but the very largest and wealthiest corporations. Even then, the accessibility of these private networks extended only to employees at company locations.

IBM was one of the first companies to offer a wide area network backbone service to businesses when it launched the IBM Information Network in 1983. This lowered the entry price to wide area network computing to a point where upper mid-sized companies could begin to expand the reach of their business systems to most North American locations. However, the prerequisite was a business system developed within IBM architectural framework. This business communications infrastructure was emerging at exactly the same time as Personal Computers burst onto the scene. In the 1980s and early 1990s, PCs fundamentally altered the rules for constructing and delivering business information systems. They also diverted the attention of MIS away from the delivery of online business transactions to IS basic survival issues.

The Internet as a Public Wide Area Network

From a business point of view, the Internet represents a low cost, worldwide data communications utility that has unmatched geographic coverage and a rapidly growing population of users. This is its primary value to businesses. The cost and other barriers to entry are so low that essentially every business can afford to exploit it. As with any major environmental change, businesses that understand the meaning of the Internet and Web technology and how to exploit it will be more likely to survive. Those that ignore it will rapidly find themselves at a serious competitive disadvantage.

Business Transactions on the Internet

Businesses create and exchange goods and services for money. The devil lies in the details. Developers of PC-based applications have been so successful in developing intuitive, easy-to-use interfaces that major businesses have now begun to entertain the possibility that the general public might just be able to order their own products, transfer their own payments, and look up their own balances. With proper designs and a robust security infrastructure, there is now an opportunity to extend online business systems directly to consumers.

What a Database Is and How It Differs from HTML Files

To understand how a business might exploit the Internet and the World Wide Web, it is important to understand the objectives and limitations of the WWW infrastructure from a business system point of view.

The World Wide Web was conceived of and designed as a mechanism for publishing information in electronic form. HTML is the media of the Web.

- If publishing a library of HTML documents addresses some portion of your business information system requirements, the Web and HTML documents are the answer for you. It is a great, low-cost, ubiquitous electronic document library system. But even as a document library system, it has some disadvantages.

- Very few businesses create formal or informal electronic documents in the form of HTML files. Most businesses create informal electronic documents in the form of OLE objects using Microsoft Office tools.

- Most businesses create formal electronic documents using professional publishing tools such as PageMaker and its companion tools from Adobe.

Disadvantages: Data Processing

Other than as an electronic document library, this technology does not support many traditional business system requirements. It is, in fact, too restrictive for most applications:

- It only supports read access to information in the library. The information is not available for update. There are no services for managing or controlling updates to the library. There is no locking mechanism or concurrency control that would enable a document to be shared for update even if an update capability existed.

- The information is in unstructured, electronic paper format. So, while there are powerful text indexing and search engines available for HTML documents, data query capabilities are severely limited. For example, the following query cannot be formulated using an HTML search engine because it cannot understand the meaning of the terms ShipToName, ShipToAddress, and so on.

    ```
    SELECT ShipToName, ShipToAddress FROM Library WHERE ShipToZip
    ➥IS BETWEEN 32256 AND 32779;
    ```

- Because the information content of the documents is unstructured, specific data content cannot easily be extracted and processed by business applications.

Data Management

Most business applications manage the creation, update, delivery, and destruction of data. As can be seen in the preceding section, this capability is not native to Web technology. It must be added.

Relational Databases

Relational databases are the de facto standard for managing business information today. Their success is no accident. Relational databases have been designed to efficiently process high volumes of short transactions involving simple alpha/numeric data. Relational databases have the flexibility to easily handle ad hoc queries and new data relationships, and they pay a lot of attention to data integrity, availability, and multi-user concurrency. They provide a robust set of functions for administrating, distributing, accessing, and updating business information. Microsoft provides two low cost, highly capable relational database products: Microsoft Access and Microsoft SQL Server, which are discussed in the next chapter.

SQL

In the late 1960s, early 1970s, Dr. E. F. Codd developed a mathematics for performing relational operations against well-formed tables. He also specified the rules for creating well-formed tables (called *normalization*) and proved that virtually any query could be specified in and resolved by his relational algebra.

Relational databases and normalization rules provided a well reasoned structure for analyzing and designing the data aspects of business applications. Once data is structured into these well formed tables, SQL enables applications and end-users reliable access to business information.

For example, you could set up a table called Advertisements with the following columns:

> Contact
>
> EmailAddress
>
> Title
>
> Manufacturer
>
> Model
>
> ModelYear
>
> AskingPrice

You could then use SQL to perform the following searches:

To get a list of all 1990 Toyotas offered at a price between $10,000 and $20,000, the SQL would be:

```
Select Title, Contact, EmailAddress Model, ModelYear FROM
➥Advertisements where Manufacturer = 'Toyota' and ModelYear = 1990
➥and AskingPrice between 10000 and 20000;
```

Note

These types of searches are not possible against HTML documents using WAIS search engines.

Object-Oriented Databases

Relational databases are today's standard for managing business information and are the preferred database technology choice when extending our online business systems to new user populations through the Internet. However, leading edge information technology has moved on. Early adopters are now exploiting object-oriented technology for business application development. This chapter uses the OMG definition of Objects, not the Microsoft OLE definition. OLE objects are discussed in the next chapter.

Complex Information

Dr. Codd's normalization rules constrain the structure of information in such a way that relational algebra works. His promise is that, so long as the information is structured according to the rules, all requests for information (queries) can be satisfied by applying relational algebra. However, the very rules that provide this benefit also inhibit the management of information in an object-oriented way.

Object-oriented databases have been developed that enable business applications to treat objects as if they were persistent. That is, the next time an application sees an instance of a particular object, it will be in the same state as it was when the program left it (unless some other application overtly changed its state in the meantime).

Navigational

Object technology describes the world differently than relational technology does. While it is difficult to grasp by those who have grown up with file and relational based applications, there is no distinction between function and data in the world of objects. Information is semantically richer because it embodies both the state of the real-world object and its behavior.

A positive side effect of this view of the world is that this information model directly supports navigation from object to object in much the same way hypertext links support navigation from document to document. In fact, a document could easily be an object. Therefore, the object-oriented model of information is more in concert with the WWW model of information than is the relational model.

Limited Queries

While object-oriented databases support direct navigation from object to object, the structure of the information they manage is not constrained by

V

Applications

Dr. Codd's normalization rules. Therefore, relational algebra and, consequently, SQL cannot reliably be applied to information stored in object-oriented databases. Today, there is no blend of relational and object-oriented databases that enables both the query capability of SQL and the navigational capability of object databases.

Why Use a Database for Web Page Publishing?

WWW server software is fairly simple in concept. It receives a request (GET) for a named resource, finds the named resource, and sends the retrieved resource to the requester, including imbedding images. Most WWW server software assumes the resource is a file, and relies on the operating system's file system to resolve the name (path) to the file so that it can be read. A major drawback of this implementation is that the name of the resource is also its address. It cannot be moved without changing its name.

Servers do not need to be implemented this way. For example, the server could assume the name is constructed of three parts:

- A data source name (database)
- A table name
- A record id

and use a relational database engine to find and deliver the record. For example, HTML could be stored in a MEMO column in an Access database. This implementation would provide a mechanism for recording additional information (properties) about the document.

A Brief Introduction to ODBC

Open Database Connectivity is a protocol that allows other applications to access and manipulate databases. This feature allows for some very powerful interactive functions on the Internet. For example, you can retrieve inventory information and create guest books and dynamically updatable Web pages. The Web browser becomes a front-end to a database. A Macintosh user can access the information in a database as easily as a Windows or UNIX user.

ODBC is a subject by itself and will not be addressed fully in this book.

> **Note**
>
> Before trying any of these examples, make sure you have WebQuest and ODBC properly installed and configured.

Integrating Your Web Page and a Database

Adding database information to your Web page is simple and straightforward using WebQuest. WebQuest has added a couple of HTML tags within SSI+ that allow the user to connect to an existing database, retrieve information from the database, and modify that information. Using SQL, it is also possible to create complex queries of the data and include that on a page.

Before you can use ODBC, make sure it is properly installed. The methodology for accessing a database from a Web page is:

- Define the data source,

- Use a form on an HTML page to request information from the user,

- Send the information request to a SHT page,

- The SHT page connects to the data source, retrieves the information, and displays it.

▶ For more information about ODBC installation see "ODBC Database Layout," p. 179

Getting Ready

The CD-ROM contains all the files that you will need to have to run these examples. They are zipped up into the following files: ODBC.ZIP and NWIND.ZIP. Copy them into a temp directory, extract them, and move them into the /webspace directory on your hard drive. The NWIND.MDB has been modified slightly to allow for ODBC connectivity. ODBC does not support field names that include a space. The tables have been modified by changing the field name from Contact Name to ContactName. Also, there are two ways of manipulating databases custom to WebQuest. You will examine the easiest way, using SSI+ ODBC tags. The more complicated process involving Dynamic Link Libraries (.DLL) is demonstrated at the WebQuest home page:

http://www.questar.com/webquest.htm

Getting Ready

Note

All of the following examples use the NWIND.MDB database that is included as a sample database with Access 2.0. While you do not need to have Access 2.0 to use the database, you need to have the database to run these examples.

The first action you need to take is to define NWIND.MDB as a data source with ODBC. To do this, double-click the ODBC control panel (located under the Main group and in Control Panel) to open ODBC. The Data Source dialog box appears on-screen. Click Add, Microsoft Access (MDB) driver, and OK.

This brings you to the Setup dialog box. Use the Select button to find the NWIND.MDB database on your hard drive (the database must be on a hard drive on the local system of the Web server). Type **nwind** as the Data Source name. Accuracy is very important because ODBC is case-sensitive. When connecting to ODBC, you define the name of the *data source*, not the name of the database. Click Advanced and set the password to simple with the Login name admin. Again this is important, ODBC will not connect to a data source unless this information is accurate.

How To Perform a Simple Query on a Database

Now you have defined a data source and database you can access using ODBC. The query takes place in two stages: in the first stage, you request a query from the user; in the second stage, you display the results of the query. The front end is a standard HTML page (NWIND.HTM), with a form. The form method is specified as "GET" because that works best with WebQuest (see listing 19.1).

Listing 19.1   Query Front End Page

```
<HTML>
<HEAD>
<!-- This file name is: NWIND.HTM -->
<TITLE>Dynamic Query look up Using NWIND.MDB</TITLE>
</HEAD>
<BODY>
<CENTER><H1>Dynamic Query Using NWIND.MDB</H1></CENTER>
<HR>
Please type in the City you want to query.<BR>
<FORM METHOD = "GET" ACTION="odbcnwnd.sht">
City: <INPUT TYPE="text" NAME="Cityname"><BR>
<INPUT TYPE=SUBMIT VALUE="Place Request">
<INPUT TYPE=RESET VALUE="Rest Form"? <BR>
</FORM>
</BODY>
</HTML>
```

This page requests the user to input the name of a city (this example uses London,) and then sends the name of the city as the variable name `Cityname` to the file ODBCNWIND.SHT, which processes the query.

Note

While an SHT file is a nonstandard HTML file, it is a standard SSI file. SSI+, which allows users this ease of database integration, is not an Internet standard, though it will be proposed as such in the summer of 1996.

The back end of this query is a nonstandard HTML page with an SHT extension (ODBCNWIND.SHT) (see listing 19.2). This extension alerts the Web server to parse or examine the contents of the file for any special actions. All files that contain SSI+ tags must be saved as SHT files or the server will not perform the action asked for by the tag.

Listing 19.2   Query Back End Page with Line Numbers Shown for Reference

```
1. <HTML><HEAD>
2. <!-- This file name is: NWIND.SHT -->
3. <TITLE>Query Results from NWIND.MDB</TITLE>
4. </HEAD>
5. <BODY>
6. <H1>Query Results from NWIND.MDB</H1>
7. Using a variable: Cityname: <!--#echo var="Cityname"-->
8. <!--#odbc connect="nwind,admin,simple"-->
9. <!--#odbc format="<P>Customer ID is %s, Contact Name is %s,
   ➥City is %s</P>"-->
10.<!--#odbc statement="SELECT CustomerID, ContactName, City FROM
   ➥Customers WHERE City LIKE '&&Cityname&&'"-->
11.<HR>
12.</BODY>
13.</HTML>
```

This page is a little more complicated, as several unusual actions are taking place:

- Line 7 places the name of the city that the user typed into a form. This doesn't affect the database; it simply reminds the user what city name they used as a query.

- Line 8 tells the Web server to connect to the datasource nwind with the login of admin and the password of simple. Note all of these three parameters are case-sensitive. To access a database, you must first connect to it through the ODBC define datasource.

- Line 9 defines the format for the data retrieved from the database. In this example, you are defining three fields (CustomerID, ContactName, and City), to be displayed on one line (the <P> tags). These fields need to be consistent with the fields on the next line and with the fields available to query in the database. If any of this is inaccurate, the query will fail and the server will return an --SSI+ ERROR--. The data from the database will be placed where the percent signs are located in the format.

▶ For more information about HTML forms. see Chapter 14 "HTML Forms," p. 393

V

Applications

■ Line 10 is where the actual work takes place. In this example, you have connected to the data source nwind, which in turn is connected to NWIND.MDB. Now you will SELECT all the data from the fields: CustomerID, ContactName, and City in the Customers Table if the data in the City field is LIKE London. There are a number of instances that fit this query (see fig. 19.1).

Fig. 19.1
Results of Query.

```
Customer ID is AROUT, Contact Name is Thomas Hardy, City is London
Customer ID is BSBEV, Contact Name is Victoria Ashworth, City is
➥London
Customer ID is CONSH, Contact Name is Elizabeth Brown, City is
➥London
Customer ID is EASTC, Contact Name is Ann Devon, City is London
Customer ID is NORTS, Contact Name is Simon Crowther, City is
➥London
Customer ID is SEVES, Contact Name is Hari Kumar, City is London
```

The words SELECT, FROM, WHERE, and LIKE are all part of the SQL language. Any SQL-based query or command can be used with SSI+. SQL is an extremely powerful and complex technology. There are several examples in this chapter. As a demonstration of the power of SQL, go back and run the example again. This time instead of typing in "London" as the city name, type in **L%n**. The % acts as a wildcard, so SQL looks for all instances in the City field where the Cityname starts with "L" and ends with "n." Notice Lyon is now listed with London. The LIKE statement allows for this kind of wildcard search.

Tip

If you want to use the power of SQL, you can create the query using Access 2.0 on the database. When you are satisfied with the query, click on the SQL button. Access will generate the SQL statement for you. Cut and paste the statement into your SHT file.

When customizing this and the other examples, keep in mind that none of the variable names are arbitrary. They are defined by the database. The most common error users make when customizing these examples is changing one of the field names—by misspelling, using the wrong case, omitting a letter, or by using the wrong field name.

Performing a Variable Search on a Selected Field

In the next example, the user can query any of the fields of the Customers table of the NWIND.MDB database. The fields are coded into a pull-down menu. This example is essentially the same as the previous example except the field name becomes a variable and instead of using Cityname as a variable, you are using Content.

Listing 19.3 Variable Query Front End Page

```
<HTML>
<HEAD>
<!-- This file name is: NWIND1.HTM -->
<TITLE>Dynamic Query of NWIND.MDB Customers Table</TITLE>
</HEAD>
<BODY>
<CENTER><H1>Dynamic Query of NWIND.MDB Customers Table</H1></CENTER>
<HR>
Please Select the Field you want to query.<BR>
<FORM ACTION="nwind.sht" METHOD="Get">

<SELECT NAME="Fields">
<OPTION VALUE="CompanyName">CompanyName
<OPTION VALUE="ContactName">ContactName
<OPTION VALUE="ContactTitle">ContactTitle
<OPTION VALUE="Address">Address
<OPTION VALUE="City" SELECTED>City
<OPTION VALUE="Region">Region
<OPTION VALUE="PostalCode">PostalCode
<OPTION VALUE="Country">Country
<OPTION VALUE="Phone">Phone
<OPTION VALUE="Fax">Fax
</SELECT>
<BR>
What do you want to search for?  <INPUT NAME="Content"
TYPE="text"><BR>
<BR>
<INPUT TYPE=submit value="Place Request"> <INPUT TYPE=reset
value="Reset Form"><BR>
</FORM>
</BODY>
</HTML>
```

The field to search on and what to search for are sent to NWIND.SHT for processing. NWIND.SHT, like ODBCNWIND.SHT, echoes the variable for the user, connects to the datasource, sets the format, queries the database, and displays the returned data. In the previous example, the data was formatted onto separate lines. In this example, the data is formatted into a table, as shown in figure 19.2.

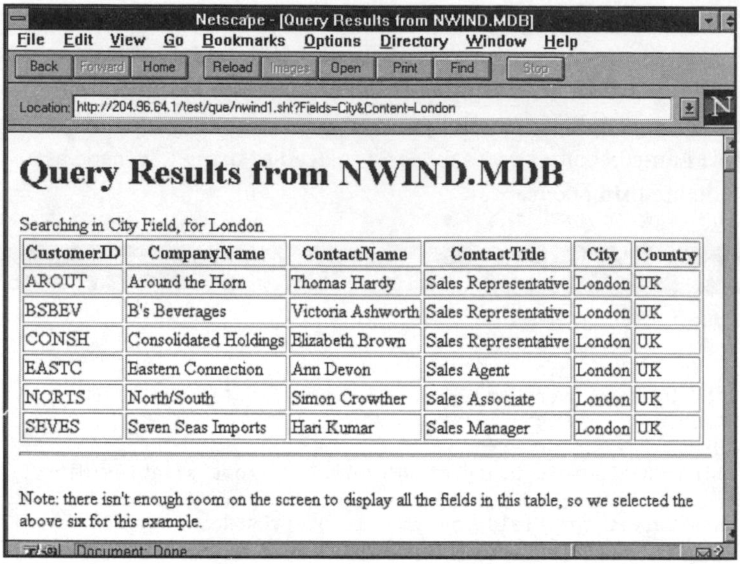

Fig. 19.2
The displayed
results in table
format.

Now the data is placed into a table cell where %s are located. You will notice six fields are listed in the table header. There are six %s and the SELECT statement selects six fields. Everything must be consistent.

Listing 19.4   Variable Query Back End Page

```
<HTML>
<HEAD>
<!-- This file name is: NWIND1.SHT -->
<TITLE>Query Results from NWIND1.MDB</TITLE>
</HEAD>
<BODY>
<H1>Query Results from NWIND.MDB</H1>
Searching in <!--#echo var="Fields"--> Field, for <!--#echo
var="Content"-->
<!--#odbc connect="nwind,admin,simple"-->
<TABLE BORDER=1>
<TR><TH>CustomerID</TH><TH>CompanyName</TH><TH>ContactName</TH>
<TH>ContactTitle</TH><TH>City</TH><TH>Country</TH></TR>
<!--#odbc format="<TR><TD>%s</TD><TD>%s</TD><TD>%s</TD><TD>%s</
TD><TD>%s</TD>
<TD>%s</TD></TR>"-->
<!--#odbc statement="SELECT CustomerID, CompanyName, ContactName,
ContactTitle, City, Country FROM Customers WHERE &&Fields&& LIKE
'&&Content&&'"-->
</TABLE>
<HR>
<P>Note: there isn't enough room on the screen to display all the
fields in this table, so we selected the above six for this example.
</P>
</BODY>
</HTML>
```

This page will return data FROM the Customers table WHERE the variable Fields is LIKE the variable Content. The two & signs define the word as a variable.

Editing and Updating Data within an Existing Database

Interactive manipulation of data is where the real power of ODBC is demonstrated. In this next example, you will connect to the Products table in NWIND.MDB using an SHT file to start instead of a standard HTML file. Also you'll introduce a new SSI+ tag to these examples as the config errmsg tag. This tag allows you to customize error responses when an error occurs.

Listing 19.5   Editing and Updating Front End Page

```
<HTML>
<HEAD>
<!--This file name is EDIT.SHT -->
<TITLE>Edit Item in Products Table from NWIND.MDB</TITLE>
</HEAD>
<BODY>
<CENTER><H1>Edit Item in Products Table from NWIND.MDB</H1></CENTER>
<CENTER><H2><I>URL Link Based</I></H2></CENTER>
<HR>
<!--#config errmsg="<CENTER><H3>An error has occurred while
connecting to the database...  Please try again later...</H3></
center>"-->
<!--#odbc connect="nwind,admin,simple"-->
<TABLE border=1>
<TR><TH>Product ID</TH><TH>Product Name</TH><TH>English Name</TH>
<TH>Quantity
Per Unit</TH><TH>Unit Price</TH><TH>Units In Stock</TH></TR>
<!--#odbc format="<TR><TD>%s</TD><TD><A HREF="edititem.sht?ID=%s">
%s</A></TD>
<TD>%s</TD><TD>%s</TD><TD>%s</TD><TD>%s</TD></TR>"-->
<!--#odbc statement="SELECT ProductID, ProductID, ProductName,
EnglishName, QuantityPerUnit, UnitPrice, UnitsInStock FROM
Products"-->
</TABLE>
</BODY>
</HTML>
```

The page shown in listing 19.5 connects to the nwind data source, formats your data into a table, runs the query, and displays the data. In this case, you are displaying all the data from the table and there are no conditional statements in the SQL query. Also notice that the data in the ProductName field is returned as a link: "edititem.sht?ID=%s". When you click one of these links, you are sent to the edititem.sht page (see listing 19.6).

V

Applications

Listing 19.6   Editing Page

```
<HTML>
<HEAD>
<!--This file name is: EDITITEM.SHT -->
<TITLE>Edit Form for Item in Products Table from NWIND.MDB</TITLE>
</HEAD>
<BODY>
<CENTER><H1>Edit Form Item in Products Table from NWIND.MDB</H1></
CENTER>
<FORM action="updateitem.sht" METHOD="GET">
<HR>
<!--#config errmsg="<CENTER><H3>An error has occurred while
connecting to the database...  Please try again later...</H3></
center>"-->
<!--#odbc connect="nwind,admin,simple"-->
<!--#odbc format="<INPUT type=hidden name=ID value="%s">Product
ID:<BR>%s<BR>
Category ID:<br><INPUT name=CategoryID size=10 value="%s"><BR>Product
Name: <BR><INPUT type=text name=ProductName size=40
Value="%s"><BR>English Name: <BR><INPUT type=text name=EnglishName
size=40 value="%s"><BR>Quantity Per Unit:<BR><INPUT name=Quantity
size=30 value="%s"><BR>Unit Price:<BR><INPUT name=UnitPrice size=10
value="%s"><BR>Units In Stock:<BR><INPUT name=UnitsInStock size=10
value="%s"><br>"-->
<!--#odbc statement="SELECT ProductID, ProductID, CategoryID,
ProductName,
EnglishName, QuantityPerUnit, UnitPrice, UnitsInStock FROM Products
WHERE
ProductID = &&ID&&"-->
<HR>
<INPUT TYPE=submit value="Update Product"> <INPUT TYPE =reset
value="Reset
Form"><BR>
</FORM>
</BODY>
</HTML>
```

Once the user has selected the product to update or edit (see fig. 19.3), that information is sent to a page that displays the information about the product formatted as a form.

The user can change any displayed content, submit the changes, and the changes will be displayed on a third page. Note that the key field, `ProductID` is not available to change; you cannot change the key field. This page may be a little overwhelming, but if you look closely, you will see that it is simply a standard HTML form with four embedded SSI+ tags. The form sends the updated information to a third page for updating the database and viewing the changes.

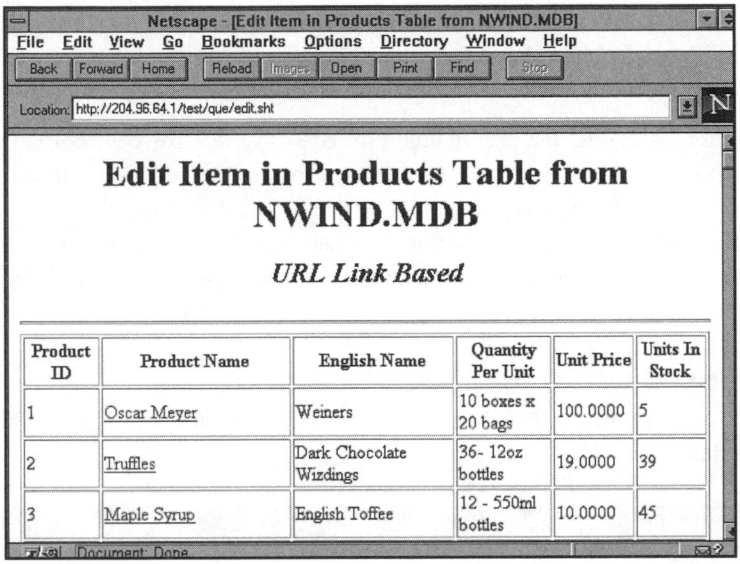

Fig. 19.3
The edit.sht HTML
interface.

Listing 19.7   Updating and Display Page

```
<!--This file name is: UPDATEITEM.SHT -->
<CENTER><H1>Update Item in Products Table from NWIND.MDB</H1></
CENTER>
<!--#odbc connect="nwind,admin,simple"-->
<!--#odbc statement="UPDATE Products SET CategoryID = &&CategoryID&&,
ProductName = '&&ProductName&&', EnglishName = '&&EnglishName&&',
QuantityPerUnit = '&&Quantity&&', UnitPrice = &&UnitPrice&&,
UnitsInStock = &&UnitsInStock&& WHERE ProductID = &&ID&&"-->

<FORM>
<!--#odbc format="Product ID:<br><INPUT name=f1 size=5 type=text
value="%s"> <br>Category ID:<br><INPUT name=f2 size=5 type=text
value="%s"><br>Product Name:<br><INPUT name=f3 size=40 type=text
value="%s"><br>English Name:<br><INPUT name=f4 size=40 type=text
value="%s"><br>Quantity Per Unit:<br><INPUT name=f5 type=text
value="%s"><br>Unit Price:<br><INPUT name=f6 type=text value=

"%s"><br>Units In Stock:<br><INPUT name=f7 type=text
value="%s"><br>"--><!--#odbc statement="SELECT ProductID, CategoryID,
ProductName, EnglishName, QuantityPerUnit, UnitPrice, UnitsInStock
FROM Products WHERE ProductID = &&ID&&"-->
</FORM>
```

On this last page, listing 19.7, the actual data in the database is changed using UPDATE in the odbc statement. In this example, every record except the
key field ProductID is updated. As another way of looking at this, the entire

entry in the database is overwritten WHERE ProductID matches the variable &&ID&&. Then all the updated data is displayed in the same form format for verification.

All of these example files are included on the CD-ROM for your convenience. These examples are only one of many ways to accomplish the same task. These examples work and you can use them as building blocks for your own Internet applications. The power of database integration is harnessed by the joining of these technologies to produce very powerful manipulation of data and databases.

Advanced ODBC and SQL Statements

SQL is too large a topic to cover here, but we will provide one more example of the flexibility of this system.

Listing 19.8   Complex Query Strings

```
<!--#odbc connect="nwind,admin,simple"-->
<TABLE border=1>
<TR><TH>CustomerID</TH><TH>CompanyName</TH><TH>Cont
actName</TH><TH>ContactTitle</TH><TH>City</TH><TH>Countr
y</TH></TR>
<!--#odbc
format="<TR><TD>%s</TD><TD>%s</TD><TD>%s</TD><
TD>%s</TD><TD>%s</TD><TD>%s</TD></TR>"-->
<!--#odbc statement="SELECT CustomerID, CompanyName, ContactName,
ContactTitle, City, Country FROM Customers WHERE &&Field&&
&&SString&&"-->
</TABLE>
```

Notice the odbc statement. WHERE is followed by two variables: Field and Sstring. The user is asked which field to query (Field), and what query to perform (Sstring). Any legal SQL WHERE statement can be used.

Note

Online documentation of the syntax of SQL can be found at **http:// www.questar.com/sql_help.sht**.

Tip

If you are having problems with the ODBC SSI+ tags and you are using the DEBUG tag, open up the ODBC control Data Source dialog box and click Options. This will allow you to log all the ODBC calls made and track down the problem. Turn this off as soon as possible, however, or else the log file will grow to fill your hard drive.

> **Note**
>
> Time stamping a database entry from an SHT file using the date/time format with Access 2.0 does not allow any formatting. There is only one format available YYYY-MM-DD HH:MM:SS.

Advantages

A primary advantage to using a relational database engine instead of a file system is the ability to attach structured data (properties) to each document, such as the Author, Version, Subject, and so on. This enables you to understand more about the document and to deliver documents based upon the values of the document's properties. For example, a CGI script can easily deliver a list of all documents written by a specific author within a specified time period. No external indexing or search engine is required.

A database can also provide a richer set of functions managing this information. Various levels of authorization, versioning, distribution, replication, and locking can be applied to tables for better control and to ensure data security and integrity.

Disadvantages

An immediate drawback of this approach is that the tools used to create electronic documents are designed to run on top of file systems. When you create an HTML file, image, video clip, and so on with any existing tool, it will be saved as a file. Therefore, additional work will be imposed on authors to get their material into and out of the database.

Second, database engines have much more limited text indexing and search capability than WAIS engines. SQL does very well at finding records based upon specific values in small character or numeric fields. But documents would be stored in long, variable-length character fields. Wildcard characters are very limited and Boolean operators are not available for these types of fields. In fact, you cannot search for anything beyond the first 255 characters of a document stored in an Access memo field.

Finally, database engines are optimized to store large numbers of (relatively) small records while file systems are designed to store (relatively) small numbers of large files. A database implementation could end up being slower than a file system implementation.

For example, when you search the Yahoo library for "good places to surf," it replies with a list of home pages with ratings of how good they match your search criteria. It rates the results through complex indexing algorithms. These algorithms do not run against the library files themselves. Rather, they run against a set of indices built by offline utilities that have analyzed the library's text.

Some of these text search engines let you specify even more powerful queries. The Dialog search engines let you specify the distance between keywords. An example might be:

```
FIND BUDGET(10N)SENATE
```

which would find all documents with the word BUDGET within 10 words of the word SENATE.

```
FIND (FEMALE or WOMEN) and (WEIGHT TRAIN? OR WEIGHT LIFT? OR
WEIGHTLIFT?)/ENG
```

which would find English language documents regarding female weightlifting articles. None of these capabilities are offered in Relational database engines.

Why Use the Web Technology for Database Applications?

This is a more pertinent question. The Internet offers companies a low cost wide area network utility. Some aspects of the World Wide Web technology enable companies to exploit this utility. The key is reaching a broader population of potential customers over a wider geographic area. While HTML enables you to construct electronic documents and publish them on the Web, most business applications have nothing to do with publishing. They manage the processing of data to conduct business.

Structured Information

Business applications process structured information. The fields in an HTML form structure data values into named fields. The values entered into an HTML form can be extracted and stored into a relational table's rows and columns.

When information is named and structured, it can be processed. An application can verify that a field contains numbers when it should and that the numbers are entered in a valid format. Once validated, the value of a field can be added, subtracted, averaged, and so on. These are the kinds of things business applications do.

Complex Queries

It may take a very complex query to locate the precise information a person needs for a business activity; for example, "Find all the people who entered orders for black wingtip shoes in the month of December last year." If the information is stored in an SQL database, the above request might be satisfied by the following SQL select statement:

```
SELECT Name, Address FROM CustomerOrders WHERE Item = 'SHOE' and
➥Style = 'WINGTIP' and OrderDate >= '#12/01/1995' and OrderDate
➥< '#1/1/1996';
```

> **Note**
>
> Indexing engines and Web crawlers do not have any visibility to information stored in a database that is reached this way.

Updates

By its nature, a business transaction changes the state of information in the business system. An order is placed, a payment is made, and the order is shipped. HTML and file systems do not provide the necessary structure, concurrency controls, or transaction support to meet these requirements.

Platform Independent User Interface

Traditional business transactions were implemented using dumb terminals, such as IBM 3270s, 5250s, 3101s, DEC VT100s, VT220s and VT320s. These character-based devices were all that was necessary to enable people to retrieve, enter, update, and delete business information. Business transactions were designed and coded specifically to the company's dumb terminal type. An application coded to run on an IBM 3270 could not be delivered to an operator on a DEC VT100.

HTML forms provide an operator interface and level of function similar to the IBM 3270. The primary difference is that an application can be designed and coded to interact with an HTML form rather than any specific piece of hardware. Web browsers interpret the form and present it to the operator regardless of whether it is running on a UNIX workstation, an IBM PC, or an Apple Macintosh. This Web technology isolates the business application developer from hardware implementation concerns. The application is developed to a form abstraction rather than to a hardware implementation.

V

Applications

This makes Web technology attractive to business application developers regardless of whether or not they ever expect to deliver their applications across the Internet. Web browsers and HTML forms provide a low-cost, high-function delivery mechanism that isolates their investment in application code from workstation, operating system, and hardware changes.

User Interface Distribution

Before the advent of Web technology (specifically graphical browsers), a company wanting to present a business application to PC users had only two choices:

- Put a dumb terminal emulator on each PC and make them operate like an IBM 3270 or DEC VT100. This approach would allow companies to continue to run the same application code they had. Any off-the-shelf emulator would do.

- Develop some PC-based code that would replace the old application or at least present a new Graphical User Interface (GUI) to the old code. However, this would mean that the company had to deliver its own code to be installed on each PC.

For the most part, the first option isolates applications from the chronic migration to new hardware and operating system levels. PC users upgrading to Windows 95 or NT could upgrade or replace the emulator code if necessary, without impact to the business applications at all. The drawback is that users have became unimpressed with the old, dumb terminal user interface. Its "un-usability" and "un-friendliness" are contrasted with ever improving windows based Graphical User Interfaces (GUIs).

The second option brought MIS into a new world of complexity. Programming, configuration management, and control (keeping the distributed application code current and in sync with hardware and OS changes) were significantly more complex.

Web technology is a middle ground that enables a company to present an acceptable user interface to a wide population of users who have an unknown configuration in a cost effective way.

HTML and the browser provide some elements of a GUI interface. No company application code needs to be installed on the user's configuration and programming to an HTML interface is relatively easy.

Multimedia Support

Some business information is graphical in nature (X-rays) and some is best understood when rendered as a graphic (trend charts). Web technology enables applications to deliver these forms of information simply and effectively, something that dumb terminal emulators cannot do.

Business Transactions on the Web

Web technology enables the use of the Internet as a low-cost, wide area network utility. It provides an acceptable user interface to a broad population of users. It isolates the company's application code from distribution and configuration issues. Are there any drawbacks or inhibitors? To find out, let's explore the nature of a business transaction.

What Is a Transaction?

A computerized business transaction is a dialog between a human and one or more applications that results in a change to the state of the business system.

Atomic Transactions

An atomic transaction consists of a single exchange of information between an operator and an application:

1. An operator retrieves, updates, and sends (posts) a form to an application.
2. The application processes the form, performs its function, and replies to the operator.

Conversational Transactions

On the other hand, a conversational transaction consists of multiple exchanges of information between an operator and one or more applications:

1. An operator retrieves, updates, and sends a form to the application.
2. The application processes the form, extracts some information, remembers some of the information, retrieves some additional information from persistent storage, and sends it to the operator along with a new form.
3. The operator looks at the new information, makes some decisions, updates the form, and sends it back to the application.

4. Steps 2-3 are repeated an undetermined number of times.

5. The application processes the form, performs its function, and replies to the operator.

An example might be an ever narrowing search for information where the operator enters some broad parameters about lease agreements, the application responds with a list of hits, the operator enters additional search constraints to be applied against the already qualified results, and so on. The operator finally finds the set of interesting lease agreements and wants them deleted.

The application for the atomic transaction does not need to know anything beyond the information contained in the single form it received. It contains the necessary and sufficient information for the application to completely perform its function. In contrast, the application in the conversational transaction is much more complex. It needs to know where it is in the conversation and the information it gathered earlier in the conversation before it can determine what it should do next. Additionally, it can be conversing with several users at the same time. In order to hold a conversation with an operator, an application needs three pieces of information when it receives a form to process:

- To which conversation does this form belong?

- Where am I in the life of this conversation?

- What information do I have from the earlier parts of the conversation?

While HyperText Transport Protocol (HTTP) can easily support atomic transactions, it does not provide the necessary support for conversational transactions.

Limitations of HyperText Transport Protocol

HTTP coupled with CGI scripts, is a sessionless protocol. When an application completes processing a form and sends a new form to the operator in reply, the TCP/IP connection is closed. When the new form is posted to the application, it is a complete connection. The information presented to the application by the server and the browser does not provide an application with enough information for it to identify which conversation a form belongs to, or even whether or not the form is part of a conversation. Without this vital piece of information, the application does not have a way hold a conversation. This problem is now solved with Microsoft's new ISAPI. The ISAPI allows an application to hold a conversation with a browser by keeping the connection open. However, if you are coding to the CGI interface, you can create your own conversational protocol as described below. After comparing the work involved with either CGI solution, you will probably choose to use the ISAPI for conversational transactions.

A Solution

An application can create a protocol of its own to deal with conversations. A conversation can be reliably identified by three pieces of information:

- The Internet address of the operator's workstation
- A unique conversation identifier
- A time span

A CGI application has access to the workstation's Internet address from the server each time it receives a form. It can generate a unique conversation identifier in a variety of ways. It can also obtain a current timestamp from the operating system. The following pseudo-code outlines how an application can initialize a conversation.

1. An operator retrieves, updates, and sends the initial form to the application.

2. The application receives the form:

   - Extract the workstation's Internet address from the HTTP_USER_AGENT environment variable.

   - Obtain a unique conversation identifier.

   - Verify and extract information from the form.

   - Process the form.

   - Obtain a current timestamp.

   - Create a scratch pad record (or object). Identify it by the conversation identifier. Save the conversation identifier, workstation Internet address, and timestamp in the scratch pad.

   - Save information necessary to continue the conversation in the scratch pad.

   - Generate the reply. In the reply form, generate a HIDDEN field that contains the unique conversation identifier.

     ```
     <INPUT TYPE=HIDDEN NAME="CONVIDENT" VALUE="abcd12345">
     ```

   - Send the reply to the operator.

3. The operator receives the new information, makes some decisions, updates the form, and posts it back to the server.

4. An application receives the form:

- Extract the workstation's Internet address from the HTTP_USER_AGENT environment variable.

- Extract the conversation identifier value from the form.

- Retrieve the scratch pad from the database using the conversation identifier as the key.

- Verify that the conversation identifier is assigned to the workstation's Internet address.

- Verify that the conversation has not expired.

- Process the form.

- Obtain a current timestamp.

- Replace the scratch pad's timestamp with the current one. Save information necessary to continue the conversation into the scratch pad.

- Generate the reply. In the reply form, generate a HIDDEN field that contains the unique conversation identifier, as in step 2.8.

- Send the reply to the operator.

5. Go back and start again with step 3.

The Browser's Back Control

When it saves a page to its cache, browsers normally identify the HTML "page" by its URL. This enables it to retrieve a page out of its cache when referenced again. However, responses generated by applications do not have a complete URL. There is no file name. Some browsers use the application's name in lieu of a file name. This leads to a design problem for conversational transactions. Suppose you create one application that manages the entire conversation. Each form in the conversation is posted to the same application and each reply comes from the same application. Most browsers will overlay the prior reply with the current one. If part of your application relies on the browser's "Back" control to allow the operator to return to earlier generated HTML pages, you are in trouble. It will not work. For these browsers, each generated reply must come from a different application in order to keep the browser from overlaying earlier generated pages. The Netscape Navigator browser does not have this design flaw.

Logical Units of Work

A logical unit of work is a set of changes to the state of business information that must be completed entirely or not completed at all. If the set of changes is only partially completed, the business information in question has lost its integrity and may lead to unpredictable business and business system behaviors, which is clearly an undesirable situation.

Database systems support the concept of a logical unit of work. They provide applications with three operations to manage logical units of work:

- Begin Transaction
- Commit
- Rollback

Begin Transaction marks the start of the logical unit of work. All changes to the state of information from that point forward belong to one logical unit of work. When an application completes a transaction, it can use the Commit operation to commit the state changes to the business system, or the Rollback operation to empty the set, as if the application had never run.

> **Note**
>
> An application must issue one of these closing commands before it ends.

Atomic transactions can exploit these operations in a simple and straightforward manner. Conversational transactions cannot. The problem for conversational transactions is a consequence of the sessionless nature of HTTP and the implementation of relational database engines. When an application has completed the processing of a form and has replied to the operator, it ends. What happens to state changes it has made during that processing? Relational database engines require an application to either commit or rollback its work before it ends. Let's look at a vehicle purchase application that must update both customer information and mark a vehicle as sold.

1. In the first exchange, the operator retrieves the customer entry form and sends it to the application, including the sale price.
2. The application updates the customer file and retrieves a list of vehicles at the dealer, constructs an option list form, and sends it to the operator.
3. The operator selects the vehicle sold and sends the form to the application.
4. The application marks the vehicle as sold and links it to the customer record. It generates and sends a confirmation page to the operator.

What happens if the customer backs out of the sale between steps 2 and 3, the customer's credit check fails, the sold vehicle is not on file, or the network connection is lost? If anything unusual occurs between steps 2 and step 4, the state of the business information is incomplete. We have a customer record indicating he bought a car for a specific price, but we do not know what car he bought. This is because the application did not have a way to define a logical unit of work to the database that spanned the changes in steps 2 and 4. From the database's point of view, step 2 was one logical unit of work and so was step 4.

A Solution

One solution to this dilemma is to store all the information in the scratch pad until the last exchange has occurred. Then do all the updates within the final application execution. This is a considerable amount of development overhead, but it guarantees the atomic nature of the transaction. To be really safe, the application should also do one additional thing. It should re-read all records that have been presented to the operator and make sure that they have not changed since the operator saw them.

Suppose an account manager was looking over delinquent lease customers and came to the conclusion that a car should be repossessed based upon a customer's account history. While the account manager was reviewing the history, someone else was applying payments. The account manager repossesses the car based upon the information he/she reviewed over the past 20 minutes. However, at the time the repossession transaction completed, the customer's account had been posted with sufficient funds to make it current! This company will have one very irate customer on their hands when the car is towed away!

In order to guarantee that the repossession transaction was correct from a business point of view, the transaction should make sure that the information that the operator used to base her/his decisions on is still true.

Concurrency Control

Concurrency controls are needed when multiple people want to share the ability to update a set of resources. These controls either prevent the actions of one operator from invalidating the actions of another or they ensure that when an operator's actions have been invalidated, he/she is notified of the fact. There are two concurrency control strategies:

■ *Pessimistic Concurrency Control.*   Prohibit other applications from modifying information that is being used to base this decision upon until this logical unit of work has completed because it is likely that they will change it before this work is completed. This is useful when there is a high transaction rate against a small number of records—perhaps a pricing table in a catalog order entry application.

- *Optimistic Concurrency Control.* Allow other applications to modify information that is being used to base this decision upon until this logical unit of work is in progress because it is highly unlikely that they will change it before this work is completed.

The above solution to the conversational logical unit of a work problem uses an optimistic concurrency control strategy. It has no other choice since applications cannot hold locks on records after they end. Therefore, it is an incomplete solution because it does not permit the use of a pessimistic concurrency control strategy.

A Better Solution

There is an X/Open standard defined for managing distributed transactions called the X/Open Distributed Transaction Processing (DTP) model. It is a software architecture that allows multiple application programs to share resources provided by multiple resource managers, and allows their work to be coordinated into global transactions (ones that span multiple program executions). One type of resource manager is a database. For more information, see:

http://www.xopen.org/

In this model, a Transaction Manager (TM) assigns identifiers to transactions, monitors their progress, takes responsibility for transaction completion and for coordinating failure recovery. IBM's DB2/NT relational database product supports this architecture and provides the X/Open Resource Manager API's. Microsoft database products do not. The only NT-based X/Open Transaction Manager product on the market is Encina. For more information about Encina see:

http://www.transarc.com/afs/transarc.com/public/www/ Public/Product/Encina/index.html

Once you install a database manager that can function as an X/Open resource manager, you have two design choices: install an X/Open compliant transaction manager and use the Application-to-TM X/Open interface, or use the TM to RM interface directly to interact with the database.

Using the TM to RM interface directly is a reasonable level of effort so long as each conversation involves updates to only one RM (database). The TM to RM interface is called the XA interface. It includes xa_start(), xa_commit(), xa_end() operations that control the life of a transaction that is not specifically tied to any single application execution.

The following is a much simplified scenario of how the XA interface can be used.

1. Your application, acting as a TM, calls xa_start() in the DB2/NT database engine, passing it a new conversation identifier to start a new global transaction.

2. Your application saves that conversation identifier in its scratch-pad area.

3. The next application in the dialog reads the scratch pad and calls xa_start(), passing the existing conversation identifier to the RM to connect back up to the existing global transaction. Each application participating in the conversation can issue database update calls. Each application in the middle of the conversation issues an xa_close() before it ends. This disconnects the application from the transaction without having to commit or roll it back!

4. The final application in the dialog can issue the xa_commit() to commit all the work that was done during the conversation, or an xa_rollback() to roll it back.

By using the XA interface, the application is not burdened with all the additional logic imposed by the first solution and it can employ either concurrency control strategy (so long as it is supported by the resource manager).

An Application Architecture for the Web

There is nothing so dynamic in the computer industry today as the explosion of Internet technologies. If it is true that designing business applications for change is a primary objective of software development, it is especially true for designing business applications that use Internet technologies.

Object Technology

Object technology promises you the ability to deliver high quality, low cost, low maintenance applications that are resilient to change. This promise, however, is conditional upon the "proper" exploitation of the technology.

Application Architecture Options

Many developers use case tools that enable them to exploit technology objects (such as buttons, frames, and so on) to create nice GUI interfaces. They then write procedures that run when certain events occur. These procedures are variously called *callbacks*, or *event handlers*. The entire application is designed within the framework provided by the case tool's technology objects.

This, however, is not constructive object-oriented application development. It is procedural application development that is designed to operate within a specific object-oriented GUI framework.

The Object Management Group (OMG—the largest software consortium in the world) believes that by exploiting the constructive capabilities of the technology one can achieve its promises. That is, the characteristics and behavior of objects should be abstracted to provide a general capability over a wide range of specialized sub-classes. The abstract interface can then be used by all clients, regardless of specialized implementations.

This paradigm is generally accepted for technology objects. That is, it accepted that there should be a general interface to buttons that enables you to put a label on them or re-size them, regardless of whether they surface as a Motif button or a Microsoft Windows button. For the most part, this philosophy has not been internalized to the point of affecting how you design business objects.

Object-Oriented Application Design

Suppose you want to create a business application that uses HTML forms for its user interface. Sometime in 1996 or 1997, Java will become a deployable technology. When that happens, you will want your application to be able to dynamically determine if the browser is Java enabled, and use a Java form instead of an HTML form. When a posted Java form is received, it will require a different kind of processing. You want this technology change to occur without changing more than one or two lines of code.

In order to make this a reality, you need to write your application to an abstract object class called something like TCform. One specialized type of form might be an HTML form class called TChtmlForm, and another might be a Java form class called TCjavaForm. If the application is written to the abstract TCform interface, it has the ability to dynamically switch between an HTML user interface and a Java user interface. The code might look like:

```
p = getenv("HTTP_ACCEPT");
if (strloc(p,"Java")) myForm = new TCjavaForm;
else myForm = new TChtmlForm;
```

From that point on, all the code is the same.

Creating a Constructive Environment

Under the OMG design concept, developers first design the basic building blocks of an application and then they use these building blocks to construct applications. Using Legos as an analogy, first you need to design the Legos pieces, and then you can use the pieces to construct things. When Legos first came out, they were designed to be used to construct houses and buildings. You had about 6 basic pieces which enabled the construction of any building design (except round ones).

Embracing the OMG concept of objects and exploiting this technology successfully means you need to create a set of abstract classes that can be assembled to construct any business application. You must ask the questions, "What is the nature of a business application?" and "What building blocks are essential to its construction?"

Developing an Abstract Application Model

The following is a generalized model of business applications:

Characteristic	Definition
Static Model	The state or characteristics of a business object.
Algorithms	The business algorithms used to perform calculations.
Constraint Logic	The business logic employed to regulate state changes in the object space; sometimes known as integrity rules.
Operations	The business object's methods and interfaces to those methods.
Transactions	A controller that prescribes a dialog with an operator to accomplish a logical unit of work.
Workflows	A process for completing a set of transactions.

This table corresponds roughly to understanding that an abstract house is composed of a roof, a floor, walls, doorways, and window openings. It does not necessarily tell you what fundamental blocks are needed, but it does outline the abstract requirements you are trying to satisfy. The next step is to identify a set of abstract classes that can be used to construct this abstract application. They might include:

Component	Definition
Domains	Responsible for verifying values, rendering values in various formats and units of measure, relational operations, algebraic operations, and so on.
Attributes	Responsible for its state or value.
Objects	Responsible for knowing characteristics or attributes of some real world entity or event and for the persistent storage of their state.
Rules	Enforces constraints.

Component	Definition
Events	Can be used to trigger the execution of rules.
Forms	Responsible for rendering themselves to operators and for verifying their validity.
Transactions	Responsible for controlling the operator dialog and completing or rolling back a logical unit of work.
Workflows	Responsible for managing the process to complete a set of transactions.

This object analysis has shown that these are a sufficient set of basic abstract classes that enable the construction of Web-based business transactions.

OO Patterns

The next step is to take this analysis into object design. You used the patterns described in *Design Patterns, Elements of Reusable Object-Oriented Software* by Gamma et. al. to help design a highly reusable abstract application model. Figure 19.4 is a Booch notation chart of the resulting class structure.

> **Note**
>
> You have only implemented a subset of the above abstract classes.

V

Applications

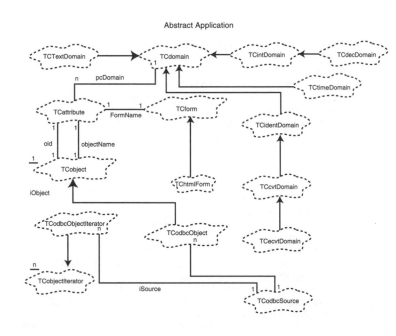

Fig. 19.4
Abstract Application model.

The abstract application model implements essentially all of the code necessary to construct an atomic business transaction using a relational database and World Wide Web technology. Listing 19.9 is an entire atomic update transaction program. This is the only logic written specifically for this transaction.

Listing 19.9   http://www.asiatown.com Site Listing Update CGI

```
// Main program
//***********************************************************************
int main(int argc, char *argv[]) {
    int ContentLength;
    char *p;
    char formBuf[MAXLEN];
    char      SMTPServer[]="ns1.ipworld.com";
    LibraryProlog();
// Read in the data from the client
    p = getenv("CONTENT_LENGTH");
    if (p != NULL) ContentLength = 1 + atoi(p);
    else ContentLength = 0;
    if (ContentLength > MAXLEN) ContentLength = MAXLEN;
    cin.get(formBuf,ContentLength);

//**************************************************
// Load the form.
    TClibraryUpdateForm form("Update WWW Listing");
    form.Input(formBuf);
// Process the form.
// 1. Verify that the form name is right.
    TCattribute *workAttribute;
    workAttribute = form.FindAttribute("FORM");
    if (workAttribute == 0) ErrorExit(0,"This form has an unknown
    ↪name.");
    if (strcmp(form.Name(),workAttribute->Value()) != 0)
        ErrorExit(0,"This is not the correct form for this
            ↪application.");
// 2. Check for required fields.
    form.CheckRequired();
// 3. If requested, perform the action.
    TCattribute *action;
    action = form.FindAttribute("ACTIONCODE");
    if (action == 0) ErrorExit(0,"Internal error. No action code
    ↪specified in this form.");
    if (*action == "PERFORM") {
        TClibraryRecord updRec("Asiatown", "Public", "Open",
        ↪"Library");
// 6. Get the name of the browser.
        workAttribute = updRec.FindAttribute("USERAGENT");
        if (workAttribute != 0) workAttribute-
        ↪>SetValue(getenv("HTTP_USER_AGENT"));
        *updRec.GetOid() = *form.FindAttribute("RECORDID");
        updRec.Update();
        cout << "<h4>Your record has been successfully updated.
        ↪Thank you.</h4>";
```

```
            form.Mail(SMTPServer);
        }
        else form.SendDisplayForm();
        LibraryEpilog();
        return 0;
    }
```

In this sample application, `TClibraryRecord` is a subclass of `TCodbcObject` and inherits all that class's methods for selecting, searching, inserting, updating, and so on. In this way, all the ODBC code is implemented in the abstract `TCodbcObject` class and is re-used by all subclasses. ❖

## CHAPTER 20

Integrating Microsoft BackOffice

Microsoft BackOffice is a family of five products: Microsoft Windows NT Server as the network foundation; Microsoft SQL Server for managing and storing data; Microsoft SNA Server for host connectivity; Microsoft Systems Management Server for managing PCs and servers; and Microsoft Mail Server for distributing information. This chapter outlines how you can apply the functions and features of these components to run your NT Web server.

In this chapter, you learn about:

- What the NT Advanced Server provides to make your Web site safe and secure
- How to use SQL Server and MS Access/95 as your database engine
- Microsoft's new Internet Information Server

Microsoft NT Server OS

The Microsoft NT Server operating system provides a robust set of functions that address many of the security, user administration, and resource sharing issues companies face when establishing an Internet presence.

Providing Internet Security

Security is one of the primary issues confronting businesses that want to use the Internet. The NT Server Operating System provides a considerable number of security features that you can use to control access to company resources. For example, the NT File System (NTFS) security can prevent access to portions of a disk (or partition). You can configure user account security to control access of the Guest account and others. Log on authentication in FTP and Telnet can prevent unauthorized users from accessing your servers. You can also audit access to your Internet servers using Event Log.

Using File System Security

If you create an FTP server, you can and should use NTFS security settings to control specific access to files and directories and to configure the behavior of files and directories. This security method requires the disk or disk partition to be formatted NTFS. It is a good idea to keep the files available through FTP on a disk or disk partition separate from your operating system, application, or personal files.

You use File Manager to set permissions on NTFS partitions. A basic use of file system security is creating read-only directories so that Internet users will not update or delete files.

One example of using file system security to control the behavior of directories is creating a drop box for your Internet customers to leave files in. If you set the permissions on the drop box directory to write only, Internet users can place files in the drop box directory, but can't see or copy any of the files left there by other customers. Only internal users with appropriate permissions can access the files.

Replicating Internet Server Files

Directory replication is a Microsoft Windows NT Server feature that allows you to set up and automatically maintain identical directory trees on multiple servers and workstations. Updates made to the files or directories on one server are periodically copied, or replicated, to other servers and workstations. When a file changes, the entire file is replicated as depicted in figure 20.1.

Fig. 20.1
Using NT file replication services to isolate your internal network from the Web.

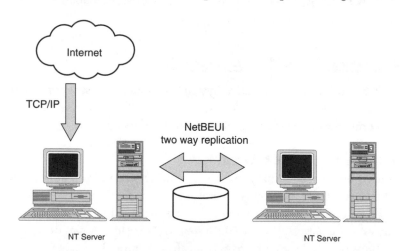

One way to isolate your internal network from the Internet is to use the Windows NT Replication Service to replicate the data on the Internet server onto another computer on the internal LAN using the Windows NT Replication service.

For example, if you're using the Internet server as a drop box for customer questions and suggestions, Internet users leave information on the Internet server, and then the Windows NT Replication service replicates the contents of the Internet server to the LAN computer. Conversely, if your LAN users need to post information to the public, users on your corporate Net copy the information to be shared to the LAN intermediary computer, and then that information is replicated to your Internet server.

You gain more control over what is brought into the LAN and permitted out of the LAN by using a replication strategy. You can check files for viruses or other problems such as excessive size before they are brought in.

There are three main components used in replication: the export server; the import computer; and the export and import directories. You can configure a Windows NT Server computer as both an export server and an import computer.

The Export Server. The computer that provides the files and directories to be replicated is called an *export server*. Files and directories can be replicated from the export server to specified computers or domains. Only computers running Windows NT Server can be export servers. They do not need to be domain controllers.

The Import Computer. Computers that receive replicated files and directories (sometimes called *updates*) from an export server are called *import computers*. Updates can be received from specified computers or domains. The following can be import computers:

Windows NT Server domain controllers and servers

Windows NT Workstations

Windows NT 3.1 Advanced Server computers

Windows NT 3.1 Workstations

LanManager OS/2 Servers and OS/2 peer servers

Export and Import Directories. The export server keeps the directories to be replicated in an export directory; by default this directory is:

    \<winnt_root>\SYSTEM32\REPL\EXPORT

This directory is shared as REPL$ when you start the Directory Replicator service for exporting. You create subdirectories under this directory for each group of files you want replicated.

Each import computer has an import directory that receives all imports; by default this directory is:

    \<winnt_root>\SYSTEM32\REPL\IMPORT

V

Applications

The Directory Replicator service automatically creates the subdirectories under this directory.

For example, to provide for replication of your drop boxes, an administrator would create the following directory on your FTP server:

```
\<winnt_root>\SYSTEM32\REPL\EXPORT\DROPBOX
```

The administrator would then configure and start the Directory Replicator service on that server. Next, the administrator would configure and start the Directory Replicator service on each of servers that the drop box directory structure should be imported to.

After directory replication occurs, the contents of the drop boxes will reside in the following directory on each domain controller:

```
\<winnt_root>\SYSTEM32\REPL\IMPORT\DROPBOX
```

When a user with access to this directory logs on to the domain, the contents of the drop boxes will be available.

Windows NT User Account Security

A primary security measure that should be observed at all times is guarding the Administrator account and administrative privilege on computers connected to the Internet. Only employees with appropriate security clearances should be given the passwords for these accounts.

If your Internet users are using any Microsoft networking client, you can use Windows NT user accounts to validate these users and define the user's permissions. These users can still access the system without a Windows NT user account using Guest or an anonymous FTP log on.

Also note that users of two computers on the Internet with Microsoft Windows-based networking software (such as Windows NT, Windows for Workgroups, LAN Manager, or MS-DOS clients) can issue net use commands, or use File Manager or Print Manager to connect to resources on the distant computer—even if that computer is on another continent. A hacker using Windows-based software could issue a net view command and then see a list of your corporate servers. Windows-based networking client security is controlled through Windows NT user account permissions and NTFS file permissions, just as it is on the local LAN.

FTP and Telnet Log On Security

The FTP and Telnet server services use the Windows NT user account database to validate users logging on.

> **Caution**
>
> Important: FTP and Telnet logons use clear-text for user names and passwords. This is a potential security weakness.

FTP always uses user-level security, meaning you must log on to use an FTP server. You can configure the FTP server service to allow only users with valid Windows NT accounts to log on. An FTP server can also be configured to permit anonymous log on. Anonymous log on requires the user to type **anonymous** as their user name and their Internet e-mail address as their password. Anonymous users access files under the Guest account. You can also allow only anonymous log on to a Windows NT FTP server. Anonymous-only log on is useful because real passwords are not used, thus, a valid password can't be revealed to network snoops.

Auditing Access with the Event Log

You can use the event log to track access to all of the Internet server services. The FTP server service and Telnet server service can be configured to record logons in the event log. Other Internet server services can create entries each time a file is downloaded.

Windows NT Router Security on TCP/IP-Based LANs

If you're using TCP/IP on your corporate network, you can create a firewall in the Internet server by disabling TCP/IP routing. This feature controls whether data is passed through the Internet server to and from the corporate network; that is, it controls whether the computer acts as a gateway. See figure 20.2.

Fig. 20.2
By disabling IP routing, you can create a firewall.

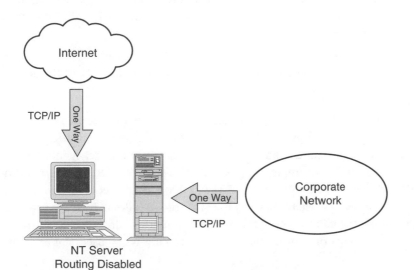

V

Applications

NT Server
Routing Disabled

The router feature works both ways. Either traffic can pass both ways or traffic can't pass through the server at all. This type of security model has all the advantages and disadvantages of the protocol isolation model discussed in the section "SNA Server," later in this chapter.

> ### Caution
>
> A major concern with this model is that the separation between the Internet and your corporate network depends on a single check box in the TCP/IP configuration dialog box (or on the associated Registry entries). Assuming an intruder somehow enters your Windows NT gateway, the intruder need only change one Registry value to expose your internal TCP/IP network.

If you use this type of security model, you also need to be especially careful to control physical and administrative access to the computer used as an Internet server. An individual familiar with Windows NT configuration tools and administrative privilege can find and change the router check box in a matter of moments.

Directory Services

You can use several tools to locate computers, directories, and files that are on the Internet. The following locator tools are included in the NT 3.51 resource kit for use with Windows NT:

- *Domain Name System (DNS)*   This system lets the user specify user-friendly computer names. DNS maps friendly computer names to numeric IP addresses. DNS servers query other DNS servers to resolve portions of the address that they can't map until the entire IP address has been built.

- *Windows Internet Name Service (WINS)*   This service maps the computer names of computers running Windows or Windows NT to IP addresses.

DNS Server

The Domain Name System is a protocol and system used throughout the Internet to map IP addresses to user-friendly names. A major advantage of this service is that the name of a computer can remain the same, even if the address changes. For example, suppose the Web site provided by Internet Productions, Inc., had the IP address 204.117.200.2. Most people would reach this computer by specifying www.ipworld.com. Besides being easier to remember, the name is more reliable. The numeric address could change for any of a number of reasons, but the name can always be used. For example, you might want to move your Web site from a server in New York to one in California because the connection rates are cheaper. However, your company has assigned the 204.117.200 zone to the New York office and 119.564.100 to California. Since Internet users access your site by www.ipworld.com, you can freely move it to California, give it a new IP address of 119.564.100.111 and no one will know the difference.

The IP address that matches this name is found by DNS servers on the Internet. This address is then used for communication with the target computer for the remainder of the session. The client software for DNS (called the *resolver*) is built into the TCP/IP software that ships with Windows NT.

You will want to provide your own DNS server if you have your own domain on the Internet or if you want to access DNS from your LAN, rather than going through your Internet provider. You should also assign the task to at least two computers: a primary and a secondary name server. Data should be replicated from the primary name server to the secondary name server. This lets the Internet-wide DNS locate computers on your network even if one of the name servers is down. How often you schedule replication will depend on how often names change in your domain. Replicate often enough that changes are known to both servers. Excessive replication can tie up your network and servers unnecessarily.

WINS Service

The Windows Internetwork Name Service (WINS) is used to resolve names on a network of computers running any combination of Windows NT and other Windows-family operating systems. WINS can be used in conjunction with DNS to resolve names on your Windows Internet for Internet users.

Setting Up WINS Name Resolution

The Windows NT DNS Server service can use the WINS service to resolve the names of computers running Windows or Windows NT. Use the WINS service to avoid double administration of a TCP/IP based NT network configuration.

Let's say you want a set of your computers to be known to the Internet as machinename.place.com. Set up the DNS service that manages the place.com zone on the domain controller for the set of machines you want exposed. DNS queries for testcomputer.place.com would come to your DNS server (ns1.place.com for example). The DNS service would resolve to the zone place.com and then hand it off to WINS. WINS lookup would find testcomputer in its domain and return its IP address.

> ### Caution
>
> Windows NT servers that run DNS and also provide WINS lookup must not be configured to use DNS for Windows name resolution. This setting is reached by choosing Network from the Control Panel, and going to the advanced configuration settings for the TCP/IP protocol. The Use DNS for Windows Name Resolution check box should be cleared.
>
> Do not put the $WINS line in reverse-lookup (IN-ADDR.ARPA.) domains.

Other Internet Tools

Windows NT TCP/IP provides FTP client and server services, and the TELNET client service, when you install the TCP/IP protocol. FTP is a character-based utility used to connect client computers to FTP servers and to list and transfer files that are on the FTP servers. The TELNET client service is a dumb terminal emulator (ansi, vt100, etc.) application that lets you log in to remote computers and issue commands as if you were at the computer's keyboard. See NTCMDS.HLP for a complete list of the other TCP/IP character-based network tools available with Windows NT. Many variations of FTP, TELNET, and other programs based on earlier Internet standards are also available on the Internet or commercially. Several can be found in the CICA library at **ftp:// ftp.cdrom.com/pub/cica/pc/win3/util**.

MS Exchange

SMTP is the generic name applied to how Internet mail is transferred. The Internet has long used several e-mail standards published as *Request For Comments (RFCs)*. *RFC 821,* also known as the *Simple Mail Transport Protocol* or *SMTP,* defines how Internet mail is transferred. *RFC 822* defines the message content for plain text messages. *RFC 1521,* also known as *Multipurpose Internet Mail Extensions* or *MIME,* extends the definition of message content to include multipart textual and nontextual body parts. Microsoft Exchange Server supports these RFCs through the Exchange Server Internet Mail Connector.

The Microsoft Exchange Server Internet Mail Connector connects Exchange Server to other mail systems that use SMTP to transfer mail. This component is called the *Internet Mail Connector* because it refers to the format of the Internet messages that are sent over the SMTP transport. In addition to SMTP and MIME, the Internet Mail Connector supports RFC 1154, which is used by the existing Microsoft Mail gateway to SMTP.

Microsoft Mail users can access the Internet via the Microsoft Exchange Server Internet Mail Connector. Messages pass through the Exchange Server's Microsoft Mail Connector to the Internet.

The Microsoft Exchange Server Internet Mail Connector connects an Exchange Server site to the Internet or another system that uses SMTP for message exchange. Microsoft Mail Server users connected to the Microsoft Exchange Server site with the Microsoft Mail Connector can also connect to the SMTP messaging system through the Exchange Server Internet Mail Connector.

Companies can use the Microsoft Exchange Server Internet Mail Connector and the Microsoft Mail Gateway to SMTP to connect Exchange Server sites to a Microsoft Mail Server post office. This gives Microsoft Exchange Server users access to the SMTP messaging system, the Microsoft Mail Server post office, and any foreign messaging systems that are accessible through the post office.

Administration

The Microsoft Exchange Server Internet Mail Connector is very easy to install, set up, and administer. It's an integral component of Microsoft Exchange Server that is installed with the Exchange Server setup program and is administered through the Exchange Server Administrative program. Because it is Microsoft Exchange Server service, it can be monitored, stopped and started, and managed like any other Windows NT service.

The Internet Mail Connector provides a number of administrative options that will help the administrator manage and control their company's Internet traffic. The following table shows examples of these controls.

Control	Description
Unread limit (msgs)	Sets the maximum number of messages that can be in the Internet Mail Connector queue at any one time.
Unread time	Sets the maximum length of time a message can remain in the Internet Mail Connector queue before it is returned to the sender.
Message transfer quota	The maximum amount of disk storage that can be used by the Internet Mail Connector database.
Maximum message size	The maximum size of a message that the Internet Mail Connector will send. Messages that exceed the maximum are returned as undeliverable.

Message Format

The Internet Mail Connector supports the following three message formats: RFC 822, RFC 1521 (MIME), and RFC 1154 (Microsoft Mail 3.2 compatibility mode). Administrators can set defaults for the Internet Mail Connector and override the default behavior based on addresses.

Inbound/Outbound Connections

The Internet Mail Connector will support multiple simultaneous inbound and outbound connections. Administrators can control the number of simultaneous connections in and out of the Internet Mail Connector.

The complexity of encoded Internet messages is hidden from the user. Inbound messages are automatically resolved, whether they are sent as an RFC 822, RFC 1521, or RFC 1154 message. UUENCODE, Base 64, and Quoted Printable encoding are automatically decoded. For outbound messages, administrators can set defaults.

Because the Internet Mail Connector can also be configured to accept connections only from known IP addresses, it can be used to set up a private messaging network on the Internet.

Domain Name Service (DNS) Resolver

The Domain Name Service (DNS) Resolver can resolve Internet addresses from a DNS service and route them from the Internet address information. It can query a DNS server and route on the information received. For this reason, the Internet Mail Connector does not require additional computers for routing purposes.

SQL Server and MS Access 95

You can implement object persistence by using either a relational or object-oriented database engine. If the main thrust of your application is to extend some part of your existing business system to the Internet, you will probably want to implement persistence over a relational engine. This will limit the design complexity of your persistent objects, but it will enable you to bridge between your new object-oriented development on the Web and your existing business systems without much difficulty.

On the other hand, you may be implementing an entirely new line of business. You may be getting into complex data types, such as video, audio, compound documents, animation, arrays, geographic information, and composite objects. If so, you may want to seriously consider an object database instead of a relational one. Since object databases directly map your object class structures to persistent storage, they can provide significant productivity, performance, and functional advantages. Programmers will not have to worry about transforming complex data structures into flat, relational tables and back again. The database engine will not be burdened with the overhead of SQL retrieval because complex objects are not inherently searchable.

Relational Databases

Developers have three relational database APIs to choose from when implementing code in a Microsoft Windows NT environment. They are ODBC, DDE, and OLE. However, a fundamental design principal is to write code to industry-standard interfaces, not to vendor interfaces. In this case, ANSI SQL is the standard syntax and semantic to use for writing SQL statements. ODBC is the standard to use for interacting with relational database engines. Detractors will denigrate the ODBC interface over performance issues. However, ODBC has emerged as the industry-standard API. Every relational database vendor supports it. Concomitant with this, developers have selected it as their preferred API. Database vendors have therefore begun to tune their products to maximize the performance of their engines through this interface. For example, Microsoft recently established an industry high of 3,194 TPC-C transactions per minute on a system costing less than $1 million using the ODBC API to their Microsoft SQL Server database product.

Microsoft recently announced ODBC/DRDA drivers for Windows 3.1 and Windows NT environments. These drivers are available with SNA Server 2.11 and support connectivity to:

> DB2 for MVS
>
> SQL/DS for VM
>
> DBS/400 for OS/400

This approach enables your Web server applications to reach corporate information stored in DB/2. By using a SNA link to your corporate data, you have established a protocol-based firewall between your corporate environment and the Internet (See the section "SNA Server," later in this chapter).

ODBC

Because the use of ODBC as the API between your application to the relational database engine allows you to pick virtually any database product and change database products with minimal impact to your application, we will assume you made this choice.

Installing ODBC

An ODBC Software Development Kit is available from the Microsoft Developer's Network (MSDN) at a Level 2 subscription. A Level 2 MSDN membership provides you with the latest versions of Windows and Windows NT Workstation, including pre-release versions. It also provides you with the *Development Platform*—a set of CDs updated quarterly that contains all the software development kits (SDKs), device driver kits (DDKs), and Windows and Windows NT Workstation operating systems from Microsoft, both domestic and international versions. For information about subscribing to the MSDN, see **http://www.microsoft.com/msdn**.

The ODBC SDK provides you with the necessary header files, help files, and DLLs to implement ODBC applications. It also provides you with test utilities, trace utilities, administration and setup utilities, and sample application source code.

Setting Up an ODBC Data Source

Use the ODBC/32 administration utility provided by the ODBC/SDK to set up and identify your database as an ODBC data source. Each driver provides a different setup application. If you're using the Microsoft ODBC drive to connect to a MS Access or SQL Server database, make your database a *System Database*. This means that any user logged into this machine will be able to see and potentially use this data source. Because the data source has its own login ID and password, it is still protected.

Now for the tricky part. Some Web servers only run as system applications and also have your CGI scripts run as system applications. They are not associated with any user. Therefore, they will not have visibility to the data source you just defined unless you manually update the NT Registry so that the Default User has access to your data sources.

1. Start the Registry Edit program. It's located in the System32 directory.

2. Open the HKEY_USERS window. Inside this window you will see a DE-FAULT folder. Inside the DEFAULT folder, you will find a SOFTWARE folder.

3. Click on the SOFTWARE folder to highlight it.

4. Under Edit on the menu bar you will see the option to add a key. Select it and add a key named ODBC. Leave the Class field blank.

5. Open the HKEY_LOCAL_MACHINE window. Inside this window you will see a SOFTWARE folder. Inside the SOFTWARE folder you will find an ODBC folder.

6. Click on the ODBC folder to highlight it. Under the Registry menu bar you will find the Save Key option. Save the ODBC folder somewhere.

7. Now go back to the HKEY_USERS window and highlight the ODBC key folder you created in the DEFAULT folder.

8. Select the Registry menu bar option Restore, and restore the ODBC key you just saved over top of the empty ODBC key you created. Now your CGI script will have access to the data sources you have set up.

Replicating Internet Server Databases

Database replication facilities can be used to provide a form of protocol isolation between your network and the Internet in the same way NT's native file system replication feature was used above. A replication scenario allows more control over what is brought into the LAN and permitted out of the LAN.

SNA Server

Microsoft's SNA Server for Windows NT provides flexible SNA connectivity between LANs and IBM host computers. The SNA server can be used to provide various forms of firewall isolation between your IBM based business systems and the Internet.

Although you might want the users on your corporate network to use the Internet, and users from the Internet to access certain information, you probably do not want Internet users to have full access to your corporate network. You can use physical isolation, protocol isolation, third-party routers, and Windows NT router security in your network to provide security, although the topology you choose affects the service you provide to LAN users.

Protocol Isolation

If you want both Internet and corporate computers to see the Internet server, you can use protocol isolation security. In this model the Internet server has two network adapters. The network adapter connected to the Internet is bound to TCP/IP. The network adapter connected to the corporate network uses SNA as depicted in figure 20.3.

The key to this model is that the Internet requires use of the IP protocol. If a different protocol, such as SNA, connects your Internet server to the corporate mainframe, the corporate network can't be accessed by Internet users because they aren't using the correct protocol. Likewise, corporate network users can't directly access the Internet because they aren't using TCP/IP.

Fig. 20.3
Using different
network adapters
and protocol
bindings provides
excellent firewall
protection.

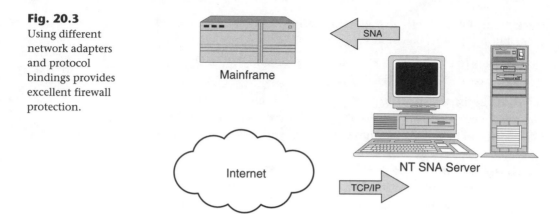

Using the ODBC/DRDA driver mentioned previously, database resources on this server are accessible from either direction, but data can't be passed through. In this way, there is a virtual barrier to passing packets through the server. Such barriers are often referred to as *firewalls*.

The advantage of the protocol isolation security model is that you can provide well-controlled access to corporate information to Internet users without exposing the corporation to unauthorized use. One disadvantage of using this type of model is that your users can't directly access the Internet. The users can't search for or retrieve Internet resources, other than those resources on the Internet server you have set up. Users also can't exchange mail with other Internet users unless you have provided the necessary Internet mail server services on the server. Another disadvantage is that, theoretically, an Internet hacker could penetrate this security model, but it's very challenging because the server does no protocol conversion.

SMS

The functions and facilities of Microsoft Systems Management Server aren't directly applicable to setting up and operating an Internet presence. They do offer your network operations group a robust set of tools for configuration management and control. It provides a set of software tools to manage networked personal computers. It supports native Microsoft NT servers, together with UNIX , LanManager, and Novell Netware servers. Macintosh computers are also supported. It enables the management of clients across the Wide Area Networks.

SMS provides:

- Automated and remote software distribution and installation via servers to clients

- Automated inventory management, collecting software and hardware configuration information from Microsoft Windows NT, LanManager, Novell Netware, and from Microsoft DOS, Windows 3.x, Windows for WorkGroups, Microsoft Windows NT, and Macintosh clients

- Remote control of clients for problem resolution—subject to user permission

- Alert and event management enables administrators to define prompts for system monitoring and enhanced fault aversion/resolution.

- Network analyzer facilities, including "Sniffer" packet tracing

- Follow-me (roving) user access to custom desktop and applications from any site

- Server load balancing

Microsoft Internet Information Server

The Microsoft Internet Information Server is now available from Microsoft via the Internet. Microsoft has announced its intention to bundle this server package with the NT Advanced Server operating system in a future release. This package includes a robust Web server plus FTP and Gopher servers. The Web server exploits many OS and BackOffice capabilities to present a comprehensive set of services that tie into the NT user, file, and machine management tools. Like other BackOffice components, this is such a comprehensive package that this chapter only gives an overview of its capabilities.

Installation

The installation of the software is as easy as running any Microsoft Setup program.

> **Caution**
>
> After Setup has completed, go into the wwwroot directory and delete everything. It's the same for the scripts directory. You don't want to be publishing sample material on the Net or running unknown scripts on your machine!

The package includes a graphical administration tool called the *Internet Service Manager*. This tool is the central location from which the Web, FTP, and Gopher services are configured and controlled. You can run the Internet Service Manager from any machine that has network connectivity to machines running these Internet services (see fig. 20.4). Only validated administrators are allowed to administer services.

Fig. 20.4

You can manage multiple Internet Servers from a central office with the Microsoft Internet Service Manager.

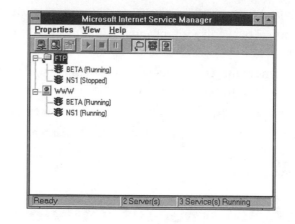

The graphical interface indicates which services are up, down, or paused. Because you can sort by server state, all stopped or paused servers can be configured to appear at the top of a report. For the FTP service, you can view current sessions from the FTP service property sheet. You can stop, start, or pause any of the services through this utility.

Each of the services can be individually configured to log information about who accessed the server and what information they accessed. This data can be useful for performance tuning, capacity planning, content assessment, and security auditing. Logging options include:

- Logging records to any file in the NT file system or any SQL database through an ODBC driver

- The Web server log can be stored in the Microsoft Professional Internet Services log format, European Microsoft Windows NT Academic Center (EMWAC) log format, or NCSA Common Log File format.

- Logging services can be configured to roll over to new log files whenever the log files achieve a particular size or whenever a day of the week, week of the month, or month changes.

Logging to SQL Server

By using the Internet Information Server database logging feature, you can store the log information directly into an SQL table. Using MS Access or SQL server query and report facilities, you can quickly analyze your site's traffic and access patterns.

Note

Database logging does increase the amount of time and resources taken to service FTP, HTTP, and Gopher requests. Sites with very heavy traffic should log to the file system for maximum performance.

User Management

Unlike other Web server software, the IIS Web server is designed to run under the security profile of an unprivileged user. The Internet Information Server builds on the Windows NT Server security model to offer straightforward and robust control over directories, documents, and executed server applications. Anonymous users (all those not required to log into the Web server) run under a user ID you specify. During installation, and later via the Service Manger, you can specify this user ID and its login password. You must use the User Manager utility to define a new user ID and password for this purpose. It's important that you protect this as securely as you would any other user ID and password on your Internet Server machine.

Caution

Do not use the default user ID that the installation process provides! Hackers will know what the default is and will only have to break the password to gain entry to your system.

If you have implemented CGIs that access an SQL database via ODBC, the anonymous user ID must have access to the Data Set Name (DSN). The easiest way to provide this access is to use the ODBC-32 utility and set the database up as a "System Database." Because this Web service is running as a normal user, the steps described below regarding how to edit the registry to establish an ODBC key under the Default profile are not needed!

> **Note**
>
> Note that the user ID that is assigned to IIS must be able to access the necessary data source ODBC.INI key information in the NT registry. If you have really restricted the resources the user ID can access, you may have inadvertently restricted its ability to access the ODBC key information. *This user ID must have more than just read access to the data source name under the ODBC.INI key in HKEY_LOCAL_MACHINE.* It must be able to Query Value, Set Value, Create Subkey, and Enumerate Subkeys. You can accomplish this by assigning "special" permissions to the user ID for the data source name key.

You may want to go beyond publishing to anonymous folks on the Net. For example, you might have a group of people in your company who want to share some sensitive documents such as product plans or designs among themselves, or a group of Internet users who have paid for a subscription to a particular set of information on your Web site. With the IIS server, you can employ NT's specific per-user and per-group access control. The same rich accounts and permissions mechanism can be applied to the Internet in these scenarios.

With client authentication, users can identify themselves to the IIS and gain access to those directories and files marked as readable only by members of the group. Because of the full-featured Windows NT Server user accounts database, any number of overlapping groups can be created and granted differing access to resources on the server.

Virtual Directories

With Microsoft Internet Information Server, administrators can distribute the files that make up their Web site across volumes of the server and even to other computers in the organization because IIS makes it possible to generate a "virtual tree" of Web aliases built from local or network directories. When HTTP, FTP, or Gopher requests are submitted to the server, it fetches files from local or network locations based on the virtual tree configuration (see fig. 20.5).

An additional benefit of using virtual directories is that it allows servers with WWW, FTP, and Gopher content to be isolated from the Internet—the Internet Information Server fetches and serves documents securely using Windows NT file-sharing while exposing other computers in the local area network to low risk of compromise by outside intruders.

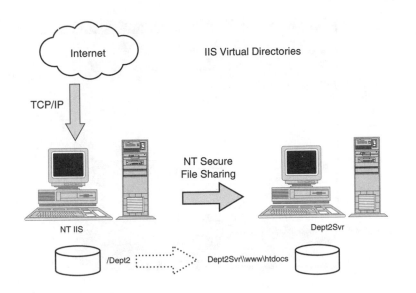

IIS Virtual Directories

Fig. 20.5
Virtual directories
let your server
reach out to
departmental
information
without exposing
them to the
Internet.

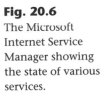

Virtual directories are configured from the Microsoft Internet Service Manager, on the "directories" pages of the FTP, WWW, and Gopher property sheets. The page lists all configured virtual directories and gives their status. If a server is configured to use multiple IP addresses and domain names, multiple separate virtual directories can be maintained.

Here's how it's done:

1. Start Microsoft Internet Service Manager (see fig. 20.6).

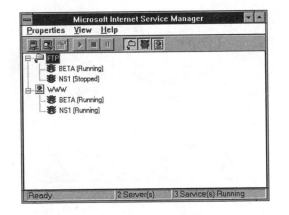

Fig. 20.6
The Microsoft
Internet Service
Manager showing
the state of various
services.

2. Bring up the property sheet for the WWW service on INETSRV12 by double-clicking the stoplight in the viewer. You should see something like the WWW Service window in figure 20.7.

V

Applications

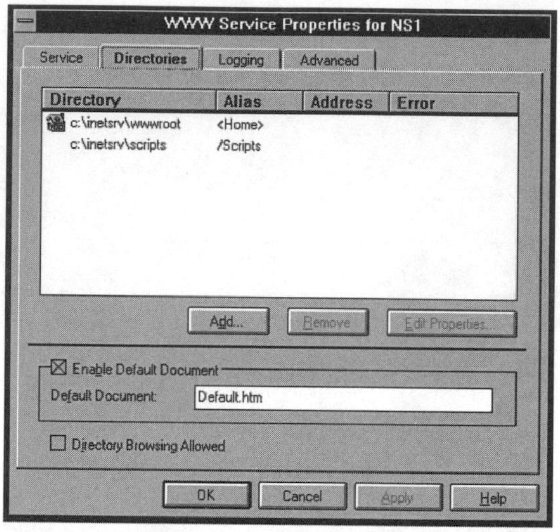

Fig. 20.7
The WWW Service
Properties menu
shows you the
home and virtual
directories defined
for this server.

3. Click the Directories tab.

4. Click the Add button to add a new root and you will see a form like the
one shown in figure 20.8.

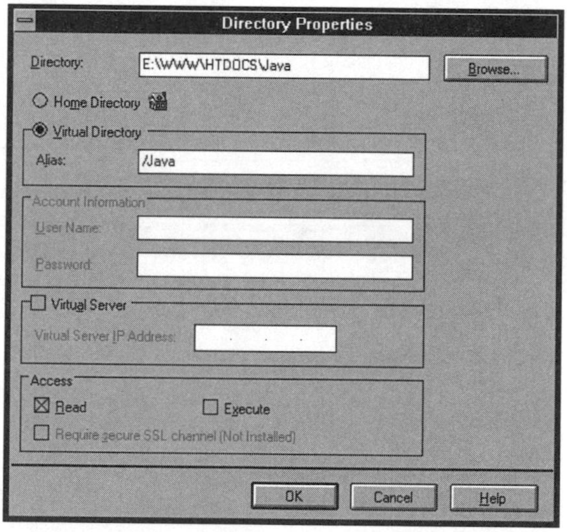

Fig. 20.8
The Directory
Properties form
enables you to
specify a virtual
directory.

5. Enter the UNC (\\servername\sharename) path to the catalog
department's pages.

6. Enter the WWW alias by which this part of the site will be known.

7. Enter the credentials that the WWW server should use to connect to the department's pages.

> **Note**
>
> Note that these credentials can override the access rights under which the request is being serviced. For more information on setting up and assigning permissions to anonymous Internet users, click Help.

Now whenever a World Wide Web client requests **http:// www.volcano.com/catalog/default.htm** or any other page from the "catalog" virtual directory, that page will be fetched and cached by the Internet Information Server from the INETSRV12 computer.

> **Caution**
>
> One check box on the dialog above, the Execute check box, deserves more explanation. World Wide Web client commands can cause programs to be executed on your machine (ISAPI and CGI scripts). To protect your environment, the Web service by default does not grant execute permission for any files except those in the "Scripts" virtual directory. This keeps an intruder who locates or places a program on the server from causing it to be executed by the server.
>
> For your site's protection, make sure this attribute is disabled in directories that shouldn't contain programs to be executed by the server in response to HTTP requests, and make sure that this attribute is enabled in directories that do.

Performance Monitoring

One of the nicest features of the IIS is its use of the NT Performance Monitor (see fig. 20.9). It comes with an extensive collection of HTTP, FTP, and Gopher-specific counters that allow for close management and precise tuning. In addition to real-time charts of service activity, the Performance Monitor provides a way to log and replay these statistics, view them as a report, or send alerts if metrics exceed or fall below preset thresholds.

A sample monitoring setup is included in the file samples/tour/msiis.pmc.

The statistics shown in table 20.1 are provided.

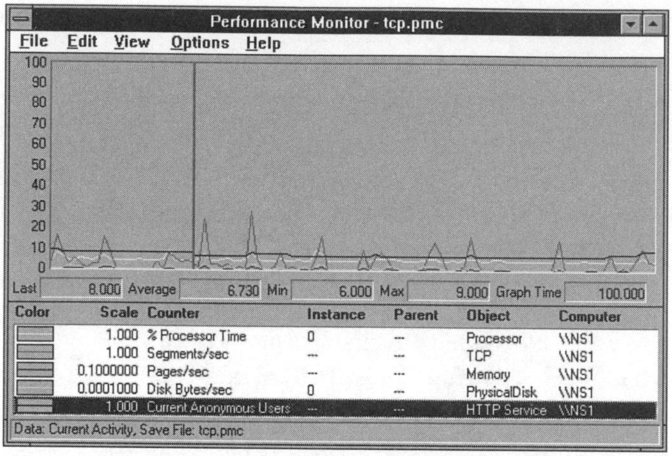

Fig. 20.9
The Microsoft IIS integrates its performance statistics into the NT performance monitor.

Table 20.1	Internet Information Server Performance Statistics
Statistic	**Description**
Cache Hits	Total (since service startup) number of times a file-open, directory-listing, or service-specific object's request was found in the IIS cache
Cache Hits %	Ratio of cache hits to all cache requests
Cache Misses	Total (since service startup) number of times a file-open, directory-listing, or service-specific object's request was not found in the cache
Cache Size	The configured maximum size of the shared HTTP, FTP, and Gopher memory cache
Cache Used	The current number of bytes containing cached data in the shared memory cache (this includes directory listings, file handle tracking, and service-specific objects)
Cached File Handles	The current number of open file handles cached by all of the Internet Information Server services
Current Blocked Async I/O Requests	The current number of async I/O requests blocked by bandwidth throttling
Directory Listings	The current number of cached directory listings cached by all of the Internet Information Server services
Measured Async I/O Bandwidth Usage	The measured bandwidth in bytes of async I/O averaged over one minute
Objects	The current number of objects cached by all of the Internet Information Server services (includes file-handle tracking objects, directory-listing objects, and service-specific objects)

Statistic	Description
Total Allowed Async I/O Requests	Total (since service startup) async I/O requests allowed by bandwidth throttling
Total Blocked Async I/O Requests	Total (since service startup) async I/O requests blocked by bandwidth throttling
Total Rejected Async I/O Requests	Total (since service startup) async I/O requests rejected by bandwidth throttling

FTP Server

Bytes Received/sec	The rate at which data bytes are received by the FTP server
Bytes Sent/sec	The rate at which data bytes are sent by the FTP server
Bytes Total/sec	Rate of total bytes transferred by the FTP server (sum of bytes sent and received)
Connection Attempts	Total number (since service startup) of connection attempts that have been made to the FTP Server
Current Anonymous Users	Current Number of anonymous users currently connected to the FTP server
Current Connections	Current number of connections to the FTP server (sum of anonymous and nonanonymous users)
Current Nonanonymous Users	Number of nonanonymous users currently connected to the FTP server
Files Received	Total files received by (uploaded to) the FTP server since service startup
Files Sent	Total files sent by (downloaded from) the FTP server since service startup
Files Total	Total files transferred by the FTP server (upload and download) since service startup
Logon Attempts	The total number of logon attempts that have been made against the FTP server since service startup
Maximum Anonymous Users	Largest number (since service startup) of anonymous users simultaneously connected to the FTP server
Maximum Connections	Largest number of simultaneous connections to the FTP server
Maximum Nonanonymous Users	Largest Number (since service startup) of nonanonymous users simultaneously connected to the FTP server
Total Anonymous Users	Total number of anonymous users who have ever connected to the FTP server since service startup
Total Nonanonymous Users	Total number of nonanonymous users who have ever connected to the FTP server since service startup

Gopher Server

Aborted Connections	Total number of connections aborted due to error or over-the-limit requests made to the Gopher server

V

Applications

(continues)

Table 20.1 Continued	
Statistic	**Description**
Gopher Server	
Bytes Received/sec	The rate at which data bytes are received by the Gopher
Bytes Sent/sec	The rate that data bytes are sent by the Gopher server
Bytes Total/sec	Total rate at which bytes are transferred by the FTP server (sum of bytes sent and received)
Connection Attempts	Total number (since service startup) of connections attempted against the Gopher service
Connections in Error	Total number of connections (since service startup) that resulted in errors when processed by the Gopher server
Current Anonymous Users	Number of anonymous users currently connected to the Gopher server
Current Connections	Number of connections to the Gopher server (sum of anonymous and nonanonymous users)
Current Nonanonymous Users	Number of nonanonymous users currently connected to the Gopher server
Directory Listings Sent	Total number of directory listings sent by the Gopher server since service startup
Files Sent	Total number of files sent by the Gopher server since service startup
Gopher Plus Requests	The total number of Gopher Plus requests received by the Gopher server since service startup
Logon Attempts	The total number of logon attempts made by the Gopher server since service startup
Maximum Anonymous Users	Maximum number of anonymous users simultaneously connected to the Gopher server since service startup
Maximum Connections	Maximum number of simultaneous connections to the Gopher server since service startup
Maximum Nonanonymous Users	The maximum number of nonanonymous simultaneously connected to the Gopher server since service startup
Searches Sent	The total number of searches performed by the Gopher server since service startup
Total Anonymous Users	Total number of anonymous users who have connected to the FTP server since service startup
Total Nonanonymous Users	Total number of nonanonymous users who have connected to the FTP server since service startup

Statistic	Description
HTTP Server	
Bytes Received/sec	The rate at which data bytes are received by the HTTP server
Bytes Sent/sec	The rate that data bytes are sent by the HTTP server
Bytes Total/sec	Total rate of bytes transferred by the HTTP server (sum of bytes sent and received)
CGI Requests	The total number of CGI requests executed since service startup; Common Gateway Interface (CGI) requests invoke custom gateway executables (EXE) that the administrator can install to add forms processing or other dynamic data sources
Connection Attempts	The number of connection attempts that have been made to the HTTP server
Connections/sec	The rate at which HTTP requests are currently being handled
Current Anonymous Users	The number of anonymous users currently connected to the HTTP service
Current CGI Requests	The current number of CGI requests simultaneously being processed by the HTTP server (includes WAIS index queries)
Current Connections	The current number of connections to the HTTP server (sum of anonymous and nonanonymous users)
Current ISAPI Extension Requests	The current ISAPI extension requests simultaneously being processed by the HTTP server
Current Nonanonymous Users	Number of nonanonymous users currently connected to the HTTP server
Files Received	The total files received by (uploaded to) the HTTP server since service startup
Files Sent	The total files sent by (downloaded from) the HTTP server since service startup
Files Total	The total files transferred by the HTTP server since service startup
Get Requests	The total number of HTTP "GET" requests received by the HTTP server; GET requests are generally used for basic file retrievals or image maps, though they can be used with forms
Head Requests	The total number of HTTP "HEAD" requests received by the HTTP server; HEAD requests generally indicate that a client is querying the state of a document they already have to see if it needs to be refreshed

(continues)

V

Applications

Table 20.1 Continued	
Statistic	**Description**
HTTP Server	
ISAPI Extension Requests	The total number of HTTP ISAPI extension requests received by the HTTP server; ISAPI Extension Requests are custom gateway Dynamic Link Libraries (DLL), which the administrator can install to add forms processing or other dynamic data sources
Logon Attempts	The number of logon attempts that have been made by the HTTP server
Maximum Anonymous Users	The largest number of anonymous users simultaneously connected to the HTTP server since service startup
Maximum BGI Requests	The largest number of BGI requests simultaneously processed by the HTTP server since service startup
Maximum ISAPI Extension Requests	The largest number of ISAPI extension requests simultaneously processed by the HTTP server since service startup
Maximum Connections	The largest number of users simultaneously connected to the HTTP server since service startup
Maximum Nonanonymous Users	The largest number of nonanonymous simultaneously connected to the HTTP server since service startup
Not Found Errors	The number of requests that couldn't be satisfied by the server because the requested document could not be found; generally reported as an HTTP 404 error code to the client
Other Request Methods	The number of HTTP requests that are not GET, POST, or HEAD methods; may include PUT, DELETE, LINK, or other methods supported by gateway applications
POST Requests	The number of HTTP requests using the POST method; generally used for forms or gateway requests
Total Anonymous Users	The total number of anonymous users who have ever connected to the HTTP server since service startup
Total Nonanonymous Users	Total number of nonanonymous users who have ever connected to the HTTP server since service startup

SNMP

Simple Network Management Protocol is used by applications and network components to provide information about abnormal events to network monitoring products. Internet Information Server includes an SNMP agent for reporting performance data to an SNMP management station. Every counter available through the Performance Monitor is also available and described by the MIB provided by the Microsoft Internet Information Server SNMP agent. SNMP MIB files are on the Microsoft Internet Information Server compact disc in the \Sdk directory.

Extensibility. The Microsoft IIS supports the following extensibility interfaces:

- *Common Gateway Interface (CGI)*   Internet Information Server supports the industry-standard CGI as well as PERL, the most common language for developing simple Web applications, such as data input forms and log analysis routines.

- *ISAPI Internet Server Applications (ISA)*   ISAs are dynamic-link libraries (DLLs) that are similar to CGI scripts. ISAs are loaded in the same address space of the HTTP server—unlike CGI, which creates a separate process for every request. This creates a back-end scripting solution that is higher performance than CGI and consumes far less memory. Not only that, but it also provides an interface that enables your application to hold onto a connection with the browser and wait for the next reply. This is the best known way to implement conversational transactions on the Web!

  ▶ See "Conversational Transactions," p. 543, to learn more about implementing conversational transactions with ISAs.

- *ISAPI HTTP Server Filters*   An HTTP filter is a replaceable DLL that the server calls on every HTTP request. When the filter is loaded, it tells the server what sort of notifications it is interested in. After that, whenever the selected events occur, the filter is called and given the opportunity to process that event.

- *ISAPI Internet Database Connector*   This allows Web browsers ODBC (Open DataBase Connectivity) database access for HTTP requests. Developers can use this feature to create Web pages with information from the database; to insert, update, and delete information in the database based on user input; and to perform other SQL commands. This is nearly the identical capability as provided by WebQuest. Only, this one is free.

  ▶ See "Integrating Your Web Page and a Database," p. 529, to learn more about the capabilities provided by WebQuest.

V

Applications

Web Technology for OLE Objects

The World Wide Web was conceived of and designed as a mechanism for publishing information in electronic form, and HyperText Markup Language is the medium used to construct documents for this library. However, very few businesses create formal or informal electronic documents in the form of HTML files. Most of our electronic document assets are in the form of OLE-enabled documents.

The following sections describe Microsoft's facilities to support the distribution of OLE enabled documents via Web technology.

Publishing OLE Document Objects

Ideally, we would like to be able to publish selective parts of this huge inventory of OLE-enabled documents as a library having the same level of functionality as Web technology has provided for HTML documents. Microsoft's BackOffice facilities will enable you to set up an electronic document library that will provide all of the above facilities and more.

- Microsoft's Front and Back Office products will provide the combined benefits of both a full text search file system and a structured storage database engine.

- They support full rich text documents.

- They support shared update of these documents.

New Storage Management with OLE 2

The OLE 2 class library provides software developers with a new way to store OLE-enabled documents. Component document integration requires the ability for many components to share a persistent storage service, be it a disk file or a record in a database, where each component needs its own bit of storage in which to save its persistent state. OLE's structured storage is the new abstraction layer for accomplishing this level of integration and can be built on top of any file or other storage system.

In structured storage, any byte array can be structured into two types of elements: *storages* and *streams*. A storage can contain any number of other storages and streams within it, just like a directory can contain files and subdirectories. Structured storage provides developers with a uniform access to OLE-enabled documents through the standard IStorage and IStream interfaces.

In essence of this is a "file system within a file" with well-defined access to data elements and the physical layout of the file being left to the system. With such a system, the application can pass individual streams or even entire storages to other components in which those components can save whatever persistent information they desire.

OLE-enabled documents can make use of the structured storage technology. To further facilitate the creation and sharing of compound documents, even between applications on different platforms, OLE 2 provides a standard implementation for storages and streams in what are called *compound files*.

A major benefit to having a single standard implementation of structured storage is that any application, including the system shell, can open and navigate through any compound file. Just as the business data stored in a relational database is accessible in a generalized way through SQL and ODBC, OLE-enabled documents and their properties are no longer hidden inside proprietary file formats. Using OLE 2 Structured Storage, applications can navigate the hierarchy of storage and stream elements. With additional naming standards and standardized stream formats for specific information, applications can access information about an OLE-enabled document without having to load the application that created it.

OLE Document Object Databases

With Structured Storage, Microsoft has created a database for OLE-enabled documents. Its initial implementation is over the three supported NT file systems. However, this new abstraction layer enables it to store OLE-enabled documents in a more robust way, a database way, which can support structured queries and the concept of logical units of work. For example, the Microsoft Exchange Server stores its shared folders in a modified Jet database engine—the same foundation used for Microsoft Access 95.

From the operator's perspective, documents are stored in the Exchange just like they are stored in the NT file system. However, the underlying database engine enables the Exchange to manage OLE-enabled documents at a much finer level of detail and with concurrency controls and transaction management. Using the Exchange Server, you can create global shared document libraries for publishing OLE-enabled documents throughout your organization.

Considering that as much as half of your company's information assets are in the form of OLE-enabled documents, this is a very significant advancement.

Databases for Implementing Business Transactions

The above discussion about Microsoft's Structured Storage database should not obscure the fact that the other half of a company's business information is not in the form of electronic documents and that Microsoft's OLE architecture and Structured Storage are not appropriate for the implementation of business transactions. Business transactions are best implemented using relational databases or OMG-defined object database services. A well-defined corporate information architecture will accommodate both forms of information assets and provide a bridge between them. This will take the form of a COM - CORBA bridge. Under such an architecture, business object views, transactions, and workflows can be implemented as OLE-enabled Windows applications that use business object methods implemented as OMG objects to perform their business functions.

(continues)

V

Applications

(continued)

When dealing with structured business information, relational databases provide higher performance for applications that primarily access data by value. Object databases provide higher performance when data access is primarily navigational via object references. The navigational characteristic of the Object paradigm more closely matches the navigational characteristic of HyperText, therefore offering the potential for high performance navigation when accessed via the COM - CORBA bridge. Object databases can also provide a significant development productivity, and functional improvements over relational databases. They enable object-oriented developers to work with persistent objects in nearly the same way as they would with any internal object. This eliminates the need to unmarshall and marshall data to and from a relational database. It enables developers to work with more complex information structures in a more natural way.

All that said, they lose some of relational technology's ability to respond to ad-hoc queries in an efficient and low-cost (programming and execution) way. They also provide additional challenges when bridging into existing business information managed by relational or prerelational engines.

If you decide to use an Object database, the fundamental design principal stated earlier still applies: write code to industry-standard interfaces, not to vendor interfaces. The standards of interest are:

- *OMG Direct Access (DA)*   This API is defined in Chapter 6 of the *OMG Common Object Services Specification (COSS)*, Volume 1. It provides a minimal set of operations that support direct access to persistent data through typed attributes organized in data objects. For more information see **http://www.omg.org/**.

- *ODMG-93*   This rigorous specification is for defining, manipulating, and querying persistent objects. The Object Database Management Group is a part of the OMG. The ODMG-93 protocol is similar to the DA protocol in that the object accesses attributes organized as data objects. The DA interface is a subset of the ODMG-93 interface. For more information see **http://www.odmg.org/**.

As with ODBC, most object database vendors are converging on these standards and have commitments to provide them by the end of 1996.

OLE Document Object Browsing. Windows 95 provides operators with an OLE-enabled document browser that reveals the properties stored in an IStream named "Summary Information." This OLE-defined stream is where applications store information such as creation and modification times, author, title, subject, revision number, keywords, and so forth. Because it's defined by the OLE 2 standard, it enables the browser to provide users with a means to sort, browse, and search for documents of interest just like Access provides us for traditional data. Summary Information property-aware tools for searching and browsing include the Exchange client in Windows 95, the Windows 95 Properties command, and the File Open dialog box in any Microsoft Office of Windows 95 application. Office 95 products also provide operators with the ability to create custom document properties that support several data types including Text, Date, Number, and Boolean.

Extensible Document Properties

When a document stored in Structured Storage is mailed to someone, the Structured Storage properties go with it. It's like sending a database record that contains the Summary Information properties, document-specific properties and the document itself as database columns. Therefore, when you open your mail using the Exchange client, you can see the document's properties without having to launch the application that created it. You can also navigate down into linked documents and see their properties without having to launch their applications. This will also allow you to search through and filter your e-mail based upon property values.

With Structured Storage and the Windows 95, Microsoft has provided us with a container browser. To understand the power of this function, imagine entering a real-world library and having a card catalog that not only enables you to locate any publication by author, date, title, subject, but that also provides you with a full table of contents. It also provides you with the capability to drill down into the category (author, date, title, subject, and so on) of an illustration on a certain page in a book, select it, and view it without opening the book! This function is way beyond what Web technology provides.

Full Context Searching. As noted above, Structured Storage creates a logical document database that can be implemented over file systems or database engines. What is implemented today as a file system folder today can easily be implemented as an OLE container tomorrow. In fact, MS Exchange "Folders" are just that. When OLE-enabled documents are stored in Structured Storage, applications can drill down into linked documents in a uniform way. Thus, WAIS-like indexing engines can now be built over OLE-enabled documents. And in fact, one has.

The Windows 95 Find Fast utility located in the Control Panel is a full-text indexing system that also indexes the Summary Information properties. Operators can build and maintain indexes to local and network drives and subtrees by using this utility. The File Open command with Windows 95 utilizes the Find Fast search engine to find documents quickly based upon content or properties.

V

Applications

When you add all this together, you end up with container browsing and document property searching, which is not available with Web technology, and Web-like full text searching. All of these capabilities work within the context of an OLE Document Object database. But what about publishing OLE Document Objects on the Internet?

Publishing OLE Document Objects

The Microsoft Internet Explorer 3.0 is based upon Microsoft's Internet client architecture called *Sweeper*. Sweeper will be a set of redistributable modules that can be used by any Windows-based application. It will be split into a set of components and services that will become an integral part of the Windows 95 and NT operating systems, making these services available to all developers of Windows-based applications.

Sweeper includes a broad set of client system services and APIs (including Hyperlinks described above) that allow developers to Internet-enable their Windows applications. Sweeper also includes OLE controls which will enable Internet Explorer 3.0 to be extensible in much the same way as HotJava was extensible through Java classes.

OLE Document Objects. With Sweeper, OLE Document Objects are formally defined as a set of OLE interfaces that are built on top of the standard OLE in-place activation interfaces. An OLE Document Object (DocObject) server owns the entire client area of the DocObject container in which it is running. You can now extend the ability of the Internet Explorer to browse any type of document (not just HTML).

Let's look at an example. Suppose you want to publish a document in its native format (DOC, XLS, TIF, JPG, ANY). When a DocObject-enabled browser tries to view that document, it downloads (with the user's permission, of course) the *.any DocObject server and runs it. The *.any DocObject server takes over the browser's entire client area and displays the *.any file. To end users, this is completely seamless; they use the same tool to browse anything on the Internet, regardless of the format. If you publish documents on the Internet, this means that you are not restricted to publishing in HTML. You can use any format you choose, so long as your constituency is running a Sweeper-enabled browser like IE 3.0.

DocObjects also enable a browser to launch a specific application when it gets to a page; the browser acts as a navigation tool to find and launch an Internet application.

Hyperlinking. With Sweeper, Microsoft has published a new set of OLE system services and interfaces called *OLE Hyperlinks*. The differences between Hyperlinks and traditional OLE document links are:

■ Hyperlinks have a two-part name, identifying the linked resource within the context of the network as opposed to an absolute or relative location within the local file system.

■ Hyperlinks are manually activated by the operator, not automatically activated by the container.

■ When a Hyperlink is activated, it communicates with a browser context that enables operator navigation controls such as History, Favorites, Go Back, Go Forward, and Go Home.

■ Hyperlink navigation is asynchronous, allowing for slow service times across communications channels.

OLE Hyperlinks may be references to a location in:

■ The same document

■ A different (top-level or embedded) document of the same class

■ A different (top-level or embedded) document of a different class

OLE document objects can be stored in file-system files, any arbitrary IStorage location, or machines on the Internet (referred to by URLs). Microsoft's vision is that there can be three flavors of Hyperlink containers and Hyperlink sources:

■ Top level documents on the local machine

■ Microsoft Network based OLE document objects in an "Office Binder like" application as described in the previous section "OLE Document Object Browsing"

> **Note**
>
> The Office Binder does not support OLE in-place activation / Document Object server functionality, hence an activated Hyperlink can't be shown in-place in the Browser.

■ Internet based OLE document objects in a browser like Internet Explorer 3.0

Hyperlink containers that provide a browser context are called *HyperLink Frames*. With the implementation of Hyperlinks, Microsoft will have exceeded the functionality that Web technology provides for HTML documents. It will do so over a far richer content base—your electronic document assets.

OLE Control and Control Container Guidelines. These Microsoft guidelines define the exact interfaces and methods that are required of well-behaved OLE Control and Control Container desktop applications. Sweeper proposes two new OLE Control component categories—Internet and multimedia/run time only—specifically to address Internet-enabled and multimedia controls.

OLE Scripting. This is a syntax- and language-neutral architecture that allows scripting vendors to "plug-in" and perform automation between components. OLE Scripting provides an infrastructure that will allow developers to plug any scripting engines into their applications. Microsoft's scripting solution, called Visual Basic Script, will use OLE Scripting and include a compiler and run time.

Internet Extensions for Win32. This API set abstracts Gopher, FTP, and HTTP protocols into easy-to-use, task-focused interfaces that simplify access to the Internet significantly.

URL Monikers. URL monikers are an implementation of asynchronous monikers, which can perform binding asynchronously to OLE objects via URLs. URL monikers encapsulate protocols: An application simply binds to the URL moniker. The moniker works with the appropriate protocol to activate the OLE object and go to the specified Internet location.

Persistent Cache API. This API is used by clients that need persistent caching services. Persistent caching allows the caller to save data in the local file system for later use. This is useful when access to the data is over a low-bandwidth link or the access is not available at all.

Pluggable Protocols and Data Formats. Given the dynamic nature of the Internet world, it is highly likely that new file formats and protocols will emerge. Sweeper uses "Quartz" (an architecture for the processing of streams of multimedia data) Filter Graphs to handle new media types and the IBind* interfaces for plugging in new protocols. ❖

CHAPTER 21
Financial Transactions

Many of the Web sites in development today are a result of the dreams and hard work of the entrepreneurs of the Internet, *infopreneurs*. If you're interested in conducting commerce via your Web site, this chapter is a must read.

This chapter covers one of the most important and quickly developing areas of Internet technology: adding secure financial transactions to your Web site. There are a number of different approaches and the chapter reviews the current high profile systems: eCash, First Virtual, CyberCash, Secure Pay, and Web900. It would be an understatement to say that security plays an important role when discussing finances and personal information. You take a look at how you can provide your customers the security they desire when transacting business with you. Some Web servers have built-in security and this chapter covers them briefly. Finally, this chapter offers you some alternative methods of transacting commerce.

In this chapter, you learn about:

- A brief history of online commerce
- Network security measures
- Electronic cash/credit equivalents
- How to become an electronic merchant
- Software commerce systems for your Web site

When reviewing and discussing secure financial transactions, you need a basic familiarity with the concepts of Internet security implementations; that is this chapter's first topic.

Development of Financial Transactions on the Internet

Internet Financial transactions began with the market for commercial online services such as Prodigy, CompuServe, and America Online. Early on, the concept of an "Electronic Mall" was introduced first by Prodigy and later implemented by the other commercial online services. In fact, Prodigy was envisioned initially to be little more than a convenient place to shop! The Prodigy Electronic Mall was the result of a joint effort involving CBS, Sears, and IBM. It allowed Prodigy customers to order a wide variety of products, ranging from groceries and flowers to automobiles and other high-ticket items. Transactions were done by credit card and the purchases were delivered to the buyer. In this transaction, Prodigy acted as a broker between the vendor and buyer. Each vendor's orders were sent to them by Prodigy at regular intervals. Prodigy received a percentage of the sales and garnered additional profits by selling advertising space.

An entirely new business concept was created! The Prodigy system is a considerable success and is a credible model for infopreneurs around the globe. However, there is a key difference between Prodigy and your Web site on the Internet. Prodigy is a closed service that its users connect directly to via modem. This means that the security of the connection is guaranteed.

The strength of the Internet (and its weakness where commerce is concerned) is that it is an open system. This means that your connection can be "listened to" by snooping ears. But because the lure of online commerce is so powerful, many large companies are working hard to implement a secure system for their own version of the Electronic Mall. The main forces driving the development of Secure Internet Protocols are the companies striving to reduce costs and increase profits by selling their products and services through the Internet. You will probably begin to hear many people talk of the "frictionless economy" where Internet technology removes all barriers to commerce regardless of time or space.

Another force is the promise to banks and merchants of cheaper, Electronic Data Interchange (EDI), the system currently used for credit card validation and commerce between large companies. EDI has been in use for years and generally requires dedicated communication lines and equipment. The Internet strategy is inherently simpler and less expensive to use. When banks accept and begin using an Internet version of EDI, their operating costs and the costs to merchants for credit card validation will drop.

Currencies

The Internet is an international phenomenon; it's not nationally specific to the United States. Someone anywhere in the world can reach anywhere else in the world easily and seamlessly. Not so in the "real world" where there are borders, nationalities, languages, and currencies. When selling products or services on the Internet, you may have to contend with different currencies and exchange rates. Most Web sites specify in U.S. currency (US$45) the prices of their merchandise; this is a good strategy. The buyer then must deal with the trouble of differing currencies. Many e-cash systems will eliminate this burden as well by converting currencies when funds are transferred into a special e-cash account.

Online Purchasing

The Internet, in general, and the World Wide Web, in particular, offer a convenient outlet for selling products and services. As the Web matures, more and more merchants are including some way for visitors to purchase from them. A number of strategies are in use, from some version of an electronic money, secure transmission of credit card numbers, taking orders and shipping them COD, to requiring visitors to establish an "account" with the merchant prior to purchasing a product or service. Using electronic money or secure transmission of credit card numbers both require new implementation of technology; this chapter focuses on those strategies.

The introduction of electronic, virtual money has raised some serious concerns for everyone involved. The nature of this electronic money is digital, ones and zeros, and instantly simple to reproduce and defraud. The companies involved in creating digital money have created elaborate systems to prevent fraud.

The transmission of secure financial information raises more concerns. How do you prevent the information from being picked up by the wrong person and unencrypted? Technically, most of the systems currently in place are as secure as the current credit card validation system used in almost every store in the western world. The robustness of the security system is not enough, the customer needs to feel that it is secure. It becomes a marketing issue.

Security Concerns

The Internet is an inherently insecure system. Data is available to anyone with the will to retrieve it. Every week, you hear or read about someone breaking into, hacking, a "secure" computer system, like the Department of Defense. It is worthwhile to remain cautious when dealing with secure information and computers. Commonly accepted "secure" systems will eventually be exposed with weaknesses and will then be enforced or retired in favor of the next "secure" system. The best security is not a powerful encryption, it is diligence. If you keep careful track of your transactions, maintain adequate security within your company, and follow common secure practices (like using passwords), you will be less likely to be the victim of some kind of fraud.

As a transactor of electronic commerce, you must be concerned with two areas of computer security:

- You must provide a way for your users to exchange information with you in a secure manner.
- The data you receive from your customers must be protected from falling into the wrong hands.

Your data can become vulnerable through sociological hacking, Brute Force hacking, keyboard readers, and the ever popular "packet sniffing."

Sociological Hacking

If you know a lot about somebody, it is often fairly easy to figure out passwords. A favorite pet, a child's name, or activity are all commonly used as passwords. You may have given passwords and private keys to coworkers and friends or you may leave that kind of information near the computer. Many instances of people breaking into "secure" systems wasn't through some marvel of computer hacking, it was the result of being observant and nosy. All administrative personnel at your site must have proper account names and passwords.

Brute Force

It's possible to decipher any encrypted message given enough time. Computers are wonderful tools for deciphering. They can scan through every possible combination of an encryption until they find the code that unlocks the message. This process is referred to as a *Brute Force*. For many years, a 40-bit RSA encryption was considered invulnerable. With the increased power of computers and the advancements in mathematical algorithms, it was broken. Computers will keep getting more powerful and mathematicians will keep coming up with new ways of code breaking.

Keyboard Readers

While not common, it is possible to "read" the keystrokes entered into a keyboard using a simple program that attaches to the keyboard driver. This program reads unencoded keystrokes and saves them into a file for later reference, thus defeating any encryption placed on the inputted information.

Packet Sniffing

Packet sniffing is the process of attaching a piece of hardware or software to an existing network and watching the packets flow through. Data transmitted across the Internet is broken into packets. Each of these packets is vulnerable to sniffing. Packet sniffing is not illegal; it is used to diagnose network problems. Misuse of the information is illegal but it is extremely difficult to detect a packet sniffer.

Public Network Security

There are two general kinds of networks, private and public. The Internet is a public network and this chapter covers only security systems for a public network. Network security spans three concerns: privacy, message authentication, and signatures.

- Privacy in transmission over public networks is accomplished by encrypting the sensitive data with one of three private key algorithms: RC4, IDEA, and DES.

- Message authentication proves that the data was not tampered with. The message is encoded with a one-way hash (an irreversible encoding) and the hash is encrypted with the sender's private key. The result is a message digest. The message digest can be opened with the sender's public key and compared to the hash of the received message. Current message digests include MD4, MD5, and SHS.

- A signature is proof of origin of the message. A signature is a bunch of information about the sender encrypted with a private key. The matching public key can be used to unlock the signature. Associated with signatures are certificates. Certificates are messages signed by a trusted central authority's private key that validate the sender and the public key of the sender for the current message. Certificates can be opened with the central authority's well-known public key.

An online reference for Internet security is the World Wide Web Consortium. Visit its security area at **http://www.w3.org/pub/WWW/Security/**.

Session Negotiation Protocols

Session Negotiation protocols allow two parties engaged in a secure transaction to negotiate and establish the encryption algorithm and protocol that will be used for the session. For example, Client A has SSL and SHTTP available and Client B has SHTTP and PCT available. Within the negotiation, they will establish SHTTP as the session protocol. All this negotiation exists within the client/server software; users do not need to worry about how to negotiate for session protocols. Three session negotiation protocols are used: SSL version 3.0 supported by Netscape and Microsoft; S-HTTP supported by Spry & NCSA; and PCT supported by Microsoft. These three protocols all function basically in the same way: they provide for negotiating what security protocols and algorithms will be used for the session. They all depend on a public key algorithm, of which there are three to choose: RSA, Diffie-Hellman, and DSS.

- *SSL version 3.0 (Secure Socket Layer)*   Netscape Communications Corporation has introduced and implemented SSL into its ubiquitous browser and Commerce Server. SSL provides privacy and a secure connection between the client and server. For online information about SSL, visit **http://proto.netscape.com/newsref/ref/ netscape-security.html**.

- *S-HTTP (Secure HyperText Transport Protocol)*   Verifone Inc. based in Menlo Park, CA has created and proposed the S-HTTP standard. S-HTTP uses the RSA public key cryptography and features end-to-end secure transactions. S-HTTP is an extension to the existing standard HTTP. For online information about S-HTTP, visit **http://www.ncsa.uiuc.edu/ InformationServers/WebSecurity/index.html**.

- *PCT (Private Communication Technology)*   Microsoft developed PCT as an enhancement and replacement of Netscape's SSL. It is designed for general purpose business and personal communications. PCT supports privacy, authentication, and mutual identification. For more information about PCT, visit **http://pct.microsoft.com/**.

Encryption Algorithms

Encryption has been around for a long time. It involves taking a piece of data and making it unreadable. Encryption algorithms actually garble the data. They are used instead of public key encryption because they are much faster. Once the data is encrypted, it will appear as digital garbage to anyone that doesn't have the proper "key" to unlock or decode the data. Over a public network, encryption allows the transmission of secure information. The security of the data is only as good as the encryption algorithm. Three robust encryption algorithms are available for use: DES, RC4, and IDEA. For online information about encryption and cryptography, visit **http://axion.physics.ubc.ca/crypt.html**.

- *DES (Digital Encryption Standard)*   Developed in the 1950s by IBM, this is the standard used in ATM "PIN" numbers. DES uses only 56 bits in the encryption so is more susceptible to a brute force attack than RSA. DES is the standard accepted by the U.S. government.

- *RC4 (Ron's Code 4)*   Ron Rivest of RSA developed RC4. It is marketed by RSA Inc. RSA claims that RC4 is 10 times faster than DES and it uses a variable key size in the algorithm.

- *IDEA (International Data Encryption Algorithm)*   Xuejia Lai and James L. Massey of ETH Zuria created IDEA. It uses a 128-bit key algorithm.

Public Key Algorithms

The implementation of Public Key Algorithms resolves the problem of encryption key management. When a piece of data is encrypted, a key is created to unencrypt the information. As long as you have the key, you can read the file. If you have multiple encrypted files, it would be possible to have a number of "keys" that you would have to keep associated with the appropriate data. One way around this is to create two keys. One key is used to encrypt the data and the other is used to decrypt it. The key that encrypted the data cannot decrypt it. One key is called your private key, the other is your public key. If someone wants to send you an encrypted message, he or she needs to use your public key to encrypt it. Your public key is by nature, public, available to anyone who wants it. Any data encrypted with your public key can only be decrypted by your private key. This way you only ever need one key.

Digital signatures ensure that the data is from the sender that the data says it is from and that the data has not been changed or modified enroute. To create a digital signature, you encrypt information about yourself with your private key. Anyone with your public key can decrypt and thus check your signature. A one-way hash is created by sending the sensitive message through a function that results in some "number," and then encrypting that number with your private key. Anyone with your public key can decrypt and thus check the enclosed hash against the hash of message received. The following may be used in the creation of public signature algorithms: RSA, Diffie-Hellman, and DSS.

- *RSA (Rivet-Shamir-Adleman)*   This algorithm was developed by three mathematicians: Rivet, Shamir, and Adleman. RSA is the most commonly used public encryption algorithm. It is online at **http://www.rsa.com/**.

- *Diffie-Hellman*   This is the first public key-based encryption algorithm. Proposed by Whitfield Diffe and Martin Hellman, Diffe-Hellman is the basis of a number of implementations such as Pretty Good Privacy (PGP).

- *DSS (Digital Signature Standard)*   National Institute of Standards and Technology created this standard. DSS employs Digital Signature Algorithm (DSA) as the algorithm. DSA is much slower than RSA and it uses between 512 to 1024 bits for the encryption key.

eCash

eCash uses the concept of an electronic "coin." The coin retains its value before, during, and after a transaction. Each coin is actually a registered serial number with an associated value. The bank that created the coin maintains a database of its serial numbers to ensure no duplicates are created. Part of the serial number points to the specific minting bank. To make a purchase, the buyer sends sufficient electronic coins to the vendor. The vendor either deposits them into a bank account, or stores them for later use. Currently, the only bank to support eCash by exchanging it for "real money" is Mark Twain Bank. eCash requires that proprietary software be installed on both the customers' and merchants' computers. eCash uses a simple graphic interface that stays resident on the client's computer and acts as a kind of virtual Automatic Teller Machine (ATM). When the client asks to buy something, the merchant's eCash software will send a request to the client to confirm the purchase (see fig. 21.1).

When the client agrees to the payment by clicking on Yes, the payment amount, in this case, $0.02 is transferred from the client to the server. The display for the client will decrease to $34.98 and the server's balance will increase by the same amount.

This is a very simple, clean strategy for providing online shopping. However, there are some disadvantages:

- The client must be running Windows 95 or Windows NT.
- The seller's choice of Web server is limited to roughly one dozen servers.
- eCash only supports two national currencies, U.S. dollars and Finnish Markars.

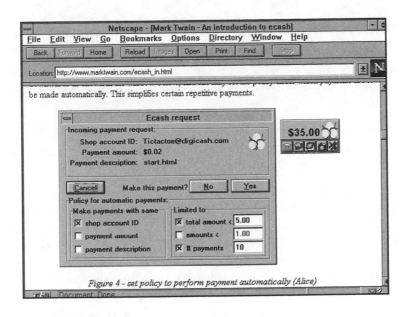

Fig. 21.1
Example of the
eCash interface.

Mark Twain Bank

Currently, Mark Twain Bank is the only bank that will convert eCash into
real money. Mark Twain Bank is in partnership with DigiCash providing
eCash for financial transactions. Mark Twain Bank is located in St. Louis, Mis-
souri. It is listed with the FDIC and it offers online services beyond eCash.

Mark Twain Bank maintains a Web space with information about eCash. We
recommend its online tutorial located at **http://www.marktwain.com/
ecash_in.html**.

Who Uses eCash

A number of companies are currently using eCash to enable online shopping
from their Web sites. The following is a partial list of these merchants.

- AUTO-NET is an online forum to buy and sell used vehicles.
- Royal Copenhagen sells fine jewelry from Denmark.
- Products from Zale sells steel framed homes, water filtration systems,
  books, food, and jewelry.
- BioNet offers herbs, homeopathies, vitamins, natural cosmetics, and
  other healthful products.

Setting Up Shop-Server on Windows

Enabling someone to purchase from your Web site using eCash requires the server component of eCash called "shop-server." eCash has set up a server with the shop-server software, so a merchant can have its Web site hosted on the eCash server.

eCash works with the shop-server in the same way Netscape works with a Web server. eCash can only interact with a Web site that has the shop-server software installed and running.

If you have set up and are managing your own Web server, and you're leasing Web hosting from an Internet Service Provider, you may have problems setting up shop-server. Shop-server requires a CGI bin to be set up and available. eCash has a set of CGI files created that, once installed, allows a customer with the installed client software to purchase products from you. The shop-server works very simply: when the client requests a hyperlink that you have designated as one that costs money, the shop-server sends a request to the client for payment. When the client accepts the request, the transaction takes place and the client receives or will receive the product. DigiCash has posted complete instructions for installing and setting up the shop-server on a number of different servers. Currently, a limited number of servers are known to be able to run shop-server.

DigiCash has a well-designed and informative Web site that describes eCash and offers all the component pieces needed to add eCash to your Web site (see fig. 21.2). Go to **http://www.digicash.com/**.

Fig. 21.2
DigiCash home page.

These are the Web servers that can implement eCash:

> EMWAC HTTPS server
>
> WebSite
>
> WebHub
>
> Netscape Communications Server
>
> Netscape Commerce Server
>
> Netscape FastTrack Server
>
> Microsoft Internet Information Server
>
> Process Software Corporation Purveyor
>
> Internet Factory Commerce Builder

Microsoft Merchant Server is a Web server that will soon be able to implement eCash.

First Virtual

First Virtual is a small company that acts as a transaction broker. No custom software is required, unlike with eCash and CyberCash. All transactions are done through e-mail and then through regularly accepted channels. Neither the buyer nor the seller need to worry about data encryption, key management, or other security concerns. First Virtual bills the merchant a fee for every processed transaction, similar to credit card companies.

How First Virtual Works

First Virtual acts as a transaction broker; when someone completes the process of buying a product from you, First Virtual will bill the buyer's credit card for the purchase. Generally these billings are every ten days and are a part of the regular credit card billing. If a buyer makes a series of small purchases that total less than US$10, First Virtual will wait ten days before posting them. After the buyer has paid his or her credit card bill and First Virtual has received the money from the credit card company (Visa or MasterCard), the money is held by First Virtual for 91 days before it is deposited into the seller's account. This holding period is designed to protect First Virtual from buyers who might contest the purchases and from the credit card company which might bill First Virtual for reimbursement.

The First Virtual-based transactions are fairly straightforward, but time-consuming. The buyer requests an item for purchase by entering a VirtualPIN; the seller tells First Virtual, which then sends an e-mail to the buyer to confirm the transaction. Once confirmed by the buyer, the transaction is processed by First Virtual.

All buyers must have a VirtualPIN to make purchases with the First Virtual system. The VirtualPIN is a buyer identifier. It does not contain any sensitive information such as credit card numbers. With First Virtual, no financial information is sent across the Internet.

To become a seller using First Virtual, you will need each of the following:

A private e-mail account

A Visa or MasterCard

A checking account that accepts direct deposits through the United States ACH system

A VirtualPIN (supplied by First Virtual)

To use InfoHaus:

All buyers must have a VirtualPIN.

To make a purchase using First Virtual:

1. The buyer selects the product or item to purchase.

2. The server asks for and optionally confirms the validity of the buyer's VirtualPIN.

3. The server notifies First Virtual of the transaction.

4. An e-mail is sent by First Virtual to the buyer to confirm the transaction.

5. The buyer then does one of three things: replies "Yes" to confirm the purchase; replies "No" to decline the purchase; or replies "Fraud" if it did not make the original purchase request.

6. When the buyer replies with a "Yes," his or her credit card is debited the amount of the purchase and the funds are direct deposited into the seller's bank account.

Encryption System

First Virtual doesn't require any new or Internet-based encryption systems. First Virtual uses already established transaction systems for the transactions. Money changes hands through credit card billing and direct deposits between the credit card companies, First Virtual, and the seller. The only information needed is the VirtualPIN, which carries no financial information.

Who Uses First Virtual

There are a lot of companies using First Virtual. The following is a partial list of these merchants.

- *Reuters New Media*   Download detailed investor reports on a wide variety of publicly traded companies.

- *The Autoseller*   Buy/sell cars, trucks, motorcycles, RVs, boats, and parts. The ads stay online until the vehicle sells.

- *The Washington Weekly*   The U.S. national politics electronic news magazine.

- *Internet Society*   The Internet Society is the nongovernmental International Organization for global cooperation and coordination for the Internet and its internetworking technologies and applications.

Setting Up a First Virtual Account

To set up an account as a seller, you will need to get a VirtualPIN. To make it easy for a seller to get one, First Virtual maintains an online application form, at **http://www.fvcom/newacct/index.html**. Fill out this form and First Virtual will send you an e-mail with a 12-digit application number and instructions on mailing your bank information to First Virtual. You will receive an e-mail with your new seller's VirtualPIN when your account is set up. This application costs US$10. This process will work anywhere in the world, but all payments between you and First Virtual will be in U.S. dollars. Once you have received your VirtualPIN, you can sign up with the InfoHaus, an online shopping mall (see fig. 21.3 and the next section). First Virtual offers an FV-API for adding this system to a Web server. An API is an "application programming interface" that allows a programmer to build applications using the technology built in to the specific API. In this case, the FV-API is First Virtual's technology bundled to allow creation of more applications using First Virtual. But the FV-API is currently only available to UNIX servers. It does do include source code, so it is possible to port over Windows NT, though there is no reference that this has been done by anyone.

> **Note**
>
> There are two types of VirtualPIN numbers, one for buyers and one for sellers. The buyer's VirtualPIN costs US$2, the seller's VirtualPIN costs US$10. To be a seller, you must have a seller's VirtualPIN.

For more information about becoming a seller with First Virtual, visit **http://www.firstvirtual.com/info/sellerindex.html**.

Fig. 21.3
The First Virtual
logo indicates a
Web site that
accepts payments
using First Virtual.

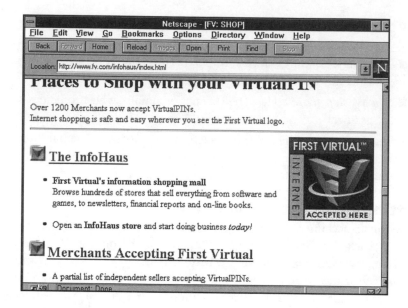

Welcome to the InfoHaus

The InfoHaus is First Virtual's shopping mall using its transaction system.
You can sell anything legal through the InfoHaus: information, goods, and
services. The InfoHaus supports both FTP and World Wide Web (HTTP)
protocols.

Becoming an InfoHaus Merchant

Once you have your seller's VirtualPIN, you'll need to establish a commercial presence for yourself within the InfoHaus. You will need to send the
InfoHaus a list of information including your business name, your
VirtualPIN, the private e-mail account that is associated with your VirtualPIN,
your preferred currency (currently your only choice is U.S. dollars), your preferred language (currently English is your only choice), and a brief description of your business. This information can be sent to the InfoHaus either
as a highly structured e-mail, (see its documentation located at: **http://
www.fv.com/pubdocs/infohaus-guide-5.txt**) or it can be telnetted to
them.

The InfoHaus maintains a structured directory of all the merchants who are
set up with InfoHaus. Your listing can be a complete Web space with all the
various HTML tricks or it can be a simple text listing of your services. The
process for setting up a Web space with the InfoHaus is fairly involved and
somewhat difficult given the choices of e-mailing or telnetting the information. It would be advisable to get a decent Telnet program for Windows NT if

you want to set up and maintain a Web-based commercial presence within the InfoHaus. The InfoHaus bills for hosting your Web pages at a rate of $1.50 per megabyte of information per month. Additionally there is a $0.29 per transaction fee plus 2 percent of the transaction amount. There is a huge amount of information about the InfoHaus in the form of FAQs (Frequently Asked Questions). While it is not very structured, all the information is available for viewing. Navigating through FAQs is not a simple process. For more information about becoming an InfoHaus merchant, visit its Web site at: **http://www.infohaus.com/infohaus.html**.

Resources Available within the InfoHaus

There are already a large number of businesses which have signed up within the InfoHaus, and that number is growing. While lacking a real search engine, the InfoHaus has divided up the listings into four different listings. A potential buyer can search by Topic, Business Name, Keyword, or Date. In addition to the FAQs mentioned above, the InfoHaus has created a Seller's guide, the InfoHaus Helpmeister, and a newsletter. All of these are available from the InfoHaus home page: **http://www.infohaus.com/**.

Who Uses InfoHaus

There are hundreds of merchants using the InfoHaus. The following is a sample of some of them.

- *LandWare Inc.*   Publisher of high-quality Mac, Newton, and Windows software.
- *PSYCHIC FRIENDS OF THE WEB*   This business offers live 24-hour professional psychic consultation.
- 1ST INFOHAUS CONSULTING   This business can help get an InfoHaus page started.

For more information about the InfoHaus, visit **http://www.infohaus.com/index.html**.

CyberCash

CyberCash is short for the CyberCash Wallet, which is the result of a cooperative agreement between CyberCash and VeriSign. The CyberCash Wallet gives a buyer the ability to purchase goods and services over the Web, and using a worldwide license of a 768-bit RSA encryption algorithm, CyberCash provides a secure channel for the transaction. The Wallet is a free software program, like eCash, that, when installed on a computer, allows CyberCash transactions.

How CyberCash Works

CyberCash works with the same basic structure as eCash and First Virtual. Figure 21.4 shows the six steps of this process. The process starts with a buyer requesting some product or service (step 1). The merchant's server sends a confirmation message to the buyer (step 2). When the buyer confirms the purchase, the merchant's server sends the transaction to CyberCash (step 3). CyberCash reformats the transaction data and sends it via regular dedicated lines to the merchant's bank (step 4). The merchant's bank then sends an authorization request to the credit card company for the transaction authorization. When the approval (or denial) is complete, it is sent back to CyberCash with the approval code (step 5). CyberCash then sends the approval code to the merchant who then forwards it to the buyer (step 6). This entire process takes between 15 and 20 seconds.

Fig. 21.4
The CyberCash transaction diagram.

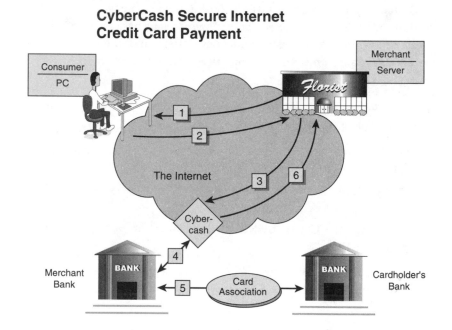

Requirements

CyberCash, like eCash and First Virtual, requires both the buyer and seller to set themselves up for using it. The following are the requirements for both buyers and sellers wishing to use CyberCash.

- Buyers will need the CyberCash Wallet, available for Windows 3.1, 95 and NT, Macintosh, and PowerPC

- Merchants will need a merchant credit card account with their existing bank
- A Terminal ID from the merchants bank for accepting Internet transactions
- CyberCash Wallet

CyberCash Wallet is compatible with the following Web browsers:

FTP & Spyglass Enhanced NCSA Mosaic Version 1.15.111.0

FTP & Spyglass Enhanced NCSA Mosaic Version 2.0

Internet In A Box—Spry AirMosaic Version 03.0A.01.04

InternetWorks Version 1.0.3

NCSA Mosaic Version 2.0.0b4

Netscape Version 1.1b3 and Version 1.1

O'Reilly and Associates Enhanced NCSA Mosaic Release 1

QuarterDeck Mosaic Prerelease 4

Setting Up a CyberCash Account

Setting yourself up as a merchant using CyberCash is relatively easy; there are explicit instructions online (see fig. 21.5 or go to **http://www.cybercash.com/cybercash/how/merch_setup.html**). There is an online application form at **http://www.cybercash.com/cybercash/how/merchantapplform.html** that you will need to fill out. After your application has been processed, CyberCash will contact you and begin setting up your online storefront, either on its or your server.

If your Web browser is not on the list of supported browsers, you will have to manually configure it to work with the CyberCash Wallet. CyberCash has instructions for doing this manual configuration.

Who Uses CyberCash

CyberCash is being used by some fairly large Internet players; the following is a partial list of companies using it.

- *ElectroWeb*   A reseller of CD-ROM software, hardware, computer peripherals, consumer electronics, music, and video games
- *Novell*   Novell's BrainShare '96 Web site. Learn about the latest Novell technologies.
- *Oracle*   Database development software
- *Price Online*   Price Club online

V

Applications

Fig. 21.5
You can get
detailed informa-
tion online.

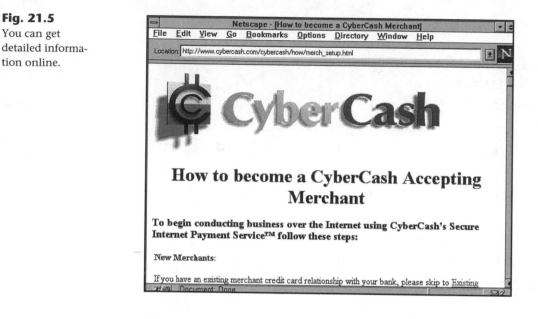

For more information about CyberCash, go to **http://www.cybercash.com**.

Also, CyberCash has submitted RFC1898, a technical review of CyberCash Credit Card Protocol Version 0.8. This document describes in complete detail the workings of CyberCash. This and other RFCs are available online at **http://ds.internic.net/ds/dspg1intdoc.html**.

Type the RFC number (**RFC1898**) into the searchable field, and it will retrieve your requested RFC. An *RFC* is an Internet term meaning Request For Comments. When a new protocol is introduced to the Internet community, generally, an RFC is submitted.

Secure Pay

Secure Pay allows for purchasing products through checks. This system has been created by Redi-Check, based in Salt Lake City, Utah. Both CyberCash and First Virtual require the buyer or client to have a credit card. Secure Pay doesn't have this requirement. The buyer sets up an account with Secure Pay, giving it his or her checking account information at Secure Pay's secure Web site and then chooses an account name and password. When the buyer wants to buy something, he or she enters his or her unique account name and password, which Secure Pay then validates. The buyer does not need any additional software. With Secure Pay, no financial information is transmitted over the Internet, so no security system is needed, (other than the initial sign up, which is secure).

Requirements

Secure Pay requires both the buyer and merchant to have bank accounts that will accept checks paid in U.S. funds. No additional hardware or software is required.

How Secure Pay Works

Secure Pay is a fairly simple structure. A buyer purchases a product or service from your Secure Pay enabled site. The buyer will have entered his or her account name and password to make the purchase. This information along with the transaction is re-sent to Redi-Check for verification. When verified, Redi-Check sends back a confirmation and then prints a check drawn against the buyer's checking account and sends the check to the merchant via regular mail. The funds are available 24 hours after the purchase was made because Secure Pay cuts checks daily.

How To Set Up a Secure Pay Account

The first step to enabling Secure Pay as a merchant is to create a merchant account with Secure Pay (see fig. 21.6). It has set up an online order form at **http://www.redi-check.com/merchant/online.html**.

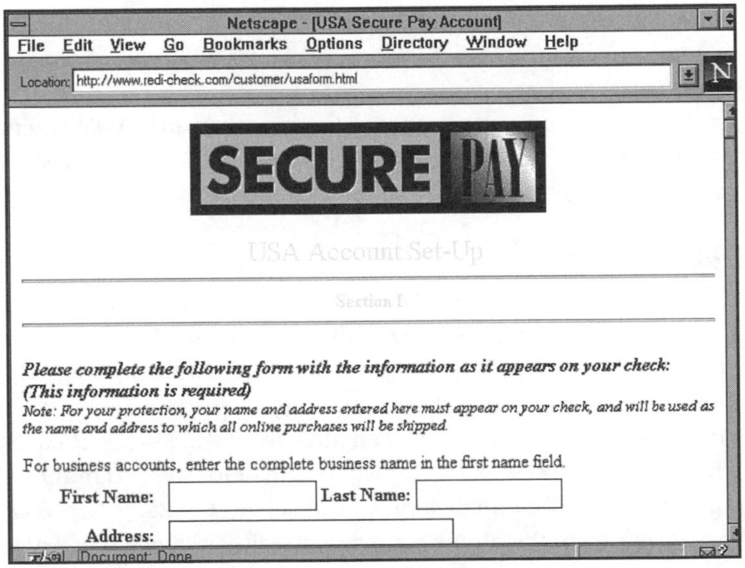

Fig. 21.6
Fill out this form to set up a Secure Pay account.

You will need to complete this form. The form allows Redi-Check to withdraw US$250 from your checking account as a one-time application and setup fee. Thereafter, there is a processing fee per transaction of 2 percent. After you have completed the application, Secure Pay will contact you to complete the process. Your account will be set up within two working days of submitting the application. Currently, Secure Pay can only handle U.S. and Canadian funds; this affects the buyer more than the merchant.

Visit the Secure Pay home page for information and applications at **http:// www.redi-check.com**.

The following is a sample of the merchants using Redi-Check's services.

- Access Market Square Internet Shopping Mall
- Icentral's ShopSite
- Mentor and Associates
- Windows95.com

Web900

Web900 is a unique approach to online purchasing. Using the existing 900 number phenomenon for billing, the merchant can easily charge for online products. This strategy is designed more for selling "digital information" than durable goods. If you have a piece of software, you could sell it online very easily with this system.

Requirements

There are no special requirements for the buyer with Web900. The merchant needs to have a server that can run CGI scripts with either PERL version 4.0 or Visual Basic.

How Web900 Works

When a buyer wants to purchase something from you, he or she is shown a page that requests a redemption code. This code is available by calling a 900 number. When the buyer calls the number, the body of the message could simply be the redemption code. The buyer then enters that code into a CGI form which validates the code against an already existing block of codes the merchant has on its server. The buyer will be billed for the 900 number call on his or her phone bill in increments of US$10 and US$25. When Web900 receives payment from the phone company, it will forward 80 percent of the total to the merchant, keeping 20 percent as a transaction fee. See figure 21.7.

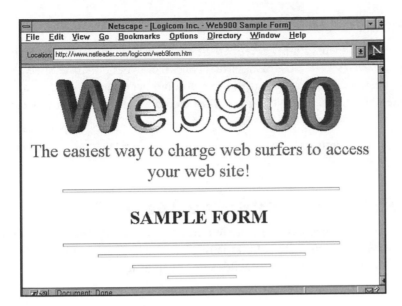

Fig. 21.7
Web900 sample
form.

How To Set Up a Web900 Account

You will need to fill out the service agreement and fax it to Web900.
The form is located at **http://www.netleader.com/logicom/
webagree.htm**. While you're getting the form, follow the links to "Sample
CGI Script" and download the CGI scripts for your system. Use the Visual
Basic-based CGI script if you are using a WINS directory; use the other PERL-
based CGI scripts if you are using a CGI-Bin directory. Web900 has created
the form to use for requesting the redemption code. Follow the links to and
download a copy of this form. Make sure you keep its information intact on
the form because Web900 requires it.

After it has received your agreement, Web900 will send redemption codes to
you as an e-mail attachment. Also, it will have created your account. With
the codes copied to the appropriate directory, the CGI script will work. If you
have problems setting up the CGI script or placing the code file, you can contact Web900; it will walk you through the setup.

Web900 processes checks on the 15th of every month for 45 days prior. For
example, the transactions that occurred in February will be processed on
April 15th.

You can find Web900 online at **http://www.netleader.com/logicom/
web900.htm**.

V

Applications

Secure Web Servers

▶ For additional secure Web servers see "Overview of WWW Server Software," p. 75

Many infopreneurs simply accept credit cards over the Internet by utilizing a secure Web server. No e-cash, virtual checks, or cyber-dollars are needed. Your customers will likely demand that you protect their financial details by implementing a secure Web server. Most credible Web server software companies have either delivered a secure server or are about to.

This chapter discusses a few of the high profile secure Web servers but be sure to review the list in Chapter 5.

Netscape Commerce Server

Netscape has implemented a complete commerce strategy based on its Commerce server and browser. Additionally, Netscape has created the following resources for commercial transactions on the Internet:

> Merchant System
>
> Publishing System
>
> Community System
>
> IStore

Each of these software packages is based on the Netscape Commerce server. Each streamlines the creation of an online business. These are all complete solutions tailored for different business needs. The Merchant system is designed to provide all the necessary tools and support structures for large businesses to create online shopping malls or large online retail stores. The Publishing system allows for online subscription-based publications.

The Community system allows for the integration of bulletin boards, real-time chat services, and private groups. IStore is the basic package that allows merchants to create an online store with sample templates.

The Commerce Server is designed to allow secure commercial transactions. All of the security features are built into the server and are available through the administration utilities. The Commerce Server uses the Secure Socket Layer (SSL) protocol to provide security. SSL sits between the TCP/IP stack and the HTTP protocol. There, SSL can provide a number of security features including server authentication, data encryption, and verifiable data integrity.

Who Uses Netscape Commerce Server

The following organizations are using some or all of Netscape's Merchant System:

- *Cybersuperstores* **http://www.cybersuperstores.com/cyber.html**
- *ISN (Internet Shopping Network)* **http://www.internet.net/**
- *Bank of America* **http://www.bankamerica.com**
- *Disney.com* **http://www2.disney.com/**
- *The Wall Street Journal on the Web* **http://www.wsj.com**

Client Software

The Netscape Commerce strategy relies on the client's use of Netscape's Web browser version 2.0. No additional software is required for the customer.

You can find more information about Netscape's support of commercial transactions on the Internet at **http://home.netscape.com/comprod/ products/iapps/index.html**.

WebQuest Secure Server

When this book is published, the WebQuest server by Questar Microsystems should have a secure Web server available to the public. This server will support Microsoft's security protocol PCT. Some of the advantages of the WebQuest server are price, roughly a tenth the price of the Netscape package, ease of use and installation, and its support of additional Internet protocols.

Client Software

WebQuest's secure server supports both Netscape 2.0 and Internet Explorer 2.0. It will also support NCSA Mosaic's secure client (version 3.0) when it is released.

For more information on how Questar's WebQuest has implemented PCT and to download a copy of the server, visit the WebQuest home page at **http://www.questar.com/webquest.htm**.

Microsoft Internet Information Server

Microsoft's Internet Information Server supports secure transactions over the Internet through SSL and RSA encryption. Currently, Microsoft's IIS SSL only works with Microsoft's Internet Explorer 2.0.

Microsoft is working on a suite of applications similar to Netscape's Merchant System. This suite will be a combination of: Microsoft's Merchant server, a server linked to databases, which will allow secure financial transactions; the

Merchant workbench, similar to Netscape's IStore; and a client "shopping utility" which will make online shopping easier and more consistent for the buyer. All these products will be available from Microsoft some time in mid-1996. Microsoft has not established pricing for these software packages, though they will probably be significantly less expensive than Netscape's current prices.

Visit Microsoft home page at **http://www.microsoft.com** and follow the link to "Search," and there search for "Electronic Retailing" and "Internet Information Server."

Shopping Carts/Shopping Malls

In addition to the online shopping malls discussed previously, InfoHaus and the IStore, there are a number of online shopping malls. The following is a short list found by using Yahoo:

- **http://www.opse.com/mallistings/**
- **http://malls.com/**
- **http://www.hummsoft.com/hummsoft/shopper.html**
- **http://worldshopping.com/**

As a merchant, you have the option of using an existing "shopping mall" for hosting your Web site. The above listing will give you a place to start. Look for a "shopping mall" that supports a search engine and is easy to navigate.

CGI Scripts

Some companies have built their own CGI scripts that allow them to sell online. Buyers are asked to post their credit card information when buying products. This strategy is fairly easy to implement and also fairly easy to break. The best way to implement this strategy is with a secure server like Netscape's Commerce Server. That way the connection between the client and server is encrypted and secure, making fraud very difficult. The actual implementation of the CGI will depend on what resources are available with your system, PERL, C++, Visual Basic, and on the abilities of the CGI programmer.

There is a large body of information online about CGI scripts. A good place to start is **http://the-inter.net/www/future21/cgia.html**.

Alternatives

In addition to the strategies reviewed above, there are other, in some ways simpler, ways of handling online commerce. Some companies allow people to place orders over the Internet and then deal with billing through common interfaces.

Taking Orders (COD)

One of the most common ways of offering products for sale over the Internet is to take orders and then deliver products COD. This approach has some very distinct advantages. The interface is very simple to create. A basic HTML form that posts the order information to your e-mail account or some sort of database is easy and quick to create. Sending product COD resolves all concerns about security and fraud, by using an existing "secure" system. The other obvious benefit is that customers without checks can purchase products from you. A twist on this is to send customers a "bill" before sending out the merchandise. When the customer has paid the bill, you send out the product. These implementations are simply a carryover from mail-order catalogs.

Establishing Accounts

Another strategy commonly used is to require customers to establish an account with the merchant. Anyone can order over the Internet, again from a Web page form, but only those customers with an account will receive the products or services. You can require a potential customer to call you with his or her credit card number to establish an account, or require that he or she send you a check for a set amount and require him or her to maintain a minimum balance. A merchant using this strategy would ship only to people with established accounts. One advantage to this is existing systems are used to process transactions. People are used to giving out their credit card number over the phone. And depending on the implementation, creating an "account" is not unfamiliar to the general public.

Summary

The frictionless economy is on its way. There are clearly many companies racing to develop a clean and secure interface for buying on the Internet. A standard has yet to be set, but many opportunities are available to the resourceful infopreneur.

V

Applications

Merchants who opt for setting up on the Internet will likely reap many benefits in both the savings they will see and the volume of business they will transact. It can certainly be much cheaper to set up a virtual store than a real one. Your virtual store will have many of the same challenges as a "real" store. You will need to market and promote to attract customers and assure them of a safe, secure place to shop. This chapter covered a lot of material; from here, use the Net to continue your explorations and craft a solution that is appropriate for your business and vision. ❖

CHAPTER 22

Interactive and Live Applications

In previous chapters, you have explored Web interaction on the most basic of levels: TXT, DOC, and HTML file transfer and forms, usage counters, and other elemental forms of information exchange. This chapter is devoted to the exploration of the next generation of interactivity and the advent *live* applications—applications that integrate aural and visual response or information exchange.

The first section of this chapter examines the state-of-the-art audio and video usage in interactive and live applications and advanced interactive concepts, such as live video conferencing. Commercial and noncommercial applications, tools, and peripherals, and sites for both resources and interaction are described or provided.

The second section of this chapter presents techniques for expanding the interactivity of the Web. This section includes discussions of the proposed methods for implementing new interactive concepts, such as Auralview, W3Vision, and WebStage sessions. It also covers the fast growing area of virtual reality interactivity.

This chapter's vision of this new interactivity is not limited to only existing technology. It turns outward and examines where you can go and what the near and not-too-distant future may have in store for those who travel the Information Superhighway.

In this chapter, you learn about:

- Live applications to add multimedia to your Web site
- Tools for implementing advanced interactive applications
- Virtual reality engines and applications
- Resource sites for sound bites, video clips, and more

Interactive and Live Application Concepts

This section examines state-of-the-art audio and video toolsets and development technology, interactive applications, and example sites. Some advanced interactive concepts under discussion are: audio and video servers and clients and real-time video conferencing. Commercial and noncommercial tools and peripherals, applications, and sites covering both resources and example interaction will be described and/or provided.

To enjoy a firm footing in the coming discussion, it is necessary to have an understanding of certain basic concepts. Within this section, the concept of *server* and *client* appears. It is not unlike the standard references to client/server in use today.

A *server* is a system that consists of both hardware and software that can offer an exchange of information and access to the services, software, or supplies required by the server's Web site visitor. Because the information transactions that are described in this section are audio, video, or a combination of both, the amount of information that needs to be exchanged is usually quite large. Add to this the security issues involved and because some of the servers on the Net are actually companies or organizations that are in the business of supplying these information transactions for a fee, the necessity arises for a controlled method for accessing this information—the *client*.

The client is also a combination hardware and software system. The software application is responsible for any security or access issues, but must also provide an acceptable method for transferring large files across the Net in a timely manner. The problem is greatly enhanced for applications that transfer large amounts of information that must be delivered in real-time.

Hardware issues also determine the *lag* time encountered with these transactions. Even having the highest speed connection (ISDN or T1) doesn't ensure that a timely transaction can occur.

During the design phase of your Web site, it is imperative that you define what type of hardware and software you expect your users to have. This will aid you in developing the look, feel, and content of the information you supply.

The toolsets, resource sites, and information supplied in this section deal with these subjects.

Audio Tools/Applications and Example Sites

One of the most popular options that you can add to your developing Web site is *streaming* or *on-demand audio*. On-demand audio allows visitors to your site to have access to audio that is transferred across the Net at speeds that allow the visitor to listen to audio in real time.

How do you supply audio in real time? The secret to transferring the vast amount of information required for real-time audio is to use data compression techniques. This is a fast developing area of Internet technology and there are several methods that can be used to accomplish compression.

However, prior to selecting a satisfactory compression technique, it is imperative to ensure the *quality* of the audio offered to your Web site visitor. Taking a simple series of steps can ensure that you develop a high level of quality for your audio.

The First Step to Quality Audio

There are a few simple rules that you should follow to achieve the highest quality sound. It is very important to achieve a high level of quality because, as you will read shortly, the method that you use to encode the audio permanently alters the quality.

Use a High-Quality Original Source and Quality Equipment. Perhaps the single greatest factor in determining the level of audio quality is the audio source. The source that you use is determined by the equipment available to you. Some of the best sources of quality audio are listed in the following table.

Source	Quality Level
Audio compact discs (CDs)	High
Digital audio tapes (DATs)	High
Analog cassettes (pre-mastered)	Medium
Vinyl records	Low

To develop quality sound from scratch, you can use the sources in the following table.

Source	Quality Level
Professional high quality microphones	Highest quality

(continues)

(continued)

Source	Quality Level
Condenser microphones	Lowest quality
Professional recording equipment or facilities (i.e., multichannel recorders, sound rooms, mixing boards)	Highest quality
Home variety recording equipment or facilities (i.e., cassette tape recorders, bathrooms, ironing boards)	Lowest quality

---

Tip

One of the best resource lists for professional audio equipment can be found at **http://www.magicnet.net/rz/world_of_audio/gear/gear1.html**.

Try to encode your audio from 16-bit source files that were digitized with a 22.05 kHz sampling rate. Most compression techniques accept multiple other forms of source files (such as 8-bit or µLaw).

When you're creating audio sources, keep in mind that you can use any production resource. However, the encoding done by the compression algorithm can cause hiss and distortion.

Source files that were recorded at either 8000 Hz or 11000 Hz are also acceptable, but, once again, remember the favorite saying of computer geeks everywhere—GIGO, which stands for Garbage In, Garbage Out. If you want quality, start with the optimum quality available.

Remember, high-quality equipment will produce high-quality results. This is true for every element in the recording chain, from the input source to the audio capture device to the software used for capturing and editing. A little forethought about your audio source file's origin can save you headaches down the road. If you intend to provide commercial audio services at your Web site, you ought to invest in professional audio equipment. This type and level of equipment doesn't have to break your bank, but it is professional equipment that should be acquired from a professional recording equipment dealer, rather than from a fly-by-night Gadget Supply or your local computer/hi-fi/appliance store.

Control the Recording Level. Create an audio source file for use on your Web site by using an internal soundcard. There are many manufacturer's of sound cards on the market. One of the Creative Labs' SoundBlaster is the de facto standard for the industry. Selecting the type of sound card you use should be based on the criteria previously listed concerning the quality of the audio source file required and the type of computer system that performs the sound capture.

> **Tip**
>
> One of the best resource lists for audio equipment and other sources is located at **http://www.music.mcgill.ca**.

Regardless of which card you use, setting the correct level of input to your sound card is critical. When an input signal exceeds the full range of amplitude available to your sound card (or any other piece of audio equipment), the result is a level that *crowns* the input amplifier. Crowning the input amplifier causes a flattening of the input that results in a clipped signal. Clipping is audible in the resulting source file as a high frequency, crackling noise.

Digitizing with your sound card requires a simple but methodical approach to achieve the finest, quality results. Using your selected audio source, you should perform several *test runs* adjusting your input level until it approaches but doesn't exceed the maximum level for the sound card input amplifier.

> **Tip**
>
> Most sound card manufacturers supply a set of utilities that perform specific tasks on their card. The input level of the various sources of audio being supplied to the sound card can usually be adjusted using a mixer utility.

> **Note**
>
> Look for an adjustment labeled Input Level or Recording Level. Most mixer utilities use some sort of visual display to provide you with either the level of sound coming in or a paddle control that is used to adjust the sound level. Ensure that no peaks above maximum occur. Generally, these excursions are indicated by a red light or red band in the case of Visual VU Meters. Be conservative with your level adjustments; you never know when an unexpected volume increase can occur.

Audio source files that do not use the optimum range of input amplitude ultimately produce unsatisfactory compressed files.

Digital Audio Editors. Once you have either created a sound file or received a sound file, you can manipulate and edit this file using a Windows-based editor.

In addition to your sound card manufacturer's set of utilities, an Audio Editor can be used to correct errors that may have crept into your audio source file. An amplitude range that is too low can be increased or normalized; hisses and pops and other forms of distortion can be erased, and the overall time of the audio recording can be changed. You can also change the file to add sound effects and even merge multiple sound files together.

Transmission Bandwidth versus Audio Type. Live audio compression techniques optimize compressed files according to the type of audio recorded and being transmitted. Speech delivery can usually be performed adequately at a transmission rate of 14.4 Kbps. Delivering music at 14.4 Kbps is a much more difficult challenge.

Encoding music for transmission to users that are connected to the Internet at 14.4 Kbps requires forethought in your music selection. It is important to remember that when transmitting audio, or video for that matter, a certain amount of bandwidth is required to do the original source justice. Transmitting a live version of the Podunk International Symphony Orchestra's version of Rossini's *Overture to William Tell* might be a wonderful service your Web site could supply; however, if you attempt to transmit this harmonically complex signal over a 14.4 Kbps modem, you cannot do the piece justice. Applications where the ultimate fidelity of the music is not as important as other contents, such as using music as a background for advertisements where the vocal message is the primary purpose of the audio source, result in a much more successful application.

As you can imagine then, using a system that uses 28.8 Kbps analog modems or ISDN and T1 digital modems, result in higher bandwidth and, therefore, in greater capabilities. Increasing your bandwidth allows for greatly improved frequency response, a greater dynamic audio range, and a decrease in the number of *artifacts*—holes in a decompressed file that cause audio noise and video flutter.

The Second Step to Quality Audio

Creating compressed files that meet the requirements discussed in the previous section requires the use of quality software that can encode the files using algorithms that make guesses as to what is most important in the audio source file. The algorithm encoder contains a predefined list of elements within a sound stream. All elements are weighted against each other and then are used to modify the stream according to each element's weight. The common elements used by encoders consist of the following:

- Transmission Bandwidth—usually either 14,4 Kbps or 28.8 Kbps
- Audio Compression
- Audio Equalization
- Noise Gating
- Audio Normalization

Transmission Bandwidth. As previously discussed, the transmission bandwidth is selected when you are determining what type of audio sources you plan to offer as a service. The encoding software uses this information to determine how much time it has in which to put the preprocessed audio source information. The overall reproduction fidelity and quality of your decompressed files will be determined by the bandwidth available for determining various audio signal qualities.

Audio Compression. Have you ever noticed a weird rumbling noise, low frequency hum, or other strange form of distortion in an audio file that you were playing? The cause of that sound is not faulty playback software or cheap hardware, rather it is due to a side effect of encoding/compressing an audio signal—an *artifact*. This is a sound that wasn't there before encoding or compressing.

The suppression of audio artifacts is one reason that you want to supply the loudest signal possible to your soundcard. Audio artifact signals are relatively low volume sounds. It doesn't really matter whether the original sound file is loud or quiet. Louder files tend to mask artifacts. Although your desire is to supply the loudest source file possible to the compression algorithm, you are limited by the amplitude of the loudest sound in the source. It only stands to reason that if you could control the variation between the loudest and softest signals you were compressing, you could effectively turn up the overall volume of the source file. This is where audio compression techniques enter the picture.

Audio compression reduces the difference between the loudest and softest areas of an incoming source file. What the audio compressor does is to use a predefined threshold to determine which input signal levels should be turned down and which should be left alone. How much control there is for turning areas of the source signal file up or down depends on how much compression is used.

Compression guidelines are rough at best and algorithmic guesses are based on years of experience. There are general rules-of-thumb, however, that should be helpful in most situations:

- Speech compression ratios at 14.4 Kbps—moderate to extreme, 4:1 to 10:1. This guarantees that the signal is loud enough to mask artifacts that are more apparent at this transmission rate.

- Speech compression ratios at 28.8 Kbps—low to moderate, 2:1 to 4:1. With a transmission rate of 28.8 Kbps, the dynamic range is greatly increased and the artifacts greatly reduced.

- Music compression ratios at 14.4 Kbps—moderate to moderately high, 4:1 to 6:1. Again, determined by the increase in artifacts and also the limited dynamic range of the supported audio.

- Music compression ratios at 28.8 Kbps—extremely low to moderate, 1:1 to 3:1. With the greater dynamic range, even a symphony orchestra would reproduce excellently.

Noise Gating. Noise gating is a function of audio compression. Simply put, it is the act of eliminating unwanted background noise that becomes audible during gaps in an audio signal. As in audio compression, noise gating is determined by setting a specific volume level above which signal amplitude is left alone but below which the signal is turned down or off. Even the least expensive compressors usually have some form of noise gating built-in.

Audio Equalization. Equalization is a bit of a mystery to most people. Even though their automobile and home audio systems usually have some form of equalization control, most people have no idea what equalization is meant for or how to determine what changes to make in the settings that came set from the factory.

Simply stated, equalization changes the frequency formula of an audio signal. This is accomplished by boosting (turning up) or cutting (turning down) certain frequencies or frequency ranges. Ultimately, equalization is meant to compensate for frequency variations in the surrounding space. The response characteristics of your apartment or your car can be compensated by using equalization. In addition, using specialized equalization systems, you can also compensate for some slight variations in the flat response curve of your speakers.

Attempting to use equalization for its intended purpose with sound files that you intend to supply over the Net is ludicrous, at best. However, you can use equalization to control another aspect of an audio signal—clarifying the signal. Clarifying the signal is essentially suppressing or filtering unwanted background noise or annoying frequencies. Using equalization, you can boost frequencies where the important content is and cut frequencies where the noise or unwanted sound is.

Some simple equalization systems only define ranges that it offers equalization for (that is low-, mid-, and high-range). Some systems allow you to choose which frequency to boost, other systems are preset at the factory. If you can select the boost frequency, or if you are using a graphic equalizer or audio processing software, begin the mid-range boost at 2.5 kHz. This mid-range boost, coupled with cutting out the high- and low-range signals, provides the desired clarifying effect.

Advanced graphic equalizers offer far more range selections and control. Whatever system you have, remember that the amount for each range depends on your equipment and source file. Experiment.

Audio Normalization. The last process that you can use to create the ultimate audio source is normalization. This is normally a software process included in most audio recording and editing software. In this process, the computer calculates how much the volume of a sound file can be turned up without causing distortion. This allows you to be conservative with your recording input levels and lets your audio recording or editing software normalization function adjust the signal levels. Just remember the following:

- Don't normalize your sound file and then perform any other form of control on your file or you'll end up with distortion.

- Never normalize at 100 percent; it may cause compression algorithms to fail. Normalizing at 90 to 95 percent will work effectively in most cases.

The Final Step to Quality Live Audio
You can now focus on your task at hand. How do you add quality audio services to your Web site? Using the guidelines described previously, you can

develop applications that provide live audio feeds to your Web site visitors or you can subscribe to one of the existing methodologies.

Luckily, developing interactive and live application sites on the Internet has become quite a bit easier. Several companies have stepped forward to offer development technology to enable the Web site creator easily implemented methods for creating audio servers that provide on-demand audio services to new users, subscribers, and visitors. In addition, each of these server applications comes with multiple platform client pairs that can be downloaded from the server or from any number of similar sites on the Web.

The audio tools described below are three of the most popular client-server pairs currently available. As previously mentioned, new toolsets and development tools are appearing all the time.

Tip

Before committing to any one audio client-server system for your particular Web site, put your search engine to work by searching for "Audio" and doing some exploration on your own. This area of technology is growing quickly.

RealAudio

RealAudio is currently the most popular *client-server* pair development tool available. RealAudio provides a complete set of on-demand audio software products including: audio servers, audio clients, and encoders.

RealAudio's home page is at **http://www.realaudio.com/** (see fig. 22.1). This home page provides download access for all RealAudio software products.

Selecting the RealAudio receiver download hypertext link opens another Web page that allows you to order the RealAudio Receiver software for several different operating systems: Windows 3.x, Windows 95/Windows NT, Mac, and a Japanese version.

Selecting the RealAudio server hypertext link opens another Web page that allows you to either order the RealAudio Server software or receive an evaluation copy that you can use to determine if the RealAudio Server system fits your specific Web site requirements.

Selecting the RealAudio Encoder hypertext link opens another Web page that lets you order the RealAudio Encoder software for several different operating systems: Windows 3.x, Windows 95/Windows NT, and several versions for the Mac.

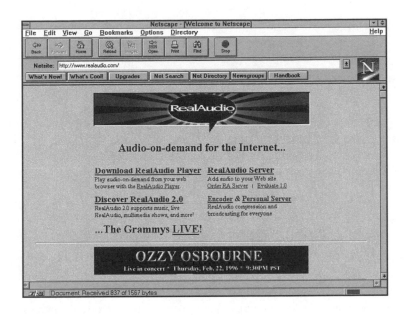

Fig. 22.1
The RealAudio
home page where
you can download
software.

V

Applications

TrueSpeech

TrueSpeech, available from DSP Group, Inc., is a new presence in the world of
on-demand audio. The TrueSpeech system is being used by a growing number
of live radio sites that are cropping up on the Net. An example of TrueSpeech
being used for live radio and music sources is discussed later at the San Francisco Audio Network site (refer to the section on example sites). The DSP
Group, Inc.'s home page is at **http://www.dspg.com/** (see
fig. 22.2).

Fig. 22.2
The DSP Group,
Inc.'s TrueSpeech
home page.

This home page provides download access for their software products. To gain access to the download page, you double-click the TrueSpeech button, which opens another Web page where you can download the TrueSpeech Audio Receiver or view the TrueSpeech video across the Net.

Double-clicking the TrueSpeech logo opens an additional page where you can download the TrueSpeech Receiver for several versions of Windows, a couple of versions for the Mac, and a Japanese language version.

StreamWorks

StreamWorks, available from Xing Technology Corporation, is one of the fastest growing live audio programs. Part of the reason for this is undoubtedly its presence in the world of real-time video (refer to later in this chapter for a discussion of the real-time video sources). Xing Technology Corporation also provides a complete set of on-demand audio software products including audio servers and audio receivers. Xing Technology Corporation's home page is at **http://www.xingtech.com/** (see fig. 22.3). This page gives you download access for all Xing software products. To gain access to the download page, double-click the StreamWorks logo.

Fig. 22.3
This is Xing Technology Corporation's home page.

Once you have double-clicked the StreamWorks logo, you go to a page where you can download StreamWorks Audio Server information, order the StreamWorks on-demand audio client software for any version of Windows, MAC, or UNIX OSs, or test drive a StreamWorks audio server running at Xing Technology Corporation Headquarters.

Interactive Audio Sites

Having the desire to provide live audio across the Net, the next question should be, how do you present it to your visitor? There are a number of excellent interactive audio sites. These sites can provide methods that you can use to set up an audio server. These sites also show you how to offer various services: the ability to explore new music; obtain sound bites, obtain freeware, shareware, and commercial demos of applications; and so on.

For an example of a site that uses the RealAudio Server, visit Computer Express's home page at **http://www.dspg.com/allplyr.htm** (see fig. 22.4). Computer Express supplies computer hardware and software and uses audio on-demand for advertising purposes, one of the many applications for audio on the Net.

Fig. 22.4
Computer Express: An Example site using RealAudio's RealAudio Server.

For an example of a site that uses the DSP Group's TrueSpeech Audio Server, visit the San Francisco Audio Network home page at **http://www.sfaudio.net/sfan_logo.html**. The San Francisco Audio Network supplies a wide variety of audio services to its subscribers including the ability to sample new audio CDs and listen to live radio.

For an example of a site that uses the Xing Technologies StreamWorks Audio Server, visit Xing Technology Corporation's Test Drive page at **http://www.xingtech.com/streams/streams.html**. The StreamWorks Test

Drive offers visitors sample uses of their Audio Server: live radio broadcasts from KWBR FM 95.3 at 16 Kbps, classical music on ISDN's 112 Kbps, and a talk radio sports program from KKAL at 10 Kbps. These are prime examples of the types of functions that on-demand audio can offer over the Net.

Xing Technologies StreamWorks Test Drive page provides the perfect segue into the next subject: live video. The Test Drive page provides a sample of the StreamWorks audio/visual server.

Video Tools, Applications, and Sites

Auralview technologies are rapidly encroaching on the Internet's back country. Daily, you find that ASCII domination is being strongly challenged by Internet auralview capabilities. Live audio servers, video servers, and video conferencing systems are appearing almost daily. And while some may find it necessary to run their Internet applications on a Sun SPARCstation with an MBONE feed, your average, run-of-the-mill, garden variety Windows NT machines certainly give them a run for their money.

Live video provides visitors to your Web site access to video information that can be transferred across the Net at speeds that are approaching real time. The underlying technology for live video is developing rapidly, the hardware is becoming less expensive, and both are available to the business and home user. Before deciding to supply video resources to your Web site, however, there are several items that must be defined and certain resources acquired.

The following sections outline a series of steps that you can take to ensure that you develop a high-quality suite of video information and provide that to your Web site visitor.

Use High Quality Original Sources and Quality Equipment

One of the greatest factors in determining the level of video quality is using high-quality video sources. The source that you use is, of course, determined by your access to required equipment, however, here a few of the better sources of quality video:

Video CDs	Highest quality
Professional video cassette tapes	High quality
Video Captured AVI Files	Unknown quality
Home-made video cassette tapes	Lowest quality

For developing quality video from scratch, you can use:

Professional video cameras	Highest quality
Computer video cameras	High quality
Home video cameras	Lowest quality
Professional recording equipment and facilities	Highest quality
Home variety recording equipment or facilities	Lowest quality

High-quality equipment will produce high-quality results. This is true for every element in the recording chain, from the input source to the video capture device to the software used for capturing and editing. Remember, a little forethought into your video source file's origin can save you headaches down the road. If you intend to add commercial video services to your Web site, you should invest in professional video equipment. Don't try to obtain professional equipment from anyone but a professional recording equipment dealer. Should your desire to provide video services outweigh your pocketbook, remember to get the highest-rated devices within your budget, and put extra effort into acquiring quality source material.

Control the Color

Control of the color spectrum in your video source is of prime importance. The following are a few hints usually followed in the video production community:

■ When selecting still backgrounds or color highlights, always use color spectrums that are easily duplicable on a SVGA color monitor. You should attempt to preview your image through NTSC/PAL/HDTV output devices.

■ Don't place saturated complementary (blue/yellow, black/white) colors next to each other since they may color-bleed.

■ Don't use highly saturated colors, especially red; they tend to color-bleed.

■ Remember, the human eye is better at distinguishing differences in intensity than it is in distinguishing differences in hue. Use intensity as the primary variable and then hue, reserving saturation for more subtle differences.

■ Control brightness and contrast.

■ High saturation background colors should be especially avoided. Dark blue is a good background color.

Color differences are important within a single image or an animated image. Don't move the camera quickly, change from bright sunlight to shadow, or change between strikingly different subject matter. You must be sure not to change colors too quickly. This can result in a disturbing visual flickering.

Adding Textual Information

If you plan to edit your video and add textual information, make sure that your image and text are both contained within the expected screen size. In other words, don't let your text information get too close to the edge of your image. A good rule of thumb is don't place text closer than 1/10 of the overall screen size to any screen edge.

If you plan on changing the text displayed on the screen, allow for adequate delay time. This delay should be proportional to the text's complexity. Two to three seconds is fine for a word or two or a short sentence. Longer times are appropriate for more text; however, dense text should be avoided. Time yourself reading the text displayed and then add a few extra seconds. Also, text should not exceed twenty characters per line and you should use large font sizes (greater than 30 pt) for titles.

Applying Shapes and Frames

If you intend to add shapes such as circles, squares, frames, or other non-linear shapes, don't use single pixel-wide lines. If you do, you most likely will find that vertical lines lose their color and horizontal lines flicker. Both result in an annoying video. Most video editors allow you to set line width sizes; choose a line width of at least two pixels.

Motion Video, Animation, and Other Moving Bodies

Animated subjects are worthy of great detailed explanations. It is not within the scope of this book to approach that depth of discussion; however, a few hints certainly can't hurt.

If you plan on using a revolving or moving object, time your motion correctly. Rotating objects should complete a revolution within three to eight seconds, depending on the complexity of the rotating shape. You should test this on yourself and colleagues. If you make the motion too slow, the end result may be very boring; make it too fast and the motion won't seem realistic or might be difficult for the eye to follow. For moving objects, be sure that the speed of the motion is not too slow to put the viewer to sleep and is fast enough to hold the viewer's interest. Don't make your viewers' heads spin with excessive motion. Effective frame rate can be slowed down to achieve different visual effects. If you play a video at five to six frames per second (fps), the end result is a "slow motion" look. Increasing the speed to nine to ten fps results in a "jittery" video. Full motion for the human eye is 30 fps. Control your effects carefully because their results on your video can be immense.

Miscellaneous

The image aspect ratio of your finished video is also an important factor to remember. If you have ever tried to watch a movie that was shot in VistaVision on your standard television, you have run into the problem of improper aspect ratio. Be sure that your final video image conforms to the aspect ratio of the viewing device; the SVGA monitor your visitors are using.

> **Note**
>
> The correct aspect ratios for NTSC, PAL, and HDTV are 4:3, 4:3, and 16:9, respectively. Computer displays, as a rule, do not conform to these ratios. As a result, video images with these aspect ratios appear distorted when viewed.

When recording your video masters, or when selecting masters that have been prerecorded, choose the highest resolution video format available. Any and all subsequent videos can then be dubbed from this master.

> **Note**
>
> When comparing the resolution of various video source standards, use the following guide. Resolution increases from left to right in the following formats:
>
> **VHS -> SVHS -> Hi8 -> BetaCam SP -> D2 Digital**

Video Transmission Bandwidth

Since you have already determined the transmission bandwidth of our video server, you need not concern yourself with the concept of fps transfer rates. Your only concern at this time should be with compression.

Compress or Don't Compress: Your Two Options

Taking a quick trip around the Internet and the World Wide Web in search of live video results in some startling revelations. If you attempt to run uncompressed video in a full motion mode, using a 14.4 Kbps modem, the time such running takes is incredibly long. This is certainly not full motion video. Choosing to use one of the available video servers or video conferencing servers that are available has to be a determining factor in both your equipment decisions (that is, going to an ISDN modem and supporting analog modems) and in your choice of Web site server. These are choices that you have to make based on need, funds, available equipment, and target audience.

A *video codec* is the device that physically performs the act of compressing and decompressing video images for transmission across a LAN or WAN. The current freeware CU-SeeMe application, offered by Cornell University, supports a codec that produces grayscale images compatible with the existing software

Adding Quality Live Video to Your Web Site

Using the previously described guidelines, you can develop applications that provide live video feeds to your Web site visitors, or you can subscribe to one of the existing methodologies that are available today.

Just as in advanced audio techniques, there are also several companies that have stepped up to offer development technology to enable the Web site creator to add either a video server or video conferencing services to new users, subscribers, and visitors. Again, each of these video applications comes with multiple platform receiver pairs that can be downloaded from your Web site or from any number of similar sites on the Web.

The video tools described in the following sections are several of the more prominent Windows NT video applications currently available. Each of these applications serve as video teleconferencing servers. If you think about it, the step between a pure video service, such as the one offered by InterneTV (found at **http://www.crs4.it/~france/TV/** and where their viewers are allowed to watch Italian television with video and sound), to offer fully interactive video conferencing is a small one.

> ### Tip
>
> Before committing to any one video system, put your search engine (refer to Chapter 17, "Search Engines and Annotation Systems," for information on search engines) to work by looking for "Live Video" across the Net and then doing some exploration on your own.

FreeVue

FreeVue provides complete video teleconferencing products. The FreeVue home page is at **http://www.freevue.com/** (see fig. 22.5) and provides download access for their video conferencing software.

Selecting the FreeVue software hypertext link opens another Web page where you can download the FreeVue teleconferencing software for Windows NT.

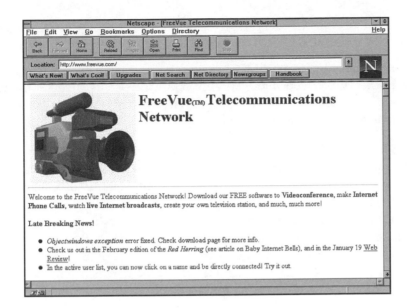

Fig. 22.5
This is the FreeVue home page.

StreamWorks

StreamWorks, available from Xing Technology Corporation, supplies several products for the world of Internet real-time video services. They provide video conferencing software and MPEG players. The Xing Technology Corporation home page is at **http://www.xingtech.com/** (see fig. 22.6). This page provides download access for all of their software products. To gain access to the download page, you double-click the StreamWorks logo.

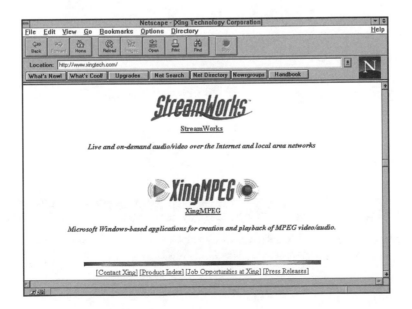

Fig. 22.6
Xing Technology Corporation's home page where you can download StreamWorks software.

Double-clicking the Xing MPEG logo opens another Web page where you can download StreamWorks' MPEG player.

Double-clicking the StreamWorks logo launches an additional selection screen where you can download StreamWorks' Video Conferencing software or test drive an example of the StreamWorks server that is running at Xing Technology Corporation headquarters.

CineVideo/Direct

CineVideo/Direct, a product of CineCom, is another popular video conferencing software products for the world of Internet real-time video services. The CineCom home page is at **http://www.cinecom.com/ CineCom/cinvdrct.html** (see fig. 22.7). This page provides download access for CineVideo/Direct, a list of current connection sites, and a ListServer for easy access to these sites. They also provide a history of the product for those interested. Selecting the CineVideo/Direct Software hypertext link downloads the CineVideo//Direct software (currently available for Windows NT).

Fig. 22.7
This is CineCom's home page where you can download CineVideo/Direct.

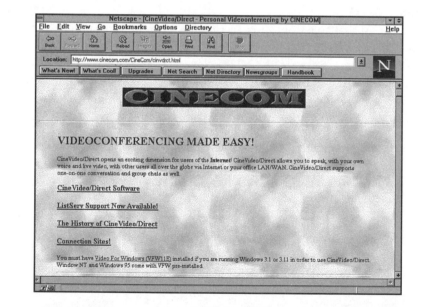

Tip

Additional technical information about CineVideo/Direct is available at **http:// www.cinecom.com/CineCom/directtech.html**.

CU-SeeMe

One of the more definitive video conferencing packages available is CU-SeeMe. This software package is a product of research being conducted at Cornell University and is available via anonymous FTP from their site at **ftp://gated.cornell.edu/pub/video**.

A commercial variation of CU-SeeMe, Enhanced CU-SeeMe, is available from White Pine Software, Inc. at **http://goliath.wpine.com/cudemowin.htm** (see fig. 22.8). Here, you can download a 30-day demo version of the Enhanced CU-SeeMe video conferencing software. You are first required to obtain a Registered DEMO Serial Number. The form for this registration can be found at **http://goliath.wpine.com/cuserial.htm**.

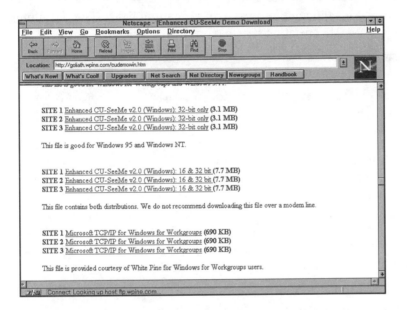

Fig. 22.8
This is where you can download Enchanced CU-SeeMe.

V

Applications

> **Note**
>
> White Pine Software, Inc. has been selected by Cornell Research Foundation as master licensee of Cornell's CU-SeeMe desktop video conferencing technology. White Pine's charter is to create low-cost, commercially enhanced and supported versions of CU-SeeMe and make it available to Internet users worldwide, bringing the advent of everyday video telecommunications one step closer.

> **Tip**
>
> White Pine Software, Inc. can be reached at **http://www.cu-seeme.com**.

CU-SeeMe provides Windows NT users with person-to person or group video teleconferencing. To provide the computing horsepower and equipment muscle necessary for video conferencing, CU-SeeMe connects each user in a group to a reflector site. A reflector site is usually a UNIX-based computer powerhouse, such as a Sun SPARCstation with an MBONE feed, that facilitates multi-participant conferencing. Although UNIX-based machines were the powerhouses of the past few years, the arrival of relatively inexpensive (less than $10,000) multi-processor, Intel Pentium-based systems running the Windows NT/MP operating system has turned the tide.

> **Tip**
>
> If you want to be placed on the CU-SeeMe mailing list, send an e-mail message with `subscribe cu-seeme-1` and your name to **listserv@cornell.edu**.

After installing your CU-SeeMe software and performing some relatively trivial configuration, you can open a receive or send/receive connection to the numerical address of another participant or the reflector site. Once connected, a split screen appears that contains the live video of each person connected to the reflector. You can never tell exactly what you might find when connecting to the reflectors. Connect and you might find yourself in the middle of a multi-window conference—or staring at a test pattern or empty office.

Available Reflector Sites. The following is a list of the reflectors that are available for public use:

- www.cu-seeme.com (192.233.34.5)
- goliath.wpine.com (192.233.34.20)
- reflector.cit.cornell.edu (132.236.91.204)
- isis.dccs.upenn.edu (130.91.72.36)
- hilda.ncsc.org (128.109.178.103)
- NASA (139.88.27.43)

Windows NT Computer Hostname. Your Windows NT computer may need a hostname. If so and you don't already have a hostname, contact your network administrator. One quick way to provide a hostname is to make an entry into the hosts file, which is in the directory that contains your Windows Sockets stack.

A host file entry uses the following syntax:

> <your IP address> <name for your PC>

If, for example, you have selected a hostname of VIDcon_Server and your IP address is 228.232.6.4, the hosts file entry is

> <228.232.6.4><VIDcon_Server

Recommended Hardware and Peripherals

You need an i486 DX/133 or Pentium-based (preferably multi-processor) system running Windows NT (Windows NT/MP for multi-processors) with a WinSock-compliant TCP/IP stack. The system should contain at least 32 MB of RAM, several gigabytes of HDD storage, an SVGA monitor capable of 1024×768 resolution and 256-colors minimum (16 million true color is preferred), and an ISDN connection supporting a telephone company connection. ISDN
modems are currently available for under $300, and typical telephone company charges are around $25 per month for an ISDN line. (Make sure that you check with your local telephone company on current prices and availability). Be aware that in some areas ISDN incurs per-minute charges in addition to monthly fees.

To create videos and to support video conferencing, you also need a Microsoft Video for Windows-compatible video board, a video capture card, a sound card, and a camera.

The Near Future: Virtual Reality

The following section presents techniques for expanding the interactivity of the Web so that directly experiencing or interacting with images and people could easily occur. You could star in your own WWW stageplay. This section also discusses virtual shopping malls.

Virtual Worlds: Tools, Applications, and Sites

The current state-of-the-art of virtual reality (VR) technology for the Internet community is Virtual Reality Modeling Language (VRML). This language is the basis of almost all VR participation on the Net today. The following sections discuss both VRML and other variations on this theme and an VR site, and a site where you can obtain one of several VRML Browser's that are currently available.

While most VRML experiences are not truly "live"—that capability coming quickly.

VRML (Virtual Reality Modeling Language)

The Virtual Reality Modeling Language has a support Web site called the VRML Technical Forum that is located at **http://vrml.wired.com/vrml.tech/** (see fig. 22.9). This support site provides downloadable copies of the VRML Version 1.0 Specification and the VRML Programming Library Version 1.0 beta 1.

Fig. 22.9

This is the VRML home page.

The-inter.Net VR Site

One of the more interesting VR sites on the Net is The-inter.Net VR network. Not only does this site offer VR-based chat and search capability, it also supplies the Windows NT CHAT application and sample VR GIF files. The-inter.Net Chat Home Page is at **http://vrml.nauticon.net/www/future21/vc**. This page supplies access to the Virtual Chat server, as well as, access to the Web page from which you can download the Windows NT version of the WinCHAT application. At this point you can download WCHAT08B.EXE, a self-extracting archive for the WinCHAT application.

The-inter.Net Screen Shots home page is at **http://vrml.nauticon.net/www/future21/screen.html**.

VRML Browsers

There are several VRML browsers. The Squirrel Virtual VRML site (see fig. 22.10) is a jumping point to other Web pages that have VRML browser. The Squirrel Virtual VRML site is at **http://www.squirrel.com.au/ virtualreality/getbrow.html.**

At this site you can find hot links to

> WebFX (**http://www.paperinc.com/**)
>
> WorldView (**http://www.webmaster.com/vrml/**)
>
> WebSpace (**http://www.sd.tgs.com/~template/WebSpace/ monday.html**)

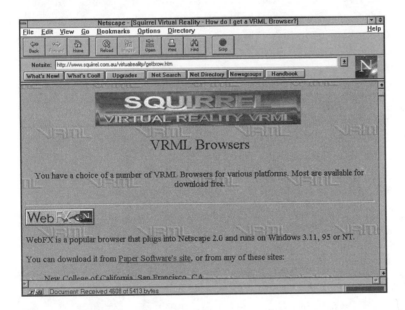

Fig. 22.10
Use the Squirrel Virtual Reality VRML's home page to access VRML browsers.

V

Applications

Live VR Worlds

There are a number of interactive world applications in development today. These worlds combine a 3-D experience with real-time person-to-person interaction. This section introduces you to three of the more advanced systems with the caveat that these sites are more than just Web site additions. These new worlds are a new technology on a par with Web technology; they represent the next generation of Internet technology.

Worlds Chat

Worlds Chat is the revolutionary 3-D, virtual chat, and entertainment environment. Worlds Chat allows users from all over cyberspace to meet and interact in a virtual space station. The chatting is done via keyboard, and the users create Avatars (digital actors) to represent themselves. Careful, it's addictive! To check it out, go to **www.worlds.net/products/wchat/**.

AlphaWorld

AlphaWorld is perhaps the first true online society. You can stake your claim and build your own site in this multiuser VR land. That's right, the users actually build the world! As of this writing, AlphaWorld is very much in beta, and very amazing. AlphaWorld is a creation of the same company as Worlds Chat. You will probably notice the visual similarities. Go to **www.worlds.net/products/alphaworld/**.

Traveler

OnLive! Technologies has developed software that allows real-time multipoint voice chat within 3-D virtual environments. What's that mean to you? It means you can talk—using your voice, not your fingers—to groups of people from all over the Internet. This is an interesting twist to the Chat scenario. The avatars have facial expressions and your avatar's mouth moves when you speak. This is certainly one of the most entertaining Internet technologies you will see anytime soon. Go to **www.onlive.com**.

The Not-Too-Distant Future: Auralview, W3Vision, and the WebStage

The not-to-distant future offers many possibilities—possibilities that are Works In Progress. This section defines some of the future applications and concepts introduced earlier in this chapter.

Auralview

The world of auralview is only slightly different from where we are today. Auralview is really an extension of the concepts of video conferencing. This future application area of Internet interaction not only has true full motion video (live, 3-D animated, or both), but it also has 3-D sound. The applications are endless: from Internet telephones, to interactive entertainment services; from distributed, industrial training films, to K-12 educational video shows. This is a world of interactive classroom-less colleges—a world in which talking to your computer is no longer a sign of mental illness.

W3Vision

The World of World Wide Web (W3) Vision is a world of endless Video and sound access from strategic places around the world, and out of this world—a place where, by simply "dialing" in a requested location you can explore the ocean seas, floors, canyon, and volcanoes. You can observe the Earth as it spins on its axis, in real time and from any one of several hundreds or thousands of views. You can enjoy a trip to the surface of the Moon, Mars, or Venus.

WebStage

The WebStage is a place where you can truly be a part of the action. Participation of world events, sporting events, plays, game shows, and training seminars takes place at your office desk, or in front of the home Multi-purpose AuralView Interface System (MAVIS). This is the Internet's future—a future you, as Web site developers, owners, and maintenance personnel, will help to define, refine, and direct. ❖

Index

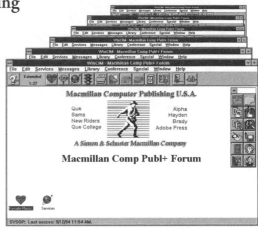

Complete and Return this Card for a *FREE* Computer Book Catalog

Thank you for purchasing this book! You have purchased a superior computer book written expressly for your needs. To continue to provide the kind of up-to-date, pertinent coverage you've come to expect from us, we need to hear from you. Please take a minute to complete and return this self-addressed, postage-paid form. In return, we'll send you a free catalog of all our computer books on topics ranging from word processing to programming and the internet.

Mr. ☐   Mrs. ☐   Ms. ☐   Dr. ☐

Name (first) ☐☐☐☐☐☐☐☐☐☐   (M.I.) ☐   (last) ☐☐☐☐☐☐☐☐☐☐☐☐☐☐☐☐☐

Address ☐☐☐☐☐☐☐☐☐☐☐☐☐☐☐☐☐☐☐☐☐☐☐☐☐☐☐☐☐☐☐

City ☐☐☐☐☐☐☐☐☐☐☐☐☐☐   State ☐☐   Zip ☐☐☐☐☐ ☐☐☐☐

Phone ☐☐☐ ☐☐☐ ☐☐☐☐   Fax ☐☐☐ ☐☐☐ ☐☐☐☐

Company Name ☐☐☐☐☐☐☐☐☐☐☐☐☐☐☐☐☐☐☐☐☐☐☐☐☐☐☐☐☐

E-mail address ☐☐☐☐☐☐☐☐☐☐☐☐☐☐☐☐☐☐☐☐☐☐☐☐☐☐☐☐☐

1. Please check at least (3) influencing factors for purchasing this book.

Front or back cover information on book ☐
Special approach to the content ☐
Completeness of content ☐
Author's reputation ☐
Publisher's reputation ☐
Book cover design or layout ☐
Index or table of contents of book ☐
Price of book ☐
Special effects, graphics, illustrations ☐
Other (Please specify): _____ ☐

2. How did you first learn about this book?

Saw in Macmillan Computer Publishing catalog ☐
Recommended by store personnel ☐
Saw the book on bookshelf at store ☐
Recommended by a friend ☐
Received advertisement in the mail ☐
Saw an advertisement in: _____ ☐
Read book review in: _____ ☐
Other (Please specify): _____ ☐

3. How many computer books have you purchased in the last six months?

This book only ☐   3 to 5 books ☐
2 books ☐   More than 5 ☐

4. Where did you purchase this book?

Bookstore ☐
Computer Store ☐
Consumer Electronics Store ☐
Department Store ☐
Office Club ☐
Warehouse Club ☐
Mail Order ☐
Direct from Publisher ☐
Internet site ☐
Other (Please specify): _____ ☐

5. How long have you been using a computer?

☐ Less than 6 months   ☐ 6 months to a year
☐ 1 to 3 years   ☐ More than 3 years

6. What is your level of experience with personal computers and with the subject of this book?

	With PCs	With subject of book
New	☐	☐
Casual	☐	☐
Accomplished	☐	☐
Expert	☐	☐

Source Code ISBN: 0-7897-0763-2

7. Which of the following best describes your job title?

Administrative Assistant .... ☐
Coordinator .... ☐
Manager/Supervisor .... ☐
Director .... ☐
Vice President .... ☐
President/CEO/COO .... ☐
Lawyer/Doctor/Medical Professional .... ☐
Teacher/Educator/Trainer .... ☐
Engineer/Technician .... ☐
Consultant .... ☐
Not employed/Student/Retired .... ☐
Other (Please specify): _____ ☐

8. Which of the following best describes the area of the company your job title falls under?

Accounting .... ☐
Engineering .... ☐
Manufacturing .... ☐
Operations .... ☐
Marketing .... ☐
Sales .... ☐
Other (Please specify): _____ ☐

9. What is your age?

Under 20 .... ☐
21-29 .... ☐
30-39 .... ☐
40-49 .... ☐
50-59 .... ☐
60-over .... ☐

10. Are you:

Male .... ☐
Female .... ☐

11. Which computer publications do you read regularly? (Please list)

_____
_____
_____
_____
_____
_____
_____
_____
_____
_____

Comments: _____
_____
_____

Fold here and scotch-tape to mail.

END-USER LICENSE AGREEMENT FOR MICROSOFT SOFTWARE

IMPORTANT—READ CAREFULLY: This Microsoft End-User License Agreement ("EULA") is a legal agreement between you (either an individual or a single entity) and Microsoft Corporation for the Microsoft software accompanying this EULA, which includes computer software and associated media and printed materials, and may include "on-line" or electronic documentation ("SOFTWARE PRODUCT" or "SOFTWARE"). By opening the sealed packet(s) OR exercising your rights to make and use copies of Internet Assistant, you agree to be bound by the terms of this EULA. If you do not agree to the terms of this EULA, promptly return this package to the place from which you obtained it.

SOFTWARE PRODUCT LICENSE

The Internet Assistant is protected by copyright laws and international copyright treaties, as well as other intellectual property laws and treaties. The Internet Assistant is licensed, not sold.

1. GRANT OF LICENSE. This EULA grants you the following rights:

- **Installation and Use.** You may install and use an unlimited number of copies of the Internet Assistant.
- **Reproduction and Distribution.** You may reproduce and distribute an unlimited number of copies of the Internet Assistant; provided that each copy shall be a true and complete copy, including all copyright and trademark notices, and shall be accompanied by a copy of the EULA. The copies may be distributed as a stand-alone product or included with your own product.

2. DESCRIPTION OF OTHER RIGHTS AND LIMITATIONS.

- **Limitations on Reverse Engineering, Decompilation, and Disassembly.** You may not reverse-engineer, decompile, or disassemble the Internet Assistant, except and only to the extent that such activity is expressly permitted by applicable law notwithstanding this limitation.
- **Separation of components.** The Internet Assistant is licensed as a single product. Its component parts may not be separated for use on more than one computer.
- **Software Transfer.** You may permanently transfer all of your rights under this EULA, provided the recipient agrees to the terms of this EULA.
- **Termination.** Without prejudice to any other rights, Microsoft may terminate this EULA if you fail to comply with the terms and conditions of this EULA. In such event, you must destroy all copies of the Internet Assistant and all of its component parts.

3. COPYRIGHT. All titles and copyrights in and to the Internet Assistant (including but not limited to any images, photographs, animations, video, audio, music, text, and "applets" incorporated into the Internet Assistant), the accompanying printed materials, and any copies of the Internet Assistant are owned by Microsoft or its suppliers. The SOFTWARE PRODUCT is protected by copyright laws and international treaty provisions. Therefore, you must treat the SOFTWARE PRODUCT like any other copyrighted material.

4. U.S. GOVERNMENT RESTRICTED RIGHTS. The Internet Assistant and documentation are provided with RESTRICTED RIGHTS. Use, duplication, or disclosure by the Government is subject to restrictions as set forth in subparagraph (c)(1)(ii) of the Rights in Technical Data and Computer Software clause at DFARS 252.227-7013 or subparagraphs (c)(1) and (2) of the Commercial Computer Software—Restricted Rights at 48 CFR 52.227-19, as applicable. Manufacturer is Microsoft Corporation/One Microsoft Way/Redmond, WA 98052-6399.

(continues)

LIMITED WARRANTY

NO WARRANTIES. Microsoft expressly disclaims any warranty for the Internet Assistant. The Internet Assistant and any related documentation is provided "as is" without warranty of any kind, either express or implied, including, without limitation, the implied warranties or merchantablility, fitness for a particular purpose, or noninfringement. The entire risk arising out of use or performance of the Internet Assistant remains with you.

NO LIABILITY FOR CONSEQUENTIAL DAMAGES. In no event shall Microsoft or its suppliers be liable for any damages whatsoever (including, without limitation, damages for loss of business profits, business interruption, loss of business information, or any other pecuniary loss) arising out of the use of or inability to use this Microsoft product, even if Microsoft has been advised of the possibility of such damages. Because some states/jurisdictions do not allow the exclusion or limitation of liability for consequential or incidental damages, the above limitation may not apply to you.

MISCELLANEOUS

If you acquired this product in the United States, this EULA is governed by the laws of the State of Washington.

If this product was acquired outside the United States, then local laws may apply.

Should you have any questions concerning this EULA, or if you desire to contact Microsoft for any reason, please contact the Microsoft subsidiary serving your country, or write: Microsoft Sales Information Center/ One Microsoft Way/Redmond, WA 98052-6399

This program was reproduced by Macmillan Computer Publishing under a special arrangement with Microsoft Corporation. For this reason, Macmillan Computer Publishing is responsible for the product warranty and for support. If your CD is defective, please return it to Macmillan Computer Publishing, which will arrange for its replacement. PLEASE DO NOT RETURN IT TO MICROSOFT CORPORATION. End users of this Microsoft program shall not be considered "registered owners" of a Microsoft product and therefore shall not be eligible for upgrades, promotions, or other benefits available to "registered Owners" of Microsoft Products.

Before using any of the software on the disc, you need to install the software you plan to use. If you have problems with the NETCD95, please contact Macmillan Technical Support at (317)581-3833. We can be reached by e-mail at **support@mcp.com** or by Compuserve at **GO QUEBOOKS**.

READ THIS BEFORE OPENING SOFTWARE

By opening this package, you are agreeing to be bound by the following:

This software is copyrighted and all rights are reserved by the publishers and its licensors. You are licensed to use this software on a single computer. You may copy the software for backup or archival purposes only. Making copies of the software for any other purpose is a violation of United States copyright laws. THIS SOFTWARE IS SOLD AS IS, WITHOUT WARRANTY OF ANY KIND, EITHER EXPRESSED OR IMPLIED, INCLUDING BUT NOT LIMITED TO THE IMPLIED WARRANTIES OF MERCHANTABILITY AND FITNESS FOR A PARTICULAR PURPOSE. Neither the publisher, nor its dealers and distributors, nor its licensors assume any liability for any alleged or actual damages arising from the use of this software. (Some states do not allow exclusion of implied warranties, so the exclusion may not apply to you.)

The entire contents of this disc and the compilation of the software are copyrighted and protected by United States copyright laws. The individual programs on the disc are copyrighted by the authors or owners of each program. Each program has its own use permissions and limitations. To use each program, you must follow the individual requirements and restrictions detailed for each. Do not use a program if you do not agree to follow its licensing agreement.

Before using any of the software on this disc, you need to install the software you plan to use. If you have problems with the WebmasterCD, please contact Macmillan Technical Support at (317)581-3833. We can be reached by e-mail at **support@mcp.com** or by CompuServe at **GO QUEBOOKS**.

The WebmasterCD has a simple HTML interface to point you to the right directories for the right software. Start your favorite Web browser and open the file START.HTM right from the CD.

Microsoft Internet Explorer for Windows 95 is located on the CD-ROM from the root directory; the file name is:

msie20.exe.

Microsoft Internet Explorer 1.5 for NT is located in the subdirectory:

CLIENT\

NOTE: Microsoft Internet Explorer 1.5 for NT will not allow you to run a setup program from within the Web browser; you will need to run setup programs from within File Manager or Explorer.

Have fun!